THE
TOP
10
OF
EVERYTHING

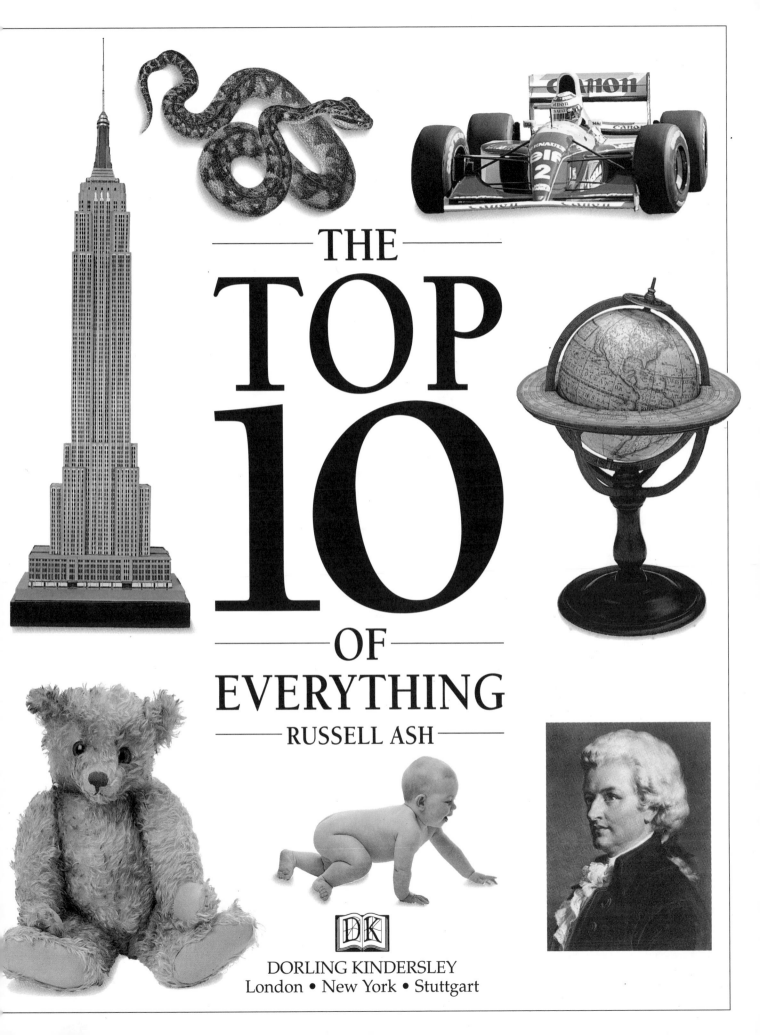

THE
TOP
10
OF
EVERYTHING

— RUSSELL ASH —

DORLING KINDERSLEY
London • New York • Stuttgart

A DORLING KINDERSLEY BOOK

Designed by The Bridgewater Book Company

Art Director Terry Jeavons

Designer James Lawrence

Editor Ian Whitelaw

Page make-up John Christopher

US Editor Jill Hamilton

Additional editorial assistance

Julee Binder, Camela Decaire, Ray Rogers

First American Edition, 1994

2 4 6 8 10 9 7 5 3 1

Published in the United States by
Dorling Kindersley Publishing, Inc.,
95 Madison Avenue,
New York, New York 10016

Library of Congress Cataloging-in-Publication Data

Ash, Russell.
    The top ten of everything / by Russell Ash. --1st American ed.
        p.   cm.
    Includes index.
    ISBN 1-56458-721-5 (hardcover). -- ISBN 1-56458-703-7 (paperback)
    1. Curiosities and wonders. 2. Questions and answers. I. Title.
AG243.A7   1994
031.02--dc20   94-6324
                                                         CIP

Reproduction by HBM Print Ltd, Singapore
Printed and bound in the United States by R R Donnelley & Sons Company

CONTENTS

INTRODUCTION

Although *The Top 10 of Everything* has been published annually in Britain since 1989, and in such countries as France and Australia, this is the first time it has appeared in the US. Creating a special edition for American readers has been both a pleasure and a challenge. It has opened many new doors to previously untapped sources of information, but garnering the data for the lists that follow has produced many surprises: a number of official organizations have been unwilling to provide material that is routinely available in the UK, while bodies that either do not exist or will not cooperate in Britain are not only accessible in the US, but could not have been more generous with their time and expertise.

The lists represent a personal selection covering a wide range of exclusively quantitative superlatives. they are not anyone's "10 Bests" (which are qualitative judgements), although there are some "10 Worst," in the case of accidents and disasters, since these can be measured by numbers of victims. Occasionally – in sections on names (of dogs, cats, and people,) for example, or in the comparative lists of lost property in New York and London – I have deliberately placed UK lists alongside their US counterparts, with often revealing results. There are also some "Progressive" lists, like that of the world land speed record or largest ocean liners, each of the entries representing a record-breaker that was in its day the fastest, the biggest, or whatever – until it was overtaken by the next one, and so on up to the present holder. There are some occasional ancillary lists, including those featuring the "10 First," or lists of the bestselling albums of each year of a decade, which offer sidelights in the form of a time-shaft of the 10-year period, as well as additional information in the form of "Did You Know?" features.

THE PACE OF CHANGE

My principal challenge is to keep abreast of recent changes: ever taller skyscrapers are erected (increasingly, outside the US); art auction records are constantly overtaken (though less often than they used to be); the richest people get richer (and sometimes poorer); sporting records are broken (the "Fastest Men on Earth" list gained a new No. 1 while this book was in preparation): and films such as *Jurassic Park* and *Mrs. Doubtfire* rapidly achieve "blockbuster" status, affecting various Top 10 lists. Even lists that one might expect to be "fixed," such as that of the world's tallest mountains, may be modified as measuring techniques are improved. The breakup of the former USSR and reunification of Germany call for statistics on the new countries that are not yet available, or sufficiently reliable, posing further problems. Countries appear and disappear, or change their names: Burma officially became Myanmar in 1989, but hardly anyone yet calls it by its new name. (Abbreviated names of country affiliations, incidentally – especially in sporting lists – follow customary practice, except for the use of "Aut" for Austria, to distinguish it from Australia, and "SA" for South Africa). Figures for country and city populations are based on the latest available census, in most instances that of 1990, with estimates for increases where officially available – with sometimes surprising consequences: the last census held in Nigeria showed that the country had 23,000,000 fewer inhabitants than had been estimated, and hence its population projection for the year 2000 has been down-rated by a staggering 40,000,000. In theory at least, with the passing of time and increasing availability of information, especially electronically, such figures should become more accurate and up to date. However, in many instances, especially with official or government figures, there is a delay in their being published, and certain figures may thus be as much as two years old. All the lists are in a constant revision, but certain examples may never satisfy purists: a list of the first fliers, for instance, has been revised in the light of more precise dating of early flights, but there may still remain some argument about the precise difference between a "flight" and a "hop."

FACT AND FICTION

By their nature, all reference book compilers enjoy facts and strive for 100% accuracy, and almost all fail to achieve it. In dealing with so much material, gathered from a vast range of international sources, I am perhaps more aware than most just how easy it is to make mistakes, and sometimes I do myself. I gain consolation (or *Schadenfreude*) in spotting the slips of others: my favorites this year are the book that describes the planet "Juniper," and a book on words that claims that the longest is 185 letters long (only 1,000 letters off,) while a reputable Sunday newspaper recently assured its readers that every British person annually consumes 7.7 tons of laundry detergent (more than the weight of an African elephant) and Turkey's population 2.2 tons a head (a mere hippopotamus-weight.) A clean story, but clearly fallacious.

During the past six years, many readers have written to me about *The Top 10 of Everything*, often suggesting ideas for new lists. Your comments are always welcomed and will help me to improve each new edition. I hope you will keep reading and continue to enjoy.

THE UNIVERSE & EARTH

THE TEN

STARS NEAREST TO THE EARTH
(*Excluding the Sun*)

	Star	Light-years*	km	miles
1	Proxima Centauri	4.22	39,923,310,000,000	24,792,500,000,000
2	Alpha Centauri	4.35	41,153,175,000,000	25,556,250,000,000
3	Barnard's Star	5.98	56,573,790,000,000	35,132,500,000,000
4	Wolf 359	7.75	73,318,875,000,000	45,531,250,000,000
5	Lalande 21185	8.22	77,765,310,000,000	48,292,500,000,000
6	Luyten 726-8	8.43	79,752,015,000,000	49,526,250,000,000
7	Sirius	8.65	81,833,325,000,000	50,818,750,000,000
8	Ross 154	9.45	89,401,725,000,000	55,518,750,000,000
9	Ross 248	10.40	98,389,200,000,000	61,100,000,000,000
10	Epsilon Eridani	10.80	102,173,400,000,000	63,450,000,000,000

* *One light-year = 5.875 x 10^{12} miles/9.4605 x 10^{12} km*

A spaceship traveling at 25,000 mph/40,237 km/h – which is faster than any human has yet reached in space – would take more than 113,200 years to reach the Earth's closest star, Proxima Centauri.

TOP 10

MOST FREQUENTLY SEEN COMETS

	Comet	Orbit period (years)
1	Encke	3.302
2	Grigg-Skjellerup	4.908
3	Honda-Mrkós-Pajdusáková	5.210
4	Tempel 2	5.259
5	Neujmin 2	5.437
6=	Brorsen	5.463
6=	Tuttle-Giacobini-Kresák	5.489
8	Tempel-L. Swift	5.681
9	Tempel 1	5.982
10	Pons-Winnecke	6.125

NATURAL PHENOMENON
This painting depicts the sighting of a comet in 1858.

COMETS COMING CLOSEST TO THE EARTH

	Comet	Date*	Distance (AU)#
1	Lexell	Jul 1, 1770	2.3
2	Tempel-Tuttle	Oct 26, 1366	3.4
3	Halley	Apr 10, 837	5.0
4	Biela	Dec 9, 1805	5.5
5	Grischow	Feb 8, 1743	5.8
6	Pons-Winnecke	Jun 26, 1927	5.9
7	La Hire	Apr 20, 1702	6.6
8	Schwassmann-Wachmann	May 31, 1930	9.3
9	Cassini	Jan 8, 1760	10.2
10	Schweizer	Apr 29, 1853	12.6

* Of closest approach to the Earth
# Astronomical units: 1AU = mean distance from the Earth to the Sun (92,955,900 miles/149,598,200 km

MOST RECENT OBSERVATIONS OF HALLEY'S COMET

1 1986
Japanese, Soviet, and European probes were all sent to investigate the comet. All were heavily battered by dust particles, and it was concluded that Halley's comet is composed of dust bonded by water and carbon dioxide ice.

2 1910
Predictions of disaster were widely published, with many people convinced that the world would come to an end.

3 1835
Widely observed, but dimmer than in 1759.

4 1759
The comet's first return, as predicted by Halley, proving his calculations correct.

5 1682
Observed in Africa and China, and in Europe, where it was observed from September 5 to 19 by Edmund Halley, who successfully calculated its orbit and predicted its return.

6 1607
Seen extensively in China, Japan, Korea, and Europe; described by German astronomer Joannes Kepler; and its position accurately measured by amateur Welsh astronomer Thomas Harriot.

7 1531
Observed in China, Japan, and Korea, and in Europe, where Peter Appian, German geographer and astronomer, noted that comets' tails point away from the Sun.

8 1456
Observed in China, Japan, Korea, and Europe. When Papal forces defeated the invading Turks, it was seen as a portent of their victory.

9 1378
Observed in China, Japan, Korea, and Europe.

10 1301
Seen in Iceland, parts of Europe, China, Japan, and Korea.

LARGEST REFLECTING TELESCOPES IN THE WORLD

	Telescope name	Location	Opened*	(m)
1	Keck Telescope	Mauna Kea Observatory, Hawaii	1992	10.0
2	Bolshoi Teleskop Azimutal'ny	Special Astrophysical Observatory of the Russian Academy of Sciences, Mount Pastukhov, Russia	1976	6.0
3	Hale Telescope	Palomar Observatory, California	1948	5.0
4	William Herschel Telescope	Observatorio del Roque de los Muchachos, La Palma, Canary Islands	1987	4.2
5=	Mayall Telescope#	Kitt Peak National Observatory, Arizona	1973	4.0
5=	4-meter Telescope#	Cerro Tololo Inter-American Observatory, Chile	1976	4.0
7	Anglo-Australian Telescope	Siding Spring Observatory, New South Wales, Australia	1974	3.9
8=	ESO 3.6-meter Telescope	European Southern Observatory, La Silla, Chile	1975	3.6
8=	Canada-France-Hawaii Telescope	Mauna Kea Observatory, Hawaii	1970	3.6
8=	United Kingdom Infrared Telescope	Mauna Kea Observatory, Hawaii	1979	3.6

* Dedicated or regular use commenced
# Northern/southern hemisphere "twin" telescopes

COMPUTING COMETS
Astronomer Royal Edmund Halley (1656–1742) computed the orbits of no fewer than 24 comets. In 1759 the dramatic return of the comet he had observed in 1682 established the science of cometary observation.

If the Keck Telescope at No. 1 is discounted because its "mirror" is not in one piece, but consists of 36 hexagonal segments slotted together, then the 10th entry in the list becomes the 3.5-meter New Technology Telescope at the European Observatory, La Silla, Chile, which started operations in 1990. The Multiple Mirror Telescope at the Fred Lawrence Whipple Observatory, Arizona, opened in 1979, has six linked 1.8-meter mirrors, together equivalent to a 4.5-meter telescope. These are being replaced by a single 6.5-meter mirror which is currently under construction.

THE PLANETS

T O P   1 0

LONGEST DAYS IN THE SOLAR SYSTEM

	Body	Length of day* days	hours	mins
1	Venus	244	0	0
2	Mercury	58	14	0
3	Sun	25#	0	0
4	Pluto	6	9	0
5	Mars		24	37
6	Earth		23	56
7	Uranus		17	14
8	Neptune		16	7
9	Saturn		10	39
10	Jupiter		9	55

* Period of rotation, based on Earth day.
\# Variable.

T O P   1 0

LONGEST YEARS IN THE SOLAR SYSTEM

	Body	Length of year* years	days
1	Pluto	247	256
2	Neptune	164	298
3	Uranus	84	4
4	Saturn	29	168
5	Jupiter	11	314
6	Mars	1	322
7	Earth		365
8	Venus		225
9	Mercury		88
10	Sun		0

* Period of orbit round the Sun, in Earth years/days

INHOSPITABLE
The surface of Venus is extremely hot, with high atmospheric pressure and clouds of sulfuric acid.

T O P   1 0

BODIES FARTHEST FROM THE SUN

(In the Solar System, excluding satellites and asteroids)

	Body	Average distance from the Sun km	miles
1	Pluto	5,914,000,000	3,675,000,000
2	Neptune	4,497,000,000	2,794,000,000
3	Uranus	2,871,000,000	1,784,000,000
4	Chiron	2,800,000,000	1,740,000,000
5	Saturn	1,427,000,000	887,000,000
6	Jupiter	778,300,000	483,600,000
7	Mars	227,900,000	141,600,000
8	Earth	149,600,000	92,900,000
9	Venus	108,200,000	67,200,000
10	Mercury	57,900,000	36,000,000

GAS GIANT
Jupiter, seen here with two of its moons, is composed almost entirely of hydrogen and helium.

DID YOU KNOW

THE MYSTERY PLANETS

Chiron, named after the centaur who ascended to heaven after being accidentally slain by Hercules, is a "mystery object" that may be either a comet or an asteroid. It was discovered on November 1, 1977 by American astronomer Charles Kowal, measures 125–190 miles/200–300 km in diameter, and orbits between Saturn and Uranus. Another mystery, so-called "Planet X," is believed by some to orbit beyond Pluto. When Pluto was discovered, it was realized that such a small planet could not cause the irregularities noticed in the orbits of Uranus and Neptune. It was concluded that there must be another as yet undiscovered planet. However, the IRAS (Infrared Astronomical Satellite) failed to detect it, while data sent back by *Voyager 2* seemed to offer explanations for Neptune's orbit without the influence of a mysterious tenth planet. Its existence remains in doubt.

T O P   1 0

LARGEST BODIES IN THE SOLAR SYSTEM

	Name	Maximum diameter km	miles
1	Sun	1,392,140	865,036
2	Jupiter	142,984	88,846
3	Saturn	120,536	74,898
4	Uranus	51,118	31,763
5	Neptune	49,532	30,778
6	Earth	12,756	7,926
7	Venus	12,103	7,520
8	Mars	6,794	4,222
9	Ganymede	5,268	3,273
10	Titan	5,150	3,200

Most of the planets are visible with the naked eye and have been observed since ancient times. The exceptions are Uranus, discovered on March 13, 1781 by the British astronomer Sir William Herschel; Neptune, found by German astronomer Johann Galle on September 23, 1846 (Galle was led to his discovery by the independent calculations of the French astronomer Urbain Leverrier and the British mathematician John Adams); and, outside the Top 10, Pluto, located using photographic techniques by American astronomer Clyde Tombaugh. The announcement of its discovery came on March 13, 1930; its diameter remains uncertain, but it is thought to be approximately 1,430 miles/2,302 km.

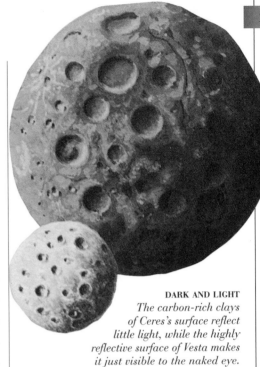

LARGEST PLANETARY MOONS

	Moon	Planet	Diameter km	Diameter miles
1	Ganymede	Jupiter	5,268	3,273

Discovered by Galileo in 1609–10 and believed to be the largest moon in the Solar System, Ganymede – one of Jupiter's 16 satellites – is thought to have a surface of ice about 60 miles/97 km thick.

2	Titan	Saturn	5,150	3,200

Titan, the largest of Saturn's 18 confirmed moons, is actually larger than Mercury or Pluto. It was discovered by the Dutch astronomer Christian Huygens in 1655.

3	Callisto	Jupiter	4,820	2,995

Similar in composition to Ganymede, Callisto is heavily pitted with craters, perhaps more so than any other body in the Solar System.

4	Io	Jupiter	3,632	2,257

Most of what we know about Io was reported back by the 1979 Voyager probe, which revealed a crust of solid sulfur with massive volcanic eruptions in progress.

5	Moon	Earth	3,475	2,159

Our own satellite is a quarter of the size of the Earth and the 5th largest in the Solar System. To date it is the only one that has been explored by humans.

6	Europa	Jupiter	3,126	1,942

Europa's fairly smooth, icy surface is covered with mysterious black lines, some of them 40 miles/64 km wide and resembling canals.

7	Triton	Neptune	2,750	1,708

Discovered in 1846 by British brewer and amateur astronomer William Lassell, Triton is unique in that it revolves around its planet in the opposite direction to the planet's rotation.

8	Titania	Uranus	1,580	982

The largest of Uranus's 15 moons, Titania was discovered by William Herschel (who had discovered the planet six years earlier) in 1787 and has a snowball-like surface of ice.

9	Rhea	Saturn	1,530	951

Saturn's second largest moon was discovered in the 17th century by Italian-born French astronomer Giovanni Cassini.

10	Oberon	Uranus	1,516	942

Oberon was discovered by Herschel and given the name of the fairy king husband of Queen Titania; both are characters in Shakespeare's A Midsummer Night's Dream.

LARGEST ASTEROIDS

	Name	Year discovered	Diameter km	Diameter miles
1	Ceres	1801	936	582
2	Pallas	1802	607	377
3	Vesta	1807	519	322
4	Hygeia	1849	450	279
5	Euphrosyne	1854	370	229
6	Interamnia	1910	349	217
7	Davida	1903	322	200
8	Cybele	1861	308	192
9	Europa	1858	288	179
10	Patienta	1899	275	171

Asteroids, sometimes known as "minor planets," are fragments of rock orbiting between Mars and Jupiter. There are perhaps 45,000 of them, but fewer than 10 percent have been named. The first (and largest) to be discovered was Ceres, which was found by Giuseppe Piazzi (1746–1826), director of the Palermo observatory in Sicily, on New Year's Day, 1801. All have been numbered according to the order in which they were discovered. Some have only code numbers, but most also have names: women's names are especially popular and include Hilda (No. 153), Bertha (No. 154), Marilyn (No. 1,486), Sabrina (No. 2,264), and Samantha (No. 3,147). Among asteroids named after men are Mark Twain (No. 2,362) and Mr. Spock from *Star Trek* (No. 2,309).

DARK AND LIGHT
The carbon-rich clays of Ceres's surface reflect little light, while the highly reflective surface of Vesta makes it just visible to the naked eye.

COLDEST BODIES IN THE SOLAR SYSTEM*

	Planet	Lowest temperature °F	Lowest temperature °C
1	Pluto	–382	–230
2	Uranus	–369	–223
3	Neptune	–364	–220
4	Mercury	–328	–200
5	Saturn	–256	–160
6	Jupiter	–229	–145
7	Mars	–220	–140
8	Earth	–128	–89
9	Venus	+867	+464
10	Sun	+9,932	+5,500

* Excluding satellites.

Absolute zero, which has almost been reached on Earth under laboratory conditions, is –459.67°F/–273.15°C, only 68.67°F below the surface temperature of Triton, a moon of Neptune. At the other extreme, it has been calculated theoretically that the core of Jupiter attains 54,000°F, more than five times the boiling point of tungsten, while the Sun's core reaches almost 28,000,000°F.

SATURN'S LARGEST MOON
NASA and the European Space Agency plan to send a space probe to Titan in April 1996. It should reach Titan in October 2002.

REACHING FOR THE MOON

FIRST ANIMALS IN SPACE

	Animal	Country of origin	Date
1	Laika	USSR	Nov 3, 1957

Name used by Western press – actually the name of the breed to which the dog named Kudryavka, a female Samoyed husky, belonged. Died in space.

2=	Laska and		
2=	Benjy (mice)	US	Dec 13, 1958

Re-entered the Earth's atmosphere, but not recovered.

4=	Able (female rhesus monkey) and		
4=	Baker (female squirrel monkey)	US	May 28, 1959

Successfully returned to Earth.

6=	Otvazhnaya (female Samoyed husky) and		
6=	An unnamed rabbit	USSR	Jul 2, 1959

Recovered.

8	Sam (male rhesus monkey)	US	Dec 4, 1959

Recovered.

9=	Belka and		
9=	Strelka (female Samoyed huskies)	USSR	Aug 19, 1960

First to orbit and return safely.

The first animal to be sent up in a rocket – but not into space – was Albert, a male rhesus monkey, in a US Air Force converted German V2 rocket in 1948. He died during the test, as did a monkey and 11 mice in a US *Aerobee* rocket in 1951. The earliest Soviet experiments with launching animals in rockets involved monkeys, dogs, rabbits, cats, and mice, most of whom died as a result. Laika, the first dog in space, went up with no hope of coming down alive. Able and Baker, launched in a *Jupiter* missile, were the first animals to be recovered (although Able died a few days later). Prior to the first US manned spaceflight, on November 29, 1961, Enos, a male chimpanzee, successfully completed two orbits and returned safely to the Earth.

LARGEST CRATERS ON THE MOON

(Near, or visible side only)

	Crater	Diameter km	miles
1	Bailly	303	188
2	Deslandres	234	145
3	Schickard	227	141
4	Clavius	225	140
5	Grimaldi	222	138
6	Humboldt	207	129
7	Belkovich	198	123
8	Janssen	190	118
9	Schiller	179	111
10=	Gauss	177	110
10=	Petavius	177	110

The most characteristic features of the lunar landscape are its craters, many of which are named after famous astronomers and scientists. On the near side of the Moon there are some 300,000 craters with diameters greater than 0.6 mile/1 km, 234 of them larger than 62 miles/100 km. Those larger than about 37 miles/60 km are correctly known as "walled plains." The walled plains and smaller craters have been continually degraded by meteorite bombardment over millions of years and as a result, many contain numerous further craters within them. Bailly (named after Jean Sylvain Bailly, astronomer and Mayor of Paris, who was guillotined soon after the French Revolution) is the largest crater on the visible side, with walls rising to 14,000 ft/4,267 m.

FIRST PEOPLE IN SPACE

	Name	Age	Orbits	Duration hr:min	Spacecraft/ country of origin	Date
1	Fl. Major Yuri Alekseyivich Gagarin	27	1	1:48	*Vostok I* USSR	Apr 12, 1961
2	Major Gherman Stepanovich Titov	25	17	25:18	*Vostok II* USSR	Aug 6–7, 1961
3	Lt.-Col. John Herschel Glenn	43	3	4:56	*Friendship 7* US	Feb 20, 1962
4	Lt.-Col. Malcolm Scott Carpenter	37	3	4:56	*Aurora 7* US	May 24, 1962
5	Major Andrian Grigoryevich Nikolayev	32	64	94:22	*Vostok III* USSR	Aug 11–15, 1962
6	Col. Pavel Romanovich Popovich	31	48	70:57	*Vostok IV* USSR	Aug 12–15, 1962
7	Cdr. Walter Marty Schirra	39	6	9:13	*Sigma 7* US	Oct 3, 1962
8	Major Leroy Gordon Cooper	36	22	34:19	*Faith 7* US	May 15–16, 1963
9	Lt.-Col. Valeri Fyodorovich Bykovsky	28	81	119:60	*Vostok V* USSR	Jun 14–19, 1963
10	Jr. Lt. Valentina Vladimirovna Tereshkova	26	48	70:50	*Vostok VI* USSR	Jun 16–19, 1963

No. 10 was the first woman in space. Among early pioneering flights, neither Alan Shepard (May 5, 1961: *Freedom 7*) nor Gus Grissom (July 21, 1961: *Liberty Bell 7*) actually entered space, achieving altitudes of only 115 miles/185 km and 118 miles/190 km respectively, and neither flight lasted more than 15 minutes. Glenn was the first American to orbit the Earth.

**COMMAND AND
SERVICE MODULE**

FIRST MOONWALKERS

	Astronaut	Birthdate	Spacecraft	Total EVA* hr:min	Mission dates
1	Neil A. Armstrong	Aug 5, 1930	*Apollo 11*	2:32	Jul 16–24, 1969
2	Edwin E. ("Buzz") Aldrin	Jan 20, 1930	*Apollo 11*	2:15	Jul 16–24, 1969
3	Charles Conrad Jr.	Jun 2, 1930	*Apollo 12*	7:45	Nov 14–24, 1969
4	Alan L. Bean	Mar 15, 1932	*Apollo 12*	7:45	Nov 14–24, 1969
5	Alan B. Shepard	Nov 18, 1923	*Apollo 14*	9:23	Jan 31–Feb 9, 1971
6	Edgar D. Mitchell	Sep 17, 1930	*Apollo 14*	9:23	Jan 31–Feb 9, 1971
7	David R. Scott	Jun 6, 1932	*Apollo 15*	19:08	Jul 26–Aug 7, 1971
8	James B. Irwin	Mar 17, 1930	*Apollo 15*	18:35	Jul 26–Aug 7, 1971
9	John W. Young	Sep 24, 1930	*Apollo 16*	20:14	Apr 16–27, 1972
10	Charles M. Duke	Oct 3, 1935	*Apollo 16*	20:14	Apr 16–27, 1972

* Extra Vehicular Activity (i.e. time spent out of the lunar module on the Moon's surface)

Six US *Apollo* missions resulted in successful Moon landings (*Apollo 13*, April 11–17, 1970, was aborted after an oxygen tank exploded). During the last of these (*Apollo 17*, December 7–19, 1972), Eugene A. Cernan (b. March 14, 1934) and Harrison H. Schmitt (b. July 3, 1935) became the only other astronauts to date who have walked on the surface of the Moon, both spending a total of 22:04 hours in EVA. No further Moon landings are planned by the US. Although Russian scientists recently proposed sending a series of unmanned probes to land on Mars, which, if successful, would have led to a follow-up manned mission between 2005 and 2010, the entire Russian space program is suffering from such severe financial problems that its current missions appear to be in jeopardy.

SATURN V
This launch vehicle was built to send astronauts to the Moon.

FIRST ARTIFICIAL SATELLITES

	Satellite	Country of origin	Launch date
1	*Sputnik 1*	USSR	Oct 4, 1957
2	*Sputnik 2*	USSR	Nov 3, 1957
3	*Explorer 1*	US	Feb 1, 1958
4	*Vanguard 1*	US	Mar 17, 1958
5	*Explorer 3*	US	Mar 26, 1958
6	*Sputnik 3*	USSR	May 15. 1958
7	*Explorer 4*	US	Jul 26, 1958
8	*Score*	US	Dec 18, 1958
9	*Vanguard 2*	US	Feb 17, 1959
10	*Discoverer 1*	US	Feb 28, 1959

Artificial satellites for use as radio relay stations were first proposed by the British science-fiction writer Arthur C. Clarke, in the October 1945 issue of *Wireless World*, but it was 12 years before his fantasy became reality with the launch of *Sputnik 1*, the first-ever artificial satellite to enter the Earth's orbit. A 184-lb/83.6-kg metal sphere, it transmitted signals back to the Earth for three weeks before its batteries failed, although it continued to be tracked until it fell back to the Earth and burned up on January 4, 1958. Its early successors were similarly short-lived, destroyed on re-entry (although *Vanguard 1* is destined to remain in orbit for the next 275 years and *Vanguard 2* for 125 years). *Sputnik 2* carried the first animal into space, and *Explorer 1* first detected the radiation zone known as the Van Allen belts. *Explorer 2* failed to enter the Earth's orbit. *Score* (the Signal Communications Orbit Relay Experiment) transmitted a pre-recorded Christmas message from President Eisenhower. *Discoverer 1*, the first to be launched in a polar orbit, was a military satellite.

FIRST UNMANNED MOON LANDINGS

	Name	Country of origin	Date (launch/impact)
1	*Lunik 2*	USSR	Sep 12/14, 1959
2	*Ranger 4**	US	Apr 23/26, 1962
3	*Ranger 6*	US	Jan 30/Feb 2, 1964
4	*Ranger 7*	US	Jul 28/31, 1964
5	*Ranger 8*	US	Feb 17/20, 1965
6	*Ranger 9*	US	Mar 21/24, 1965
7	*Luna 5**	USSR	May 9/12, 1965
8	*Luna 7**	USSR	Oct 4/8, 1965
9	*Luna 8**	USSR	Dec 3/7, 1965
10	*Luna 9*	USSR	Jan 31/Feb 3, 1966

In addition to these 10, debris left on the surface of the Moon includes the remains of several more *Luna* craft, including unmanned sample-collectors and *Lunakhod 1* and *2* (1966–71; all Soviet), seven *Surveyors* (1966–68), five *Lunar Orbiters* (1966–67), and the descent stages of six *Apollo* modules (all US) – to which one may add the world's most expensive used cars, the three Lunar Rovers used on *Apollo* missions Nos. 15 to 17 and worth $6,000,000 each.

* Crash landing

ASTRONAUTS

COUNTRIES WITH MOST SPACEFLIGHT EXPERIENCE

(To January 1, 1994)

	Country	Missions	Host country	Total duration of missions day	hr	min	sec
1	USSR	72	–	3,835	8	16	44
2	US	89	–	738	3	57	25
3	Russia	4	–	710	6	23	5
4	France	5	1 US/3 USSR/1 Russia*	74	4	43	36
5	Germany	5	3 US/2 USSR	41	4	33	3
6	Canada	3	US	26	3	34	31
7	Japan	2	1 US/1 USSR	15	20	26	11
8	Bulgaria	2	USSR	11	19	11	6
9	Belgium	1	US	8	22	9	25
10	Afghanistan	1	USSR	8	20	27	0

** Russia became a separate independent
state on December 25, 1991.*

FIRST MANNED ORBIT
*On April 12, 1961 Soviet cosmonaut
Yuri Gagarin became the first person in
space when he completed one orbit of
the Earth in his capsule, Vostok 1.*

FIRST SPACEWALKERS

	Astronaut	Spacecraft	EVA* hr:min	Launch date
1	Alexei Leonov	*Voshkod 2*	0:12	Mar 18, 1965
2	Edward H. White	*Gemini 4*	0:23	Jun 3, 1965
3	Eugene A. Cernan#	*Gemini 9*	2:08	Jun 3, 1966
4	Michael Collins	*Gemini 10*	1:30	Jul 18, 1966
5	Richard F. Gordon	*Gemini 11*	1:57	Sep 12, 1966
6	Edwin E. ("Buzz") Aldrin**	*Gemini 12*	5:37	Nov 11, 1966
7	Alexei Yeleseyev	*Soyuz 5*	‡	Jan 15, 1969
8	Yevgeny Khrunov	*Soyuz 5*	‡	Jan 15, 1969
9	David R. Scott##	*Apollo 9*	1:01	Mar 3, 1969
10	Russell L. Schweickart	*Apollo 9*	1:07	Mar 3, 1969

* Extra Vehicular Activity.
 # December 7, 1972 – first to walk in space four times.
**July 16, 1969 – first to walk in space twice.
##July 26, 1971 – first to walk in space three times.
‡ Short duration EVA transfer to Soyuz 4.

FIRST IN-FLIGHT SPACE FATALITIES

1 Vladimir M.
Komarov   (b. Mar 16, 1927)

*Launched on April 24, 1967, Soviet spaceship
Soyuz 1 experienced various technical
problems during its 18th orbit. After a
successful reentry, the capsule parachute was
deployed at 23,000 ft/7,010 m, but its lines
became tangled and it crash-landed near Orsk
in the Urals, killing Komarov (the survivor of a
previous one-day flight on October 12, 1964),
who thus became the first-ever space fatality.*

2= Georgi T.
Dobrovolsky   (b. Jun 1, 1928)
2= Viktor I.
Patsayev   (b. Jun 19, 1933)
2= Vladislav N.
Volkov   (b. Nov 23, 1933)

*After a then-record 23 days in space, and a
linkup with the Salyut space station, the
Soviet Soyuz 9 mission ended in disaster on
June 29, 1971 when the capsule depressurized
during reentry. Although it landed intact, all
three cosmonauts – who were not wearing
spacesuits – were found dead. Their ashes were
buried, along with those of Yuri Gagarin and
Vladimir Komarov, at the Kremlin, in Moscow.
Spacesuits have been worn during reentry on
all subsequent missions.*

5= Gregory B.
Jarvis   (b. Aug 24, 1944)
5= Sharon C.
McAuliffe   (b. Sep 2, 1948)
5= Ronald E.
McNair   (b. Oct 21, 1950)
5= Ellison S.
Onizuka   (b. Jun 24, 1946)
5= Judith A.
Resnik   (b. Apr 5, 1949)
5= Francis R.
Scobee   (b. May 19, 1939)
5= Michael J.
Smith   (b. Apr 30, 1945)

*Challenger STS-51-L, the 25th Space Shuttle
mission, exploded on takeoff from Cape
Canaveral, Florida, on January 28, 1986. The
cause was determined to have been leakage of
seals in the joint between rocket sections. The
disaster, which was watched by thousands on
the ground and millions on television, halted
the US space program until a full review of
engineering problems and safety methods had
been undertaken, and it was not until
September 29, 1988 that the next Space
Shuttle, Discovery STS-26, was launched.*

The 11 cosmonauts and astronauts in this
list are, to date, the only in-flight space
fatalities. They are not, however, the only

victims of other accidents during the space programs of the former USSR and the US. On October 24, 1960, five months before the first manned flight, Field Marshal Mitrofan Nedelin, the commander of the USSR's Strategic Rocket Forces, and an unknown number of other personnel (a total of 165 according to some authorities) were killed in the catastrophic launchpad explosion of an unmanned space rocket at the Baikonur cosmodrome, but the precise circumstances remain secret. Another explosion, during the refueling of a *Vostok* rocket at the Plesetsk Space Center on March 18, 1980, left some 50 dead. During a test countdown of *Apollo 1* on January 27, 1967, Roger B. Chaffee, Virgil I. "Gus" Grissom, veteran of the US's second and seventh space missions, and Edward H. White (who flew in the eighth US mission) were killed in a fire, probably caused by an electrical fault. This tragedy led to greatly improved capsule design and safety procedures.

A number of former astronauts and cosmonauts have also been killed in accidents during other activities: Yuri Gagarin, the first man in space, was killed on March 27, 1968 in an airplane crash. The same fate befell a number of American astronauts who trained for but were killed before their space missions: Charles A. Bassett, Theodore C. Freeman, Elliot M. See, and Clifton C. Williams all died during training in T-38 jet crashes in 1964–67. Stephen D. Thorne was killed in a 1986 airplane accident, and Edward G. Givens in a 1967 car crash. John L. Swigert, who had survived the ill-fated *Apollo 13* mission in 1970, died of cancer on December 27, 1982, thus becoming the first American space explorer to die of natural causes. James B. Irwin, who died on August 8, 1991 as a result of a heart attack, became the first moonwalker to die.

T O P 1 0

MOST EXPERIENCED SPACEMEN

(To January 1, 1994)

	Name	Missions	Total duration of missions			
			days	hr	min	sec
1	Musa Manarov	2	541	0	31	18
2	Sergei Krikalyov	2	463	7	11	0
3	Yuri Romanenko	3	430	18	21	30
4	Alexander Volkov	3	391	11	54	0
5	Anatoli Solovyov	3	377	20	0	0
6	Leonid Kizim	3	374	17	57	42
7	Vladimir Titov	2	367	22	56	48
8	Vladimir Solovyov	2	361	22	50	0
9	Valeri Ryumin	3	361	21	31	57
10	Vladimir Lyakhov	3	333	7	48	37

All the missions listed were undertaken by the USSR (and, more recently, Russia). The durations of Soviet/Russian cosmonauts' space missions are far ahead of those of the US, whose closest rivals are the three *Skylab 4* astronauts Gerald P. Carr, Edward G. Gibson, and William R. Pogue. Each of them clocked up a total of 84 days 1 hr 15 min 31 sec in space (November 16, 1973 to February 8, 1974) giving all three the equal US record for space experience. The four Space Shuttle missions of Daniel C. Brandenstein (*SST-8*, *STS-51-G*, *STS-32*, and *STS-49*) make him the most experienced Shuttle astronaut, with a total time in space of 32 days 21 hr 5 min 16 sec.

T O P 1 0

MOST EXPERIENCED SPACEWOMEN

(To January 1, 1994)

	Name*	Missions	Total duration of missions			
			days	hr	min	sec
1	Shannon W. Lucid	4	34	22	53	14
2	Bonnie J. Dunbar	3	31	17	15	33
3	Kathryn C. Thornton	3	23	41	15	30
4	Margaret Rhea Seddon	2	23	2	27	54
5	Kathryn D. Sullivan	3	22	4	48	39
6	Svetlana Savitskaya	2	19	17	7	0
7	Tamara E. Jernigan	2	18	23	10	33
8	Marsha S. Ivins	2	18	20	15	43
9	Ellen S. Baker	2	17	43	9	4
10	Sally K. Ride	2	14	7	47	43

* *All US except Savitskaya (USSR).*

THE FACE OF THE EARTH

LARGEST METEORITE CRATERS IN THE WORLD

	Crater	Diameter km	miles
1=	Sudbury, Ontario, Canada	140	87
1=	Vredefort, South Africa	140	87
3=	Manicouagan, Québec, Canada	100	62
3=	Popigai, Russia	100	62
5	Puchezh-Katunki, Russia	80	50
6	Kara, Russia	60	37
7	Siljan, Sweden	52	32
8	Charlevoix, Québec, Canada	46	29
9	Araguainha Dome, Brazil	40	25
10	Carswell, Saskatchewan, Canada	37	23

The jury is still out on the Earth's notable meteor craters: unlike those on the Solar System's other planets and moons, many astroblemes (collision sites) on the Earth have been weathered over time and obscured, and one of the ongoing debates in geology is thus whether or not certain craterlike structures are of meteoric origin or the remnants of long-extinct volcanoes. The Vredefort Ring, for example, long thought to be meteoric, was declared in 1963 to be volcanic, but has since been claimed as a definite meteor crater, as are all the giant meteorite craters in the Top 10, which are listed as such (along with 106 others) by the International Union of Geological Sciences Commission on Comparative Planetology. The relatively small Barringer Crater in Arizona (0.79 miles/1.265 km) is the largest that *all* scientists agree is definitely meteoric in origin.

LARGEST ISLANDS IN THE WORLD

	Island	Location	Approx. area* sq km	sq miles
1	Greenland (Kalaatdlit Nunaat)	Arctic Ocean	2,175,590	840,000
2	New Guinea	West Pacific	789,900	304,980
3	Borneo	Indian Ocean	751,000	289,961
4	Madagascar (Malagasy Republic)	Indian Ocean	587,041	226,657
5	Baffin Island, Canada	Arctic Ocean	507,451	195,926
6	Sumatra, Indonesia	Indian Ocean	422,200	163,011
7	Honshu, Japan	Northwest Pacific	230,092	88,839
8	Great Britain	North Atlantic	218,041	84,186
9	Victoria Island, Canada	Arctic Ocean	217,290	83,896
10	Ellesmere Island, Canada	Arctic Ocean	196,236	75,767

* *Mainlands, including areas of inland water, but excluding offshore islands*

Australia is regarded as a continental land mass rather than an island; otherwise it would rank 1st, at 2,941,517 sq miles/7,618,493 sq km, or 35 times the size of Great Britain.

LARGEST DESERTS IN THE WORLD

	Desert	Location	Approx. area sq km	sq miles
1	Sahara	North Africa	9,000,000	3,500,000
2	Australian	Australia	3,800,000	1,470,000
3	Arabian	Southwest Asia	1,300,000	502,000
4	Gobi	Central Asia	1,040,000	401,500
5	Kalahari	Southern Africa	520,000	201,000
6	Turkestan	Central Asia	450,000	174,000
7	Takla Makan	China	327,000	125,000
8=	Sonoran	US/Mexico	310,000	120,000
8=	Namib	Southwest Africa	310,000	120,000
10=	Thar	Northwest India/Pakistan	260,000	100,000
10=	Somali	Somalia	260,000	100,000

HOT AND BARREN
The Gobi Desert, in the dry heart of central Asia, occupies most of Mongolia and part of China. In recent years, exciting finds of fossil bones and dinosaur eggs have been unearthed there.

T O P   1 0

LARGEST ISLANDS IN THE US

	Island	Approx area sq km	sq miles
1	Hawaii, Hawaii	4,037	10,456
2	Kodiak, Alaska	3,672	9,510
3	Puerto Rico	3,459	8,959
4	Prince of Wales, Alaska	2,587	6,700
5	Chicagof, Alaska	2,085	5,400
6	Saint Lawrence, Alaska	1,710	4,430
7	Admiralty, Alaska	1,649	4,270
8	Nunivak, Alaska	1,625	4,210
9	Unimak, Alaska	1,606	4,160
10	Baranof, Alaska	1,598	4,140

Long Island, New York (1,396 sq miles/ 3,630 sq km) falls just outside the Top 10. Manhattan, New York, measures just 22 sq miles/57 sq km.

D I D   Y O U   K N O W

ISLANDS LOST AND FOUND

• The South Atlantic Saxemberg Island and the Aurora Islands, allegedly discovered in 1762 by the crew of the *Aurora*, and once marked by marine charts, do not actually exist.

• Bouvet Island, also in the South Atlantic, was discovered in 1739 but then lost. It was sought by Captain Cook and other explorers and was rediscovered in 1808.

• One of the world's newest islands is the volcanic Surtsey, which emerged from the sea southwest of Iceland in November 1963.

T O P   1 0

LONGEST CAVES IN THE WORLD

	Cave	Location	Total known length m	ft
1	Mammoth cave system	Kentucky, US	560,000	1,837,270
2	Optimisticeskaja	Ukraine	178,000	583,989
3	Hölloch	Switzerland	137,000	449,475
4	Jewel Cave	South Dakota, US	127,000	416,667
5	Siebenhengsteholensystem	Switzerland	110,000	360,892
6	Ozernaya	Ukraine	107,300	352,034
7	Réseau de la Coume d'Hyouernede	France	90,500	296,916
8	Sistema de Ojo Guarena	Spain	89,100	292,323
9	Wind Cave	South Dakota, US	88,500	290,354
10	Fisher Ridge cave system	Kentucky, US	83,000	273,950

T O P   1 0

DEEPEST DEPRESSIONS IN THE WORLD

	Depression	Maximum depth below sea level m	ft
1	Dead Sea, Israel/Jordan	400	1,312
2	Turfan Depression, China	154	505
3	Qattâra Depression, Egypt	133	436
4	Poluostrov Mangyshlak, Kazakhstan	132	433
5	Danakil Depression, Ethiopia	117	383
6	Death Valley, US	86	282
7	Salton Sink, US	72	235
8	Zapadny Chink Ustyurta, Kazakhstan	70	230
9	Prikaspiyskaya Nizmennost', Kazakhstan/Russia	67	220
10	Ozera Sarykamysh, Turkmenistan/Uzbekistan	45	148

The shore of the Dead Sea is the lowest exposed ground below sea level. However, the bed of the Sea, at 2,388 ft/728 m below sea level, is only half as deep as that of Lake Baikal, Russia, which is 4,872 ft/ 1,485 m below sea level. Much of Antarctica is also below sea level (some as low as 8,326 ft/2,538 m), but the land there is covered by an ice cap.

D I D   Y O U   K N O W

HOW LOW CAN YOU GO?

The greatest depth below ground level on land, that of the world's deepest mine, is far exceeded by the greatest chasm in the sea bed. The Marianas Trench in the Pacific Ocean plunges to a depth of 35,813 ft/10,916 m – 28.65 times the height of the Empire State Building. The bottom of the trench was reached on January 23, 1960 by Jacques Piccard and Donald Walls in the bathyscape *Trieste*.

ON TOP OF THE WORLD

TOP 10

HIGHEST MOUNTAINS IN THE WORLD

(Height of principal peak; lower peaks of the same mountain are excluded)

	Mountain	Country	m	ft
1	Everest	Nepal/Tibet	8,846	29,022
2	K2	Kashmir/China	8,611	28,250
3	Kanchenjunga	Nepal/Sikkim	8,598	28,208
4	Lhotse	Nepal/Tibet	8,501	27,890
5	Makalu I	Nepal/Tibet	8,470	27,790
6	Dhaulagiri I	Nepal	8,172	26,810
7	Manaslu I	Nepal	8,156	26,760
8	Cho Oyu	Nepal	8,153	26,750
9	Nanga Parbat	Kashmir	8,126	26,660
10	Annapurna I	Nepal	8,078	26,504

Many of the Top 10 mountains have alternative names: in Tibetan, Everest is known as Chomolungma ("Goddess Mother of the World"). K2 (so called because it was the second mountain in the Karakoram range counting from the Kashmir end) is also referred to by the local name Chogori, and sometimes as Godwin-Austen (after Lieutenant Henry Haversham Godwin-Austen (1834–1923), who first surveyed it in 1865). Manaslu is also known as Kutang I, and Nanga Parbat as Diamir.

TOP 10

HIGHEST MOUNTAINS IN THE US

	Mountain	m	ft
1	McKinley (Denali)	6,194	20,320
2	St. Elias	5,489	18,008
3	Foraker	5,304	17,400
4	Bona	5,044	16,550
5	Blackburn	4,996	16,390
6	Kennedy	4,964	16,286
7	Sanford	4,949	16,237
8	South Buttress	4,842	15,885
9	Vancouver	4,785	15,700
10	Churchill	4,766	15,638

All 10 tallest mountains in the US are in Alaska or on the Alaska/Canada border. Mt. Logan in Canada is the second tallest peak in the North American continent at 19,850 ft/6,050 m. Colorado and California also have a number of mountains over 14,000 ft/4,267 m. Only one other state – Washington – has a mountain in the Top 80: Mt. Rainier at 14,410 ft/4,392 m.

JAGGED PEAKS
Apart from Mts. Fujiyama and Kilimanjaro, which are both volcanoes, these mountains belong to geologically young ranges (less than 70 million years old), so have not had time to undergo extensive erosion.

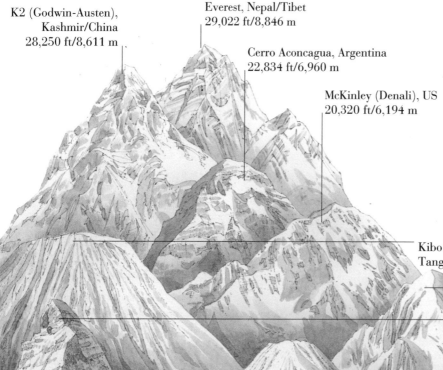

K2 (Godwin-Austen), Kashmir/China 28,250 ft/8,611 m

Everest, Nepal/Tibet 29,022 ft/8,846 m

Cerro Aconcagua, Argentina 22,834 ft/6,960 m

McKinley (Denali), US 20,320 ft/6,194 m

Kibo (Kilimanjaro), Tanganyika/Tanzania 19,340 ft/5,895 m

Mont Blanc, France/Italy 15,770 ft/4,807 m

Matterhorn, Italy/Switzerland 14,691 ft/4,478 m

Fujiyama, Japan 12,388 ft/3,776 m

T O P 1 0

HIGHEST MOUNTAINS IN AFRICA

	Mountain	Country	m	ft
1	Kibo (Kilimanjaro)	Tanganyika/Tanzania	5,895	19,340
2	Batian (Kenya)	Kenya	5,199	17,058
3	Ngaliema	Uganda/Zaïre	5,109	16,763
4	Duwoni	Uganda	4,896	16,062
5	Baker	Uganda	4,843	15,889
6	Emin	Zaïre	4,798	15,741
7	Gessi	Uganda	4,715	15,470
8	Sella	Uganda	4,627	15,179
9	Ras Dashen	Ethiopia	4,620	15,158
10	Wasuwameso	Zaïre	4,581	15,030

HOW HIGH?
The height of Everest was estimated in the 19th century as 29,002 ft/8,840 m. This was later revised to 29,029 ft/ 8,848 m, but on April 20, 1993, using the latest measuring techniques, the height was revised to the current "official" figure.

T O P 1 0

HIGHEST MOUNTAINS IN OCEANIA

	Mountain	m	ft
1	Jaya	5,030	16,500
2	Daam	4,920	16,150
3	Pilimsit	4,800	15,750
4	Trikora	4,750	15,580
5	Mandala	4,700	15,420
6	Wilhelm	4,690	15,400
7	Wisnumurti	4,590	15,080
8	Yamin	4,530	14,860
9	Kubor	4,360	14,300
10	Herbert	4,270	14,000

T O P 1 0

HIGHEST MOUNTAINS IN SOUTH AMERICA

	Mountain	Country	m	ft
1	Cerro Aconcagua	Argentina	6,960	22,834
2	Ojos del Salado	Argentina/Chile	6,885	22,588
3	Bonete	Argentina	6,873	22,550
4	Pissis	Argentina/Chile	6,780	22,244
5	Huascarán	Peru	6,768	22,205
6	Llullaillaco	Argentina/Chile	6,723	22,057
7	Libertador	Argentina	6,721	22,050
8	Mercadario	Argentina/Chile	6,670	21,884
9	Yerupajá	Peru	6,634	21,765
10	Tres Cruces	Argentina/Chile	6,620	21,720

T O P 1 0

HIGHEST MOUNTAINS IN NORTH AMERICA

	Mountain	Country	m	ft
1	McKinley (Denali)	US	6,194	20,320
2	Logan	Canada	6,050	19,850
3	Citlaltépetl (Orizaba)	Mexico	5,700	18,700
4	St. Elias	US/Canada	5,489	18,008
5	Popocatépetl	Mexico	5,452	17,887
6	Foraker	US	5,304	17,400
7	Ixtaccihuatl	Mexico	5,286	17,343
8	Lucania	Canada	5,226	17,147
9	King	Canada	5,173	16,971
10	Steele	Canada	5,073	16,644

RIVERS AND WATERFALLS

TOP 10

LONGEST RIVERS IN EUROPE
(Excluding former USSR)

	River	Countries	km	miles
1	Danube	Germany/Austria/Slovakia/ Hungary/Yugoslavia (Serbia)/ Romania/Bulgaria	2,842	1,766
2	Rhine	Switzerland/Germany/ Holland	1,368	850
3	Elbe	Czechoslovakia/Germany	1,167	725
4	Loire	France	1,014	630
5	Tagus	Portugal	1,009	627
6	Meuse	France/Belgium/Holland	950	590
7	Ebro	Spain	933	580
8	Rhône	Switzerland/France	813	505
9	Guadiana	Spain/Portugal	805	500
10	Seine	France	776	482

TOP 10

LONGEST RIVERS IN SOUTH AMERICA

	River	Countries	km	miles
1	Amazon	Peru/Brazil	6,448	4,007
2	Plata–Paraná	Brazil/Paraguay/ Argentina/Uruguay	4,000	2,485
3	Madeira–Mamoré– Grande	Bolivia/Brazil	3,380	2,100
4	Purus	Peru/Brazil	3,207	1,993
5	São Francisco	Brazil	3,198	1,987
6	Orinoco	Colombia/Venezuela	2,736	1,700
7	Tocantins	Brazil	2,699	1,677
8	Paraguay	Paraguay/Brazil/ Argentina/Bolivia	2,549	1,584
9	Japura–Caquetá	Colombia/Brazil	2,414	1,500
10	Negro	Colombia/Venezuela/ Brazil	2,253	1,400

TOP 10

LONGEST RIVERS IN THE WORLD

	River	Countries	km	miles
1	Nile	Tanzania/Uganda/ Sudan/Egypt	6,670	4,145
2	Amazon	Peru/Brazil	6,448	4,007
3	Yangtze–Kiang	China	6,300	3,915
4	Mississippi–Missouri– Red Rock	US	5,971	3,710
5	Yenisey–Angara–Selenga	Mongolia/Russia	5,540	3,442
6	Huang Ho (Yellow River)	China	5,464	3,395
7	Ob'–Irtysh	Mongolia/Kazakhstan/Russia	5,410	3,362
8	Zaïre (Congo)	Angola/Zaïre	4,700	2,920
9	Lena–Kirenga	Russia	4,400	2,734
10	Mekong	Tibet/China/Myanmar (Burma)/ Laos/Cambodia/Vietnam	4,350	2,703

TOP 10

LONGEST RIVERS IN NORTH AMERICA

	River	Country	km	miles
1	Mackenzie– Peace	Canada	4,241	2,635
2	Missouri– Red Rock	US	4,088	2,540
3	Mississippi	US	3,779	2,348
4	Missouri	US	3,726	2,315
5	Yukon	US	3,185	1,979
6	St. Lawrence	Canada	3,130	1,945
7	Rio Grande	US	2,832	1,760
8	Nelson	Canada	2,575	1,600
9	Arkansas	US	2,348	1,459
10	Colorado	US	2,334	1,450

The Mississippi, Missouri, and Red Rock Rivers are often combined, thus becoming the 4th longest river in the world at 3,710 miles/5,971 km.

BRINGER OF LIFE
For thousands of years, since the time of the ancient Egyptians, the Nile has attracted the peoples of northeast Africa to its fertile banks.

GREATEST WATERFALLS IN THE WORLD

(Based on volume of water)

	Waterfall	Country	Average flow (m³/sec)
1	Boyoma (Stanley)	Zaïre	17,000
2	Khône	Laos	11,610
3	Niagara (Horseshoe)	Canada/US	5,830
4	Grande	Uruguay	4,500
5	Paulo Afonso	Brazil	2,890
6	Urubupungá	Brazil	2,750
7	Iguaçu	Argentina/ Brazil	1,700
8	Maribondo	Brazil	1,500
9	Churchill (Grand)	Canada	1,390
10	Kabalega (Murchison)	Uganda	1,200

THE CRYSTAL MOUNTAIN

In 1594 Sir Walter Raleigh journeyed up the Orinoco river in search of the legendary city of Eldorado. The climate, powerful currents, and dwindling supplies forced him to abandon his quest, but before turning back he saw at a distance a waterfall that resembled a "Mountain of Crystal . . . like a white church tower of an exceeding height." Raleigh had almost certainly discovered the world's highest waterfall, which subsequent Spanish explorers also reported seeing, but without naming it. The falls were named in honor of American adventurer James Angel, who was prospecting for gold in the Guiana Highlands. On November 14, 1933 he first spotted the falls from the air, later crash-landing his airplane on a nearby plateau. He survived and made his way back to civilization.

HIGHEST WATERFALLS IN THE US

	Waterfall	River/state	Drop m	ft
1	Ribbon (Yosemite)	Ribbon Creek, California	1,612	491
2	Upper Yosemite	Yosemite Creek, California	1,430	436
3	Widow's Tears	Meadow Brook, California	1,170	357
4	Middle Cascade	Yosemite Creek, California	909	277
5	Fairy	Stevens Creek, Washington	700	213
6	Feather	Fall River, California	640	195
7	Bridalveil	Bridalveil Creek, California	620	189
8	Nevada	Merced, California	594	181
9	Multnomah	Multnomah Creek, Oregon	542	165
10	Sentinel	Sentinel Creek, California	500	152

HIGHEST WATERFALLS IN THE WORLD

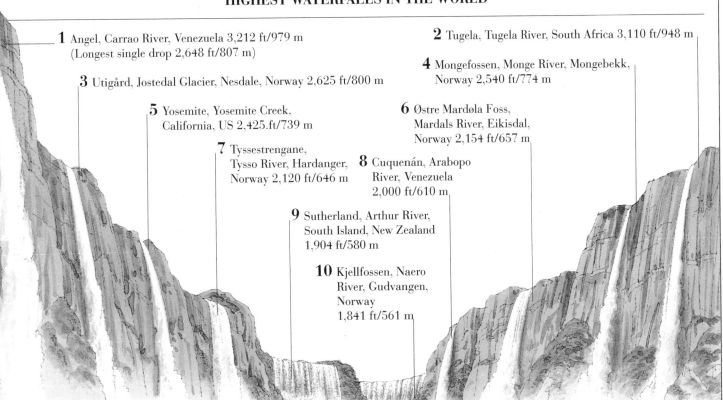

1 Angel, Carrao River, Venezuela 3,212 ft/979 m (Longest single drop 2,648 ft/807 m)

2 Tugela, Tugela River, South Africa 3,110 ft/948 m

3 Utigård, Jostedal Glacier, Nesdale, Norway 2,625 ft/800 m

4 Mongefossen, Monge River, Mongebekk, Norway 2,540 ft/774 m

5 Yosemite, Yosemite Creek, California, US 2,425.ft/739 m

6 Østre Mardøla Foss, Mardals River, Eikisdal, Norway 2,154 ft/657 m

7 Tyssestrengane, Tysso River, Hardanger, Norway 2,120 ft/646 m

8 Cuquenán, Arabopo River, Venezuela 2,000 ft/610 m

9 Sutherland, Arthur River, South Island, New Zealand 1,904 ft/580 m

10 Kjellfossen, Naero River, Gudvangen, Norway 1,841 ft/561 m

SEAS AND LAKES

TOP 10

LARGEST OCEANS AND SEAS IN THE WORLD

	Ocean/sea	Approx. area sq km	sq miles
1	Pacific Ocean	165,241,000	63,800,000
2	Atlantic Ocean	82,439,000	31,830,000
3	Indian Ocean	73,452,000	28,360,000
4	Arctic Ocean	13,986,000	5,400,000
5	Arabian Sea	3,864,000	1,492,000
6	South China Sea	3,447,000	1,331,000
7	Caribbean Sea	2,753,000	1,063,000
8	Mediterranean Sea	2,505,000	967,000
9	Bering Sea	2,269,000	876,000
10	Bay of Bengal	2,173,000	839,000

TOP 10

LAKES WITH THE GREATEST VOLUME OF WATER

	Lake	Location	Volume cubic km	cubic miles
1	Caspian Sea	Azerbaijan/Iran/Kazakhstan/ Russia/Turkmenistan	89,600	21,497
2	Baikal	Russia	22,995	5,517
3	Tanganyika	Burundi/Tanzania/Zaïre/Zambia	18,304	4,392
4	Superior	Canada/US	12,174	2,921
5	Nyasa (Malawi)	Malawi/Mozambique/Tanzania	6,140	1,473
6	Michigan	US	4,874	1,169
7	Huron	Canada/US	3,575	858
8	Victoria	Kenya/Tanzania/Uganda	2,518	604
9	Great Bear	Canada	2,258	542
10	Great Slave	Canada	1,771	425

TOP 10

DEEPEST OCEANS AND SEAS IN THE WORLD

TOP 10

DEEPEST DEEP-SEA TRENCHES

	Name	Ocean	Deepest point m	ft
1	Mariana	Pacific	10,924	35,837
2	Tonga*	Pacific	10,800	35,430
3	Philippine	Pacific	10,497	34,436
4	Kermadec*	Pacific	10,047	32,960
5	Bonin	Pacific	9,994	32,786
6	New Britain	Pacific	9,940	32,609
7	Kuril	Pacific	9,750	31,985
8	Izu	Pacific	9,695	31,805
9	Puerto Rico	Atlantic	8,605	28,229
10	Yap	Pacific	8,527	27,973

Some authorities consider these parts of the same feature.

The eight deepest ocean trenches would be deep enough to submerge Mount Everest, which is 29,022 ft/ 8,846 m above sea level.

	Ocean/sea	Average depth m	ft		Ocean/sea	Average depth m	ft
1	Pacific Ocean	4,028	13,215	6	Bering Sea	1,547	5,075
2	Indian Ocean	3,963	13,002	7	Gulf of Mexico	1,486	4,874
3	Atlantic Ocean	3,926	12,880	8	Mediterranean Sea	1,429	4,688
4	Caribbean Sea	2,647	8,685	9	Japan Sea	1,350	4,429
5	South China Sea	1,652	5,419	10	Arctic Ocean	1,205	3,953

T O P 1 0

LARGEST LAKES IN THE WORLD

	Lake	Location	Approx. area sq km	Approx. area sq miles
1	Caspian Sea	Azerbaijan/Iran/ Kazakhstan/Russia/ Turkmenistan	378,400	146,101
2	Superior	Canada/US	82,100	31,699
3	Victoria	Kenya/Tanzania/Uganda	62,940	24,301
4	Huron	Canada/US	59,580	23,004
5	Michigan	US	57,700	22,278
6	Aral Sea	Kazakhstan/Uzbekistan	40,000	15,444
7	Tanganyika	Burundi/Tanzania/ Zaïre/Zambia	31,987	12,350
8	Baikal	Russia	31,494	12,160
9	Great Bear	Canada	31,153	12,028
10	Great Slave	Canada	28,570	11,031

Lake Superior is the world's largest freshwater lake. Lake Baikal (or Baykal) in Siberia, with a depth of as much as 1.02 miles/1.63 km in parts, is the world's deepest. It has been calculated that, as a result of two feeder rivers being diverted for irrigation, between 1973 and 1989 the area of the Aral Sea fell by so much that it dropped from 4th to 6th place and is in danger of becoming nonexistent.

UNIQUELY RICH
Probably the world's oldest lake, Baikal is home to a remarkable range of plants and animals, including at least 1,300 species that are found nowhere else on the Earth. Lake Baikal contains approximately 20 percent of the Earth's supply of freshwater.

T O P 1 0

DEEPEST FRESHWATER LAKES IN THE WORLD

	Lake	Location	Greatest depth m	Greatest depth ft
1	Baikal	Russia	1,637	5,371
2	Tanganyika	Burundi/ Tanzania/ Zaïre/ Zambia	1,471	4,825
3	Malawi	Malawi/ Mozambique/ Tanzania	706	2,316
4	Great Slave	Canada	614	2,015
5	Matana	Celebes, Indonesia	590	1,936
6	Crater	Oregon, US	589	1,932
7	Toba	Sumatra, Indonesia	529	1,736
8	Hornindals	Norway	514	1,686
9	Sarez	Tajikistan	505	1,657
10	Tahoe	California/ Nevada, US	501	1,645

T O P 1 0

LARGEST FRESHWATER LAKES IN THE US
(Excluding those partly in Canada)

	Lake	State	Approx. area sq km	Approx. area sq miles
1	Michigan	Illinois/ Indiana/ Michigan/ Wisconsin	57,700	22,278
2	Iliamna	Alaska	2,590	1,000
3	Okeechobee	Florida	1,813	700
4	Becharof	Alaska	1,186	458
5	Red	Minnesota	1,168	451
6	Teshepuk	Alaska	816	315
7	Naknek	Alaska	627	242
8	Winnebago	Wisconsin	557	215
9	Mille Lacs	Minnesota	536	207
10	Flathead	Montana	510	197

NATURAL DISASTERS

24

SEARCHING FOR SURVIVORS
After Colombia's worst landslide, rescuers struggle to release victims from the mud and rubble.

T O P 1 0

WORST AVALANCHES AND LANDSLIDES OF THE 20TH CENTURY
(Excluding those where most deaths resulted from flooding caused by avalanches or landslides)

	Location	Incident	Date	Estimated no. killed
1	Yungay, Peru	Landslide	May 31, 1970	17,500
2	Italian Alps	Avalanche	Dec 13, 1916	10,000
3	Huarás, Peru	Avalanche	Dec 13, 1941	5,000
4	Mount Huascaran, Peru	Avalanche	Jan 10, 1962	3,500
5	Medellin, Colombia	Landslide	Sep 27, 1987	683
6	Chungar, Peru	Avalanche	Mar 19, 1971	600
7	Rio de Janeiro, Brazil	Landslide	Jan 11, 1966	550
8=	Northern Assam, India	Landslide	Feb 15, 1949	500
8=	Grand Rivière du Nord, Haiti	Landslide	Nov 13/14, 1963	500
10	Blons, Austria	Avalanche	Jan 11, 1954	411

The worst incident of all, the destruction of Yungay, Peru, in May 1970, was only part of a much larger cataclysm. The landslide, which wiped out the town and left just 2,500 survivors out of a population of 20,000, followed on the heels of an earthquake and widespread flooding that left a total of up to 70,000 dead.

T O P 1 0

WORST EARTHQUAKES IN THE WORLD

	Location	Date	Estimated no. killed
1	Near East/Mediterranean	May 20, 1202	1,100,000
2	Shenshi, China	Feb 2, 1556	820,000
3	Calcutta, India	Oct 11, 1737	300,000
4	Antioch, Syria	May 20, 526	250,000
5	Tang-shan, China	Jul 28, 1976	242,419
6	Nan-shan, China	May 22, 1927	200,000
7	Yeddo, Japan	1703 (exact date unknown)	190,000
8	Kansu, China	Dec 16, 1920	180,000
9	Messina, Italy	Dec 28, 1908	160,000
10	Tokyo/Yokohama, Japan	Sep 1, 1923	142,807

There are some discrepancies between the "official" death tolls in many of the world's worst earthquakes and the estimates of other authorities: a figure of 750,000 is sometimes quoted for the the Tang-shan earthquake of 1976, for example, and totals ranging from 58,000 to 250,000 for the quake that devastated Messina in 1908. Several other earthquakes in China and Turkey resulted in deaths of 100,000 or more. In recent times, the Armenian earthquake of December 7, 1988 and that which struck northwest Iran on June 21, 1990 resulted in the deaths of more than 55,000 (official estimate 28,854) and 50,000 respectively. One of the most famous earthquakes, the one that destroyed San Francisco on April 18, 1906, killed between 500 and 1,000 people – mostly in the fires that resulted from broken gas pipes and electricity cables following the shock.

T O P 1 0

WORST TSUNAMIS ("TIDAL WAVES") IN THE WORLD

	Location	Year	Estimated no. killed
1	Atlantic coast (Morocco, western Europe, West Indies)	1775	60,000
2	Sumatra, Java	1883	36,000
3=	Japan	1707	30,000
3=	Italy	1783	30,000
5	Japan	1896	27,122
6	Chile, Hawaii	1868	25,000
7	Ryukyu Islands	1771	11,941
8	Japan	1792	9,745
9=	Japan	1498	5,000
9=	Japan	1611	5,000
9=	Peru	1756	5,000
9=	Chile, Hawaii, Japan	1960	5,000
9=	Philippines	1976	5,000

TOP 10

WORST VOLCANIC ERUPTIONS IN THE WORLD

1 Tambora, Indonesia — Apr 5–12, 1815 — 92,000

The cataclysmic eruption of Tambora killed about 10,000 islanders immediately, with a further 82,000 dying subsequently from disease and famine resulting from crops being destroyed. An estimated 1,900,000 tons of ash were hurled into the atmosphere. This blocked out the sunlight and affected the weather over large areas of the globe during the following year. One effect of this was to produce brilliantly colored sunsets, depicted strikingly in paintings from the period, especially in the works of J.M.W. Turner. It even had an influence on literary history: kept indoors by inclement weather at the Villa Diodati on Lake Geneva, Lord Byron and his companions amused themselves by writing horror stories, one of which was Mary Shelley's classic, Frankenstein.

2 Miyi-Yama, Java — 1793 — 53,000

Miyi-Yama, the volcano dominating the island of Kiousiou, erupted during 1793, engulfing all the local villages in mudslides and killing most of the rural population.

3 Mont Pelée, Martinique — May 8, 1902 — 40,000

After lying dormant for centuries, Mont Pelée began to erupt in April 1902. Assured that there was no danger, the 30,000 residents of the main city, St. Pierre, stayed in their homes and were there when the volcano burst apart and showered the port with molten lava, ash, and gas, destroying all life and property. Some 50 people were killed by deadly fer-de-lance snakes, disturbed by the eruption.

4 Krakatoa, Sumatra/Java — Aug 26–27, 1883 — 36,380

After a series of eruptions over several days, the uninhabited island of Krakatoa exploded with what may have been the biggest bang ever heard by humans, recorded clearly 3,000 miles/4,800 km away. Some sources put the deaths as high as 200,000, most of them killed by subsequent tidal waves up to 100 ft/30 m high. The events were portrayed in the 1969 film Krakatoa, East of Java, but purists should note that Krakatoa is actually west of Java.

2 Nevado del Ruiz, Colombia — Nov 13, 1985 — 22,940

The Andean volcano gave warning signs of erupting, but by the time it was decided to evacuate the local inhabitants, it was too late. The hot steam, rocks, and ash ejected from mudslide engulfed the town of Armero.

6 Mount Etna, Italy — Mar 11, 1669 — more than 20,000

Europe's largest volcano (10,760 ft/3,280 m) has erupted frequently, but the worst instance occurred in 1669 when the lava flow engulfed the town of Catania, killing at least 20,000.

7 Laki, Iceland — Jan–Jun 1783 — 20,000

Iceland is one of the most volcanically active places on Earth but, being sparsely populated, eruptions seldom result in major loss of life. The worst exception took place at the Laki volcanic ridge, culminating on June 11 with the largest ever recorded lava flow. It engulfed many villages in a river of lava up to 50 miles/80 km long and 100 ft/30 m deep, releasing poisonous gases that killed those who managed to escape the lava.

8 Vesuvius, Italy — Aug 24, 79 — 16–20,000

When the previously dormant Vesuvius erupted suddenly, the Roman city of Herculaneum was engulfed by a mudflow while Pompeii was buried under a vast layer of pumice and volcanic ash – which ironically preserved it in a near-perfect state that was not uncovered until excavations by archaeologists in the 19th and 20th centuries.

9 Vesuvius, Italy — Dec 16–17, 1631 — 18,000

Although minor eruptions occurred at intervals after that of AD 79, the next major cataclysm was almost as disastrous, when lava and mudflows gushed down onto the surrounding towns, including Naples.

10 Mount Etna, Italy — 1169 — more than 15,000

Large numbers died in Catania cathedral where they believed they would be safe, and more were killed when a tidal wave hit the port of Messina.

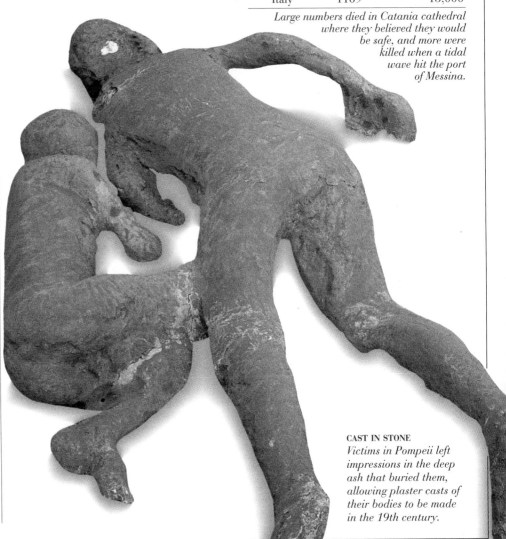

CAST IN STONE
Victims in Pompeii left impressions in the deep ash that buried them, allowing plaster casts of their bodies to be made in the 19th century.

WEATHER EXTREMES

COLDEST AND HOTTEST INHABITED PLACES IN THE WORLD (AVERAGE TEMPERATURES)

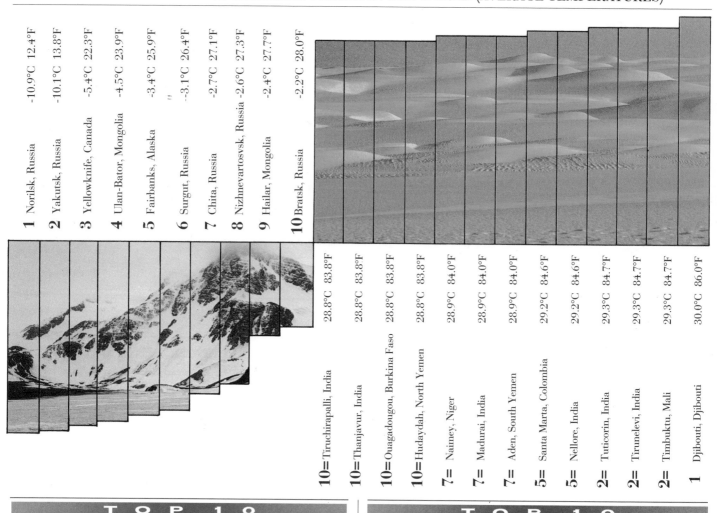

	Location	Temperature
1	Norilsk, Russia	-10.9°C 12.4°F
2	Yakutsk, Russia	-10.1°C 13.8°F
3	Yellowknife, Canada	-5.4°C 22.3°F
4	Ulan-Bator, Mongolia	-4.5°C 23.9°F
5	Fairbanks, Alaska	-3.4°C 25.9°F
6	Surgut, Russia	-3.1°C 26.4°F
7	Chita, Russia	-2.7°C 27.1°F
8	Nizhnevartovsk, Russia	-2.6°C 27.3°F
9	Hailar, Mongolia	-2.4°C 27.7°F
10	Bratsk, Russia	-2.2°C 28.0°F

	Location	Temperature
10=	Tiruchirapalli, India	28.8°C 83.8°F
10=	Thanjavur, India	28.8°C 83.8°F
10=	Ouagadougou, Burkina Faso	28.8°C 83.8°F
10=	Hudaydah, North Yemen	28.8°C 83.8°F
7=	Naimey, Niger	28.9°C 84.0°F
7=	Madurai, India	28.9°C 84.0°F
7=	Aden, South Yemen	28.9°C 84.0°F
5=	Santa Marta, Colombia	29.2°C 84.6°F
5=	Nellore, India	29.2°C 84.6°F
2=	Tuticorin, India	29.3°C 84.7°F
2=	Tirunelevi, India	29.3°C 84.7°F
2=	Timbuktu, Mali	29.3°C 84.7°F
1	Djibouti, Djibouti	30.0°C 86.0°F

WETTEST INHABITED PLACES IN THE WORLD

	Location	Average annual rainfall mm	in
1	Buenaventura, Colombia	6,743	265.47
2	Monrovia, Liberia	5,131	202.01
3	Pago Pago, American Samoa	4,990	196.46
4	Moulmein, Myanmar (Burma)	4,852	191.02
5	Lae, Papua New Guinea	4,465	182.87
6	Baguio, Luzon Island, Philippines	4,573	180.04
7	Sylhet, Bangladesh	4,457	175.47
8	Conakry, Guinea	4,341	170.91
9=	Padang, Sumatra Island, Indonesia	4,225	166.34
9=	Bogor, Java, Indonesia	4,225	166.34

The total annual rainfall of the Top 10 locations is equivalent to 26 6-ft/1.83-m adults standing on top of each other.

DRIEST INHABITED PLACES IN THE WORLD

	Location	Average annual rainfall mm	in
1	Aswan, Egypt	0.5	0.02
2	Luxor, Egypt	0.7	0.03
3	Arica, Chile	1.1	0.04
4	Ica, Peru	2.3	0.09
5	Antofagasta, Chile	4.9	0.19
6	Minya, Egypt	5.1	0.20
7	Asyut, Egypt	5.2	0.20
8	Callao, Peru	12.0	0.47
9	Trujilo, Peru	14.0	0.54
10	Fayyum, Egypt	19.0	0.75

The total annual rainfall of the Top 10 inhabited places is just 2.5 in/64.8 mm – the length of an adult little finger.

TOP 10

COLDEST CITIES IN THE US

	City	Mean temperature °C	°F
1	International Falls, Minnesota	2.4	36.4
2	Duluth, Minnesota	3.4	38.2
3	Caribou, Maine	3.8	38.9
4	Marquette, Michigan	4.0	39.2
5	Sault Ste. Marie, Michigan	4.3	39.7
6	Fargo, North Dakota	4.7	40.5
7	Williston, North Dakota	4.9	40.8
8	Alamosa, Colorado	5.1	41.2
9	Bismarck, North Dakota	5.2	41.3
10	Saint Cloud, Minnesota	5.2	41.4

TOP 10

WARMEST CITIES IN THE US

	City	Mean temperature °C	°F
1	Key West, Florida	25.4	77.7
2	Miami, Florida	24.2	75.6
3	West Palm Beach, Florida	23.7	74.6
4=	Fort Myers, Florida	23.3	73.9
4=	Yuma, Arizona	23.3	73.9
6	Brownsville, Texas	23.1	73.6
7=	Orlando, Florida	22.4	72.4
7=	Vero Beach, Florida	22.4	72.4
9	Corpus Christi, Texas	22.3	72.1
10	Tampa, Florida	22.2	72.0

Source: National Climatic Data Center

These are constantly updated mean figures kept by individual climatic data centers from the beginning of their records, the origins of which vary (some began collecting data over 100 years ago), and include readings complete up to November 1993. (The figures do not include Hawaii and Alaska.)

TOP 10

DRIEST CITIES IN THE US

	City	Mean annual precipitation mm	ins
1	Yuma, Arizona	67	2.65
2	Las Vegas, Nevada	106	4.19
3	Bishop, California	142	5.61
4	Bakersfield, California	145	5.72
5	Phoenix, Arizona	180	7.11
6	Alamosa, Colorado	181	7.13
7	Reno, Nevada	190	7.49
8	Winslow, Arizona	194	7.64
9	El Paso, Texas	199	7.82
10	Winnemucca, Nevada	200	7.87

TOP 10

WETTEST CITIES IN THE US

	City	Mean annual precipitation mm	in
1	Quillayute, Washington	2,654	104.50
2	Astoria, Oregon	1,768	69.60
3	Blue Canyon, California	1,724	67.87
4	Mobile, Alabama	1,642	64.64
5	Tallahassee, Florida	1,641	64.59
6	Pensacola, Florida	1,553	61.16
7	New Orleans, Louisiana	1,517	59.74
8	West Palm Beach, Florida	1,516	59.72
9	Miami, Florida	1,513	59.55
10	Tupelo, Mississippi	1,425	56.12

TOP 10

WINDIEST CITIES IN THE US

	City	Mean wind speed km/h	mph
1	Blue Hill, Massachusetts	24.8	15.4
2	Dodge City, Kansas	22.5	14.0
3	Amarillo, Texas	21.7	13.5
4	Rochester, Minnesota	21.1	13.1
5=	Cheyenne, Wyoming	20.8	12.9
5=	Casper, Wyoming	20.8	12.9
7	Great Falls, Montana	20.4	12.7
8	Goodland, Kansas	20.3	12.6
9	Boston, Massachusetts	20.1	12.5
10	Lubbock, Texas	20.0	12.4

TOP 10

SNOWIEST CITIES IN THE US

	City	Mean annual snowfall mm	in
1	Blue Canyon, California	6,116	240.8
2	Marquette, Michigan	3,266	128.6
3	Sault Ste. Marie, Michigan	2,964	116.7
4	Syracuse, New York	2,835	111.6
5	Caribou, Maine	2,804	110.4
6	Mount Shasta, California	2,664	104.9
7	Lander, Wyoming	2,604	102.5
8	Flagstaff, Arizona	2,537	99.9
9	Sexton Summit, Oregon	2,484	97.8
10	Muskegon, Michigan	2,464	97.0

LIFE ON EARTH

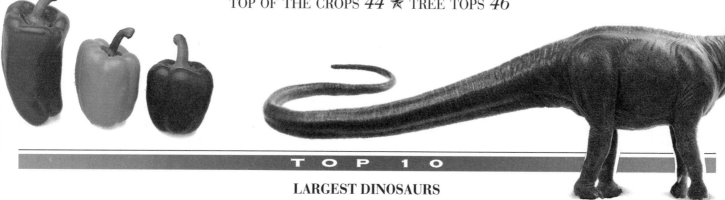

T O P 1 0

LARGEST DINOSAURS

1 *"Seismosaurus"*
Length: 98–119 ft/30–36 m
Estimated weight: 55–90 tons

A single skeleton of this colossal plant-eater was excavated in 1985 near Albuquerque, New Mexico, by American paleontologist David Gillette and given an unofficial name (i.e. one that is not yet an established scientific name) that means "earth-shaking lizard." It is currently being studied by the New Mexico Museum of Natural History.

2 *Supersaurus*
Length: 80–100 ft/24–30 m
Height: 54 ft/16 m
Estimated weight: 55 tons

The remains of Supersaurus were found in Colorado in 1972 (like those of Ultrasaurus, by James A. Jensen). Some scientists have suggested a length of up to 138 ft/42 m and a weight of 80–110 tons.

3 *Antarctosaurus*
Length: 60–98 ft/18–30 m
Estimated weight: 40–55 tons

Named Antarctosaurus ("southern lizard") by German paleontologist Friedrich von Huene in 1929, this creature's thigh bone alone measures 7 ft 6 in/2.3 m.

4 *Barosaurus*
Length: 75–90 ft/23–27.5 m
Height and weight uncertain

Barosaurus (meaning "heavy lizard," so named by American paleontologist Othniel C. Marsh in 1890) has been found in both North America and Africa, thus proving the existence of a land link in Jurassic times (205–140 million years ago).

5 *Mamenchisaurus*
Length: 89 ft/27 m
Height and weight uncertain

An almost complete skeleton discovered in 1972 showed it had the longest neck of any known animal, composing more than half of its total body length – perhaps up to 49 ft/15 m. It was named by Chinese paleontologist Young Chung Chien after the place in China where it was found.

6 *Diplodocus*
Length: 75–89 ft/23–27 m
Estimated weight: 13 tons

As it was long and thin, Diplodocus was a relative lightweight in the dinosaur world. It was also probably one of the most stupid dinosaurs, having the smallest brain in relation to its body size. Diplodocus was given its name (which means "double beam") in 1878 by Marsh. One skeleton was named Diplodocus carnegii, in honor of Scottish-American millionaire Andrew Carnegie, who financed the excavations that discovered it.

7 *"Ultrasaurus"*
Length: Over 82 ft/25 m
Height: 52 ft/16 m
Estimated weight: 55 tons

Discovered by US paleontologist James A. Jensen in Colorado in 1979, it has not yet been fully studied. Some authorities put its weight at an unlikely 110–150 tons. Confusingly, although its informal name (which means "ultra lizard") was widely recognized, another, smaller dinosaur has been given the same official name.

8 *Brachiosaurus*
Length: 82 ft/25 m
Height: 52 ft/16 m
Estimated weight: 55 tons

Its name (given to it in 1903 by US paleontologist Elmer S. Riggs) means "arm lizard." Some have put the weight of Brachiosaurus as high as 210 tons, but this seems improbable, in the light of theories of maximum weights of terrestrial animals.

9 *Pelorosaurus*
Length: 80 ft/24 m
Weight
uncertain

The first fragments of Pelorosaurus ("monstrous lizard") were found in Sussex and named by British doctor and geologist Gideon Algernon Mantell as early as 1850.

10 *Apatosaurus*
Length: 66–70 ft/
20–21m

Estimated weight:
20–30 tons

Apatosaurus (its name, coined by Marsh, means "deceptive lizard") is better known by its former name of Brontosaurus ("thunder reptile"). The bones of the first one ever found, in Colorado in 1879, caused great confusion for many years because its discoverer attached a head from a different species to the rest of the skeleton.

The Top 10 is based on the most reliable recent evidence of their lengths and indicates the probable ranges, although these are undergoing constant revision. Lengths have often been estimated from only a few surviving fossilized bones, and there is much dispute even among experts about these and even more about the weights of most dinosaurs. Some, such as *Diplodocus* were long but not immensely heavy.

Everyone's favorite dinosaur, *Tyrannosaurus rex* ("tyrant lizard"), does not appear in the Top 10 list because although it was one of the fiercest flesh-eating dinosaurs, it was not as large as many of the herbivorous ones. However, measuring a probable 39 ft/12 m and weighing more than 6 tons, it certainly ranks as one of the largest flesh-eating animals yet discovered. Bones of an earlier dinosaur called *Epanterias* were found in Colorado in 1877 and 1934, but incorrectly identified until recently, when studies suggested that this creature was possibly larger than *Tyrannosaurus*.

To compare these sizes with living animals, note that the largest recorded crocodile measured 20 ft 4 in/6.2 m and the largest elephant 35 ft/10.7 m from trunk to tail and weighed about 12 tons. The largest living creature ever measured is the blue whale at 110 ft/33.6 m – slightly smaller than the size claimed for *Seismosaurus*.

T O P   1 0
FIRST DINOSAURS TO BE NAMED

	Name	Meaning	Named by	Year
1	*Megalosaurus*	Great lizard	William Buckland	1824
2	*Iguanodon*	Iguana tooth	Gideon Mantell	1825
3	*Hylaeosaurus*	Woodland lizard	Gideon Mantell	1832
4	*Macrodontophion*	Large tooth snake	A. Zborzewski	1834
5=	*Thecodontosaurus*	Socket-toothed lizard	Samuel Stutchbury and H. Riley	1836
5=	*Palaeosaurus*	Ancient lizard	Samuel Stutchbury and H. Riley	1836
7	*Plateosaurus*	Flat lizard	Hermann von Meyer	1837
8=	*Cladeiodon*	Branch tooth	Richard Owen	1841
8=	*Cetiosaurus*	Whale lizard	Richard Owen	1841
10	*Pelorosaurus*	Monstrous lizard	Gideon Mantell	1850

T O P   1 0
FINAL DATES WHEN 10 SPECIES WERE LAST SEEN ALIVE

1 Aurochs   1627

This giant wild ox was last recorded in central Europe, after the advance of agriculture forced it to retreat from its former territory, which once stretched west as far as Britain.

2 *Aepyornis*   1649

Also known as the "Elephant bird," the 10-ft/3-m wingless bird was a native of Madagascar.

3 Dodo   1681

Discovered by European travelers in 1507, the last Dodo seen alive was on the island of Mauritius in 1681. Its name comes from the Portuguese for "stupid," and its lack of flight, tameness, and taste made it extremely vulnerable to being caught and eaten.

4 Steller's sea cow   1768

A large marine mammal named after its 1741 discoverer, German naturalist Georg Wilhelm Steller, it was hunted to extinction. The Spectacled Cormorant, which Steller also found, became extinct at about the same time.

5 Great auk   1844

The last example of this flightless North Atlantic seabird breeding in Britain was in 1812, when one was nesting in the Orkneys, and the last seen in Britain in 1821 when one was killed for food on St. Kilda. The last surviving pair in the world was killed on June 4, 1844 on Eldey island (Iceland) on behalf of a collector called Carl Siemsen. A stuffed specimen was sold at Sotheby's, London, in 1971.

6 Tarpan   1851

The European wild horse was last seen in the Ukraine. Another wild horse thought to be extinct, Przewalski's horse, has been rediscovered in Mongolia and new captive-bred stock has been reintroduced into its former range around the Gobi Desert.

7 Quagga   1883

This zebralike creature found in South Africa, first recorded in 1685, was hunted by European settlers for food and leather to such an extent that by 1870 the last specimen in the wild had been killed. The last example, a female in Amsterdam Zoo, died on August 12, 1883.

8 Guadalupe Island Caracara   1900

On December 1, 1900, the last-ever example of this large brown hawk was sighted.

9 Passenger pigeon   1914

This is an example of a creature whose last moment can be stated precisely, when at 1:00 pm on September 1, 1914 at Cincinnati Zoo, a 29-year-old bird named Martha expired. Her stuffed body is displayed by the Smithsonian Institution, Washington DC. Totals ran a staggering five to nine billion in the 19th century, but they were remorselessly killed for food and to protect farm crops in the US.

10 Carolina parakeet   1918

Like Martha the Passenger Pigeon, the last of this colorful species died at Cincinnati Zoo on February 21, 1918.

COMMON AND RARE

MOST ABUNDANT CLASSES OF ANIMAL

1   Insects and spiders

At least 5,000,000,000,000,000 individuals. Among the most common insects are ants, fleas, flies, and the little-known springtails, which inhabit moist topsoil the world over. The latter alone probably outnumber the human race.

2   Crustaceans

Besides crabs, sowbugs, and so on, this class also includes the krill and other tiny shrimp-like creatures that form a major ingredient in plankton, the mainstay of life in the oceans.

3   Worms

Earthworms and other tubelike animals, including parasitic worms, can occur in great numbers in some habitats: more than 1,000,000 earthworms were counted in 1 acre/0.4 hectare of British farmland. But their distribution is variable compared with the teeming arthropods higher up the list.

4   Fish

Total fish population of the world's oceans has been estimated at around 838,000,000 tons – at least 100,000,000,000,000 individuals.

5   Mollusks

Includes snails, slugs, most shellfish, squids and octopus, and many tiny animals in the plankton horde.

6   Amphibians

Frogs, toads, newts, and the like: an estimated trillion (1,000,000,000,000) creatures.

7   Birds

Many birds share human habitats yet avoid conflict with us, so have the edge in numbers over most other larger wildlife outside the oceans. There are probably about 100,000,000,000 birds in the world and the most common must include poultry species and town inhabitants such as the sparrows.

8   Mammals (excluding humans)

Despite exploding human numbers and heavy pressures on many rare mammal species in the wild, other mammals probably still outnumber humans by at least four to one, boosted by the huge numbers of herd animals, pets, and "commensal" or scavenging animals such as rats and mice that share our habitat.

9   Humans

The baby that pushed the world's human population meter past the 5,000,000,000 mark was in all probability born in 1987.

10   Reptiles

Reptiles never recovered from the unknown cataclysm that finished off the dinosaurs, well before Homo sapiens arrived on the scene. Now largely through conflict and competition with humans, the world's snakes, lizards, turtles, crocodiles, and other scaly-skinned beasts are once more in decline and may number fewer than 2,000,000,000 individuals at present.

Microbes exist in staggering numbers: some nine trillion (9,000,000,000,000) of medium size could be packed into a box with sides 1 in/2.5 cm long. But whether they are plants, animals, both, or neither is a matter of endless debate and we shall therefore disregard them.

Of animals that can be seen without a microscope, insects unquestionably top the numbers league: there are at least 1,000,000 insects for each of the Earth's 5,554,552,000 humans. Put together, they would weigh at least 12 times as much as the human race and at least three times more than the combined weight of all other living animals.

Estimates of the populations of other classes are at best "guesstimates," and this Top 10 should be viewed as a general picture of the relative numbers of each type of animal.

GROUPS WITH MOST KNOWN SPECIES

	Group	Approx. no. of known species
1	Insects	750–800,000
2	Higher plants	248,000
3	Noninsect arthropods (crustaceans, spiders, etc.)	123,000
4	Fungi	69,000
5	Mollusks	50,000
6	Algae	27,000
7=	Roundworms	12,000
7=	Flatworms	12,000
7=	Earthworms	12,000
10	Birds	9,000

The total number of known species is about 1,400,000. Approximately 27,000 species become extinct annually, principally in rainforests.

TOP 10

MOST ENDANGERED MAMMALS IN THE WORLD

Mammal	Number
1= Tasmanian wolf	?
1= Halcon fruit bat	?
1= Ghana fat mouse	?
4 Kouprey	10
5 Javan rhinoceros	50
6 Iriomote cat	60
7 Black lion tamarin	130
8 Pygmy hog	150
9 Tamaraw	200
10 Indus dolphin	400

The first three mammals on the list have not been seen for many years and may well be extinct, but zoologists are hopeful of the possibility of their survival: the Tasmanian wolf, for example, has been technically extinct since the last specimen died in a zoo in 1936, but occasional unconfirmed sightings suggest that there may still be animals in the wild, and a 1,601,240-acre/ 648,000-hectare nature reserve has been set aside for it in Tasmania in the expectation that it will be found again. The only Halcon fruit bat that has ever been seen is one that was discovered in the Philippines in 1937. (Another bat, the Tanzanian woolly bat, was discovered in the 1870s but has not been observed since, and is assumed to be extinct.)

All the species on this list, which is ranked in order of rarity, face global extinction – unlike many species that may be at serious risk in one area but flourishing elsewhere. Some species that would once have been on the "most endangered" list, such as the Arabian oryx, were "extinct" in the wild, but have been successfully bred in captivity and reintroduced into their natural habitats.

TOP 10

RAREST MARINE MAMMALS

Mammal	Estimated no.
1 Caribbean monk seal	200
2 Mediterranean monk seal	300–400
3 Juan Fernandez fur seal	750
4 West Indian manatee	1,000
5 Guadeloupe fur seal	1,600
6 New Zealand fur seal	2,000
7= Hooker's sea lion	4,000
7= Right whale	4,400
9 Fraser's dolphin	7,800
10 Amazon manatee	8,000

The hunting of seals for their fur and of whales for oil and other products, combined in many instances with the depletion of their natural food resources by the fishing industry, has resulted in a sharp decline in the population of many marine mammals. Populations of some species of seal formerly numbering in the millions have shrunk to a few thousand and it has been estimated that the world population of humpback whales has dwindled from 100,000 to 10,000.

TOP 10

COUNTRIES WITH THE MOST ELEPHANTS

Country	Elephants
1 Zaïre	195,000
2 Tanzania	100,000
3 Gabon	76,000
4 Congo	61,000
5 Botswana	51,000
6 Zimbabwe	43,000
7 Zambia	41,000
8 Sudan	40,000
9 Kenya	35,000
10 Cameroon	21,000

All the countries in the Top 10 are in Africa, which in 1987 was believed to have a total elephant population of 764,410. India's 20,000 Asian elephants just fail to enter the list and the entire surviving population of Asian elephants in the wild is only a fraction of that of Africa at between 30,000 and 55,000. In addition, about 16,000 tame elephants are found in Myanmar (Burma), India, Thailand, Vietnam, and Cambodia. Estimates of Asian elephant populations are notoriously unreliable as this species is exclusively a forest animal and its numbers cannot be sampled using aerial survey techniques. The same is true of the forest variety of African elephant, distributed in heavily wooded countries such as Gabon or Zaïre, as distinct from the savannah elephant found in the wide-open spaces of scantily wooded countries including Tanzania and Zimbabwe, and this problem may account for widely varying estimates of elephant populations in such countries.

CREATURES GREAT AND SMALL

Diversity is one of the most impressive features of the animal kingdom, and even within a single species huge variations in size can be encountered. There are practical problems that make measurement difficult – it is virtually impossible to weigh an elephant in the wild, or to estimate the flight speed of a speeding bird, for example. The lists therefore represent "likely averages" based on the informed observations of specialized researchers, rather than individual assessments or rare and extreme record-breaking cases.

T O P 1 0

HEAVIEST PRIMATES

	Primate	Length* cm	in	Weight kg	lb
1	Gorilla	200	79	220	485
2	Man	177	70	77	170
3	Orangutan	137	54	75	165
4	Chimpanzee	92	36	50	110
5=	Baboon	100	39	45	99
5=	Mandrill	95	37	45	99
7	Gelada baboon	75	30	25	55
8	Proboscis monkey	76	30	24	53
9	Hanuman langur	107	42	20	44
10	Siamang gibbon	90	35	13	29

* Excluding tail.

The largest primates (including Man) and all the apes are rooted in the Old World (Africa, Asia, and Europe): only one member of a New World species of monkeys (the Guatemalan howler at 36 in/91 cm; 20 lb/9 kg) is a close contender for the Top 10. The difference between the prosimians (primitive primates), great apes, lesser apes, and monkeys has more to do with shape than size, although the great apes top most of the list anyway. Lower down the list, the longer, skinnier, and lighter forms of the lemurs, langurs, gibbons, and monkeys, designed for serious monkeying around in trees, send the length column haywire.

T O P 1 0

HEAVIEST TERRESTRIAL MAMMALS

	Mammal	Length m	ft	Weight kg	lb
1	African elephant	7.2	23.6	5,000	11,023
2	Great Indian rhinoceros	4.2	13.8	4,000	8,818
3	Hippopotamus	4.9	16.1	2,000	4,409
4	Giraffe	5.8	19.0	1,200	2,646
5	American bison	3.9	12.8	1,000	2,205
6	Grizzly bear	3.0	9.8	780	1,720
7	Arabian camel (dromedary)	3.0	9.8	600	1,323
8	Moose	3.0	9.8	595	1,312
9	Tiger	2.8	9.2	300	661
10	Gorilla	2.0	6.6	220	485

The list excludes domesticated cattle and horses. It also avoids comparing close kin such as the African and Indian elephants, highlighting instead the sumo stars within distinctive large mammal groups such as the bears, deer, big cats, primates, and bovines (oxlike mammals). Sizes are not necessarily the top of the known range: records exist, for instance, of African elephant specimens weighing more than 13,228 lb/6,000 kg.

T O P 1 0

LARGEST CARNIVORES

	Animal	Length m	ft	in	Weight kg	lb
1	Southern elephant seal	6.5	21	4	3,500	7,716
2	Walrus	3.8	12	6	1,200	2,646
3	Steller sea lion	3.0	9	8	1,100	2,425
4	Grizzly bear	3.0	9	8	780	1,720
5	Polar bear	2.5	8	2	700	1,543
6	Tiger	2.8	9	2	300	661
7	Lion	1.9	6	3	250	551
8	American black bear	1.8	6	0	227	500
9	Giant panda	1.5	5	0	160	353
10	Spectacled bear	1.8	6	0	140	309

Of the 273 species in the mammalian order Carnivora or meat-eaters, many (including its largest representatives on land, the bears) are in fact omnivorous and around 40 specialize in eating fish or insects. All, however, share a common ancestry indicated by the butcher's-knife form of their canine teeth. As the Top 10 would otherwise consist exclusively of seals and related marine carnivores, only three representatives have been included in order to enable the terrestrial heavyweight division to make an appearance. The polar bear is probably the largest land carnivore if shoulder height (when the animal is on all fours) is taken into account: it tops an awesome 5 ft 3 in/1.60 m, compared with the 4 ft/1.20 m of its nearest rival, the grizzly. The common (or least) weasel is probably the smallest carnivore: small specimens are less than 7 in/17 cm long, not counting the tail, and can weigh less than 3 oz (about 80 g).

T O P   1 0

LONGEST ANIMALS

	Animal	Length m	ft	in
1	Blue whale	33.5	110	0
2	Royal python	10.7	35	0
3	Tapeworm	10.0	32	10
4	Whale shark	9.8	32	2
5	African elephant	7.2*	23	7
6	Crocodile	5.9	19	5
7	Giraffe	5.8	19	0
8	Hippopotamus	4.9	16	1
9	Arabian camel (dromedary)	4.1	13	6
10=	Indian bison	3.4	11	2
10=	White rhinoceros	3.4	11	2

* *Trunk to tail.*

The lion's mane jellyfish, which lives in the Arctic Ocean, has tentacles as long as 131 ft/40 m trailing behind it, but its "body" is relatively small, and it has thus not been included. Only one fish (the whale shark is a fish, not a true whale) and one snake have been included.

T O P   1 0

SMALLEST MAMMALS

	Mammal	Weight g	oz	Length cm	in
1	Kitti's hognosed bat	2.0	0.07	2.9	1.1
2	Pygmy shrew	1.5	0.05	3.6	1.4
3	Pipistrelle bat	3.0	0.11	4.0	1.6
4	Little brown bat	8.0	0.28	4.0	1.6
5	Masked shrew	2.4	0.08	4.5	1.8
6	Southern blossom bat	12.0	0.42	5.0	2.0
7	Harvest mouse	5.0	0.18	5.8	2.3
8	Pygmy glider	12.0	0.42	6.0	2.4
9	House mouse	12.0	0.42	6.4	2.5
10	Common shrew	5.0	0.18	6.5	2.5

The pygmy glider and another that does not quite make the Top 10, the pygmy possum, are marsupials, more closely related to kangaroos than to anything else in this list. Some classifications exclude marsupials from the mammal class. Among other contenders for the small world are the water shrew (0.42 oz/12.0 g; 2.8 in/7.0 cm) and bank vole (0.53 oz/15.0 g; 3.2 in/8.0 cm). The Kitti's hognosed bat is represented only by a few specimens in museum collections, so it may well have been short-changed.

T O P   1 0

LONGEST SNAKES

	Snake	Maximum length m	ft
1	Royal python	10.7	35
2	Anaconda	8.5	28
3	Indian python	7.6	25
4	Diamond python	6.4	21
5	King cobra	5.8	19
6	Boa constrictor	4.9	16
7	Bushmaster	3.7	12
8	Giant brown snake	3.4	11
9	Diamondback rattlesnake	2.7	9
10	Indigo or gopher snake	2.4	8

Although the South American anaconda is sometimes claimed to be the longest snake, this has not been authenticated and it seems that the python remains entitled to claim preeminence.

GIANT OF THE SEAS
Probably the largest animal that ever lived, the Blue whale dwarfs even the other whales.

T O P   1 0

HEAVIEST MARINE MAMMALS

	Mammal	Length m	ft	Weight (tons)
1	Blue whale	33.5	110.0	145.0
2	Fin whale	25.0	82.0	50.0
3	Right whale	17.5	57.4	45.0
4	Sperm whale	18.0	59.0	40.0
5	Gray whale	14.0	46.0	36.0
6	Humpback whale	15.0	49.2	29.0
7	Baird's whale	5.5	18.0	12.0
8	Southern elephant seal	6.5	21.3	4.0
9	Northern elephant seal	5.8	19.0	3.7
10	Pilot whale	6.4	21.0	3.2

ANIMAL RECORD-BREAKERS

DEADLIEST SNAKES IN THE WORLD

	Species	Native region
1=	Taipan	Australia and New Guinea

Mortality is nearly 100 percent unless antivenin is administered promptly.

	Species	Native region
1=	Black mamba	Southern and Central Africa

Mortality nearly 100 percent without antivenin.

	Species	Native region
3	Tiger snake	Australia

Very high mortality without antivenin.

	Species	Native region
4	Common krait	South Asia

Up to 50 percent mortality even with antivenin.

	Species	Native region
5	Death adder	Australia

Over 50 percent mortality without antivenin.

	Species	Native region
6	Yellow or Cape cobra	Southern Africa

The most dangerous type of cobra, with high mortality.

	Species	Native region
7	King cobra	India and Southeast Asia

At 16 ft/4.9 m long, the King cobra is the largest poisonous snake in the world. It also injects the most venom into its victims.

	Species	Native region
8=	Bushmaster	Central and South America
8=	Green mamba	Africa
10	Coral snake	North, Central, and South America

Most people fear snakes, but only a few dozen of the 3,000-odd snake species that exist can cause serious harm and many more are beneficial because they prey on vermin and on other snake species of worse repute. The strength of a snake's venom can be measured, but this does not indicate how dangerous it may be: the Australian smooth-scaled snake, for example, is believed to be the most venomous land snake, but no human victims have ever been recorded. The Top 10 takes into account the degree of threat posed by those snakes that have a record of causing fatalities. This is approximate, since such factors as the amount of venom injected and the victim's resistance can vary greatly.

MAMMALS WITH THE LARGEST LITTERS

	Mammal	Average litter
1	Tailless tenrec	21
2	Golden hamster	11
3	Ermine	10
4	Coypu	8.5
5=	European hedgehog	7
5=	African hunting dog	7
7=	Meadow vole	6.5
7=	Wild boar	6.5
9=	Wolf	6
9=	Black-backed jackal	6

These are averages; extreme examples, for instance of pigs with litters of 30 or more, have been recorded. Although the tiny tenrec from Madagascar has similarly produced as many as 31 in a single litter, average mammalian litter sizes are minute when compared with those of other animals. Fish commonly lay more than 10,000 eggs at a time and many amphibians more than 1,000. The most staggeringly prolific creature of all is probably the Ocean sunfish, which lays as many as 300,000,000 eggs.

MAMMALS WITH THE LONGEST GESTATION PERIODS

	Mammal	Average gestation (days)
1	African elephant	660
2	Asian elephant	600
3	Baird's beaked whale	520
4	White rhinoceros	490
5	Walrus	480
6	Giraffe	460
7	Tapir	400
8	Arabian camel (dromedary)	390
9	Fin whale	370
10	Llama	360

The 480-day gestation of the walrus includes a delay of up to five months while the fertilized embryo is held as a blastocyst (a sphere of cells) but is not implanted until later in the wall of the uterus. This option enables offspring to be produced at the most favorable time of the year. Human gestation (ranging from 253 to 303 days) is exceeded not only by the Top 10 mammals but also by others including the porpoise, horse, and water buffalo.

MAMMALS WITH THE SHORTEST GESTATION PERIODS

	Mammal	Average gestation (days)
1	Short-nosed bandicoot*	12
2	Opossum*	13
3	Shrew	14
4	Golden hamster	15
5=	Lemming	20
5=	Mouse	20
7	Rat	21
8	Gerbil	24
9=	Mole	28
9=	Rabbit	28

* *These animals are marsupials. Their young are not fully developed when they are born and they are transferred into a "pouch" to continue their development.*

TOP 10

FASTEST MAMMALS IN THE WORLD

Mammal	Maximum recorded speed km/h	mph		Mammal	Maximum recorded speed km/h	mph
1 Cheetah	105	65		**5=** Thomson's gazelle	76	47
2 Pronghorn antelope	89	55		**7** Brown hare	72	45
3= Mongolian gazelle	80	50		**8** Horse	69	43
3= Springbok	80	50		**9=** Greyhound	68	42
5= Grant's gazelle	76	47		**9=** Red deer	68	42

Although some authorities have alleged higher speeds, this list is based on data from reliable sources using accurate methods of measurement. In addition to these speeds, estimated over distances of up to ¼ mile/0.4 km, charging lions can achieve 50 mph/ 80 km/h over very short distances, while various members of the antelope family, wildebeests, elks, dogs, coyotes, foxes, hyenas, zebras, and Mongolian wild asses have all been credited with unsustained spurts of 64 km/h/40 mph or more. Just failing to make the list is the Sei whale, the fastest of the large sea mammals at 40.2 mph/64 km/h.

TOP 10

FASTEST FISH IN THE WORLD

Fish	Maximum recorded speed km/h	mph
1 Sailfish	110	68
2 Marlin	80	50
3 Bluefin tuna	74	46
4 Yellowfin tuna	70	44
5 Blue shark	69	43
6 Wahoo	66	41
7= Bonefish	64	40
7= Swordfish	64	40
9 Tarpon	56	35
10 Tiger shark	53	33

TOP 10

LONGEST-LIVED ANIMALS

(*Excluding humans*)

Animal	Maximum age (years)
1 Quahog (marine clam)	up to 200
2 Giant tortoise	150
3 Greek tortoise	110
4 Killer whale	90
5 European eel	88
6 Lake sturgeon	82
7 Sea anemone	80
8 Elephant	78
9 Freshwater mussel	75
10 Andean condor	70

The ages of animals in the wild are difficult to determine with accuracy since the precise birth and death dates of relatively few long-lived animals have ever been recorded. There are clues, such as annual growth of shells, teeth, and, in the case of whales, even ear wax. The Top 10 represents documented maximum ages of animals attained by more than one example – although there may well be extreme cases of animals exceeding these life spans. Although there are alleged instances of parrots living to ages of 80 years or more, few stand up to scrutiny.

TOP 10

LAZIEST ANIMALS IN THE WORLD

Animal	Average hours of sleep
1 Koala	22
2 Sloth	20
3= Armadillo	19
3= Opossum	19
5 Lemur	16
6= Hamster	14
6= Squirrel	14
8= Cat	13
8= Pig	13
10 Spiny anteater	12

The list excludes periods of hibernation, which can last up to several months among creatures such as the ground squirrel, marmot, and brown bear. At the other end of the scale comes the frantic shrew, which has to hunt and eat constantly or perish: it literally has no time for sleep. The incredible swift contrives to sleep on the wing, "turning off" alternate halves of its brain for shifts of two hours or more. Flight control is entrusted to whichever hemisphere is on duty at the time.

TOP 10

MOST INTELLIGENT MAMMALS

1	Man
2	Chimpanzee
3	Gorilla
4	Orangutan
5	Baboon
6	Gibbon
7	Monkey
8	Smaller toothed whale
9	Dolphin
10	Elephant

This list is based on research conducted by Edward O. Wilson, Professor of Zoology at Harvard University, who defined intelligence as speed and extent of learning performance over a wide range of tasks, also taking into account the ratio of the animal's brain size to its body bulk. It may come as a surprise that the dog does not make the Top 10, and that if Man is excluded, No. 10 becomes the pig.

BIRDS

FASTEST BIRDS IN THE WORLD

	Bird	Maximum recorded speed km/h	mph
1	Spine-tailed swift	171	106
2	Frigate bird	153	95
3	Spur-winged goose	142	88
4	Red-breasted merganser	129	80
5	White-rumped swift	124	77
6	Canvasback duck	116	72
7	Eider duck	113	70
8	Teal	109	68
9=	Mallard	105	65
9=	Pintail	105	65

Until airplane pilots cracked 190 mph/ 306 km/h/ in 1919, birds were the fastest animals on Earth: stooping (diving) peregrine falcons clock up speeds approaching 185 mph/298 km/h. However, most comparisons of air speed in birds rule out diving or wind-assisted flight: most small birds in migration can manage a ground speed of 60 mph/97 km/h to 70 mph/113 km/h if there is even a moderate following wind. This list therefore picks out star performers among the medium- to large-sized birds (mainly waterfowl) that do not need help from wind or gravity to hit their top speed.

RAREST BIRDS IN THE WORLD

	Bird	Pairs reported
1	Echo parakeet (Mauritius)	1
2	Mauritius kestrel	3
3	Mauritius parakeet	4
4	Cuban ivory-billed woodpecker	8
5	Madagascar sea eagle	10
6=	Pink pigeon (Mauritius)	12
6=	Magpie robin (Seychelles)	12
8	Imperial Amazon parrot	15
9	Siberian crane	25
10	Tomba bowerbird (Papua New Guinea)	30

Several rarer bird species are known from single sightings but are assumed to be extinct in the absence of records of breeding pairs. With nowhere to seek refuge, rare species come under pressure on islands such as Mauritius, where the dodo met its fate in the 18th century. Petrels spend much of their lives far from land, so their numbers are virtually impossible to determine.

LARGEST FLIGHTED BIRDS

	Bird	Weight kg	lb	oz
1	Great bustard	20.9	46	1
2	Trumpeter swan	16.8	37	1
3	Mute swan	16.3	35	15
4=	Wandering albatross	15.8	34	13
4=	Whooper swan	15.8	34	13
6	Manchurian crane	14.9	32	14
7	Kori bustard	13.6	30	0
8	Gray pelican	13.0	28	11
9	Black vulture	12.5	27	8
10	Griffon vulture	12.0	26	7

Wing size does not necessarily correspond to weight in flighted birds. The 13-ft/4-m wingspan of the marabou stork beats all the birds listed here, yet its body weight is usually no heavier than any of these. When laden with a meal of carrion, however, the marabou can double its weight and needs all the lift it can get to take off. It usually has to wait until dinner is digested.

TOP 10

LARGEST FLIGHTLESS BIRDS

	Bird	Weight			Height	
		kg	lb	oz	cm	in
1	Ostrich	156.5	345	0	274.3	108.0
2	Emu	40.0	88	3	152.4	60.0
3	Cassowary	33.5	73	14	152.4	60.0
4	Rhea	25.0	55	2	137.1	54.0
5	Kiwi	29.0	63	15	114.3	45.0
6	Emperor penguin	29.4	64	13	114.0	44.9
7	King penguin	15.8	34	13	94.0	37.0
8	Gentoo penguin	5.4	11	14	71.0	28.0
9=	Adelie penguin	4.9	10	13	71.0	28.0
9=	Magellanic penguin	4.9	10	13	71.0	28.0

There are 46 living and 16 recently extinct flightless birds on record. The largest bird in recorded history was the flightless "elephant bird" (*Aepyornis*) of Madagascar. It weighed around 966 lb/438 kg and stood 10 ft/3 m tall. Its eggs were nearly 15 in/38 cm long and weighed over 40 lb/18 kg. The smallest known bird, the bee hummingbird, weighs 0.06 oz/1.7 g and measures 2.5 in/6.4 cm from beak to tail. Almost 100,000 bee hummingbirds would be needed to balance one ostrich on a pair of scales.

OSTRICH
An ostrich, when running, can reach a speed of 40 mph/64 km/h.

TOP 10

HIGHEST-FUNDED BIRD RECOVERY PROGRAMS IN THE US

	Bird	Amount spent ($)*
1	Bald eagle	24,651,000
2	Florida scrub jay	19,733,000
3	Northern spotted owl	12,856,000
4	Red-cockaded woodpecker	7,063,000
5	American peregrine falcon	5,986,000
6	Least Bell's vireo	2,363,000
7	Whooping crane	2,331,000
8	Masked bobwhite	2,140,000
9	California clapper rail	1,783,000
10	Brown pelican	1,704,000

* Fiscal year 1991
Source: US Fish and Wildlife Service

SPIRIT OF A NATION
The bald eagle, a national symbol of the United States, is protected under the National Emblem Act (1940).

TOP 10

MOST COMMON BREEDING BIRDS IN THE US

	Bird
1	Red-winged blackbird
2	House sparrow
3	Mourning dove
4	European starling
5	American robin
6	Horned lark
7	Common grackle
8	American crow
9	Western meadowlark
10	Brown-headed cowbird

This list, based on research carried out by the Breeding Bird Survey of the US Fish and Wildlife Service, ranks birds breeding in the US, with the red-winged blackbird (*Agelaius phoeniceus*) heading the list. Found throughout the United States, except in extreme desert and mountain regions, its population has grown from 25,6000,000 estimated in 1983 to more than 30,000,000 today.

CATS, DOGS, AND OTHER PETS

MOST POPULAR DOG BREEDS IN THE US

	Breed	No. registered by American Kennel Club, Inc. (1992)
1	Labrador Retriever	120,879
2	Rottweiler	95,445
3	Cocker Spaniel	91,925
4	German Shepherd	76,941
5	Poodle	73,449
6	Golden Retriever	69,850
7	Beagle	60,661
8	Dachshund	50,046
9	Shetland Sheepdog	43,449
10	Chow chow	42,670

DOGS' NAMES IN THE UK

	Female	Male
1	Sheba	Ben
2	Sam(antha)	Max
3	Bess	Sam
4	Gemma	Pip
5	Rosie	Duke
6	Megan	Prince
7	Lucky	Captain
8	Sandy	Tyson
9	Bonnie	Butch
10	Cindy	Oscar

It is interesting to note the difference in favorite dogs' names in the UK and the US; Prince and Sam are the only two that are common to both countries.

DOGS' NAMES IN THE US

1	Lady
2	King
3	Duke
4	Peppy
5	Prince
6	Pepper
7	Snoopy
8	Princess
9	Heidi
10=	Sam
10=	Coco

The names on this list come from a recent study of male and female names on US dog licenses. The same list also revealed several bizarre names, including Beowulf, Bikini, Fag, Rembrandt, and Twit. Lassie, popularized by films from 1942 onward, has declined to 82nd position, while Rover is in a humble 161st place.

MOST POPULAR PETS IN THE US

	Pet	% of US households
1	Dogs	36.5
2	Cats	30.9
3	Birds	5.7
4=	Fish	2.8
4=	Horses	2.8
6	Rabbits	1.5
7	Hamsters	1.0
8	Guinea pigs	0.5
9	Gerbils	0.3
10	Ferrets	0.2

While this survey indicates numbers of households owning companion pets, owners frequently have more than one: the average is 1.5 in the case of dogs, and 2.0 for cats, and hence the estimated populations for each are 52,500,000 and 57,000,00 respectively, cats thereby outnumbering dogs.

Source: American Veterinary Medical Association

TRICKS BY DOGS IN THE US

	Trick	Dogs performing
1	Sit	5,313,105
2	Shake paw	3,795,075
3	Roll over	2,884,257
4	"Speak"	2,681,853
5=	Lie down	1,872,237
5=	Stand on hind legs	1,872,237
7	Beg	1,821,636
8	Dance	1,543,331
9	"Sing"	759,015
10	Fetch newspaper	430,508

A survey conducted by the Pet Food Institute and a US pet food manufacturer produced these astonishingly precise statistics for the tricks performed by 25,300,500 of the alleged 41,361,183 dogs in the country. Surprisingly for such a religious nation, only 379,508 were claimed to "say prayers."

DID YOU KNOW

THE WORLD'S LONGEST WALKIES

Fortean Times, "The Journal of Strange Phenomena", conducted an investigation into stories of dogs walking huge distances to return to their owners. They considered many well-documented cases such as that of Spook, a German Shepherd lost overboard off the coast of British Columbia in 1976, who not only swam ashore but walked back to his owners' former home in Sacramento, California, but their long-distance champion was a collie named Bobbie. On August 15, 1923, Bobbie, from Silverton, Oregon, was lost during a visit to Wolcott, Indiana. Exactly six months later, he turned up in Silverton, disheveled and exhausted after having trekked about 3,000 miles over some of the harshest terrain in America.

TOP 10

CATS' NAMES IN THE US

	Female	Male		Female	Male
1	Samantha	Tiger/Tigger	6	Angel/Angela	Snoopy
2	Misty	Smokey	7	Ginger	Morris
3	Patches	Pepper	8	Tiger/Tigger	Mickey
4	Cali/Calico	Max/Maxwell	9	Princess	Rusty/Rusti
5	Muffin	Simon	10	Punkin/Pumpkin	Boots/Bootsie

TOP 10

LIVE PARROT TRADERS IN THE WORLD

	IMPORTERS				EXPORTERS	
	Country	No. per annum			Country	No. per annum
1	US	305,997		1	Argentina	177,992
2	Germany*	60,564		2	Tanzania	84,220
3	UK	34,520		3	Indonesia	58,832
4	Netherlands	27,822		4	Guyana	30,324
5	Japan	27,790		5	Sierra Leone	28,430
6	Belgium	20,357		6	Uruguay	20,967
7	France	18,843		7	Peru	17,032
8	Sweden	16,454		8	Honduras	15,816
9	Spain	11,406		9	India	15,445
10	Canada	9,551		10	Malaysia	15,012

Includes figures for the former German Democratic Republic (65 imports and 3,263 exports)

TOP 10

PEDIGREE CAT BREEDS IN THE US

	Breed	Total registered
1	Persian	48,010
2	Maine Coon	3,549
3	Siamese	2,979
4	Abyssinian	2,360
5	Exotic Shorthair	1,388
6	Scottish Fold	1,282
7	Oriental Shorthair	1,219
8	American Shorthair	1,140
9	Birman	932
10	Burmese	930

The biggest increase in popularity over the past 10 years has been for the Exotic Shorthair, which has leaped from 14th in 1982 to its current No. 5 position.

Source: Cat Fancier's Association

DID YOU KNOW

PITY POLLY...

Parrots are popular pets, but some species are growing rare in the wild as more and more birds are captured and exported each year. Amsterdam used to be a major import route until the Netherlands joined CITES (Convention on International Trade in Endangered Species) in 1984; over 33,000 live parrots passed through Schiphol Airport in 18 months during 1980–81. Many do not survive the often inhumane conditions in which they are transported. Trade in live parrots (apart from those listed as threatened under CITES) is not illegal so long as numbers are reported, but abuses are rife.

TOP 10

MOST INTELLIGENT DOGS

1	Border Collie		6	Shetland Sheepdog
2	Poodle		7	Labrador Retriever
3=	German Shepherd (Alsatian)		8	Papillon
3=	Golden Retriever		9	Rottweiler
5	Doberman Pinscher		10	Australian Cattle Dog

For his 1994 book *The Intelligence of Dogs*, psychology professor and pet trainer Stanley Coren put 133 breeds through a series of work and obedience tests. Surprise results included the bloodhound's lowly 128th place, while the Afghan Hound was bottom of the class.

TOP 10

CATS' NAMES IN THE UK

(Based on an RSPCA survey conducted during National Pet Week, 1991)

1	Sooty
2	Tigger
3	Tiger
4	Smokey
5	Ginger
6	Tom
7	Fluffy
8	Lucy
9	Sam
10	Lucky

LIVESTOCK

T O P 1 0

TYPES OF LIVESTOCK IN THE WORLD

	Animal	World total
1	Chickens	11,279,000,000
2	Cattle	1,284,188,000
3	Sheep	1,138,363,000
4	Pigs	864,096,000
5	Ducks	580,000,000
6	Goats	574,181,000
7	Turkeys	259,000,000
8	Buffaloes	147,520,000
9	Horses	60,843,000
10	Donkeys	44,270,000

The world chicken population is more than double the human population, while the world's cattle population outnumbers the population of China. There are more pigs in the world than the entire population of India, and enough turkeys for every single American citizen to have one each for Thanksgiving.

T O P 1 0

CHICKEN COUNTRIES

	Country	Chickens
1	China	2,179,000,000
2	US	1,437,000,000
3	Russia	628,000,000
4	Indonesia	600,000,000
5	Brazil	570,000,000
6	India	410,000,000
7	Japan	335,000,000
8	Mexico	282,000,000
9	Ukraine	233,000,000
10	France	208,000,000
	World total	11,279,000,000

The Top 10 countries have 61 percent of the world's chicken population. In the US the estimated chicken population outnumbers the human population more than five times over.

T O P 1 0

CATTLE COUNTRIES

	Country	Cattle
1	India	192,650,000
2	Brazil	153,000,000
3	US	99,559,000
4	China	82,760,000
5	Russia	54,677,000
6	Argentina	50,020,000
7	Ethiopia	31,000,000
8	Mexico	30,157,000
9	Colombia	24,772,000
10=	Bangladesh	23,700,000
10=	Ukraine	23,700,000
	World total	1,284,188,000

The Top 10 – or in this instance 11 – countries own almost 60 percent of the world's cattle. The cattle population of the US is equivalent to more than one animal for every three people.

T O P 1 0

GOAT COUNTRIES

	Country	Goats
1	India	117,000,000
2	China	95,032,000
3	Pakistan	38,564,000
4	Nigeria	24,000,000
5	Iran	23,500,000
6	Sudan	18,700,000
7	Ethiopia	18,100,000
8	Bangladesh	18,000,000
9	Brazil	12,000,000
10	Indonesia	11,400,000
	World total	574,181,000

The goat is one of the most widely distributed of all domesticated animals, because its resilience to diseases such as the tuberculosis that affect cattle and its adaptability to harsh conditions make it ideally suited to less developed countries.

T O P 1 0

TURKEY COUNTRIES

	Country	Turkeys
1	US	90,000,000
2	France	32,000,000
3	Russia	24,000,000
4	Italy	23,000,000
5=	Ukraine	10,000,000
5=	UK	10,000,000
7=	Brazil	6,000,000
7=	Mexico	6,000,000
7=	Portugal	6,000,000
10=	Argentina	5,000,000
10=	Canada	5,000,000
	World total	259,000,000

Some 88 percent of the world's turkeys are found in the Top 10 countries – with the largest number, appropriately, in the US, their area of origin.

T O P 1 0

BUFFALO COUNTRIES

	Country	Buffaloes
1	India	78,550,000
2	China	21,983,000
3	Pakistan	18,273,000
4	Thailand	4,793,000
5	Indonesia	3,400,000
6	Nepal	3,058,000
7	Egypt	3,036,000
8	Vietnam	2,867,000
9	Philippines	2,569,000
10	Myanmar (Burma)	2,099,000
	World total	147,520,000

More than 95 percent of the world's total buffalo population resides in the Top 10 countries. Only two European countries have significant herds: Romania with 180,000 and Italy (where buffalo milk is used to make mozzarella cheese) with 83,000.

TOP 10

SHEEP COUNTRIES

	Country	Sheep
1	Australia	146,820,000
2	China	111,143,000
3	New Zealand	53,500,000
4	Russia	52,535,000
5	Iran	45,000,000
6	India	44,407,000
7	Turkey	40,433,000
8	Kazakhstan	33,908,000
9	South Africa	32,100,000
10	UK	28,932,000
	World total	*1,138,363,000*

This is one of the few world lists in which the UK ranks considerably higher than the US, which has only 10,750,000 head of sheep. The Falkland Islands have 713,000 sheep to a human population of 2,121 (336 sheep per person), followed by New Zealand (16 sheep per person).

TOP 10

PIG COUNTRIES

	Country	Pigs
1	China	379,739,000
2	US	57,684,000
3	Russia	35,384,000
4	Brazil	33,050,000
5	Germany	26,063,000
6	Poland	22,086,000
7	Ukraine	17,800,000
8	Spain	17,240,000
9	Mexico	16,502,000
10	Netherlands	13,727,000
	World total	*864,096,000*

The distribution of the world's pig population is determined by cultural, religious, and dietary factors – few pigs are found in African and Islamic countries, for example – so there is a disproportionate concentration of pigs in those countries that do not have such prohibitions.

TOP 10

DUCK COUNTRIES

	Country	Ducks
1	China	381,000,000
2=	India	30,000,000
2=	Vietnam	30,000,000
4	France	18,000,000
5	Thailand	17,000,000
6	Bangladesh	12,000,000
7	Philippines	9,000,000
8	Egypt	8,000,000
9=	Mexico	7,000,000
9=	Poland	7,000,000
	World total	*580,000,000*

While it is extraordinary to consider that 66 percent of the world's domestic ducks live in China, an examination of the menu of any Chinese restaurant reveals the duck's major role in oriental cuisine. In contrast, British ducks number barely 2,000,000.

TOP 10

HORSE COUNTRIES

	Country	Horses
1	China	10,201,000
2	Brazil	6,200,000
3	Mexico	6,180,000
4	US	5,450,000
5	Argentina	3,300,000
6	Ethiopia	2,750,000
7	Russia	2,610,000
8	Mongolia	2,300,000
9	Colombia	2,006,000
10	Kazakhstan	1,523,000
	World total	*60,843,000*

Mongolia makes an appearance in few Top 10 lists – but here it scores doubly since it is also the only country in the world where humans are outnumbered by horses. Throughout the world the horse population has declined as they have been replaced by motor vehicles.

TOP 10

DONKEY COUNTRIES

	Country	Donkeys
1	China	11,200,000
2	Ethiopia	5,200,000
3	Pakistan	3,650,000
4	Mexico	3,189,000
5	Iran	1,935,000
6	Egypt	1,550,000
7	India	1,500,000
8	Brazil	1,350,000
9	Afghanistan	1,300,000
10	Nigeria	1,000,000
	World total	*44,270,000*

The donkey is used extensively throughout the world as a beast of burden, although its role in such countries as the UK (with an estimated donkey population of around 10,000) has been largely reduced to providing rides for children.

DID YOU KNOW

"THE SHIP OF THE DESERT": CAMEL FACTS

The camel is outside the livestock Top 10, but has a respectable world population of over 17,000,000.

There are over 10,000,000 camels in the top five countries – Somalia, Sudan, India, Pakistan, and Ethiopia.

Camels were native to North America about 2,000,000 years ago and in the 19th century lived in the wild in the southwest and western US, descendants of a herd introduced by the government in 1856.

"The straw that broke the camel's back" is a graphic but untrue saying: camels can carry enormous loads but if they are overladen will simply refuse to get up.

Camel-hair brushes are made not from camel hair but the hair from squirrels' tails.

The camel is a relative of the South American llama.

FRUIT SALAD

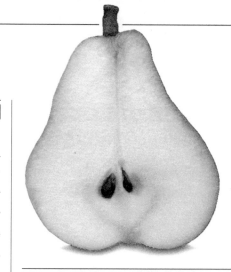

TOP 10
FRUIT CROPS IN THE WORLD

Crop	Annual production (metric tonnes)
1 Grapes	60,655,000
2 Bananas	49,630,000
3 Apples	43,087,000
4 Coconuts	41,044,000
5 Plantains	26,797,000
6 Mangoes	16,987,000
7 Pears	10,692,000
8 Pineapples	10,490,000
9 Peaches and nectarines	10,076,000
10 Oranges	8,465,000

TOP 10
COCONUT-PRODUCING COUNTRIES

Country	Annual production (metric tonnes)
1 Indonesia	13,015,000
2 Philippines	8,465,000
3 India	7,430,000
4 Sri Lanka	1,750,000
5 Thailand	1,353,000
6 Malaysia	1,087,000
7 Vietnam	1,050,000
8 Mexico	989,000
9 Brazil	878,000
10 Papua New Guinea	780,000
World total	*41,044,000*

TOP 10
PEAR-PRODUCING COUNTRIES

Country	Annual production (metric tonnes)
1 China	2,830,000
2 Italy	1,135,000
3 US	862,000
4 Spain	602,000
5 Germany	537,000
6 Japan	452,000
7 Argentina	420,000
8 Turkey	415,000
9 France	394,000
10 Turkey	370,000
World total	*10,692,000*

TOP 10
GRAPE-PRODUCING COUNTRIES

Country	Annual production (metric tonnes)
1 Italy	10,178,000
2 France	8,514,000
3 Spain	5,676,000
4 US	5,508,000
5 Turkey	3,460,000
6 Argentina	1,821,000
7 Iran	1,650,000
8= Portugal	1,450,000
8= South Africa	1,450,000
10 Greece	1,300,000
World total	*60,655,000*

TOP 10
BANANA-PRODUCING COUNTRIES

Country	Annual production (metric tonnes)
1 India	7,000,000
2 Brazil	5,650,000
3 Philippines	3,900,000
4 Ecuador	3,600,000
5 Indonesia	2,500,000
6 China	2,200,000
7 Colombia	1,900,000
8 Burundi	1,645,000
9 Costa Rica	1,633,000
10 Thailand	1,630,000
World total	*49,630,000*

TOP 10
MANGO-PRODUCING COUNTRIES

Country	Annual production (metric tonnes)
1 India	10,000,000
2 Mexico	1,120,000
3 Pakistan	800,000
4 Indonesia	700,000
5= China	615,000
5= Thailand	615,000
7 US	597,000
8 Brazil	400,000
9 Philippines	290,000
10 Haiti	230,000
World total	*16,987,000*

T O P 1 0

APPLE-PRODUCING COUNTRIES

	Country	Annual production (metric tonnes)
1	US	4,876,000
2	China	4,817,000
3	Former USSR#	4,500,000
4	Germany	3,206,000
5	Italy	2,402,000
6	France	2,324,000
7	Turkey	2,000,000
8	Poland	1,570,000
9	Iran	1,520,000
10=	Argentina	1,110,000
10=	India	1,110,000
	World total	43,087,000

Figures for post-dissolution USSR not yet available.

Spain and Japan are the only other countries in the world with annual apple production of more than 1,000,000 tonnes. Having steadily declined during the 1980s in the face of cheap imports, the UK's commercial production of apples has recently increased again and in 1992 totalled 377,000 tonnes.

ORANGE-PRODUCING COUNTRIES

	Country	Annual production (metric tonnes)
1	Brazil	19,640,000
2	US	8,038,000
3	China	5,090,000
4	Mexico	2,850,000
5	Spain	2,724,000
6	India	1,900,000
7	Italy	1,803,000
8	Egypt	1,690,000
9	Iran	1,300,000
10	Pakistan	1,150,000
	World total	57,048,000

During the 1980s, orange production progressively increased from a world total of less than 40,000,000 tonnes. China's production, in particular, rocketed up almost sevenfold during the decade, from under 800,000 tonnes to its present 3rd position in the world league table.

PINEAPPLE-PRODUCING COUNTRIES

	Country	Annual production (metric tonnes)
1	Thailand	1,900,000
2	Philippines	1,170,000
3	China	1,000,000
4	India	820,000
5	Brazil	800,000
6	Vietnam	500,000
7	US	499,000
8	Indonesia	380,000
9	Colombia	347,000
10	Mexico	299,000
	World total	43,087,000

PEACH- AND NECTARINE-PRODUCING COUNTRIES

	Country	Annual production (metric tonnes)
1	Italy	1,886,000
2	US	1,419,000
3	Greece	1,120,000
4	Spain	964,000
5	China	932,000
6	France	520,000
7	Former USSR	350,000
8	Turkey	270,000
9	Argentina	250,000
10	Chile	223,000
	World total	10,076,000

PLANTAIN-PRODUCING COUNTRIES

	Country	Annual production (metric tonnes)
1	Uganda	8,099,000
2	Rwanda	2,900,000
3	Colombia	2,745,000
4	Zaïre	1,830,000
5	Nigeria	1,350,000
6	Ghana	1,200,000
7	Ivory Coast	1,170,000
8	Ecuador	930,000
9	Cameroon	860,000
10	Tanzania	794,000
	World total	26,797,000

TOP OF THE CROPS

TOP 10

FOOD CROPS IN THE WORLD

	Country	Annual production (metric tonnes)
1	Sugar cane	1,104,580,000
2	Wheat	563,649,000
3	Corn	526,410,000
4	Rice	525,475,000
5	Sugar beet	279,991,000
6	Potatoes	268,492,000
7	Barley	160,134,000
8	Cassava	152,218,000
9	Sweet potatoes	128,016,000
10	Soybeans	114,011,000

TOP 10

SUGAR CANE-GROWING COUNTRIES IN THE WORLD

	Country	Annual production (metric tonnes)
1	Brazil	270,672,000
2	India	249,300,000
3	China	77,548,000
4	Cuba	58,000,000
5	Thailand	46,805,000
6	Mexico	39,955,000
7	Pakistan	38,865,000
8	Australia	29,300,000
9	Colombia	28,930,000
10	Philippines	27,300,000
	World total	*1,104,580,000*

TOP 10

WHEAT-GROWING COUNTRIES IN THE WORLD

	Country	Annual production (metric tonnes)
1	China	101,003,000
2	US	66,920,000
3	India	55,084,000
4	Russia	46,000,000
5	France	32,600,000
6	Canada	29,870,000
7	Ukraine	19,473,000
8	Turkey	19,318,000
9	Kazakhstan	18,500,000
10	Pakistan	15,684,000
	World total	*563,649,000*

TOP 10

CORN-GROWING COUNTRIES IN THE WORLD

	Country	Annual production (metric tonnes)
1	US	240,774,000
2	China	95,340,000
3	Brazil	30,619,000
4	Mexico	14,997,000
5	France	14,613,000
6	Argentina	10,699,000
7	India	9,740,000
8	Indonesia	7,947,000
9	Italy	7,170,000
10	Romania	6,829,000
	World total	*526,410,000*

TOP 10

RICE-GROWING COUNTRIES IN THE WORLD

	Country	Annual production (metric tonnes)
1	China	188,150,000
2	India	109,511,000
3	Indonesia	47,770,000
4	Bangladesh	27,400,000
5	Vietnam	21,500,000
6	Thailand	18,500,000
7	Myanmar (Burma)	13,771,000
8	Japan	13,225,000
9	Brazil	9,961,000
10	Philippines	9,185,000
	World total	*525,475,000*

THE STAFF OF LIFE
Developed over millenia from wild grasses, wheat is the second largest food crop in the world. Bread wheat is ground up to make flour that has a high gluten content. This produces an elastic dough that makes light and airy bread. It is the most widely grown form of modern wheat.

TOP 10

SUGAR BEET-GROWING COUNTRIES IN THE WORLD

	Country	Annual production (metric tonnes)
1	France	31,334,000
2	Ukraine	28,546,000
3	Germany	27,150,000
4	US	26,170,000
5	Russia	25,500,000
6	China	15,010,000
7	Turkey	14,800,000
8	Italy	14,300,000
9	Poland	11,052,000
10	UK	8,500,000
	World total	*279,991,000*

TOP 10

POTATO-GROWING COUNTRIES IN THE WORLD

	Country	Annual production (metric tonnes)
1	Russia	37,800,000
2	China	33,937,000
3	Poland	23,388,000
4	Ukraine	20,427,000
5	US	18,671,000
6	India	15,500,000
7	Germany	10,975,000
8	Belarus	8,000,000
9	UK	7,882,000
10	Netherlands	7,595,000
	World total	*268,492,000*

TOP 10

BARLEY-GROWING COUNTRIES IN THE WORLD

	Country	Annual production (metric tonnes)
1	Russia	25,500,000
2	Germany	12,196,000
3	Canada	10,919,000
4	France	10,474,000
5	Ukraine	10,106,000
6	US	9,936,000
7	Kazakhstan	8,000,000
8	UK	7,386,000
9	Turkey	6,900,000
10	Spain	5,995,000
	World total	*160,134,000*

TOP 10

CASSAVA-GROWING COUNTRIES IN THE WORLD

	Country	Annual production (metric tonnes)
1	Brazil	22,652,000
2	Thailand	21,130,000
3	Nigeria	20,000,000
4	Zaïre	18,300,000
5	Indonesia	16,318,000
6	Tanzania	7,111,000
7	India	5,200,000
8	Ghana	4,000,000
9	Uganda	3,780,000
10	China	3,358,000
	World total	*152,218,000*

TOP 10

SWEET POTATO-GROWING COUNTRIES IN THE WORLD

	Country	Annual production (metric tonnes)
1	China	109,200,000
2	Indonesia	2,172,000
3	Vietnam	2,110,000
4	Uganda	1,752,000
5	Japan	1,300,000
6	India	1,220,000
7	Rwanda	770,000
8	Brazil	705,000
9	Burundi	701,000
10	Philippines	670,000
	World total	*128,016,000*

TOP 10

SOYBEAN-GROWING COUNTRIES IN THE WORLD

	Country	Annual production (metric tonnes)
1	US	59,780,000
2	Brazil	19,161,000
3	Argentina	11,315,000
4	China	9,707,000
5	India	2,950,000
6	Indonesia	1,881,000
7	Italy	1,434,000
8	Canada	1,387,000
9	Paraguay	1,315,000
10	Mexico	670,000
	World total	*114,011,000*

TREE TOPS

T O P 1 0

MOST FORESTED COUNTRIES IN THE WORLD
(By percent forest cover)

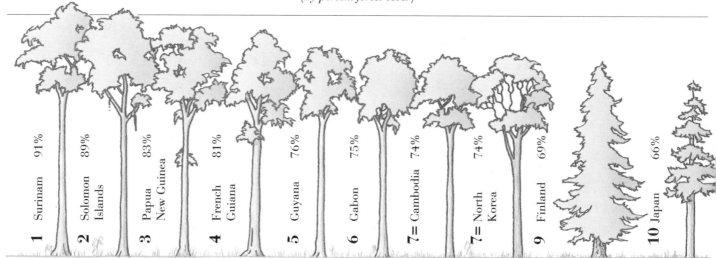

1 Surinam 91%
2 Solomon Islands 89%
3 Papua New Guinea 83%
4 French Guiana 81%
5 Guyana 76%
6 Gabon 75%
7= Cambodia 74%
7= North Korea 74%
9 Finland 69%
10 Japan 66%

TOP 10

TALLEST TREES IN THE US

(The tallest known example of each of the 10 tallest species)

	Tree	Location	m	ft
1	Coast redwood	Humboldt Redwoods State Park, California	110.6	363
2	Coast Douglas fir	Coos County, Oregon	100.27	329
3	General Sherman giant sequoia	Sequoia National Park, California	83.8	275
4	Noble fir	Mount St. Helens National Monument, Washington	82.9	272
5	Sugar pine	Yosemite National Park, California	82.3	270
6	Western hemlock	Olympic National Park, Washington	73.5	241
7	Port-Orford cedar	Siskiyou National Forest, Oregon	66.8	219
8	Sitka spruce	Seaside, Oregon	62.8	206
9	Swamp chestnut (Basket) oak	Fayette County, Alabama	61.0	200
10	Pignut hickory	Robbinsville, North Carolina	57.9	190

The 363-ft/110.6-m champion coast redwood stands just 2 ft/ 0.60 m shorter than the cross on the dome on St. Paul's Cathedral, London. A close rival, known as the Dyerville Giant (from Dyerville, California), stood 362 ft/110.3 m high but fell in a storm on March 27, 1991. Several extinct types of Australian eucalyptus exceeded 400 ft/122 m.

TOP 10

TALLEST TREES IN THE UK

(The tallest known example of each of the 10 tallest species)

	Tree	Location	m	ft
1	Grand fir	Strone House, Argyll, Strathclyde	63.4	208
2	Douglas fir	The Hermitage, Dunkeld, Tayside	62.5	205
3	Sitka spruce	Private estate, Strath Earn, Tayside	61.6	202
4=	Giant sequoia	Castle Leod, Strathpeffer, Highland	53.0	174
4=	Low's fir	Diana's Grove, Blair Castle, Strathclyde	53.0	174
6	Norway spruce	Moniack Glenn, Highland	51.8	170
7=	Western hemlock	Benmore Younger Botanic Gardens, Argyll, Strathclyde	51.0	167
7=	Noble fir	Ardkinglas House, Argyll, Strathclyde	51.0	167
9	European silver fir	Armadale Castle, Skye, Highland	50.0	164
10	London plane	Bryanston School, Blandford, Dorset	48.0	157

Based on data supplied by *The Tree Register of the British Isles*

LARGEST NATIONAL FORESTS IN THE US

	Forest/location	Area (sq miles)
1	Tongass National Forest, Sitka, Alaska	6,455,577
2	Chugach National Forest, Anchorage, Alaska	2,086,655
3	Toiyabe National Forest, Sparks, Nevada	1,240,248
4	Tonto National Forest, Phoenix, Arizona	1,109,886
5	Boise National Forest, Boise, Idaho	1,022,298
6	Humboldt National Forest, Elko, Nevada	956,800
7	Challis National Forest, Challis, Idaho	951,558
8	Shoshone National Forest, Cody, Wyoming	940,866
9	Flathead National Forest, Kalispess, Montana	909,081
10	Payette National Forest, McCall, Idaho	897,005

The forest at No. 1 on this list is actually larger than the area of all 10 of the smallest US states together with the District of Columbia. Even the much smaller No. 2 is larger than Massachusetts, and No. 10 covers an area greater than that of Delaware and Rhode Island combined.

THE LARGEST LIVING THING ON EARTH

Founded in 1890, the Sequoia National Park in Northern California is the home of the General Sherman, a giant sequoia believed to be the planet's most colossal living thing. Some nine percent bigger than its nearest rival, another sequoia known as the General Grant, the tree has a circumference of 998 in and an average crown spread of 107 ft, and is 275 ft tall. Weighing some 1,400 tons (as much as nine blue whales or 360 elephants), it has been calculated that it is 266,000,000,000 times heavier than the seed from which it sprouted some 2,600 years ago. The General Sherman is gaining 40 cubic feet, or one ton, of wood a year, making it the world's fastest-growing organism. Its volume is 52,508 cubic feet: if this amount of lumber were made into pencils, laid end to end they would reach around the equator, a distance of 24,901.46 miles/40,075.02 km. The tree, which was held sacred by the Mono Indians, was formerly named the Karl Marx by a Utopian community that once dwelled in the area. It was renamed in 1879 by pioneer cattleman James Wolverton, who had served under General Sherman in the Civil War.

BIGGEST TREES IN THE US

(The biggest known example of each of the 10 biggest species)

	Species	Location/state	Points
1	General Sherman giant sequoia	Sequoia National Park, California	1,300
2	Coast redwood	Humboldt Redwoods State Park, California	1,017
3	Western red cedar	Forks, Washington	924
4	Sitka spruce	Olympic National Forest, Washington	922
5	Coast Douglas fir	Coos County, Oregon	762
6	Common bald cypress	Cat Island, Louisiana	748
7	Sycamore	Jeromesville, Ohio	737
8	Port-Orford cedar	Siskiyou National Forest, Oregon	680
9	Sugar pine	Yosemite National Park, California	635
10	Incense cedar	Marble Mountains Wilderness, California	626

The American Forestry Association operates a *National Register of Big Trees*, which is constantly updated as new "champion trees" are nominated. Their method of measurement, which produces this Top 10 by species, is not based solely on height, but also takes account of the thickness of the trunk and the spread of the crown (the upper branches and leaves), and expresses this information in "points." The formula used to calculate the number of points for a tree involves adding the circumference in inches of the tree at 4½ feet above the ground, the total height of the tree in feet, and one-quarter of the average crown spread in feet.

MOST COMMON TREES IN THE US

1	Ponderosa pine	6	Black cherry
2	Green ash	7	Red mulberry
3	Eastern cottonwood	8	Eastern redcedar
4	Black willow	9	American sycamore
5	Silver maple	10	Boxelder

This Top 10 is based on the American Forestry Association's estimates of the relative numbers of those trees that make up the largest ranges in the US. A range is defined as an area in which the species grows "naturally and well."

THE HUMAN WORLD

T O P   1 0

LONGEST BONES IN THE HUMAN BODY

	Bone	Average length cm	in
1	Femur (thighbone – upper leg)	50.50	19.88
2	Tibia (shinbone – inner lower leg)	43.03	16.94
3	Fibula (outer lower leg)	40.50	15.94
4	Humerus (upper arm)	36.46	14.35
5	Ulna (inner lower arm)	28.20	11.10
6	Radius (outer lower arm)	26.42	10.40
7	Seventh rib	24.00	9.45
8	Eighth rib	23.00	9.06
9	Innominate bone (hipbone – half pelvis)	18.50	7.28
10	Sternum (breastbone)	17.00	6.69

These are average dimensions of the bones of an adult male measured from their extremities (ribs are curved, and the pelvis measurement is taken diagonally). The same bones in the female skeleton are usually 6 to 13 percent smaller, with the exception of the sternum, which is virtually identical.

T O P   1 0

LARGEST HUMAN ORGANS

	Organ		Average weight g	oz
1	Liver		1,560	55.0
2	Brain	male	1,408	49.7
		female	1,263	44.6
3	Lungs	right	580	20.5
		left	510	18.0
		total	1,090	38.5
4	Heart	male	315	11.1
		female	265	9.3
5	Kidneys	left	150	5.3
		right	140	4.9
		total	290	10.2
6	Spleen		170	6.0
7	Pancreas		98	3.5
8	Thyroid		35	1.2
9	Prostate	male only	20	0.7
10	Adrenals	left	6	0.2
		right	6	0.2
		total	12	0.4

This list is based on average immediate post-mortem weights, as recorded by St. Bartholomew's Hospital, London, and other sources during a 10-year period. Instances of organs far larger than the average have been recorded, including male brains of over 70.6 oz./2,000 g According to some definitions, the skin may be considered an organ, and since it can comprise 16 percent of a body's total weight (384 oz/ 10,886 g in a person weighing 150 lb/68 kg), it would head the Top 10.

THE BODY

T O P 1 0

MOST COMMON BLOOD GROUPS IN THE UK

	Group	Percentage*			Group	Percentage*
1	O+	37.4		7	AB+	3.4
2	A+	35.7		8	B-	1.5
3	B+	8.5		9	A2-	1.26
4	A2+	7.14		10	AB-	0.6
5	O-	6.6				
6	A-	6.3				

* Total less than 100 percent as a result of rounding off and existence of rare sub-groups.

This list presents a breakdown for blood groups in 10 categories: a US equivalent is unavailable, since US methods divide blood into eight groups, but the proportions are very similar (the percentage of O+ and O- are in fact absolutely identical), emphasising the common racial stock of the two countries.

T O P 1 0

MOST COMMON PHOBIAS

	Object of phobia	Medical term
1	Spiders	Arachnephobia or arachnophobia
2	People and social situations	Anthropophobia or sociophobia
3	Flying	Aviatophobia
4	Open spaces	Agoraphobia, cenophobia, or kenophobia
5	Confined spaces	Claustrophobia, cleisiophobia, cleithrophobia, or clithrophobia
6	Heights	Acrophobia, altophobia, hypsophobia, or hypsiphobia
7	Cancer	Carcinomaphobia, carcinophobia, carcinomatophobia, cancerphobia, or cancerophobia
8	Thunderstorms	Brontophobia or keraunophobia; related phobias are those associated with lightning (astraphobia), cyclones (anemophobia), and hurricanes and tornadoes (lilapsophobia)
9	Death	Necrophobia or thanatophobia
10	Heart disease	Cardiophobia

A phobia is a morbid fear that is out of all proportion to the object of the fear. Many people would admit to being uncomfortable about these principal phobias, as well as others, such as snakes (ophiophobia), injections (trypanophobia), or ghosts (phasmophobia), but most do not become obsessive about them nor allow such fears to rule their lives. True phobias often arise from some incident in childhood when a person has been afraid of some object and has developed an irrational fear that persists into adulthood. Nowadays, as well as the valuable work done by the Phobics Society and other organizations, phobias can be cured by taking special desensitization courses, for example, to conquer one's fear of flying.

T O P 1 0

MOST COMMON ALLERGENS

(Substances that cause allergies)

Food		Environmental
Nuts	1	House dust mite (*Dermatophagoldes pteronyssinus*)
Shellfish/seafood	2	Grass pollens
Milk	3	Tree pollens
Wheat	4	Cats
Eggs	5	Dogs
Fresh fruit (apples, oranges, strawberries, etc)	6	Horses
Fresh vegetables (potatoes, cucumber, etc)	7	Molds (*Aspergillus fumigatus, Alternaria,Cladosporium*, etc.)
Cheese	8	Birch pollen
Yeast	9	Weed pollen
Soy protein	10	Wasp/bee venom

An allergy has been defined as "an unpleasant reaction to foreign matter, specific to that substance, which is altered from the normal response and peculiar to the individual concerned." Allergens are commonly foods but may also be environmental agents, pollen as a cause of hay fever being one of the best known. Reactions to them can result in symptoms ranging from severe mental or physical disability to minor irritations such as mild headache in the presence of fresh paint. "Elimination dieting" to pinpoint and avoid food allergens and the identification and avoidance of environmental allergens can result in complete cures from many allergies.

MATTERS OF LIFE AND DEATH

T O P 1 0

COUNTRIES WITH THE MOST HOSPITALS

	Country	Beds per 10,000	Hospitals
1	China	23	63,101
2	Brazil	37	28,972
3	India	8	25,452
4	Russia	135	12,711
5	Nigeria	9	11,588
6	Vietnam	25	10,768
7	Pakistan	6	10,673
8	Japan	136	10,096
9	North Korea	135	7,924
10	US	47	6,738

T O P 1 0

COUNTRIES WITH THE MOST DOCTORS

	Country	Patients per doctor	Doctors
1	China	648	1,808,000
2	Russia	226	657,800
3	US	416	614,000
4	India	2,337	365,000
5	Germany	313	251,877
6	Italy	228	249,704
7	Ukraine	226	228,900
8	Japan	583	211,797
9	Brazil	848	169,500
10	Spain	257	153,306

Comparing countries, their declared number of doctors, and hence the ratios of patients to doctors, is fraught with problems, especially since some countries, such as Russia and the Ukraine, include dentists with their doctors. China also includes practitioners of the traditional Chinese medicine.

T O P 1 0

COUNTRIES WITH THE HIGHEST MALE LIFE EXPECTANCY

	Country	Life expectancy at birth (years)
1	Japan	75.9
2=	Iceland	75.1
2=	Macau	75.1
4	Hong Kong	75.0
5	Israel	74.9
6	Sweden	74.6
7	Spain	74.4
8	Switzerland	74.1
9=	Andorra	74.0
9=	Netherlands	74.0
9=	Norway	74.0
	US	72.0

The generally increasing life expectancy for males in the Top 10 countries contrasts sharply with that in many underdeveloped countries, particularly the majority of African countries, where it rarely exceeds 45 years. Sierra Leone is at the bottom of the league with 41.4 years.

T O P 1 0

COUNTRIES WITH THE HIGHEST FEMALE LIFE EXPECTANCY

	Country	Life expectancy at birth (years)
1	Japan	81.8
2=	France	81.0
2=	Andorra	81.0
4	Switzerland	80.9
5	Iceland	80.8
6=	Hong Kong	80.3
6=	Macau	80.3
8=	Sweden	80.2
8=	Netherlands	80.2
10	Norway	80.0
	US	79.0

Female life expectancy in all the Top 10 countries equals or exceeds 80 years. This represents the average: as many women are now living beyond this age as die before attaining it. The comparative figure for such Third World countries as Sierra Leone, where it is 44.6 years for women, makes for less encouraging reading.

T O P 1 0

MOST COMMON REASONS FOR VISITS TO THE DOCTOR

These figures show consulting rates in the UK, and give an indication of major complaints in an industrialized country. The Royal College of General Practitioners considers that these statistics represent the average number of consultations per condition that a doctor with a typical practice of 2,500 patients might expect to deal with in a year. These relatively common problems contrast with others that are extremely rare: on average a doctor might expect to see a person with a dislocated hip only once every 20 years, or a patient with phenylketonuria (a metabolic disorder) just once in 200 years.

	Condition	Consulting rate per 2,500 patients
1	Upper respiratory tract infections	600
2	Nonspecific "symptoms"	375
3	Skin disorders	350
4=	Psychiatric problems	250
4=	High blood pressure	250
4=	Minor accidents	250
7	Gastrointestinal conditions	200
8	Rheumatic aches and pains	150
9=	Chronic rheumatism	100
9=	Acute throat infections	100
9=	Acute bronchitis	100
9=	Lacerations	100
9=	Eczema/dermatitis	100

T O P   1 0

BESTSELLING PRESCRIPTION DRUGS IN THE WORLD

	Brand name	Manufacturer	Prescribed for	Annual revenue (US $)
1	Zantac	Glaxo	Ulcers	3,023,000,000
2	Vasotec	Merck & Co.	High blood pressure, etc.	1,745,000,000
3	Capoten	Bristol-Myers-Squibb	High blood pressure, etc.	1,580,000,000
4	Voltaren	Ciba-Geigy	Arthritis	1,185,000,000
5	Tenormin	ICI	High blood pressure	1,180,000,000
6	Adalat	Bayer	Angina; high blood pressure	1,120,000,000
7	Tagamet	SmithKline Beecham	Ulcers	1,097,000,000
8	Mevacor	Merck & Co.	High fat level in blood	1,090,000,000
9	Naproxen	Syntex	Arthritis	954,000,000
10	Ceclor	Eli Lilly	Infections	935,000,000

In 1991 the total revenue of the top 25 drug companies was $94,598,000,000. Fewer than 25 countries in the world have a gross domestic product (the total production of goods and services of the entire country) of more than this figure (which is approximately equivalent to the GDP of Norway). Of this total, the Top 10 drugs alone accounted for earnings of $13,909,000,000.

T O P   1 0

PRESCRIPTION DRUGS IN THE US

	Generic drug	Drug type	Prescribed for	No. of new prescriptions (1993)
1	Amoxycillin trihydrate	Antibiotic	Infections	33,588,000
2	Penicillin VK	Antibiotic	Infections	11,152,000
3	Prednisone	Steroid	Inflammation	9,629,000
4	Doxycycline hyciate	Antibiotic	Infections, acne	6,517,000
5	Cephalexin	Antibiotic	Infections	5,890,000
6	Ibuprofen*	Analgesic, nonsteroidal anti-inflammatory	Inflammation	4,878,000
7	Ampicillin	Antibiotic	Infections	4,025,000
8	Tetracycline HCI	Antibiotic	Infections, acne	3,391,000
9	Acetaminophen/cod	Analgesic	Pain relief	3,381,000
10	Hydrochlorothiazide	Diuretic	Water retention, high blood pressure	3,184,000

Also available over the counter

This list of the 10 drugs most frequently prescribed in the US is dominated by various antibiotics; these, along with anti-inflammatories and analgesics (pain-relieving drugs), make up a total of 85,635,000 new prescriptions for the Top 10 alone. In 1993, the leading 30 products accounted for 120,282,000 prescriptions.

T O P   1 0

MOST COMMON CAUSES OF DEATH IN THE US

	Cause of death	US total
1	Diseases of the heart	720,480
2	Cancer	521,090
3	Cerebrovascular diseases	143,640
4	Chronic obstructive pulmonary diseases and allied conditions	91,440
5	Accidents and adverse effects*	86,310
6	Pneumonia and influenza	76,120
7	Diabetes	50,180
8	Human Immune deficiency Virus infection	33,590
9	Suicide	29,760
10	Homicide and legal intervention	26,570

* *Comprises motor vehicle accidents (41,470) and all other accidents and adverse affects (44,600)*

Source: National Center for Health Statistics

Figures are for 1992 based on a total number of 2,177,000 deaths estimated in the US for that year.

FOR BETTER OR FOR WORSE

Marriage rates for most Western countries have been steadily declining: there were 533,900 marriages in the UK's peak year of 1940, but only 349,739 in 1991. Although high divorce rates are a relatively modern phenomenon, national censuses taken around the turn of the century show that the US was already the world leader with 199,500 people (114,930 women and 84,570 men) recorded as divorced. The annual average for divorces in England and Wales – as in most other Western countries – has risen inexorably: in the period from 1871 to 1875 it numbered 357, by 1896–1900 it had reached 980, and by 1907 it stood at 1,288. The number of divorces more than doubled over the period from 1970 to 1991, reaching 158,745 in England and Wales, 12,399 in Scotland, and 2,344 in Northern Ireland.

TOP 10

COUNTRIES WITH THE HIGHEST DIVORCE RATE

	Country	Divorces per 1,000 p.a.
1	Maldives	25.5
2	Liechtenstein	7.3
3	Peru	6.0
4	US	4.7
5	Puerto Rico	3.9
6	Ukraine	3.7
7	Cuba	3.6
8	Former USSR	3.4
9	Canada	3.1
10	Denmark	3.0

MARRIAGE IN THE MOVIES

The commercial success and critical acclaim of the British film *Four Weddings and a Funeral* (1994) places it in a long line of comedy films with weddings as their central theme. *Father of the Bride* (1991), itself a remake of a 1950 film with the same title, is one of the highest-earning, while *Lovers and Other Strangers* (1970), *A Wedding* (1978), and *Betsy's Wedding* (1990) have all been box-office hits. Weddings that are thwarted are another Hollywood staple, as in *The Philadelphia Story* (1940) and *The Graduate* (1967). Both of them, like the original *Father of the Bride*, were nominated for "Best Picture" Oscars – although all were jilted at the altar . . . .

TOP 10

COUNTRIES WITH THE HIGHEST MARRIAGE RATE

	Country	Marriages*
1	Northern Mariana Islands	31.2
2	US Virgin Islands	18.0
3	Bermuda	15.2
4	Benin	12.8
5	Guam	12.0
6	Bangladesh	11.6
7	Mauritius	10.7
8	Azerbaijan	10.4
9=	Kazakhstan	10.0
9=	Cayman Islands	10.0
9=	Uzbekistan	10.0
	US	9.4

* Per 1,000 p.a., during latest period for which figures available

The apparent world record marriage rate in the Northern Mariana Islands, which has a population of under 44,000, may be a statistical "blip" resulting from the recording of marriages by visitors, which has the effect of distorting the national pattern.

TOP 10

MONTHS FOR WEDDINGS IN THE US

	Month	Weddings		Month	Weddings
1	June	256,000	6	October	221,000
2	August	242,000	7	December	184,000
3	May	231,000	8	April	175,000
4	July	228,000	9	November	174,000
5	September	227,000	10	February	166,000

Source: National Center for Health Statistics

Figures are for 1992 from a US total of some 2,362,000 weddings, a decrease of 9,000 from 1991. March is at No. 11 with 145,000, and January is last with 112,000.

TOP 10

MOST COMMON CAUSES OF MARITAL DISCORD AND BREAKDOWN

1	Lack of communication		7	Work (usually one partner devoting excessive time to work)
2	Continual arguments			
3	Infidelity		8	Children (whether to have them; attitudes toward their upbringing)
4	Sexual problems			
5	Physical or verbal abuse		9	Addiction (to drinking, gambling, spending, etc.)
6	Financial problems, recession, and fear of being laid off		10	Step-parenting

T O P 1 0

STATES WITH THE MOST WEDDINGS

	State*	Weddings (1992)
1	Texas	182,997
2	New York	156,252
3	Florida	138,129
4	Nevada	114,223
5	Illinois	93,500
6	Ohio	92,156
7	Pennsylvania	80,424
8	Tennessee	70,905
9	Michigan	70,700
10	Virginia	69,694

T O P 1 0

STATES WITH THE MOST DIVORCES

	State*	Divorces (1992)
1	Texas	98,960
2	Florida	87,074
3	New York	57,038
4	Ohio	53,535
5	Illinois	43,612
6	Pennsylvania	39,864
7	Georgia	39,586
8	Michigan	39,424
9	North Carolina	36,150
10	Tennessee	33,939

Figures are not available for California. Source: National Center for Health Statistics

T O P 1 0

PROFESSIONS OF COMPUTER DATING MEMBERS

Men		Women
Teachers	1	Teachers
Civil servants	2	Secretaries
Engineers	3	Nurses
Company directors	4	Women at home
Accountants	5	Civil servants
Students	6	Clerks
Self-employed	7	Students
Computer programmers	8	Social workers
Managers	9	Receptionists
Farmers	10	Sales staff

Based on figures supplied by Dateline, the UK's largest and oldest-established computer dating agency.

THE FIRST 10 WEDDING ANNIVERSARY GIFTS

1	Cotton
2	Paper
3	Leather
4	Fruit and flowers
5	Wood
6	Sugar (or iron)
7	Wool (or copper)
8	Bronze (or electrical appliances)
9	Pottery (or willow)
10	Tin (or aluminum)

The custom of celebrating each wedding anniversary with a specific type of gift has a long tradition, but has changed much over the years – for example in the association of electrical appliances with the 8th anniversary. It varies considerably from country to country: in the US and UK many of the earlier themes are often disregarded in favor of the "milestone" anniversaries: the 25th (silver), 40th (ruby), 50th (gold), and 60th (diamond). Actually, the 75th anniversary is the "diamond," but few married couples live long enough to celebrate it, so it is usually commemorated as the 60th.

WHAT'S IN A NAME?

TOP 10

GIRLS' AND BOYS' NAMES IN THE US

Girls		Boys
Brittany	**1**	Michael
Ashley	**2**	Christopher
Jessica	**3**	Matthew
Amanda	**4**	Joshua
Sarah	**5**	Andrew
Megan	**6**	James
Caitlin	**7**	John
Samantha	**8**	Nicholas
Stephanie	**9**	Justin
Katherine	**10**	David

American name fashions are highly volatile, and vary considerably according to the child's ethnic background and the influences of popular culture. Jennifer, for example, rose to No. 2 position because the heroine of the book and 1970 film *Love Story* had this name, and Tiffany entered the Top 10 in 1980 in the wake of the TV series, *Charlie's Angels*, and its character Tiffany Welles. Ashley rose to prominence only in the 1980s: by 1984 it was already being noted as the girl's name of the year, (just as Angela had been 10 years earlier), and by 1990 had reached No. 1. This pattern has been mirrored in the 1990s with Brittany, a name that does not even make an appearance among the Top 100 of British girls' names; only Jessica and Katherine (or, rather, Catherine with a "C") appear in the Top 10s of both countries. In contrast, six of the Top 10 US boys' names (Michael, Christopher, Matthew, Joshua, Andrew, and James) also appear in the British Top 10. Michael has topped every US list for 30 years, while Joshua appeared in the Top 10 for the first time in 1983. Richard plummeted from the ranking after Richard Nixon's disgrace in the Watergate scandal, and has not regained its former popularity.

TOP 10

MOST COMMON SURNAMES IN THE US

	Surname	Number
1	Smith	2,382,509
2	Johnson	1,807,263
3	Williams/Williamson	1,568,939
4	Brown	1,362,910
5	Jones	1,331,205
6	Miller	1,131,205
7	Davis	1,047,848
8	Martin/Martinez/ Martinson	1,046,297
9	Anderson/Andersen	825,648
10	Wilson	787,825

The United States Social Security Administration last published its survey of the most common surnames 20 years ago, based on the number of people for whom it had more than 10,000 files, which covered a total of 3,169 names. The SSA has not repeated the exercise, but it is probable that the ranking order has remained very similar.

TOP 10

MOST COMMON NAMES OF FILM CHARACTERS

	Name	Characters
1	Jack	126
2	John	104
3	Frank	87
4	Harry	72
5	David	63
6	George	62
7=	Michael	59
7=	Tom	59
9	Mary	54
10	Paul	53

Based on Simon Rose's *One FM Essential Film Guide* (1993) survey of feature films released in the period 1983–93.

TOP 10

MOST COMMON US SURNAMES DERIVED FROM OCCUPATIONS

1	Smith
2	Miller
3	Taylor
4	Clark (cleric)
5	Walker (cloth worker)
6	Wright (workman)
7	Baker
8	Carter (driver or maker of carts)
9	Stewart (steward)
10	Turner (woodworker)

It is reckoned that about one in six US surnames – especially among families of European origin – recalls the occupation of the holder's ancestors. Several US Presidents have borne such surnames, including Zachary Taylor and Jimmy Carter, both of which feature in the Top 10. Less obvious is that of 19th President Rutherford Hayes, since Hayes was the name once given to a person in charge of hedges.

TOP 10

INITIAL LETTERS OF SURNAMES IN THE US

RAREST				MOST COMMON	
%	Letter			Letter	%
0.1	X	**1**		S	9.8
0.3	Q	**2**		B	7.0
0.9	U	**3**		M	6.5
1.2	I	**4**		K	6.4
1.3	Y	**5**		D	5.9
2.0	J	**6**		C, P	5.5
2.2	Z	**7**		G	5.2
2.5	E	**8**		L	5.0
2.6	O	**9**		A	4.8
2.7	N, V	**10**		T	4.6

The frequency of the in-between initial letters is: H and R – 4.4%, F – 3.3%, and W – 3.1%.

TOP 10

MOST COMMON SURNAMES OF EUROPEAN ORIGIN IN THE US

(As recorded by the US Social Security Administration, 1974)

	German*	Irish	Italian	Scottish	Welsh
1	Myers	Murphy	Russo	Morrison	Williams
2	Schmidt	Kelly#**	Lombardo/Lombardi	Scott	Jones
3	Hoffman(n)	Sullivan	Romano	Campbell	Davis
4	Wagner#	Kennedy**	Marino	Stewart	Thomas
5	Meyer	Bryant	Lorenzo‡‡	Ross	Lewis
6	Schwarz	Kelley#**	Costa‡‡	Graham	Evans
7	Schneider	Burke	Luna	Hamilton	Rogers
8	Zimmerman(n)	Riley	Rossi/Rossini	Murray	Morgan
9	Keller	O'Brien	Esposito	Kennedy##	Hughes
10	Klein	McCoy	Gallo	Gordon	Price

* *Excluding those that have been anglicized, such as Schmidt/Smith*
# *Sometimes of English origin*
** *Sometimes of Scottish origin*
‡‡ *Sometimes of Spanish/Portuguese origin*
May also be of Irish origin

As a result of migration within Great Britain, it is often as likely that a US family with a Welsh surname actually came from England. Welsh surnames appear in relatively high numbers, all those in the Top 10 featuring among the 100 most common surnames in the US. This partly reflects the limited number of surnames in use in Wales, where entire communities often bear only a handful of different names.

The SSA's method of enumerating names was based on the first six letters, so that the count of some names may be distorted – the Morrisons by those with the surname Morris, for instance. The highest number recorded for a Mc or Mac surname is that of Mackinnon (98,162 examples).

TOP 10

MOST COMMON US SURNAMES OF HISPANIC ORIGIN

1	Rodriguez	6	Martinez
2	Gonzalez	7	Hernandez
3	Garcia	8	Perez
4	Lopez	9	Sanchez
5	Rivera	10	Torres

THE TEN

LAST NAMES IN THE SAN FRANCISCO PHONE BOOK

1	Zytron First Image Management Co
2	Zyzinski, John
3	Zyzzyva
4	Zzcor, W.
5	Zzoble, N.
6	Zzyzx Group
7	Zzzzonzo, Z.
8	Zzzzyux
9	Zzzzzz, Bob
10	Zzzzzz, Otto

TOP 10

MOST COMMON SURNAMES IN THE MANHATTAN TELEPHONE DIRECTORY

1	Smith
2	Brown/Browne
3	Williams/Williamson
4	Cohen (and variant spellings)
5	Lee
6	Johnson
7	Rodriguez
8	Green/Greene
9	Davis
10	Jones

TOP 10

MOST COMMON PATRONYMS IN THE US

1	Johnson ("son of John")
2	Williams/Williamson ("son of William")
3	Jones ("son of John")
4	Davis ("son of Davie/David")
5	Martin/Martinez/Martinson ("son of Martin")
6	Anderson/Andersen ("son of Andrew")
7	Wilson ("son of Will")
8	Harris/Harrison ("son of Harry")
9	Thomas ("son of Thomas")
10	Thomson/Thompson ("son of Thomas")

Patronyms are names recalling a father or other ancestor. Up to one-third of all US surnames may be patronymic in origin.

ORGANIZATIONS

TOP 10

MEMBERSHIP ORGANIZATIONS IN THE US

	Organization	Approx. membership
1	American Automobile Association	34,000,000
2	American Association of Retired Persons	32,700,000
3	YMCA of the USA	12,781,793
4	National Right to Life Committee	12,000,000
5	National Geographic Society	10,800,000
6	National Parents and Teachers Association	6,800,000
7	National Committee to Preserve Social Security and Medicare	6,000,000
8	National Wildlife Federation	5,600,000
9	4-H Program	5,478,826
10	Boy Scouts of America	5,300,000

TOP 10

LARGEST LABOR UNIONS IN THE US

	Union	Membership
1	International Brotherhood of Teamsters, Chauffeurs, Warehousemen and Helpers of America	1,316,000
2	American Federation of State, County and Municipal Employees	1,167,000
3	United Food and Commercial Workers' International Union	997,000
4	Service Employees International Union	919,000
5	International Union of Automobile, Aerospace and Agricultural Implement Workers of America	771,000
6	International Brotherhood of Electrical Workers	710,000
7	American Federation of Teachers	574,000
8	International Association of Machinists and Aerospace Workers	474,000
9	Communications Workers of America	472,000
10	United Steelworkers of America	421,000

The total membership of labor unions has declined from its peak years in the 1970s, when it approached 20,000,000, to fewer than 16,000,000 today. Alongside the great US labor unions are several smaller ones, such as the Distillery, Wine & Allied Workers International Union, with fewer than 15,000 members. However, none rival the miniscule size of some of their UK counterparts, among which are such tiny organizations as the Military and Orchestral Musical Instrument Makers' Trade Society (48 members) and the Sheffield Wool Shearers' Union (14).

Source: AFL–CIO, Washington, DC

TOP 10

ENVIRONMENTAL ORGANIZATIONS IN THE US

	Organization	Membership
1	National Wildlife Federation	5,600,000
2	Greenpeace	1,600,000
3	World Wildlife Fund	1,200,000
4	Nature Conservancy	724,000
5	National Audubon Society	600,000
6	Sierra Club	550,000
7	National Parks and Conservation Association	450,000
8	The Wilderness Society	330,000
9	Environmental Defense Fund	250,000
10	Natural Resources Defense Council	170,000

TOP 10

CITY OF LONDON LIVERY COMPANIES

1	Mercers
2	Grocers
3	Drapers
4	Fishmongers
5	Goldsmiths
6=	Merchant Taylors
6=	Skinners
8	Haberdashers
9	Salters
10	Ironmongers

London's livery companies, so called from the distinctive costume, or livery, worn by their members, grew out of the city craft guilds of the 14th century, but today they function more as charitable, educational, and social institutions than as trade associations. At one time all had halls with collections of art treasures and often extensive grounds, but as companies such as the Bonnet Makers, Virginals Makers, and Heumers (helmet makers) were disbanded or absorbed and buildings were destroyed (many of them in the Second World War) or sold to raise funds, the number of halls dwindled to fewer than 40. Today the liverymen elect the sheriffs of London and the Lord Mayor. In the time of Henry VIII (1509–47), the Court of Aldermen established a list in order of precedence, headed by the "Great Twelve." These were the ones given in this list; the Vintners (wine-sellers) at No. 11; and the Clothworkers at No. 12. A dispute over precedence between the Skinners and Merchant Taylors was resolved by their order switching in alternate years. Over the centuries, many companies have left and new ones joined, such as the Guild of Air Pilots and Navigators (81st), Environmental Cleaners (97th), and Information Technologists (100th).

TOP 10

MEMBERSHIP ORGANIZATIONS IN THE UK

	Organization	Membership
1	Trades Union Congress	7,646,832
2	Automobile Association	7,600,000 #
3	National Alliance of Women's Organizations	6,000,000
4	Royal Automobile Club	5,050,000
5	National Trust	2,173,875
6	UNISON	1,486,984
7	Transport & General Workers Union	1,036,586
8	Amalgamated Engineering and Electrical Union	884,463
9	Royal Society for the Protection of Birds	870,000
10	GMB (formerly General, Municipal, Boilermakers and Allied Trades Union)	830,743

Unlike the list of Top 10 Membership Organizations in the US, trade unions (labor unions) feature quite prominently here, at Nos. 1, 6, 7, 8, and 10.

TOP 10

COUNTRIES WITH THE HIGHEST GIRL GUIDE AND GIRL SCOUT MEMBERSHIP

	Country	Membership
1	US	3,510,313
2	Philippines	1,250,928
3	India	758,575
4	UK	707,651
5	South Korea	184,993
6	Pakistan	101,634
7	Indonesia	98,656
8	Malaysia	92,539
9	Japan	88,331
10	Australia	87,331

The Girl Guide Movement was started in 1910 by Sir Robert Baden-Powell and his sister, Agnes (1858–1945). Today the World Association of Girl Guides and Girl Scouts has 128 national member organizations with a total membership of 8,500,000.

TOP 10

COUNTRIES WITH THE HIGHEST BOY SCOUT MEMBERSHIP

	Country	Membership
1	US	4,625,800
2	Philippines	2,350,710
3	India	2,272,700
4	Indonesia	2,134,368
5	UK	657,466
6	Bangladesh	368,063
7	Pakistan	326,753
8	South Korea	309,460
9	Thailand	274,123
10	Canada	269,425

Following an experimental camp held from July 29 to August 9, 1907 on Brownsea Island, Dorset, England, Sir Robert Baden-Powell (1857–1941), a former general in the British army, launched the Scouting Movement. There are now more than 25,000,000 Scouts in 211 countries and territories. There are believed to be just 13 countries in the world where Scouting either does not exist or is forbidden for political reasons, among which China is the largest.

BOY SCOUTS
The Boy Scouts organization, founded in 1908, accepts boys between 11 and 15 years of age. It combines an emphasis on moral values with enjoyable and challenging physical activities.

TOP 10

US WOMEN'S ORGANIZATIONS

	Organization	Membership
1	National Organization for Women	280,000
2	National Organization for Female Executives	250,000
3	Daughters of the American Revolution	204,000
4	Association of Junior Leagues International	190,000
5	International Ladies Garment Workers Union	173,000
6	American Association of University Women	135,000
7	National Federation of Business and Professional Women's Clubs	125,000
8	National Women's Political Caucus	75,000
9	National Council of Negro Women	40,000
10	Women's Campaign Fund	23,000

TOP 10

US STATES WITH THE MOST GIRL SCOUTS

	State	Girl Scouts
1	California	226,399
2	New York	177,456
3	Illinois	155,799
4	Texas	151,364
5	Pennsylvania	151,351
6	Ohio	147,726
7	Michigan	117,878
8	Florida	96,712
9	New Jersey	94,759
10	Missouri	87,188

The Girl Guides of the United States of America was founded by Juliet Gordon Low in Savannah, Georgia, on March 12, 1912, taking the British Girl Guides, founded in 1910, as its model, and was renamed Girl Scouts in 1913. There are now 2,613,036 girl members and 826,692 adult members.

PEOPLE IN POWER

MRS. INDIRA GANDHI
Unrelated to Mahatma Gandhi, but daughter of India's first Prime Minister Jawaharlal Nehru, Indira Gandhi died in office, shot by Sikh extremists. She was succeeded by her son Rajiv, who was later assassinated by Tamil Tigers.

TOP 10
FIRST COUNTRIES TO GIVE WOMEN THE VOTE

	Country	Year
1	New Zealand	1893
2	Australia (South Australia 1894; Western Australia 1898; Australia united 1901)	1902
3	Finland (then a Grand Duchy under the Russian Crown)	1906
4	Norway (restricted franchise; all women over 25 in 1913)	1907
5	Denmark and Iceland (a Danish dependency until 1918)	1915
6=	Netherlands	1917
6=	USSR	1917
8=	Austria	1918
8=	Canada	1918
8=	Germany	1918
8=	Great Britain and Ireland (Ireland was part of the UK until 1921. At first, vote was given only to women over 30 – voting age lowered to 21 in 1928)	1918
8=	Poland	1918

Although not a country, the Isle of Man was the first place to give women the vote, in 1880. Until 1920 the only other European countries to enfranchise women were Sweden in 1919 and Czechoslovakia in 1920. Certain states of the US gave women the vote at earlier dates (Wyoming in 1869, Colorado in 1894, Utah in 1895, and Idaho in 1896), but it was not granted nationally until 1920. A number of countries, such as France and Italy, did not give women the vote until 1945. Switzerland did not allow women to vote in elections to the Federal Council until 1971, and Liechtenstein was one of the last to relent, in 1984. In certain countries, such as Saudi Arabia, women are not allowed to vote at all – but neither are men.

TOP 10
FIRST NATIONS TO RATIFY THE UN CHARTER

	Country	Date
1	Nicaragua	Jul 6, 1945
2	US	Aug 8, 1945
3	France	Aug 31, 1945
4	Dominican Republic	Sep 4, 1945
5	New Zealand	Sep 19, 1945
6	Brazil	Sep 21, 1945
7	Argentina	Sep 24, 1945
8	China	Sep 28, 1945
9	Denmark	Oct 9, 1945
10	Chile	Oct 11, 1945

In New York on June 26, 1945, only weeks after the end of the Second World War in Europe, 50 nations signed the World Security Charter. Each of the individual signatories ratified the Charter individually over the ensuing months, and the UN came into effect on October 24.

TOP 10
LONGEST-SERVING PRESIDENTS IN THE WORLD TODAY

	President	Country	Took office
1	Marshal Mobutu Sésé Séko	Zaïre	November 24, 1965
2	Dr. Hastings Kamuzu Banda*	Malawi	July 6, 1966
3	General Suharto	Indonesia	March 27, 1967
4	General Gnassingbé Eyadéma	Togo	April 14, 1967
5	El Hadj Omar Bongo	Gabon	December 2, 1967
6	Colonel Mu'ammar Gadhafi	Libya	September 1, 1969
7	Lt.-General Hafiz al-Asad	Syria	February 22, 1971
8	Didier Ratsiraka	Madagascar	June 15, 1975
9	Fidel Castro	Cuba	December 2, 1976
10	France Albert René	Seychelles	June 5, 1977

* *Created President for Life, July 6, 1971*

Félix Houphouët-Boigny, President of the Ivory Coast, died on December 7, 1993 after serving as leader of his country since November 27, 1960. Having been born on October 18, 1905, he was, at 88, the oldest president in the world. President Kim Il-sung of North Korea was president from December 28, 1972 until his death on July 8, 1994. Alhaji Sir Dawda Kairaba Jawara, president of The Gambia from April 24, 1970, was ousted by a military coup on July 23, 1994.

TOP 10

US PRESIDENTS WITH THE GREATEST NUMBER OF POPULAR VOTES

	President	Year	Votes
1	Ronald W. Reagan	1984	54,455,075
2	George H.W. Bush	1988	48,886,097
3	Richard M. Nixon	1972	47,169,911
4	William J. Clinton	1992	44,909,889
5	Ronald W. Reagan	1980	43,899,248
6	Lyndon B. Johnson	1964	43,129,484
7	James E. Carter	1976	40,830,763
8	Dwight D. Eisenhower	1956	35,590,472
9	John F. Kennedy	1960	34,226,731
10	Dwight D. Eisenhower	1952	33,936,234

Despite population increases and the enfranchisement of 18- to 21-year-olds in 1972, the Top 10 ranking shows that it is not the most recent Presidential elections that have attracted the greatest number of popular votes for the winning candidate. Also, many Presidents have won with less than 50 percent of the total popular vote: in 1824, John Quincy Adams achieved only 108,740 votes – 30.5 percent of the total, and in 1860 Abraham Lincoln had 1,865,593 – 39.8 percent.

TOP 10

STATE LEGISLATURES WITH MOST WOMEN

	State	Women legislators (%)
1	Washington	39.5
2	Colorado	35.0
3	Vermont	33.9
4	New Hampshire	33.5
5	Arizona	33.3
6	Maine	31.7
7	Idaho	30.5
8	Kansas	29.1
9	Wisconsin	27.3
10	Nevada	27.0

In 1994, 1,529 (an average of 20.6 percent) of the 7,424 state legislators in the US are women. Twenty-five years ago, the comparative figures were 301 seats, or 4.0 percent of the total.

TOP 10

WORLD'S FIRST FEMALE PRIME MINISTERS AND PRESIDENTS

	Name	Country	Period in office
1	Sirimavo Bandaranaike (PM)	Ceylon (Sri Lanka)	1960–64/1970–77
2	Indira Gandhi (PM)	India	1966–84
3	Golda Meir (PM)	Israel	1969–74
4	Maria Estela Perón (President)	Argentina	1974–75
5	Elisabeth Domitien (PM)	Central African Republic	1975
6	Margaret Thatcher (PM)	UK	May 1979–Nov 1990
7	Dr. Maria Lurdes Pintasilgo (PM)	Portugal	Aug–Nov 1979
8	Vigdís Finnbogadóttir (President)	Iceland	Jun 1980–
9	Mary Eugenia Charles (PM)	Dominica	Jul 1980–
10	Gro Harlem Brundtland (PM)	Norway	Feb–Oct 1981/ May 1986–Oct 1989

The first ten have been followed by Corazón Aquino, who became President of the Philippines in 1986, Benazir Bhutto, Prime Minister of Pakistan (1988–90), Violeta Barrios de Chamorro, President of Nicaragua (1990–), Ertha Pascal-Trouillot, President of Haiti (1990–), and Mary Robinson, President of the Irish Republic (1990–). Since 1990, several other countries have appointed female Prime Ministers, including France (Edith Cresson), Canada (Kim Campbell), Burundi (Sylvie Kinigi), and Turkey (Tansu Çiller).

MRS. (NOW LADY) THATCHER

ALL THE PRESIDENTS

THE TEN

FIRST PRESIDENTS OF THE US

	President (dates)	Period of office
1	George Washington (1732–99)	1789–97
2	John Adams (1735–1826)	1797–1801
3	Thomas Jefferson (1743–1826)	1801–09
4	James Madison (1751–1836)	1809–17
5	James Monroe (1758–1831)	1817–25
6	John Quincy Adams (1767–1848)	1825–29
7	Andrew Jackson (1767–1845)	1829–37
8	Martin Van Buren (1782–1862)	1837–41
9	William H. Harrison (1773–1841)	1841
10	John Tyler (1790–1862)	1841–45

TOP 10

TALLEST US PRESIDENTS

	President	Height m	ft in
1	Abraham Lincoln	1.93	6 4
2	Lyndon B. Johnson	1.91	6 3
3=	William J. Clinton	1.89	6 2½
3=	Thomas Jefferson	1.89	6 2½
5=	Chester A. Arthur	1.88	6 2
5=	George H.W. Bush	1.88	6 2
5=	Franklin D. Roosevelt	1.88	6 2
5=	George Washington	1.88	6 2
9=	Andrew Jackson	1.85	6 1
9=	Ronald W. Reagan	1.85	6 1

ABRAHAM LINCOLN
Lincoln is most famous for having preserved the Union during the Civil War and for the emancipation of the American slaves. He is perhaps less well known for being the tallest of the US Presidents!

TOP 10

LONGEST-SERVING US PRESIDENTS

	President	Period in office years days
1	Franklin D. Roosevelt	12 39
2=	Grover Cleveland	8*
2=	Dwight Eisenhower	8*
2=	Ulysses S. Grant	8*
2=	Andrew Jackson	8*
2=	Thomas Jefferson	8*
2=	James Madison	8*
2=	James Monroe	8*
2=	Ronald W. Reagan	8*
2=	Woodrow Wilson	8*

* Two four-year terms — now the maximum any US President may remain in office

TOP 10

SHORTEST-SERVING US PRESIDENTS

	President	Period in office years	days
1	William H. Harrison		32
2	James A. Garfield		199
3	Zachary Taylor	1	128
4	Gerald R. Ford	2	150
5	Warren G. Harding	2	151
6	Millard Fillmore	2	236
7	John F. Kennedy	2	306
8	Chester A. Arthur	3	166
9	Andrew Johnson	3	323
10	John Tyler	3	332

TOP 10

SHORTEST US PRESIDENTS

	President	Height m	ft in
1	James Madison	1.63	5 4
2=	Benjamin Harrison	1.68	5 6
2=	Martin Van Buren	1.68	5 6
4=	John Adams	1.70	5 7
4=	John Quincy Adams	1.70	5 7
4=	William McKinley	1.70	5 7
7=	William H. Harrison	1.73	5 8
7=	James K. Polk	1.73	5 8
7=	Zachary Taylor	1.73	5 8
10=	Ulysses S. Grant	1.74	5 8½
10=	Rutherford B. Hayes	1.74	5 8½

THE TEN

LAST US PRESIDENTS AND VICE-PRESIDENTS TO DIE IN OFFICE

	Name/date	Office
1	John F. Kennedy* November 22, 1963	President
2	Franklin D. Roosevelt April 12, 1945	President
3	Warren G. Harding August 2, 1923	President
4	James S. Sherman October 30, 1912	Vice-President
5	William McKinley* September 14, 1901	President
6	Garret A. Hobart November 21, 1899	Vice-President
7	Thomas A. Hendricks November 25, 1885	Vice-President
8	James A. Garfield* September 19, 1881	President
9	Henry Wilson November 10, 1875	Vice-President
10	Abraham Lincoln* April 15, 1865	President

* Assassinated

TOP 10

LONGEST-LIVED US PRESIDENTS

	President	Age at death years	months
1	John Adams	90	8
2	Herbert Hoover	90	2
3	Harry S Truman	88	7
4	James Madison	85	3
5	Thomas Jefferson	83	2
6	Richard M. Nixon	81	3
7	John Quincy Adams	80	7
8	Martin Van Buren	79	7
9	Dwight D. Eisenhower	78	5
10	Andrew Jackson	78	2

TOP 10

YOUNGEST US PRESIDENTS

	President	Age at inauguration years	days
1	Theodore Roosevelt	42	322
2	John F. Kennedy	43	236
3	William Clinton	46	154
4	Ulysses S. Grant	46	236
5	Grover Cleveland	47	351
6	Franklin Pierce	48	101
7	James A. Garfield	49	105
8	James K. Polk	49	122
9	Millard Fillmore	50	184
10	John Tyler	51	8

TOP 10

OLDEST US PRESIDENTS

	President	Age at inauguration years	days
1	Ronald W. Reagan	69	349
2	William H. Harrison	68	23
3	James Buchanan	65	315
4	George H.W. Bush	64	223
5	Zachary Taylor	64	100
6	Dwight D. Eisenhower	62	98
7	Andrew Jackson	61	354
8	John Adams	61	125
9	Gerald R. Ford	61	26
10	Harry S Truman	60	339

DID YOU KNOW

THE WEIGHT OF OFFICE

While James Madison, the shortest US President, weighed just 100 lb/ 45 kg, Howard Taft (in office 1909–13) is believed to have been the heaviest at 332 lb/150 kg. He was so large that a special bath tub had to be installed in the White House for him. Bill Clinton has attained 235 lb/107 kg, making him probably the third heaviest President after Grover Cleveland.

JOHN F. KENNEDY
As well as being one of the youngest men ever to be elected President, Kennedy was also the first Roman Catholic ever to hold this office.

ROYAL HIGHNESSES

TOP 10

FIRST ROMAN EMPERORS

	Caesar	Born	Acceded	Died	Fate
1	Julius Caesar	Jul 12, 100 BC	48 BC	Mar 15, 44 BC	Assassinated
2	Augustus	Sep 23, 63 BC	27 BC	Aug 19, AD 14	Died
3	Tiberius	Nov 16, 42 BC	14 BC	Mar 16, AD 37	Died
4	Caligula	Aug 31, AD 12	AD 37	Jan 24, AD 41	Assassinated
5	Claudius	Aug 1, AD 10	AD 41	Oct 13, AD 54	Assassinated
6	Nero	Dec 15, AD 37	AD 54	Jun 9, AD 68	Suicide
7	Galba	Dec 24, AD 3	AD 68	Jan 15, AD 69	Assassinated
8	Otho	Apr 28, AD 32	AD 69	Apr 16, AD 69	Suicide
9	Vitellius	Sep 24, AD 15	AD 69	Dec 22, AD 69	Assassinated
10	Vespasian	Nov 18, AD 9	AD 69	Jun 23, AD 79	Died

TOP 10

SHORTEST-REIGNING BRITISH MONARCHS

	Monarch	Reign	Duration
1	Jane	1553	14 days
2	Edward V	1483	75 days
3	Edward VIII	1936	325 days
4	Richard III	1483–85	2 years
5	James II	1685–88	3 years
6	Mary I	1553–58	5 years
7	Mary II	1689–94	5 years
8	Edward VI	1547–53	6 years
9	William IV	1830–37	7 years
10	Edward VII	1901–10	9 years

TOP 10

WORLD'S LONGEST-REIGNING MONARCHS

	Monarch	Country	Reign	Age at accession	Reign years
1	Louis XIV	France	1643–1715	5	72
2	John II	Liechtenstein	1858–1929	18	71
3	Franz-Josef	Austria–Hungary	1848–1916	18	67
4	Victoria	UK	1837–1901	18	63
5	Hirohito	Japan	1926–89	25	62
6	George III	UK	1760–1820	22	59
7	Louis XV	France	1715–74	5	59
8	Pedro II	Brazil	1831–89	6	58
9	Wilhelmina	Netherlands	1890–1948	10	58
10	Henry III	England	1216–72	9	56

TOP 10

LONGEST-REIGNING QUEENS IN THE WORLD*

	Queen	Country	Reign	Reign years
1	Victoria	UK	1837–1901	63
2	Wilhelmina	Netherlands	1890–1948	58
3	Wu Chao	China	655–705	50
4	Salote Tubou	Tonga	1918–65	47
5	Elizabeth I	England	1558–1603	44
6	Elizabeth II	UK	1952–	42
7	Maria Theresa	Hungary	1740–80	40
8	Maria I	Portugal	1777–1816	39
9	Joanna I	Italy	1343–81	38
10=	Suiko Tenno	Japan	593–628	35
10=	Isabella II	Spain	1833–68	35

Some authorities have claimed a 73-year reign for Alfonso I of Portugal, but his father, Henry of Burgundy, who conquered Portugal, ruled as Count, and it was this title that Alfonso inherited on April 30, 1112, at the age of two. His mother, Theresa of Castile, ruled until he took power in 1128, but he did not assume the title of king until July 25, 1139, during the Battle of Ourique at which he vanquished the Moors. He thus ruled as king for 46 years until his death on December 6, 1185. More extravagant claims are sometimes made for long-reigning monarchs in the ancient world. One example is the alleged 94 years of Phiops II, a Sixth Dynasty Egyptian pharaoh, but since his dates of birth and death are uncertain, he has not been included.

* *Queens and empresses who ruled in their own right, not as consorts of kings or emperors*

As well as being the longest-reigning queen, Victoria is among the longest-reigning monarchs in the world. She also holds first place as the British monarch who occupied the throne for the longest time, beating her nearest rival, George III, by some four years.

LE ROI SOLEIL
Nicknamed the "Sun King" because of the splendor of his court, Louis XIV began his reign at five years of age, but he was not crowned until he was 16 years old.

T O P 1 0

YOUNGEST BRITISH MONARCHS

(Since the Norman Conquest)

	Monarch	Reign	Age at accession years	months
1	Henry VI	1422–61	0	8
2	Henry III	1216–72	9	1
3	Edward VI	1547–53	9	3
4	Richard II	1377–99	10	5
5	Edward V	1483	12	5
6	Edward III	1327–77	14	2
7	Jane	1553	15	8
8	Henry VIII	1509–47	17	10
9	Victoria	1837–1901	18	1
10	Charles II	1660–85	18	8

Henry VI was born on December 6, 1421 and became King of England on September 1, 1422, the day after the death of his father, Henry V. At the age of 10 months (following the death of his grandfather, Charles VI, on October 21, 1422), he also became King of France. Before the Norman Conquest, Edward the Martyr became king in 975 when aged about 12 and Ethelred II ("the Unready") in 978 at the age of about 10.

T O P 1 0

LONGEST-REIGNING BRITISH MONARCHS

	Monarch	Reign	Age at accession	Age at death	Reign years
1	Victoria	1837–1901	18	81	63
2	George III	1760–1820	22	81	59
3	Henry III	1216–72	9	64	56
4	Edward III	1327–77	14	64	50
5	Elizabeth I	1558–1603	25	69	44
6	Elizabeth II	1952–	25	–	42
7	Henry VI	1422–61 (deposed, d.1471)	8 months	49	38
8	Henry VIII	1509–47	17	55	37
9	Charles II	1660–85	19	54	36
10	Henry I	1100–35	31–32*	66–67*	35

* Henry I's birthdate is unknown, so his age at accession and death are uncertain.

This list excludes the reigns of monarchs before 1066, so it omits such rulers as Ethelred II who reigned for 37 years. Queen Elizabeth II overtook Henry VI's reign (38 years and 185 days) in August 1990 and is on target to pass that of her namesake Queen Elizabeth I in June 1996. If she is still on the throne on September 11, 2015, she will have beaten Queen Victoria's record by one day. She will then be 89 years old, and will be the UK's oldest ruler.

QUEEN VICTORIA
After her father's brothers, George IV and William IV, died, Princess Alexandrina Victoria became Queen of Great Britain and Ireland, and Empress of India.

T O P 1 0

OLDEST MONARCHS TO ASCEND THE BRITISH THRONE

	Monarch	Reign	Age at accession
1	William IV	1830–37	64
2	Edward VII	1901–10	59
3	George IV	1820–30	57
4	George I	1714–27	54
5	James II	1685–88	51
6	George V	1910–36	44
7	George II	1727–60	43
8	Edward VIII	1936	41
9	George VI	1936–52	40
10	William I	1066–87	39

T O P 1 0

LONGEST-REIGNING LIVING MONARCHS IN THE WORLD

(Including hereditary rulers of principalities, dukedoms, etc.)

	Monarch	Country	Date of birth	Accession
1	Bhumibol Adulyadej	Thailand	Dec 5, 1927	Jun 9, 1946
2	Rainier III	Monaco	May 31, 1923	May 9, 1949
3	Elizabeth II	UK	Apr 21, 1926	Feb 6, 1952
4	Hussein	Jordan	Nov 14, 1935	Aug 11, 1952
5	Hassan II	Morocco	Jul 9, 1929	Feb 26, 1961
6	Isa bin Sulman al-Khalifa	Bahrain	Jul 3, 1933	Nov 2, 1961
7	Malietoa Tanumafili II	Western Samoa	Jan 4, 1913	Jan 1, 1962
8	Jean	Luxembourg	Jan 5, 1921	Nov 12, 1964
9	Taufa'ahau Tupou IV	Tonga	Jul 4, 1918	Dec 16, 1965
10	Qaboos bin Said	Oman	Nov 18, 1942	Jul 23, 1970

There are 25 countries that have emperors, kings, queens, princes, dukes, sultans, or other hereditary rulers as their heads of state. Malaysia, uniquely, has an elected monarchy.

EXPLORATION AND ENDEAVOR

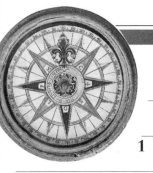

TOP 10

FIRST EXPLORERS TO LAND IN THE AMERICAS

	Explorer	Nationality	Discovery/ exploration	Year
1	Christopher Columbus	Italian	West Indies	1492
2	John Cabot	Italian/ English	Nova Scotia/ Newfoundland	1497
3	Alonso de Hojeda	Spanish	Brazil	1499
4	Vicente Yañez Pinzón	Spanish	Amazon	1500
5	Pedro Alvarez Cabral	Portuguese	Brazil	1500
6	Gaspar Corte Real	Portuguese	Labrador	1500
7	Rodrigo de Bastidas	Spanish	Central America	1501
8	Vasco Nuñez de Balboa	Spanish	Panama	1513
9	Juan Ponce de León	Spanish	Florida	1513
10	Juan Díaz de Solís	Spanish	Río de la Plata	1515

After his pioneering voyage of 1492, Columbus made three subsequent journeys to the West Indies and South America. Following him, several expeditions landed on the same islands of the West Indies (these have not been included as new explorations). Although Hojeda (or Ojeda) was the leader of the 1499 expedition, Amerigo Vespucci, after whom America is named, was also on the voyage. Of the three voyages that arrived in 1500, that of Pinzón (who had also been with Columbus on his 1492 voyage) takes precedence as he landed on January 26. Cabral followed in April, while Corte Real, who is thought to have landed late in 1500, disappeared on the voyage.

TOP 10

FIRST MOUNTAINEERS TO CLIMB EVEREST

	Mountaineer	Nationality	Date
1	Edmund Hillary	New Zealander	May 29, 1953
2	Tenzing Norgay	Nepalese	May 29, 1953
3	Jürg Marmet	Swiss	May 23, 1956
4	Ernst Schmied	Swiss	May 23, 1956
5	Hans-Rudolf von Gunten	Swiss	May 24, 1956
6	Adolf Reist	Swiss	May 24, 1956
7	Wang Fu-chou	Chinese	May 25, 1960
8	Chu Ying-hua	Chinese	May 25, 1960
9	Konbu	Tibetan	May 25, 1960
10=	Nawang Gombu	Indian	May 1, 1963
10=	James Whittaker	American	May 1, 1963

Nawang Gombu and James Whittaker are 10th equal because, neither man wishing to deny the other the privilege of being the first to reach the summit, they ascended the last few feet together, side by side.

CAPTAIN WEBB AND THE FIRST CROSS-CHANNEL SWIM

Captain Matthew Webb (1848–83) was one of the most celebrated men in Victorian England. The son of a Shropshire doctor and one of 12 children, he went to sea at the age of 12 and soon became renowned for his strength and stamina in the water, saving the lives of swimmers – including one of his brothers – and winning medals for bravery. Yet his fame derived largely from a single exploit, when in 1875 he became the first person to swim the English Channel.

During the next 36 years no fewer than 71 people, 22 of them women, tried to emulate Webb's cross-Channel swim, but it was not until 1911 that 37-year-old Thomas William Burgess of Rotherham, Yorkshire, finally succeeded in becoming the second man to swim the Channel. It was to be an additional 16 years before the tally reached 10, three of them women.

T O P   1 0

FIRST CROSS-CHANNEL SWIMMERS

	Swimmer	Nationality	Time hr:min	Date
1	Matthew Webb	British	21:45	Aug 24–25, 1875
2	Thomas Burgess	British	22:35	Sep 5–6, 1911
3	Henry Sullivan	American	26:50	Aug 5–6, 1923
4	Enrico Tiraboschi	Italian	16:33	Aug 12, 1923
5	Charles Toth	American	16:58	Sep 8–9, 1923
6	Gertrude Ederle	American	14:39	Aug 6, 1926
7	Millie Corson	American	15:29	Aug 27–28, 1926
8	Arnst Wierkotter	German	12:40	Aug 30, 1926
9	Edward Temme	British	14:29	Aug 5, 1927
10	Mercedes Gleitze	British	15:15	Oct 7, 1927

The first three crossings were from England to France, the rest from France to England. Gertrude Ederle was the first woman to swim the Channel, and on September 11, 1951 American Florence Chadwick became the first woman to swim from England to France. In 1934 Edward Temme also swam from England to France, becoming the first person to cross successfully in both directions. The Channel has been swum underwater (by Fred Baldasare in 1962), and by an 11-year-old girl. The record for the fastest crossing was held at one time by a 16-year-old American girl, Lynne Cox. It is now held by another American, Penny Dean, who crossed in 7 hr 40 min on July 29, 1978.

T O P   1 0

FASTEST CROSS-CHANNEL SWIMMERS

	Swimmer	Nationality	Year	Time hr: min
1	Penny Lee Dean	American	1978	7:40
2	Philip Rush	New Zealander	1987	7:55
3	Richard Davey	British	1988	8:05
4	Irene van der Laan	Dutch	1982	8:06
5	Paul Asmuth	American	1985	8:12
6	Anita Sood	Indian	1987	8:15
7	Monique Wildschutt	Dutch	1984	8:19
8	Eric Johnson	American	1985	8:20
9	Susie Maroney	Australian	1990	8:29
10	Lyndon Dunsbee	British	1984	8:34

T O P   1 0

FIRST PEOPLE TO REACH THE SOUTH POLE

	Name	Nationality	Date
1=	Roald Amundsen*	Norwegian	Dec 14, 1911
1=	Olav Olavsen Bjaaland	Norwegian	Dec 14, 1911
1=	Helmer Julius Hanssen	Norwegian	Dec 14, 1911
1=	Helge Sverre Hassel	Norwegian	Dec 14, 1911
1=	Oscar Wisting	Norwegian	Dec 14, 1911
6=	Robert Falcon Scott*	British	Jan 17, 1912
6=	Henry Robertson Bowers	British	Jan 17, 1912
6=	Edgar Evans	British	Jan 17, 1912
6=	Lawrence Edward Grace Oates	British	Jan 17, 1912
6=	Edward Adrian Wilson	British	Jan 17, 1912

* Expedition leader

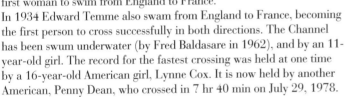

SCOTT'S TELESCOPE

Just 33 days separated the first two expeditions to reach the South Pole. Although several voyages had sailed close to Antarctica, no one had set foot on the mainland until the 19th century. Robert Falcon Scott, a young naval lieutenant, first landed in the Antarctic in 1902 and examined the feasibility of reaching the South Pole. In 1909 Ernest Shackleton marched to within 113 miles/182 km of the Pole, and a multination race for its conquest began. A British Antarctic Expedition, led by Scott, was organized in 1910 with the goal "to reach the South Pole and to secure for the British Empire the honour of this achievement," but on his arrival in Australia, Scott learned that the Norwegian Roald Amundsen had also embarked on an expedition to the Pole. After reaching the Antarctic, Scott undertook scientific research and acclimatized his team to local conditions. His party, leaving later than Amundsen's, suffered severe weather and, after problems with motor sleds, ponies, and dogs, relied entirely on man-hauled sleds. Amundsen, in contrast, depended exclusively on dogs, and even used them as part of his team's food supply, viewing them as a "mobile larder" (which the British expedition considered barbaric). When Scott finally reached the Pole, his party found that the Norwegians had beaten them. Plagued by illness, hunger, bad weather, and exhaustion, they began the journey back to their base during which Evans died after injuring himself. Realizing that they had insufficient rations, Oates stepped out into a blizzard in a famous act of self-sacrifice. At precisely the time that Amundsen's achievement was being reported to the world, the remaining three died in their tent.

CROSS-COUNTRY SKIS
These heavy wooden cross-country skis were used by Scott on his first Antarctic expedition.

NOBEL PRIZES

T O P 1 0

NOBEL PRIZE WINNING COUNTRIES

	Country	Phy	Che	Ph/Med	Lit	Pce	Eco	Total
1	US	57	38	70	10	17	21	213
2	UK	20	23	23	8	10	6	90
3	Germany	19	27	14	6	4	–	70
4	France	11	7	7	12	9	1	47
5	Sweden	4	4	7	7	5	2	29
6	Switzerland	2	5	5	2	3	–	17
7	USSR	7	1	2	3	2	1	16
8	Stateless institutions	–	–	–	–	14	–	14
9	Italy	3	1	3	5	1	–	13
10=	Denmark	3	–	5	3	1	–	12
10=	Netherlands	6	2	2	–	1	1	12

Phy – Physics; Che – Chemistry; Ph/Med – Physiology or Medicine; Lit – Literature; Pce – Peace; Eco – Economic Sciences

A century ago, on November 27, 1895, the Swedish scientist Alfred Nobel signed his will in which he left the major part of his fortune of 31,600,000 Swedish kroner, amassed through his invention of dynamite, to establish a trust fund, now estimated to be worth over $225,000,000. Nobel died the following year, but interest earned from this money has enabled annual prizes to be awarded since 1901 to those who have achieved the greatest common good in the fields of Physics, Chemistry, Physiology or Medicine, Literature, Peace, and, since 1969, Economic Sciences. All the award ceremonies take place in Stockholm, Sweden, with the exception of the Peace Prize, which is awarded in Oslo, Norway.

T H E T E N

FIRST US WINNERS OF THE NOBEL PRIZE FOR PHYSIOLOGY OR MEDICINE

	Winner	Prize year
1	Thomas Hunt Morgan (1866–1945)	1933
2	George Hoyt Whipple (1879–1976)	1934
3	George Richards Minot (1885–1950)	1934
4	William Parry Murphy (1892–1987)	1934
5	Edward Adelbert Doisy* (1893–1986)	1943
6	Joseph Erlanger (1874–1965)	1944
7	Herbert Spencer Gasser (1888–1963)	1944
8	Hermann Joseph Muller (1890–1967)	1946
9	Carl Ferdinand Cori*# (1896–1984)	1947
10	Gerty Theresa Cori, née Radnitz*# (1896–1957)	1947

* Prize shared with other nationalities
 # Joint award to husband and wife; both born in Prague, then part of Austria

T H E T E N

FIRST US WINNERS OF THE NOBEL PEACE PRIZE

	Winner	Prize year
1	Theodore Roosevelt (1858–1919)	1906
2	Elihu Root (1845–1937)	1912
3	Thomas Woodrow Wilson (1856–1924)	1919
4	Charles Gates Dawes* (1865–1951)	1925
5	Frank Billings Kellogg (1856–1937)	1929
6	Jane Addams (1860–1935)	1931
7	Nicholas Murray Butler (1862–1947)	1931
8	Cordell Hull (1871–1955)	1945
9	John Raleigh Mott (1865–1955)	1946
10	Emily Greene Balch (1867–1961)	1946

* Prize shared with other nationalities

In 1962, the American Linus Carl Pauling (1901–94), winner of the 1954 Chemistry Prize, became the only person to win two unshared Prizes in separate categories, Martin Luther King Jr. (1929–68), won in 1964, and Henry Kissinger (b. 1923), was joint prize-winner in 1973 with Vietnamese statesman Le Duc Tho (1911–90).

T H E T E N

FIRST US WINNERS OF THE NOBEL PRIZE FOR PHYSICS

	Winner	Prize year
1	Albert Abraham Michelson (1852–1931)	1907
2	Robert Andrews Millikan (1868–1953)	1923
3	Carl David Anderson* (1905–91)	1936
4	Clinton Joseph Davisson* (1881–1958)	1937
5	Ernest Orlando Lawrence (1901–58)	1939
6	Otto Stern# (1888–1969)	1943
7	Isidor Isaac Rabi** (1898–1988)	1944
8	Percy Williams Bridgman (1882–1961)	1946
9	Felix Bloch (1905–1983)‡	1952
10	Edward Mills Purcell (1912–)	1952

* Prize shared with other nationalities
 # German-born
**Austrian-born
‡ Swiss-born

T H E   T E N

FIRST WOMEN TO WIN A NOBEL PRIZE

	Winner	Nationality	Prize	Year
1	Marie Curie* (1867–1934)	Polish	Physics	1903
2	Bertha von Suttner (1843–1914)	Austrian	Peace	1905
3	Selma Lagerlöf (1858–1940)	Swedish	Literature	1909
4	Marie Curie (1867–1934)	Polish	Chemistry	1911
5	Grazia Deledda (1875–1936)	Italian	Literature	1926 #
6	Sigrid Undset (1882–1949)	Norwegian	Literature	1928
7	Jane Addams** (1860–1935)	American	Peace	1931
8	Irène Joliot-Curie‡ (1897–1956)	French	Chemistry	1935
9	Pearl Buck (1892–1973)	American	Literature	1938
10	Gabriela Mistral (1899–1957)	Chilean	Literature	1945

The American writer, Pearl Buck (1892–1973), won the Nobel Prize for Literature in 1938. Until 1924 she spent most of her life in China, from which she drew the inspiration for many of her novels and plays. Her most famous works include *East Wind: West Wind* (1930), *The Good Earth* (1931; Pulitzer Prize), *Dragon Seed* (1942), *Imperial Woman* (1956), and *Mandala*(1976).

* *Shared half with husband Pierre Curie; other half to Henri Becquerel*
\# *Awarded 1927*
** *Shared with Nicholas Murray Butler*
‡ *Shared with husband Frédéric Joliot-Curie*

T H E   T E N

FIRST US WINNERS OF THE NOBEL PRIZE FOR CHEMISTRY

	Winner	Prize year
1	Theodore William Richards (1868–1928)	1914
2	Irving Langmuir (1881–1957)	1932
3	Harold Clayton Urey (1893–1981)	1934
4	James Batcheller Sumner (1887–1955)	1946
5	John Howard Northrop (1891–1987)	1946
6	Wendell Meredith Stanley (1904–1971)	1946
7	William Francis Giauque (1895–1982)	1949
8	Edwin Mattison McMillan (1907–1991)	1951
9	Glenn Theodore Seaborg (1912–)	1951
10	Linus Carl Pauling (1901–94)	1954

The scientific bias of the Nobel Prizes reflects the fact that Alfred Nobel was himself a chemist and inventor of note, with a total of 355 patents in his name, and the founder of the first multinational chemicals companies.

T H E   T E N

FIRST US WINNERS OF THE NOBEL PRIZE FOR ECONOMIC SCIENCES

	Winner	Prize year
1	Paul Anthony Samuelson (1915–)	1970
2	Simon S. Kuznets (1901–1985)	1971
3	Kenneth Joseph Arrow* (1921–)	1972
4	Wassily Leontief# (1906–)	1973
5	Tjalling Charles Koopmans* (1910–1985)**	1975
6	Milton Friedman (1912–)	1976
7	Herbert Alexander Simon (1916–)	1978
8	Theodore William Schultz* (1902–)	1979
9	Lawrence R. Klein (1920–)	1980
10	James Tobin (1918–)	1981

* *Prize shared with other nationalities*
\# *Russian-born*
**Dutch-born

This award – officially designated the Prize in Economic Sciences in Memory of Alfred Nobel – was instituted by the Bank of Sweden at the time of its tercentenary in 1968 and first awarded the following year.

T H E   T E N

FIRST US WINNERS OF THE NOBEL PRIZE FOR LITERATURE

	Winner	Prize year
1	Sinclair Lewis (1885–1951)	1930
2	Eugene O'Neill (1888–1953)	1936
3	Pearl Buck (1892–1973)	1938
4	William Faulkner (1897–1962)	1949
5	Ernest Hemingway (1899–1961)	1954
6	John Steinbeck (1902–1968)	1962
7	Saul Bellow (1915–)	1976
8	Isaac Bashevis Singer (1904–1991)	1978
9	Czeslaw Milosz* (1911–)	1980
10	Joseph Brodsky# (1940–)	1987

* *Polish-born*
\# *Russian-born*

The most recent US recipient of the Nobel Prize for Literaure is Toni Morrison (b. 1931), awarded the prize in 1993.

THE GOOD & THE BAD

TOP 10

ORGANIZED RELIGIONS IN THE WORLD

	Religion	Followers
1	Christianity	1,869,751,000
2	Islam	1,014,372,000
3	Hinduism	751,360,000
4	Buddhism	334,002,000
5	Sikhism	19,853,000
6	Judaism	18,153,000
7	Confucianism	6,230,000
8	Baha'ism	5,742,000
9	Jainism	3,927,000
10	Shintoism	3,336,800

This list excludes the followers of various tribal and folk religions, new religions, and shamanism. Since reforms in the former USSR, many who practiced Christianity in secret while following the Communist anti-religion line in public have now declared their faith openly. The list is based on the work of David B. Barrett, who has been monitoring world religions for many years.

TOP 10

LARGEST HINDU POPULATIONS IN THE WORLD

	Country	Total Hindu population
1	India	700,900,000
2	Nepal	17,240,000
3	Bangladesh	13,960,000
4	Sri Lanka	2,730,000
5	Pakistan	1,930,000
6	Malaysia	1,340,000
7	Mauritius	580,000
8	South Africa	430,000
9	UK	410,000
10	US	340,000

TOP 10

LARGEST BUDDHIST POPULATIONS IN THE WORLD

	Country	Total Buddhist population
1	Japan	97,090,000 *
2	China	71,000,000
3	Thailand	54,570,000
4	Vietnam	47,260,000
5	Myanmar (Burma)	39,900,000
6	South Korea	15,990,000
7	Sri Lanka	12,210,000
8	Taiwan	9,000,000
9	Cambodia	8,210,000
10	Hong Kong	4,380,000#

* Including many who also practice Shintoism
 # Buddhist and Taoist

TOP 10

LARGEST MUSLIM POPULATIONS IN THE WORLD

	Country	Total Muslim population
1	Indonesia	164,140,000
2	Pakistan	123,870,000
3	Bangladesh	99,710,000
4	India	99,000,000
5	Turkey	59,390,000
6	Iran	55,000,000
7	Egypt	51,400,000
8	Nigeria	41,200,000
9	China	28,000,000
10	Algeria	26,890,000

TOP 10

LARGEST JEWISH POPULATIONS IN THE WORLD

	Country	Total Jewish population
1	US	5,981,000
2	Israel	4,240,000
3	Former USSR	2,236,000
4	France	640,000
5	Canada	350,000
6	UK	315,000
7	Argentina	220,000
8	Brazil	183,000
9	South Africa	120,000
10	Australia	80,000

The Diaspora or scattering of Jewish people has been in progress for nearly 2,000 years, and as a result Jewish communities are found in virtually every country in the world. In 1939 it was estimated that the total world Jewish population was 17,000,000. Some 6,000,000 fell victim to Nazi persecution, reducing the figure to about 11,000,000, but by 1993 it was estimated to have grown again, and now exceeds 18,000,000.

TOP 10

RELIGIOUS AFFILIATIONS IN THE US

	Religion/organization	Membership
1	Roman Catholic Church	58,267,424
2	Southern Baptist Convention	15,232,347
3	United Methodist Church	8,785,135
4=	Muslim	8,000,000 *
4=	National Baptist Convention, USA, Inc.	8,000,000 *
6	Jews	5,981,000 #
7	Church of God in Christ	5,499,875
8	Evangelical Lutheran Church in America	5,245,177
9	Church of Jesus Christ of Latter-day Saints (Mormons)	4,336,000
10	Presbyterian Church	3,788,358

* Estimated
# Combined membership of several groups

It is claimed that out of the total US population of 248,709,873 (1990 census), 156,336,384, or 62.86 percent, are active members of a religious organization. Those represented in the Top 10 are the principal sects of often larger groups.

TOP 10

CHRISTIAN DENOMINATIONS IN THE WORLD

Denomination	Adherents
1 Roman Catholic	872,104,646
2 Slavonic Orthodox	92,523,987
3 United (including Lutheran/ Reformed)	65,402,685
4 Pentecostal	58,999,862
5 Anglican/Episcopalian	52,499,051
6 Baptist	50,321,923
7 Lutheran (excluding United)	44,899,837
8 Reformed (Presbyterian)	43,445,520
9 Methodist	31,718,508
10 Disciples (Restorationists)	8,783,192

TOP 10

LARGEST CHRISTIAN POPULATIONS IN THE WORLD

	Country	Total Christian population
1	US	223,240,000
2	Brazil	136,100,000
3	Former USSR	105,469,000
4	Mexico	85,080,000
5	Germany	61,340,000
6	Philippines	56,900,000
7	UK	50,470,000
8	Italy	47,560,000
9	Nigeria	44,860,000
10	France	44,080,000

Although Christian communities are found in almost every country in the world, it is difficult to put a precise figure on nominal membership rather than active participation, and these figures therefore represent only approximations.

The Top 10 is based on mid-1980s estimates supplied by MARC Europe, a Christian research and information organization. A subsequent estimate by the Vatican increased the figure for Roman Catholics to 911,000,000 while retaining the 52,000,000 figure for Anglicans – which indicates something of the problem of arriving even at "guesstimates" when it comes to global memberships. More recent estimates are not yet available.

THE CHRISTIAN FAITH

THE TEN
COMMANDMENTS

1 Thou shalt have no other gods before Me.

2 Thou shalt not make unto thee any graven image.

3 Thou shalt not take the name of the Lord thy God in vain.

4 Remember the sabbath day, to keep it holy.

5 Honor thy father and thy mother.

6 Thou shalt not kill.

7 Thou shalt not commit adultery.

8 Thou shalt not steal.

9 Thou shalt not bear false witness against thy neighbor.

10 Thou shalt not covet thy neighbor's house, thou shalt not covet thy neighbor's wife, nor his manservant, nor his maidservant, nor his ox, nor his ass, nor any thing that is thy neighbor's.

Exodus 20:3 (taken from the King James Bible)

CATHOLIC TASTES
A young girl in traditional white kneels to receive Holy Communion for the first time.

TOP 10
ANIMALS MOST MENTIONED IN THE BIBLE

	Animal	OT*	NT*	Total
1	Sheep	155	45	200
2	Lamb	153	35	188
3	Lion	167	9	176
4	Ox	156	10	166
5	Ram	165	0	165
6	Horse	137	27	164
7	Bullock	152	0	152
8	Ass	142	8	150
9	Goat	131	7	138
10	Camel	56	6	62

* *Occurrences in verses in the King James Bible (Old and New Testaments), including plurals*

The sheep are sorted from the goats (itself a biblical expression – "a shepherd divideth his sheep from the goats," in Matthew 25:32) in this Top 10 list of animals regarded as the most significant in biblical times, either economically or symbolically. Several generic terms are also found: beast (337 references), cattle (153), fowl (90), fish (56), and bird (41). Some creatures are mentioned only once, in Leviticus 11, which contains a list of animals that are considered "unclean" (the weasel, chameleon, and tortoise, for example). There are 40 references to the dog, but the cat is not mentioned once.

TOP 10
NAMES MOST MENTIONED IN THE BIBLE

	Name	OT*	NT*	Total
1	Jesus (984) Christ (576)	0	1,560	1,560
2	David	1,005	59	1,064
3	Moses	767	80	847
4	Jacob	350	27	377
5	Aaron	347	5	352
6	Solomon	293	12	305
7=	Joseph	215	35	250
7=	Abraham	176	74	250
9	Ephraim	182	1	183
10	Benjamin	162	2	164

* *Occurrences in verses in the King James Bible (Old and New Testaments), including possessive uses, such as "John's"*

The name Judah also appears 816 times, but the total includes references to the land as well as the man with that name. At the other end of the scale there are many names that appear only once or twice, among them Berodach-baladan and Tiglath-pileser. "God" is mentioned 4,105 times (2,749 Old Testament, 1,356 New Testament). The most mentioned place names produce few surprises: Israel (2,600 references) heads the list, followed by Jerusalem (814), Egypt (736), Babylon (298), and Assyria (141).

TOP 10
WORDS MOST MENTIONED IN THE BIBLE

	Word	OT*	NT*	Total
1	The	52,948	10,976	63,924
2	And	40,975	10,721	51,696
3	Of	28,518	6,099	34,617
4	To	10,207	3,355	13,562
5	That	9,152	3,761	12,913
6	In	9,767	2,900	12,667
7	He	7,348	3,072	10,420
8	For	6,690	2,281	8,971
9	I	6,669	2,185	8,854
10	His	7,036	1,437	8,473

A century before computers were invented, Thomas Hartwell Horne (1780–1862), a dogged Biblical researcher, undertook a manual search of the King James Bible to work out the frequency of occurrence of particular words. He concluded that the word "and" appeared a total of 35,543 times in the Old Testament and 10,684 times in the New Testament. He was fairly close on the latter – but he clearly missed quite a few instances in the Old Testament, as a recent computer search of the King James Bible indicates.

* *Occurrences in verses in the King James Bible (Old and New Testaments)*

T O P 1 0

FIRST POPES

1	Saint Peter
2	Saint Linus
3	Saint Anacletus
4	Saint Clement I
5	Saint Evaristus
6	Saint Alexander I
7	Saint Sixtus I
8	Saint Telesphorus
9	Saint Hyginus
10	Saint Pius I

The first 10 popes all lived during the first 150 years of the Christian Church. As well as all being revered as martyrs, they have one other feature in common: virtually nothing is known about any of them.

UNENVIABLE RECORD
Pope Urban VII died of malaria before his coronation, 12 days after being elected.

T O P 1 0

NATIONALITIES OF POPES

	Nationality	No.
1	Roman/Italian	208–209*
2	French	15–17#
3	Greek	15–16**
4	Syrian	6
5	German	4–6#
6	Spanish	5
7	African	2–3*
8	Galilean	2
9=	Dutch	1
9=	English	1
9=	Polish	1
9=	Portuguese	1

* *Gelasius I was Roman, but of African descent; it is unknown whether Miltiades was African or Roman.*
\# *The Franco-German frontier was variable at the births of two popes, hence their nationalities are uncertain.*
** *Theodore I was of Greek descent, but born in Jerusalem.*

Before John Paul II (the only Polish pope to date) took office, the last non-Italian pope was Hadrian VI, a Dutchman, who reigned from 1522 to 1523. Nicholas Breakspear, who took the name Hadrian IV in 1154, was the only English pope to date.

T O P 1 0

LONGEST-SERVING POPES

	Pope	Period in office	Years
1	Pius IX	Jun 16, 1846– Feb 7, 1878	31
2	Leo XIII	Feb 20, 1878– Jul 20, 1903	25
3	Peter	c. 42–67	c. 25
4	Pius VI	Feb 15, 1775– Aug 29, 1799	24
5	Adrian I	Feb 1, 772– Dec 25, 795	23
6	Pius VII	Mar 14, 1800– Aug 20, 1823	23
7	Alexander III	Sep 7, 1159– Aug 30, 1181	21
8	Sylvester	Jan 31, 314– Dec 31, 335	21
9	Leo I	Sep 29, 440– Nov 10, 461	21
10	Urban VIII	Aug 6, 1623– Jul 29, 1644	20

If he is still in office, the present pope, John Paul II, will enter the Top 10 in 1999 and could top it in 2010, when he will be 90 years old.

T O P 1 0

SHORTEST-SERVING POPES

	Pope	Year in office	Duration (days)
1	Urban VII	1590	12
2	Valentine	827	c. 14
3	Boniface VI	896	15
4	Celestine IV	1241	16
5	Sisinnius	708	20
6	Sylvester III	1045	21
7	Theodore II	897	c. 21
8	Marcellus II	1555	22
9	Damasus II	1048	23
10=	Pius III	1503	26
10=	Leo XI	1605	26

Many of those in this list were already elderly and in poor health when they were elected. Boniface VI and Sylvester III were deposed, and Damasus II possibly poisoned. Pope Johns have been particularly unlucky: John XXI lasted nine months but was killed in 1277 when a ceiling collapsed on him, while John XII was beaten to death by the husband of a woman with whom he was having an affair. In modern times, John Paul I was pontiff for just 33 days in 1978.

T O P 1 0

MOST COMMON NAMES OF POPES

	Name	No.
1	John	23
2	Gregory	16
3	Benedict	15
4	Clement	14
5=	Innocent	13
5=	Leo	13
7	Pius	12
8	Boniface	9
9=	Alexander	8
9=	Urban	8

CRIME

COUNTRIES WITH THE HIGHEST CRIME RATES

Country	Reported crime rate per 100,000 population
1 Dominica	22,432
2 Suriname	17,819
3 St. Kitts and Nevis	15,468
4 Sweden	14,188
5 New Zealand	13,247
6 Canada	11,443
7 Greenland	10,339
8 Denmark	10,270
9 Gibraltar	10,039
10 Guam	9,229
England and Wales	*8,986*
US	*5,820*

These figures are based on reported crimes: the reporting of crimes is not solely a response to lawlessness, but also relates to the public confidence in the ability of the police. There are many countries in which crime is so commonplace and law enforcement so inefficient or corrupt that many incidents go unreported, since victims know that doing so would achieve no result.

COUNTRIES WITH MOST BURGLARIES

Country	Annual burglaries per 100,000 population
1 Netherlands	2,621.8
2 Bahamas	2,580.4
3 Israel	2,483.0
4 New Zealand	2,447.6
5 Denmark	2,382.9
6 Bermuda	2,092.3
7 England and Wales	1,991.2
8 Australia	1,962.8
9 Malta	1,907.1
10 Sweden	1,801.8
US	*1,235.9*

COUNTRIES WITH THE LOWEST CRIME RATES

Country	Reported crime rate per 100,000 population	Country	Reported crime rate per 100,000 population
1 Togo	11.0	6 Guinea	32.4
2 Bangladesh	16.8	7 Mali	33.0
3 Nepal	29.1	8 Burkina Faso	41.0
4= Congo	32.0	9 Syria	73.0
4= Niger	32.0	10 Burundi	87.0

COUNTRIES WITH MOST CAR THEFTS

Country	Annual thefts per 100,000 population	Country	Annual thefts per 100,000 population
1 Switzerland	1,504.6 *	6 USA	657.8
2 New Zealand	1,026.4	7 Norway	608.7
3 England and Wales	977.4	8 Denmark	575.9
4 Sweden	879.0	9 Italy	546.0
5 Australia	770.6	10 France	519.6

* Including motorcycles and bicycles.

US STATES WITH THE HIGHEST CRIME RATES

State	Crimes per 100,000	State	Crimes per 100,000
1 District of Columbia	11,407.0	6 Louisiana	6,546.5
2 Florida	8,358.2	7 New Mexico	6,434.1
3 Texas	7,057.9	8 Georgia	6,405.4
4 Arizona	7,028.6	9 Maryland	6,224.6
5 California	6,679.5	10 Nevada	6,203.8

US STATES WITH THE LOWEST CRIME RATES

State	Crimes per 100,000	State	Crimes per 100,000
1 West Virginia	2,609.7	6 Pennsylvania	3,392.7
2 North Dakota	2,903.3	7 Vermont	3,410.0
3 South Dakota	2,998.9	8 Maine	3,523.6
4 New Hampshire	3,080.6	9 Iowa	3,957.1
5 Kentucky	3,323.5	10 Idaho	3,996.2

TOP 10
WORST YEARS FOR CRIME IN THE US

	Year	Crimes per 100,000
1	1980	5,950.0
2	1991	5,897.8
3	1981	5,858.2
4	1990	5,820.3
5	1989	5,741.0
6	1988	5,664.2
7	1992	5,660.2
8	1982	5,603.6
9	1979	5,565.4
10	1987	5,550.0

This list, which relates numbers of crimes reported to the population, and hence factors in population increases, tends to refute the notion that the United States crime rate increases inexorably from year to year, by indicating that 1980 was the worst year on record, with 13,408,300 crimes reported in a population of 225,349,264. However, the general postwar trend is up, and we may look back with nostalgia to the 1960–62 period, when the US population was 179,323,175 and there were 1,946,500 crimes reported nationwide – a rate of just 1,085.5 per 100,000.

TOP 10
TYPES OF PROPERTY THEFT IN THE US

	Property	Total value ($)
1	Motor vehicles	7,332,195,000
2	Jewelry and precious metals	1,257,043,000
3	TVs, radios, stereos, etc.	1,135,415,000
4	Currency, notes, etc.	918,797,000
5	Clothing and furs	408,539,000
6	Office equipment	320,220,000
7	Household goods	249,138,000
8	Firearms	129,290,000
9	Consumable goods	113,020,000
10	Livestock	18,200,000

Along with the category "Miscellaneous," worth an estimated $2,725,799,000 in 1992 a total of $14,607,656,000 worth of property was stolen in the US – more than the entire Gross Domestic Product of some developing countries. Overall, some $5,202,203,000 worth, or 35.6 percent of the items stolen, was recovered, with motor vehicles the most likely to be retrieved ($4,681,303,000 worth, or 63.8 percent of those stolen), and jewelry the least likely ($56,698,000/4.5 percent).

TOP 10
COUNTRIES' EMBASSIES IN THE US WITH THE MOST UNPAID PARKING FINES

	Country	Unpaid fines ($)*
1	Russia	2,768,635
2	Former USSR	1,661,535
3	Nigeria	195,860
4	Cameroon	72,940
5	Egypt	65,935
6	South Korea	58,980
7	India	58,610
8	China	53,730
9	Spain	53,100
10	Ukraine	49,135

* As of April 1994

The use of diplomatic immunity by embassy staff to evade both serious criminal offences and misdemeanors, including parking fines, is an international problem, with some embassies appearing prominently in such lists in different parts of the world: the Soviet Union consistently headed the comparative list in the UK, for example, although its place has now been taken by Nigeria. (The US Embassy in London has not always had an unblemished record, but in 1993 failed to pay just three parking fines.)

TOP 10
CARS MOST VULNERABLE TO THEFT IN THE US

1	Mercedes SL convertible
2	Volkswagen cabriolet
3	Ford Mustang convertible
4	Ford Mustang
5	Chevrolet Corvette convertible
6	BMW 318i/325i convertible
7	Nissan 300ZX
8	Nissan 300ZX 2+2
9	BMW 525i/535i
10	BMW 318i/325i 2-Door

TOP 10
LARGEST FEDERAL CORRECTIONAL INSTITUTIONS IN THE US
(By population)

	Institution	Location	Rated capacity
1	US Penitentiary	Atlanta, Georgia	1,819
2	US Penitentiary	Leavenworth, Kansas	1,436
3	US Penitentiary	Lompoc, California	1,305
4	Federal Correctional Institution	Fort Dix, New Jersey	1,300
5	Federal Correctional Institution	Jessup, Georgia	1,140
6	Federal Correctional Institution,	Sheridan, Oregon	1,094
7	US Penitentiary	Terre Haute, Indiana	1,088
8	Federal Correctional Institution,	Marianna, Florida	1,033
9	Federal Correctional Institution	El Reno, Oklahoma	1,026
10	Federal Correctional Institution	Manchester, Kentucky	1,000

MURDER FACTS

TOP 10
COUNTRIES WITH THE HIGHEST MURDER RATES

	Country	Murders p.a. per 100,000 population
1	Swaziland	87.8
2	Bahamas	52.6
3	Lesotho	51.1
4	Colombia	40.5
5	Aruba	37.5
6	Sudan	30.5
7	Philippines	30.1
8	Guernsey	27.4
9	Nauru	25.0
10	Greenland	23.5
	US	*9.1*
	England	*1.3*

TOP 10
WORST CITIES FOR MURDER IN THE US

	City	Murders
1	New York	1,995
2	Los Angeles	1,094
3	Chicago	939
4	Detroit	595
5	Houston	465
6	Washington DC	443
7	Philadelphia	425
8	Dallas	387
9	Baltimore	335
10	New Orleans	279

The identity of America's 10 murder capitals remains fairly consistent from year to year, with only some slight adjustment to the order. The figures here are for 1992, when the Top 10 accounted for 6,957, or 31 percent, of the total 22,540 murders committed in the US.

THE POINT OF THE MATTER
Contrary to press reports, killings involving guns in England and Wales have actually declined from a 1987 peak of 78, while homicides caused by sharp instruments have become more widespread.

TOP 10
MOST COMMON MURDER WEAPONS/METHODS IN ENGLAND AND WALES

	Weapon/method	Victims
1	Sharp instrument	226
2	Hitting and kicking	140
3	Strangulation and asphyxiation	80
4	Shooting	52
5	Blunt instrument	51
6	Burning	24
7	Drowning	15
8	Poison and drugs	14
9	Motor vehicle	9
10	Explosives	4

According to Home Office statistics, there were 622 homicides in 1992 in England and Wales (382 male and 240 female victims). In addition to those in the list, the apparent method in five incidents is described as "other" and two of unknown cause. This represents a fall from the previous year, but the general trend has been one of increase – although it should be noted that some offenses first recorded as homicides were later reclassified. The number of victims first exceeded the 400 mark in 1952, 500 in 1974, and 600 in 1979. Based on the 1992 statistic, however, England and Wales are still relatively safe countries: the odds of being murdered in England and Wales are one in 79,090. One is more than six times as likely to be killed in the US.

TOP 10
WORST YEARS FOR GUN MURDERS IN THE US

	Year	Victims
1	1992	15,377
2	1991	14,265
3	1980	13,650
4	1990	12,847
5	1981	12,523
6	1974	12,474
7	1975	12,061
8	1989	11,832
9	1982	11,721
10	1986	11,381

DID YOU KNOW
US CRIME CLOCK

The murder rate in the US (1992 statistics) is equivalent to one murder every 23 minutes. More common crimes produce equally alarming statistics: there is a robbery every 47 seconds, a motor vehicle theft every 20 seconds, and a burglary every 11 seconds.

WORST YEARS FOR MURDER IN THE US

	Year	Victims
1	1992	22,540
2	1980	21,860
3	1991	21,505
4	1981	20,053
5	1990	20,045
6	1982	19,485
7	1986	19,257
8	1989	18,954
9	1983	18,673
10	1975	18,642

MOST COMMON MURDER WEAPONS/METHODS IN THE US

	Weapon/method	Victims
1	Handguns	12,489
2	Knives or cutting instruments	3,265
3	"Personal weapons" (hands, feet, fists, etc.)	1,114
4	Shotguns	1,104
5	Firearms (type not stated)	1,086
6	Blunt objects (hammers, clubs, etc.)	1,029
7	Rifles	698
8	Strangulation	313
9	Fire	203
10	Asphyxiation	114

Less common methods include drowning (27 cases), explosives (19), and poison (13). The total number of murders for 1992 amounted to 22,540 – or one person in every 11,034. The order of the weapons has not changed much in recent years, but the numbers have increased dramatically: in 1965, for example, there were 8,773 murder victims in the US, with firearms used in 5,015 cases. By 1992 the figure had risen by 257 percent, with 15,377, or 68 percent, committed using firearms.

GUN MURDERS
Handguns are the number one murder weapon in the US while shooting ranks only fourth as a method of killing in the UK.

ENGLAND AND WALES CRIME CLOCK

Based on 1992 crime figures for England and Wales, a murder is committed, on average, every 14 hours, a robbery every 10 minutes, a violent crime every three minutes, a motor vehicle theft every 53 seconds, and a burglary every 23 seconds. If comparing with the US crime clock (see opposite), one should keep in mind that the population of the US is almost five times that of England and Wales.

RELATIONSHIPS OF HOMICIDE VICTIMS TO PRINCIPAL SUSPECTS IN THE US

	Relationship	Victims
1	Acquaintance	6,102
2	Stranger	3,053
3	Wife	913
4	Friend	843
5	Girlfriend	519
6	Husband	383
7	Son	325
8	Boyfriend	240
9	Daughter	235
10	Neighbor	217

In addition to these offenses, which accounted for 22,540 murders in 1992, FBI statistics recorded 8,818 murders where the victim's relationship to the suspect was unknown, 393 "other family members" (those not specified elsewhere), 169 fathers, 167 brothers, 121 mothers, and 42 sisters.

WORST STATES FOR MURDER IN THE US

	State	Firearms used	Total murders
1	California	2,851	3,921
2	New York	1,760	2,370
3	Texas	1,627	2,239
4	Illinois	832	1,217
5	Florida	712	1,176
6	Michigan	655	934
7	North Carolina	450	708
8	Pennsylvania	450	684
9	Georgia	443	671
10	Louisiana	507	659

Of the 14,579 murders committed in the Top 10 states in 1992, firearms were used in 10,287, or 70.6 percent. In that year, there were more murders in Pennsylvania, ranked 8th in the list, and with an estimated 1992 resident population of 12,009,000, than in the whole of England and Wales, with more than four times as many inhabitants. The top three states all had murder rates of close to 13.0 per 100,000 of the population, while of those appearing in the Top 10, the highest murder rate (15.4 per 100,000) occurred in Louisiana and the lowest (5.7 per 100,000) in Pennsylvania.

MURDER MOST FOUL

TOP 10

MOST PROLIFIC SERIAL KILLERS OF THE 20TH CENTURY

Serial killers are mass murderers who kill repeatedly, often over long periods, in contrast to the so-called "spree killers" who have been responsible for massacres on single occasions, usually with guns, and other perpetrators of single outrages, often by means of bombs, resulting in multiple deaths. Because of the secrecy surrounding their horrific crimes, and the time-spans involved, it is almost impossible to calculate the precise numbers of serial killers' victims. The numbers of murders attributed to these criminals should be taken as "best estimates" based on the most reliable evidence available. Such is the magnitude of the crimes of some of them, however, that some of the figures may be underestimates.

1 Pedro Alonzo (or Armando) López

After he was captured in 1980, López, known as the "Monster of the Andes," led police to 53 graves, but had probably murdered a total of more than 300 young girls in Colombia, Ecuador, and Peru. He was sentenced to life imprisonment.

2 Henry Lee Lucas

The subject of the film, Henry, Portrait of a Serial Killer, Lucas (b.1937) may have

ANDREI CHIKATILO
Chikatilo successfully led a double life as a married father and schoolteacher and Communist party member for the 12 years he preyed on the citizens of Rostov-on-Don.

committed up to 200 murders. In 1983 he admitted to 360 and was convicted of 11, and is now on Death Row in Huntsville, Texas. His full toll of victims will probably never be known.

3 Bruno Lüdke

Lüdke (b.1909) was a German who confessed to murdering 86 women between 1928 and January 29, 1943. Declared insane, he was incarcerated in a Vienna hospital where he was subjected to medical experiments, apparently dying on April 8, 1944 after a lethal injection.

4 Delfina and Maria de Jesús Gonzales

After abducting girls to work in their Mexican brothel, Rancho El Angel, the Gonzales sisters murdered as many as 80 of them, and an unknown number of their customers, and buried them in the grounds. In 1964 the two were sentenced to 40 years' imprisonment.

5 Daniel Camargo Barbosa

Eight years after the arrest of Lopez (see No. 1) in Ecuador, Barbosa, another Ecuadorean, was captured after a similar series of horrific child murders – with a probable total of 71 victims. He was sentenced to just 16 years in prison.

6 Kampatimar Shankariya

Caught after a two-year spree during which he killed as many as 70 times, Shankariya was hanged in Jaipur, India, on May 16, 1979.

TOP 10

MOST PROLIFIC MURDERERS IN THE US

1 Henry Lee Lucas

Lucas ranks as America's worst serial killer, with anything up to 200 victims (see No. 2 in The 10 Most Prolific Serial Killers of the 20th Century).

2 Herman Webster Mudgett

Mudgett (b. 1860), regarded as America's first mass murderer, was believed to have lured over 150 women to his "castle" on 63rd Street, in Chicago, which was fully equipped for torturing and murdering them and disposing of their bodies. Arrested in 1894 and found guilty of murder, he confessed to killing 27. He was hanged at Moyamensing Prison, Philadelphia, on May 7, 1896.

3 Julio Gonzalez

On the morning of Sunday March 25, 1990, following an argument with his girlfriend, Lydia Feliciano, Gonzalez, a 36-year-old Cuban refugee who had lived in the US for 10 years, firebombed her place of employment, Happy Land, which was an illegal discotheque in the Bronx, New York. He killed 87 people, although Ms. Feliciano was one of six survivors.

4 Randolph Kraft

(see No. 7 in the previous list)

5 Donald Harvey

(see No. 9 in the previous list)

6 John Gilbert Graham

In order to claim on six life insurance policies, Graham put a time bomb in the luggage of his mother, Daisy King, as she boarded a DC-6B airliner in Denver, Colorado, on November 1, 1955; it blew up, killing all 44 on board. On January 11, 1957, Graham was found guilty – only of his mother's murder – and executed in the gas chamber of Colorado State Penitentiary.

7 Daniel Burke

On a flight from Los Angeles to San Francisco on December 7, 1987, a Pacific Southwest Airlines commuter jet crashed, killing 43. In the wreckage the FBI found a .44 Magnum and a note from a passenger, Daniel Burke, an aggrieved former airline employee, from which they concluded that he had shot the pilot.

8 Bella Poulsdatter Sorensen Gunness

Bella, or Belle Gunness (1859–1908?), a Norwegian-born immigrant to the US, is believed to have murdered her husband Peter Gunness for his life insurance (she claimed that an ax had fallen from a shelf and onto his head). After this, she lured between 16 and 28 suitors through "lonely hearts" advertisements, as well as numerous others – as many as 42 – to her Laporte, Indiana, farm, where she murdered them. On April 28, 1908 her farm was burned to the ground. A headless corpse found in the ruins was declared to be Gunness, killed – along with her three children – by her accomplice Ray Lamphere, but it seems likely that she faked her own death and disappeared.

9 Ted Bundy

After spending nine years on death row, Bundy (b.1947) was executed by electrocution at Florida State Prison on January 24, 1989. During his last hours he confessed to 23 murders. Police linked him conclusively to the murders of 36 girls, and he once admitted that he might have killed as many as 100 times.

7 Randolph Kraft

From 1972 until his arrest on May 14, 1983, Kraft is thought to have murdered 67 men. On November 29, 1989 he was found guilty on 16 counts and was sentenced to death in the San Quentin gas chamber.

8 Dr. Marcel André Henri Felix Petiot

Dr. Marcel Petiot (b.1897), once mayor of Villeneuve, is known to have killed at least 27 but admitted to 63 murders at his Paris house during the Second World War. He claimed that they were Nazi collaborators, but it is probable that they were wealthy Jews whom he robbed and killed after pretending to help them escape from occupied France. Petiot was guillotined on May 26, 1946.

9 Donald Harvey

Working as an orderly in hospitals in Kentucky and Ohio, Harvey is believed to have murdered some 58 patients up to the time of his arrest in March 1987. He pleaded guilty to 24 murders for which he received multiple life sentences, later confessing to further charges and receiving additional sentences.

10 Andrei Chikatilo

Russia's worst serial killer was convicted in Rostov-on-Don in 1992 of killing 52 women and children between 1978 and 1990. He was executed by a firing squad at Novocherkassk prison on February 14, 1994.

10 John Wayne Gacy

On March 13, 1980 John Wayne Gacy (b.1942) was sentenced to death by electrocution for the Chicago murders of 34 men. He was executed on May 10, 1994.

This list covers individual murderers rather than killings by bandits, groups, and gangs. There have also been other, unconfirmed, reports of mass murders. On July 17, 1961, William Estel Brown claimed that on March 18, 1937, he had deliberately loosened the gas pipes in his school basement in New London, Texas, causing an explosion that killed 297 children and teachers. If true, he would qualify for the No. 1 position in this grim list. The claims of some authorities that Johann Otto Hoch, executed in 1906, had killed as many as 50 women, and modern serial killer Randall Brent Woodfield (known as the "I-5 Killer") up to 44, are – along with with those for various other candidates – unlikely ever to be confirmed.

TOP 10

WORST GUN MASSACRES OF ALL TIME

(By individuals, excluding terrorist and military actions; totals exclude perpetrator)

Perpetrator/location/date circumstances	Killed
1 Woo Bum Kong Sang-Namdo, South Korea, April 28, 1982	57

Off-duty policeman Woo Bum Kong (or Wou Bom-Kon), 27, went on a drunken rampage with rifles and hand grenades, killing 57 and injuring 38 before blowing himself up.

2 Baruch Goldstein Hebron, Occupied West Bank, Israel, February 25, 1994	29

Goldstein, a 42-year-old US immigrant doctor, carried out a gun massacre of Palestinians at prayer at the Tomb of the Patriarchs before being beaten to death by the crowd.

3= James Oliver Huberty San Ysidro, California, July 18, 1984	22

Huberty, aged 41, opened fire in a McDonald's restaurant, killing 21 before being shot dead by a SWAT marksman. A further 19 were wounded, one of whom died the following day.

3= George Hennard Killeen, Texas, October 16, 1991	22

Hennard drove his pickup truck through the window of Luby's Cafeteria and, in 11 minutes, killed 22 with semiautomatic pistols before shooting himself.

5= Charles Joseph Whitman, Austin, Texas, July 31–August 1, 1966	16

25-year-old ex-Marine marksman Whitman killed his mother and wife. The following day he took the elevator to the 27th floor of the campus tower and ascended to the observation deck at the University of Texas at Austin, from where he shot 14 and wounded 34 before being shot dead by police officer Romero Martinez.

5= Michael Ryan, Hungerford, Berkshire, UK, August 19, 1987	16

Ryan, 26, shot 14 dead and wounded 16 others (two of whom died later) before shooting himself.

5= Ronald Gene Simmons Russellville, Arkansas, December 28, 1987	16

47-year-old Simmons killed 16, including 14 members of his own family, by shooting or strangling. He was caught and on February 10, 1989 was sentenced to death.

Perpetrator/location/date circumstances	Killed
8= Wagner von Degerloch Muehlhausen, Germany, September 3–4, 1913	14

Wagner von Degerloch, a 39-year-old schoolteacher, murdered his wife and four children before embarking on a random shooting spree, as a result of which nine more were killed and 12 injured. Regarded as one of the first "spree killers," von Degerloch was committed to a mental asylum where he died in 1938.

8= Patrick Henry Sherrill Edmond, Oklahoma, August 20, 1986	14

Sherrill, aged 44, shot 14 dead and wounded six others at the post office where he worked before killing himself.

8= Christian Dornier Luxiol, Doubs, France, July 12, 1989	14

Dornier, a 31-year-old farmer, went on a rampage leaving 14 dead and nine injured, including several children, before being wounded and caught by police.

8= Marc Lépine Montreal University, Canada, December 6, 1989	14

In Canada's worst gun massacre, Lépine, a 25-year-old student, went on an armed rampage, firing only at women, then shot himself.

GEORGE HENNARD
Police found over 100 spent cartridges in the carnage that spree killer Hennard left behind.

POLICE AND PRISONS

T O P 1 0

US CITIES WITH LARGEST POLICE FORCES

	City	State	No. of police officers
1	New York	New York	28,249
2	Chicago	Illinois	12,238
3	Los Angeles	California	7,800
4	Philadelphia	Pennsylvania	6,233
5	Washington	District of Columbia	4,224
6	Houston	Texas	4,201
7	Detroit	Michigan	3,845
8	Dallas	Texas	2,882
9	Baltimore	Maryland	2,844
10	Milwaukee	Wisconsin	2,002

In 1992 there were 544,309 law enforcement officers (plus 204,521 civilians) serving the US, a national average of 2.2 per 1,000 of the population. Of these, 91 percent were male and 9 percent female. A bill announced in August 1993 provided funds for a further 50,000 officers as the first step toward an additional 100,000. In the period from 1980 to 1992 an average of 146 officers a year were killed in the line of duty, either feloniously or as a result of accidents.

T O P 1 0

MOST COMMON REASONS FOR HIRING PRIVATE DETECTIVES

1	Tracing debtors
2	Serving subpoenas
3	Locating assets
4	Assessing accident cases
5	Tracing missing persons
6	Insurance claims
7	Matrimonial
8	Countering industrial espionage
9	Criminal cases
10	Checking personnel

This Top 10 derives from a survey carried out in the UK, but is representative of the range of private detectives' activities on both sides of the Atlantic. The affinities have a long history; the most famous American detective, Allan Pinkerton, was actually British.

DID YOU KNOW

A MAN OF MANY PARTS

The original model for Sherlock Holmes, the most famous of all fictional detectives, is claimed to have been Dr. Joseph Bell (1837–1911), an Edinburgh surgeon whose methods of deducing details of his patients' lives from their appearance was observed first-hand by Arthur Conan Doyle when he was a medical student. Others have also been credited with providing elements of Holmes's character, among them another Scottish doctor, Professor Sir Robert Christison, called as an expert witness in the Burke and Hare body-snatching trial, and Wendel Scherer, a real-life "consulting detective." His first name may come from the cricketer Mordecai Sherlock, and Holmes is perhaps a tribute to the American author and physician Oliver Wendell Holmes. Features such as Holmes's famous deerstalker hat were invented by the illustrators and actors who first portrayed him.

T O P 1 0

US STATES WITH THE MOST PRISON INMATES, 1980/1991

	State	1980	1991
1	California	24,569	101,808
2	New York	21,815	57,862
3	Texas	29,892	51,677
4	Florida	20,735	46,533
5	Michigan	15,124	36,423
6	Ohio	13,489	35,744
7	Illinois	11,899	29,115
8	Georgia	12,178	23,644
9	New Jersey	5,884	23,483
10	Pennsylvania	8,171	23,388
	US Total	*319,821*	*824,133*

At the end of 1991 there were 752,525 inmates in State prisons and 71,608 in Federal institutions in the United States. Of the total, 776,550 were men and 47,583 women. The state with the fewest prisoners over the same period was North Dakota, with 253 in 1980 and 492 in 1991. No state experienced a decline, but West Virginia had the smallest increase in prisoner numbers, from 1,257 in 1980 to 1,502 in 1991. The nationwide prison population in 1991 was two-and-a-half times greater than that in 1980, but that of certain states increased to an even greater extent: California's, for example, grew more than fourfold. Even factoring in the population increase over the period, the proportion of prisoners almost trebled, from 1.46 per 1,000 inhabitants in 1980 to 3.27 per 1,000 in 1991.

T O P   1 0

COUNTRIES WITH MOST POLICE OFFICERS PER CAPITA

	Country	Population per police officer		Country	Population per police officer
1	Angola	14*	7=	Antigua and Barbuda	120
2	Kuwait	80	7=	Mongolia	120
3	Nicaragua	90*	7=	Seychelles	120
4	Brunei	100	10=	Iraq	140
5=	Nauru	110	10=	United Arab Emirates	140
5=	Cape Verde	110		US	345
				UK	420

* Including civilian militia

DID YOU KNOW

INSIDE STORIES

Perhaps the most productive of prison industries, at least in terms of literature, has been authorship, for many famous books have been penned by prisoners. While in prison in Spain, Miguel de Cervantes wrote *Don Quixote* (1605); Sir Walter Raleigh's *History of the World* (1614) was written during his stay in the Tower of London; and John Bunyan's *The Pilgrim's Progress* was written after he was thrown into jail in 1660 for preaching without a license.

T O P   1 0

COUNTRIES WITH FEWEST POLICE OFFICERS PER CAPITA

	Country	Population per police officer		Country	Population per police officer
1	Maldives	35,710	6	Benin	3,250
2	Canada	8,640	7	Madagascar	2,900
3	Rwanda	4,650	8	Central African Republic	2,740
4	Ivory Coast	4,640	9	Bangladesh	2,560
5	Gambia	3,310	10	Niger	2,350*

* Including paramilitary forces

T O P   1 0

MOST COMMON REASONS FOR ARREST IN THE US

	Offense	Arrests
1	Driving under the influence	1,624,500
2	Larceny/theft	1,504,500
3	Drug-abuse violations	1,066,400
4	Drunkenness	832,300
5	Disorderly conduct	753,100
6	Aggravated assault	507,210
7	Fraud	424,200
8	Burglary	424,000
9	Vandalism	323,100
10	Weapons*	239,300

* Carrying, possessing, etc.

The total number of arrests in the US in 1992, including those for offenses not appearing in the Top 10, was 14,075,100 – equivalent to 5.5 percent of the population. Of these, 81 percent were males – although larceny/theft was the crime for which most females were arrested, and accounted for the greatest number of arrests for both sexes among those under the age of 18. Six percent of all those arrested in the US were aged under 15, 16 percent under 18, 29 percent under 21, and 45 percent under 45. Under-25s accounted for 46 percent of arrests in city areas, 41 percent in suburban counties, and 38 percent in rural counties.

CAPITAL PUNISHMENT

TOP 10

FIRST COUNTRIES TO ABOLISH CAPITAL PUNISHMENT

	Country	Abolished
1	Russia	1826
2	Venezuela	1863
3	Portugal	1867
4=	Brazil	1882
4=	Costa Rica	1882
6	Ecuador	1897
7	Panama	1903
8	Norway	1905
9	Uruguay	1907
10	Colombia	1910

Although Russia was the first country to abolish capital punishment, it brought back the death penalty at a later date. Some countries abolished capital punishment in peacetime only, or for all crimes except treason, generally extending it totally in more recent years. Others retained it on their statute books, but effectively abolished it: the last execution in Liechtenstein, for example, took place in 1795, in Mexico in 1946, and in Belgium in 1950.

TOP 10

FIRST EXECUTIONS BY LETHAL INJECTION IN THE US

	Victim	Execution
1	Charles Brooks	December 7, 1982
2	James Autry	March 14, 1984
3	Ronald O'Bryan	March 31, 1984
4	Thomas Barefoot	October 30, 1984
5	Doyle Skillern	January 16, 1985
6	Stephen Morin	March 13, 1985
7	Jesse De La Rosa	May 15, 1985
8	Charles Milton	June 25, 1985
9	Henry Porter	July 9, 1985
10	Charles Rumbaugh	September 11, 1985

Although Oklahoma was the first state to legalize execution by lethal injection, the option was not taken there until 1990. All of the above were executed in Texas (where, curiously, death row inmates with the first name of Charles figure prominently). Over the past ten years, this option has become the most common form of execution in states that allow its use.

Source: Death Penalty Information Center

TOP 10

STATES WITH THE MOST EXECUTIONS, 1930-1992

	Decade	Executions
1	Georgia	381
2	Texas	351
3	New York	329
4	California	293
5	North Carolina	268
6	Florida	199
7	Ohio	172
8	South Carolina	166
9	Mississippi	158
10	Louisiana	153

Eight states (Wisconsin, Rhode Island, North Dakota, Minnesota, Michigan, Maine, Hawaii, and Alaska) had no executions during this period: several in fact had abolished the death penalty at an earlier date. Michigan was the first to do so, in 1847, followed by Wisconsin in 1853, Maine in 1887, and Minnesota in 1911. A total of 20 states have carried out executions since 1977, led by Texas with 64 in the years from 1977 to 1992.

THE HOT SEAT
This form of capital punishment was first adopted by New York State, and the first person to be executed in this way was William Kemmler, on August 6, 1890, in Auburn Prison.

THE TEN

NAZI WAR CRIMINALS HANGED AT NUREMBERG
(Following the International Military Tribunal trials, November 20, 1945 to August 31, 1946)

	Name	Age
1	Joachim Von Ribbentrop	53

Former Ambassador to Great Britain and Hitler's last Foreign Minister (the first to be hanged, at 1:02 am)

	Name	Age
2	Field Marshal Wilhelm Von Keitel	64

Keitel had ordered the killing of 50 Allied air force officers after the Great Escape

	Name	Age
3	General Ernst Kaltenbrunner	44

SS and Gestapo leader

	Name	Age
4	Reichminister Alfred Rosenburg	53

Ex-Minister for Occupied Eastern territories

	Name	Age
5	Reichminister Hans Frank	46

Ex-Governor of Poland

	Name	Age
6	Reichminister Wilhelm Frick	69

Former Minister of the Interior

	Name	Age
7	Gauleiter Julius Streicher	61

Editor of anti-Semitic magazine Die Stürmer

	Name	Age
8	Reichminister Fritz Sauckel	52

Ex-General Plenipotentiary for the Utilization of Labor (the slave-labor program)

	Name	Age
9	Colonel-General Alfred Jodl	56

Former Chief of the General Staff

	Name	Age
10	Gauleiter Artur Von Seyss-Inquart	

Governor of Austria and later Commissioner for Occupied Holland (the last to be hanged)

LAST GASP
On February 8, 1924, at the Nevada State Penitentiary at Carson City, Gee Jon (right), a Chinese man, was the first person to be executed by lethal gas. This method was an experiment in executions; scientists tried it out first on a cat, and declared it to be more painless than hanging. Thomas Russell, who went to the gas chamber along with Gee Jon, is shown on the left.

TEN
US EXECUTION FIRSTS

1 First to be hanged

John Billington, for the shooting murder of John Newcomin, Plymouth, Massachusetts, September 30, 1630

2 First to be hanged for witchcraft

Achsah Young, in Massachusetts, May 27, 1647

3 First to be hanged for treason

Jacob Leisler, for insurrection, City Hall Park, New York, May 16, 1691

4 First to be hanged for slave trading

Captain Nathaniel Gordon, Tombs Prison, New York, February 21, 1862

5 First US civilian to be hanged for treason

William Bruce Mumford, for tearing down the American flag in New Orleans, June 7, 1862

6 First man to be electrocuted

William Kemmler, alias John Hart, for the ax murder of Matilda Ziegler, Auburn Prison, New York, August 6, 1890

7 First woman to be electrocuted

Martha M. Place, for murdering her step-daughter Ida, Sing Sing Prison, New York, March 20, 1899

8 First to be executed in the gas chamber

Gee Jon, for murder, Carson City, Nevada, February 8, 1924

9 First to be electrocuted for treason

Julius and Ethel Rosenberg, Sing Sing, New York, June 19, 1953

10 First to be executed by lethal injection

Charles Brooks, for murder, Department of Corrections, Huntsville, Texas, December 6, 1982

TOP 10
CAPITAL PUNISHMENT STATES IN THE US

	State	Death penalty now in force	No. of people executed 1930–87
1	Georgia	Electrocution	378
2	New York	None	329
3	Texas	Lethal injection	323
4	California	Lethal gas	292
5	North Carolina	Lethal gas or injection	266
6	Florida	Electrocution	187
7	Ohio	Electrocution	172
8	South Carolina	Electrocution	164
9	Mississippi	Lethal injection	157
10	Pennsylvania	Electrocution	152

TOP 10
STATES WITH THE MOST PRISONERS ON DEATH ROW

	State	No. under death sentence
1	Texas	344
2	California	332
3	Florida	312
4	Pennsylvania	153
5	Illinois	145
6	Alabama	124
7	Ohio	121
8	Oklahoma	120
9	Arizona	103
10	Georgia	101

There are 34 states in the Federal Prison System which still operate death penalty laws. As of December 31, 1992, there were 2,575 inmates on death row.

Source: Department of Justice

TOP 10
DECADES FOR EXECUTIONS IN THE US

	Decade	Executions		Decade	Executions
1	1930–39	1,670	**6**	1910–19	1,042
2	1940–49	1,287	**7**	1950–59	719
3	1890–1900	1,215	**8**	1960–69	192
4	1900–09	1,190	**9**	1980–89	117
5	1920–29	1,169	**10**	1970–79	3

These are the total number of executions under civil authority (local, state, or federal), excluding lynchings which were common around the turn of the century. The 1970s was a relatively good decade to be on death row, when the Furman Decision in the Supreme Court meant that individual states were forced to relegislate their death penalty laws, resulting in lengthy delays in executions.

Source: Department of Justice

THE WORLD AT WAR

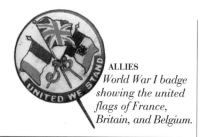

ALLIES
World War I badge showing the united flags of France, Britain, and Belgium.

T O P 1 0

LARGEST ARMED FORCES OF WORLD WAR I

	Country	Personnel*
1	Russia	12,000,000
2	Germany	11,000,000
3	British Empire	8,904,467
4	France	8,410,000
5	Austria-Hungary	7,800,000
6	Italy	5,615,000
7	US	4,355,000
8	Turkey	2,850,000
9	Bulgaria	1,200,000
10	Japan	800,000

* *Total at peak strength*

DID YOU KNOW

THE WORST WARS OF THE 20TH CENTURY

While the military fatalities of the First and Second World Wars were the worst of the 20th century, several other wars of the past 60 years have resulted in horrifically high levels of casualties. The Korean War of 1950–53 produced an estimated 1,893,100 military deaths, while the Sino-Japanese War (1937–41) and the Biafra-Nigeria Civil War (1967–70) are each believed to have caused 1,000,000 losses, and the Spanish Civil War (1936–39) an estimated 611,000. The Vietnam War (1961–73) produced 546,000, and some 200,000 were sustained in each of three other campaigns: the India-Pakistan War (1947), the USSR's invasion of Afghanistan (1979–89), and the Iran-Iraq War (1980–88).

T O P 1 0

COUNTRIES SUFFERING THE GREATEST MILITARY LOSSES IN WORLD WAR I

	Country	Killed
1	Germany	1,773,700
2	Russia	1,700,000
3	France	1,357,800
4	Austria-Hungary	1,200,000
5	British Empire*	908,371
6	Italy	650,000
7	Romania	335,706
8	Turkey	325,000
9	US	116,516
10	Bulgaria	87,500

The number of battle fatalities and deaths from other causes among military personnel varied enormously from country to country: Romania's death rate was highest of all, at 45 percent of its total mobilized forces; Germany's was 16 percent, Austria-Hungary's and Russia's 15 percent, and the British Empire's 10 percent, with the US's 2 percent and Japan's 0.04 percent among the lowest.

* *Including Australia, Canada, India, New Zealand, South Africa, etc.*

AFTERMATH
A forest strewn with dead Russian soldiers after a First World War battle.

BELGIAN ARMS AND FLAG

T O P 1 0

COUNTRIES WITH THE MOST PRISONERS OF WAR, 1914–18

	Country	Captured		Country	Captured
1	Russia	2,500,000	6	Turkey	250,000
2	Austria-Hungary	2,200,000	7	British Empire	191,652
3	Germany	1,152,800	8	Serbia	152,958
4	Italy	600,000	9	Romania	80,000
5	France	537,000	10	Belgium	34,659

TOP 10

SMALLEST ARMED FORCES OF WORLD WAR II

	Country	Personnel*
1	Costa Rica	400
2	Liberia	1,000
3=	El Salvador	3,000
3=	Honduras	3,000
3=	Nicaragua	3,000
6	Haiti	3,500
7	Dominican Republic	4,000
8	Guatemala	5,000
9=	Bolivia	8,000
9=	Paraguay	8,000
9=	Uruguay	8,000

* Total at peak strength

Several of the South American countries entered the Second World War at a very late stage: Argentina, for example, did not declare war on Germany and Japan until March 27, 1945. The smallest European armed force was that of Denmark, with a maximum strength of 15,000. Just 13 Danish soldiers were killed during the one-day German invasion of April 9, 1940, when Denmark became the second country after Poland to be occupied.

TOP 10

LARGEST ARMED FORCES OF WORLD WAR II

	Country	Personnel*
1	USSR	12,500,000
2	US	12,364,000
3	Germany	10,000,000
4	Japan	6,095,000
5	France	5,700,000
6	UK	4,683,000
7	Italy	4,500,000
8	China	3,800,000
9	India	2,150,000
10	Poland	1,000,000

* Total at peak strength

TOP 10

TANKS OF WORLD WAR II

	Tank/country/(introduced)	Weight (US tons)	No. produced
1	Sherman, US (1942)	34.7	41,530
2	T34 Model 42, USSR (1940)	31.9	35,120
3	T34/85, USSR (1944)	35.8	29,430
4	M3 General Stuart, US (1941)	13.7	14,000
5	Valentine II, UK (1941)	19.6	8,280
6	M3A1 Lee/Grant, US (1941)	30.0	7,400
7	Churchill VII, UK (1942)	44.8	5,640
8=	Panzer IVD, Germany (pre-war)	22.4	5,500
8=	Panzer VG, Germany (1943)	50.2	5,500
10	Crusader I, UK (1941)	21.3	4,750

TOP 10

COUNTRIES SUFFERING THE GREATEST MILITARY LOSSES IN WORLD WAR II

	Country	Killed
1	USSR	13,600,000
2	Germany	3,300,000
3	China	1,324,516
4	Japan	1,140,429
5	British Empire* (of which UK	357,116 264,000)
6	Romania	350,000
7	Poland	320,000
8	Yugoslavia	305,000
9	US	292,131
10	Italy	279,800

* Including Australia, Canada, India, New Zealand, etc.

The actual numbers killed in the Second World War have been the subject of intense argument for nearly 50 years. The immense level of the military casualty rate of the USSR in particular is hard to comprehend. It is included here at its lowest likely level, but most authorities now believe that of the 30,000,000 Soviets who bore arms, as many as 8,500,000 died in action and up to 2,500,000 of wounds received in battle and disease. Some 5,800,000 were taken prisoner, of which perhaps 3,300,000 may have died in captivity. It should also be kept in mind that these were military losses: to these should be added many untold millions of civilian war deaths.

MOUNTAIN GUN
The WWII 3.7-in howitzer was ideal for use in hilly terrain, as the barrel could be raised high enough to fire over peaks. This "pack howitzer" could be broken down into eight pieces for transporting by mules.

ACES HIGH

The term "ace" was first used during the First World War for a pilot who had brought down at least five enemy aircraft; the British regarded the tally for an "ace" as varying from three to ten aircraft. The first reference in print to an air "ace" appeared in an article in *The Times* (September 14, 1917). The names of French pilots who achieved this feat were recorded in official communiqués, but while US and other pilots followed the same system, the British definition of an "ace" was never officially approved, remaining an informal concept during both world wars. The German equivalent of the air "ace" was *Oberkanone*, which means "top gun."

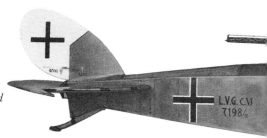

LVG CVI, 1917
This German aircraft, fitted with guns and able to carry bombs, was one of the most versatile of the First World War airplanes.

T O P 1 0

BRITISH AND COMMONWEALTH AIR ACES OF WORLD WAR I

	Pilot	Nationality	Kills claimed
1	Edward Mannock	British	73
2	William Avery Bishop	Canadian	72
3	Raymond Collishaw	Canadian	60
4	James Thomas Byford McCudden	British	57
5=	Anthony Wetherby Beauchamp-Proctor	British	54
5=	Donald Roderick MacLaren	British	54
7	William George Barker	Canadian	53
8	Robert Alexander Little	Australian	47
9=	Philip Fletcher Fullard	British	46
9=	George Edward Henry McElroy	Irish	46

This Top 10 takes account of British Empire pilots belonging to the Royal Flying Corps, the Royal Naval Air Service, and (after April 1, 1918) the Royal Air Force. The total of Edward "Mick" Mannock (1887–1918) may actually be greater than those definitely credited to him. Similarly, British pilot Albert Ball is generally credited with 44 kills (and hence not in the Top 10), but with the qualification that his total may have been greater. If this list were extended to include French pilots it would have (at No. 1) René Paul Fonck (1894–1953) with 75 kills and Georges-Marie Ludovic Jules Guynemer (1894–1917) with 54.

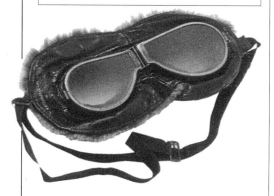

T O P 1 0

GERMAN AIR ACES OF WORLD WAR I

	Pilot	Kills claimed
1	Manfred von Richthofen*	80
2	Ernst Udet	62
3	Erich Loewenhardt	53
4	Werner Voss	48
5	Fritz Rumey	45
6	Rudolph Berthold	44
7	Paul Bäumer	43
8=	Josef Jacobs	41
8=	Bruno Loerzer	41
10=	Oswald Boelcke	40
10=	Franz Büchner	40
10=	Lothar Freiherr von Richthofen*	40

* *Brothers*

Top First World War "ace" Rittmeister Manfred, Baron von Richthofen's claim of 80 kills has been disputed, since only 60 of them have been completely confirmed. Richthofen, known as the "Red Baron" and leader of the so-called "Flying Circus" (because the aircraft of his squadron were painted in distinctive bright colors), shot down 21 Allied fighters in the single month of April 1917. His own end a year later, on April 21, 1918, has been the subject of controversy ever since, and it remains uncertain whether his Fokker triplane was shot down in aerial combat with British pilot Captain A. Roy Brown (who was credited with the kill) or by shots from Australian machine gunners on the ground.

THE "RED BARON"
Baron von Richthofen has passed into legend as the greatest air ace of the First World War.

T O P   1 0

US AIR ACES OF WORLD WAR I

Pilot	Kills claimed
1 Edward Vernon Rickenbacker	26
2 Frank Luke Jr.	21
3 Gervais Raoul Lufbery	17
4 George Augustus Vaughn Jr.	13
5= Field E. Kindley	12
5= David Endicott Putnam	12
5= Elliot White Springs	12
8= Reed Gresham Landis	10
8= Jacques Michael Swaab	10
10= Lloyd Andrews Hamilton	9
10= Chester Ellis Wright	9

Edward ("Eddie") Rickenbacker
(1890–1973) first achieved fame in the US
as a champion racing-car driver. A visit to
England in 1917 encouraged his interest in
flying and when the US entered the First
World War (April 6, 1917) he enlisted,
serving initially as chauffeur to General
Pershing before transferring to active
service as a pilot. On March 19, 1918
Rickenbacker took part in the first-ever
US patrol over enemy lines and on April 29
shot down his first airplane. A month later,
with five kills to his credit, he became an
acknowledged "ace," eventually achieving a
total of 26 kills (22 aircraft and four
balloons) and winning the US Congressional
Medal of Honor, the country's highest
award. Rickenbacker also served in the
Second World War and later became CEO
of Eastern Airlines. He died in 1973. As well
as the 151 kills credited to the pilots in the
Top 10, a further 76 US pilots each shot
down between five and nine enemy aircraft.
Frank Leaman Baylies had 12 kills, but
served solely with the French air force and
hence is not included in the US list.

BRITISH AND COMMONWEALTH AIR ACES OF WORLD WAR II

Pilot	Nationality	Kills claimed
1 Marmaduke Thomas St. John Pattle	South African	41
2 James Edgar "Johnny" Johnson	British	38
3 Adolf Gysbert "Sailor" Malan	South African	35
4 Brendan "Paddy" Finucane	Irish	32
5 George Frederick Beurling	Canadian	31⅓
6= John Robert Daniel Braham	British	29
6= Robert Roland Stanford Tuck	British	29
8 Neville Frederick Duke	British	28⅞
9 Clive Robert Caldwell	Australian	28½
10 Frank Reginald Carey	British	28⅓

Kills that are expressed
as fractions refer to
those that were shared
with others, the number
of fighters involved
and the extent of each
pilot's participation
determining the
proportion allocated
to him. As a result of
this precise reckoning,
British pilot James
Harry "Ginger" Lacey,
with 28 kills, just misses
sharing 10th place
with Frank Reginald
Carey by ⅓ of a kill.

LUFTWAFFE ACES OF WORLD WAR II

Pilot	Kills claimed
1 Eric Hartmann	352
2 Gerhard Barkhorn	301
3 Günther Rall	275
4 Otto Kittel	267
5 Walther Nowotny	255
6 Wilhelm Batz	237
7 Erich Rudorffer	222
8 Heinrich Baer	220
9 Herman Graf	212
10 Heinrich Ehrler	209

Although these apparently high claims have
been dismissed by some military historians
as inflated for propaganda purposes, it is
worth noting that many of them relate to
kills on the Eastern Front, where the
Luftwaffe was undoubtedly superior to its
Soviet opponents. Few have questioned the
so-called "Blond Knight" Eric Hartmann's
achievement, however, and his victories
over Soviet aircraft so outraged the USSR
that after the war he was arrested and
sentenced to 25 years in a Russian labor
camp. He was released in 1955, returned to
serve in the West German air force, and
died on September 20, 1993.

MISSING
*Most of "Pat" Pattle's kills were made flying an
ancient Gladiator biplane. On April 22, 1941,
after three kills, he was himself shot down over
the Aegean and was never seen again.*

US AIR ACES OF WORLD WAR II

Pilot	Kills claimed
1 Richard I. Bong	40
2 Thomas B. McGuire	38
3 David McCampbell	34
4 Frances S. Gabreski	31
5= Gregory Boyington	28
5= Robert S. Johnson	28
7 Charles H. MacDonald	27
8= George E. Preddy	26
8= Joseph J. Foss	26
10 Robert M. Hanson	25

AIR WARFARE

COUNTIES RECEIVING THE MOST V2 HITS

	County	V2s
1	London	517
2	Essex	378
3	Kent	64
4	Hertfordshire	34
5	Norfolk	29
6	Suffolk	13
7	Surrey	8
8	Sussex	4
9	Bedfordshire	3
10	Buckinghamshire	2

The weapon originally called the Fi-103 (from Fiesler, its main manufacturer) or Flakzeitlgerät 76 ("antiaircraft aiming device 76") or FZG 76, eventually became known to the Germans as the V1 (from Vergeltungswaffe Eins – "vengeance weapon 1"), and to its British victims as the "flying bomb," "buzz bomb," or "doodlebug." These pilotless jet-propelled aircraft, measuring 25 ft 4½ in/7.7 m, were made of sheet steel and plywood and carried 1,874 lb/850 kg of high explosive. Using 420 gallons/1,591 liters of gasoline oxidized by compressed air, they achieved an average speed of 350 mph/563 km/h and a range of about 130 miles/209 km, which they reached in 20–25 minutes. Their engines then cut out, and eyewitnesses tell of the "ominous silence" before the explosion some 12 seconds later. The first ten V1 rockets were launched against England on June 13, 1944. In subsequent months more than 8,000 were launched. Many were erratic and strayed off course or crashed, and of those that continued toward London, a large proportion were brought down by barrage balloons, antiaircraft fire, and particularly by fighter pilots. Nonetheless, they managed to cause over 23,000 casualties.

The V1 was the precursor of the far deadlier V2. Masterminded by Werner von Braun (1912–77), later leader of the US space program, the 46 ft/14 m V2 rocket (known to its German developers as the "A4") was more accurate and far more powerful than the V1. It produced a thrust of 56,000 lb/25,400 kg capable of carrying 1 ton of explosive up to 225 miles/362 km, while its speed of 3,600 mph/5,794 km/h made it virtually impossible to combat with antiaircraft fire or to intercept with fighter aircraft. V2 technology was used by the US to develop missiles suitable for carrying nuclear bombs.

LANDING ON JAPANESE SOIL
In 1945, after over a year of bombing raids carried out by the US and involving napalm fire bombs and, finally, atomic bombs, Japan surrendered to the Allies. In September 1945, General MacArthur accepted Japan's formal surrender, on board the US flagship Missouri *in Tokyo Bay, while Allied troops occupied the forts guarding the bay. Under MacArthur, the Allies went on to occupy the country.*

ALLIED AIRCRAFT OF WORLD WAR II

	Model	Type	No. produced
1	Illyushin Il-2m3 (USSR)	Ground-attack	36,200
2	Supermarine Spitfire (UK)	Fighter	20,350
3	Consolidated Liberator (US)	Bomber	18,500
4	Yakolev Yak-9D (USSR)	Fighter	16,800
5	Republic Thunderbolt (US)	Fighter	15,630
6	North American Mustang (US)	Fighter	15,470
7	Hawker Hurricane (UK)	Fighter	14,230
8	Curtis Kittyhawk (US)	Fighter-bomber	13,740
9	Vought Corsair (US)	Carrier-fighter	12,740
10	Boeing Flying Fortress (US)	Bomber	12,700

MONTHS FOR AIR STRIKES AGAINST JAPAN*

	Month/ year	Bombs (tons) High explosive	Incendiary	Total
1	Jul 1945	9,388	33,163	42,551
2	Jun 1945	9,954	22,588	32,542
3	May 1945	6,937	17,348	24,285
4	Aug 1945	8,438	12,591	21,029
5	Apr 1945	13,209	4,283	17,492
6	Mar 1945	4,105	11,138	15,243
7	Feb 1945	2,401	1,619	4,020
8	Dec 1944	3,051	610	3,661
9	Jan 1945	2,511	899	3,410
10	Nov 1944	1,758	447	2,205

Attacks on Japan by the US Twentieth Air Force began in June 1944, originally flying B-29 bombers from bases in India. After the capture of the nearer Marianas islands, raids with 500 or more B-29s flew from there, attacking military and civilian targets in Japan, including major cities, with increasing frequency. Only a fraction of the tonnage of bombs dropped on Germany was used, but casualties, especially from fires in populated areas, were much higher. A total of 28,826 sorties were flown by the US Twentieth Air Force alone (US Navy and other aircraft flew fewer), dropping 64,190 tons of high explosive bombs and 105,446 tons of incendiary bombs. As the list shows, the raids grew in intensity toward the closing months of the war, culminating in the dropping of atomic bombs on the cities of Hiroshima on August 6 and Nagasaki on August 9, and resulting in the Japanese surrender on August 15, 1945.

* *By US Twentieth Air Force, June 1944 to August 1945*

TOP 10
LUFTWAFFE AIRCRAFT OF WORLD WAR II

	Model	Type	No. produced
1	Messerschmitt Me 109	Fighter	30,480
2	Focke-Wulf Fw 190	Fighter	20,000
3	Junkers Ju 88	Bomber	15,000
4	Messerschmitt Me 110	Fighter-bomber	5,762
5	Heinkel He 111	Bomber	5,656
6	Junkers Ju 87	Dive bomber	4,881
7	Junkers Ju 52	Transport	2,804
8	Fiesler Fi 156	Communications	2,549
9	Dornier Do 217	Bomber	1,730
10	Heinkel He 177	Bomber	1,446

More than 60 years after its first flight, the Junkers Ju 52 is still in service as a transport airplane in South America.

TOP 10
FASTEST FIGHTER AIRCRAFT OF WORLD WAR II

	Aircraft	Country	mph	km/h
1	Messerschmitt Me 163	Germany	596	959
2	Messerschmitt Me 262	Germany	560	901
3	Heinkel He 162A	Germany	553	890
4	P-51-H Mustang	US	487	784
5	Lavochkin La11	USSR	460	740
6	Spitfire XIV	UK	448	721
7	Yakolev Yak-3	USSR	447	719
8	P-51-D Mustang	US	440	708
9	Tempest VI	UK	438	705
10	Focke-Wulf FW190D	Germany	435	700

Maximum speed columns: mph and km/h.

Also known as the *Komet*, the Messerschmitt Me 163 was a short-range rocket-powered interceptor brought into service in 1944–45. During this time, the aircraft scored a number of victories over its slower Allied rivals. The Messerschmitt Me 262 was the first jet in operational service.

TOP 10
MOST HEAVILY BLITZED CITIES IN THE UK

	City	Major raids	Tonnage of high explosive dropped
1	London	85	23,949
2	Liverpool/Birkenhead	8	1,957
3	Birmingham	8	1,852
4	Glasgow/Clydeside	5	1,329
5	Plymouth/Devonport	8	1,228
6	Bristol/Avonmouth	6	919
7	Coventry	2	818
8	Portsmouth	3	687
9	Southampton	4	647
10	Hull	3	593

The list, which is derived from official German sources, is based on total tonnage of high explosives dropped in major night attacks during the "Blitz" period, from September 7, 1940 to May 16, 1941.

TOP 10
CITIES MOST BOMBED BY THE RAF AND USAAF, 1939–45

	City	Estimated civilian deaths
1	Dresden	100,000+
2	Hamburg	55,000
3	Berlin	49,000
4	Cologne	20,000
5	Magdeburg	15,000
6	Kassel	13,000
7	Darmstadt	12,300
8=	Heilbronn	7,500
8=	Essen	7,500
10=	Dortmund	6,000
10=	Wuppertal	6,000

The high level of casualties in Dresden resulted principally from the saturation bombing and the firestorm that ensued after Allied raids on the lightly defended city. The scale of the raids was massive: 775 British bombers took part in the first night's raid, on February 13, 1945, followed the next day by 450 US bombers, with a final attack by 200 US bombers on February 15.

TOP 10
AREAS OF EUROPE MOST BOMBED BY ALLIED AIRCRAFT*, 1939–45

	Area	Bombs dropped (tonnes)
1	Germany	1,350,321
2	France	583,318
3	Italy	366,524
4	Austria, Hungary, and the Balkans	180,828
5	Belgium and Netherlands	88,739
6	Southern Europe and Mediterranean	76,505
7	Czechoslovakia and Poland	21,419
8	Norway and Denmark	5,297
9	Sea targets	564
10	British Channel Islands	93

* *British and US*

Between August 1942 and May 1945 alone, Allied air forces (Bomber Command plus 8 and 15 US Air Forces) flew 731,969 night sorties (and Bomber Command a further 67,598 day sorties), during which time they dropped a total of 1,850,919 tons of bombs.

WAR AT SEA

T O P   1 0

LARGEST BATTLESHIPS OF WORLD WAR II

	Name	Country	Status	Length ft/m	Tonnage*
1=	*Musashi*	Japan	Sunk Oct 25, 1944	862/263	72,809
1=	*Yamato*	Japan	Sunk Apr 7, 1945	862/263	72,809
3=	*Iowa*	US	Still in service with US Navy	887/270	55,710
3=	*Missouri*	US	Still in service with US Navy	887/270	55,710
3=	*New Jersey*	US	Still in service with US Navy	887/270	55,710
3=	*Wisconsin*	US	Still in service with US Navy	887/270	55,710
7=	*Bismarck*	Germany	Sunk May 27, 1941	823/251	50,153
7=	*Tirpitz*	Germany	Sunk Nov 12, 1944	823/251	50,153
9=	*Jean Bart*	France	Survived WWII, later scrapped	812/247	47,500
9=	*Richelieu*	France	Survived WWII, later scrapped	812/247	47,500

* *A ship's tonnage is always measured in metric tonnes.*

COUNTRIES SUFFERING THE GREATEST MERCHANT SHIPPING LOSSES IN WORLD WAR I

	Country	Vessels sunk Number	Tonnage
1	UK	2,038	6,797,802
2	Italy	228	720,064
3	France	213	651,583
4	US	93	372,892
5	Germany	188	319,552
6	Greece	115	304,992
7	Denmark	126	205,002
8	Netherlands	74	194,483
9	Sweden	124	192,807
10	Spain	70	160,383

COUNTRES SUFFERING THE GREATEST MERCHANT SHIPPING LOSSES IN WORLD WAR II

	Country	Vessels sunk Number	Tonnage
1	UK	4,786	21,194,000
2	Japan	2,346	8,618,109
3	Germany	1,595	7,064,600
4	US	578	3,524,983
5	Norway	427	1,728,531
6	Netherlands	286	1,195,204
7	Italy	467	1,155,080
8	Greece	262	883,200
9	Panama	107	542,772
10	Sweden	204	481,864

During 1939–45, Allied losses in the Atlantic alone totalled 3,843 ships (16,899,147 tonnes). June 1942 was the worst period of the war, with 131 vessels (652,487 tonnes) lost in the Atlantic and 42 (181,709 tonnes) lost elsewhere.

BRAZILIAN BATTLESHIP
In the early 20th century, Dreadnought-type vessels incorporating the latest advances in steam propulsion, gunnery, and armor plating revolutionized sea warfare.

UP PERISCOPE
As submarines are enhanced with nuclear power and the ability to fire long-range missiles underwater, tacticians increasingly consider them the most important of all strategic weapons.

TOP 10
U-BOAT COMMANDERS OF WORLD WAR II

	Commander	U-boats commanded	Ships sunk
1	Otto Kretschmer	U-23, U-99	45
2	Wolfgang Luth	U-9, U-138, U-43, U-181	44
3	Joachim Schepke	U-3, U-19, U-100	39
4	Erich Topp	U-57, U-552	35
5	Victor Schutze	U-25, U-103	34
6	Heinrich Leibe	U-38	30
7	Karl F. Merten	U-68	29 *
8	Günther Prien	U-47	29 *
9	Johann Mohr	U-124	29 *
10	Georg Lassen	U-160	28

* Gross tonnage used to determine ranking order

Günther Prien (born January 16, 1908, killed in action March 7, 1941) performed the remarkable feat of penetrating the British naval base at Scapa Flow on October 14, 1939 and sinking the Royal Navy battleship *Royal Oak* at anchor. For this exploit he was awarded the Knight's Cross, the first of 318 to be won by members of the German navy during the Second World War. Prien was killed when U-47 was sunk.

DID YOU KNOW

OLD WAR-HORSE

One ship that survived the Japanese attack on the US fleet at Pearl Harbor (December 7, 1941) was the USS *Phoenix*. After serving through the rest of the war, she was sold to Argentina in 1951 and renamed the *General Belgrano*. On May 2, 1982, during the Falklands War, she was sunk by a British submarine, with the loss of 368 lives.

TOP 10
NAVIES 100 YEARS AGO

	Country	Guns	Men	Ships*
1	UK	3,631	94,600	659
2	France	1,735	70,600	457
3	Russia	710	31,000	358
4	Italy	611	23,000	267
5	Germany	608	16,500	217

	Country	Guns	Men	Ships*
6	Austria	309	9,000	168
7	Netherlands	256	10,000	140
8	Spain	305	16,700	136
9	Turkey	382	23,000	124
10	US	284	10,000	95

* Battleships, cruisers, gun-boats, and torpedo-boats

TOP 10
US NAVY SUBMARINE COMMANDERS OF WORLD WAR II

	Commander	Submarines commanded	Ships sunk
1	Richard H. O'Kane	*Tang*	31
2	Eugene B. Fluckley	*Barb*	25
3	Slade D. Cutter	*Seahorse*	21
4	Samuel D. Dealey	*Harder*	20½ #
5	William S. Post Jr.	*Gudgeon* and *Spot*	19
6	Reuben T. Whitaker	*S-44* and *Flasher*	18½ #
7	Walter T. Grifith	*Bowfin* and *Bullhead*	17 *
8	Dudley W. Morton	*R-5* and *Wahoo*	17 *
9	John E. Lee	*S-12*, *Grayling*, and *Croaker*	16
10	William B. Sieglaff	*Tautog* and *Tench*	15

 # ½ refers to shared "kills"
* Gross tonnage used to determine ranking order.

TOP 10
SUBMARINE FLEETS OF WORLD WAR II

	Country	Submarines
1	Japan*	163
2	US*	112
3	France	77
4	USSR	75
5	Germany	57
6	UK	38
7	Netherlands	21
8	Italy	15
9	Denmark	12
10	Greece	6

Strength at December 1941

The list shows submarine strengths at the outbreak of the war. During hostilities, the belligerent nations increased their production prodigiously: from 1939 to 1945, the Axis powers (Germany, Italy, and Japan) commissioned a further 1,337 submarines (1,141 by Germany alone). The Allies commissioned 422.

MODERN MILITARY

TOP 10

LONGEST-SERVING JOINT CHIEFS OF STAFF

	Name/Rank	Branch of Armed Forces	Length of time served Years	Months	Took office	Left office
1	General Earle G. Wheeler	US Army	6	–	Jul 3, 1964	Jul 2, 1970
2	Admiral Arthur W. Radford	US Navy	4	–	Aug 15, 1953	Aug 15, 1957
3=	General of the Army Omar N. Bradley	US Army	4	–	Aug 16, 1949	Aug 15, 1953
3=	Admiral William J. Crowe Jr.	US Navy	4	–	Oct 1, 1985	Sep 30, 1989
3=	Admiral Thomas H. Moorer	US Navy	4	–	Jul 2, 1970	Jul 1, 1974
3=	General Colin L. Powell	US Army	4	–	Oct 1, 1989	Sep 30,1993
7	General David C. Jones	US Air Force	4	–	Jun 21, 1978	Jun 18, 1982
8	General George S. Brown	US Air Force	4	–	Jul 1, 1974	Jun 20, 1978
9	General John W. Vessey Jr.	US Army	3	3	Jun 18, 1982	Sep 30, 1985
10	General Nathan F. Twining	US Air Force	3	1	Aug 15, 1957	Sep 30, 1960

TOP 10

RANKS OF THE US NAVY, ARMY, AND AIR FORCE

	Navy	Army	Air Force
1	Admiral	General	General
2	Vice-Admiral	Lieutenant-General	Lieutenant-General
3	Rear Admiral (Upper Half)	Major-General	Major-General
4	Rear-Admiral (Lower Half)	Brigadier-General	Brigadier-General
5	Captain	Colonel	Colonel
6	Commander	Lieutenant-Colonel	Lieutenant-Colonel
7	Lieutenant Commander	Major	Major
8	Lieutenant	Captain	Captain
9	Lieutenant (Junior Grade)	First Lieutenant	First Lieutenant
10	Ensign	Second Lieutenant	Second Lieutenant

TOP 10

COUNTRIES WITH THE LARGEST DEFENSE BUDGETS

	Country	Budget ($)
1	US	323,500,000,000
2	Russia	52,500,000,000
3	UK	42,000,000,000
4	Germany	39,500,000,000
5	Japan	36,700,000,000
6	France	33,100,000,000
7	Italy	22,700,000,000
8	China	15,000,000,000
9	Saudi Arabia	14,500,000,000
10	South Korea	12,600,000,000

TOP 10

SMALLEST ARMED FORCES IN THE WORLD*

	Country	Estimated total active forces		Country	Estimated total active forces
1	Belize	660	6=	Cape Verde	1,300
2	Luxembourg	800	6=	The Seychelles	1,300
3	The Bahamas	850	8	Malta	1,650
4	The Gambia	900	9	Suriname	2,200
5	Equatorial Guinea	1,100	10	Trinidad and Tobago	2,650

* *Excluding those countries not declaring a defense budget*

TOP 10

20TH-CENTURY WARS WITH MOST MILITARY FATALITIES

	War	Years	Military fatalities
1	Second World War	1939–45	15,843,000
2	First World War	1914–18	8,545,800
3	Korean War	1950–53	1,893,100
4=	Sino-Japanese War	1937–41	1,000,000
4=	Biafra-Nigeria Civil War	1967–70	1,000,000
6	Spanish Civil War	1936–39	611,000
7	Vietnam War	1961–73	546,000
8=	India-Pakistan War	1947	200,000
8=	USSR invasion of Afghanistan	1979–89	200,000
8=	Iran-Iraq War	1980–88	200,000

TOP 10

COUNTRIES WITH THE LARGEST UN PEACEKEEPING FORCES

	Country	Personnel numbers Civilian police	Troops	Military observers	Total
1	France	63	7,316	70	7,449
2	Pakistan	–	7,057	82	7,139
3	India	–	5,835	29	5,864
4	UK	–	3,868	33	3,901
5	Jordan	100	3,085	88	3,273
6	Bangladesh	72	3,007	185	3,264
7	Malaysia	43	2,447	82	2,572
8	Canada	45	2,194	66	2,305
9	Netherlands	11	2,154	76	2,241
10	Egypt	31	2,095	66	2,192

TOP 10

LARGEST ARMED FORCES IN THE WORLD

	Country	Estimated active forces Army	Navy	Air	Total
1	China	2,300,000	260,000	470,000	3,030,000
2	Russia	1,400,000	320,000	300,000	2,720,000*
3	US	586,200	693,600#	449,900	1,729,700
4	India	1,100,000	55,000	110,000	1,265,000
5	North Korea	1,000,000	45,000	82,000	1,127,000
6	Vietnam	700,000	42,000	115,000	857,000
7	South Korea	520,000	60,000	53,000	633,000
8	Pakistan	510,000	22,000	45,000	577,000
9	Turkey	370,000	50,000	80,900	500,900
10	Taiwan	312,000	59,300	70,000	442,000
	UK	133,058	58,513	79,341	270,912

* Balance of total comprises Strategic Deterrent Forces, Paramilitary, National Guard, etc.
# Navy 546,650, Marines 193,000

In addition to the active forces listed here, many of the world's foremost military powers have considerable reserves on standby. South Korea's are estimated at some 4,500,000, Vietnam's 3–4,000,000, Russia's 3,000,000, the US's 1,784,050, China's 1,200,000, and Turkey's 1,107,000.

TOP 10

US MEDAL OF HONOR CAMPAIGNS

	Campaign	Years	Medals awarded
1	Civil War	1861–65	1,520
2	Second World War	1941–45	433
3	Indian Wars	1861–98	428
4	Vietnam War	1965–73	238
5	Korean War	1950–53	131
6	First World War	1917–18	123
7	Spanish–American War	1898	109
8	Philippines/Samoa	1899–1913	91
9	Boxer Rebellion	1900	59
10	Mexico	1914	55

The Congressional Medal of Honor, the highest military award in the US, was first issued in 1863. In addition to the medal itself, recipients receive such benefits as a $200 per month pension for life, free air travel, and the right to be buried in the Arlington National Cemetery.

TOWN AND COUNTRY

TOP 10

SMALLEST COUNTRIES IN THE WORLD

	Country	Area sq km	sq miles
1	Vatican City	0.44	0.17
2	Monaco	1.81	0.7
3	Gibraltar	6.47	2.5
4	Macao	16.06	6.2
5	Nauru	21.23	8.2
6	Tuvalu	25.90	10.0
7	Bermuda	53.35	20.6
8	San Marino	59.57	23.0
9	Liechtenstein	157.99	61.0
10	Antigua	279.72	108.0

The "country" status of several of these microstates is questionable, since their government, defense, currency, and other features are often intricately linked with those of larger countries – the Vatican City with Italy, and Monaco with France, for example, while Gibraltar and Bermuda are dependent territories of the UK.

TOP 10

LARGEST COUNTRIES IN THE WORLD

	Country	Area sq km	sq miles
1	Russia	17,070,289	6,590,876
2	Canada	9,970,537	3,849,646
3	China	9,596,961	3,705,408
4	US	9,372,614	3,618,787
5	Brazil	8,511,965	3,286,488
6	Australia	7,686,848	2,967,909
7	India	3,287,590	1,269,346
8	Argentina	2,766,889	1,068,302
9	Kazakhstan	2,716,626	1,048,895
10	Sudan	2,505,813	967,500

World total 136,597,770 52,740,700

The breakup of the former USSR has effectively introduced two new countries, with Russia taking preeminent position while Kazakhstan, which enters in 9th position, ousts Algeria from the bottom of the list.

TOP 10

LONGEST FRONTIERS IN THE WORLD

	Country	km	miles
1	China	22,143	13,759
2	Russia	20,139	12,514
3	Brazil	14,691	9,129
4	India	14,103	8,763
5	US	12,248	7,611
6	Zaïre	10,271	6,382
7	Argentina	9,665	6,006
8	Canada	8,893	5,526
9	Mongolia	8,114	5,042
10	Sudan	7,697	4,783

The 7,611 miles/12,248 km of the US's frontiers include those shared with Canada (3,987 miles/6,416 km of which comprise the longest continuous frontier in the world), the 1,539-mile/2,477-km boundary between Canada and Alaska, that with Mexico (2,067 miles/3,326 km), and between the US naval base at Guantánamo and Cuba (18 miles/29 km).

WORLD COUNTRIES

TOP 10

COUNTRIES WITH MOST NEIGHBORS

	Country/neighbors	No. of neighbors
1	China	16

Afghanistan, Bhutan, Hong Kong, India, Kazakhstan, Kyrgyzstan, Laos, Macao, Mongolia, Myanmar (Burma), Nepal, North Korea, Pakistan, Russia, Tajikistan, Vietnam

2	Russia	14

Azerbaijan, Belarus, China, Estonia, Finland, Georgia, Kazakhstan, Latvia, Lithuania, Mongolia, North Korea, Norway, Poland, Ukraine

3	Brazil	10

Argentina, Bolivia, Colombia, French Guiana, Guyana, Paraguay, Peru, Suriname, Uruguay, Venezuela

4=	Germany	9

Austria, Belgium, Czech Republic, Denmark, France, Luxembourg, Netherlands, Poland, Switzerland

4=	Sudan	9

Central African Republic, Chad, Egypt, Eritrea, Ethiopia, Kenya, Libya, Uganda, Zaïre

4=	Zaïre	9

Angola, Burundi, Central African Republic, Congo, Rwanda, Sudan, Tanzania, Uganda, Zambia

7=	Austria	8

Czech Republic, Germany, Hungary, Italy, Liechtenstein, Slovakia, Slovenia, Switzerland

7=	France	8

Andorra, Belgium, Germany, Italy, Luxembourg, Monaco, Spain, Switzerland

7=	Saudi Arabia	8

Iraq, Jordan, Kuwait, Oman, People's Democratic Republic of Yemen, Qatar, United Arab Emirates, Yemen Arab Republic

7=	Tanzania	8

Burundi, Kenya, Malawi, Mozambique, Rwanda, Uganda, Zaïre, Zambia

7=	Turkey	8

Armenia, Azerbaijan, Bulgaria, Georgia, Greece, Iran, Iraq, Syria

TOP 10

COUNTRIES WITH THE LONGEST COASTLINES

	Country	km	miles
1	Canada	243,791	151,485
2	Indonesia	54,716	33,999
3	Greenland	44,087	27,394
4	Russia	37,653	23,396
5	Philippines	36,289	22,559
6	Australia	25,760	16,007
7	Norway	21,925	13,624
8	US	19,924	12,380
9	New Zealand	15,134	9,404
10	China	14,500	9,010

TOP 10

LARGEST COUNTRIES IN ASIA

	Country	Area sq km	Area sq miles
1	China	9,596,961	3,705,408
2	India	3,287,590	1,269,346
3	Kazakhstan	2,716,626	1,049,155
4	Saudi Arabia	2,149,640	830,000
5	Indonesia	1,904,569	735,358
6	Iran	1,648,000	636,296
7	Mongolia	1,565,000	604,250
8	Pakistan	803,950	310,407
9	Turkey (in Asia)	790,200	305,098
10	Myanmar (Burma)	676,552	261,218

TOP 10

LARGEST COUNTRIES IN EUROPE

	Country	Area sq km	Area sq miles
1	Russia (in Europe)	4,710,227	1,818,629
2	Ukraine	603,700	233,090
3	France	547,026	211,208
4	Spain	504,781	194,897
5	Sweden	449,964	173,732
6	Germany	356,999	137,838
7	Finland	337,007	130,119
8	Norway	324,220	125,182
9	Poland	312,676	120,725
10	Italy	301,226	116,304

TOP 10

LARGEST COUNTRIES IN AFRICA

	Country	Area sq km	Area sq miles
1	Sudan	2,505,813	967,500
2	Algeria	2,381,741	919,595
3	Zaïre	2,345,409	905,567
4	Libya	1,759,540	679,362
5	Chad	1,284,000	495,755
6	Niger	1,267,080	489,191
7	Angola	1,246,700	481,354
8	Mali	1,240,000	478,791
9	Ethiopia	1,221,900	471,778
10	South Africa	1,221,031	471,445

WORLD POPULATIONS

TOP 10

WORLD POPULATION

Year	Estimated total
1000	254,000,000
1500	460,000,000
1600	579,000,000
1700	679,000,000
1800	954,000,000
1850	1,094,000,000
1900	1,633,000,000
1950	2,515,312,000
1960	3,019,376,000
1970	3,697,918,000
1980	4,450,210,000
1985	4,853,848,000
1993	5,554,552,000

World population is believed to have exceeded 5,000,000 before 8000 BC, and surpassed 5,000,000,000 in 1987. The United Nations has estimated the future growth of world population within three ranges – "low," "medium," and "high," depending on the extent of birth control measures and other factors during the coming decades. The high scenario, which assumes that few additional checks are placed on population expansion, implies a 78 percent global increase by the year 2025. Estimates suggest that by the turn of the century more than 60 percent of the world's population will be in Asia.

Year	Low	Medium	High
1995	5,679,685,000	5,765,861,000	5,854,986,000
2000	6,088.506,000	6,251,055,000	6,410,707,000
2005	6,463,211,000	6,728,574,000	6,978,754,000
2010	6,805,064,000	7,190,762,000	7,561,301,000
2015	7,109,736,000	7,639,547,000	8,167,357,000
2020	7,368,995,000	8,062,274,000	8,791,432,000
2025	7,589,731,000	8,466,516,000	9,422,749,000

TOP 10

MOST HIGHLY POPULATED COUNTRIES 100 YEARS AGO

	Country	Population
1	China	360,250,000
2	India	286,696,960
3	Russia	108,843,192
4	US	62,981,000
5	Germany	49,421,803
6	Austria	41,345,329
7	Japan	40,072,020
8	France	38,343,192
9	UK	37,888,153
10	Turkey	32,978,100

In the 1890s many national boundaries were quite different from their present form: for example, India encompassed what are now Pakistan and Bangladesh, Poland was part of Russia, and Austria and Turkey were extensive empires that included all their territories in their censuses. The 1891 census of the UK indicated that the population of England and Wales was 29,001,018. The estimated total population of the entire British Empire at this time was 340,220,000, making it second only to China's.

TOP 10

MOST HIGHLY POPULATED COUNTRIES IN THE WORLD

	Country	Population* 1983	1993
1	China	1,008,175,288	1,177,585,000
2	India	683,880,051	903,159,000
3	US	226,545,805	258,104,000
4	Indonesia	153,000,000	197,232,000
5	Brazil	119,098,922	156,664,000
6	USSR/Russia	271,203,000	149,300,000
7	Pakistan	83,780,000	125,314,000
8	Japan	118,390,000	124,712,000
9	Bangladesh	94,700,000	122,255,000
10	Nigeria	85,000,000	95,060,000

* Based on closest census or most recent estimate

During the 1980s world population increased from 4,450,000,000 at the beginning of the decade to 5,292,000,000 at the end – a growth of almost 19 percent. The figures for the past 10 years show that the population of China now represents over 21 percent of the total population of the world in 1993 (now estimated to be more than 5,554,552,000). Although differential rates of population increase result in changes in the order, the members of the Top 10 remain largely the same from year to year: the population of Pakistan, for example, only recently overtook that of Japan. Despite the anomaly that the USSR no longer exists, Russia, its largest former component state, maintains an independent place in the ranking.

T O P 1 0

COUNTRIES WITH THE HIGHEST ESTIMATED POPULATION IN THE YEAR 2000

	Country	Population
1	China	1,260,154,000
2	India	1,018,105,000
3	US	275,327,000
4	Indonesia	219,496,000
5	Brazil	169,543,000
6	Russia	151,460,000
7	Pakistan	148,540,000
8	Bangladesh	143,548,000
9	Japan	127,554,000
10	Nigeria	118,620,000

Asia contains many of the countries with the highest estimated populations in the year 2000. The part of the territory of the former USSR in Asia previously placed the USSR as one of the most populated countries in Asia. Following the breakup of the Soviet Union, no one of its individual states has such a high population. The largest country at present, Uzbekistan, has a population of 22,128,000.

T O P 1 0

LEAST POPULATED COUNTRIES IN THE WORLD

	Country	Population
1	Vatican City	738
2	Falkland Islands	1,916
3	Nauru	8,100
4	Tuvalu	8,229
5	Wallis and Fortuna	14,800
6	Cook Islands	17,185
7	San Marino	22,361
8	Monaco	28,000
9	Liechtenstein	28,181
10	Gibraltar	28,848

T O P 1 0

MOST DENSELY POPULATED COUNTRIES AND COLONIES IN THE WORLD

	Country/colony	Area sq km	sq miles	Population	Population per sq mile
1	Macau	16.06	6.2	479,000	77,249
2	Monaco	1.81	0.7	28,000	40,067
3	Hong Kong	1,037.29	400.5	5,900,000	14,732
4	Singapore	619.01	39.0	2,826,000	11,823
5	Gibraltar	6.47	2.5	28,848	11,549
6	Vatican City	0.44	0.17	738	4,343
7	Malta	313.39	121.0	362,950	2,999
8	Bermuda	53.35	20.6	58,460	2,839
9	Bangladesh	143,998.15	55,598.0	122,255,000	2,199
10	Bahrain	675.99	261.0	568,000	2,176
	US	9,372,614.90	3,618,787.0	258,104,000	73
	UK	244,046.79	94,227.0	57,970,000	616
	World total	135,597,770.00	52,509,600.0	5,554,552,000	average 105

T O P 1 0

COUNTRIES WITH THE HIGHEST BIRTH RATE

	Country	Birth rate*
1	Rwanda	58.0
2	Malawi	54.3
3	Yemen	53.6
4	Uganda	51.9
5	Ethiopia	50.4
6	Niger	50.2
7	Mali	50.1
8	Burundi	50.0
9	Afghanistan	49.0
10	Tanzania	47.7

* Live births per annum per 1,000 population

The 10 countries with the highest birth rate during the 1990s to date correspond very closely with those countries that have the highest fertility rate (the average number of children born to each woman in that country). In the case of Rwanda, the fertility rate is 8.29.

T O P 1 0

COUNTRIES WITH THE LOWEST BIRTH RATE

	Country	Birth rate*
1	Italy	10.0
2=	Greece	10.7
2=	Japan	10.7
4	Spain	11.4
5	Austria	11.5
6	Germany	11.7
7=	Hong Kong	12.1
7=	Hungary	12.1
9=	Denmark	12.4
9=	Portugal	12.4

* Live births per annum per 1,000 population

As with the highest birth rate, there is a close correlation between the countries that have the lowest birth rate and those with the lowest fertility rate. Fertility rates of less than 2.0 effectively imply that the woman and her partner are not replacing themselves, which means that the population is declining.

WORLD CITIES

Calculating the populations of the world's cities is fraught with difficulties, not least that of determining whether the city is defined by its administrative boundaries or by its continuously expanding built-up areas or conurbations. Since different countries adopt different methods, and some have populations concentrated in city centers while others are spread out in suburbs sprawling over hundreds of square miles, it has been impossible to compare them meaningfully. In order to resolve this problem, the US Bureau of the Census has adopted the method of defining cities as population clusters or "urban agglomerations" with densities of more than 5,000 inhabitants per square mile (1,931 per sq km). Totals based on this system will differ considerably from those of other methods: according to this system,

for example, the hugely spread-out city of Shanghai has a population of 6,936,000, compared with the total of 12,670,000 estimated for its metropolitan area. On this basis, the city in the Top 10 with the greatest area is New York (1,274 sq miles/3,300 sq km) and the smallest Bombay (95 sq miles/246 sq km) – which also means that Bombay has the greatest population density, 127,379 inhabitants per sq mile/49,191 per sq km – more than 12 times that of London.

One recent change to note in the Top 10 is the inexorable rise in the population of Brazil's second-largest city, Rio de Janeiro, the total of which has now overtaken that of Buenos Aires. These two remain the most populous cities in the Southern Hemisphere, with Jakarta, Indonesia, the runner-up (9,882,000 in 1991, using this method of calculation).

TOP 10

MOST HIGHLY POPULATED CITIES IN THE WORLD

	City/Country	Population
1	Tokyo/Yokohama, Japan	27,245,000
2	Mexico City, Mexico	20,899,000
3	São Paulo, Brazil	18,701,000
4	Seoul, South Korea	16,792,000
5	New York, US	14,625,000
6	Osaka-Kobe-Kyoto, Japan	13,872,000
7	Bombay, India	12,101,000
8	Calcutta, India	11,898,000
9	Rio de Janeiro, Brazil	11,688,000
10	Buenos Aires, Argentina	11,657,000

TOP 10

FIRST CITIES IN THE WORLD WITH POPULATIONS OF MORE THAN ONE MILLION

	City	Country
1	Rome	Italy
2	Angkor	Cambodia
3	Hangchow	China
4	London	UK
5	Paris	France
6	Peking	China
7	Canton	China
8	Berlin	Germany (Prussia)
9	New York	US
10	Vienna	Austria

Rome's population was reckoned to have exceeded 1,000,000 some time in the second century BC, and both Angkor and Hangchow had reached this figure by about AD 900 and 1200 respectively, although all three subsequently declined (Angkor was completely abandoned in the 15th century). No other city attained 1,000,000 until London in the early years of the 19th century. The next cities to pass the million mark did so between about 1850 and the late 1870s. Now at least 130 cities have populations of 1,000,000 or more.

TOP 10

MOST HIGHLY POPULATED CITIES IN THE WORLD 100 YEARS AGO

	City	Population
1	London	4,231,431
2	Paris	2,423,946
3	Peking	1,648,814
4	Canton (Kwangchow)	1,600,000
5	Berlin	1,579,244
6	Tokyo	1,552,457
7	New York	1,515,301
8	Vienna	1,364,548
9	Chicago	1,099,850
10	Philadelphia	1,046,964

In 1890 Nanking in China was the only other city in the world with a population of more than 1,000,000, with another Chinese city, Tientsin (now Tianjin), close behind. Several other cities, including Constantinople, St. Petersburg, and Moscow, all had populations in excess of 750,000. It is remarkable that in 1890, Brooklyn, with a population 806,343, was marginally larger than Bombay (804,470 in 1891), whereas Bombay's present population of 12,571,720 is more than five times that of the whole of Kings County, New York.

TOP 10

MOST HIGHLY POPULATED CITIES IN NORTH AMERICA

	City	Country	Population
1	Mexico City	Mexico	20,899,000
2	New York	US	14,625,000
3	Los Angeles	US	10,130,000
4	Chicago	US	6,529,000
5	Philadelphia	US	4,003,000
6	San Francisco	US	3,987,000
7	Miami	US	3,471,000
8	Guadalajara	Mexico	3,370,000
9	Toronto	Canada	3,145,000
10	Detroit/Windsor	US/Canada	2,969,000

The method used by the US Bureau of the Census for calculating city populations (see introduction, above) takes into account the often widely spread "urban agglomerations" – in the instance of Detroit and Windsor giving rise to the anomaly of a "city" that straddles two countries.

TOP 10

MOST HIGHLY POPULATED CITIES IN EUROPE

	City	Country	Population
1	Moscow*	Russia	10,446,000
2	London*	UK	9,115,000
3	Paris*	France	8,720,000
4	Essen	Germany	7,452,000
5	Istanbul#	Turkey	6,678,000
6	Milan	Italy	4,749,000
7	St. Petersburg	Russia	4,672,000
8	Madrid*	Spain	4,513,000
9	Barcelona	Spain	4,227,000
10	Manchester	UK	4,030,000

* Capital city
\# Located in Turkey in Europe

The problem of defining a city's boundaries means that population figures generally relate to "urban agglomerations," which often include suburbs sprawling over very large areas. The US Bureau of the Census method of identifying city populations (see introduction) produces this list – although one based on cities minus their suburbs would present a very different picture.

TOP 10

LARGEST CITIES IN THE WORLD IN THE YEAR 2000

	City/Country	Estimated population 2000*
1	Tokyo-Yokohama, Japan	29,971,000
2	Mexico City, Mexico	27,872,000
3	São Paulo, Brazil	25,354,000
4	Seoul, South Korea	21,976,000
5	Bombay, India	15,357,000
6	New York, US	14,648,000
7	Osaka-Kobe-Kyoto, Japan	14,287,000
8	Tehran, Iran	14,251,000
9	Rio de Janeiro, Brazil	14,169,000
10	Calcutta, India	14,088,000

* Based on US Bureau of the Census method of calculating city populations; this gives a list that differs from that calculated by other methods, such as those used by the United Nations.

GROWING ALL THE TIME
Tokyo's bustling streets will be busier than ever if, as predicted, the city's population increases by over two and a half million before the year 2000.

TOP 10

MOST DENSELY POPULATED CITIES IN THE WORLD

	City	Country	Population per sq mile
1	Hong Kong	Hong Kong	247,501
2	Lagos	Nigeria	142,821
3	Jakarta	Indonesia	130,026
4	Bombay	India	127,379
5	Ho Chi Minh City	Vietnam	120,168
6	Ahmadabad	India	115,893
7	Shenyang	China	109,974
8	Tianjin	China	98,990
9	Cairo	Egypt	97,106
10	Bangalore	India	96,041

TOP 10

LARGEST NONCAPITAL CITIES IN THE WORLD

	City	Population	Country	Capital/population
1	Shanghai	12,670,000	China	Beijing 10,860,000
2	Bombay	12,571,000	India	Delhi 8,375,188
3	Calcutta	10,916,272	India	Delhi 8,375,188
4	São Paulo	10,063,110	Brazil	Brasília 1,803,478
5	New York	7,322,564	US	Washington DC 604,000
6	Rio de Janeiro*	6,603,388	Brazil	Brasília 1,803,478
7	Karachi*	6,500,000	Pakistan	Islamabad 350,000
8	Tianjin	5,700,000	China	Beijing 10,860,000
9	St. Petersburg*	5,020,000	Russia	Moscow 8,967,000
10	Alexandria	5,000,000	Egypt	Cairo 14,000,000

* Former capital

Based on comparison of population within administrative boundaries – hence not comparable with the list of The 10 Largest Cities in the World.

THE STATES OF THE UNION

TOP 10

LARGEST STATES IN THE US

	State	Area* sq km	sq miles
1	Alaska	1,700,139	656,427
2	Texas	695,676	268,602
3	California	424,002	163,708
4	Montana	380,850	147,047
5	New Mexico	314,939	121,599
6	Arizona	295,276	114,007
7	Nevada	286,368	110,567
8	Colorado	269,620	104,101
9	Oregon	254,819	98,386
10	Wyoming	253,349	97,819

Total, including water

Alaska, the largest state, has the second smallest population (587,000; Wyoming is the smallest with 453,588). Alaska also has the greatest area of inland water of any state: 222,871 sq miles/86,051 sq km. By comparison, the UK (94,227 sq miles/244,046 sq km) is smaller than Wyoming, the 10th largest state.

TOP 10

SMALLEST STATES IN THE US

	State	Area* sq km	sq miles
1	Rhode Island	4,002	1,545
2	Delaware	6,447	2,489
3	Connecticut	14,358	5,544
4	New Jersey	22,590	8,722
5	New Hampshire	24,219	9,351
6	Vermont	24,903	9,615
7	Massachusetts	27,337	10,555
8	Hawaii	28,313	10,932
9	Maryland	32,135	12,407
10	West Virginia	62,759	24,231

Total, including water

The District of Columbia has a total area of 69 sq miles/179 sq km.

TOP 10

FIRST STATES OF THE US

	State	Entered Union		State	Entered Union
1	Delaware	December 7, 1787	6	Massachusetts	February 6, 1788
2	Pennsylvania	December 12, 1787	7	Maryland	April 28, 1788
3	New Jersey	December 18, 1787	8	South Carolina	May 23, 1788
4	Georgia	January 2, 1788	9	New Hampshire	June 21, 1788
5	Connecticut	January 9, 1788	10	Virginia	June 25, 1788

The names of two of these states commemorate early colonists. Delaware was named after Thomas West, Lord De La Warr, a governor of Virginia. Pennsylvania was called "Pensilvania," or "Penn's woodland," in its original charter, issued in 1681 to the Quaker leader William Penn. He had acquired the territory as part settlement of a debt of £16,000 owed to his father by King Charles II. Two states were named after places with which their founders had associations: New Jersey was the subject of a deed issued in 1644 by the Duke of York to John Berkeley and Sir George Carteret, who came from Jersey in the Channel Islands, and New Hampshire was called after the English county by settler Captain John Mason. Two names are of native American origin: Connecticut after the Algonquin Indian name "kuenihtekot," meaning "long river at" (the extra letter "c" was probably added by a writer who had "connect" in mind); and Massachusetts, which is believed to be native American for "high hill, little plain," the name of a place and of a tribe. The remaining four states' names have royal connections. Virginia was named after Queen Elizabeth I, the "Virgin Queen," and Georgia received its name from English soldier and politician James Oglethorpe in honor of King George II. The colony of Maryland was named after Queen Henrietta Maria, wife of Charles I. South Carolina was originally a French settlement called La Caroline after the French king Charles IX, but the tract of land was issued in 1619 to Sir Robert Heath, who renamed it Carolina after the English king Charles I.

TOP 10

LAST STATES OF THE US

	State	Entered Union		State	Entered Union
1	Hawaii	August 21, 1959	6	Utah	January 4, 1896
2	Alaska	January 3, 1959	7	Wyoming	July 10, 1890
3	Arizona	February 24, 1912	8	Idaho	July 3, 1890
4	New Mexico	January 6, 1912	9	Washington	November 11, 1889
5	Oklahoma	November 16, 1907	10	Montana	November 8, 1889

TOP 10

COUNTRIES OUTSIDE THE US WITH THE MOST RESIDENT US CITIZENS

	Country	US citizens		Country	US citizens
1	Mexico	425,400	6	Italy	83,400
2	Canada	259,700	7	Israel	77,200
3	UK	170,100	8	Australia	67,000
4	Germany	152,300	9	Spain	61,400
5	Philippines	120,600	10	Greece	54,000

TOP 10

MOST HIGHLY POPULATED STATES IN THE US

	State	Population 1900	1990
1	California	1,485,053	29,760,021
2	New York	7,268,894	17,990,455
3	Texas	3,048,710	16,986,510
4	Florida	528,542	12,937,926
5	Pennsylvania	6,302,115	11,881,643
6	Illinois	4,821,550	11,430,602
7	Ohio	4,157,545	10,847,115
8	Michigan	2,420,982	9,295,297
9	New Jersey	1,883,669	7,730,188
10	North Carolina	1,893,810	6,628,637

According to the Census of each year, the total population of the US in 1900 was 76,212,168 – about 31 percent of its 1990 population of 248,709,873. It has undergone a 63 times expansion in the 200 years since 1790, when it was just 3,929,214. Some states continue to grow faster than others: between 1980 and 1989 the population of Florida increased by 30 percent and that of California grew by more than 20 percent.

TOP 10

ANCESTRIES OF THE US POPULATION

	Ancestry group	Number
1	German	57,947,873
2	Irish	38,735,539
3	English	32,651,788
4	African-American	23,777,098
5	Italian	14,664,550
6	American	12,395,999
7	Mexican	11,586,983
8	French	10,320,935
9	Polish	9,366,106
10	American Indian	8,708,220

The 1990 US Census asked people to identify the ancestry group to which they believed themselves to belong: while 23.3 percent were able to claim German ancestry, 15.6 Irish, and so on, 5 percent were unable to define their family origin more precisely than "American." Many claimed multiple ancestry, and some reported broad racial origins, such as "White" (1,799,711 respondents), "European" (466,718), and "Asian" (107,172).

TOP 10

LARGEST AMERICAN INDIAN TRIBES

	Tribe	Population
1	Cherokee	308,132
2	Navajo	219,198
3	Chippewa	103,826
4	Sioux	103,255
5	Choctaw	82,299
6	Pueblo	52,939
7	Apache	50,051
8	Iroquois	49,038
9	Lumbee	48,444
10	Creek	43,550

The total American Indian population was 1,878,285 according to the 1990 Census. Different authorities have estimated that at the time of the first European arrivals in 1492, it was anything from 1,000,000 to 10,000,000. This declined to a low of some 90,000 in 1890, but has increased over the past century: according to the Census it had risen to 357,000 in 1950, 793,000 in 1970, and 1,479,000 in 1980.

TOP 10

FOREIGN BIRTHPLACES OF THE US POPULATION*

	Birthplace	Number
1	Mexico	4,298,014
2	Philippines	912,674
3	Canada	744,830
4	Cuba	736,971
5	Germany	711,929
6	UK	640,145
7	Italy	580,592
8	Korea	568,397
9	Vietnam	543,262
10	China	529,837

* US Bureau of the Census 1990 figures

TOP 10

COUNTRIES OF ORIGIN OF US IMMIGRANTS, 1820–1993

	Country	Number
1	Germany	7,117,192
2	Italy	5,419,285
3	Great Britain	5,178,264
4	Mexico*	5,177,422
5	Ireland	4,755,172
6	Canada	4,380,955
7	Austria/Hungary #	4,354,085
8	Former USSR**	3,572,281
9	West Indies	3,035,898
10	Sweden ‡	1,288,763

* Unreported 1886–93
# Unreported before 1861; combined 1861–1905; separately 1905–, but cumulative total included here; Austria included with Germany 1938–45
** Russia before 1917
‡ Figures combined with Norway 1820–68

TOP 10

LARGEST AMERICAN INDIAN RESERVATIONS

	Reservation	State	Population
1	Navajo	Arizona/New Mexico/Utah	143,405
2	Pine Ridge	Nevada/ South Dakota	11,182
3	Fort Apache	Arizona	9,825
4	Gila River	Arizona	9,116
5	Papago	Arizona	8,480
6	Rosebud	South Dakota	8,043
7	San Carlos	Arizona	7,110
8	Zuni Pueblo	Arizona/ New Mexico	7,073
9	Hopi	Arizona	7,061
10	Blackfeet	Montana	7,025

PLACE NAMES

T O P 1 0

LONGEST PLACE NAMES IN THE WORLD

(Including single-word, hyphenated, and multiple names)

	Name	Letters
1	Krung thep mahanakhon bovorn ratanakosin mahintharayutthaya mahadilok pop noparatratchathani burirom udomratchanivetma hasathan amornpiman avatarnsa thit sakkathattiyavisnukarmprasit	167

When the poetic name of Bangkok, capital of Thailand, is used, it is usually abbreviated to "Krung Thep" (City of Angels).

	Name	Letters
2	Taumatawhakatangihangakoauau- otamateaturipukakapikimaunga- horonukupokaiwhenuakitanatahu	85

This is the longer version (the other has a mere 83 letters) of the Maori name of a hill in New Zealand. It translates as "The place where Tamatea, the man with the big knees, who slid, climbed, and swallowed mountains, known as land-eater, played on the flute to his loved one."

	Name	Letters
3	Gorsafawddacha'idraigodanhed- dogleddollônpenrhynareur- draethceredigion	67

A name contrived by the Fairbourne Steam Railway, Gwynedd, North Wales, for publicity purposes and in order to outdo its rival, No. 4. It means "The Mawddach station and its dragon teeth at the Northern Penrhyn Road on the golden beach of Cardigan Bay."

	Name	Letters
4	Llanfairpwllgwyngyllgogerychwyrn- drobwllllantysiliogogogoch	58

This is the place in Gwynedd famed especially for the length of its railway tickets. It means "St. Mary's Church in the hollow of the white hazel near to the rapid whirlpool of Llantysilio of the Red Cave." Its authenticity is suspect, since its official name consists of only the first 20 letters, and the full name appears to have been invented as a hoax in the 19th century by local inhabitant John Evans.

	Name	Letters
5	El Pueblo de Nuestra Señora la Reina de los Angeles de la Porciuncula	57

The site of a Franciscan mission and the full Spanish name of Los Angeles; it means "the town of Our Lady the Queen of the Angels of the Little Portion." Now it is customarily known by its initial letters "LA," making it also one of the shortest-named cities in the world.

	Name	Letters
6	Chargoggagoggmanchauggagogg- chaubunagungamaugg	45

America's longest place name, a lake near Webster, Massachusetts. Its Indian name, loosely translated, means "You fish on your side, I'll fish on mine, and no one fishes in the middle." It is pronounced "Char-gogg-a-gogg (pause) man-chaugg-a-gogg (pause) chau-bun-a-gung-a-maugg."

	Name	Letters
7=	Lower North Branch Little Southwest Miramichi	40

The longest place name in Canada belongs – rather incongruously – to a short river in New Brunswick.

	Name	Letters
7=	Villa Real de la Santa Fe de San Francisco de Asis	40

The full Spanish name of Santa Fe, New Mexico, translates as "Royal city of the holy faith of St. Francis of Assisi."

	Name	Letters
9	Te Whakatakangaotengarehuote- ahiatamatea	38

The Maori name of Hammer Springs, New Zealand; like the second name in this list, it refers to a legend of Tamatea, explaining how the springs were warmed by "the falling of the cinders of the fire of Tamatea."

	Name	Letters
10	Meallan Liath Coire Mhic Dhubhghaill	32

The longest multiple name in Scotland belongs to this place near Aultanrynie, Highland. The alternative spelling is Meallan Liath Coire Mhic Dhughaill.

T O P 1 0

LONGEST PLACE NAMES IN THE UK

(Single and hyphenated only)

	Name	Letters
1	Gorsafawddacha'idraigodanhed- dogleddollônpenrhynareur- draethceredigion (*see* The 10 Longest Place Names in the World)	67
2	Llanfairpwllgwyngyllgogerych- wyrndrobwllllantysiliogogogoch (*see* The 10 Longest Place Names in the World)	58
3	Sutton-under-Whitestonecliffe, North Yorkshire	27
4	Llanfihangel-yng-Ngwynfa, Powys	22
5=	Llanfihangel-y-Creuddyn, Dyfed	21
5=	Llanfihangel-y-traethau, Gwynedd	21

	Name	Letters
7	Cottonshopeburnfoot, Northumberland	19
8=	Blakehopeburnhaugh, Northumberland	18
8=	Coignafeuinternich, Inverness-shire	18
10=	Claddach-baleshare, North Uist, Outer Hebrides	17
10=	Claddach-knockline, North Uist, Outer Hebrides	17

Runners-up include Combeinteignhead, Doddiscombsleigh, Moretonhampstead, Stokeinteignhead, and Woolfardisworthy (pronounced "Woolsery"), all of which are in Devon and have 16 letters. The longest multiple name in England is North Leverton with Habblesthorpe, Nottinghamshire (30 letters), followed by Sulhampstead Bannister Upper End, Berkshire (29). In Wales the longest are Lower Llanfihangel-y-Creuddyn, Dyfed (26) followed by Llansantffraid Cwmdeuddwr, Powys (24), and in Scotland Meallan Liath Coire Mhic Dhughaill, Highland, (32), a loch on the island of Lewis called Loch Airidh Mhic Fhionnlaidh Dhuibh (31), and Huntingtower and Ruthvenfield (27). If the parameters are extended to include Ireland, Castletownconyersmaceniery (26), Co. Limerick, Muikeenachidirdhashaile (24), and Muckanaghederdauhalia (21), both in Co. Galway, are scooped into the net. The shortest place name in the UK is Ae in Dumfries and Galloway, Scotland.

TOP 10

COUNTRIES WITH THE LONGEST OFFICIAL NAMES

	Official name	Common English name	Letters
1	al-Jamāhīrīyah al-ʿArabīya al-Lībīyah ash-Shaʿbīyah al-Ishtirākīyah	Libya	56
2	al-Jumhūrīyah al-Jazāʾirīyah ad-Dīmuqrāṭīyah ash-Shaʿbīyah	Algeria	49
3	United Kingdom of Great Britain and Northern Ireland	United Kingdom	45
4	Sri Lankā Prajathanthrika Samajavadi Janarajaya	Sri Lanka	43
5	Jumhūrīyat al-Qumur al-Ittihādīyah al-Islāmīyah	The Comores	41
6=	al-Jumhūrīyah al-Islāmīyah al-Mūrītānīyah	Mauritania	36
6=	The Federation of St. Christopher and Nevis	St. Kitts and Nevis	36
8	Jamhuuriyadda Dimuqraadiga Soomaaliya	Somalia	35
9	al-Mamlakah al-Urdunnīyah al-Hāshimīyah	Jordan	34
10	Repoblika Demokratika n'i Madagaskar	Madagascar	32

TOP 10

MOST COMMON STREET NAMES IN THE US

1	Second Street	6	First Street
2	Park Street	7	Sixth Street
3	Third Street	8	Seventh Street
4	Fourth Street	9	Washington Street
5	Fifth Street	10	Maple Street

The list continues with Oak, Eighth, Elm, Lincoln, Ninth, Pine, Walnut, Tenth, and Cedar. Curiously, First is not first, because many streets that would be so designated are instead called Main.

TOP 10

MOST COMMON PLACE NAMES IN THE US

	Name	No. of occurrences		Name	No. of occurrences
1	Midway	207	6	Centerville	109
2	Fairview	192	7	Mount Pleasant	108
3	Oak Grove	150	8	Riverside	106
4	Five Points	145	9	Bethel	105
5	Pleasant Hill	113	10	New Hope	98

TOP 10

MOST COMMON PLACE NAMES OF BIBLICAL ORIGIN IN THE US

	Name/meaning/original location	US occurrences
1	Salem	95

"Peace"; this was the kingdom of Melchizidek, supposedly Jerusalem.

2	Eden	61

"Pleasure"; principally meaning the place where mankind began, it is also the name given to a market in Mesopotamia.

3	Bethel	47

"House of God"; this was a city in Palestine, or a town in South Judah.

4	Lebanon	39

"White"; in the Bible this was originally the name of two mountain ranges. Today it is the name of a country.

5	Sharon	38

"Plain"; this was the plain on the Mediterranean coast between Judah and Caesarea. It was also the name of a place in east Jordan.

6	Goshen	33

"Drawing near"; as well as being the northern province of Egypt, this was also the name of part of southern Palestine, and of a city in Judah.

7	Jordan	27

"Descender"; this was the principal river of Palestine.

8	Hebron	26

"Friendship"; this could be either a person or a place. In the Bible, the son of Kohath was called Hebron, and this was also the name of a city in Judah.

9	Zion	24

"Mount, sunny"; this was a mountain in Jerusalem, or the sacred capital of the Jewish people generally.

10=	Antioch	18

Named for Antiochus, king of Syria, this was the capital of the Greek kings of Syria. There was also a city of Pisidia with the same name.

10=	Paradise	18

"Pleasure ground"; this is another name for the Garden of Eden, or heaven.

10=	Shiloh	18

"Peace"; this possibly signified the Messiah, and was the name of a city in Ephraim.

Research conducted by John Leighley surveyed a substantial sampling (61,742) of US place names, from which he concluded that 101 different names, comprising a total of 803 occurrences, were of biblical origin.

US CITIES

TOP 10

LARGEST CITIES IN THE US

	City	State	Population
1	New York	New York	7,322,564
2	Los Angeles	California	3,485,398
3	Chicago	Illinois	2,783,726
4	Houston	Texas	1,630,553
5	Philadelphia	Pennsylvania	1,585,577
6	San Diego	California	1,110,549
7	Detroit	Michigan	1,027,974
8	Dallas	Texas	1,006,877
9	Phoenix	Arizona	983,403
10	San Antonio	Texas	935,933

Based on the 1990 Census, these are estimates for central city areas only, not for the total metropolitan areas that surround them, which may be several times as large.

TOP 10

LARGEST CITIES IN THE US IN 1900

Rank 1900	1990	City	State	1900 population
1	(1)	New York	New York	3,437,202
2	(3)	Chicago	Illinois	1,698,575
3	(5)	Philadelphia	Pennsylvania	1,293,697
4	(34)	St. Louis	Missouri	575,238
5	(20)	Boston	Massachusetts	560,892
6	(13)	Baltimore	Maryland	508,957
7	(24)	Cleveland	Ohio	381,768
8	(50)	Buffalo	New York	352,387
9	(14)	San Francisco	California	342,782
10	(45)	Cincinnati	Ohio	325,902

Only the first three cities are in the present Top 10, the rest having been overtaken by seven others that had relatively small populations at the turn of the century: Los Angeles (102,479 in 1900), Houston (44,633), San Diego (17,700), Detroit (285,704), Dallas (42,638), Phoenix (5,444) and San Antonio (53,321). The population of Buffalo has actually declined from 352,387 in 1900 to 328,123 today.

TOP 10

US CITIES WITH THE GREATEST POPULATION DECLINE, 1980-1990

	City	Population 1980	1990	Percentage decline
1	Gary, Indiana	151,968	116,646	23.2
2	Newark, New Jersey	329,248	275,221	16.4
3	Detroit, Michigan	1,203,368	1,027,974	14.6
4	Pittsburgh, Pennsylvania	423,960	369,879	12.8
5	St Louis, Missouri	452,801	396,685	12.4
6	Cleveland, Ohio	573,822	505,616	11.9
7	Flint, Michigan	159,611	140,761	11.8
8	New Orleans, Louisiana	557,927	496,638	10.9
9	Warren, Michigan	161,134	144,864	10.1
10	Chattanooga, Tennessee	169,514	152,494	10.0

During the 1980s, many of the great industrial cities suffered shrinkage as the country's manufacturing base declined in favor of high-tech businesses, service industries, and imports – especially of motor vehicles. Detroit, Philadelphia, and Chicago may still be numbered among the 10 largest cities in the US, but the populations of all three dwindled between 1980 and 1990, whereas those of cities such as Los Angeles and Dallas expanded during the same period.

TOP 10

FASTEST-GROWING CITIES IN THE US, 1980–1990

	City	Population 1980	1990	Percentage increase
1	Moreno Valley, California	28,309	118,779	319.6
2	Mesa, Arizona	152,404	288,104	89.0
3	Rancho Cucamonga, California	55,250	101,409	83.5
4	Plano, Texas	72,231	128,885	78.5
5	Irvine, California	62,134	110,330	77.6
6	Escondido, California	64,355	108,635	66.8
7	Oceanside, California	76,698	128,154	67.1
8	Santa Clarita, California	66,730	110,690	65.9
9	Bakersfield, California	105,611	174,820	65.5
10	Arlington, Texas	160,113	261,721	63.5

The majority of fastest-growing US cities (seven of the Top 10 and 11 in the Top 20) are located in California, with Texas the closest runner-up. The enduring appeal of the Golden State to those relocating, plus natural increase, added 6,092,257 to its population between the 1980 and 1990 censuses, and as a result it now has 11.97 percent of the entire US population.

NEW YORK SKYLINE
Although its skyscrapers give it a sharply modern look, New York has a wealth of historic locations.

TOP 10

US CITIES WITH THE MOST HISTORIC PLACES

	City	Historic places*
1	New York, New York	624
2	Philadelphia, Pennsylvania	470
3	Washington DC	336
4	Chicago, Illinois	223
5	Cincinnati, Ohio	222
6	Boston, Massachusetts	196
7=	Baltimore, Maryland	176
7=	Cleveland, Ohio	176
9	Providence, Rhode Island	126
10	Richmond, Virginia	120

* As designated in the National Register of Historic Places

TOP 10

HIGHEST CITIES IN THE US

	City	Highest point m	ft
1	Colorado Spings, Colorado	1,873	6,145
2	Denver, Colorado	1,667	5,470
3	Albuquerque, New Mexico	1,632	5,354
4	Los Angeles, California	1,549	5,081
5	Salt Lake City, Utah	1,319	4,327
6	Honolulu, Hawaii	1,227	4,025
7	El Paso, Texas	1,147	3,762
8	Lubbock, Texas	988	3,241
9	Phoenix, Arizona	835	2,740
10	Tucson, Arizona	728	2,390

This list is based on the highest points within the city limits of US cities with populations of more than 150,000. Some of these cities are otherwise generally low-lying, but there are much smaller settlements that are wholly at higher elevations, such as, in Colorado, the habitation of Climax (11,560 ft/3,523 m).

TOP 10

MOST DENSELY POPULATED CITIES IN THE US*

(Cities with populations of 100,000+ only)

	City	Population per sq km	sq mile
1	New York	9,151	23,701
2	Paterson, New Jersey	6,445	16,693
3	San Francisco, California	5,985	15,502
4	Jersey City, New Jersey	5,922	15,337
5	Chicago, Illinois	4,730	12,251
6	Inglewood, California	4,626	11,952
7	Boston, Massachusetts	4,579	11,860
8	Philadelphia, Pennsylvania	4,531	11,734
9	Newark, New Jersey	4,461	11,554
10	El Monte, California	4,315	11,175

The New York figure is for the metropolitan area as a whole. Three boroughs, though – Manhattan, Brooklyn, and the Bronx – have even higher population densities.

TOP 10

CITIES WITH THE GREATEST AREA

	City	State	Area sq km	sq miles
1	Anchorage	Alaska	4,397.0	1,697.7
2	Jacksonville	Florida	1,965.0	758.7
3	Oklahoma City	Oklahoma	1,575.2	608.2
4	Houston	Texas	1,398.3	539.9
5	Nashville-Davidson	Tennessee	1,225.8	473.5

	City	State	Area sq km	sq miles
6	Los Angeles	California	1,215.5	469.3
7	Phoenix	Arizona	1,087.5	419,9
8	Indianapolis	Indiana	936.8	361.7
9	Dallas	Texas	886.8	342.4
10	Chesapeake	Virginia	882.4	340.7

NATIONAL PARKS

THE TEN

FIRST NATIONAL MONUMENTS IN THE US

	National monument	Established
1	Devils Tower, Wyoming	Sep 24, 1906
2	Montezuma Castle, Arizona	Dec 8, 1906
3	Gila Cliff Dwellings, New Mexico	Nov 16, 1907
4	Tonto, Arizona	Dec 19, 1907
5	Muir Woods, California	Jan 9, 1908
6	Grand Canyon, Arizona	Jan 11, 1908
7	Pinnacles, California	Jan 16, 1908
8	Jewel Cave, South Dakota	Feb 7, 1908
9	Natural Bridges, Utah	Apr 16, 1908
10	Navajo, Arizona	Mar 20, 1909

There are some 76 National Monuments in the US, covering a total of 4,787,744 acres. Some sites were identified as of special historical importance earlier than those in the Top 10, but were not officially designated as National Monuments until later dates, among them the Custer Battlefield, Montana (the site of the Battle of Little Big Horn, June 25–26, 1876), which was established as a national cemetery on January 29, 1879, but did not become a National Monument until an Act of Congress dated March 22, 1946.

THE TEN

FIRST NATIONAL HISTORIC SITES IN THE US

	National historic site	Established*
1	Ford's Theatre, Washington DC	Apr 7, 1866
2	Abraham Lincoln Birthplace, Kentucky	Jul 17, 1916
3	Andrew Johnson Memorial Tennessee	Aug 29, 1935
4	Jefferson National Expansion Memorial, Missouri	Dec 20, 1935
5	Whitman Mission, Washington	Jun 29, 1936
6	Salem Maritime, Massachusetts	Mar 17, 1938
7	Fort Laramie, Wyoming	Jul 16, 1938
8	Hopewell Furnace, Pennsylvania	Aug 3, 1938
9	Vanderbilt Mansion, New York	Dec 18, 1940
10	Fort Raleigh, North Carolina	Apr 5, 1941

* Dates include those for locations originally assigned other designations but later authorized as Historic Sites.

Jimmy Carter's birthplace in Georgia (1987) and a site commemorating the Brown *v* Board of Education case of 1954, (1992) are two recent Historic Sites. This case, originating in Kansas, ruled that racial segregation in public schools was unconstitutional.

THE TEN

FIRST NATIONAL PARKS IN THE US

	National Park	Established
1	Yellowstone, Wyoming/ Montana/Idaho	Mar 1, 1872
2	Sequoia, California	Sep 25, 1890
3=	Yosemite, California	Oct 1, 1890
3=	General Grant, California*	Oct 1, 1890
5	Mount Rainier, Washington	Mar 2, 1899
6	Crater Lake, Oregon	May 22, 1902
7	Wind Cave, South Dakota	Jan 9, 1903
8	Mesa Verde, Colorado	Jun 29, 1906
9	Glacier, Montana	May 11, 1910
10	Rocky Mountain, Colorado	Jan 26, 1915

* Name changed to Kings Canyon National Park, March 4, 1940.

These are the first National Parks established as such in the US. Several others, founded under different appellations at earlier dates, and later redesignated as National Parks, could also claim a place in the list. For example, Hot Springs, Arkansas, established as early as April 20, 1832 as Hot Springs Reservation, became a public park on June 16, 1880, but was not made a National Park until March 4, 1921. Similarly, Petrified Forest, Arizona, was made a National Monument on December 8, 1906, but did not become a National Park until December 9, 1962.

THE TEN

FIRST NATIONAL BATTLEFIELDS IN THE US

	National Battlefield	Battle	Established*
1	Chickamauga and Chattanooga, Georgia/Tennessee	Sep 19–20, 1863	Aug 19, 1890
2	Antietam, Maryland	Sep 17, 1862	Aug 30, 1890
3	Shiloh, Tennessee	Apr 6–7, 1862	Dec 27, 1894
4	Gettysburg, Pennsylvania	Jul 1–3, 1863	Feb 11, 1895
5	Vicksburg, Mississippi	Jan 9–Jul 4, 1863	Feb 21, 1899
6	Big Hole, Montana	Aug 9, 1877	Jun 23, 1910
7	Guilford Courthouse, North Carolina	Mar 15, 1781	Mar 2, 1917
8	Kennesaw Mountain, Georgia	Jun 20–Jul 2, 1864	Apr 22, 1917
9	Moores Creek, North Carolina	Feb 27, 1776	Jun 2, 1926
10	Petersburg, Virginia	Jun 15, 1864–Apr 3, 1865	Jul 3, 1926

There are in all 24 National Battlefields, National Battlefield Parks, and National Military Parks, but just one National Battlefield Site – Brices Cross Roads, Mississippi (the scene of a Civil War engagement on Jun 10, 1864, the Site was established on Feb 21, 1929). The earliest battle to be so commemorated is Fort Necessity, Pennsylvania (July 3, 1754; National Battlefield established Mar 4, 1931), the opening hostility in the French and Indian War, in which the militia led by George Washington, then a 22-year-old Lt.-Colonel, was defeated and captured.

* Dates include those for locations originally assigned other designations but later authorized as National Battlefields, National Battlefield Parks, and National Military Parks.

T O P 1 0

LARGEST NATIONAL PARKS IN THE US

	National Park	Established	Area sq km	Area sq miles
1	Wrangell-St. Elias, Alaska	Dec 2, 1980	33,716	13,018
2	Gates of the Arctic, Alaska	Dec 2, 1980	30,448	11,756
3	Denali (formerly Mt. McKinley), Alaska	Feb 26, 1917	19,088	7,370
4	Katmai, Alaska	Dec 2, 1980	15,037	5,806
5	Glacier Bay, Alaska	Dec 2, 1980	13,054	5,040
6	Lake Clark, Alaska	Dec 2, 1980	10,671	4,120
7	Yellowstone, Wyoming/Montana/Idaho	Mar 1, 1872	8,982	3,468
8	Kobuk Valley, Alaska	Dec 2, 1980	7,084	2,735
9	Everglades, Florida	May 30, 1934	5,662	2,186
10	Grand Canyon, Arizona	Feb 26, 1919	4,931	1,904

Yellowstone National Park was established on March 1, 1872 as the first national park in the world with its role "as a public park or pleasuring ground for the benefit and enjoyment of the people." There are now some 1,200 national parks in more than 100 countries. There are 49 National Parks in the US, with a total area of more than 73,816 sq miles/191,183 sq km. This is more than double the area they covered before 1980 (when large tracts of Alaska were added). With the addition of various National Monuments, National Historic Parks, National Preserves, and other specially designated areas under the aegis of the National Park Service, the total area is 124,378 sq miles/322,138 sq km, and is visited by almost 300,000,000 people a year.

T O P 1 0

MOST-VISITED NATIONAL PARKS IN THE US

	Park/location	Visitors (1993)
1	Great Smoky Mountains National Park, North Carolina/Tennessee	9,283,848
2	Grand Canyon National Park, Arizona	4,575,602
3	Yosemite National Park, California	3,839,645
4	Yellowstone National Park, Wyoming	2,912,193
5	Rocky Mountains, Colorado	2,780,342
6	Olympic National Park, Washington	2,679,598
7	Acadia National Park, Maine	2,656,034
8	Grand Teton, Wyoming	2,568,689
9	Mammoth Cave, Kentucky	2,396,234
10	Zion National Park, Utah	2,391,580

RIVER DEEP, MOUNTAIN HIGH
Yellowstone is the oldest National Park in the US. Its attractions include the spectacular Grand Canyon of the Yellowstone and the dramatic scenery of the Yellowstone River, which plunges over 400 ft/122 m from two waterfalls below Yellowstone Lake before it enters the canyon. Volcanic rock formations, fossil forests, and geysers are among the park's other amazing natural features.

WORLD'S TALLEST BUILDINGS

TOP 10

TALLEST BUILDINGS ERECTED MORE THAN 100 YEARS AGO

	Building	Location	Year completed	Height m	ft
1	Eiffel Tower	Paris, France	1889	300	984
2	Washington Memorial	Washington DC, US	1885	169	555
3	Ulm Cathedral	Ulm, Germany	1890	161	528
4	Lincoln Cathedral	Lincoln, England	c.1307 (destroyed 1548)	160	525
5	Cologne Cathedral	Cologne, Germany	1880	156.4	513
6	Notre-Dame	Rouen, France	1530	156	512
7	St. Pierre Church	Beauvais, France	1568 (collapsed 1573)	153	502
8	St. Paul's Cathedral	London, England	1315 (destroyed 1561)	149	489
9	Rouen Cathedral	Rouen, France	1876	148	485
10	Great Pyramid	Giza, Egypt	c.2580 BC	146.5	481

TOP 10

TALLEST HABITABLE BUILDINGS IN THE WORLD

	Building	Location	Year completed	Stories	Height m	ft
1	Sears Tower with spires	Chicago, US	1974	110	443 520	1,454 1,707
2	World Trade Center*	New York City, US	1973	110	417	1,368
3	Empire State Building with spire	New York City, US	1931	102	381 449	1,250 1,472
4	Amoco Building	Chicago, US	1973	80	346	1,136
5	John Hancock Center with spire	Chicago, US	1968	100	343 450	1,127 1,476
6	Yu Kyong Hotel	Pyongyang, North Korea	1992	105	320	1,050
7	Central Plaza with spire	Hong Kong	1992	78	309 374	1,015 1,228
8	First Interstate World Center	Los Angeles, US	1990	73	310	1,017
9	Texas Commerce Tower	Houston, US	1981	75	305	1,002
10	Bank of China Tower with spires	Hong Kong	1989	70	305 368	1,001 1,209

* Twin towers; the second tower, completed in 1973, has the same number of stories but is slightly smaller at 1,362 ft/415 m – although its spire takes it up to 1,710 ft/521 m.

Heights do not include TV and radio antennae and uninhabited extensions. This list is scheduled to change in 1996, when the 95-story Petronas Tower, Kuala Lumpur (1,476 ft/450 m) becomes the "world's tallest," while further skyscrapers will join the Top 10 list soon after.

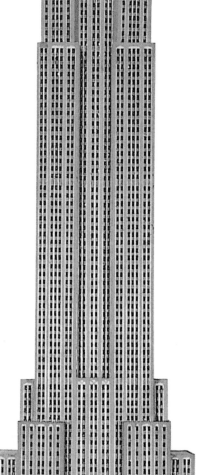

EMPIRE STATE BUILDING
Located on New York's Fifth Avenue, this huge skyscraper held the record of tallest building for more than 40 years. The upper part was built as a mooring site for airships, though it was never used as such.

TOP 10

TALLEST CHIMNEYS IN THE WORLD

	Chimney/location	Height m	ft
1	Ekibastuz Power Station, Kazakhstan	420	1,377
2	International Nickel Company, Sudbury, Ontario, Canada	381	1,250
3	Pennsylvania Electric Company, Homer City, Pennsylvania, US	371	1,216
4	Kennecott Copper Corporation, Magna, Utah, US	370	1,215
5	Ohio Power Company, Cresap, West Virginia, US	368	1,206
6	Zasavje Power Station, Trbovlje, Slovenia	360	1,181
7	Empresa Nacional de Electricidad SA, Puentes de Garcia Rodriguez, Spain	356	1,169
8	Appalachian Power Company, New Haven, West Virginia, US	336	1,103
9	Indiana & Michigan Electric Company, Rockport, Indiana, US	316	1,037
10	West Penn Power Company, Reesedale, Pennsylvania, US	308	1,012

Nos. 2 to 5 and 7 to 10 were all built by Pullman Power Products Corporation (formerly a division of M.W. Kellogg), an American engineering company that has been in business since 1902 and has built many of the world's tallest chimneys. The largest internal volume is No. 7 – 6,700,000 cubic feet. The diameter of No. 1, completed in 1991, tapers from 144 ft/44 m at the base to 47 ft/14 m at the top; the outside diameter of No. 4, built in 1974 and formerly the world's largest, is 124 ft/38 m at the base, tapering to 40 ft/12 m.

TOP 10

TALLEST TELECOMMUNICATIONS TOWERS IN THE WORLD

	Tower/location	Year completed	Height m	ft
1	CN Tower, Toronto, Canada	1975	553	1,815
2	Ostankino Tower, Moscow, Russia	1967	537	1,762
3	Alma-Ata Tower, Kazakhstan	1983	370	1,214
4	TV Tower, Berlin, Germany	1969	365	1,198
5	TV Tower, Tashkent, Uzbekistan	1983	357	1,171
6	Tokyo Tower, Tokyo, Japan	1959	333	1,093
7	TV Tower, Frankfurt, Germany	1977	331	1,086
8	National Transcommunications Transmitter, Emley Moor, West Yorkshire, UK	1971	329	1,080
9	Eiffel Tower, Paris, France	1889	321	1,053
10	Sydney Tower, Sydney, Australia	1981	305	1,001

All the towers listed are self-supporting, rather than masts braced with guy wires, and all have observation facilities, the highest being that in the CN Tower, Toronto (the world's tallest self-supporting structure of any kind) at 1,467 ft/447 m. Towers new to the Top 10, both currently under construction and due for completion in 1995, will be the KL Tower, Kuala Lumpur, Malaysia (1,378 ft/420 m) and the Sky Tower, Auckland, New Zealand (1,076 ft/328 m). As a result, the Eiffel Tower will drop out of the Top 10 and the Vegas World Tower, Las Vegas, US (1,012 ft/309 m), also scheduled for completion in 1995, will not achieve Top 10 status.

TOP 10

TALLEST STRUCTURES THAT ARE NO LONGER STANDING

	Structure	Location	Completed	Destroyed	Height m	ft
1	Warszawa Radio Mast	Konstantynow, Poland	1974	1991	646	2,120
2	KSWS TV Mast	Roswell, New Mexico, US	1956	1960	491	1,610
3	IBA Mast	Emley Moor, UK	1965	1969	385	1,265
4	No. 6 Flue (chimney), Matla Power Station	Kriel, South Africa	1980	1981	275	902
5	Singer Building	New York, US	1908	1970	200	656
6	New Brighton Tower	Merseyside, UK	1900	1919	171	562
7	Lincoln Cathedral	Lincoln, England	c.1307	1548	160	525
8	St. Pierre Church	Beauvais, France	1568	1573	153	502
9	St. Peter's	Louvain, Flanders	1497	1606	152	500
10	Lin-He Pagoda	Hang Zhou, China	970	1121	150	492

The Matla Power Station chimney was never fully operational and, following an accident that resulted in two fatalities, was demolished. If excluded for this reason, the 10th entry is the 410-ft/125-m Legal & General Building, Sydney, Australia, built in 1977 and dismantled floor by floor in nine months during 1991.

BIGGEST BUILDINGS – US

REACHING FOR THE SKY: 100 YEARS OF "WORLD'S TALLEST" HABITABLE BUILDINGS

World's tallest building	Year	Stories	Height m	ft
American Surety Building, New York (remodeled 1975 as Bank of Tokyo)	1895	21	90	300
Saint Paul Building, New York	1899	16	94	310
Park Row Building, New York	1899	29	118	386
Singer Building, New York (demolished 1970)	1908	41	200	656
Metropolitan Life, New York	1909	50	212	700
Woolworth Building, New York	1914	60	241	791
40 Wall Street, New York	1930	70	283	927
Chrysler Building, New York	1930	77	319	1,046
Empire State Building, New York *with spire*	1931	102	381 *449*	1,250 *1,472*
World Trade Center, New York	1973	110	417	1,368
Sears Tower, Chicago *with spires*	1974	110	443 *520*	1,454 *1,707*
Petronas Tower, Kuala Lumpur, Malaysia	UC/1996	95	450	1,475
Chongqing Tower, Chongqing, China	UC/1997	114	457	1,500
Nina Tower, Hong Kong *with spire*	UC/1998	100	468 *520*	1,535 *1,705*

UC *under construction/expected completion year.*

T O P 1 0

TALLEST HABITABLE BUILDINGS IN THE US

	Building	Location	Year completed	Storeys	m	ft
1	Sears Tower *with spires*	Chicago, Illinois	1974	110	443 *520*	1,454 *1,707*
2	World Trade Center*	New York, New York	1973	110	417	1,368
3	Empire State Building *with spire*	New York, New York	1931	102	381 *449*	1,250 *1,472*
4	Amoco Building	Chicago, Illinois	1973	80	346	1,136
5	John Hancock Center *with spires*	Chicago, Illinois	1968	100	343 *450*	1,127 *1,476*
6	First Interstate World Center	Los Angeles, California	1990	73	310	1,017
7	Texas Commerce Tower	Houston, Texas	1981	75	305	1,002
8	Allied Bank Plaza	Houston, Texas	1983	71	302	992
9	311 South Wacker Drive	Chicago, Illinois	1990	65	296	970
10	Columbia Center	Seattle, Washington	1986	76	291	954

* *Twin towers; the second tower, completed in 1974, has the same number of stories but is slightly smaller at 1,362 ft/415 m – although its spire takes it up to 1,710 ft/521 m.*

In the decade before the construction of the American Surety Building, the world's tallest habitable building (cathedrals and structures such as the Eiffel Tower excluded) was the 20-story Auditorium Building, Chicago, completed in 1889 and measuring 270 ft/82 m; the Masonic Temple Building, also in Chicago and with the same number of stories, completed in 1891, just beat it at 274 ft/84 m. Since then, each successive world record holder was a New York City skyscraper, until the Sears Tower regained the crown for Chicago. However, as the table shows, a succession of tall buildings scheduled for completion before the end of the century will take the title of "world's tallest" from the US and establish it firmly in the Far East.

DIZZYING HEIGHTS
Chicago contains some of the tallest buildings in the US, including the twin-spired John Hancock Center.

TOP 10

TALLEST REINFORCED CONCRETE BUILDINGS IN THE WORLD

	Building	Location	Year completed	Stories	Height m	ft
1	Central Plaza with spire	Hong Kong	1992	78	309 374	1,015 1,228
2	311 South Wacker Drive	Chicago, US	1990	65	296	970
3	2 Prudential Plaza with spire	Chicago, US	1990	64	275 303	901 994
4	NCNB	Charlotte, US	1992	60	265	871
5	Water Tower Place	Chicago, US	1975	74	262	859
6	Messeturm	Frankfurt, Germany	1990	70	256	841
7	Citispire	New York, US	1989	72	245	802
8	Rialto Tower	Melbourne, Australia	1985	60	242	794
9	Tun Abdul Rasak Building	Penang, Malaysia	1985	61	232	761
10	Carnegie Hall Tower	New York, US	1990	59	230	756

Reinforced concrete was patented in France by Joseph Monier (1823–1906) on March 16, 1867, and developed by another Frenchman, François Hennebique (1842–1921). The first American buildings constructed from it date from a century ago, since when it has become one of the most important of all building materials. Steel bars set within concrete slabs expand and contract at the same rate as the concrete, providing great tensile strength and fire resistance, making it the ideal material for huge structures such as bridge spans and skyscrapers.

TOP 10

LARGEST HOTELS IN THE US

	Hotel	Rooms
1	MGM Grand Casino, Las Vegas	5,012
2	Excalibur, Las Vegas	4,032
3	Hilton Flamingo, Las Vegas	3,530
4	Mirage, Las Vegas	3,049
5	Treasure Island, Las Vegas	2,900
6	Hilton Hotel, Las Vegas	2,877
7	Bally Grand Hotel, Las Vegas	2,832
8	Circus Circus, Las Vegas	2,793
9	Imperial Palace, Las Vegas	2,637
10	Lumor Hotel, Las Vegas	2,533

Source: American Hotel/Motel Association

TOP 10

NORTH AMERICAN CITIES WITH MOST SKYSCRAPERS

	City	Skyscrapers
1	New York, New York	131
2	Chicago, Illinois	46
3	Houston, Texas	26
4	Los Angeles, California	20
5	Dallas, Texas	17
6	San Francisco, California	15
7=	Atlanta, Georgia	13
7=	Boston, Massachusetts	13
9	Seattle, Washington	11
10	Toronto, Ontario, Canada	10

This list covers habitable buildings of more than 500 ft/152 m.

TOP 10

HIGHEST PUBLIC OBSERVATORIES IN THE WORLD

	Observatory	Location	Year completed	Height m	ft
1	CN Tower, Toronto, Canada	Space deck	1975	447	1,465
2	World Trade Center, New York, US	Roof top Tower B	1973	415	1,360
3	Sears Tower, Chicago, US	103rd floor	1974	412	1,353
4	Empire State Building, New York, US	102nd floor	1931	381	1,250
5	Ostankino Tower, Moscow, Russia	5th floor turret	1967	360	1,181
6	John Hancock Center, Chicago, US	94th floor	1968	322	1,056
7	Central Plaza, Hong Kong	75th floor	1992	280	918
8	Eiffel Tower, Paris, France	Observatory level 3	1889	274	900
9	Transco Tower, Houston, US	64th floor	1986	260	852
10	RCA Center, New York, US	70th floor	1933	259	850

While seven of the world's 10 highest observatories or public viewing platforms are in North America, viewing facilities are a feature of towers and buildings the world over. The Eiffel Tower, constructed for this purpose and as a symbol of the technological skills of the French people, was built between 1887 and 1889 as the centerpiece of the Paris Exhibition, providing the world's highest viewing platform in a manmade structure for 42 years, until the opening of the Empire State Building. From the 1930s onward, US observatories dominated the world, but have been steadily losing ground to Asian buildings such as the KL Tower, Kuala Lumpur, Malaysia, currently under construction and with a public observatory at 906 ft/276 m.

BRIDGES AND TUNNELS

T O P 1 0

LONGEST SUSPENSION BRIDGES IN THE WORLD

	Bridge	Completed	Length of main span m	ft
1	Akashi-Kaikyo, Japan	UC/1998	1,990.0	6,529
2	Great Belt East Bridge, Denmark	UC/1997	1,624.0	5,328
3	Humber Estuary, UK	1980	1,410.0	4,626
4	Verrazano Narrows, New York, NY	1964	1,298.5	4,260
5	Golden Gate, San Francisco, California	1937	1,280.2	4,200
6	Mackinac Straits, Michigan, Missouri	1957	1,158.2	3,800
7	Bosphorus, Istanbul, Turkey	1973	1,074.1	3,524
8	George Washington, New York, NY	1931	1,066.8	3,500
9	Ponte 25 Abril (Ponte Salazar), Lisbon, Portugal	1966	1,012.9	3,323
10	Forth Road Bridge, UK	1964	1,005.8	3,300

UC *Under construction/expected completion year*

The Messina Strait Bridge, planned to stretch between Sicily and Calabria in southern Italy, remains a speculative project, but if constructed according to plan it will have by far the longest center span of any bridge (although at 12,828 ft/3,910 m the Akashi-Kaikyo bridge will be the world's longest overall). If only completed bridges are included, the Humber Estuary Bridge heads the list. No. 9 is another British structure, the Severn Bridge (completed 1966; 3,240 ft/987.6 m). No. 10 then becomes the Tacoma Narrows II, Washington (completed 1950; 2,800 ft/853.4 m).

T O P 1 0

LONGEST CANTILEVER BRIDGES IN THE WORLD

	Bridge	Completed	Longest span m	ft
1	Pont de Québec, Canada	1917	548.6	1,800
2	Firth of Forth, Scotland	1890	521.2	1,710
3	Minato, Osaka, Japan	1974	509.9	1,673
4	Commodore John Barry, New Jersey/Pennsylvania	1974	494.4	1,622
5	Greater New Orleans, Louisiana	1958	480.1	1,575
6	Howrah, Calcutta, India	1943	457.2	1,500
7	Transbay, San Francisco	1936	426.7	1,400
8	Baton Rouge, Louisiana	1969	376.4	1,235
9	Tappan Zee, Tarrytown, New York	1955	369.4	1,212
10	Longview, Oregon/Washington	1930	365.8	1,200

T O P 1 0

LONGEST BRIDGES IN THE US

	Bridge	Year completed	Length of main span m	ft
1	Verrazano Narrows, New York	1964	1,298	4,260
2	Golden Gate, San Francisco, California	1937	1,280	4,200
3	Mackinac Straits, Michigan, Missouri	1957	1,158	3,800
4	George Washington, New York	1931	1,067	3,500
5	Tacoma Narrows II, Washington	1950	853	2,800
6	Transbay, San Francisco, California	1936	704	2,310
7	Bronx-Whitestone, New York	1939	701	2,300
8=	Delaware Memorial, Wilmington, Delaware (twin)	1951/68	655	2,150
8=	Seaway Skyway, Ogdensburg, New York	1960	655	2,150
10=	Melville Gas Pipeline, Atchafalaya River, Louisiana	1951	610	2,000
10=	Walt Whitman, Philadelphia, Pennsylvania	1957	610	2,000

T O P 1 0

LONGEST ROAD AND RAILROAD TUNNELS IN THE US
(*Excluding subways*)

	Tunnel/location	Type	Completed	Length km	miles
1	Cascade, Washington	Rail	1929	12.54	7.79
2	Flathead, Montana	Rail	1970	12.48	7.78
3	Moffat, Colorado	Rail	1928	10.00	6.21
4	Hoosac, Massachusetts	Rail	1875	7.56	4.70
5	BART Trans-Bay Tubes, San Francisco, California	Rail	1974	5.79	3.60
6	Brooklyn-Battery, New York	Road	1950	2.78	1.73
7	E. Johnson Memorial, Colorado	Road	?	2.74	1.70
8	Eisenhower Memorial, Colorado*	Road	1973	2.72	1.69
9	Holland Tunnel, New York	Road	1927	2.61	1.62
10	Lincoln Tunnel I, New York	Road	1937	2.51	1.56

* *The highest-elevation highway tunnel in the world*

At 9.13 miles/14.70 km, Canadian Mount McDonald railroad tunnel, on the Canadian Pacific line, is the longest transportation tunnel in North America. The US Air Force is reported to have built an experimental missile transportation tunnel 3.73 miles/6 km long beneath the Arizona desert. The New York City West Delaware water tunnel (105 miles/168.98 km) is the longest tunnel of any kind in the world.

GOLDEN GATE BRIDGE
This magnificent suspension bridge spans the Golden Gate waterway that links San Francisco Bay with the Pacific Ocean.

T O P 1 0

LONGEST ROAD TUNNELS IN THE WORLD

	Tunnel/country	Year completed	Length km	miles
1	St. Gotthard, Switzerland	1980	16.32	10.14
2	Arlberg, Austria	1978	13.98	8.69
3	Fréjus, France/Italy	1980	12.90	8.02
4	Mont-Blanc, France/Italy	1965	11.60	7.21
5	Gudvangen, Norway	1992	11.40	7.08
6	Leirfjord, Norway	UC	11.11	6.90
7	Kan-Etsu, Japan	1991	11.01	6.84
8	Kan-Etsu, Japan	1985	10.93	6.79
9	Gran Sasso, Italy	1984	10.17	6.32
10	Plabutsch, Austria	1987	9.76	6.06

UC *Under construction.*

All the road tunnels in the Top 10 were built during the past 30 years. Previously, the record for "world's longest" had been held by the 3.13-mile/5.04-km Viella Tunnel, Cataluña, Spain, which was opened in 1941. This tunnel itself overtook the 2.13-mile/3.43-km Mersey Tunnel connecting Liverpool and Birkenhead, built in 1925–34.

T O P 1 0

LONGEST RAILROAD TUNNELS IN THE WORLD

	Tunnel/country	Year completed	Length km	miles
1	Seikan, Japan	1988	53.90	33.49
2	Channel Tunnel, France/England	1994	49.94	31.03
3	Moscow Metro (Medvedkovo/ Belyaevo section), Russia	1979	30.70	19.07
4	London Underground (East Finchley/Morden Northern Line), UK	1939	27.84	17.30
5	Dai-Shimizu, Japan	1982	22.17	13.78
6	Simplon II, Italy/Switzerland	1922	19.82	12.31
7	Simplon I, Italy/Switzerland	1906	19.80	12.30
8	Shin-Kanmon, Japan	1975	18.68	11.61
9	Apennine, Italy	1934	18.49	11.49
10	Rokko, Japan	1972	16.25	10.10

The first specifically built passenger rail tunnel was the 2,514-ft/766-m Tyler Hill Tunnel, Kent, opened on May 4, 1830. The longest rail tunnel built in the 19th century is the 9.32-mile/15-km St. Gotthard Tunnel, Switzerland, opened on May 20, 1882.

OTHER STRUCTURES

PENT-UP POWER
The Hoover Dam is located in Black Canyon on the Colorado River. Its functions include flood and silt control, irrigation, providing power, and supplying water for domestic and industrial use.

TOP 10

LARGEST VOLUME* DAMS IN THE WORLD

	Dam	Location	Completed	Volume (m³)
1	Syncrude Tailings	Alberta, Canada	1992	540,000,000
2	Pati	Paraná, Argentina	1990	230,180,000
3	New Cornelia Tailings	Ten Mile Wash, Arizona	1973	209,500,000
4	Tarbela	Indus, Pakistan	1976	105,922,000
5	Fort Peck	Missouri River, Montana	1937	96,050,000
6	Lower Usuma	Usuma, Nigeria	1990	93,000,000
7	Atatürk	Euphrates, Turkey	1990	84,500,000
8	Yacyreta-Apipe	Paraná, Paraguay/ Argentina	1991	81,000,000
9	Guri (Raul Leoni)	Caroni, Venezuela	1986	77,971,000
10	Rogun	Vakhsh, Tajikstan	1987	75,500,000

* *Material used in construction – earth, rocks, concrete, etc.*

Despite the recent cancellation of several dams on environmental grounds, such as two in the Cantabrian Mountains, Spain, numerous major projects are in development for completion by the end of the century, when this Top 10 will contain some notable new entries. Among several in Argentina is the Chapeton dam under construction on the Paraná, and scheduled for completion in 1998; it will have a volume of 296,200,000 m³ and will thus become the second largest dam in the world. The Pati, also on the Paraná, will be 238,180,000 m³. The Cipasang dam, under construction on the Cimanuk, Indonesia, will have a volume of 90,000,000 m³.

TOP 10

LARGEST VOLUME DAMS IN THE US

(Material used in construction – earth, rocks, concrete, etc.)

	Dam	Location	Completed	Volume (m²)
1	New Cornelia Tailings	Ten Mile Wash, AZ	1973	209,500,000
2	Fort Peck	Missouri River, MT	1937	96,050,000
3	Oahe	Missouri River, SD	1958	70,339,000
4	Oroville	Feather, CA	1968	59,635,000
5	San Luis	San Luis Creek, CA	1967	59,559,000
6	Garrison	Missouri River, ND	1953	50,843,000
7	Cochiti	Rio Grande, NM	1975	50,228,000
8	Earthquake Lake	Madison, MT	1959	38,228,000
9	Fort Randall	Missouri River, SD	1952	38,200,000
10	Castaic	Castaic Creek, CA	1973	33,640,000

TOP 10

HIGHEST DAMS IN THE US

	Dam/lake	Location	Completed	Height m	ft
1	Oroville	Feather, CA	1968	230	755
2	Hoover	Colorado River, AZ/NV	1936	221	725
3	Dworshak	North Fork of Clearwater, ID	1973	219	717
4	Glen Canyon	Colorado River, AZ	1966	216	709
5	New Bullard's Bar	North Yuba, CA	1970	194	637
6	New Melones	Stanislaus, CA	1979	191	625
7	Swift	Lewis, WA	1958	186	610
8	Mossyrock	Cowlitz, WA	1968	185	607
9	Shasta	Sacramento, CA	1945	183	602
10	Don Pedro	Tuolumnne, CA	1971	173	568

Hailed as one of the great engineering achievements of the era, the Boulder Dam, whch was built in 21 months at a cost of $175,000,000, was renamed the Hoover Dam in 1947, in honor of the president who authorized its construction. It was the tallest in the world until the 778-ft/237-m Mauvoisin, Switzerland, was completed in 1957. The Grand Coulee, on the Columbia River, Washington (completed 1942; 551 ft/168 m), is the largest concrete dam, and also holds the record as the largest concrete construction of any kind in the world. Currently, the world's tallest dam is the Nurek on the River Vakhsh, Tajikstan, which was completed in 1980 and measures 984 ft/ 300 m. Under construction on the same river, but behind schedule as a result of financial problems consequent to the breakup of the former Soviet Union, is the Rogun Dam, which is planned to attain 1,099 ft/335 m.

TOP 10

LARGEST MAN-MADE LAKES IN THE WORLD

(Includes only those formed as a result of dam construction)

	Dam/lake	Location	Year completed	Volume (m³)
1	Owen Falls	Uganda	1954	204,800,000,000
2	Kariba	Zimbabwe	1959	181,592,000,000
3	Bratsk	Russian Federation	1964	169,270,000,000
4	High Aswan	Egypt	1970	168,000,000,000
5	Akosombo	Ghana	1965	148,000,000,000
6	Daniel Johnson	Canada	1968	141,852,000,000
7	Guri (Raul Leoni)	Venezuela	1986	136,000,000,000
8	Krasnoyarsk	Russian Federation	1967	73,300,000,000
9	Bennett	Canada	1967	70,309,000,000
10	Zeya	Russian Federation	1978	68,400,000,000

TOP 10

LARGEST BELLS IN THE WESTERN WORLD

	Bell/location	Year cast	Weight (tons)
1	*Tsar Kolokol*, Kremlin, Moscow, Russia	1735	222.56
2	*Voskresenskiy (Resurrection)*, Ivan the Great Bell Tower, Kremlin, Moscow, Russia	1746	72.20
3	*Petersglocke*, Cologne Cathedral, Germany	1923	28.00
4	Lisbon Cathedral, Portugal	post-1344	26.90
5	St. Stephen's Cathedral, Vienna, Austria	1957	23.58
6	Bourdon, Strasbourg Cathedral, France	1521	22.05
7	*Savoyarde*, Sacre-Coeur Basilica, Paris, France	1891	20.78
8	Bourdon, Riverside Church, New York	1931	20.44
9	Olmütz (Olomouc), Czech Republic	1931	20.05
10	*Campagna gorda*, Toledo Cathedral, Spain	1753	19.04

The largest bell in the world is the *Tsar Kolokol*, cast in Moscow for the Kremlin, which is 20 ft 2 in/6.14 m high and 21 ft 8 in/6.6 m in diameter. It cracked before it was installed and has remained there, unrung, ever since. New York's Riverside Church bell (the largest ever cast in England) is the bourdon (that sounding the lowest note) of the Laura Spelman Rockefeller Memorial carillon. This bell, with a diameter of 10 ft 2 in/3.10 m, is one of the 74-bell carillon, the world's largest, the total weight of which is 114.24 tons.

TOP 10

OLDEST CHURCHES IN THE US

	Church/location	Built
1	Cervento de Porta Coeli, San German, Puerto Rico*	1609
2	San Estevan del Rey Mission, Valencia County, New Mexico	1629
3	St. Luke's Church, Isle of Wight County, Virginia	1632
4	First Church of Christ and the Ancient Burying Ground, Hartford County, Connecticut	1640
5	St. Ignatius Catholic Church, St. Mary's County, Maryland	1641
6	Merchant's Hope Church, Prince George County, Virginia	1657
7	Flatlands Dutch Reformed Church, King's County, New York	1660
8=	Claflin-Richards House, Essex County, Massachusetts	1661
8=	Church San Blas de Illesces of Coamo, Ponce, Puerto Rico*	1661
8=	St. Mary's Whitechapel, Lancaster County, Virginia	1661

* *Not US territory when built, but now US National Historic Sites*

Source: US Department of the Interior, National Register of Historic Places

THE BELL THAT NEVER RANG

The Tsar Kolokol ("Emperor Bell"), cast in 1733, is still the world's largest bell. However, during a fire in 1737 water was thrown onto it, causing it to crack, and a 12.7-ton fragment broke off it. As a result, this mighty bell has never been rung.

CULTURE & LEARNING

ΣΑΕ

TOP 10

LARGEST UNIVERSITIES IN THE WORLD

	University	Students
1	State University of New York	369,318
2	University of Calcutta, India	300,000
3	University of Mexico, Mexico	271,358
4	University of Paris, France	263,680
5	University of Buenos Aires, Argentina	248,453
6	University of Bombay, India	222,713
7	University of Guadalajara, Mexico	214,986
8	University of Rajasthan, India	192,039
9	University of Rome, Italy	180,000
10	University of California	157,331

Several other universities in the US, India, Egypt, and Italy have more than 100,000 students. Where universities are divided into numerous separate campuses, figures are for the totals of all campuses.

TOP 10

LARGEST UNIVERSITIES IN THE US

	University	Enrollments 1992/93
1	University of Minnesota (Twin Cities), Minnesota	54,671
2	Ohio State University (Main Campus), Ohio	52,179
3	Miami Dade Community College, Florida	51,768
4	University of Texas (Austin), Texas	49,253
5	Arizona State University, Arizona	43,628
6	University of Wisconsin (Madison), Wisconsin	41,824
7	Texas A&M University, Texas	41,710
8	Michigan State University, Michigan	39,138
9	Pennsylvania State University (Main Campus), Pennsylvania	38,446
10	University of Illinois (Urbana Campus), Illinois	38,396

Source: National Center For Educational Statistics

TOP 10

COUNTRIES WITH MOST UNIVERSITIES

	Country	Universities
1	India	7,301
2	US	3,559
3	Mexico	1,832
4	Argentina	1,540
5	Japan	1,114
6	China	1,075
7	France	1,062
8	Bangladesh	997
9	Brazil	918
10	Indonesia	900
	UK	*86*

As a result of the 1992 Further and Higher Education Acts, the United Kingdom increased its tally of universities from 48 to 86 by reclassifying former polytechnics and colleges of further education. Of the present total, 70 are in England, 12 in Scotland, two in Wales, and two in Northern Ireland.

PENNSYLVANIA
STATE
UNIVERSITY

TOP 10

US STATES WITH THE HIGHEST HIGH SCHOOL GRADUATION RATES

	State	Rate (%)
1	Minnesota	89.5
2	North Dakota	86.7
3	Nebraska	86.3
4	Iowa	85.9
5	Montana	84.9
6	South Dakota	84.2
7	Wisconsin	82.5
8	New Jersey	82.1
9	Wyoming	81.7
10	Kansas	81.1
	US average	*71.2*

TOP 10

US STATES WITH THE LOWEST HIGH SCHOOL GRADUATION RATES

	State	Rate (%)
1	Louisiana	54.3
2	District of Columbia	59.5
3=	Florida	61.2
3=	South Carolina	61.2
5	Mississippi	61.7
6	Georgia	64.0
7	New York	64.4
8	Alabama	65.6
9	Texas	65.9
10	California	67.7

TOP 10

OLDEST UNIVERSITIES AND COLLEGES IN THE US

	University	Year chartered
1	Harvard University, Massachusetts	1636
2	College of William & Mary, Virginia	1692
3	Yale University, Connecticut	1701
4	University of Pennsylvania, Pennsylvania	1740
5	Moravian College, Pennsylvania	1742
6	Princeton University, New Jersey	1746
7	Washington & Lee University, Virginia	1749
8	Columbia University, New York	1754
9	Brown University, Rhode Island	1764
10	Rutgers, The State University of New Jersey	1766

Source: National Center For Educational Statistics

DID YOU KNOW

300 YEARS OF THE COLLEGE OF WILLIAM AND MARY

The College of William and Mary in Williamsburg, Virginia, one of America's oldest universities, was granted its charter by King William III and Queen Mary II of England on February 8, 1693. The foundations of the original building (designed, it is thought, by Sir Christopher Wren, the genius behind London's St. Paul's Cathedral) were laid in August 1695, and it remains the oldest academic building in use in the US. In 1776 the College was the birthplace of the first fraternity, Phi Beta Kappa, and it numbers among its alumni four signers of the Declaration of Independence, three US Presidents (Thomas Jefferson, James Monroe, and John Taylor), actress Glenn Close, and Buffalo Bills player Mark Kelso.

TOP 10

BACHELOR'S DEGREE MAJORS AT US UNIVERSITIES AND COLLEGES

	Degree	Degrees
1	Business	256,603
2	Social Sciences/History	133,974
3	Education	108,006
4	Psychology	63,513
5	Health professions	61,720
6	Engineering	61,206
7	English Language, Literature & Letters	54,951
8	Communications	54,257
9	Visual & Performing Arts	46,522
10	Biological & Life Sciences	42,941

Figures are as at June 1992 for Bachelor's Degrees obtained after at least four years of undergraduate study.

Source: National Center For Educational Statistics

TOP 10

MOST EXPENSIVE US UNIVERSITIES AND COLLEGES

	University	1992/93 tuition fees ($)
1	Bennington College, VT	19,780
2	Brown University, RI	18,392
3	Massachusetts Institute of Technology, MA	18,000
4	Amherst University, MA	17,900
5	Tufts University, MA	17,897
6	Williams College, MA	17,840
7	Princeton University, NJ	17,750
8	Brandeis University, MA	17,726
9	Gettysburg College, PA	17,650
10	Swarthmore College, PA	17,646

All of these are in the northeastern states. The most expensive institution in the West is Pitzer College in California at $17,170.

Source: National Center For Educational Statistics

LIBRARIES

T O P 1 0

LARGEST LIBRARIES IN THE WORLD

	Library	Location	Founded	Books
1	Library of Congress	Washington, DC	1800	28,000,000
2	British Library	London, UK	1753*	18,000,000
3	Harvard University Library	Cambridge, Massachusetts	1638	12,394,894
4	Russian State Library #	Moscow, Russia	1862	11,750,000
5	New York Public Library	New York, New York	1848	11,300,000 **
6	Yale University Library	New Haven, Connecticut	1701	9,937,751
7	Biblioteca Academiei Romane	Bucharest, Romania	1867	9,397,260
8	Bibliothèque Nationale	Paris, France	1480	9,000,000
9	University of Illinois	Urbana, Illinois	1867	8,096,040
10	National Library of Russia‡	St. Petersburg, Russia	1795	8,000,000

LIBRARY OF CONGRESS
Originally founded in 1800, to make books available to members of Congress, the Library of Congress in Washington, DC is in effect the national library of the US. The world's largest collection of books and pamphlets, manuscripts, photographs, maps, and music has been amassed through purchase, exchanges, gifts, and copyright deposits.

* *Founded as part of the British Museum 1753; became an independent body 1973*
# *Founded as Rumyantsev Library; formerly State V.I. Lenin Library*
** *Reference holdings only, excluding books in lending library branches*
‡ *Formerly M.E. Saltykov-Shchedrin State Public Library*

T O P 1 0

LARGEST UNIVERSITY LIBRARIES IN THE US

	Library	Location	Founded	Books
1	Harvard University	Cambridge, Massachusetts	1638	12,394,894
2	Yale University	New Haven, Connecticut	1701	9,173,981
3	University of Illinois	Urbana, Illinois	1867	8,096,040
4	University of California	Berkeley, California	1868	7,854,630
5	University of Texas	Austin, Texas	1883	6,680,406
6	University of Michigan	Ann Arbor, Michigan	1817	6,598,574
7	Columbia University	New York, New York	1754	6,262,162
8	University of California	Los Angeles, California	1868	6,247,320
9	Stanford University	Stanford, California	1885	6,127,388
10	Cornell University	Ithaca, New York	1865	5,468,870

T O P 1 0

LARGEST PUBLIC LIBRARIES IN THE US

	Library	Location	Founded	Books
1	Queens Borough Public Library	Queens, New York	1896	9,271,960
2	Chicago Public Library	Chicago, Illinois	1872	8,166,421
3	Boston Public Library	Boston, Massachusetts	1852	6,000,000
4	Los Angeles County	Los Angeles, California	1912	5,784,785
5	Brooklyn Public Library	Brooklyn, New York	1896	5,474,809
6	Free Library of Philadelphia	Philadelphia, Pennsylvania	1891	5,062,771
7	Cincinnati and Hamilton County Public Library	Cincinnati, Ohio	1853	4,423,432
8	New York Public Library	New York, New York	1848*	4,400,000#
9	Denver Public Library	Denver, Colorado	1889	4,243,162
10	Houston Public Library	Houston, Texas	1901	3,982,539

Peterboro Public Library, New Hampshire, founded on April 9, 1833 with 700 volumes, was the first public library (in that it was supported by local taxes) in the United States. New York's Astor Library, founded in 1848 with a $400,000 bequest from America's richest man, John Jacob Astor, opened to the public in February 1, 1854 – although it did not permit books to be borrowed. In 1895 it was merged with the Lenox Library (founded by philanthropist James Lenox) and the Tilden Trust (based on the fortune of the presidential candidate Samuel Jones) to form the New York Public Library.

* Astor Library founded 1848; consolidated with Lenox Library and Tilden Trust to form New York Public Library, 1895

Lending library holdings only; excluding reference collections, for which see The 10 Largest Libraries in the World

BRITISH LIBRARY
This is now the second largest library in the world. Use of the library is restricted to people involved in research.

WORDS AND LANGUAGE

T O P 1 0

LONGEST WORDS IN THE ENGLISH LANGUAGE

1 Acetylseryltyrosylserylisoleucylthreonylserylprolylserylglutaminylphenylalanylvalylphenylalanylleucylserylserylvalyltryptophylalanylaspartylprolylisoleucylglutamylleucylleucyllasparaginylvalylcysteinylthreonylserylserylleucylglyclasparaginylglutaminylphenylalanylglutaminylthreonylglutaminylglutaminylalanylarginylthreonylthreonylglutaminylvalylglutaminylglutaminylphenylalanylserylglutaminylvalyltryptophyllysylprolylphenylalanylprolylglutaminylserylthreonylvalylarginylphenylalanylprolylglycylaspartylvalyltyrosyllsyslvalyltyrosylarginyltyrosylasparaginylalanylvalylleucylaspartylprolylleucylisoleucylthreonylalanylleucylleucylglycylthreonylphenylalanylaspartylthreonylarginylasparaginylarginylisoleucylisoleucylglutamylvalylglutamylasparaginylglutaminylglutaminylserylprolylthreonylthreonylalanylglutamylthreonylleucylaspartylalanylthreonylarginylarginylvalylaspartylaspartylalanylthreonylvalylalanylisoleucylarginylserylalanylasparaginylisoleucylasparaginylleucylvallasparaginylglutamylleucylvalylarginylglycylthreonylglycylleucyltyrosylasparaginylglutaminylasparaginylthreonylphenylalanylglutamylserylmethionylserylglycylleucylvalyltryptophylthreonylserylalanylprolylalanylserine   (1,185 letters)

The word for the Tobacco Mosaic Virus, Dahlemense Strain, qualifies as the longest word in English because it has actually been used in print (in the American Chemical Society's Chemical Abstracts – and in the first British edition of The Top 10 of Everything (1989), where a typesetting error robbed it of a single "l", which surprisingly went unnoticed by its readers), whereas certain even longer words for chemical compounds, which have been cited in such sources as the Guinness Book of Records, are bogus in the sense that they have never been used by scientists or appeared in full in print. Long words for chemical compounds may be regarded by purists as cheating, since such words as trinitrophenyl-methylnitramine (29 letters) – a type of explosive – can be created by linking together the scientific names of their components. Other words that are also discounted are those that have been invented with the sole intention of being long words, such as a 100-letter word used by James Joyce in Finnegans Wake.

2 Aopadotenachoselachogaleokranioleipsanodrimhipotrimmatosilphioparaomelitokatakechymenokichlepikossyphophattoperisteralektryonoptekephalliokigklopeleiolagoiosiraiobaphetraganopterygon (182 letters)

This is the English transliteration of a 170-letter Greek word that appears in The Ecclesiazusae (a comedy on government by women) by the Greek playwright Aristophanes (c.448–380 BC) as a description of a 17-ingredient dish.

3 Aequeosalinocalcalinosetaceoaluminosocupreovitriolic (52 letters)

Invented by a medical writer, Dr. Edward Strother (1675–1737), this word was used to describe the spa waters at Bath.

4 Asseocarnisanguineoviscericartilaginonervomedullary (51 letters)

Coined by writer and East India Company official Thomas Love Peacock (1785–1866), this was used in his satire Headlong Hall (1816) to describe the structure of the human body.

5 Pneumonoultramicroscopicsilicovolcanoconiosis (45 letters)

It first appeared in print (though ending in "-koniosis") in F. Scully's Bedside Manna [sic] (1936), then found its way into Webster's Dictionary and is now in the Oxford English Dictionary – but with the note that it occurs "…chiefly as an instance of a very long word." It is said to mean a lung disease caused by breathing very fine dust.

6 Hepaticocholangiocholecystenterostomies (39 letters)

These are surgical operations to create channels of communication between gall bladders and hepatic ducts or intestines.

7= Pseudoantidisestablishmentarianism (34 letters)

This word, meaning "false opposition to the withdrawal of state support from a Church," was derived from that perennial favorite long word, antidisestablishmentarianism (a mere 28 letters). Another composite made from it (though usually hyphenated) is ultra-antidisestablishmentarianism, which means "extreme opposition to the withdrawal of state support from a Church" (33 letters).

7= Supercalifragilisticexpialidocious (34 letters)

Although an invented word, perhaps it is now eligible since it has appeared in the Oxford English Dictionary. It was popularized by the song of this title in the film Mary Poppins (1964) where it is used to mean "wonderful," but it was originally written in 1949 in an unpublished song by Parker and Young who spelt it "supercalafajalistickespialadojus" (32 letters). In 1965–66, Parker and Young unsuccessfully sued the makers of Mary Poppins, claiming infringement of copyright. In summarizing the case, the US Court decided against repeating this mouthful, stating that "All variants of this tongue-twister will hereinafter be referred to collectively as 'the word.'"

9= Encephalomyeloradiculoneuritis (30 letters)

This is the name of a syndrome caused by a virus associated with encephalitis.

9= Hippopotomonstrosesquipedalian (30 letters)

Appropriately, this is a word that means "pertaining to an extremely long word."

9= Pseudopseudohypoparathyroidism (30 letters)

First used (hyphenated) in the US in 1952 and (unhyphenated) in the UK in The Lancet in 1962, it describes a medical case in which a patient appeared to have symptoms of pseudohypoparathyroidism, but with "no manifestations suggesting hypoparathyroidism." If the rules are changed and No. 1 is disqualified as a compound chemical name, and No. 2 because it is a transliteration from Greek, the next longest word is Floccinaucinihilipilification (29 letters). Alternatively spelt "Flocci-nauci-nihilipilification" or, by Sir Walter Scott, in his Journal (March 18, 1829), "Flocci-paucinihilipilification," it means the action of estimating as worthless. Until supercalifragilisticexpialidocious, floccinaucinihilipilification was the longest word in the Oxford English Dictionary. Honorificabilitudinitatibus, a 27-letter monster word, is used by Shakespeare in Love's Labour's Lost (Act V, Scene i) to mean honorably.

T O P 1 0

MOST WIDELY SPOKEN LANGUAGES IN THE WORLD

	Country	Approx. no. of speakers
1	Chinese (Mandarin)	901,000,000
2	English	451,000,000
3	Hindustani	377,000,000
4	Spanish	360,000,000
5	Russian	291,000,000
6	Arabic	207,000,000
7	Bengali	190,000,000
8	Portuguese	178,000,000
9	Malay-Indonesian	148,000,000
10	Japanese	126,000,000

According to 1992 estimates by Sidney S. Culbert of the University of Washington, there are only two other languages spoken by more than 100,000,000 individuals: French (122,000,000) and German (118,000,000). A further 10 languages are spoken by 50,000,000 to 100,000,000 people: Urdu (98,000,000), Punjabi (89,000,000), Korean (73,000,000), Telugu (70,000,000), Tamil (68,000,000), Marathi (67,000,000), Italian (63,000,000), Javanese (61,000,000), Vietnamese (60,000,000), and Turkish (57,000,000).

T O P 1 0

LANGUAGES MOST SPOKEN IN THE US

	Country	Speakers
1	English	198,601,000
2	Spanish	17,339,000
3	French	1,702,000
4	German	1,547,000
5	Italian	1,309,000
6	Chinese	1,249,000
7	Tagalog	843,000
8	Polish	723,000
9	Korean	626,000
10	Vietnamese	507,000

T O P 1 0

COUNTRIES WITH THE MOST ENGLISH LANGUAGE SPEAKERS

	Country	Approx. no. of speakers
1	US	215,000,000
2	UK	56,000,000
3	Canada	17,000,000
4	Australia	14,000,000
5	Ireland	3,300,000
6	New Zealand	3,000,000
7	Jamaica	2,300,000
8	South Africa	2,000,000
9	Trinidad and Tobago	1,200,000
10	Guyana	900,000

The Top 10 represents the countries with the greatest numbers of inhabitants who speak English as their mother tongue. After the 10th entry, the figures dive to around 250,000 in the case of both Barbados and the Bahamas, while Zimbabwe occupies 13th place with some 200,000 English speakers. In addition to these and others that make up a world total probably in excess of 451,000,000, there are perhaps as many as 1,000,000,000 who speak English as a second language.

T O P 1 0

MOST STUDIED LANGUAGES IN THE US

	Language	Registrations*
1	Spanish	533,944
2	French	272,472
3	German	133,348
4	Italian	49,699
5	Japanese	45,717
6	Russian	44,626
7	Latin	28,178
8	Chinese	19,490
9	Ancient Greek	16,401
10	Hebrew#	12,995

* *In US Institutions of Higher Education*
\# *Comprises 5,724 registrations in Biblical Hebrew and 7,271 in Modern Hebrew*

These figures are from the most recent survey conducted by the Modern Language Association of America from colleges and universities in the fall of 1990, which indicated a total of 1,184,100 foreign language registrations, the highest enrollment ever recorded since the surveys began in 1958. Japanese showed the greatest gain since the previous poll (in 1986), with a 12.3% increase.

T O P 1 0

US STATES WITH MOST NON-ENGLISH SPEAKERS

	State	Total population*	English-speakers	Non-English speakers	Non-English speakers (%)
1	New Mexico	1,390,048	896,049	493,999	35.5
2	California	27,383,547	18,764,213	8,619,334	31.5
3	Texas	15,605,822	11,635,518	3,970,304	25.4
4	Hawaii	1,026,209	771,485	254,724	24.8
5	New York	16,743,048	12,834,328	3,908,720	23.3
6	Arizona	3,374,806	2,674,519	700,287	20.8
7	New Jersey	7,200,696	5,794,548	1,406,148	19.5
8	Florida	12,095,284	9,996,969	2,098,315	17.3
9	Rhode Island	936,423	776,931	159,492	17.0
10	Connecticut	3,060,000	2,593,825	466,175	15.2

* *5+ years old, as per 1990 Census*

THE OXFORD ENGLISH DICTIONARY

Although conceived earlier, work on the *Oxford English Dictionary* started in earnest in 1879 with James Murray as editor. He and his colleagues scoured thousands of English texts for quotations representing the changing usages of English words, frequently chopping up copies of rare books, pasting extracts onto slips of paper, and filing them. The first part covering A–Ant was published in 1884 and other sections followed at intervals. Murray died in 1915, but work continued until 1928, when the first edition was complete. Its 12 volumes defined 414,825 words and phrases, with about 2,000,000 quotations providing information on the first recorded use, continuing usage, and later variations in the use of each word. Supplements were added over the ensuing years until it was decided to computerize all the material, work on which commenced in 1984. The original *Dictionary*, *Supplements*, and new entries were incorporated into a gigantic, 540 megabyte database. Over 120 keyboard operators keyed in more than 350,000,000 characters, their work checked by over 50 proofreaders. The complete second edition, costing about $15,000,000 to produce, was published in 1989. Its 20 volumes, currently priced at $2,750, contain 21,728 pages with about 60,000,000 words of text defining some 557,889 words (over 34 percent more than the first edition), together with 2,435,671 quotations. The entire dictionary is now available on CD-ROM (a single compact disc) for $895.00.

T O P 1 0

EARLIEST DATED WORDS IN THE *OXFORD ENGLISH DICTIONARY*

	Word	Source	Date
1=	town	Laws of Ethelbert	601–4
1=	priest	Laws of Ethelbert	601–4
3	earl	Laws of Ethelbert	616
4	this	Bewcastle Column	*c.*670
5	streale	Ruthwell Cross	*c.*680
6	ward	Cædmon, Hymn	680
7	thing	Laws of Hlothær and Eadric	685–6
8	theft	Laws of Ine	688–95
9	worth	Laws of Ine	695
10	then	Laws of King Wihtræd	695–6

The 10 earliest citations in the *OED* come from 7th-century Anglo-Saxon documents and stone inscriptions. All have survived as commonly used English words, with the exception of "streale," which is another name for an arrow. A few other English words can be definitely dated to before 700, among them "church" which, like "then," appears in a law of King Wihtræd.

A WORD IN EDGEWISE
This is a complete set of the Oxford English Dictionary, *the ultimate lexicon of the English language.*

T O P 1 0

LONGEST WORDS IN THE *OXFORD ENGLISH DICTIONARY*

	Word	Letters
1	pneumonoultramicroscopicsilicovolcanoconiosis	45
2	supercalifragilisticexpialidocious	34
3	pseudopseudohypoparathyroidism	30
4=	floccinaucinihilipilification	29
4=	triethylsulphonemethylmethane	29
6=	antidisestablishmentarianism	28
6=	octamethylcyclotetrasiloxane	28
6=	tetrachlorodibenzoparadioxin	28
9	hepaticocholangiogastronomy	27
10=	radioimmunoelectrophoresis	26
10=	radioimmunoelectrophoretic	26

Words that are hyphenated, including such compound words as "transformational-generative" and "tristhio-dimethyl-benzaldehyde", have not been included. There is only one unhyphenated word, the 25-letter "psychophysicotherapeutics." After this, there is a surprisingly large number of words containing 20–24 letters (radioimmunoprecipitation, spectrophotofluorometric, thyroparathyroidectomize, hypergammaglobulinaemia, roentgenkymographically and immunosympathectomized, for example) – few of which are ever used by anyone except scientists and crossword puzzle compilers.

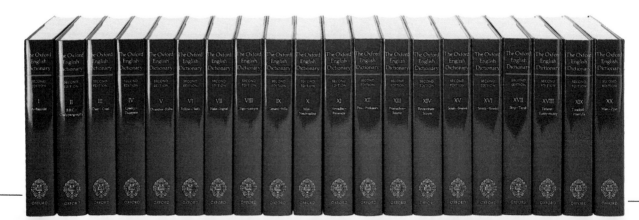

T O P 1 0

WORDS WITH MOST MEANINGS IN THE *OXFORD ENGLISH DICTIONARY*

	Word	Meanings
1	set	464
2	run	396
3	go	368
4	take	343
5	stand	334
6	get	289
7	turn	288
8	put	268
9	fall	264
10	strike	250

T O P 1 0

LETTERS OF THE ALPHABET WITH MOST ENTRIES IN THE *OXFORD ENGLISH DICTIONARY*

	Letter	Entries
1	S	34,556
2	C	26,239
3	P	24,980
4	M	17,495
5	A	15,880
6	T	15,497
7	R	15,483
8	B	14,633
9	D	14,519
10	U	12,943

This list of the 10 most common first letters does not correspond with the list of the 10 most frequently used letters in written English, which is generally held to be ETAINOSHRD. If the alphabet were restricted to just these letters, among the useful phrases that could be created – without repeating any letters – are "the inroads," "note radish," "date rhinos," and "hot sardine."

T O P 1 0

MOST-QUOTED AUTHORS IN THE *OXFORD ENGLISH DICTIONARY*

	Author	Approx. no. of references
1	William Shakespeare (1564–1616)	33,303
2	Sir Walter Scott (1771–1832)	16,659
3	John Milton (1608–74)	12,465
4	John Wyclif (c.1330–84)	11,972
5	Geoffrey Chaucer (c.1343–1400)	11,902
6	William Caxton (c.1422–91)	10,324
7	John Dryden (1631–1700)	9,139
8	Charles Dickens (1812–70)	8,557
9	Philemon Holland (1552–1637)	8,419
10	Alfred, Lord Tennyson (1809–92)	6,972

The figures given here may not be exact because of variations in the way in which sources are quoted, or in instances where more than one example is included from the same author. All those in the Top 10 are prolific "classic" British authors whose works were widely read in the late 19th century.

T O P 1 0

MOST-QUOTED SOURCES IN THE *OXFORD ENGLISH DICTIONARY*

	Source	Approx. no. of references*
1	*The Times* (UK)	19,098
2	*Cursor Mundi*#	11,035
3	*Encyclopedia Britannica*	10,102
4	*Daily News***	9,650
5	*Nature*	9,150
6	*Transactions of the Philological Society*	8,972
7	*Chronicle***	8,550
8	*Westminster Gazette*	7,478
9	*History of England***	7,180
10	*Listener*	7,139

* *These figures may not be absolutely precise because of variations in the way in which source books and journals are quoted, where there is more than one example from the same source, etc.*
# *Cursor Mundi is a long 14th-century Northumbrian poem which is extensively cited for early uses of English words.*
** *References to these may include several different works with similar titles.*

T O P 1 0

LETTERS OF THE ALPHABET WITH FEWEST ENTRIES IN THE *OXFORD ENGLISH DICTIONARY*

	Letter	Entries
1	X	152
2	Z	733
3	Q	1,824
4	Y	2,298
5	J	2,326
6	K	3,491
7	V	5,430
8	N	5,933
9	O	7,737
10	W	8,804

The number of entries beginning with "x" has increased in the past 100 years, with the introduction of such terms as "x-ray" in 1896, "X-certificate" or "X-rated" films (1950), "xerography" (the photocopying process, invented by Chester F. Carlson in 1948), and "Xerox," the proprietary name derived from it in 1952.

BOOKS AND READERS

TOP 10

MOST EXPENSIVE BOOKS AND MANUSCRIPTS EVER SOLD AT AUCTION

Book/manuscript/sale	Price ($)*
1 *The Gospels of Henry the Lion*, c.1173–75 Sotheby's, London, December 6, 1983	10,841,000

The most expensive manuscript, book, or work of art other than a painting ever sold.

2 *The Gutenberg Bible*, 1455 Christie's, New York, October 22, 1987	5,390,000

One of the first books ever printed, by Johann Gutenberg and Johann Fust in 1455, it holds the record for the most expensive printed book.

3 *The Northumberland Bestiary*, c.1250–60 Sotheby's, London, November 29, 1990	5,049,000

The highest price ever paid for an English manuscript.

4 Autographed manuscript of nine symphonies by Wolfgang Amadeus Mozart, c.1773–74 Sotheby's, London, May 22, 1987	3,854,000

The record for a music manuscript and for any postmedieval manuscript.

5 John James Audubon's *The Birds of America*, 1827–38 Sotheby's, New York, June 6, 1989	3,600,000

This collection of over 400 hand-colored engravings holds the record for a natural history book. A facsimile reprint published by Abbeville Press, New York (1985), listed at $30,000, is the most expensive book ever published.

Book/manuscript/sale	Price ($)*
6 The Bible in Hebrew Sotheby's, London, December 5, 1989	2,932,000

A manuscript written in Iraq, Syria, or Babylon in the ninth or tenth century, it holds the record for any Hebrew manuscript.

7 *The Monypenny Breviary*, illuminated manuscript, c. 1490–95, Sotheby's, London, June 19, 1989	2,639,000

The record for any French manuscript.

8 *The Hours and Psalter of Elizabeth de Bohun, Countess of Northampton*, c. 1340–45 Sotheby's, London, June 21, 1988	2,530,000
9 *Biblia Pauperum* Christie's, New York, October 22, 1987	2,200,000

This block-book bible was printed in the Netherlands in c.1460. (The pages of block-books, with text and illustrations, were printed from single carved woodblocks rather than movable type.)

10 *The Gospels of St. Hubert*, c. 860–80 Sotheby's, London, November 26, 1985	1,742,000

* *Excluding premiums*

TOP 10

BESTSELLING CHILDREN'S BOOKS OF ALL TIME IN THE US

Author/title/first published	Total sales
1 Beatrix Potter, *The Tale of Peter Rabbit* (1902)	9,000,000
2 Dr. Seuss, *Green Eggs and Ham* (1960)	6,500,000
3 Dr. Seuss, *One Fish, Two Fish, Red Fish, Blue Fish* (1960)	6,200,000
4 S.E. Hinton, *The Outsiders* (1967)	6,000,000
5 Dr. Seuss, *Hop on Pop* (1963)	5,900,000
6 Dr. Seuss, *Dr. Seuss's ABC* (1963)	5,800,000
7 Dr. Seuss, *The Cat in the Hat* (1957)	5,600,000
8 Judy Blume, *Are You There, God? It's Me, Margaret* (1970)	5,500,000
9 L. Frank Baum, *The Wonderful Wizard of Oz* (1900)	5,200,000
10 E.B. White, *Charlotte's Web* (1952)	4,900,000

Total sales are estimates for combined hardback and paperback domestic sales since first publication. Extending the list to a Top 20 would encompass further works by several of the major authors featured here, including S.E. (Susan Eloise) Hinton and Judy Blume, as well as Laura Ingalls Wilder, the author of *Little House on the Prairie* (1953) and other bestsellers. A number of enormously popular earlier American children's classics, such as Louisa May Alcott's *Little Women* (1868–69) and its sequels, and Mark Twain's *Tom Sawyer* (1876), have long been out of copyright and available in countless editions; their cumulative sales over more than a century are impossible to calculate, but could well qualify some of them for the Top 10.

BEATRIX POTTER
The animal stories of British author Beatrix Potter are as well loved in the US as they are in the UK. Her most famous book, The Tale of Peter Rabbit, *is probably the bestselling children's book in the world.*

THE TEN

LAST WINNERS OF THE NEWBERY MEDAL

Year	Author/book title
1994	Lois Lowry, *The Giver*
1993	Cynthia Rylant, *Missing May*
1992	Phyllis Reynolds Naylor, *Shiloh*
1991	Jerry Spinelli, *Maniac Magee*
1990	Lois Lowry, *Number the Stars*
1989	Paul Fleischman, *Joyful Noise: Poems for Two Voices*
1988	Russell Freedman, *Lincoln: A Photobiography*
1987	Sid Fleischman, *The Whipping Boy*
1986	Patricia MacLachlan, *Sarah, Plain and Tall*
1985	Robin McKinley, *The Hero and the Crown*

TOP TEN

LAST PULITZER PRIZEWINNERS FOR GENERAL NONFICTION

Year	Author/Book title
1993	Garry Wills, *Lincoln at Gettysburg*
1992	Daniel Yergin, *The Prize: The Epic Quest for Oil*
1991	Bert Holldobler and Edward O. Wilson, *The Ants*
1990	Dale Maharidge and Michael Williamson, *And Their Children After Them*
1989	Neil Sheehan, *A Bright Shining Lie: John Paul Vann and America in Vietnam*
1988	Richard Rhodes, *The Making of the Atomic Bomb*
1987	David K. Shipler, *Arab and Jew*
1986	Joseph Lelyveld, *Move Your Shadow*; J. Anthony Lukas, *Common Ground*
1985	Studs Terkel, *The Good War*
1984	Paul Starr, *Social Transformation of American Medicine*

THE TEN

FIRST POCKET BOOKS

	Author/book title
1	James Hilton, *Lost Horizon*
2	Dorothea Brande, *Wake Up and Live!*
3	William Shakespeare, *Five Great Tragedies*
4	Thorne Smith, *Topper*
5	Agatha Christie, *The Murder of Roger Ackroyd*
6	Dorothy Parker, *Enough Rope*
7	Emily Brontë, *Wuthering Heights*
8	Samuel Butler, *The Way of All Flesh*
9	Thornton Wilder, *The Bridge of San Luis Rey*
10	Felix Saltern, *Bambi*

All 10 Pocket Books were published in the US in 1939. Unlike their British counterparts, Penguin Books, Pocket Books titles all had pictorial covers: the first 10 were created by Isador N. Steinberg and Frank J. Lieberman (who also drew the Pocket Books logo). A survey of sales in 1957 showed that of these 10, the Shakespeare was the bestselling title with over 2,000,000 copies in print, followed by *Lost Horizon* (1,750,000), *Topper* (1,500,000), and *Wuthering Heights* (over 1,000,000).

TOP TEN

LAST PULITZER PRIZEWINNERS FOR FICTION

Year	Author/book title
1993	Robert Olen Butler, *A Good Scent from a Strange Mountain*
1992	Jane Smiley, *A Thousand Acres*
1991	John Updike, *Rabbit at Rest*
1990	Oscar Hijuelos, *The Mambo King Plays Songs of Love*
1989	Anne Tyler, *Breathing Lessons*
1988	Toni Morrison, *Beloved*
1987	Peter Taylor, *A Summons to Memphis*
1986	Larry McMurtry, *Lonesome Dove*
1985	Alison Lurie, *Foreign Affairs*
1984	William Kennedy, *Ironweed*

A STING IN THE TALE
Dorothy Parker was famed for her acid wit. She wrote short stories and a bestselling book of verse, Enough Rope, *and was also a tough reviewer of other books (such as* Winnie the Pooh*).*

TOP 10

TRADE PUBLISHERS IN THE US

	Company	Sales ($)*
1	Random House	1,015,000,000
2	Bantam Doubleday Dell	650,000,000
3=	HarperCollins	387,000,000
3=	Paramount Consumer	387,000,000
5	Penguin USA	325,000,000
6	Time Warner Trade	240,000,000
7	Putnam Berkley	212,000,000
8	Macmillan Publishing	180,000,000
9	Hearst Trade Group	160,000,000
10	St. Martin's	143,000,000

* *1992 sales*

WORLD BESTSELLERS

BESTSELLING BOOKS OF ALL TIME

1 The Bible   6,000,000,000

No one really knows how many copies of the Bible have been printed, sold, or distributed. The Bible Society's attempt to calculate the number printed between 1816 and 1975 produced the figure of 2,458,000,000. A more recent survey up to 1992 put it closer to 6,000,000,000 in more than 2,000 languages and dialects. Whatever the precise figure, it is by far the bestselling book of all time.

2 Quotations from the Works of Mao Tse-tung   800,000,000

Chairman Mao's "Little Red Book" could scarcely fail to become a bestseller: between the years 1966 and 1971 it was compulsory for every Chinese adult to own a copy. It was both sold and distributed to the people of China – though what proportion voluntarily bought it must remain open to question. Some 100,000,000 copies of his Poems *were also disseminated.*

3 *American Spelling Book by Noah Webster*   100,000,000

First published in 1783, this reference book by American man of letters Noah Webster (1758–1843) – of Webster's Dictionary *fame – remained a bestseller in the US throughout the 19th century.*

4 *The Guinness Book of Records*   74,000,000+

First published in 1955, The Guinness Book of Records *stands out as the greatest contemporary publishing achievement. In the UK there have now been 37 editions (it was not published annually until 1964), as well as numerous foreign language editions.*

5 *The McGuffey Readers* by William Holmes McGuffey   60,000,000

Published in numerous editions from 1853, some authorities have put the total sales of these educational textbooks, originally compiled by American anthologist William Holmes McGuffey (1800–73), as high as 122,000,000. It has also been claimed that 60,000,000 copies of the 1879 edition were printed, but as this is some 10,000,000 more than the entire population of the US at the time, the publishers must have been extremely optimistic about its success.

6 *A Message to Garcia by Elbert Hubbard*   40–50,000,000

Now forgotten, Hubbard's polemic on the subject of labor relations was published in 1899 and within a few years had achieved these phenomenal sales, largely because many American employers purchased bulk supplies to distribute to their employees. The literary career of Elbert Hubbard (1856–1915) was cut short in 1915 when he went down with the Lusitania, *but even in death he was a record-breaker: his posthumous* My Philosophy *(1916) was published in one of the largest-ever "limited editions," of 9,983 copies – all of them signed.*

7 *The Common Sense Book of Baby and Child Care* by Benjamin Spock   39,200,000+

Dr. Spock's 1946 manual became the bible of infant care for subsequent generations of parents. Most of the sales have been of the paperback edition of the book.

8 *World Almanac*   36,000,000+

Having been published annually since 1868 (with a break from 1876 to 1886), this wide-ranging reference book has remained a bestseller ever since.

9 *Valley of the Dolls by Jacqueline Susann*   28,712,000+

This racy tale of sex, violence, and drugs by Jacqueline Susann (1921–74), first published in 1966, is, perhaps surprisingly, the world's bestselling novel. Susann's closest rival for a bestselling work of fiction is Margaret Mitchell, whose Gone With the Wind *has achieved sales approaching 28,000,000.*

10 *In His Steps: "What Would Jesus Do?"* by Rev. Charles Monroe Sheldon   28,500,000

Though virtually unknown today, Charles Sheldon (1857–1946) achieved fame and fortune with this 1896 religious treatise.

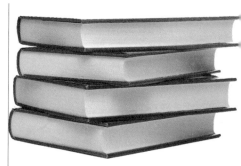

It is extremely difficult to establish precise sales even of contemporary books, and virtually impossible to do so with books published long ago. How many copies of the complete works of Shakespeare or Conan Doyle's Sherlock Holmes books have been sold in countless editions? The publication of variant editions, translations, and pirated copies all affect the global picture, and few publishers or authors are willing to expose their royalty statements to public scrutiny. As a result, this Top 10 list offers no more than the "best guess" at the great bestsellers of the past, and it may well be that there are other books with a valid claim to a place in it.

There are problems of definition: what, for example, is the status of a book that is revised and reissued annually, and what precisely is a "book"? A UNESCO conference in 1950 decided it was "a non-periodical literary publication containing 49 or more pages, not counting the covers" (which is baffling in itself, since all publications have to contain an even number of pages, while, according to this criterion, a 32-page children's book would not be regarded as a book at all). If *Old Moore's Almanac* is classified as a book rather than a periodical or a pamphlet, it would appear high on the list. Having been published annually since 1697, its total sales to date are believed to be over 112,000,000. More than 107,000,000 copies of the Jehovah's Witness tract, *The Truth That Leads to Eternal Life,* first published in 1968, are believed to have been distributed in 117 languages, usually in return for a donation to the sect, but as they were not sold it does not rank as a "bestseller."

TOP 10

WORLD'S BESTSELLING FICTION

As with the bestselling books of all time, it is virtually impossible to arrive at a definitive list of fiction bestsellers that encompasses all permutations including hardback and paperback editions, book club sales, and translations, and takes account of the innumerable editions of earlier classics such as *Robinson Crusoe* or the works of Jane Austen, Charles Dickens, or popular foreign authors such as Jules Verne. Although only Jacqueline Susann's *Valley of the Dolls* appears on the all-time list, and publishers' precise sales data remains tantalizingly elusive (it has been said that the most published fiction is publishers' own sales figures), there are many other novels that must be close contenders for the Top 10. It seems certain that all the following have sold in excess of 10,000,000 copies in hardback and paperback worldwide:

Richard Bach	*Jonathan Livingstone Seagull*
William Blatty	*The Exorcist*
Peter Benchley	*Jaws*
Erskine Caldwell	*God's Little Acre*
Joseph Heller	*Catch-22*
D.H. Lawrence	*Lady Chatterley's Lover*
Harper Lee	*To Kill a Mockingbird*
Colleen McCullough	*The Thorn Birds*
Grace Metalious	*Peyton Place*
Margaret Mitchell	*Gone With the Wind*
George Orwell	*Animal Farm*
George Orwell	*1984*
Mario Puzo	*The Godfather*
Harold Robbins	*The Carpetbaggers*
J.D. Salinger	*Catcher in the Rye*
Erich Segal	*Love Story*

There are also several prolific popular novelists whose books have achieved combined international sales of colossal proportions. The field is led by detective story authoress *extraordinaire* Agatha Christie, with total sales of more than 2,000,000,000 since 1920, followed by romantic novelist Barbara Cartland (650,000,000), Belgian detective novelist Georges Simenon (600,000,000), and American crime-writer Erle Stanley Gardner (320,000,000). If this list were extended to embrace other prolific bestselling novelists during the postwar period, it would probably include such writers as Jeffrey Archer, Catherine Cookson, Ian Fleming, Robert Ludlum, Alistair MacLean, and Mickey Spillane.

TOP 10

MOST PUBLISHED AUTHORS OF ALL TIME

	Author	Nationality
1	William Shakespeare (1564–1616)	British
2	Charles Dickens (1812–70)	British
3	Sir Walter Scott (1771–1832)	British
4	Johann Goethe (1749–1832)	German
5	Aristotle (384–322 BC)	Greek
6	Alexandre Dumas (*père*) (1802–70)	French
7	Robert Louis Stevenson (1850–94)	British
8	Mark Twain (1835–1910)	American
9	Marcus Cicero (106–43 BC)	Roman
10	Honoré de Balzac (1799–1850)	French

This Top 10 is based on a search of a major US library computer database. Shakespeare is cited over 15,000 times.

DID YOU KNOW

THE LONG AND THE SHORT OF IT

The longest single word in a book title appears in M.C.A. Kinneby's *Le "Boschmannschucrutund- kakafresserdeutschkolossal- kulturdestruktokathedralibu- sundkinden,"* published in Paris in 1915. Its longest English rival is Miles Peter Andrews's *The Baron Kinkvervankotsdorspra- kingatchdern* (1781). At the other extreme, Sir Walter Newman Flower was the author of a book published in 1925 with the title *?*.

BESTSELLING CHILDREN'S AUTHORS IN THE WORLD

René Goscinny and Albert Uderzo

René Goscinny (1926–77) and Albert Uderzo (b. 1927) created the comic-strip character Astérix the Gaul in 1959. They produced 30 books with total sales of at least 220,000,000 copies.

Hergé

Georges Rémi (1907–83), the Belgian author- illustrator who wrote under the pen name Hergé, created the comic-strip character Tintin in 1929. Appearing in book form from 1948 onward, they achieved worldwide popularity and have been translated into about 45 languages and dialects. Total sales are believe to be at least 160,000,000.

Enid Blyton

With sales of her Noddy books exceeding 60,000,000 copies and more than 700 children's books to her name (UNESCO calculated that there were 974 translations of her works in the 1960s alone), total sales of her works are believed to be over 100,000,000, making her the bestselling English language author of the 20th century.

Dr. Seuss

His books in the US Top 10 alone total about 30,000,000 copies; to this must be added those titles that have sold fewer than 5,000,000 in the US and all foreign editions of all his books, suggesting totals of more than 100,000,000.

Beatrix Potter

The Tale of Peter Rabbit (1902) was one of a series of books, the cumulative total sales of which probably exceed 50,000,000.

Lewis Carroll

Total world sales of all editions of Carroll's two classic children's books, Alice's Adventures in Wonderland and Alice Through the Looking Glass, are incalculable, but just these two books probably place him among the 20 bestselling children's authors of all time.

It is impossible to make a definitive list of the bestselling children's books in the world, but based on total sales of their entire output, these authors have produced titles that have been bestsellers – especially those in numerous translations – over a long period.

US BESTSELLERS

TOP 10

FICTON BESTSELLERS OF 1993

	Author	Title	Sales
1	Robert James Waller	*The Bridges of Madison County*	4,362,352
2	John Grisham	*The Client*	2,927,376
3	Robert James Waller	*Slow Waltz at Cedar Bend*	1,978,342
4	Tom Clancy	*Without Remorse*	1,814,173
5	Stephen King	*Nightmares and Dreamscapes*	1,328,927
6	Danielle Steele	*Vanished*	1,121,716
7	Anne Rice	*Lasher*	736,010
8	Scott Turow	*Pleading Guilty*	710,152
9	Laura Esquivel	*Like Water for Chocolate*	675,000 *
10	Robert Ludlum	*The Scorpio Illusion*	600,000 *

* *Approx. – precise figures confidential*
  Source: Publishers Weekly

Sales of the year's blockbusters were so substantial that despite achieving often impressive runs in the charts (such as the 15 weeks sustained by Richard North Patterson's *Degree of Guilt* and the 10 weeks of Susan Isaacs' *After All These Years*), a record number of 16 novels made the bestseller charts with sales of more than 150,000 copies each, and yet failed to make the year's Top 30.

BESTSELLING PROFESSOR
Writing on one of the topics least likely to top the charts, British professor of physics Stephen Hawking, of Cambridge University, has brought theoretical physics to the widest possible audience. Although his book A Brief History of Time *is no longer among the Top 10 Nonfiction Bestsellers, it has sold over 5,000,000 copies worldwide since it was first published in 1985.*

THE TEN

HARDBACK NONFICTION BESTSELLERS OF THE PAST 10 YEARS

Year	Author	Title	Publisher
1984	Lee Iacocca with William Novak	*Iacocca: An Autobiography*	Bantam Books
1985	Lee Iacocca with William Novak	*Iacocca: An Autobiography*	Bantam Books
1986	Bill Cosby	*Fatherhood*	Doubleday
1987	Bill Cosby	*Time Flies*	Doubleday/Dolphin
1988	Robert E. Kowalski	*The 8-Week Cholesterol Cure*	Harper & Row
1989	Robert Fulghum	*All I Really Need to Know I Learned in Kindergarten: Uncommon Thoughts on Common Things*	Villard
1990	Charles Kuralt	*A Life on the Road*	Putnam
1991	Katherine Hepburn	*Me: Stories of My Life*	Knopf
1992	Rush Limbaugh	*The Way Things Ought to Be*	Pocket Books
1993	Rush Limbaugh	*See, I Told You So*	Pocket Books

Source: Publishers Weekly

THE TEN

HARDBACK FICTION BESTSELLERS OF THE PAST 10 YEARS

Year	Author	Title	Publisher
1984	Stephen King and Peter Straub	*The Talisman*	Viking
1985	Jean M. Auel	*The Mammoth Hunters*	Crown
1986	Stephen King	*It*	Viking
1987	Stephen King	*The Tommyknockers*	Putnam
1988	Tom Clancy	*The Cardinal of the Kremlin*	Putnam
1989	Tom Clancy	*Clear and Present Danger*	Putnam
1990	Jean M. Auel	*The Plains of Passage*	Crown
1991	Alexandra Ripley	*Scarlett: The Sequel to Margaret Mitchell's Gone With the Wind*	Warner Books
1992	Stephen King	*Dolores Claiborne*	Viking/Penguin
1993	Robert James Waller	*The Bridges of Madison County*	Warner Books

Source: Publishers Weekly

T O P 1 0

NONFICTON BESTSELLERS OF 1993

	Author	Title	Sales
1	Rush Limbaugh	*See, I Told You So*	2,587,600
2	Howard Stern	*Private Parts*	1,228,298
3	Jerry Seinfeld	*Seinlanguage*	1,106,000
4	Betty J. Eadie with Curtis Taylor	*Embraced by the Light*	956,122
5	Deepak Chopra	*Ageless Body, Timeless Mind*	802,417
6	Susan Powter	*Stop the Insanity*	688,816
7	Clarissa Pinkola	*Women Who Run with the Wolves*	652,423
8	John Gray	*Men Are from Mars, Women Are from Venus*	582,624
9	Elizabeth Marshall Thomas	*The Hidden Life of Dogs*	548,177
10	Harvey Penick with Bud Shrake	*And If You Play Golf, You're My Friend*	509,219

Source: Publishers Weekly

T O P 1 0

ALMANACS, ATLASES, AND ANNUALS OF 1993

	Title	Sales
1	*The World Almanac and Book of Facts 1993*	2,200,000
2	*The World Almanac and Book of Facts 1994*	2,080,000
3	*J.J. Lasser's Your Income Tax 1994*	750,000
4	*Mobil Travel Guide Series 1993*	525,000
5	*Erst & Young Tax Guide 1993*	500,000
6	*Gousha's New Deluxe 1994 Road Atlas*	450,000
7	*What Color is Your Parachute? 1993*	316,189
8	*Ernst & Young Tax-Saving Strategies Guide 1993*	300,000
9	*Information Please Almanac 1994*	290,000
10	*Gousha's Interstate Road Atlas 1994*	265,000

Source: Publishers Weekly

Still the leader by a considerable margin, *The World Almanac and Book of Facts* was first published in 1868 by the *New York World*. Containing 120 pages, including 12 pages of advertisements, it originally focused on political matters such as Southern Reconstruction following the Civil War. It ceased publication in 1876, but was revived 10 years later on the personal initiative of the newspaper's publisher, Joseph Pulitzer, and has been published annually ever since.

T H E T E N

PUBLISHERS WITH THE MOST WEEKS ON THE BESTSELLER CHARTS, 1993

	Company	Hardback books	Hardback weeks	Paperback books	Paperback weeks	Total weeks
1	Random House Inc.	42	347	39	388	735
2	Putnam Berkley	17	110	22	88	668
3	Bantam Doubleday Dell	27	236	26	234	470
4	Paramount	24	212	33	249	461
5	HarperCollins	17	206	11	80	286
6	Penguin USA	10	82	17	115	197
7	Time Warner	8	108	12	72	180
8	Norton	1	2	1	48	50
9	Hearst	2	6	12	39	45
10	Macmillan	3	26	1	14	40

Source: Publishers Weekly

JAMES HILTON

Hilton was one of the bestselling popular novelists of the mid-20th century. His book Lost Horizon *was among the very first books published by Pocket Books (now owned by Paramount Consumers). This novel, and two of Hilton's other works –* Goodbye, Mr. Chips *and* Random Harvest *– were made into hugely successful films. He also created the word "Shangri-La," which first occurred in* Lost Horizon *as the name of a remote mountain land and has passed into the English language as the epitome of an unattainable paradise.*

READ ALL ABOUT IT

T O P   1 0

DAILY NEWSPAPERS IN THE WORLD

	Newspaper	Country	Average daily circulation
1	*Yomiuri Shimbun*	Japan	8,700,000
2	*Asahi Shimbun*	Japan	7,400,000
3	*People's Daily*	China	6,000,000
4	*Bild Zeitung*	Germany	5,900,000
5	*The Sun*	UK	3,851,929
6	*Daily Mirror*	UK	2,523,944
7	*Daily Mail*	UK	1,716,070
8	*Wall Street Journal*	US	1,857,131
9	*USA Today*	US	1,632,345*
10	*Daily Express*	UK	1,397,852

* National edition; Eastern edition average 798,515.

Just outside this list are another four US newspapers. The *New York Times* comes in at No. 11, with a circulation of 1,230,461; then come the *Los Angeles Times* (circulation: 1,138,353), the *Washington Post* (circulation: 855,171), and the *New York Daily News* (circulation: 769,801). The official Soviet newspaper *Pravda*, which is no longer published, formerly topped this list, with alleged daily sales peaking in May 1990 at 21,975,000 copies. If true, it would hold the world record for a daily newspaper.

T H E   T E N

OLDEST NEWSPAPERS IN THE UK

Newspaper	First published
1 The London Gazette	Nov 16, 1665

Originally published in Oxford as The Oxford Gazette, *while the royal court resided there during an outbreak of the plague. After 23 issues it moved to London with the court and changed its name.*

Newspaper	First published
2 Berrow's Worcester Journal	c.1709

Britain's oldest surviving provincial newspaper (the Norwich Post *was founded in 1701, but is defunct), it first appeared as the* Worcester Post-Man *and changed its name to* Berrow's Worcester Journal *in 1808. Its claim to have started as early as 1690 has never been substantiated.*

Newspaper	First published
3 Lincoln, Rutland and Stamford Mercury	c.1710

Originally published as the Stamford Mercury *c.1710 (allegedly 1695, and possibly in 1712), it later became the* Lincoln, Rutland and Stamford Mercury.

Newspaper	First published
4 Lloyds List	1726

Providing shipping news, originally weekly, but since 1734 Britain's oldest daily.

Newspaper	First published
5 News Letter (Belfast)	March 6, 1738

Published daily since 1855.

Newspaper	First published
6 Hampshire Chronicle	1772

Published in Winchester, it subsequently amalgamated with the Hampshire Observer.

Newspaper	First published
7 The Times	January 1, 1785

First published as the Daily Universal Register, *it changed its name to* The Times *on March 1, 1788.*

Newspaper	First published
8 Observer	December 4, 1791

The first Sunday newspaper in the UK was Johnson's British Gazette and Sunday Monitor, *which was first published on March 2, 1780. It survived until 1829, making the* Observer *the longest-running Sunday newspaper.*

Newspaper	First published
9 The Licensee	February 8, 1794

Britain's oldest trade newspaper (a daily established by the Licensed Victuallers Association to earn income for its charity), and the first national paper on Fleet Street, the Morning Advertiser *changed its name to* The Licensee *and became a twice-weekly news magazine in 1994, at the time of its 200th anniversary.*

Newspaper	First published
10 Sunday Times	February 1821

Issued as the New Observer *until March 1821 and the* Independent Observer *from April 1821 until October 21, 1822, when it changed its name to the* Sunday Times. *On February 4, 1962 it became the first British newspaper to issue a color supplement.*

The *Guardian*, a weekly from 1821 until 1855 (and called the *Manchester Guardian* until 1959), misses a place in the Top 10 by just three months.

TOP 10

SUNDAY NEWSPAPERS IN THE US

	Newspaper	Average Sunday circulation (1993)
1	Los Angeles Times	1,530,547
2	Detroit Free Press	1,191,500
3	Washington Post	1,158,329
4	Chicago Tribune	1,119,430
5	New York Times	1,116,217
6	Philadelphia Enquirer	978,223
7	Long Island Newsday	846,083
8	Boston Globe	803,376
9	San Francisco Chronicle	708,542
10	Newark Star Ledger	705,469

Source: Standard Rate & Data Service

TOP 10

COUNTRIES WITH MOST DAILY NEWSPAPERS

	Country	No. of daily newspapers
1	Russia	4,808
2	India	2,281
3	US	1,611
4	Kazakhstan	456
5	Turkey	399
6	Brazil	356
7	Germany	354
8	Mexico	285
9	Uzbekistan	279
10	Pakistan	237
	UK	104

	Country	Sales per 1,000 inhabitants
1	Latvia	1,637
2	Estonia	1,620
3	Romania	1,119
4	Lithuania	712
5	Georgia	671
6	Hong Kong	632
7	Norway	614
8	Japan	587
9	Iceland	572
10	Moldova	561
	US	250

Certain countries have large numbers of newspapers each serving relatively small areas and hence with restricted circulations: the US is the most notable example, with 1,611 daily newspapers, but only five of them with average daily sales of more than 1,000,000, while the UK, with fewer individual newspapers, also has five with circulations of over 1,000,000. If the table is arranged by total sales of daily newspapers per 1,000 inhabitants, the result is somewhat different (see following list):

"Official" figures from former Soviet Bloc countries should always be regarded with some degree of circumspection.

One curious anomaly is that of the Vatican City's one newspaper, *L'Osservatore Romano*, an average of 70,000 of which are printed. Since the population of the Vatican is only about 738, it implies a daily sale of 94,850 per 1,000, or 95 copies per head. In fact, of course, most of them are sent outside the Holy See.

TOP 10

CONSUMERS OF NEWSPRINT

	Country	Consumption per inhabitant kg	lb	oz
1	US	54.043	119	2
2	Denmark	44.928	99	1
3	New Zealand	44.475	98	1
4	Switzerland	44.041	97	1
5	Finland	38.790	85	8
6	Australia	36.828	81	3
7	Canada	34.920	77	0
8	Austria	33.022	72	13
9	Netherlands	31.979	70	8
10	UK	30.031	66	3

National consumption of newsprint – the cheap wood-pulp paper used for printing newspapers – provides a measure of the extent of newspaper sales in the Top 10 countries.

TOP 10

DAILY NEWSPAPERS IN THE US

	Newspaper	Average daily circulation (1993)
1	Wall Street Journal	1,818,562
2	USA Today	1,557,171
3	Los Angeles Times	1,170,896
4	Detroit Free Press*	1,021,941
5	Washington Post	823,449
6	New York Daily News	779,294
7	Long Island Newsday	751,942
8	New York Times	746,347
9	Chicago Tribune	727,520
10	Philadelphia Enquirer	689,735

* Includes morning and evening editions

Apart from the *Wall Street Journal*, which focuses mainly on financial news, *USA Today* remains the United States' only true national daily newspaper.

Source: Standard Rate & Data Service

MAGAZINES AND COMICS

FIRST COMIC BOOKS IN THE US

(First published commercially: earlier comic books were given away as promotional items)

	Comic	First published
1	*Famous Funnies: Series 1*	Feb 1934

35,000 copies of this 64-page comic book sold at 10 cents each mark the beginning of the comic book era.

	Comic	First published
2	*Famous Funnies* No. 1	Jul 1934

The first monthly comic ("The Nation's Comic Monthly"), it ran for 21 years, a total of 218 issues.

	Comic	First published
3	*New Fun*	Feb 1935

Became More Fun *after the 6th issue.*

	Comic	First published
4	*Micky Mouse Magazine*	Jun 1935

Became Walt Disney's Comics and Stories *from October 1940.*

	Comic	First published
5	*New Comics*	Dec 1935

Became New Adventure Comics *after No. 12.*

	Comic	First published
6	*Popular Comics*	Feb 1936
7=	*King Comics*	Apr 1936
7=	*Tip Top Comics*	Apr 1936

One of the longest-running of the early comic books, it ceased publication in May 1961 with its 225th issue.

	Comic	First published
9	*The Funnies*	Oct 1936

Became The New Funnies *from issue No. 65.*

	Comic	First published
10	*Detective Picture Stories*	Dec 1936

The first-ever thematic comic book, in July 1938 its title was changed to Keen Detective Funnies.

MAGAZINES IN THE US

	Magazine/ no. of issues a year	Circulation*
1	Modern Maturity (12)	22,453,000
2	Reader's Digest (12)	16,860,000
3	TV Guide (52)	14,967,000
4	National Geographic (12)	9,626,000
5	Better Homes and Gardens (12)	7,777,000
6	Ladies Home Journal (12)	5,370,000
7	Consumer Reports (12)	5,279,000
8	Family Circle (17)	5,099,000
9	Good Housekeeping (12)	5,045,000
10	McCall's (12)	4,796,000

* *Average for 1993*

MOST VALUABLE AMERICAN COMICS

	Comic	Value ($)*
1	*Action Comics* No.1	105,000

Published in June 1938, the first issue of Action Comics *marked the original appearance of Superman.*

	Comic	Value ($)*
2	*Detective Comics* No.27	96,000

Issued in May 1939, it is prized as the first comic to feature Batman.

	Comic	Value ($)*
3	*Marvel Comics* No.1	75,000

The Human Torch and other heroes were first introduced in the issue dated October 1939.

	Comic	Value ($)*
4	*Superman* No.1	72,000

The first comic devoted to Superman, it reprinted the original Action Comics *story and was published in summer 1939.*

	Comic	Value ($)*
5	*Detective Comics* No.1	51,000

Published in March 1937, it was the first in a long-running series.

	Comic	Value ($)*
6	*Whiz Comics* No.1	44,000

Published in February 1940 – and confusingly numbered "2" – it was the first comic book to feature Captain Marvel.

	Comic	Value ($)*
7	*All American Comics* No.16	39,000

The Green Lantern made his debut in this issue, dated July 1940.

	Comic	Value ($)*
8	*Batman* No.1	38,000

Published in Spring 1940, this was the first comic book devoted to Batman.

	Comic	Value ($)*
9	*Captain America Comics* No.1	38,000

Published in March 1941, this was the original comic book in which Captain America appeared.

	Comic	Value ($)*
10	*New Fun Comics* No.1	

Its February 1935 publication was notable as the first-ever DC comic book.

* *For example in "Near Mint" condition
Source: © Overstreet Publications Inc.*

The actual prices paid both at auction and in private transactions vary considerably, with even higher prices than these occasionally reported. All the most expensive comic books in the Top 10 come from the so-called "Golden Age" (1938-1945), and to command very high prices must be in "Very Fine" or "Near Mint" condition.

COMIC BOOK PUBLISHERS IN THE US

	Publisher	Market share %*
1	Marvel	33.51
2	D.C.	20.87
3	Image	16.58
4	Dark Horse	6.93
5	Valiant	4.73
6	Malibu	3.94
7	Wizard	1.65
8=	Defiant	1.11
8=	Topps	1.11
10	Viz	1.05
	Others total	*8.52*

* *As of August 1994*

Between August 1991 and August 1994 old-established market leaders Marvel and D.C. have seen their combined market share fall from 80.0 percent to 54.38 percent as various new kids arrive on the block – most notably the publishers of the anarchic British comic book *Viz*, emulating its stratospheric rise to bestsellerdom on the other side of the Atlantic.

THE TEN

EARLIEST-ESTABLISHED MAGAZINES IN THE US

Magazine	Founded
1 Saturday Evening Post	1821

The often-stated claim that the Saturday Evening Post was started as early as 1728 is unfounded: it is suggested that it was a descendant of the Universal Instructor in All Arts and Sciences and Pennsylvania Gazette, founded by Samuel Keimer in 1728, and bought in 1729 by Benjamin Franklin, who published it as the Pennsylvania Gazette, but this journal had ceased publication by 1815, and the Saturday Evening Post was started in Philadelphia in 1821 by Samuel C. Atkinson and Charles Alexander, neither of whom had any connection with the earlier magazine.

Magazine	Founded
2 Scientific American	1845

Began publication in New York on August 28 in a newspaper format.

Magazine	Founded
3 Town & Country	1846
4 Harper's Magazine	1850

The magazine began its life in New York as Harper's Monthly.

Magazine	Founded
5 The Atlantic	1857

Started in Boston (as the Atlantic Monthly) under editor James Russell Lowell.

Magazine	Founded
6 The Nation	1865

Founded by Irish-born Edwin Lawrence Godkin, it commenced publication in New York.

Magazine	Founded
7 Harper's Bazaar	1867

William Randoph Hearst bought the magazine in 1913 and in 1913 subtly changed its name from Harper's Bazar with one "a".

Magazine	Founded
8 Popular Science	1872

Founded in New York as Popular Science Monthly by Edward Livingston Youmans, an author and teacher who had been blind for most of his life. Its first issue, published in May and priced at 50 cents, contained articles on subjects ranging from "Science and Immortality" and "Women and Political Power" to "The Causes of Dyspepsia."

Magazine	Founded
9 American Field	1874

Magazine	Founded
10 Thoroughbred Record	1875

Appropriately, first published in the inaugural year of the Kentucky Derby.

In 1916 American bank clerk DeWitt Wallace published a booklet called Getting the Most Out of Farming, which consisted of extracts from various US Government agricultural publications. While recovering after being wounded in France during the war, he contemplated applying the same principle to a general interest magazine and in 1920 produced a sample copy of Reader's Digest. He and his wife, Lila Acheson, solicited sales by subscription and published 5,000 copies of the first issue in February 1922. It was an enormous success, rapidly becoming the US's bestselling monthly magazine. Today 41 editions are published in 17 languages. DeWitt died in 1981 and Lila Wallace in 1984.

TOP 10

WOMEN'S MAGAZINES IN THE US

Magazine/ no. of issues a year	Circulation*
1 Better Homes and Gardens (12)	7,777,000
2 Ladies Home Journal (12)	5,370,000
3 Family Circle (17)	5,099,000
4 Good Housekeeping (12)	5,045,000
5 McCall's (12)	4,796,000
6 Woman's Day (17)	4,582,000
7 Redbook (12)	3,444,000
8 Cosmopolitan (12)	2,758,000
9 Glamour (12)	2,177,000
10 New Woman (12)	1,443,000

* Average for 1993

The quintessential women's fashion magazine Vogue stands at No. 13, with an average monthly circulation of 1,244,000.

Source: Standard Rate & Data Service

TOP 10

SPECIALIST MAGAZINES IN THE US

Magazine/ no. of issues a year	Circulation*
1 TV Guide (52)	14,967,000
2 National Geographic (12)	9,626,000
3 Sports Illustrated (52)	3,815,000
4 Prevention (12)	3,416,000
5 Vegetarian Times (12)	3,164,000
6 Smithsonian (12)	2,238,000
7 Money (13)	2,226,000
8 Motorland (12)	2,127,000
9 Ebony (12)	2,034,000
10 Field And Stream (12)	2,007,000

* Average for 1993
Source: Standard Rate & Data Service

TOP 10

TRADE MAGAZINES IN THE US

Title/ no. of issues per year	Circulation
1 Independent Business (6)	609,927
2 ABA Journal, The Lawyer's Magazine (12)	402,992
3 Chief Financial Officer (12)	350,529
4 The Journal of the American Medical Association (48)	339,808
5 American Medical News (48)	321,091
6 Industry Week (24)	288,001
7 Registered Nurse (12)	284,566
8 Farm Industry News (12)	254,964
9 Soybean Digest (11)	235,882
10 PC Week (51)	231,483

Figures given are for the combined paid and unpaid average circulations for the six months ended December 1993.

Source: Business Publications Audit (BPA)

ART AT AUCTION

TOP 10

MOST EXPENSIVE PAINTINGS EVER SOLD

Artist/work/sale	Price ($)
1 Vincent van Gogh, *Portrait du Dr. Gachet* Christie's, New York, May 15, 1990	75,000,000

Sold to Ryoei Saito, head of Japanese Daishowa Paper Manufacturing.

2 Pierre-Auguste Renoir, *Au Moulin de la Galette* Sotheby's, New York, May 17, 1990	71,000,000

Also purchased by Ryoei Saito – two days later.

3 Pablo Picasso, *Les Noces de Pierrette*, Binoche et Godeau, Paris, November 30, 1989	51,700,000

Sold by Swedish financier Fredrik Roos and bought by Tomonori Tsurumaki, a property developer, bidding from Tokyo by phone.

4 Vincent van Gogh, *Irises* Sotheby's, New York, November 11, 1987	49,000,000

After much speculation, its mystery purchaser was eventually confirmed as Australian businessman Alan Bond. However, since he was unable to pay for it in full, its former status as the world's most expensive work of art has been disputed. In 1990 it was sold to the J. Paul Getty Museum, Malibu, for an undisclosed sum, with speculation ranging from $60,000,000 to as little as $35,000,000.

5 Pablo Picasso, Self Portrait: *Yo Picasso* Sotheby's, New York, May 9, 1989	43,500,000

The anonymous purchaser may have been Greek shipping magnate Stavros Niarchos.

6 Pablo Picasso, *Au Lapin Agile* Sotheby's, New York, November 15, 1989	37,000,000

The painting depicts Picasso as a harlequin at the bar of the café Lapin Agile. The owner of the café acquired the picture in exchange for food and drink at a time when Picasso was hard up. In 1989 it was bought by the Walter Annenberg Foundation.

7 Vincent van Gogh, *Sunflowers* Christie's, London, March 30, 1987	36,200,000

At the time, the most expensive picture ever sold (and still the most expensive sold in the UK), it was bought by the Yasuda Fire and Marine Insurance Company of Tokyo.

8 Pablo Picasso, *Acrobate et Jeune Arlequin* Christie's, London, November 28, 1988	35,500,000

Until the sale of Yo Picasso, *this held the world record for a 20th-century painting. It was bought by Mitsukoshi, a Japanese department store. (In Japan, many major stores have important art galleries.)*

9 Jacopo da Carucci (Pontormo), *Portrait of Duke Cosimo I de Medici* Christie's, New York, May 31, 1989	32,000,000

The world record price for an Old Master – and the only one in the Top 10 – it was bought by the J. Paul Getty Museum, Malibu.

10 Paul Cézanne, *Nature Morte – Les Grosses Pommes* Sotheby's, New York, May 11, 1993	26,000,000

Sold by one Greek shipowner, George Embiricos, and bought by another, Stavros Niarchos.

TOP 10

ARTISTS WITH MOST PAINTINGS SOLD FOR MORE THAN $1,000,000

PORTRAIT OF DR. GACHET
BY VINCENT VAN GOGH

Artist	No. of paintings sold for $1M+
1 Pablo Picasso	148
2 Auguste Renoir	142
3 Claude Monet	126
4 Edgar Degas	64
5 Marc Chagall	53
6 Camille Pissarro	49
7 Henri Matisse	45
8 Paul Cézanne	42
9 Vincent van Gogh	32
10= Jean Dubuffet	31
10= Amedeo Modigliani	31

TOP 10

MOST EXPENSIVE PAINTINGS BY WINSLOW HOMER

Work/sale	Price ($)
1 *The Signal of Distress* (1892–96) Sotheby's, New York, October 17, 1980	1,700,000
2 *The Unruly Calf* (1875) Sotheby's, New York, December 3, 1982	1,100,000
3= *Backrush* (no date) Sotheby's, New York, May 27, 1992	1,000,000
3= *The Whittling Boy* (1873) Christie's, New York, May 26, 1994	1,000,000
5 *Uncle Ned at Home* (1875) Christie's, New York, May 26, 1993	900,000
6 *Three Boys in a Dory* (1873) Christie's, New York, May 28, 1992	850,000
7 *The Initials* (1864) Sotheby's, New York, November 30, 1989	800,000
8 *In Charge of Baby* (1873) Sotheby's, New York, May 28, 1987	700,000
9 *Enchanted* (1874) Sotheby's, New York, December 5, 1985	650,000
10 *Looking Out to Sea* (1872) Sotheby's, New York, May 27, 1993	640,000

TOP 10
MOST EXPENSIVE WORKS BY FREDERIC REMINGTON

	Work	Sale/date	Price ($)
1	Attack on Supply Wagons (oil painting)	Sotheby's, New York, November 30, 1989	4,300,000
2	Coming Through the Rye (bronze)	Christie's, New York, May 25, 1989	4,000,000
3	Wounded Bunkie (bronze)	Sotheby's, New York, November 30, 1989	2,700,000
4	Wounded Bunkie equestrian group (bronze)	Sotheby's, New York, May 26, 1993	1,800,000
5	Coming Through the Rye (bronze)	Sotheby's, New York, December 2, 1993	1,100,000
6	Story of Where Sun Goes (oil painting)	Sotheby's, New York, November 30, 1989	750,000
7	The Bronco Buster (bronze)	Christie's, New York, June 1, 1984	630,000
8	The Frozen Shepherder (oil painting)	Christie's, New York, December 1, 1989	620,000
9	The Outlaw equestrian group (bronze)	Christie's, New York, December 1, 1989	600,000
10	Assault on His Dignity (oil painting)	Sotheby's, New York, May 30, 1985	570,000

TOP 10
MOST EXPENSIVE PAINTINGS BY AMERICAN ARTISTS

	Artist/work/sale	Price ($)
1	Willem de Kooning (b.1904), Interchange Sotheby's, New York, November 8, 1989	18,800,000
2	Jasper Johns (b.1930), False Start Sotheby's, New York, November 10, 1988	15,500,000
3	Jasper Johns, Two Flags Sotheby's, New York, November 8, 1989	11,000,000
4	Jackson Pollock (1912–56), Number 8, 1950 Sotheby's, New York, May 2, 1989	10,500,000
5	Willem de Kooning, July, Christie's, New York, November 7, 1990	8,000,000
6	Frederic Edwin Church (1826–1900), Home by the Lake, Scene in the Catskill Mountains, Sotheby's, New York, May 24, 1989	7,500,000
7	Robert Rauschenberg (b.1925), Rebus Sotheby's, New York, April 30, 1991	6,600,000
8	Willem de Kooning, Palisade, Sotheby's, New York, May 8, 1990	6,500,000
9	Jasper Johns, White Flag, Christie's, New York, November 9, 1988	6,400,000
10	Roy Lichtenstein (b.1923), Kiss II Christie's, New York, May 7, 1990	5,500,000

TOP 10
MOST EXPENSIVE PAINTINGS BY PABLO PICASSO

	Work/sale	Price ($)
1	Les Noces de Pierrette Binoche et Godeau, Paris, November 30, 1989	51,700,000
2	Self Portrait: Yo Picasso Sotheby's, New York, May 9, 1989	43,500,000
3	Au Lapin Agile Sotheby's, New York, November 15, 1989	37,000,000
4	Acrobate et Jeune Arlequin Christie's, London, November 28, 1988	35,500,000
5	Le Miroir Sotheby's, New York, November 15, 1989	24,000,000
6	Maternité Christie's, New York, June 14, 1988	22,500,000
7	Les Tuileries Christie's, London, June 25, 1990	22,000,000
8	Mère et Enfant Sotheby's, New York, November 15, 1989	17,000,000
9=	Famille de l'Arlequin Christie's, New York, November 14, 1989	14,000,000
9=	La Cage d'Oiseaux Sotheby's, New York, November 10, 1988	14,000,000

DID YOU KNOW
TOP 10 WOMEN ARTISTS
Seven of the ten most expensive paintings by women are by the American Impressionist Mary Cassatt (1845–1926). In first place is The Conversation, sold in 1988 for $4,100,000. Black Hollyhocks with Blue Larkspur by American Georgia O'Keeffe (1887–1986) fetched $1,800,000 in 1987. Finnish artist Helene Schjerfbeck (1862–1946) is the other woman in this list; her Balskorna – Dancing Shoe sold in 1990 for $1,600,000.

THE IMPRESSIONISTS

TOP 10
MOST EXPENSIVE PAINTINGS BY VINCENT VAN GOGH

	Painting/sale	Price ($)
1	*Portrait du Dr. Gachet* Christie's, New York, May 15, 1990	75,000,000
2	*Irises* Sotheby's, New York, November 11, 1987	49,000,000
3	*Sunflowers* Christie's, London, March 30, 1987	36,225,000
4	*Autoportrait* Christie's, New York, May 15, 1990	24,000,000
5	*Le Vieil If* Christie's, New York, November 14, 1989	18,500,000
6	*Le Pont de Trinquetaille* Christie's, London, June 29, 1987	18,400,000
7	*Adeline Ravoux* Christie's, New York, May 11, 1988	12,500,000
8	*Romans Parisiens, les Livres Jaunes* Christie's, London, June 27, 1988	10,920,000
9	*Carrière Près de Saint-Remy* Sotheby's, New York, November 15, 1989	10,500,000
10	*Paysage au Soleil Levant* Sotheby's, New York, April 24, 1985	9,000,000

TOP 10
MOST EXPENSIVE PAINTINGS BY PAUL CEZANNE

	Painting/sale	Price ($)
1	*Nature Morte – les Grosses Pommes* Sotheby's, New York, May 11, 1993	26,000,000
2	*Pommes et Serviette* Christie's, London, November 27, 1989	15,600,000
3	*Pichet et Fruits sur une Table* Sotheby's, New York, May 9, 1989	10,500,000
4	*La Côté du Galet, à Pontoise* Sotheby's, New York, May 10, 1988	8,400,000
5	*Arlequin* Sotheby's, London, November 29, 1988	7,480,000
6	*Le Jas de Bouffan* Sotheby's, New York, November 12, 1990	6,500,000
7	*Saint-Henri et la Baie de l'Estaque* Sotheby's, New York, May 10, 1988	6,200,000
8	*Carrière de Bibemus* Sotheby's, New York, November 15, 1989	6,000,000
9	*L'Homme à la Pipe* Christie's, London, November 30, 1992	5,056,000
10	*Les Reflets dans l'Eau* Sotheby's, New York, October 18, 1989	4,600,000

TOP 10
MOST EXPENSIVE PAINTINGS BY PAUL GAUGUIN

	Painting/sale	Price ($)
1	*Mata Mua – in Olden Times* Sotheby's, New York, May 9, 1989	22,000,000
2	*Te Fare Hyménée, La Maison des Chants*, Sotheby's, London, April 4, 1989	10,260,000
3	*Entre les Lys* Sotheby's, New York, November 15, 1989	10,000,000
4	*L'Allée des Alyscamps, Arles* Christie's, London, November 28, 1988	6,545,000
5	*Petit Breton a l'Oie* Sotheby's, London, November 28, 1989	6,240,000
6	*Ferme en Bretagne II* Christie's, New York, May 10, 1989	6,200,000
7	*Les Trois Huttes, Tahiti* Christie's, London, November 30, 1987	3,784,000
8	*Vaches au Bord de la Mer* Sotheby's, New York, October 18, 1989	3,600,000
9	*Mata Mua – in Olden Times* Sotheby's, New York, May 15, 1984	3,500,000
10	*Fruits Exotiques et Fleurs Rouges* Sotheby's, London, June 27, 1989	3,297,000

DID YOU KNOW

THE IMPRESSIONIST BOOM

After having their brand of art mocked and derided during their lifetimes, several of the pioneer Impressionists lived just long enough to see the public come to appreciate their work. However, since most of them had experienced years of poverty while they produced these masterpieces they would have been amazed by the escalation in the prices of their paintings. At the beginning of the 20th century, it was still possible to buy a painting by Vincent van Gogh for about $190, a Cézanne for $1,000, a Manet for $2,000, a Monet for under $5,000, and a Renoir for $10,000. Prices rose slowly but appreciably throughout the century; in 1958 van Gogh's *Public Garden in Arles* achieved a new record of $370,000 and by 1970 paintings by Impressionists including van Gogh, Monet, and Renoir had all achieved prices of more than $1,400,000. This upward trend continued: in 1980 van Gogh's *Le Jardin de Poète, Arles* was sold for $5,200,000, and in 1985 his *Paysage au Soleil Levant* made $9,000,000. A colossal price surge followed in the late 1980s, with van Gogh paintings consistently leading the way. In 1987 the sale of his *Sunflowers* trebled the previous record price for a van Gogh, and subsequently this figure was itself overtaken by *Irises* (sold later that year) and by *Portrait du Dr. Gachet* (sold in 1990). The latter is currently the most expensive painting in the world.

TOP 10

MOST EXPENSIVE PAINTINGS BY EDOUARD MANET

	Painting/sale	Price ($)
1	*La rue Mosnier aux Drapeaux* Christie's, New York, November 14, 1989	24,000,000
2	*Le Banc, le Jardin de Versailles* Christie's, New York, May 15, 1990	15,000,000
3	*La Promenade* Sotheby's, New York, November 15, 1989	13,500,000
4	*La rue Mosnier au Paveurs* Christie's, London, December 1, 1986	10,080,000
5	*Bouquet de Pivoines* Sotheby's, New York, November 13, 1990	4,000,000
6	*La Promenade* Christie's, New York, November 15, 1983	3,600,000
7	*Fleurs dans un Vase de Cristal* Christie's, New York, November 14, 1990	3,400,000
8	*Portrait de Madame Brunet* Christie's, New York, May 16, 1984	2,000,000
9	*Femme Assise au Jardin, ou Le Tricot* Christie's, London, June 27, 1988	1,848,000
10	*Les Travailleurs de la Mer* Christie's, New York, May 12, 1992	1,800,000

TOP 10

MOST EXPENSIVE PAINTINGS BY CLAUDE MONET

	Painting/sale	Price ($)
1	*Dans la Prairie* Sotheby's, London, June 28, 1988	21,840,000
2	*Le Parlement, Coucher de Soleil* Christie's, New York, May 10, 1989	13,000,000
3	*Le Pont du Chemin de Fer à Argenteuil* Christie's, London, November 28, 1988	11,594,000
4	*Le Bassin aux Nymphéas* Christie's, New York, November 11, 1992	11,000,000
5=	*Le Grand Canal* Sotheby's, New York, November 15, 1989	10,500,000
5=	*Nymphéas* Christie's, New York, November 14, 1989	10,500,000
7	*Santa Maria della Salute et le Grand Canal, Venise* Sotheby's, London, April 4, 1989	10,431,000
8	*Garden House on the Banks of the Zaan* Sotheby's, New York, May 9, 1989	10,000,000
9	*Le Parlement, Soleil Couchant* Christie's, New York, November 14, 1989	9,000,000
10	*La Jetée du Havre* Christie's, New York, May 12, 1993	8,800,000

TOP 10

MOST EXPENSIVE PAINTINGS BY PIERRE AUGUSTE RENOIR

	Painting/sale	Price ($)
1	*Au Moulin de la Galette* Sotheby's, New York, May 17, 1990	71,000,000
2=	*Jeune Fille au Chat* Sotheby's, New York, May 17, 1990	16,500,000
2=	*La Tasse de Chocolat* Sotheby's, New York, November 12, 1990	16,500,000
4	*La Promenade* Sotheby's, London, April 4, 1989	16,074,000
5	*La Liseuse* Christie's, New York, November 14, 1989	13,000,000
6	*Jeune Fille au Chapeau Garni de Fleurs des Champs* Sotheby's, New York, May 9, 1989	12,500,000
7	*La Loge* Christie's, New York, May 10, 1989	11,000,000
8	*Gabrielle à sa Coiffure* Christie's, New York, November 14, 1989	8,000,000
9	*Baigneuse, Femme en Jupe Rouge Essuyant les Pieds* Sotheby's, New York, November 11, 1988	7,750,000
10	*Jeune Fille Portant une Corbeille de Fleurs* Christie's, London, June 21, 1993	7,748,000

ART ON SHOW

TOP 10

BEST-ATTENDED EXHIBITIONS AT THE FINE ARTS MUSEUM, BOSTON

	Exhibition	Year	Attendance
1	Monet in the Nineties	1990	537,502
2	Renoir	1985	515,795
3	Pompeii	1978	432,080
4	New World: American Painting	1983	264,640
5	Pissaro	1981	235,012
6	Masters From The Cone Collection	1991	221,886
7	Rubens	1993	218,010
8	Living National Treasures of Japan	1982	197,456
9	Great Bronze Age of China	1981	192,175
10	Goya	1989	185,765

MUMMY MASK
Tutankhamun's mask was the highlight of the exhibition of his tomb treasures, which was highly successful both at the National Gallery, Washington, DC, and the Metropolitan Museum of Art, New York. The mask, which is made of solid gold and inlaid with glass and precious materials such as lapis lazuli, weighs over 22.5 lb (10.2 kg).

TOP 10

BEST-ATTENDED EXHIBITIONS AT THE NATIONAL GALLERY, WASHINGTON DC

	Exhibition	Year	Attendance
1	Rodin Rediscovered	1981–82	1,053,223
2	Treasure Houses of Britain	1985–86	990,474
3	Treasures of Tutankhamun	1976–77	835,924
4	Archaeological Finds of the People's Republic of China	1974–75	684,238
5	Ansel Adams: Classic Images	1985–86	651,652
6	The Splendor of Dresden	1978	620,089
7	The Art of Paul Gauguin	1988	596,058
8	Circa 1492: Art in the Age of Exploration	1991–92	568,192
9	Post-Impressionism: Cross Currents in European & American Painting	1980	557,533
10	Great French Paintings from The Barnes Foundation	1993	520,924

TOP 10

BEST-ATTENDED EXHIBITIONS AT THE METROPOLITAN MUSEUM OF ART, NEW YORK

	Exhibition	Year	Attendance
1	The Treasures of Tutankhamun	1978–79	1,226,467
2	The Mona Lisa	1963	1,077,000
3	The Vatican Collection: The Papacy and Art	1983	896,743
4	Seurat	1991–92	642,408
5	Van Gogh in St. Rémy and Auvers	1986–87	630,699
6	Van Gogh in Arles	1984	624,120
7	Mexico: Splendor of Thirty Centuries	1990–91	584,528
8	Masterpieces of Impressionism and Post-Impressionism: The Annenberg Collection	1991	560,734
9	Velazquez	1989–90	556,394
10	Degas	1988–89	540,363

TOP 10

BEST-ATTENDED EXHIBITIONS AT THE ART INSTITUTE OF CHICAGO

	Exhibition	Year	Attendance
1	A Century of Progress	1933	1,538,103
2	The Vatican Collection	1983	616,134
3	Pompeii AD 79	1978	489,118
4	Monet in the Nineties	1990	456,217
5	Paintings by Claude Monet	1975	384,458
6	The Art of Paul Gauguin	1988	374,477
7	A Day in the Country	1985–86	369,766
8	Half a Century of American Art	1939–40	363,093
9	Paintings by Renoir	1973	352,987
10	The Search for Alexander	1981	319,892

SYMBOL OF FREEDOM
Standing on a massive pedestal, Liberty bears a book of law and a burning torch that reaches 305 ft (93 m) above sea level.

TOP 10

MOST EXPENSIVE PHOTOGRAPHS EVER SOLD AT AUCTION

	Photographer/photograph/sale	Price ($)
1	Edward S. Curtis (American, 1868–1952), *The North American Indian**, 1907–30, Sotheby's, New York, October 7, 1993	662,500
2	Alfred Stieglitz (American, 1864–1946), *Georgia O'Keeffe: A Portrait – Hands with Thimble*, 1930, Christie's, New York, October 8, 1993	398,500
3=	Alfred Stieglitz, *Equivalents (21)**, 1920s Christie's, New York, October 30, 1989	396,000
3=	Edward S. Curtis, *The North American Indian**, 1907–30 Christie's, New York, October 13, 1992	396,000
5	Man Ray (American, 1890–1976), *Noir et Blanche**, 1926 Christie's, New York, April 21, 1994	354,500
6	Man Ray, *Hier, Demain, Aujourd'hui* (triptych), 1930–32 Christie's, New York, October 8, 1993	222,500
7	Man Ray, *Glass Tears, c.*1930 Sotheby's, London, May 7, 1993	195,000
8	Tina Modotti (Mexican, 1896–1942), *Two Callas*, 1925 Christie's, New York, October 8, 1993	189,500
9	Alexander Rodchenko (Russian, 1891–1956), *Girl with Leica*, 1934 Christie's, London, October 29, 1992	181,450
10	Tina Modotti, *Roses, Mexico*, 1925 Sotheby's, New York, April 17, 1991	165,000

* Collections; all others are single prints

TOP 10

TALLEST FREE-STANDING STATUES IN THE WORLD

	Statue	Height m	ft
1	*Chief Crazy Horse*, Thunderhead Mountain, South Dakota	172	563

Started in 1948 by Polish-American sculptor Korczak Ziolkowski and continued after his death in 1982 by his widow and eight of his children, this gigantic equestrian statue is even longer than it is high (641 ft/195 m). It is not expected to be completed until the next century.

2	*Buddha*, Tokyo, Japan	120	394

This Japan-Taiwanese project, unveiled in 1993, took seven years to complete and weighs 110 tons.

3	*The Indian Rope Trick*, Riddersberg Säteri, Jönköping, Sweden	103	337

Sculptor Calle Örnemark's 159-ton wooden sculpture depicts a long strand of "rope" held by a fakir, while another figure ascends.

4	*Motherland, 1967*, Volgograd, Russia	82	270

Unveiled in 1967, this concrete statue of a woman with raised sword commemorates the Soviet victory at the Battle of Stalingrad (1942–43).

5	*Buddha*, Bamian, Afghanistan	53	173

Near this 3rd–4th century AD statue lie the remains of the even taller Sakya Buddha, said to have measured 1,000 ft/305 m.

	Statue	Height m	ft
6	*Kannon*, Otsubo-yama, near Tokyo, Japan	52	170

The immense statue of the goddess of mercy was unveiled in 1961 in honor of the dead of the Second World War.

7	*Statue of Liberty*, New York	46	151

Designed by Auguste Bartholdi and presented to the US by the people of France, the statue was shipped in sections to Liberty (formerly Bedloes) Island where it was assembled. It was unveiled on October 28, 1886, and restored and reinaugurated on July 4, 1986. It consists of sheets of copper on an iron frame, and weighs 252 tons in total.

8	*Christ*, Rio de Janeiro, Brazil	38	125

The work of sculptor Paul Landowski and engineer Heitor da Silva Costa, the figure of Christ weighs 1,282 tons. It was unveiled in 1931 and has recently been restored.

9	*Tian Tan (Temple of Heaven) Buddha* Po Lin Monastery, Lantau Island, Hong Kong	34	112

Completed after 20 years of work and unveiled on December 29, 1993, the bronze statue weighs 275 tons and cost £6,000,000 ($9,000,000).

10	*Colossi of Memnon*, Karnak, Egypt	21	70

Two seated sandstone figures of Pharaoh Amenhotep III.

MUSIC

T O P 1 0

SINGLES OF ALL TIME WORLDWIDE

	Artist/title	Sales exceed
1	Bing Crosby, *White Christmas*	30,000,000
2	Bill Haley & His Comets, *Rock Around the Clock*	17,000,000
3	Beatles, *I Want To Hold Your Hand*	12,000,000
4=	Elvis Presley, *It's Now or Never*	10,000,000
4=	Whitney Houston, *I Will Always Love You*	10,000,000
6=	Elvis Presley, *Hound Dog/ Don't Be Cruel*	9,000,000
6=	Paul Anka, *Diana*	9,000,000
8=	Beatles, *Hey Jude*	8,000,000
8=	Monkees, *I'm a Believer*	8,000,000
10=	Beatles, *Can't Buy Me Love*	7,000,000
10=	Band Aid, *Do They Know it's Christmas?*	7,000,000
10=	USA For Africa, *We Are the World*	7,000,000

FIRST TOP 10 SINGLES CHART IN THE US

1	Tommy Dorsey, *I'll Never Smile Again*	6	Charlie Barnet, *Where Was I*
2	Jimmy Dorsey, *The Breeze and I*	7	Glenn Miller, *Pennsylvania 6-5000*
3	Glenn Miller, *Imagination*	8	Tommy Dorsey, *Imagination*
4	Kay Kyser, *Playmates*	9	Bing Crosby, *Sierra Sue*
5	Glenn Miller, *Fools Rush In*	10	Mitchell Ayres, *Make-Believe Island*

This was the first singles Top 10 compiled by *Billboard* magazine, for its issue dated July 20, 1940. Since the 7-inch 45-rpm single was still the best part of a decade in the future, all these would have been 10-inch 78-rpm disks. Note the almost total domination of big-name big bands more than a half century ago – and spare a thought for Mitchell Ayres, who crept in at the bottom of this very first chart, and then never had a hit again.

T O P 1 0

ARTISTS WITH THE LONGEST CHART CAREER RUNS, 1955–1994

	Artist	Chart span Years	Months		Artist	Chart span Years	Months
1	Aretha Franklin	33	3	6	Smokey Robinson	32	1
2	Tina Turner	33	2	7	B.B. King	31	8
3	Paul Simon	33	0	8	Dion	31	3
4	Roy Orbison	32	11	9=	Ronald Isley	30	9
5	Ray Charles	32	4	9=	Patti Labelle	30	9

The Queen Of Soul tops the list thanks to her 1994 hit *Willing to Forgive*, which stretched a US chart career that began in February 1961. Roy Orbison's achievement is even more remarkable. His career, which began in 1956, stalled in 1967. He did not chart again until 1980, and it was another nine years before his Top 10 smash, *You Got It*, made the survey just before his death.

T O P   1 0

SINGLES OF ALL TIME IN THE US

	Artist/title	Released
1	Bing Crosby, *White Christmas*	1942
2	Beatles, *I Want to Hold Your Hand*	1964
3	Elvis Presley, *Hound Dog/Don't Be Cruel*	1956
4	Elvis Presley, *It's Now or Never*	1960
5	Whitney Houston, *I Will Always Love You*	1992
6	Beatles, *Hey Jude*	1968
7	USA For Africa, *We Are the World*	1985
8	Tag Team, *Whoomp! There It Is*	1993
9	Bryan Adams, *Everything I Do (I Do It for You)*	1991
10	Chipmunks, *The Chipmunk Song*	1958

T O P   1 0

SINGLES THAT STAYED LONGEST AT NO. 1 IN THE US*

	Artist/title	Year released	Weeks at No. 1
1	Whitney Houston, *I Will Always Love You*	1992	14
2	Boyz II Men, *End of the Road*	1992	13
3=	Elvis Presley, *Don't Be Cruel/Hound Dog*	1956	11
3=	All-4-One, *I Swear*	1994	11
5=	Perez Prado, *Cherry Pink and Apple Blossom White*	1955	10
5=	Debby Boone, *You Light Up My Life*	1977	10
5=	Olivia Newton-John, *Physical*	1981	10
8=	Bobby Darin, *Mack the Knife*	1959	9
8=	Beatles, *Hey Jude*	1968	9
8=	Diana Ross and Lionel Richie, *Endless Love*	1981	9
8=	Kim Carnes, *Bette Davis Eyes*	1981	9
8=	Guy Mitchell, *Singing the Blues*	1956	9
8=	Percy Faith, *Theme from "A Summer Place"*	1960	9

* *Based on Billboard charts from 1955 when Billboard's US Top 100 was inaugurated for singles*

White Christmas is still the US's all-time most-charted single, having been a major Yuletide seller every Christmas for the 21 years from its original release in 1942. Total US sales are thought to be somewhere in the region of 15,000,000 disks, more than twice the number for the Beatles' biggest seller at No. 2, *I Want To Hold Your Hand*. The Whitney Houston release became the first single to exceed sales of 4,000,000 in the 1990s, joined in 1993 by the equally quadruple-platinum rap novelty hit by Tag Team.

T O P   1 0

YOUNGEST ARTISTS TO HAVE NO. 1 SINGLES IN THE US

	Artist/year	Age* yrs	mths
1	Michael Jackson (1970)	11	5
2	Jimmy Boyd (1952)	12	11
3	Stevie Wonder (1963)	13	2
4	Donny Osmond (1971)	13	9
5	Laurie London (1958)	14	3
6	Little Peggy March (1963)	15	1
7	Brenda Lee (1960)	15	7
8=	Paul Anka (1957)	16	1
8=	Tiffany (1987)	16	1
10=	Little Eva (1962)	17	1
10=	Lesley Gore (1963)	17	1

* *During first week of debut No. 1 US single*

T O P   1 0

OLDEST ARTISTS TO HAVE NO. 1 SINGLES IN THE US

	Artist/year	Age* yrs	mths
1	Louis Armstrong (1964)	63	10
2	Lawrence Welk (1961)	57	11
3	Morris Stoloff (1956)	57	10
4	Frank Sinatra (1967)	51	4
5	Lorne Greene (1964)	49	9
6=	Dean Martin (1964)	47	2
6=	Bill Medley (1987)	47	2
8	Sammy Davis Jr. (1972)	46	6
9	Tina Turner (1984)	45	9
10	Dionne Warwick (1986)	45	1

* *During final week of last or most recent No. 1 US single*

Five of these artists are still alive, so there is still potential for boosting their ranking.

SINGLES OF THE DECADES

TOP 10

SINGLES OF EACH YEAR OF THE 1960s IN THE US

1960	Elvis Presley, *It's Now or Never*
1961	Del Shannon, *Runaway*
1962	Ray Charles, *I Can't Stop Loving You*
1963	Jimmy Gilmer & The Fireballs, *Sugar Shack*
1964	Beatles, *I Want to Hold Your Hand*
1965	Beatles, *Help!*
1966	Staff Sergeant Barry Sadler, *The Ballad of the Green Berets*
1967	Lulu, *To Sir with Love*
1968	Beatles, *Hey Jude*
1969	Archies, *Sugar Sugar*

TOP 10

SINGLES OF EACH YEAR OF THE 1970s IN THE US

1970	Jackson 5, *I'll Be There*
1971	Three Dog Night, *Joy to the World*
1972	Roberta Flack, *The First Time Ever I Saw Your Face*
1973	Dawn, *Tie a Yellow Ribbon Round the Old Oak Tree*
1974	Barbra Streisand, *The Way We Were*
1975	Captain and Tennille, *Love Will Keep Us Together*
1976	Johnnie Taylor, *Disco Lady*
1977	Debby Boone, *You Light Up My Life*
1978	Bee Gees, *Night Fever*
1979	Gloria Gaynor, *I Will Survive*

TOP 10

SINGLES OF EACH YEAR OF THE 1980s IN THE US

1980	Queen, *Another One Bites the Dust*	1985	USA For Africa, *We Are the World*
1981	Diana Ross and Lionel Richie, *Endless Love*	1986	Dionne Warwick and Friends, *That's What Friends Are For*
1982	Survivor, *Eye of the Tiger*	1987	Whitney Houston, *I Wanna Dance with Somebody (Who Loves Me)*
1983	Kenny Rogers and Dolly Parton, *Islands in the Stream*	1988	Beach Boys, *Kokomo*
1984	Prince, *When Doves Cry*	1989	Tone Loc, *Wild Thing*

DID YOU KNOW

LISTENER'S CHOICE

The story of the jukebox began in 1889, with a hand-operated Edison phonograph with a coinbox and four listening tubes. The word "jukebox" first appeared in print in 1939. In the 1950s the launch of the 45-rpm single revolutionized jukebox design; the latest development is the introduction of compact disc-playing models.

TOP 10

SINGLES OF THE 1950s IN THE US

	Title	Artist	Year
1	*Hound Dog/Don't Be Cruel*	Elvis Presley	1956
2	*The Chipmunk Song*	Chipmunk	1958
3	*Love Letters in the Sand*	Pat Boone	1957
4	*Rock Around the Clock*	Bill Haley & His Comets	1955
5	*Tom Dooley*	Kingston Trio	1958
6	*Love Me Tender*	Elvis Presley	1956
7	*Tennessee Waltz*	Patti Page	1951
8	*Volare (Nel Blu Dipintu Di Blu)*	Domenico Modugno	1958
9	*Jailhouse Rock*	Elvis Presley	1957
10	*All Shook Up*	Elvis Presley	1957

Rock 'n' roll and Elvis Presley were the twin catalysts that ignited record sales in the US in the middle of the 1950s, and both are represented strongly in the decade's biggest sellers, the former mostly in the person of the latter. While Presley's double-sider, topping 6,000,000, was the decade's top single by a wide margin, the fastest seller was *The Chipmunk Song*, which moved a remarkable 3,500,000 copies in five weeks.

TOP 10

SINGLES OF THE 1960s IN THE US

	Title	Artist	Year
1	*I Want to Hold Your Hand*	Beatles	1964
2	*It's Now or Never*	Elvis Presley	1960
3	*Hey Jude*	Beatles	1968
4	*The Ballad of the Green Berets*	Staff Sergeant Barry Sadler	1966
5	*Love Is Blue*	Paul Mauriat	1968
6	*I'm a Believer*	Monkees	1966
7	*Can't Buy Me Love*	Beatles	1964
8	*She Loves You*	Beatles	1964
9	*Sugar Sugar*	Archies	1969
10	*The Twist*	Chubby Checker	1960

Though the 1960s are recalled as the decade in which British music invaded America, the only UK representatives among the decade's 10 biggest sellers in the US are by the leaders of that invasion, the Beatles – although they do completely dominate the list, holding Nos. 1, 3, 7, and 8. Elvis Presley's *It's Now or Never*, with sales of around 5,000,000, almost equaled his total on *Hound Dog/Don't Be Cruel* which had made it the previous decade's biggest single.

TOP 10

SINGLES OF THE 1970s IN THE US

	Title	Artist	Year
1	*You Light Up My Life*	Debby Boone	1977
2	*Le Freak*	Chic	1978
3	*Night Fever*	Bee Gees	1978
4	*Stayin' Alive*	Bee Gees	1978
5	*Shadow Dancing*	Andy Gibb	1978
6	*Disco Lady*	Johnnie Taylor	1976
7	*I'll Be There*	Jackson 5	1970
8	*Star Wars Theme/ Cantina Band*	Meco	1977
9	*Car Wash*	Rose Royce	1976
10	*Joy to the World*	Three Dog Night	1971

During the last four years of the 1970s, singles sales in the US rose to their highest-ever level, and chart-topping records were almost routinely selling over 2,000,000 copies. Also at their commercial peak in the States during this period were the Bee Gees, who appropriately have the biggest presence on this chart, both with two of their own songs and as writer/producers of younger brother Andy Gibb's *Shadow Dancing*.

TOP 10

SINGLES OF THE 1980s IN THE US

	Title	Artist	Year
1	*We Are the World*	USA For Africa	1985
2	*Physical*	Olivia Newton-John	1981
3	*Endless Love*	Diana Ross and Lionel Richie	1981
4	*Eye of the Tiger*	Survivor	1982
5	*I Love Rock 'n' Roll*	Joan Jett & The Blackhearts	1982
6	*When Doves Cry*	Prince	1984
7	*Celebration*	Kool & The Gang	1981
8	*Another One Bites the Dust*	Queen	1980
9	*Wild Thing*	Tone Loc	1989
10	*Islands in the Stream*	Kenny Rogers and Dolly Parton	1983

America's top-selling single of the 1980s was, rather fittingly, a record that included contributions from many of those artists who had become the recording élite during the decade – the charity single for Africa's famine victims, *We Are the World*. Meanwhile, three of the close runners-up – *Endless Love* (same film), *Eye of the Tiger* (from *Rocky III*), and *When Doves Cry* (from Prince's *Purple Rain*) – were all taken from movies.

CLASSIC ROCK

T O P   1 0

WHITNEY HOUSTON SINGLES IN THE US

1	*I Will Always Love You*	1992
2	*I Wanna Dance with Somebody*	1987
3	*The Greatest Love of All*	1986
4	*How Will I Know*	1986
5	*I'm Your Baby Tonight*	1990
6	*All the Man that I Need*	1991
7	*Saving All My Love for You*	1985
8	*Where Do Broken Hearts Go*	1988
9	*Didn't we Almost Have it All*	1987
10	*So Emotional*	1987

Whitney Houston is the most successful female vocalist of the past 10 years. This list comprises all of Whitney's chart-toppers, from her first, *Saving All My Love for You*, released in 1985, to her latest, 1992's *I Will Always Love You*. The latter is the bestselling single of the past 30 years in the US, as well as being the bestselling single ever by a female artiste in both the US and the world.

T O P   1 0

BEATLES SINGLES IN THE US

1	*I Want to Hold Your Hand*	1964
2	*Hey Jude*	1968
3	*Can't Buy Me Love*	1964
4	*She Loves You*	1964
5	*I Feel Fine*	1964
6	*Get Back*	1969
7	*Help!*	1965
8	*A Hard Day's Night*	1964
9	*Come Together/Something*	1969
10	*Yesterday*	1965

The top four titles on this list, all of which sold more than 3,000,000, also figure among America's 10 biggest-selling singles of the 1960s, with *I Want to Hold Your Hand*, the song with which the Beatles first made their name in the US, becoming that decade's top seller.

T O P   1 0

ROLLING STONES SINGLES IN THE US

1	*(I Can't Get No) Satisfaction*	1965
2	*Miss You*	1978
3	*Honky Tonk Women*	1969
4	*Get Off of My Cloud*	1965
5	*Ruby Tuesday*	1967
6	*Angie*	1973
7	*Brown Sugar*	1971
8	*Paint it Black*	1964
9	*19th Nervous Breakdown*	1966
10	*Jumpin' Jack Flash*	1968

Unlike in the UK, where the Stones' Top 10 sellers all occurred before 1970, the group's US successes have been more evenly spread over their career, with second-placed *Miss You* perhaps benefiting from being released during the period in 1978 when American singles sales were at their all-time height.

STILL GOING STRONG
Mick Jagger continues to be as energetic as ever on the Rolling Stones' world tours.

T O P 1 0

ELVIS PRESLEY SINGLES IN THE US

1	*Don't Be Cruel/Hound Dog*	1956
2	*It's Now or Never*	1960
3	*Love Me Tender*	1956
4	*Heartbreak Hotel*	1956
5	*Jailhouse Rock*	1957
6	*All Shook Up*	1957
7	*(Let Me Be Your) Teddy Bear*	1957
8	*Are You Lonesome Tonight?*	1960
9	*Don't*	1958
10	*Too Much*	1957

Elvis had dozens of million-selling singles, scattered throughout his career, but most of his absolute monsters were during his 1950s heyday when he was the spearhead of rock 'n' roll music. The inspired coupling of *Don't Be Cruel* and *Hound Dog*, which held the number one spot for almost a quarter of 1956, sold some 6,000,000 copies in the US alone. *It's Now or Never*, the biggest of his post-Army successes, sold in the region of 5,000,000.

THE KING
Elvis's popularity was at its zenith in the 1950s. His music still enjoys a huge following today.

T O P 1 0

MICHAEL JACKSON SINGLES IN THE US

1	*Billie Jean*	1983
2	*Rock with You*	1980
3	*Beat It*	1983
4	*Don't Stop 'Til You Get Enough*	1979
5	*Say Say Say**	1983
6	*I Just Can't Stop Loving You*	1987
7	*Black or White*	1990
8	*The Girl Is Mine**	1982
9	*Bad*	1987
10	*Man in the Mirror*	1988

* Duet with Paul McCartney

The first eight of the Top 10 titles here sold over 1,000,000 copies each in the US alone, and all the singles in the list reached No. 1 on the Hot 100.

T O P 1 0

PRINCE SINGLES IN THE US

1	*When Doves Cry*	1984
2	*Kiss*	1986
3	*Let's Go Crazy*	1984
4	*Purple Rain*	1984
5	*Batdance*	1989
6	*Cream*	1991
7	*U Got the Look*	1987
8	*Raspberry Beret*	1985
9	*The Most Beautiful Girl in the World*	1994
10	*Little Red Corvette*	1983

When Doves Cry is the only Prince single to sell over 2,000,000 units in the US, and was featured in his most successful film project, *Purple Rain*, the soundtrack of which also spawned the 1,000,000-plus selling singles at Nos. 3 and 4.

T O P 1 0

MADONNA SINGLES IN THE US

1	*Like a Virgin*	1984
2	*Vogue*	1990
3	*Like a Prayer*	1989
4	*Crazy for You*	1985
5	*Justify My Love*	1990
6	*This Used to Be My Playground*	1992
7	*Papa Don't Preach*	1986
8	*Open Your Heart*	1986
9	*Live to Tell*	1986
10	*Who's That Girl*	1987

Of these US No. 1 hits, the first five of which were 1,000,000-plus sellers, *Crazy for You* came from the film soundtrack to *Vision Quest*; *This Used to Be My Playground* featured in *A League of Their Own*; *Live To Tell* was the theme to the movie *At Close Range*; and *Who's That Girl* was the title cut from the film of that name.

RECORD BREAKERS

WHITNEY HOUSTON
Since the mid-1980s Whitney Houston has had a hugely successful career. Her single I Will Always Love You, *and the film* The Bodyguard *(in which she had a starring role), were smash hits both in the US and worldwide.*

TOP 10

SINGLES BY FEMALE VOCALISTS IN THE US

1	Whitney Houston, *I Will Always Love You*
2	Debbie Boone, *You Light Up My Life*
3	Olivia Newton-John, *Physical*
4	Joan Jett & The Blackhearts, *I Love Rock 'n' Roll*
5	Gloria Gaynor, *I Will Survive*
6	Donna Summer, *Bad Girls*
7	Samantha Sang, *Emotions*
8	Donna Summer, *Hot Stuff*
9	Lulu, *To Sir with Love*
10	Jeannie C. Riley, *Harper Valley P.T.A.*

Among these blockbusters, all of them 2,000,000-plus sellers, it is fitting that Whitney Houston's multi-platinum success from *The Bodyguard Original Soundtrack* was also written by a woman – Dolly Parton – whose original version of *I Will Always Love You* peaked in 1982 at a lowly No. 53.

TOP 10

CHRISTMAS SINGLES OF ALL TIME IN THE US

1	Bing Crosby, *White Christmas*
2	Bing Crosby, *Silent Night/Adeste Fideles*
3	Gene Autry, *Rudolph the Red-Nosed Reindeer*
4	Chipmunks, *The Chipmunk Song*
5	Jimmy Boyd, *I Saw Mommy Kissing Santa Claus*
6	Harry Simeone Chorale, *The Little Drummer Boy*
7	Band Aid, *Do They Know It's Christmas?*
8	Bing Crosby, *I'll Be Home For Christmas*
9	Elmo & Patsy, *Grandma Got Run Over By a Reindeer*
10	Bobby Helms, *Jingle Bell Rock*

Most of America's bestselling Christmas singles come from the middle years of the century, with five of this Top 10 list predating the rock era, and only two titles – Band Aid's *Do They Know It's Christmas?* and Elmo & Patsy's comedy item (which has sold over 1,000,000 in recent years without, curiously, ever making the US singles chart) – are more recent than the 1950s. Bing Crosby's *White Christmas* is the world's all-time bestselling single.

TOP 10

FOREIGN-LANGUAGE SINGLES IN THE US

1	Domenico Modugno, *Volare (Nel Blu Dipintu Di Blu)*
2	Singing Nun, *Dominique*
3	Kyu Sakamoto, *Sukiyaki*
4	Los Lobos, *La Bamba*
5	Falco, *Rock Me Amadeus*
6	Nena, *99 Luftballons*
7	Ritchie Valens, *La Bamba*
8	Lolita, *Sailor*
9	Emilio Pericoli, *Al Di La*
10	Sandpipers, *Guantanamera*

With five weeks at No. 1 and sales of over 2,000,000, Domenico Modugno's 1958 smash hit *Volare* still holds the mantle of all-time sales champion among foreign-language singles, although *La Bamba*, with a double showing here, is easily the most successful foreign-language song. The hits of the coincidentally single-named Austrian singers Falco and Lolita and the German Nena were all sung in German. Falco's and Nena's singles also reached No.1 in the UK, where the latter's was rerecorded in English as *99 Red Balloons*. There, having failed to make the charts, Lolita's 1960 *Sailor* was also translated into English and became a No.1 hit for Petula Clark.

T O P 1 0

HEAVY METAL SINGLES OF ALL TIME IN THE US

1 Survivor, *Eye of the Tiger*

2 REO Speedwagon, *Keep On Loving You*

3 Joan Jett & The Blackhearts, *I Love Rock 'n' Roll*

4 Guns N' Roses, *Sweet Child o' Mine*

5 Foreigner, *I Want to Know What Love Is*

6 Van Halen, *Jump*

7 Styx, *Babe*

8 Sheriff, *When I'm With You*

9 Bachman Turner Overdrive, *You Ain't Seen Nothing Yet/Free Wheelin'*

10 Foreigner, *Waiting for a Girl Like You*

Eye of the Tiger, which sold 2,000,000 copies, benefited not least from its exposure in the *Rocky III* movie, while the million-selling *You Ain't Seen Nothing Yet* has continued to sell since hitting US No. 1 in 1974, thanks to President Reagan's repeated use of the phrase and song at Republican political conventions during the 1980s. Despite both entries being ballads, Foreigner's huge popularity as a hard rock act has been consistent since their chart debut in 1977.

T O P 1 0

RAP SINGLES OF ALL TIME IN THE US

1 Tag Team, *Whoomp! There It Is*

2 Tone Loc, *Wild Thing*

3 Sir Mix-A-Lot, *Baby Got Back*

4 Kris Kross, *Jump*

5 Wreckx-N-Effect, *Rump Shaker*

6 Tone Loc, Funky *Cold Medina*

7 Vanilla Ice, *Ice Ice Baby*

8 Young MC, *Bust a Move*

9 DJ Jazzy Jeff & The Fresh Prince, *Parents Just Don't Understand*

10 Salt 'n' Pepa, *Push It*

Just missing the top 10, Kurtis Blow's *The Breaks*, released as far back as 1980, was the first rap single to sell over 1,000,000 copies and remains a seminal release in the history of the genre. Once written off as a musical fad, rap currently dominates the American Singles sales music scene, with the top five titles having sold over 2,000,000 units each.

T O P 1 0

COUNTRY SINGLES OF ALL TIME IN THE US

1 Dolly Parton and Kenny Rogers, *Islands in the Stream*

2 Oakridge Boys, *Elvira*

3 Billy Ray Cyrus, *Achy Breaky Heart*

4 C.W. McCall, *Convoy*

5 Jeannie C. Riley, *Harper Valley P.T.A.*

6 Johnny Cash, *A Boy Named Sue*

7 Lynn Anderson, *Rose Garden*

8 Roger Miller, *King of the Road*

9 Charlie Daniels Band, *The Devil Went Down to Georgia*

10 Crystal Gayle, *Don't it Make My Brown Eyes Blue*

Nos. 1 and 2 are the only Country singles to sell more than 2,000,000 copies in the US, although Billy Ray Cyrus' huge hit, *Achy Breaky Heart*, approached the same sales achievement in the summer of 1992. All of the other titles listed have sold over 1,000,000 copies.

T O P 1 0

INSTRUMENTAL SINGLES OF ALL TIME IN THE US

1 Paul Mauriat, *Love Is Blue*

2 Meco, *Star Wars Theme*

3 Percy Faith, Theme From *A Summer Place*

4 Anton Karas, *The Harry Lime Theme (The Third Man)*

5 Champs, *Tequila*

6 Acker Bilk, *Stranger on the Shore*

7 Perez Prado, *Cherry Pink and Apple Blossom White*

8 Tornados, *Telstar*

9 Bert Kaempfert, *Wonderland By Night*

10 Lawrence Welk, *Calcutta*

If this Top 10 reveals anything, it is that non-vocal hits are more likely to be found in the "middle-of-the-road" sector than in rock 'n' roll. Most of these pieces are the equivalent of ballads, with only *Tequila*, possibly *Telstar*, and just possibly Meco's disco adaptation of *Star Wars* qualifying as rock music.

T O P 1 0

POSTHUMOUS SINGLES OF ALL TIME IN THE US

1 John Lennon, *(Just Like) Starting Over*

2 Jim Croce, *Time in a Bottle*

3 John Lennon, *Woman*

4 Otis Redding, *(Sittin' on) The Dock of the Bay*

5 Elvis Presley, *My Way*

6 Janis Joplin, *Me and Bobby McGee*

7 John Lennon, *Nobody Told Me*

8 Roy Orbison, *You Got It*

9 Sam Cooke, *Shake*

10 Buddy Holly, *It Doesn't Matter Anymore*

While Lennon is proving to be the most popular posthumous singles artist, the greatest length of time between an artist's death and subsequent chart success is held by Nat King Cole who "duetted" with his daughter Natalie Cole on her 1991 hit *Unforgettable* (he died on February 15, 1965). The single featured Nat's vocal dubbed in from his original 1952 hit.

IS THIS A RECORD?

TOP 10

SINGLES OF ALL TIME IN THE UK BANNED BY THE BBC

1 Frankie Goes To Hollywood, *Relax*
2 Jane Birkin and Serge Gainsbourg, *Je T'Aime . . . Moi Non Plus*
3 Ricky Valance, *Tell Laura I Love Her*
4 Sex Pistols, *God Save the Queen*
5 George Michael, *I Want Your Sex*
6 Jasper Carrott, *Magic Roundabout*
7 Wings, *Hi Hi Hi*
8 Max Romeo, *Wet Dream*
9 Judge Dread, *Big Seven*
10 Judge Dread, *Big Six*

Until recently, BBC radio was prone to keep records off the airwaves if (a) their melody was a desecration of a classical piece, (b) their lyrics were deemed offensive due to a concern with sex, drugs, death, or politics, or (c) they mentioned trade names, which was reckoned to be against the BBC's charter. Most of those on this list were placed in category (b) – and yet they all became Top 10 hits regardless.

TOP 10

KARAOKE SONGS IN THE US, 1993

	Song	Original artist
1	*New York, New York*	Frank Sinatra
2	*My Way*	Frank Sinatra
3	*Love Shack*	B52s
4	*Mack the Knife*	Bobby Darin
5	*The Rose*	Bette Midler
6	*Takin' Care of Business*	Bachman-Turner Overdrive
7	*Hello Dolly!*	Louis Armstrong
8	*Friends in Low Places*	Garth Brooks
9	*Greatest Love of All*	George Benson
10	*Crazy*	Patsy Cline

This Top 10, based on data supplied by *American Karaoke Magazine*, was assembled from a survey of Karaoke DJs (or "KJs") across the US, where bars and clubs often specialize in one music genre, usually standards, pop, rock, or country.

TOP 10

JUKEBOX SINGLES OF ALL TIME IN THE US

1 Patsy Cline, *Crazy* (1962)
2 Bob Seger, *Old Time Rock 'n' Roll* (1979)
3 Elvis Presley, *Hound Dog/Don't Be Cruel* (1956)
4 Marvin Gaye, *I Heard It Through the Grapevine* (1968)
5 Bobby Darin, *Mack The Knife* (1959)
6 Bill Haley & His Comets, *Rock Around the Clock* (1955)
7 Doors, *Light My Fire* (1967)
8 Otis Redding, *(Sittin' on) The Dock of the Bay* (1968)
9 Temptations, *My Girl* (1965)
10 Frank Sinatra, *New York, New York* (1980)

This list was compiled in 1992 by the Amusement and Music Operators Association, whose members service and operate over 250,000 jukeboxes in the US, and is based on the estimated popularity of jukebox singles from 1950 to the present. The list is updated every three years: the Righteous Brothers' *Unchained Melody* was the highest new entry into the Top 40 in 1992, at No. 12 (due, in part, to its being the featured song in the movie *Ghost*).

TOP 10

ONE-HIT WONDERS OF ALL TIME IN THE US

1 USA For Africa, *We Are the World*
2 Bobby McFerrin, *Don't Worry Be Happy*
3 M, *Pop Muzik*
4 Zager & Evans, *In the Year 2525 (Exordium and Terminus)*
5 Jan Hammer, *Miami Vice* (theme)
6 Elegants, *Little Star*
7 Hollywood Argyles, *Alley-Oop*
8 Laurie London, *He's Got the Whole World (In His Hands)*
9 Morris Stoloff, *Moonglow* (theme from *Picnic*)
10 Silhouettes, *Get a Job*

All of these acts hit US No. 1 with their only American chart appearance, but never followed up with any other rock chart disc. The charity ensemble USA For Africa's only single release is by far the most successful one-hit wonder, with over 4,000,000 copies sold, while numbers two to four all sold in excess of 1,000,000 – earning the artists enough to retire without another chart appearance. Honorable mention to Tag Team's 1993 smash *Whoomp! There It Is*: although it peaked only at No. 2 on the Hot 100, it sold more than 4,000,000 copies, and, as a rap novelty, seems destined to become a notable one-off success.

TOP 10

FIRST ARTISTS TO FEATURE IN A COCA-COLA TV COMMERCIAL

	Act/Jingle	Year
1	McGuire Sisters, *Pause for a Coke*	1958
2=	Brothers Four*, *Refreshing New Feeling*	1960
2=	Anita Bryant, *Refreshing New Feeling*	1960
2=	Connie Francis, *Refreshing New Feeling*	1960
5=	Fortunes, *Things Go Better with Coke*	1963
5=	Limelighters*, *Things Go Better with Coke*	1963
7	Ray Charles, *Things Go Better with Coke*	1969
8=	Bobby Goldboro, *It's the Real Thing*	1971
8=	New Seekers*, *It's the Real Thing*	1971
10	Dottie West*, *It's the Real Thing (Country Sunshine)*	1972

* *Artist provided only the audio soundtrack.*

Coke has used music artists in its promotion since the 1900s. In the 1950s they sponsored music TV shows for the likes of Eddie Fisher and Mario Lanza. 1980s ads featured Robert Plant and Chuck Berry, and recent ads include George Michael and Paula Abdul.

MOST FREQUENTLY RECORDED SONGS IN THE US, 1900–50

	Title	Year first recorded
1	*St. Louis Blues*	1914
2	*Tea for Two*	1924
3	*Body and Soul*	1930
4	*After You've Gone*	1918
5	*How High the Moon*	1940
6	*Blue Skies*	1927
7	*Dinah*	1925
8	*Ain't Misbehavin'*	1929
9	*Honeysuckle Rose*	1929
10	*Stardust*	1929

WORST RECORDS OF ALL TIME?

1	Jimmy Cross, *I Want My Baby Back*
2	Zara Leander, *Wunderbar*
3	Legendary Stardust Cowboy, *Paralysed*
4	Pat Campbell, *The Deal*
5	Nervous Norvus, *Transfusion*
6	Jess Conrad, *This Pullover*
7	Mel & Dave, *Spinning Wheel*
8	Dickey Lee, *Laurie*
9	Mrs. Miller, *A Lover's Concerto*
10	Tania Day, *I Get So Lonely*

In 1978, London Capital Radio DJ Kenny Everett polled his listeners on their least favorite songs from the discs he regularly played in a "ghastly records" spot. From 6,000 replies, these were the Top (or Bottom) 10, which went on to headline a special "All-Time Worst" show. Mostly obscure before Everett dragged them up, several of these have since become bywords of bad taste on vinyl, particularly Jimmy Cross's 1965 tale of necrophiliac love which proudly tops this grisly list.

FIRST WORDS OF POPULAR SONGS

	Word	Incidence		Word	Incidence
1	I	226	9	Oh	48
2	My	115	10=	If	46
3	I'm	94	10=	I'll	46
4	When	93			
5	You	72			
6=	It's	58			
6=	Little	58			
8	In	55			

This Top 10 is based on a survey of about 6,500 popular songs published or released as records in the period 1900–75. If all the variants of "I" (I, I'd, I'll, I'm, and I've) are combined, the total goes up to 405.

US CHART SINGLES WITH THE LONGEST TITLES

	Title	Artist	Highest position	Year	No. of letters*
1	*Anaheim, Azusa & Cucamonga Sewing Circle, Book Review and Timing Association*	Jan & Dean	77	1964	66
2	*What Can You Get a Wookie for Christmas (When He Already Owns a Comb)?*	Star Wars Intergalactic Droid Choir & Chorale	69	1980	57
3	*Breaking Up Is Hard on You (a.k.a. Don't Take Ma Bell Away From Me)*	American Comedy Network	70	1984	53
4=	*Does Your Chewing Gum Lose Its Flavor on the Bedpost Over Night*	Lonnie Donegan	5	1961	52
4=	*Objects in the Rear View Mirror May Appear Closer Than They Are*	Meat Loaf	38	1994	52
4=	*Rhythm 'n' Blues (Mama's Got the Rhythm – Papa's Got the Blues)*	McGuire Sisters	5	1955	52
7=	*If I Said You Have a Beautiful Body Would You Hold It Against Me*	Bellamy Brothers	39	1979	51
7=	*(Sartorial Eloquence) Don't Ya Wanna Play This Game No More?*	Elton John	39	1980	51
9=	*Pink Cookies in a Plastic Bag Getting Crushed By Buildings*	L.L. Cool J	96	1993	49
9=	*First Thing Ev'ry Morning (and the Last Thing Ev'ry Night)*	Jimmy Dean	91	1965	49

* *Punctuation, excluding spaces, is counted as a single letter.*

Lonnie Donegan's 1961 single was based on a 1924 hit by Ernest Hare and Billy Jones entitled *Does The Spearmint Lose Its Flavor on the Bedpost Over Night.*

LONG PLAYERS

ALBUMS OF ALL TIME WORLDWIDE

1	Michael Jackson, *Thriller*
2	Whitney Houston/Various, Soundtrack, *The Bodyguard*
3	Various, Soundtrack, *Saturday Night Fever*
4	Beatles, *Sgt. Pepper's Lonely Hearts Club Band*
5	Various, Soundtrack, *Grease*
6	Simon and Garfunkel, *Bridge Over Troubled Water*
7	Bruce Springsteen, *Born in the USA*
8	Various, Soundtrack, *The Sound of Music*
9	Fleetwood Mac, *Rumours*
10	Dire Straits, *Brothers in Arms*

Total worldwide sales of albums are notoriously hard to gauge, but even with the huge expansion of the album market during the 1980s, and multiple million sales of many major releases, this Top 10 is still an élite company; the sales of the entries are between 20,000,000 and 25,000,000 globally, with *The Bodyguard* near 26,000,000, and the seemingly uncatchable *Thriller* on 40,000,000.

BEATLES AND FRIENDS
Originally released in 1967, Sgt. Pepper's Lonely Hearts Club Band *has clocked up sales of around 25 million copies.*

40 YEARS OF THE ALBUM

Although there were several earlier attempts to introduce "long-playing" records, the first successful product was the 12-inch 33⅓-rpm vinyl album, with 23 minutes of recorded sound on each side, perfected by Dr. Peter Goldmark and launched at the Waldorf-Astoria Hotel, New York, on June 21, 1948. The death-knell of the vinyl album was sounded on March 1, 1983, however, when the first compact disc players went on sale. Within a decade, sales of CDs had overtaken those of their predecessors, which are being progressively phased out.

ALBUMS OF ALL TIME IN THE US

1	Michael Jackson, *Thriller*	**6**	Carole King, *Tapestry*
2	Fleetwood Mac, *Rumours*	**7**	Whitney Houston/Various, Soundtrack, *The Bodyguard*
3	Eagles, *Eagles – Their Greatest Hits 1971–1975*	**8**	Led Zeppelin, *Led Zeppelin IV (Untitled)*
4	Pink Floyd, *Dark Side of the Moon*	**9**	Various, Soundtrack, *Saturday Night Fever*
5	Bruce Springsteen, *Born in the USA*	**10**	Various, Soundtrack, *Dirty Dancing*

Thriller's US sales now exceed 22,000,000, so it will take a mighty album indeed ever to catch up. The rest of this field, all of which have sold in excess of 10,000,000 copies apiece, are well behind by comparison, with second-placed *Rumours* having sold over 14,000,000 copies. A lot of these albums were originally released before the CD age, so have benefited from "second copy" buying, as people replace old vinyl copies with compact discs; a good example is Carole King's *Tapestry*, the only album on the list not to be officially certified for its 12,000,000-plus sales accomplishment.

TOP 10

FIRST MILLION-SELLING ALBUMS IN THE US

	Artist/title	Year
1	Various, *Oklahoma!* (original cast recording)	1949
2	Various, *South Pacific* (original cast recording)	1949
3	Various, Soundtrack, *An American in Paris*	1952
4	Mantovani, *Strauss Waltzes*	1953
5	Mantovani, *Christmas Carols*	1953
6	Mario Lanza, *Songs from "The Student Prince"*	1954
7	Glenn Miller Band, *The Glenn Miller Story*	1954
8	Mantovani, *Mantovani Plays the Immortal Classics*	1954
9	Bing Crosby, *Merry Christmas*	1954
10	Kermit Schafer, *Radio Bloopers*	1954

Albums in the usual sense – 12" or 10" discs played at 33⅓ rpm – first appeared in the US in 1948. Nos. 1 and 9 in this Top 10 were both originally issued prior to the dates listed as boxed-set collections of 78-rpm records.

TOP 10

ARTISTS WITH THE MOST NO. 1 CHART ALBUMS IN THE US

	Artist	No. 1 Albums
1	Beatles	15
2=	Elvis Presley	9
2=	Rolling Stones	9
4	Elton John*	8
5=	Paul McCartney	7
5=	Barbra Streisand	7
7	Led Zeppelin	6
8=	Kingston Trio	5
8=	Herb Alpert & The Tijuana Brass	5
8=	Chicago	5

* *Including* The Lion King *soundtrack (1994)*

The Rolling Stones missed the opportunity for a sole ranking in second position when their most recent release, *Voodoo Lounge*, peaked at No. 2 upon release in July 1994. A similar fate befell Frank Sinatra's last outing, his 1993 *Duets*.

TOP 10

ALBUMS THAT STAYED LONGEST ON THE US CHART

	Artist/title	Chart weeks*
1	Pink Floyd, *Dark Side of the Moon*	741
2	Johnny Mathis, *Johnny's Greatest Hits*	490
3	Various, *My Fair Lady* (original cast recording)	480
4	Various, Soundtrack, *Oklahoma!*	305
5	Carole King, *Tapestry*	302
6	Johnny Mathis, *Heavenly*	295
7=	Various, Soundtrack, *The King and I*	277
7=	Tennessee Ernie Ford, *Hymns*	277
9	Various, *The Sound of Music* (original cast recording)	276
10	Various, *Camelot* (original cast recording)	265

* *To December 31, 1993*

It is unlikely that any album in this century will match the total amassed by Pink Floyd's rock opus *Dark Side of the Moon*, which still appears occasionally in the Top 200 chart some 20 years after its original release.

TOP 10

ALBUMS THAT STAYED LONGEST AT NO. 1 IN THE US CHARTS

(*Based on* Billboard *charts to March 31, 1994*)

	Album/release year	Weeks at No. 1
1	Michael Jackson, *Thriller* (1982)	37
2=	Harry Belafonte, *Calypso* (1956)	31
2=	Fleetwood Mac, *Rumours* (1977)	31
4=	Various, Soundtrack, *Saturday Night Fever* (1978)	24
4=	Prince & The Revolution, Soundtrack, *Purple Rain* (1984)	24
6	MC Hammer, *Please Hammer Don't Hurt'Em* (1990)	21
7=	Whitney Houston/Various, Soundtrack, *The Bodyguard* (1992)	20
7=	Elvis Presley, Soundtrack, *Blue Hawaii* (1962)	20
9=	Monkees, *More of the Monkees* (1967)	18
9=	Various, Soundtrack, *Dirty Dancing* (1988)	18
9=	Garth Brooks, *Ropin' the Wind* (1991)	18

Some sources identify the soundtrack album of *West Side Story* (1962) as the longest at No. 1 on the *Billboard* chart, but its 57-week stay was in a chart solely for stereo albums – then a relatively new phenomenon. Not all of the albums from the general chart had continuous No. 1 runs: in some cases, their sojourns at the top were punctuated by briefer stays by other records. Five of the Top 10 are film soundtracks, which suggests that a successful movie tie-in may well aid sales longevity.

TOP 10

ARTISTS WITH THE MOST CHART ALBUMS IN THE US

	Artist	Chart albums
1	Elvis Presley	92
2	Frank Sinatra	66
3	Johnny Mathis	63
4=	James Brown	49
4=	Ray Coniff	49
6	Mantovani	45
7	Barbra Streisand	43
8=	Beach Boys	41
8=	Temptations	41
8=	Lawrence Welk	41

Elvis' staggering total will not be matched this century, and could even pass the 100 total by the year 2000.

ALBUMS OF THE DECADES

SIMON AND GARFUNKEL
This duo scored a hit in 1970 with Bridge Over Troubled Water, and also enjoyed astounding success with the title track from the album.

T O P 1 0

ALBUMS OF EACH YEAR OF THE 1960s IN THE US

1960	Various, *The Sound of Music* (original cast recording)
1961	Judy Garland, *Judy at Carnegie Hall*
1962	Various, Soundtrack, *West Side Story*
1963	Documentary, *John Fitzgerald Kennedy: A Memorial Album*
1964	Beatles, *Meet the Beatles*
1965	Various, Soundtrack, *Mary Poppins*
1966	Herb Alpert & The Tijuana Brass, *Whipped Cream and Other Delights*
1967	Beatles, *Sgt. Pepper's Lonely Hearts Club Band*
1968	Beatles, *The Beatles* ("White Album")
1969	Various, *Hair* (Broadway cast)

Unique in its summary of 1960s music is the J.F. Kennedy *Memorial Album*, released soon after his assassination. Based on a tribute broadcast by New York radio station WMCA, it sold 4,000,000 copies between December 7 and 12, 1963.

D I D   Y O U   K N O W

THE FIRST DECADE OF ALBUM HITS

The first 33⅓-rpm LPs were unveiled by Columbia in June 1948, and released to the buying public on September 18 of that year. By June 18, 1949, Columbia had achieved total sales of 3,500,000, and they were soon followed by other companies. During the 1950s the album became a universally popular recording medium. Movie and musical soundtracks dominated the market; the original soundtrack of *South Pacific* (1958), one of the biggest-selling albums of all time, logged 262 weeks on the chart and became the bestselling album of the 1950s. Hard on its heels were the original cast recordings of *My Fair Lady* (1956) and *The Music Man* (1958) and the soundtracks of *Gigi* (1958) and *Oklahoma* (1955). Among individual artists Harry Belafonte's album *Calypso* (1956) was the sixth highest earner of the 1950s – and in seventh position was newcomer Elvis Presley, with his 1956 album *Elvis*.

T O P 1 0

ALBUMS OF THE 1960s IN THE US

	Artist/title	Year
1	Various, Soundtrack, *West Side Story*	1961
2	Beatles, *Meet The Beatles*	1964
3	Various, Soundtrack, *The Sound of Music*	1965
4	Beatles, *Sgt Pepper's Lonely Hearts Club Band*	1967
5	Monkees, *The Monkees*	1966
6	Monkees, *More of The Monkees*	1967
7	Various, *Hair* (Broadway cast)	1968
8	Herb Alpert & The Tijuana Brass, *Whipped Cream and Other Delights*	1965
9	Various, Soundtrack, *Mary Poppins*	1964
10	Documentary, *John Fitzgerald Kennedy: A Memorial Album*	1963

While Beatles, Monkees, and Presley discs sold huge quantities in a relatively short period of time, successful film soundtracks had less dramatic sales peaks but greater longevity, often staying on the charts for years – *The Sound of Music* eventually accrued a chart residence of more than five years.

T O P 1 0

ALBUMS OF THE 1970s IN THE US

	Artist/title	Year
1	Fleetwood Mac, *Rumours*	1977
2	Various, Soundtrack, *Saturday Night Fever*	1977
3	Various, Soundtrack, *Grease*	1978
4	Carole King, *Tapestry*	1971
5	Pink Floyd, *The Dark Side of the Moon*	1973
6	Boston, *Boston*	1976
7	Peter Frampton, *Frampton Comes Alive!*	1976
8	Stevie Wonder, *Songs in the Key of Life*	1976
9	Elton John, *Goodbye Yellow Brick Road*	1973
10	Eagles, *Hotel California*	1976

In the decade when album sales really took off (*Rumours* alone sold over 13,000,000 copies), it is notable that five of these Top 10 titles were double albums.

BRUCE SPRINGSTEEN
The popularity of albums such as Born in the USA, *and his sellout concert appearances, made The Boss one of the most successful rock stars of the 1980s.*

T O P 1 0

ALBUMS OF EACH YEAR OF THE 1970s IN THE US

970	Simon and Garfunkel, *Bridge Over Troubled Water*
971	Carole King, *Tapestry*
972	Don McLean, *American Pie*
973	Pink Floyd, *Dark Side of the Moon*
974	John Denver, *John Denver's Greatest Hits*
975	Elton John, *Captain Fantastic and the Brown Dirt Cowboy*
976	Peter Frampton, *Frampton Comes Alive*
1977	Fleetwood Mac, *Rumours*
1978	Various, Soundtrack, *Saturday Night Fever*
1979	Supertramp, *Breakfast in America*

WALL OF SOUND
Pink Floyd's last multi-million-selling album was The Wall, *which took them to No. 1 in 1980 and 10th place overall in the following decade.*

T O P 1 0

ALBUMS OF EACH YEAR OF THE 1980s IN THE US

1980	Pink Floyd, *The Wall*
1981	REO Speedwagon, *Hi Infidelity*
1982	Asia, *Asia*
1983	Michael Jackson, *Thriller*
1984	Prince & The Revolution, Soundtrack, *Purple Rain*
1985	Madonna, *Like a Virgin*
1986	Whitney Houston, *Whitney Houston*
1987	Bon Jovi, *Slippery When Wet*
1988	George Michael, *Faith*
1989	Milli Vanilli, *Girl You Know It's True*

The 1980s opened with Pink Floyd's *The Wall* spending three-and-a-half months at No.1, approaching their former triumph with *Dark Side of the Moon. The Wall* eventually sold over 7,000,000 copies in the US.

T O P 1 0

ALBUMS OF THE 1980s IN THE US

	Artist/title	Year
1	Michael Jackson, *Thriller*	1982
2	Bruce Springsteen, *Born in the USA*	1984
3	Various, Soundtrack, *Dirty Dancing*	1987
4	Prince & The Revolution, Soundtrack, *Purple Rain*	1984
5	Lionel Richie, *Can't Slow Down*	1983
6	Whitney Houston, *Whitney Houston*	1985
7	Def Leppard, *Hysteria*	1987
8	Bon Jovi, *Slippery When Wet*	1986
9	Guns N' Roses, *Appetite for Destruction*	1988
10	Pink Floyd, *The Wall*	1979

On October 30, 1984, *Thriller* became the first album to receive its 20th platinum sales certificate, for sales of 20,000,000 copies in the US alone. It dominated the US charts in 1983 and early 1984, and seven of the tracks became Top 10 singles in the US; far from detracting from the album's sales, the success of each single served to re-boost its popularity. *The Wall*, although included here as a 1980s album, was actually released during the week ending December 15, 1979, but accumulated most of its sales during the following decade.

ALBUM GREATS

TOP 10

BOXED-SET ALBUMS OF THE 1990s IN THE US

(To March 31, 1994)

	Title	Artist	Year of release
1	*Led Zeppelin/Remasters*	Led Zeppelin	1990/2 *
2	*Just for the Record*	Barbra Streisand	1991
3	*Boats Beaches Bars and Ballads*	Jimmy Buffett	1992
4	*Songs of Freedom*	Bob Marley	1992
5	*Pandora's Box*	Aerosmith	1991
6	*The Complete Recordings*	Robert Johnson	1990
7	*Live Shit: Binge and Purge*	Metallica	1993
8	*Crossroads*	Eric Clapton	1988
9	*Storyteller*	Rod Stewart	1989
10	*The King Of Rock 'n' Roll – the Complete '50s Masters*	Elvis Presley	1992

* Remasters *is a 1992 edited version of the original* Led Zeppelin, *which had already sold more than 1,000,000 by the time* Remasters *came out.*

While overall back-catalog CD sales have kept the record industry alive over the past decade, boxed-set collections in particular have proved a highly profitable and popular source of revenue. Relatively inexpensive to produce, some boxed-set compilations can begin to make a profit for record companies after selling only 25,000 copies.

TOP 10

INSTRUMENTAL ALBUMS OF ALL TIME IN THE US

1	Ernest Gold and the Sinfonia of London Orchestra, Soundtrack, *Exodus*
2	Enoch Light and the Light Brigade/Terry and the All-Stars, *Persuasive Percussion*
3	Henry Mancini, Soundtrack, *Breakfast at Tiffany's*
4	Lawrence Welk, *Calcutta!*
5	Victor Young, Soundtrack, *Around the World in 80 Days*
6	Henry Mancini, *The Music from Peter Gunn*
7	Herb Alpert & The Tijuana Brass, *What Now My Love*
8	Herb Alpert & The Tijuana Brass, *Whipped Cream and Other Delights*
9	Enoch Light and the Light Brigade, *Stereo 33/MM*
10	Van Cliburn, *Tchaikovsky: Piano Concerto No. 1*

These are the most successful instrumental albums of all time in the US, based on chart performance. All of them hit No. 1, and between them logged a total of 1,076 weeks on the US Albums survey.

TOP 10

COUNTRY ALBUMS OF ALL TIME IN THE US

1	Garth Brooks, *No Fences*
2	Garth Brooks, *Ropin' the Wind*
3	Billy Ray Cyrus, *Some Gave All*
4	Garth Brooks, *Garth Brooks*
5	Garth Brooks, *The Chase*
6	Patsy Cline, *Greatest Hits*
7	Garth Brooks, *In Pieces*
8	Waylon Jennings, *Greatest Hits*
9	Randy Travis, *Always and Forever*
10	Alabama, *Feels So Right*

Each of these albums has sold more than 4,000,000 domestic copies, but Garth Brooks is in a league of his own. Exploding onto the country scene in 1990, he has become his own industry, selling over 35,000,000 albums in under four years in the US alone, and is the first country artist to sell 10,000,000 copies of one album (*No Fences*).

TOP 10

ALBUMS IN THE US, 1993

1	Whitney Houston/Various, Soundtrack, *The Bodyguard*
2	Janet Jackson, *Janet*
3	Pearl Jam, *VS*
4	Kenny G, *Breathless*
5	Mariah Carey, *Music Box*
6	Eric Clapton, *Unplugged*
7	Dr. Dre, *The Chronic*
8	Garth Brooks, *In Pieces*
9	Stone Temple Pilots, *Core*
10	Meat Loaf, *Bat out of Hell II: Back Into Hell*

Each of these albums sold over 2,500,000 copies in the US during 1993; *The Bodyguard* added over 5,500,000 to its 1992 tally.

GARTH BROOKS
Booming record sales during the 1990s have made Brooks a giant among country artists.

T O P 1 0

HEAVY METAL ALBUMS OF ALL TIME IN THE US

1 Led Zeppelin, *Led Zeppelin IV (Untitled)*

2 Def Leppard, *Hysteria*

3 Boston, *Boston*

4 AC/DC, *Back in Black*

5 Bon Jovi, *Slippery When Wet*

6 Guns N' Roses, *Appetite for Destruction*

7 Def Leppard, *Pyromania*

8 Meat Loaf, *Bat out of Hell*

9 Journey, *Escape*

10 ZZ Top, *Eliminator*

All of these albums have sold more than 7,000,000 copies each in the US alone, with *Led Zeppelin IV (Untitled)* recently certified for sales over 11,000,000. *Hysteria*'s sales performance is a particularly remarkable achievement for Def Leppard, the British band whose lineup has suffered a death (Steve Clark in 1991) and whose long-time drummer, Rick Allen, continues to perform with the band despite losing his left arm in a car accident in 1984.

EVERYTHING'S COMING UP ROSES
Packed concerts, album sales in the millions, and even bestselling T-shirts, make Guns N' Roses one of the highest-profile bands around.

T O P 1 0

ORIGINAL CAST RECORDINGS OF ALL TIME IN THE US

1	*My Fair Lady* (Broadway)	1956
2	*The Sound of Music* (Broadway)	1959
3	*The Music Man* (Broadway)	1958
4	*The Phantom of the Opera* (London)	1988
5	*Camelot* (Broadway)	1961
6	*West Side Story* (Broadway)	1958
7	*Jesus Christ Superstar**	1970
8	*Fiddler on the Roof* (Broadway)	1964
9	*Hair* (Broadway)	1968
10	*Hello, Dolly!* (Broadway)	1964

* *Although an original Broadway cast version appeared in 1972, the album that outperformed it here was a studio cast recording made in 1970 with Deep Purple vocalist Ian Gillan playing Jesus.*

The 1950s and early 1960s were clearly the golden era of musicals, when cast albums regularly outperformed the burgeoning number of rock 'n' roll artist releases.

T O P 1 0

RAP ALBUMS OF ALL TIME IN THE US

1 MC Hammer, *Please Hammer Don't Hurt 'Em*

2 Vanilla Ice, *To the Extreme*

3 Beastie Boys, *Licence to Ill*

4 Kris Kross, *Totally Krossed Out*

5 Snoop Doggy Dogg, *Doggy Style*

6 Dr. Dre, *The Chronic*

7 R. Kelly, *12 Play*

8 Run D.M.C., *Raising Hell*

9 L.L. Cool J, *Bigger and Deffer*

10 Tone Loc, *Loc'ed After Dark*

On March 7, 1987, No. 3 became the first rap album to top the US Albums Chart. The top eight albums here have each sold over 3,000,000 copies in the US alone, with the 1990s' hottest rap-producer Dr. Dre (at No. 6) also responsible for the success of the quadruple-platinum No. 5, *Doggy Style*.

T O P 1 0

CHILDREN'S ALBUMS OF ALL TIME IN THE US

1 Various, *Mickey Mouse Disco*

2 Various, *Mousercise*

3 Various, *Children's Favorites Volume 1*

4 Various, *Disney's Christmas Favorites*

5 Various, *Children's Favorites Volume 2*

6 Various, Soundtrack, *Mary Poppins*

7 Various, Soundtrack, *The Jungle Book*

8 The Muppets, *The Sesame Street Book and Record*

9 The Chipmunks, *Chipmunk Punk*

10 The Chipmunks, *Urban Chipmunk*

Released in April 1980, No. 1 became the biggest-selling children's title of all time, notching up over 2,000,000 units, tailed closely by its follow-up release, *Mousercise*. However, by the end of its peak sales and chart career, it is likely that Disney's *The Lion King* soundtrack album, released in 1994, will outperform all of the above.

MUSIC ON RADIO, TV, AND FILM

TOP 10

MOST PERFORMED BMI SONGS OF ALL TIME IN THE US

	Title/Composer(s)
1	*Yesterday*, Lennon & McCartney
2	*Never My Love*, Donald & Richard Addrisi
3	*By The Time I Get to Phoenix*, Jim Webb
4	*Gentle on My Mind*, John Hartford
5	*You've Lost That Lovin' Feelin'*, Phil Spector, Barry Mann, & Cynthia Weil
6	*More*, Norman Newell, Nino Oliviero, Riz Ortalani, & Marcello Ciorcioloni
7	*Georgia on My Mind*, Hoagy Carmichael & Stuart Gorrell
8	*Bridge Over Troubled Water*, Paul Simon
9	*Something*, George Harrison
10	*Mrs. Robinson*, Paul Simon

This list represents the most broadcast songs of all time on American radio and television, for those titles represented by the BMI (Broadcast Music Incorporated). The first five songs have all been broadcast over 5,000,000 times in the US alone.

TOP 10

BMI "MILLION-AIRS"

	Songwriter(s)	No. of Million-Airs
1	Lennon & McCartney	26
2	Barry Gibb	22
3	Paul Simon	15
4	Norman Gimbel	12
5	Holland, Dozier, Holland	10
6	Barry Mann	9
7	Cynthia Weil	8
8=	Gerry Goffin	7
8=	Daryl Hall	7
8=	Carole Bayer-Sager	7
8=	Gamble & Huff	7
8=	John & Taupin	7

These are songwriters with the greatest number of songs broadcast more then 1,000,000 times. In the repertoire of songs in the BMI (Broadcast Music Incorporated) nearly 1,000 have achieved "Million-Air" status – that is, they have been broadcast over 1,000,000 times in the United States. With each song averaging three minutes, this is equal to over 50,000 hours of broadcasting, or 5.7 years of continuous airplay. It is estimated that, at any given time, there is a Lennon & McCartney composition being played on at least one US radio station – a graphic reminder of the partnership's colossal and ongoing royalty income.

PAUL McCARTNEY AND JOHN LENNON
Their songs – cover versions as well as original recordings – are still a mainstay of music programs on US radio.

TOP 10

SONGS ON *YOUR HIT PARADE*, 1935–58

	Composer/title	Year
1	Sid Lippman, *Too Young*	1951
2	Irving Berlin, *White Christmas*	1942
3	Arthur Hammerstein & Dudley Wilson, *Because of You*	1951
4	Harry Warren, *You'll Never Know*	1943
5	Sammy Fain, *I'll Be Seeing You*	1938
6	Dorothy Stewart & Clement Scott, *Now Is the Hour*	1946
7	Fred Fisher, *Peg o' My Heart*	1947
8	Richard Rodgers, *People Will Say We're in Love*	1943
9	Bille Reid, *A Tree in the Meadow*	1948
10	Richard Rodgers, *Some Enchanted Evening*	1949

Your Hit Parade, a popular syndicated US radio program featuring the most successful sheet-music sales on a weekly basis, began broadcasting in 1935.

THE TEN

FIRST ARTISTS TO APPEAR ON *AMERICAN BANDSTAND*

	Artist/song performed	Date
1	Billy Williams, *I'm Gonna Sit Right Down and Write Myself a Letter*	Aug 5, 1957
2	Chordettes, *Just Between You and Me*	Aug 5, 1957
3	Dale Hawkins, *Susie Q*	Aug 6, 1957
4	Don Rondo, *White Silver Sands*	Aug 6, 1957
5	Paul Anka, *Diana*	Aug 7, 1957
6	Lee Andrews & The Hearts, *Long Lonely Nights*	Aug 9, 1957
7	Gene Vincent & His Blue Caps, *Lotta Lovin'/Wear My Ring*	Aug 12, 1957
8	Four Coins, *Shangri-La*	Aug 12, 1957
9	Jodi Sands, *All My Heart*	Aug 13, 1957
10	Sal Mineo, *Start Movin'/Lasting Love*	Aug 13, 1957

Notable as the first pop music TV program, *American Bandstand* began nationwide broadcasting on 67 stations on August 5, 1957.

T O P   1 0

HIGHEST-RATED TV MUSIC SHOWS IN THE US, 1980–90

	Show	Broadcast date	% of TV audience*
1	*The Grammy Awards,*	Feb 28, 1984	30.8
2	*American Music Awards*	Jan 16, 1984	27.4
3	*American Music Awards*	Jan 28, 1985	25.8
4=	*American Music Awards*	Jan 17, 1983	24.4
4=	*Country Music Awards*	Oct 11, 1982	24.4
6	*The Grammy Awards*	Feb 27, 1980	23.9
7	*The Grammy Awards*	Feb 26, 1985	23.8
8	*Country Music Awards*	Oct 13, 1980	22.9
9	*Country Music Awards*	Oct 10, 1983	22.6
10	*American Music Awards*	Jan 26, 1987	22.2

* *Percentage of US households with TV sets watching the broadcast. There are now more than 93,000,000 such households in the US.*

The Grammy Awards is primarily a music industry voting affair, while the *American Music Awards* is based on votes cast by the public and therefore tends to be a more teen-oriented broadcast. Annual music awards shows dominate American network music programming and are far more popular than, say, *Soul Train* or *Casey Kasem's American Top 10* weekly programs; they also include the *MTV Music Awards* (broadcast on cable), the *Jukebox Music Awards*, the *International Rock Awards*, the *Billboard Music Awards*, the *Rock Music Awards*, and the *Annual Country Music Awards*, a rival to the more successful *Country Music Awards* listed here.

THE PARTRIDGE FAMILY
This show, first broadcast in 1970, starred teen heart-throb David Cassidy.

T O P   1 0

FILM SOUNDTRACKS IN THE US, 1993

	Artist/title
1	Whitney Houston/Various, Soundtrack, *The Bodyguard*
2	Various, *Sleepless in Seattle*
3	Various, *Aladdin*
4	George Strait, *Pure Country*
5	Various, *Boomerang*
6	Various, *Menace II Society*
7	Various, *Last Action Hero*
8	Various, *Singles*
9	Tina Turner, *What's Love Got to Do with It?*
10	Various, *Sister Act 2*

Film soundtracks are now often popular enough in their own right to prop up the flagging fortunes of the movie itself, a notable example being George Strait's *Pure Country*, which has spent over two years on the Top 200 Albums chart with total sales exceeding 3,000,000 – a hugely successful release that continued to sell long after the film had left the movie theaters.

T O P   1 0

HIGHEST-RATED NETWORK MUSIC TV SERIES IN THE US, 1950–90

	Program/year	% of TV audience*
1	*Stop the Music* (1951)	34.0
2	*Your Hit Parade* (1958)	33.6
3	*The Perry Como Show* (1956)	32.6
4	*Name That Tune* (1958)	26.7
5	*The Dean Martin Show* (1966)	24.8
6	*The Sonny & Cher Hour* (1973)	23.3
7	*The Partridge Family* (1972)	22.6
8	*The Glen Campbell Goodtime Hour* (1968)	22.5
9	*The Johnny Cash Show* (1969)	21.8
10	*Cher* (1975)	21.3

* *Percentage of US households with TV sets watching the broadcast: the total of households rose from 3,800,000 in 1950 to 92,100,000 in 1990.*

T H E   T E N

FIRST MUSIC VIDEOS BROADCAST BY MTV IN THE US

1	Buggles, *Video Killed the Radio Star*
2	Pat Benatar, *You Better Run*
3	Rod Stewart, *She Won't Dance with Me*
4	Who, *You Better You Bet*
5	PhD, *Little Susie's on the Up*
6	Cliff Richard, *We Don't Talk Anymore*
7	Pretenders, *Brass in Pocket*
8	Todd Rundgren, *Time Heals*
9	REO Speedwagon, *Take It on the Run*
10	Styx, *Rockin' the Paradise*

This varied line-up inaugurated the world's first 24-hour music video network on August 1, 1981. Six of the 10 are British acts, there are no R & B videos, and little-known British duo PhD, who never had a US chart record, make an incongruous appearance at No. 5.

MUSIC AT AUCTION

RECORD SLEEVES
*John Lennon's
30-year-old jacket
fetched $47,900
at auction.*

T O P 1 0

MOST EXPENSIVE ITEMS OF POP MEMORABILIA EVER SOLD AT AUCTION

(Excluding rock stars' clothing – see previous list)

	Item/sale	Price ($)*
1	John Lennon's 1965 Rolls-Royce Phantom V touring limousine, finished in psychedelic paintwork Sotheby's, New York, June 29, 1985	2,299,000
2	Jimi Hendrix's Fender *Stratocaster* electric guitar Sotheby's, London, April 25, 1990	370,000
3	Acoustic guitar owned by David Bowie, Paul McCartney, and George Michael Christie's, London, May 18, 1994	330,000
4	Buddy Holly's Gibson acoustic guitar, *c.*1945, in a tooled leather case made by Holly Sotheby's, New York, June 23, 1990	242,000
5	John Lennon's 1970 Mercedes-Benz 600 Pullman four-door limousine Christie's, London, April 27, 1989	213,000
6	Elvis Presley's 1942 Martin D-18 guitar (used to record his first singles, 1954–56) Red Baron Antiques, Atlanta, Georgia, October 3, 1991 The same guitar was resold by Christie's, London, May 14, 1993 for $167,300.	180,000
7	Elvis Presley's 1963 Rolls-Royce Phantom V touring limousine Sotheby's, London, August 28, 1986	161,700
8	Buddy Holly's Fender *Stratocaster* electric guitar, 1958 Sotheby's, New York, June 23, 1990	110,000
9	John Lennon's handwritten lyrics for *A Day In The Life* Sotheby's, London, August 27, 1992	95,800
10	Elton John's 1977 Panther de Ville Coupé Sotheby's, London, August 22, 1991	78,100

* *Including 10 percent buyer's premium, where appropriate*

Pioneered particularly by Sotheby's in London, pop memorabilia has become big business – especially if it involves personal association with megastars such as the Beatles and, more recently, Buddy Holly (whose spectacles were sold by Sotheby's, New York, June 23, 1990 for $45,100). In addition to the Top 10, high prices have also been paid for other musical instruments once owned by notable rock stars, such as a guitar belonging to John Entwistle of the Who and pianos formerly owned by Paul McCartney and John Lennon.

T O P 1 0

MOST EXPENSIVE ITEMS OF ROCK STARS' CLOTHING SOLD AT AUCTION IN THE UK

	Item/sale	Price ($)*
1	Elvis Presley's one-piece "Shooting Star" stage outfit, *c.*1972 Phillips, London, August 24, 1988	48,000
2	John Lennon's black leather jacket, *c.*1960–62 Christie's, London, May 7, 1992	47,900
3	Four "super hero"-style costumes worn by glam rock group Kiss in the film *Kiss Meets the Phantom* (1978) Christie's, London, May 14, 1993	31,400
4	Michael Jackson's white rhinestone glove Christie's, London, December 19, 1991	27,900
5	Elvis Presley's one-piece stage costume, as worn on the cover of his *Burning Love* album Phillips, London, August 25, 1992	26,100
6	Elvis Presley's blue stage costume, *c.*1972 Phillips, London, August 24, 1988	25,900
7	Jimi Hendrix's black felt hat Sotheby's, London, August 22, 1991	24,200
8	Elton John's giant Dr Marten boots from the film *Tommy* Sotheby's, London, September 6, 1988	20,300
9=	Michael Jackson's black sequinned jacket Sotheby's, London, August 22, 1991	18,600
9=	Prince's *Purple Rain* stage costume, 1984 Christie's, London, December 19, 1991	18,600

* *Including 10 percent buyer's premium*

T O P   1 0

MOST EXPENSIVE MUSIC MANUSCRIPTS EVER SOLD AT AUCTION

	Manuscript/sale	Price ($)*
1	Nine symphonies by Wolfgang Amadeus Mozart Sotheby's, London, May 22, 1987	3,854,000
2	Ludwig van Beethoven's Piano Sonata in E Minor, Opus 90 Sotheby's, London, December 6, 1991	1,690,000
3	Wolfgang Amadeus Mozart's Fantasia in C Minor and Sonata in C Minor Sotheby's, London, November 21, 1990	1,496,000
4	Robert Schumann's Piano Concerto in A Minor, Opus 54 Sotheby's, London, November 22, 1989	1,240,000
5	Ludwig van Beethoven's first movement of the Sonata for Violoncello and Piano in A Major, Opus 69 Sotheby's, London, May 17, 1990	897,600
6	Johann Sebastian Bach's cantata *Auf Christi Himmelfahrt allein* Sotheby's, London, November 22, 1989	604,500
7	Igor Stravinsky's *Rite of Spring* Sotheby's, London, November 11, 1982	570,000
8	Franz Schubert's Quartet in B flat Major (No. 8) D.112, Opus 168 Christie's, London, June 24, 1992	534,600
9	Henry Purcell, 21 pieces for the harpsichord (the highest price for a British manuscript) Sotheby's, London, May 26, 1994	414,750
10	Johann Sebastian Bach's cantata *O Ewigkeit, Du Donnerwort* Sotheby's, London, November 11, 1982	361,000

* "Hammer prices" excluding premiums

The collection of nine symphonies by Mozart not only holds the record for the highest price ever paid for a music manuscript, but also for any post-medieval manuscript.

T O P   1 0

MOST EXPENSIVE MUSICAL INSTRUMENTS EVER SOLD AT AUCTION

	Instrument/sale	Price ($)*
1	"Mendelssohn" Stradivarius violin Christie's, London, November 21, 1990	1,686,700
2	"Cholmondley" Stradivarius violoncello Sotheby's, London, June 22, 1988	1,145,800
3	Steinway grand piano, decorated by Lawrence Alma-Tadema and Edward Poynter for Henry Marquand, 1884–87 Sotheby Parke Bernet, New York, March 26, 1980	390,000
4	Jimi Hendrix's Fender *Stratocaster* electric guitar Sotheby's, London, April 25, 1990	370,000
5	Acoustic guitar owned by David Bowie, Paul McCartney, and George Michael Christie's, London, May 18, 1994	330,000
6	Verne Powell platinum flute Christie's, New York, October 18, 1986	187,000
7	Flemish single-manual harpsichord made by Johan Daniel Dulken of Antwerp, 1755 Sotheby's, London, March 27, 1990	153,900
8	Kirkman double-manual harpsichord Christie's, London, June 26, 1987	126,000
9	Columnar alto recorder made by Hans van Schratt, mid-16th century Christie's, London, March 16, 1988	73,900
10	"Portable Grand Piano" made by John Isaac Hawkins, *c.*1805 (a very early example of an upright piano, considerably pre-dating the modern type, and one of only three examples known) Sotheby's, London, July 4, 1985	15,000

* Including 10 percent buyer's premium, where appropriate

This list shows the most expensive example of each type of instrument. The two harpsichords and two pianos are of different types but from the same family, so perhaps numbers 7 and 9 should be disqualified. In that case, 9 and 10 would be a pair of German kettle drums, *c.*1700, sold at Sotheby's, London, on November 21, 1974 for $9,000, and a Swiss sachbut made by J. Steimer of Zofinger in the early 18th century (Sotheby's, London, May 6, 1976, $4,800).

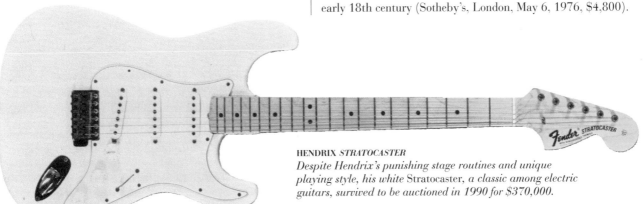

HENDRIX *STRATOCASTER*
Despite Hendrix's punishing stage routines and unique playing style, his white Stratocaster, a classic among electric guitars, survived to be auctioned in 1990 for $370,000.

CLASSICAL AND OPERA

OPERAS MOST FREQUENTLY PERFORMED AT THE METROPOLITAN OPERA HOUSE, NEW YORK

	Opera	Composer	Performances
1	La Bohème	Giacomo Puccini	716
2	Aïda	Giuseppe Verdi	709
3	La Traviata	Giuseppe Verdi	565
4	Carmen	Georges Bizet	548
5	Tosca	Giacomo Puccini	547
6	Madama Butterfly	Giacomo Puccini	497
7	Rigoletto	Giuseppe Verdi	494
8	Pagliacci	Ruggero Leoncavallo	445
9	Faust	Charles Gounod	436
10	Cavalleria Rusticana	Pietro Mascagni	415

The Metropolitan Opera House opened on October 22, 1883, with a performance of Charles Gounod's *Faust*. Such is the universality of opera that no fewer than eight of the Met's top operas also appear (though in a somewhat different order) in the Top 10 performed at London's principal venue, the Royal Opera House, Covent Garden, where *La Bohème* similarly tops the list of "most performed."

OPERAS MOST FREQUENTLY PERFORMED AT THE ROYAL OPERA HOUSE, COVENT GARDEN, LONDON 1833–1993

	Opera	Composer	First performance	Total
1	La Bohème	Giacomo Puccini	Oct 2, 1897	493
2	Carmen	Georges Bizet	May 27, 1882	478
3	Aïda	Giuseppe Verdi	Jun 22, 1876	446
4	Faust	Charles Gounod	Jul 18, 1863	428
5	Rigoletto	Giuseppe Verdi	May 14, 1853	423
6	Don Giovanni	Wolfgang Amadeus Mozart	Apr 17, 1834	373
7	Tosca	Giacomo Puccini	Jul 12, 1900	363
8	Norma	Vincenzo Bellini	Jul 12, 1833	353
9	Madama Butterfly	Giacomo Puccini	Jul 10, 1905	342
10	La Traviata	Giuseppe Verdi	May 25, 1858	339

The total number of performances is up to December 31, 1993. The records are complete back to 1847, but for the two operas premiered earlier, the figure is based on the best available evidence.

LAST WINNERS OF THE "BEST CLASSICAL ALBUM" GRAMMY AWARD

Year	Artist/title/performer
1994	Béla Bartók, *The Wooden Prince* Pierre Boulez, Chicago Symphony Orchestra and Chorus
1993	Gustav Mahler, *Symphony No. 9* Leonard Bernstein, Berlin Philharmonic Orchestra
1992	Leonard Bernstein, *Candide* Leonard Bernstein, London Symphony Orchestra
1991	Charles Ives, *Symphony No. 2 (And Three Short Works)* Leonard Bernstein, New York Philharmonic Orchestra
1990	Béla Bartók, *Six String Quartets*/Emerson String Quartet
1989	Giuseppi Verdi, *Requiem and Operatic Choruses* Robert Shaw, Atlanta Symphony Orchestra
1988	*Horowitz in Moscow*/Vladimir Horowitz
1987	*Horowitz: The Studio Recordings, New York*/Vladimir Horowitz
1986	Hector Berlioz, *Requiem* Robert Shaw, Atlanta Symphony Orchestra
1985	*Amadeus* (Original Soundtrack)/Neville Marriner, Academy of St Martin-in-the-Fields, Ambrosian Opera Chorus

The three consecutive awards to Leonard Bernstein in 1991–93 brought his overall Grammy tally to 15.

MOST PROLIFIC CLASSICAL COMPOSERS

	Composer	Dates	Nationality	Hrs
1	Joseph Haydn	1732–1809	Austrian	340
2	George Handel	1685–1759	German/English	303
3	Wolfgang Amadeus Mozart	1656–91	Austrian	202
4	Johann Sebastian Bach	1685–1750	German	175
5	Franz Schubert	1797–1828	German	134
6	Ludwig van Beethoven	1770–1827	German	120
7	Henry Purcell	1659–95	English	116
8	Giuseppe Verdi	1813–1901	Italian	87
9	Antonín Dvořák	1841–1904	Czechoslovakian	79
10=	Franz Liszt	1811–86	Hungarian	76
10=	Peter Tchaikovsky	1840–93	Russian	76

This list is based on a survey conducted by *Classical Music* magazine which ranked classical composers by the total number of hours of music each composed. If the length of the composer's working life is brought into the calculation, Schubert wins: his 134 hours were composed in a career of 18 years, giving an average of 7 hours 27 minutes per annum. The same method would put Tchaikovsky ahead of Liszt: although both composed 76 hours of music, Tchaikovsky worked for 30 years and Liszt for 51, giving them respective annual averages of 2 hours 32 minutes and 1 hour 29 minutes.

LARGEST OPERA HOUSES IN THE WORLD

	Opera house	Location	seating	Capacity standing	total
1	The Metropolitan Opera	New York, NY	3,800	265	4,065
2	Cincinnati Opera	Cincinnati, OH	3,630	–	3,630
3	Lyric Opera of Chicago	Chicago, IL	3,563	–	3,563
4	San Francisco Opera	San Francisco, CA	3,176	300	3,476
5	The Dallas Opera	Dallas, TX	3,420	–	3,420
6	Canadian Opera Company	Toronto, Canada	3,167	–	3,167
7	Los Angeles Music Center Opera	Los Angeles, CA	3,098	–	3,098
8	San Diego Opera	San Diego, CA	2,992	84	3,076
9	Seattle Opera	Seattle, WA	3,017	–	3,017
10	L'Opéra de Montréal	Montreal, Canada	2,874	–	2,874

THE PLACE TO BE SEEN
New York's Metropolitan Opera House was built in 1883 as a showcase for the world's best singers – and for the city's opera-going high society.

LARGEST OPERA HOUSES IN EUROPE

	Opera house	Location	seating	Capacity standing	total
1	Opéra Bastille	Paris, France	2,716	–	2,716
2	Gran Teatre del Liceu	Barcelona, Spain	2,700	–	2,700
3	English National Opera	London, UK	2,356	75	2,431
4	Staatsoper	Vienna, Austria	1,709	567	2,276
5	Teatro alla Scala	Milan, Italy	2,015	150	2,165
6	Bolshoi Theatre	Moscow, Russia	2,153	*	2,153
7	The Royal Opera	London, UK	2,067	42	2,109
8	Bayerische Staatsoper	Munich, Germany	1,773	328	2,101
9	Bayreuth Festspielhaus	Bayreuth, Germany	1,925	–	1,925
10	Teatro Comunale	Florence, Italy	1,890	–	1,890

* Standing capacity unspecified

LAST WINNERS OF THE "BEST OPERA RECORDING" GRAMMY AWARD

Year	Artist/title/principal soloists
1994	Handel, *Semele*/Kathleen Battle, Marilyn Horne, Samuel Ramey, Sylvia McNair, Michael Chance
1993	Richard Strauss, *Die Frau Ohne Schatten*/Placido Domingo, Jose Van Dam, Hildegard Behrens
1992	Richard Wagner, *Götterdämmerung* Hildegard Behrens, Ekkehard Wlashiha
1991	Richard Wagner, *Das Rheingold* James Morris, Kurt Moll, Christa Ludwig
1990	Richard Wagner, *Die Walküre*/Gary Lakes, Jessye Norman, Kurt Moll
1989	Richard Wagner, *Lohengrin*/Placido Domingo, Jessye Norman, Eva Randova
1988	Richard Strauss, *Ariadne Auf Naxos* Anna Tomowa-Sintow, Kathleen Battle, Agnes Baltsa, Gary Lakes
1987	Leonard Bernstein, *Candide*/Erie Mills, David Eisler, John Lankston
1986	Arnold Schoenberg, *Moses und Aron* Franz Mazura, Philip Landridge
1985	Georges Bizet, *Carmen* (Original Soundtrack)/Julia Migenes Johnson, Faith Esham, Placido Domingo

OPERA'S LONDON HOME
Built in 1858, on a site occupied by a succession of theaters since 1732, the Royal Opera House is home to the Royal Opera and Royal Ballet Companies.

STAGE & SCREEN

TOP 10

LONGEST-RUNNING SHOWS OF ALL TIME ON BROADWAY

	Show	Performances
1	A Chorus Line (1975–90)	6,137
2	Oh! Calcutta! (1976–89)	5,959
3	Cats (1982–)	4,790*
4	42nd Street (1980–89)	3,486
5	Grease (1972–80)	3,388
6	Fiddler on the Roof (1964–72)	3,242
7	Life with Father (1939–47)	3,224
8	Tobacco Road (1933–41)	3,182
9	Les Misérables (1987–)	2,943*
10	Hello Dolly! (1964–71)	2,844

Still running; total at March 31, 1994

TOP 10

LONGEST-RUNNING SHOWS OF ALL TIME IN THE UK

	Show	Performances
1	The Mousetrap	17,215
2	No Sex, Please – We're British	6,761*
3	Cats	5,390
4	Starlight Express	4,163*
5	Oliver!	4,125*
6	Oh! Calcutta!	3,918
7	Les Misérables	3,449
8	Jesus Christ, Superstar	3,357*
9	The Phantom of the Opera	3,190
10	Evita	2,900*

* *Still running; total at March 31, 1994*

All the longest-running shows in the UK have been London productions. "West End" theater shows are regarded by most visitors to London as being among the main attractions, and the long runs of many have been sustained through tourist audiences, principally from the US.

TOP 10

LONGEST-RUNNING CAMERON MACKINTOSH PRODUCTIONS

	Production	Performances
1	Cats (London)	5,390
2	Cats (New York)	4,790
3	Les Misérables (London)	3,449
4	The Phantom of the Opera (London)	3,190
5	Les Misérables (New York)	2,943
6	The Phantom of the Opera (New York)	2,576
7	Miss Saigon (London)	1,981
8	Five Guys Named Moe (London)	1,330
9	Miss Saigon (New York)	1,272
10	Oliver! (London)	1,139

All still running except No. 10; total at March 31, 1994

IN THE LONG RUN

NINE LIVES
Cats *has been a huge success both in the US and worldwide.*

TOP 10

LONGEST-RUNNING MUSICALS OF ALL TIME IN THE UK

	Show	Performances
1	Cats	5,390 *
2	Starlight Express	4,163 *
3	Les Misérables	3,449 *
4	Jesus Christ, Superstar	3,357
5	Phantom of the Opera	3,190 *
6	Evita	2,900
7	The Sound of Music	2,386
8	Salad Days	2,283
9	My Fair Lady	2,281
10	Miss Saigon	1,981 *

* *Still running; total at March 31, 1994*

TOP 10

LONGEST-RUNNING NONMUSICALS OF ALL TIME IN THE UK

	Show	Performances
1	The Mousetrap	17,215 *
2	No Sex, Please – We're British	6,761
3	Oh! Calcutta!#	3,918
4	Run for Your Wife	2,638
5	There's a Girl in My Soup	2,547
6	Pyjama Tops	2,498
7	Sleuth	2,359
8	Boeing Boeing	2,035
9	Blithe Spirit	1,997
10	Worm's Eye View	1,745

* *Still running; total at March 31, 1994*
\# *A revue with music, rather than a musical*

TOP 10

LONGEST-RUNNING COMEDIES OF ALL TIME IN THE UK

	Show	Performances
1	No Sex Please – We're British	6,761
2	Run for Your Wife	2,638
3	There's a Girl in My Soup	2,547
4	Pyjama Tops	2,498
5	Boeing Boeing	2,035
6	Blithe Spirit	1,997
7	Worm's Eye View	1,745
8	Dirty Linen	1,667
9	Reluctant Heroes	1,610
10	Seagulls Over Sorrento	1,551

TOP 10

LONGEST-RUNNING MUSICALS OF ALL TIME ON BROADWAY

	Show	Performances
1	A Chorus Line (1979–90)	6,137
2	Cats (1982–)	4,790 *
3	42nd Street (1980–89)	3,486
4	Grease (1972–80)	3,388
5	Fiddler on the Roof (1964–72)	3,242
6	Les Misérables (1987–)	2,943 *
7	Hello Dolly! (1964–71)	2,844
8	My Fair Lady (1956–62)	2,717
9	The Phantom of the Opera (1988–)	2,576 *
10	Annie (1977–83)	2,377

* *Still running; total at March 31, 1994*

Off Broadway, the musical show *The Fantasticks* by Tom Jones and Harvey Schmidt has been performed continuously at the Sullivan Street Playhouse, New York, since May 3, 1960 – a total of more than 13,500 performances.

VIVE LA REVOLUTION
With almost 6,500 performances so far in New York and London, Les Misérables *is proving to be another smash hit for Cameron Mackintosh.*

TOP 10

LONGEST-RUNNING NONMUSICALS OF ALL TIME ON BROADWAY

	Show	Performances
1	Oh! Calcutta! (1976–89)	5,959
2	Life with Father (1939–47)	3,224
3	Tobacco Road (1933–41)	3,182
4	Abie's Irish Rose (1922–27)	2,327
5	Deathtrap (1978–82)	1,792
6	Gemini (1977–81)	1,788
7	Harvey (1944–49)	1,775
8	Born Yesterday (1946–49)	1,642
9	Mary, Mary (1961–65)	1,572
10	Voice of the Turtle (1943–47)	1,557

More than half the longest-running nonmusical shows on Broadway began their runs before the Second World War; the others all date from the period up to the 1970s, before the long-running musical completely dominated the Broadway stage. Off Broadway, these records have all been broken by *The Drunkard*, which was performed at the Mart Theater, Los Angeles, from July 6, 1933 to September 6, 1953, and then reopened with a musical adaption and continued its run from September 7, 1953 until October 17, 1959 – a grand total of 9,477 performances seen by some 3,000,000 people.

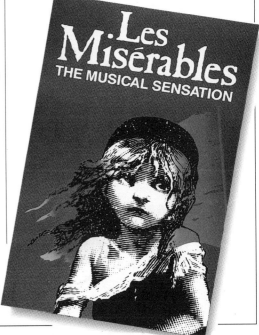

ALL THE WORLD'S A STAGE

THE TEN

LAST TONY AWARDS FOR A PLAY

1994	*Angels in America Part II: Perestroika*
1993	*Angels in America Part I: Millenium Approaches*
1992	*Dancing at Lughnasa*
1991	*Lost in Yonkers*
1990	*The Grapes of Wrath*
1989	*The Heidi Chronicles*
1988	*M. Butterfly*
1987	*Fences*
1986	*I'm Not Rappaport*
1985	*Biloxi Blues*

The Tony Awards, established by the American Theater Wing in 1947 to honor outstanding Broadway plays and musicals, are named for the actress and director Antoinette Perry (1888–1946), who headed the American Theater Wing during the Second World War.

THE TEN

LAST TONY AWARDS FOR A MUSICAL

1994	*Passion*
1993	*Kiss of the Spider Woman*
1992	*Crazy for You*
1991	*The Will Rogers Follies*
1990	*City of Angels*
1989	*Jerome Robbins's Broadway*
1988	*The Phantom of the Opera*
1987	*Les Misérables*
1986	*The Mystery of Edwin Drood*
1985	*Big River*

THE TEN

LAST TONY AWARDS FOR AN ACTOR

1994	Stephen Spinella, *Angels in America Part II: Perestroika*
1993	Ron Leibman, *Angels in America Part I: Millenium Approaches*
1992	Judd Hirsch, *Conversations with My Father*
1991	Nigel Hawthorne, *Shadowlands*
1990	Robert Morse, *Tru*
1989	Philip Bosco, *Lend Me a Tenor*
1988	Ron Silver, *Speed-the-Plow*
1987	James Earl Jones, *Fences*
1986	Judd Hirsch, *I'm Not Rappaport*
1985	Derek Jacobi, *Much Ado About Nothing*

THE TEN

LAST TONY AWARDS FOR AN ACTRESS

1994	Diana Rigg, *Medea*
1993	Madeline Kahn, *The Sisters Rosensweig*
1992	Glenn Close, *Death and the Maiden*
1991	Mercedes Ruehl, *Lost in Yonkers*
1990	Maggie Smith, *Lettice and Lovage*
1989	Pauline Collins, *Shirley Valentine*
1988	Joan Allen, *Burn This*
1987	Linda Lavin, *Broadway Bound*
1986	Lily Tomlin, *The Search for Signs of Intelligent Life in the Universe*
1985	Stockard Channing, *A Day in the Death of Joe Egg*

TOP 10

THEATER-GOING COUNTRIES IN THE WORLD

	Country	Annual theater attendance per 1,000 population
1	Cuba	2,559
2	Mongolia	1,700
3	Vietnam	1,000
4	UK	720
5	Iceland	658
6	Bulgaria	650
7	Luxembourg	613
8	Albania	590
9	Romania	578
10	Netherlands	575
	US	*170*

THE TEN

FIRST PULITZER DRAMA AWARDS

1918	Jesse Lynch Williams, *Why Marry?*
1920	Eugene O'Neill, *Beyond the Horizon*
1921	Zona Gale, *Miss Lulu Bett*
1922	Eugene O'Neill, *Anna Christie*
1923	Owen Davis, *Icebound*
1924	Hatcher Hughes, *Hell-Bent for Heaven*
1925	Sidney Howard, *They Knew What They Wanted*
1926	George Kelly, *Craig's Wife*
1927	Paul Green, *In Abraham's Bosom*
1928	Eugene O'Neill, *Strange Interlude*

The Pulitzer Drama Award is made for "an American play, preferably original and dealing with American life."

THE TEN

MOST RECENT PULITZER DRAMA AWARDS

1994	Edward Albee, *Three Tall Women*
1993	Tony Kushner, *Angels in America: Millennium Approaches*
1992	Robert Schenkkan, *The Kentucky Cycle*
1991	Neil Simon, *Lost in Yonkers*
1990	August Wilson, *The Piano Lesson*
1989	Wendy Wasserstein, *The Heidi Chronicles*
1988	Alfred Uhry, *Driving Miss Daisy*
1987	August Wilson, *Fences*
1986	No award
1985	Stephen Sondheim and James Lapine, *Sunday in the Park with George*

TOP 10

WORST DISASTERS AT THEATER AND ENTERTAINMENT VENUES

(19th and 20th centuries, excluding sports stadiums and racetracks)

	Location	Venue	Date	No. killed
1	Canton, China	Theater	May 25, 1845	1,670
2	Shanghai, China	Theater	June 1871	900
3	Lehmann Circus, St Petersburg, Russia	Circus	February 14, 1836	800
4	Antoung, China	Cinema	February 13, 1937	658
5	Ring Theater, Vienna	Theater	December 8, 1881	620
6	Iroquois Theater, Chicago	Theater	December 30, 1903	591
7	Coconut Grove Night Club, Boston	Night Club	November 28, 1942	491
8	Abadan, Iran	Theater	August 20, 1978	422
9	Niteroi, Brazil	Circus	December 17, 1961	323
10	Brooklyn Theater, New York	Theater	December 5, 1876	295

All of the world's worst disasters at theaters have been caused by fire. The figure given for the first entry in this list is a conservative estimate; some sources put it as high as 2,500, but, even in recent times, reports from China are often unreliable. The figure for the Ring Theater fire also varies greatly according to source, some claiming it to be as high as 850. The worst circus fire in the United States (which caused a stampede) was at Ringling Brothers' Circus, Hartford, Connecticut, on July 6, 1944, when 168 people lost their lives and 480 were injured.

DID YOU KNOW

IN THE SHORT RUN

For every long-running show, there are many that last for only a few nights. On Broadway, *Frankenstein* (1981) closed after a single night, while *Carrie* closed on May 17, 1988 after five performances, reputedly losing the visiting Royal Shakespeare Company $7,000,000. The short runner has a long international history: on December 18, 1816 the only performance of J.R. Ronden's *The Play Without an A* took place at the Paris Théâtre des Variétés. The total absence of words containing the letter "a" was trying for both actors and audience, who rioted and did not allow it to finish. *The Intimate Revue* opened and closed at the Duchess Theatre, London, on Tuesday, March 11, 1930. A disaster from start to finish, the scenery changes took so long that seven scenes were abandoned to allow the long-suffering audience to go home before midnight. The musical *Roza*, scheduled to open at the Adelphi Theatre, London, in June 1984, failed to get even that far, closing on the day rehearsals were due to start.

THE IMMORTAL BARD

SHAKESPEARE'S MOST PRODUCED PLAYS

	Play	Productions
1	*As You Like It*	64
2=	*Hamlet*	58
2=	*The Merchant of Venice*	58
2=	*Twelfth Night*	58
5=	*Much Ado About Nothing*	56
5=	*The Taming of the Shrew*	56
7	*A Midsummer Night's Dream*	49
8=	*Macbeth*	47
8=	*The Merry Wives of Windsor*	47
8=	*Romeo and Juliet*	47

This list, which is based on an analysis of Shakespearean productions from December 31, 1878 to January 1, 1994 at Stratford-on-Avon, and by the Royal Shakespeare Company in London, provides a reasonable picture of his most popular plays. Records do not, however, indicate the total number of individual performances during each production.

WILLIAM SHAKESPEARE (1564–1616)
England's best-known poet, actor, and playwright was born in Stratford-on-Avon, Warwickshire, the town to which he returned at the end of a life spent in the theatrical world of London.

SHAKESPEARE'S FIRST PLAYS

	Play	Approx. year written
1	*Titus Andronicus*	1588–90
2	*Love's Labour's Lost*	1590
3	*Henry VI, Parts I–III*	1590–91
4=	*The Comedy of Errors*	1591
4=	*Richard III*	1591
4=	*Romeo and Juliet*	1591
7	*The Two Gentlemen of Verona*	1592–93
8	*A Midsummer Night's Dream*	1593–94
9	*Richard II*	1594
10	*King John*	1595

Few authorities agree on the precise dating of Shakespeare's plays. There are only scant contemporary records of their early performances, and only half of them appeared in print in his lifetime – and even those that were published before his death in 1616 were generally much altered from his originals. It was not until after 1623, with the publication of the so-called "Folios," that Shakespeare's complete works were progressively published. There is much argument over the dating of *Romeo and Juliet* in particular, which may have been written as early as 1591 or as late as 1596–97; if the latter, it would be predated by Nos. 7–10 on the list and by *The Merchant of Venice* (c. 1596).

SHAKESPEARE'S LONGEST PLAYS

	Play	Lines
1	*Hamlet*	3,901
2	*Richard III*	3,886
3	*Coriolanus*	3,820
4	*Cymbeline*	3,813
5	*Othello*	3,672
6	*Antony and Cleopatra*	3,630
7	*Troilus and Cressida*	3,576
8	*Henry VIII*	3,450
9	*Henry V*	3,368
10	*The Winter's Tale*	3,354

DID YOU KNOW

SHAKESPEARE ON FILM

Kenneth Branagh's 1993 version of *Much Ado About Nothing* continues a tradition of adapting Shakespeare's plays as films, which began in the silent era. There are more than 50 versions of *Hamlet*; the 1990 remake, starring Mel Gibson, is the highest-earning. Franco Zeffirelli's *Romeo and Juliet* (1968) remains the most commercially successful adaptation of a Shakespeare play.

TOP 10

POLONIUS'S PRECEPTS FOR LAERTES

1 *Give thy thoughts no tongue,*
Nor any unproportioned
thought his act.

2 *Be thou familiar, but by no*
means vulgar.

3 *Those friends thou hast,*
and their adoption tried,
Grapple them to thy soul with
hoops of steel;

4 *But do not dull thy palm*
with entertainment
Of each new-hatch'd,
unfledged comrade.

5 *Beware of entrance to a*
quarrel, but being in,
Bear't that the opposed may
beware of thee.

6 *Give every man thy ear,*
but few thy voice;

7 *Take each man's censure,*
but reserve thy judgment.

8 *Costly thy habit as thy*
purse can buy,
But not express'd in fancy;
rich, not gaudy;
For the apparel oft
proclaims the man,
And they in France of the best
rank and station
Are of a most select and
generous chief in that.

9 *Neither a borrower nor*
a lender be;
For loan oft loses both
itself and friend,
And borrowing dulls the
edge of husbandry.

10 *This above all: to thine*
ownself be true,
And it must follow, as the
night the day,
Thou canst not then be false
to any man.

In Act I, Scene iii of *Hamlet*, Polonius, the Lord Chamberlain and father of Hamlet's friend Laertes, gives his son these 10 pieces of advice before Laertes sets sail for France.

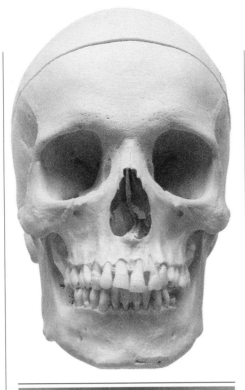

TOP 10

SHAKESPEARE'S MOST DEMANDING ROLES

	Role	Play	Lines
1	Hamlet	*Hamlet*	1,422
2	Falstaff	*Henry IV, Parts I and II*	1,178
3	Richard III	*Richard III*	1,124
4	Iago	*Othello*	1,097
5	Henry V	*Henry V*	1,025
6	Othello	*Othello*	860
7	Vincentio	*Measure for Measure*	820
8	Coriolanus	*Coriolanus*	809
9	Timon	*Timon of Athens*	795
10	Antony	*Antony and Cleopatra*	766

Hamlet's role comprises 11,610 words – over 36 percent of the total number of lines spoken in the play, but if multiple plays are considered, he is beaten by Falstaff who, as well as appearing in *Henry IV, Parts I and II*, also appears in *The Merry Wives of Windsor* where he has 436 lines. His total of 1,614 lines thus makes him the most talkative of all Shakespeare's characters. By the same criterion, Henry V appears (as Prince Hal) in *Henry IV Part I*, where he speaks 117 lines, making his total 1,142.

TOP 10

WORDS MOST USED BY SHAKESPEARE

	Word	Frequency
1	The	27,457
2	And	26,285
3	I	21,206
4	To	19,938
5	Of	17,079
6	A	14,675
7	You	14,326
8	My	13,075
9	That	11,725
10	In	11,511

In his complete works, William Shakespeare wrote a total of 884,647 words – 118,406 lines comprising 31,959 separate speeches. He used a total vocabulary of 29,066 different words, some – such as "America" – appearing only once (*The Comedy of Errors*, III.ii), while at the other end of the scale the Top 10 accounts for all those words that he used on more than 10,000 occasions. Perhaps surprisingly, their relative frequency is not dissimilar to what we might encounter in modern usage: supposedly "Shakespearean" words such as "prithee" and "zounds!" actually make a poor showing in the frequency table. Another 18 words appear more than 5,000 times, in descending order: is, not, me, for, it, with, be, his, this, your, he, but, have, as, thou, so, him, and will. It should be noted that these statistics are derived from a computer analysis of Shakespeare's works conducted in the late 1960s – which, although comprehensive, was rather ahead of its time, since the software for such a monumental task was much less sophisticated than it would be today – and it is possible that the odd instance of a word's use may have slipped through the net. Reports of missing examples will be gratefully received.

100 YEARS OF MOVIES

Firsts in 1895 include:

March 22: First film screened: Workers Leaving the Lumière Factory, shown to an engineering society in Paris (earlier films were viewed individually, in "peep-show" machines).

March 30: First film of a public sporting event: the Oxford and Cambridge boat race, London, by British pioneer Birt Acres (1854–1918).

April 21: First movie shown in the US: at Woodville Latham's Pantoptikon, New York.

May 20: First film screened publicly: a boxing match ("Young Griffo" *v* "Battling (Charles) Barnett"), filmed at Madison Square Garden on May 5 and shown at 153 Broadway, New York.

June 20: First news film: Birt Acres' "newsreel" of the opening of the Kiel Canal, Hamburg, by Kaiser Wilhelm II. This, and other films by Acres, were first shown in London on January 14, 1896.

December 28: First film in Europe shown to a paying audience: by Louis and Auguste Lumière, at the Grand Café, Paris.

TOP 10

MOVIE REMAKES

	Original film	Remake
1	*Father of the Bride* (1950)	1991
2	*The Ten Commandments* (1923)	1956
3	*A Star Is Born* (1954)	1976
4	*Ben Hur* (1926)	1959
5	*King Kong* (1933)	1976
6	*Dragnet* (1954)	1987
7	*The Three Musketeers* (1948)	1974
8	*Hamlet* (1964)	1990
9	*The Postman Always Rings Twice* (1946)	1981
10	*King Solomon's Mines* (1950)	1985

This Top 10 lists the 10 most lucrative remakes and only includes remakes with the identical title. Hence such retitled remakes as *Anna and the King of Siam* (1946)/*The King and I* (1956) and *Dracula* (1979)/*Bram Stoker's Dracula* (1992) are ineligible. The "original" film is the last significant Hollywood version of a film, but many subjects have been remade on more than one occasion – *The Three Musketeers* and *Hamlet* being notable examples.

TOP 10

MOST EXPENSIVE ITEMS OF FILM MEMORABILIA SOLD AT AUCTION

	Item/sale	Price ($)*
1	James Bond's Aston Martin DB5 from *Goldfinger* Sotheby's, New York, June 28, 1986	275,000
2	Herman J. Mankiewicz's scripts for *Citizen Kane* and *The American* Christie's, New York, June 21, 1989	231,000
3	Judy Garland's ruby slippers from *The Wizard of Oz* Christie's, New York, June 21, 1988	165,000
4	Piano from the Paris scene in *Casablanca* Sotheby's, New York, December 16, 1988	154,000
5	Charlie Chaplin's hat and cane Christie's, London, December 11, 1987 (£82,500) (resold at Christie's, London, December 17, 1993 for £55,000/$82,500)	135,300
6	Clark Gable's script from *Gone With the Wind* Sotheby's, New York, December 16, 1988	77,000
7	Charlie Chaplin's boots Christie's, London, December 11, 1987 (£38,500)	63,100
8	A 1932 Universal poster for *The Old Dark House*, starring Boris Karloff Christie's, New York, December 9, 1991	48,400
9	A special effects painting of the Emerald City from *The Wizard of Oz* Camden House, Los Angeles, April 1, 1991	44,000
10	16mm film of the only meeting between Danny Kaye and George Bernard Shaw Christie's, London, April 27, 1989 (£20,900)	32,400

* *$/£ conversion at rate then prevailing*

This list excludes animated film celluloids or "cels" – the individually painted scenes that are shot in sequence to make up cartoon films – which are now attaining colossal prices: just one of the 150,000 color cels from *Snow White* (1937) was sold in 1991 for $209,000 and in 1989 $286,000 was reached for a black-and-white cel depicting Donald Duck in *Orphan's Benefit* (1934). If memorabilia relating to film stars is included, Orson Welles' annotated script from the radio production of *The War of the Worlds* ($143,000/£90,500 in 1988) would qualify for the Top 10, while near-misses are the witch's hat from *The Wizard of Oz* ($33,000 in 1988) and Marilyn Monroe's "shimmy" dress from *Some Like it Hot* ($32,300 in 1988).

TOP 10

FILMS OF THE SILENT ERA

1	*The Birth of a Nation*	1915
2	*The Big Parade*	1925
3	*Ben Hur*	1926
4	*The Ten Commandments*	1923
5=	*What Price Glory?*	1926
5=	*The Covered Wagon*	1923
7=	*Way Down East*	1921
7=	*Hearts of the World*	1918
9=	*Wings*	1927
9=	*The Four Horsemen of the Apocalypse*	1921

The Birth of a Nation is not only at the top of the list, but, having earned almost twice as much as *The Big Parade*, is ranked as the most successful film made before 1937, when *Snow White and the Seven Dwarfs* took the crown. All the films in this list were black and white, with the exception of *Ben Hur*, which, despite its early date, contains a color sequence.

TOP 10

BLACK-AND-WHITE FILMS

1	*Young Frankenstein*	1974
2	*Schindler's List*	1993
3	*Black Rain*	1990
4	*Paper Moon*	1973
5	*Manhattan*	1979
6	*Mom and Dad*	1944
7	*Who's Afraid of Virginia Woolf?*	1966
8	*Easy Money*	1983
9	*The Last Picture Show*	1971
10	*From Here to Eternity*	1953

Perhaps surprisingly, all the most successful black-and-white films date from the modern era, when the choice of filming in color or monochrome was available and the decision to use just black-and-white was thus deliberate.

YOUNG FRANKENSTEIN
Marty Feldman brings a comic slant to the classic tale of Frankenstein's monster.

TOP 10

FEES EARNED BY ACTORS IN *CASABLANCA*

	Actor	Part	Fee ($)
1	Humphrey Bogart	Rick Blaine	36,667
2=	Ingrid Bergman	Ilse Lund	25,000
2=	Paul Henreid	Victor Laszlo	25,000
2=	Conrad Veidt	Major Strasser	25,000
5	Claude Rains	Captain Louis Renault	22,000
6	Sydney Greenstreet	Ferrari	7,500
7	Dooley Wilson	Sam	3,500
8	S.Z. Sakall	Carl	2,600
9	Peter Lorre	Ugarte	2,333
10	Leonid Kinskey	Sascha	2,267

YOU MUST REMEMBER THIS
Humphrey Bogart and Ingrid Bergman feature in a scene in Rick's Bar, in the classic film Casablanca.

These are the budgeted fees that formed a major component of the total cost of the 1942 film. It was budgeted at $878,000, but actually cost $950,000 to make. After being nominated for eight Academy Awards and winning three ("Best Picture," "Best Director," and "Best Screenplay"), *Casablanca* went on to achieve both commercial success and critical acclaim, many considering it the greatest Hollywood movie of all time.

TOP 10

YEARS FOR FILM RELEASES IN THE US

	Year	US produced	Imported	Total released
1	1928	641	193	884
2	1921	854	0	854
3	1918	841	0	841
4	1920	796	0	796
5	1937	538	240	778
6	1938	455	314	769
7	1935	525	241	766
8	1939	483	278	761
9	1922	748	0	748
10	1927	678	65	743

As this list indicates, the prewar years were Hollywood's most prolific period – although from the late 1920s onward, the proportion of home-grown to imported films gradually declined (imports actually overtook home-produced films for the first time in 1958, and it was not until 1975 that the trend was reversed). The total number of films released into the US marketplace reached an all-time low of 354 in 1978.

TOP 10

YEARS FOR FILM PRODUCTION IN THE UK

	Year	Films produced
1	1936	192
2	1937	176
3	1935	165
4	1920	155
5	1934	145
6	1921	137
7	1938	134
8	1962	126
9	1919	122
10	1933	115

The peak year for the British movie industry was almost 60 years ago, and apart from a curious "blip" in 1962, it has never recovered the eminence it once attained in this "golden age." British film production declined steadily, hitting triple figures for the last time in 1970 (when 103 films were produced in the UK), and dipping to an all-time low of 27 in 1988, with 42 (including co-productions) in 1992.

FILM HITS AND MISSES

Films that appear in the lists of "10 Most Successful" for various categories and Top 10s of films in which various stars have appeared are ranked according to the total rental fees paid to distributors by cinemas in North America (US and Canada). This is regarded by the film industry as a reliable guide to what a film has earned in those markets, while as a rough rule of thumb – also used by the industry itself – doubling the North American rental receipts gives a very approximate world total.

Rental income is not the same as "box office gross," another commonly used way of comparing the success of films. While the latter method is certainly valid over a short period – for example, to compare films released in the same year – it indicates what the movie theaters rather than the films themselves earned and it varies according to ticket price.

Inflation is a key factor in calculating "success." As movie theater ticket prices go up, so do box office income and the rental fees charged by distributors. This means that the biggest earners tend to be among the most recent releases. If inflation is taken into account, the most successful film ever is *Gone With the Wind*; while it has earned actual rental fees of almost $80,000,000 (ranking it only 40th in the all-time list), inflation since the film's release in 1939 makes this worth more than $500,000,000 in today's money.

T O P 1 0

FILMS RELEASED IN THE US IN 1993

	Film	Distributor	1993 release	Box office gross ($)*
1	*Jurassic Park*	Universal	Jun 11	349,531,892
2	*Mrs. Doubtfire*	Twentieth Century-Fox	Nov 24	219,195,051
3	*The Fugitive*	Warner Bros.	Aug 6	183,875,760
4	*The Firm*	Paramount	Jun 30	158,340,292
5	*Sleepless in Seattle*	TriStar	Jun 25	126,670,704
6	*Indecent Proposal*	Paramount	Apr 7	106,614,059
7	*In the Line of Fire*	Columbia	Jul 9	102,243,874
8	*The Pelican Brief*	Warner Bros.	Dec 17	100,768,056
9	*Schindler's List*	Universal	Dec 15	96,003,638
10	*Cliffhanger*	TriStar	May 28	84,049,211

* *Ongoing earnings through August 11, 1994*

Source: © 1994 Entertainment Data, Inc.

T O P 1 0

MOST EXPENSIVE FILMS EVER MADE

(*All US-made unless otherwise stated*)

	Film	Year	Cost ($)
1	*True Lies*	1994	110,000,000
2	*Inchon* (US/Korea)	1981	102,000,000
3	*War and Peace* (USSR)	1967	100,000,000
4	*Terminator 2: Judgment Day*	1991	95,000,000
5	*Total Recall*	1990	85,000,000
6	*The Last Action Hero*	1993	82,500,000
7	*Batman Returns*	1992	80,000,000
8	*Alien³*	1992	75,000,000
9=	*Who Framed Roger Rabbit*	1988	70,000,000
9=	*Die Hard 2*	1990	70,000,000
9=	*Hook*	1991	70,000,000

* *Excluding James Bond films*
\# *Academy Award for "Best Picture"*

T O P 1 0

FILM RENTAL BLOCKBUSTERS OF ALL TIME

1	*E.T. The Extra-Terrestrial*	1982
2	*Jurassic Park*	1993
3	*Star Wars*	1977
4	*Return of the Jedi*	1983
5	*Batman*	1989
6	*The Empire Strikes Back*	1980
7	*Home Alone*	1990
8	*Ghostbusters*	1984
9	*Jaws*	1975
10	*Raiders of the Lost Ark*	1981

The first two films in this list have each earned more than $200,000,000 in North American rentals alone, while the rest of this elite group have all earned in excess of $100,000,000. Only seven other films have ever earned more than $100,000,000: *Indiana Jones and the Last Crusade* (1989), *Terminator 2* (1991), *Indiana Jones and the Temple of Doom* (1984), *Beverly Hills Cop* (1984), *Back to the Future* (1985), *Home Alone 2: Lost in New York* (1993), and *Batman Returns* (1992).

T O P 1 0

BRITISH FILMS OF ALL TIME*

1	*Chariots of Fire#*	1981
2	*2001: A Space Odyssey*	1968
3	*Revenge of the Pink Panther*	1978
4	*Gandhi#*	1982
5	*Greystoke: The Legend of Tarzan*	1984
6	*Time Bandits*	1981
7	*Lawrence of Arabia#*	1962
8	*Return of the Pink Panther*	1975
9	*The Pink Panther Strikes Again*	1976
10	*Murder on the Orient Express*	1974

T O P 1 0

FILM SEQUELS OF ALL TIME

1 *Star Wars/The Empire Strikes Back/ Return of the Jedi*

2 *Raiders of the Lost Ark/ Indiana Jones and the Temple of Doom/ Indiana Jones and the Last Crusade*

3 *Rocky I–VI*

4 *Star Trek I–VI*

5 *Batman /Batman Returns*

6 *Home Alone 1–2*

7 *Back to the Future I–III*

8 *Jaws I–IV*

9 *Ghostbusters I–II*

10 *Superman I–IV*

Based on total earnings of the original film and all its sequels up to the end of 1993, the *Star Wars* trilogy stands head and shoulders above the rest, having made more than $500,000,000 in the North American market alone. All the other films in the Top 10 have achieved total earnings of around $200,000,000 or more, with *Lethal Weapon 1–3* and *Beverly Hills Cop I–II* lagging just outside the Top 10. A successful film does not guarantee a successful sequel, however: although their total earns them a place in the Top 10, each of the four *Superman* films actually earned less than the previous one, with *Superman IV* earning just one-tenth of the original. *Smokey and the Bandit Part III* earned just one-seventeenth of the original, and while the 1973 film *The Sting* was a box-office blockbuster, its 1983 sequel earned less than one-fifteenth as much, and *Grease 2* less than one-tenth of the original *Grease*. On the other hand, *Terminator 2* has already earned six times as much as its "prequel."

The James Bond films are not presented as sequels, but if they were taken into account, their total earnings would place them in 2nd position in this list.

T O P 1 0

BIGGEST FILM FLOPS OF ALL TIME

	Film	Year	Loss ($)
1	*The Adventures of Baron Münchhausen*	1988	48,100,000
2	*Ishtar*	1987	47,300,000
3	*Hudson Hawk*	1991	47,000,000
4	*Inchon*	1981	44,100,000
5	*The Cotton Club*	1984	38,100,000
6	*Santa Claus – The Movie*	1985	37,000,000
7	*Heaven's Gate*	1980	34,200,000
8	*Billy Bathgate*	1991	33,000,000
9	*Pirates*	1986	30,300,000
10	*Rambo III*	1988	30,000,000

Since the figures shown here are based upon North American rental earnings balanced against the films' original production cost, some in the list may eventually recoup a proportion of their losses via overseas earnings, video, and TV revenue, while for others, such as *Inchon* and *Pirates*, time has run out. The recent entry of *Hudson Hawk* and *Billy Bathgate*, two newcomers to the "flops" league table, means that the British-produced *Raise the Titanic* (1980), reputed to have lost $29,200,000, has finally sunk from the Top 10.

T O P 1 0

FILM SEQUELS THAT EARNED THE GREATEST AMOUNT MORE THAN THE ORIGINAL

	Original	Outearned by
1	*Alien*	*Aliens*
2	*Die Hard*	*Die Hard 2*
3	*First Blood*	*Rambo: First Blood Part II/Rambo III*
4	*48 Hours*	*Another 48 Hours*
5	*Lethal Weapon*	*Lethal Weapon 2 / Lethal Weapon 3*
6	*A Nightmare on Elm Street*	*A Nightmare on Elm Street 2, 3, 4, 5*
7	*The Pink Panther*	*Return of the Pink Panther/ The Pink Panther Strikes Again/ Revenge of the Pink Panther/*
8	*Rocky*	*Rocky III/Rocky IV*
9	*Star Trek*	*Star Trek IV: The Voyage Home*
10	*Terminator*	*Terminator 2: Judgment Day*

AVENGING ANGEL
Arnold Schwarzenegger starred in both the original Terminator *film and the even more successful* Terminator 2: Judgment Day.

FILMS OF THE DECADE

T O P 1 0

FILMS OF THE 1930s

	Film	Year
1	Gone With the Wind*	1939
2	Snow White and the Seven Dwarfs	1937
3	The Wizard of Oz	1939
4	King Kong	1933
5	San Francisco	1936
6=	Mr Smith Goes to Washington	1939
6=	Lost Horizon	1937
6=	Hell's Angels	1930
9	Maytime	1937
10	City Lights	1931

* Winner of "Best Picture" Academy Award

Both Gone With the Wind and Snow White and the Seven Dwarfs have generated considerably more income than any other prewar films, appearing respectively within the Top 40 and the Top 60 films of all time – although if the income of Gone With the Wind is adjusted to allow for inflation in the period since its release, it could with some justification be regarded as the most successful film ever. Gone With the Wind and The Wizard of Oz both celebrated their 50th anniversaries in 1989, and the extra publicity generated by these events further enhanced their rental income. The Academy Award-winning Cavalcade (1932) is a potential contender for a place in this Top 10, but its earnings have been disputed.

T O P 1 0

FILMS OF THE 1940s

	Film	Year
1	Bambi	1942
2	Fantasia	1940
3	Cinderella	1949
4	Pinocchio	1940
5	Song of the South	1946
6	Mom and Dad	1944
7	Samson and Delilah	1949
8=	The Best Years of Our Lives*	1946
8=	Duel in the Sun	1946
10	This Is the Army	1943

* Winner of "Best Picture" Academy Award

With the top four films of the decade classic Disney cartoons (and Song of the South part animated/part live action), the 1940s may truly be regarded as the "golden age" of the animated film. The genre was especially appealing in this era as colorful escapism during and after the drabness and grim realities of the war years. The songs from two of these films – "When You Wish Upon a Star" from Pinocchio and "Zip-A-Dee-Doo-Dah" from Song of the South – won "Best Song" Academy Awards. The cumulative income of certain of the Disney cartoons has increased as a result of their systematic re-release in movie theaters and as bestselling videos. Samson and Delilah heralded the epic movies of the 1950s.

T O P 1 0

FILMS OF THE 1950s

	Film	Year
1	The Ten Commandments	1956
2	Lady and the Tramp	1955
3	Peter Pan	1953
4	Ben Hur*	1959
5	Around the World in 80 Days*	1956
6	Sleeping Beauty	1959
7=	South Pacific	1958
7=	The Robe	1953
9	Bridge on the River Kwai*	1957
10	This Is Cinerama	1952

* Winner of "Best Picture" Academy Award

While the popularity of animated films continued with Lady and the Tramp, Peter Pan, and Sleeping Beauty, the 1950s were outstanding as the decade of the "big" picture. Many of the most successful films were enormous in terms of cast (Around the World in 80 Days boasted no fewer than 44 stars, most in cameo performances) and scale (Ben Hur, with its vast sets, broke all records by costing a staggering $4,000,000 to make, while The Robe was the first picture to offer the wide screen of Cinemascope). They were also enormous in the magnitude of the subjects they tackled. Three of these were major biblical epics. Bridge on the River Kwai was unusual in that it was a British-made success, with primarily British stars.

WIND-FALL!
Vivien Leigh and Clark Gable are shown in a scene from Gone With the Wind. In cash terms, the film has earned almost 20 times the then record $4,230,000 it cost to make – but indexing its earnings over the 55 years since its release would establish it as Hollywood's all-time money earner.

TOP 10

FILMS OF THE 1960s

	Film	Year
1	The Sound of Music*	1965
2	101 Dalmatians	1961
3	The Jungle Book	1967
4	Doctor Zhivago	1965
5	Butch Cassidy and the Sundance Kid	1969
6	Mary Poppins	1964
7	The Graduate	1968
8	My Fair Lady*	1964
9	Thunderball	1965
10	Funny Girl	1968

During the 1960s the growth in popularity of soundtrack record albums and featured singles often matched the commercial success of the films from which they were derived. Four of the Top 10 films of the decade were avowed musicals, while all had a high musical content, every one of them generating either an album or a hit single or two. *The Sound of Music*, the highest-earning film of the decade, produced the fastest-selling album ever, with over half a million sold in two weeks – as well as the first million-selling tape cassette. *Mary Poppins* was a No. 1 album, as were albums of *The Jungle Book* and *Doctor Zhivago*.

* Winner of "Best Picture" Academy Award

TOP 10

FILMS OF THE 1990s

	Film	Year
1	Jurassic Park	1993
2	Home Alone	1990
3	Terminator 2	1991
4	Home Alone 2: Lost in New York	1992
5	Batman Returns	1992
6	Mrs Doubtfire	1993
7	Ghost	1990
8	The Fugitive	1993
9	Robin Hood: Prince of Thieves	1991
10	Aladdin	1992

TOP 10

FILMS OF THE 1970s

	Film	Year
1	Star Wars	1977
2	Jaws	1975
3	Grease	1978
4	The Exorcist	1973
5	The Godfather*	1972
6	Superman	1978
7	Close Encounters of the Third Kind	1977/80
8	The Sting*	1973
9	Saturday Night Fever	1977
10	National Lampoon's Animal House	1978

* Winner of "Best Picture" Academy Award

In the 1970s the arrival of the two prodigies, Steven Spielberg and George Lucas, set the scene for the high adventure blockbusters whose domination has continued ever since. Lucas directed his first science-fiction film, *THX 1138*, in 1970 and went on to write and direct *Star Wars* (and wrote the two sequels, *The Empire Strikes Back* and *Return of the Jedi*). Spielberg directed *Jaws* and wrote and directed *Close Encounters* (which derives its success from the original release and the 1980 "Special Edition").

TOP 10

FILMS OF THE 1980s

	Film	Year
1	E.T. The Extra-Terrestrial	1982
2	Return of the Jedi	1983
3	Batman	1989
4	The Empire Strikes Back	1980
5	Ghostbusters	1984
6	Raiders of the Lost Ark	1981
7	Indiana Jones and the Last Crusade	1989
8	Indiana Jones and the Temple of Doom	1984
9	Beverly Hills Cop	1984
10	Back to the Future	1985

The 1980s were clearly the decade of the adventure film, with George Lucas and Steven Spielberg continuing to assert their control of Hollywood, carving up the Top 10 between them. Lucas produced 2 and 4, and Spielberg directed 1, 6, 7, 8, and 10. Paradoxically, despite their colossal box office success, they consistently failed to match this with a "Best Picture" Academy Award. *E.T.* and *Raiders of the Lost Ark* were both nominated, but neither they nor any of the other high-earning films of the 1980s won this Oscar. By way of compensation, each made more than $100,000,000 in North American rentals.

HOME ALONE
This film, starring the young Macaulay Culkin, is not only one of the highest-earning films of the early 1990s but is ranked among the 10 most successful ever. So far, it has earned over $100,000,000 in North American rentals alone.

Just four years into the decade, all 10 of these films have amassed rental income from the North American market alone in excess of $80,000,000, an achievement matched by only 15 films in the whole of the 1980s and just seven in the 1970s. *Home Alone* has been so successful that it now ranks as one of the Top 10 films of all time. The sequel, *Home Alone 2: Lost in New York*, which was made in 1992, is now ranked 16th in the list of all-time top films. A further 22 films released since 1990, including several released as recently as 1993, have each earned more than $50,000,000.

MOVIE MAGIC

TOP 10

ANIMATED FILMS

1	*Aladdin*	1992
2	*Who Framed Roger Rabbit?**	1988
3	*Beauty and the Beast*	1991
4	*One Hundred and One Dalmatians*	1961
5	*Snow White and the Seven Dwarfs*	1937
6	*Jungle Book*	1967
7	*Bambi*	1942
8	*Fantasia*	1940
9	*Cinderella*	1949
10	*Pinocchio*	1940

* *Part-animated, part-live action*

For more than 50 years the popularity of animated films has been so great that they stand out among the most successful films of each decade: *Snow White* was the second highest-earning film of the 1930s (after *Gone With the Wind*); *Bambi, Fantasia,* and *Cinderella* – and, through the success of its recent re-release, *Pinocchio* – were the four most successful films of the 1940s. *Lady and the Tramp*, though just outside the Top 10, was the second most successful of the 1950s (after *The Ten Commandments*). *One Hundred and One Dalmatians* and *Jungle Book* were the second and third most successful films of the 1960s (after *The Sound of Music*).

Runners-up include, in descending order: *Lady and the Tramp* (1955); *The Little Mermaid* (1989); *Peter Pan* (1953); *The Rescuers* (1977); *The Fox and the Hound* (1981); the part-animated *Song of the South* (1946); *The Aristocats* (1970); *Oliver and Company* (1988); *The Land Before Time* (1988); *An American Tail* (1986); and *Sleeping Beauty* (1989).

TOP 10

SCIENCE-FICTION AND FANTASY FILMS

1	*E.T. The Extra-Terrestrial*	1982
2	*Star Wars*	1977
3	*Return of the Jedi*	1983
4	*Batman*	1989
5	*The Empire Strikes Back*	1980
6	*Ghostbusters*	1984
7	*Terminator 2*	1991
8	*Back to the Future*	1985
9	*Batman Returns*	1992
10	*Ghost*	1990

Reflecting our taste for escapist fantasy adventures, the first six in this list also appear in the all-time Top 10, and all 10 are among the 17 most successful films ever, having earned more than $80,000,000 each from North American rentals alone. Eight more contenders just outside the Top 10 also achieved rental income in excess of $60,000,000: *Close Encounters of the Third Kind*; *Gremlins*; *Honey, I Shrunk the Kids*; *Back to the Future, Part II*; *Teenage Mutant Ninja Turtles*; *Superman II*; *Total Recall*; and *Ghostbusters II*.

TOP 10

COMEDY FILMS

1	*Home Alone*	1990
2	*Mrs Doubtfire*	1993
3	*Beverly Hills Cop*	1984
4	*Ghost*	1990
5	*Home Alone 2: Lost in New York*	1992
6	*Tootsie*	1982
7	*Pretty Woman*	1990
8	*Three Men and a Baby*	1987
9	*Beverly Hills Cop II*	1987
10	*The Sting*	1973

The two *Beverly Hills Cop* films are regarded by certain purists as "action thrillers" rather than comedies. If they are excluded, Nos. 9 and 10 become *National Lampoon's Animal House* (1978) and *Crocodile Dundee* (1986). If *Ghost* and *Pretty Woman*, which are arguably either comedies or romances with comedy elements, are also excluded, the next two on this list are *Look Who's Talking* (1989) and *Coming to America* (1988). Other high-earning comedy films include *Sister Act* (1992), *City Slickers* (1991), *Nine to Five* (1980), *Smokey and the Bandit* (1977), *Stir Crazy* (1980), *Crocodile Dundee II* (1988), and *The Addams Family* (1991).

WHO FRAMED ROGER RABBIT?
Bob Hoskins faces his co-star in this part-animated, part-live action film.

TOP 10

CHILDREN'S FILMS

(Excluding animated films)

1	*Honey, I Shrunk the Kids*	1989
2	*Hook*	1991
3	*Teenage Mutant Ninja Turtles*	1990
4	*The Karate Kid Part II*	1986
5	*Mary Poppins*	1964
6	*The Karate Kid*	1984
7	*Teenage Mutant Ninja Turtles II*	1991
8	*War Games*	1983
9	*The Muppet Movie*	1979
10	*The Goonies*	1985

Some of the most successful films of all time, such as *E.T.*, *Star Wars* and its two sequels, the two *Ghostbusters* films, *Home Alone* and *Home Alone 2: Lost in New York*, have been those that are unrestricted by classification, appeal to the broadest possible base of the "family audience," and consequently attract the greatest revenue. This list, however, is of films that are aimed primarily at a young audience – though some are undoubtedly also appreciated by accompanying adults.

TOP 10

MUSICAL FILMS

1	*Grease*	1978
2	*The Sound of Music*	1965
3	*Saturday Night Fever*	1977
4	*American Graffiti*	1973
5	*The Best Little Whorehouse in Texas*	1982
6	*Mary Poppins*	1964
7	*Fiddler on the Roof*	1971
8	*Annie*	1982
9	*A Star Is Born*	1976
10	*Flashdance*	1983

Traditional musicals (films in which the cast actually sings) and films in which a musical soundtrack is a major component of the film are included. Several other musical films have also each earned in excess of $30,000,000 in North American rentals; among them *Coalminer's Daughter* (1980), *The Rocky Horror Picture Show* (1975), *Footloose* (1984), *The Blues Brothers* (1980), and *Purple Rain* (1984), but it would appear that the era of the blockbuster musical film is over.

TOP 10

DISASTER FILMS

1	*Die Hard 2*	1990
2	*The Towering Inferno*	1975
3	*Airport*	1970
4	*The Poseidon Adventure*	1972
5	*Die Hard*	1988
6	*Earthquake*	1974
7	*Airport 1975*	1974
8	*Airport '77*	1977
9	*The Hindenburg*	1975
10	*Black Sunday*	1977

Disasters involving blazing buildings, natural disasters such as volcanoes, earthquakes and tidal waves, train and air crashes, sinking ships, and terrorist attacks have long been a staple of Hollywood films, of which these are the most successful. Firemen fighting fires are also part of the theme of *Backdraft* (1991), which, if included, would enter at No. 5. *The China Syndrome* (1979) would appear in seventh place, except that the threatened nuclear diasaster that provides the story line is actually averted.

TOP 10

BIBLICAL FILMS

1	*The Ten Commandments*	1956
2	*Ben Hur*	1959
3	*The Robe*	1953
4	*Jesus Christ Superstar*	1973
5	*Quo Vadis*	1951
6	*Samson and Delilah*	1949
7	*Spartacus*	1960
8	*Jesus*	1979
9	*The Greatest Story Ever Told*	1965
10	*King of Kings*	1961

Biblical subjects have been standard Hollywood fare since the pioneer days, but are now less fashionable – Martin Scorsese's controversial *The Last Temptation of Christ* (1988) actually earned less than silent versions of *Ben Hur* (1926) and *The Ten Commandments* (1923).

TOP 10

HORROR FILMS

1	*Jurassic Park*	1993
2	*Jaws*	1975
3	*The Exorcist*	1973
4	*Jaws II*	1978
5	*Bram Stoker's Dracula*	1992
6	*Aliens*	1986
7	*Alien*	1979
8	*Poltergeist*	1982
9	*King Kong*	1976
10	*The Amityville Horror*	1979

This list encompasses supernatural and science-fiction horror and monsters (including dinosaurs, gorillas, and oversized sharks), but omits science-fiction films that do not have a major horrific component.

TOP 10

FILMS FEATURING DINOSAURS

1	*Jurassic Park*	1993
2	*Fantasia*	1940
3	*The Land Before Time**	1988
4	*Baby… Secret of the Lost Legend*	1985
5	*One of Our Dinosaurs is Missing*	1975
6	*Journey to the Center of the Earth*	1959
7	*King Kong*	1933
8	*At the Earth's Core*	1976
9	*One Million Years BC*	1966
10	*When Dinosaurs Ruled the Earth*	1970

* *Animated*

TOUGH GUYS

JAMES BOND FILMS

	Film	Year	Bond actor
1	Octopussy	1983	Roger Moore
2	Moonraker	1979	Roger Moore
3	Thunderball	1965	Sean Connery
4	Never Say Never Again	1983	Sean Connery
5	The Living Daylights	1987	Timothy Dalton
6	For Your Eyes Only	1981	Roger Moore
7	A View to a Kill	1985	Roger Moore
8	The Spy Who Loved Me	1977	Roger Moore
9	Goldfinger	1964	Sean Connery
10	Diamonds Are Forever	1967	Sean Connery

Ian Fleming's 12 James Bond novels have miraculously become the basis of 18 films. After his death in 1964, *For Your Eyes Only*, *Octopussy*, and *The Living Daylights* were developed by other writers from his short stories; *Never Say Never Again* was effectively a remake of *Thunderball*, while *A View to a Kill* and *Licence to Kill* (1989, in 11th place) were written without reference to Fleming's writings. *Casino Royale*, the 13th highest-earning Bond film, featuring 56-year-old David Niven as the retired spy Sir James Bond, is an oddity in that it was presented as an avowed comedy, rather than an adventure with comic elements. Outside the Top 10, George Lazenby played Bond in a single film, *On Her Majesty's Secret Service*, which ranks next to bottom in the earnings league; the very first Bond film, *Dr. No* (1963), has earned the least – less, in fact, than *Chitty Chitty Bang Bang*, the film based on Ian Fleming's children's book of this title.

PRISON AND PRISON ESCAPE FILMS*

1	Stir Crazy	1980
2	Papillon	1973
3	Escape from Alcatraz	1979
4	Ernest Goes to Jail	1990
5	Breakout	1975
6	Cool Hand Luke	1967
7	We're No Angels	1989
8	Chained Heat	1983
9	Penitentiary	1980
10	Jailhouse Rock	1957

* *Excluding war films with prison scenes (such as* The Dirty Dozen*) or prisoner-of-war movies (*The Great Escape, Stalag 17, *etc.).*

AL PACINO
Although best known for his roles in Scarface *and the* Godfather *films, Al Pacino did not receive an Oscar for any of them. His first "Best Actor" award was for* Scent of a Woman *(1992).*

COP FILMS

1	Beverly Hills Cop	1984
2	Beverly Hills Cop II	1987
3	Lethal Weapon 3	1993
4	Lethal Weapon 2	1989
5	Die Hard 2	1990
6	Dick Tracy	1990
7	Basic Instinct	1992
8	Naked Gun 2½: The Smell of Fear	1991
9	Another 48 Hrs	1990
10	Police Academy	1984

This list includes only films in which policemen or detectives are the central characters. *The Silence of the Lambs* (1991) and *The Untouchables* (1987) earned enough to qualify, but the main characters in both are with the FBI rather than police officers. A close runner-up is *Turner & Hooch* (1989), where it is arguable whether the cop or the dog is the star. *Lethal Weapon 2* and *3* feature prominently in this list, along with *Another 48 Hrs*, but what happened to the original films? Like *The Terminator* / *Terminator 2*, they are classic examples of originals out-earned by their sequels – in the instance of *Lethal Weapon*, each of the successors made more than twice as much as the prototype. Each of the five *Police Academy* sequels, on the other hand, earned progressively less than its predecessor.

MAFIA FILMS

1	The Godfather	1972
2	The Firm	1993
3	The Godfather, Part III	1990
4	The Untouchables	1987
5	The Godfather, Part II	1974
6	Scarface	1983
7	Goodfellas	1990
8	Prizzi's Honor	1985
9	The Cotton Club	1984
10	Married to the Mob	1988

T O P   1 0

WESTERNS

1	*Dances with Wolves*	1990
2	*Butch Cassidy and the Sundance Kid*	1969
3	*Unforgiven*	1992
4	*Jeremiah Johnson*	1972
5	*How the West Was Won*	1962
6	*Pale Rider*	1985
7	*Young Guns*	1988
8	*Young Guns II*	1990
9	*Bronco Billy*	1980
10	*Little Big Man*	1970

Clint Eastwood is in the unusual position of directing and starring in a film that has forced another of his own films out of the Top 10, since the recent success of *Unforgiven* has ejected *The Outlaw Josey Wales* (1976). Although it has a Western setting, *Back to the Future, Part III* (1990) is essentially a science-fiction film (if it were a true Western, it would rate in 2nd place). According to some criteria, *The Last of the Mohicans* (1992) qualifies as a Western; if included, it would be in 4th position.

SETTING THE STAGE
Films are either shot on location or in a studio set. Hollywood westerns inevitably included a dusty frontier town, and usually featured a confrontation scene in the saloon.

T O P   1 0

WAR FILMS

1	*Platoon*	1986
2	*Good Morning, Vietnam*	1987
3	*Apocalypse Now*	1979
4	*M*A*S*H*	1970
5	*Patton*	1970
6	*The Deer Hunter*	1978
7	*Full Metal Jacket*	1987
8	*Midway*	1976
9	*The Dirty Dozen*	1967
10	*A Bridge Too Far*	1977

Surprisingly few war films have appeared in the high-earning bracket in recent years, which suggests that the days of big-budget films in this genre may be over. This list, however, excludes successful films that are not technically "war" films but that have military themes, such as *A Few Good Men* (1992), *The Hunt for Red October* (1990), and *An Officer and a Gentleman* (1982), which would otherwise be placed in the top five. Another such film is *Top Gun* (1986), which would actually head the list, just beating *Rambo: First Blood 2* (1985), a post-Vietnam war action film that is also disqualified.

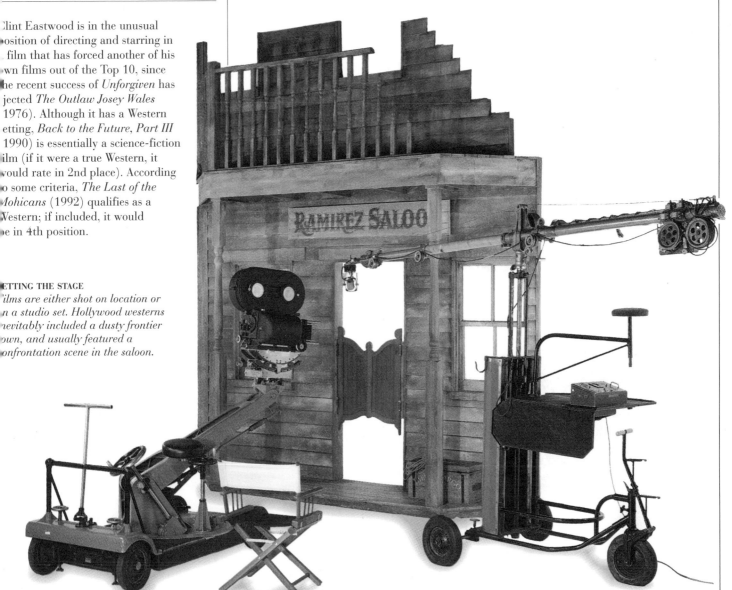

OSCAR WINNERS – FILMS

T O P 1 0

FILMS NOMINATED FOR THE MOST OSCARS

(Oscar® is a registered trademark)

	Film	Year	Awards	Nominations
1	*All About Eve*	1950	6	14
2=	*Gone With the Wind*	1939	8*	13
2=	*From Here to Eternity*	1953	8	13
2=	*Mary Poppins*	1964	5	13
2=	*Who's Afraid of Virginia Woolf?*	1966	5	13
6=	*Mrs Miniver*	1942	6	12
6=	*The Song of Bernadette*	1943	4	12
6=	*Johnny Belinda*	1948	1	12
6=	*A Streetcar Named Desire*	1951	4	12
6=	*On the Waterfront*	1954	8	12
6=	*Ben Hur*	1959	11	12
6=	*Becket*	1964	1	12
6=	*My Fair Lady*	1964	8	12
6=	*Reds*	1981	3	12
6=	*Dances with Wolves*	1990	7	12
6=	*Schindler's List*	1993	7	12

* *Plus two special awards*

The Turning Point (1977) and *The Color Purple* (1985) suffered the ignominy of receiving 11 nominations without a single win.

T O P 1 0

FILMS TO WIN MOST OSCARS

	Film	Year	Awards
1	*Ben Hur*	1959	11
2	*West Side Story*	1961	10
3=	*Gigi*	1958	9
3=	*The Last Emperor*	1987	9
5=	*Gone With the Wind*	1939	8
5=	*From Here to Eternity*	1953	8
5=	*On the Waterfront*	1954	8
5=	*My Fair Lady*	1964	8
5=	*Cabaret*	1972	8
5=	*Gandhi*	1982	8
5=	*Amadeus*	1984	8

Going My Way (1944), *The Best Years of Our Lives* (1946), *The Bridge on the River Kwai* (1957), *Lawrence of Arabia* (1962), *Patton* (1970), *The Sting* (1973), *Out of Africa* (1985), *Dances with Wolves* (1990), and *Schindler's List* (1993) all won seven Oscars each.

T O P 1 0

"BEST PICTURE" OSCAR WINNERS AT THE BOX OFFICE

1	*Rain Man*	1988
2	*The Godfather*	1972
3	*Dances with Wolves*	1990
4	*The Sound of Music*	1965
5	*Gone With the Wind*	1939
6	*The Sting*	1973
7	*Platoon*	1986
8	*Kramer* vs *Kramer*	1979
9	*One Flew Over the Cuckoo's Nest*	1975
10	*The Silence of the Lambs*	1991

Winning the Academy Award for "Best Picture" is no guarantee of box-office success: the award is given for a picture released the previous year, and by the time the Oscar ceremony takes place, the filmgoing public has already effectively decided on the winning picture's fate. Receiving the Oscar may enhance a successful picture's continuing earnings, but it is generally too late to revive a film that may already have been judged mediocre.

T O P 1 0

"BEST PICTURE" OSCAR WINNERS OF THE 1960s

Year	Film
1960	*The Apartment*
1961	*West Side Story*
1962	*Lawrence of Arabia*
1963	*Tom Jones*
1964	*My Fair Lady*
1965	*The Sound of Music*
1966	*A Man for All Seasons*
1967	*In the Heat of the Night*
1968	*Oliver!*
1969	*Midnight Cowboy*

The 1960 winner, *The Apartment*, was the last black-and-white film to receive a "Best Picture" Oscar until Steven Spielberg's *Schindler's List* in 1993.

TOP 10

"BEST PICTURE" OSCAR WINNERS OF THE 1930s

Year	Film
1930	All Quiet on the Western Front
1931	Cimarron
1932	Grand Hotel
1933	Cavalcade
1934	It Happened One Night*
1935	Mutiny on the Bounty
1936	The Great Ziegfeld
1937	The Life of Emile Zola
1938	You Can't Take it With You
1939	Gone With the Wind

* Winner of Oscars for "Best Director," "Best Actor," "Best Actress," and "Best Screenplay"

The first Academy Awards, popularly known as Oscars, were presented at a ceremony at the Hollywood Roosevelt Hotel on May 16, 1929, and were for films released in the period 1927–28. A second ceremony held at the Ambassador Hotel on October 31 of the same year was for films released in 1928–29.

TOP 10

"BEST PICTURE" OSCAR WINNERS OF THE 1970s

Year	Film
1970	Patton
1971	The French Connection
1972	The Godfather
1973	The Sting
1974	The Godfather, Part II
1975	One Flew Over the Cuckoo's Nest*
1976	Rocky
1977	Annie Hall
1978	The Deer Hunter
1979	Kramer vs Kramer

* Winner of Oscars for "Best Director," "Best Actor," "Best Actress," and "Best Screenplay"

TOP 10

"BEST PICTURE" OSCAR WINNERS OF THE 1940s

Year	Film
1940	Rebecca
1941	How Green Was My Valley
1942	Mrs Miniver
1943	Casablanca
1944	Going My Way
1945	The Lost Weekend
1946	The Best Years of Our Lives
1947	Gentleman's Agreement
1948	Hamlet
1949	All the King's Men

TOP 10

"BEST PICTURE" OSCAR WINNERS OF THE 1980s

Year	Film
1980	Ordinary People
1981	Chariots of Fire
1982	Gandhi
1983	Terms of Endearment
1984	Amadeus
1985	Out of Africa
1986	Platoon
1987	The Last Emperor
1988	Rain Man
1989	Driving Miss Daisy

The winners of "Best Picture" Oscars during the 1990s are: 1990 Dances With Wolves; 1991 The Silence of the Lambs – which also won Oscars for "Best Director," "Best Actor," "Best Actress," and "Best Screenplay;" 1992 Unforgiven; and 1993 Schindler's List – which also won six other awards. These were for "Best Director," "Best Adapted Screenplay," "Best Film Editing," "Best Art Direction," "Best Cinematography," and "Best Original Score."

TOP 10

"BEST PICTURE" OSCAR WINNERS OF THE 1950s

Year	Film
1950	All About Eve
1951	An American in Paris
1952	The Greatest Show on Earth
1953	From Here to Eternity
1954	On the Waterfront
1955	Marty
1956	Around the World in 80 Days
1957	The Bridge on the River Kwai
1958	Gigi
1959	Ben Hur

GOLDEN IDOL
Standing 13.5 in 30 cm high, gold-plated "Oscar" was reputedly named for his resemblance to a film librarian's Uncle Oscar.

DID YOU KNOW

LANDMARKS

Wings (1927), the first film to receive a "Best Picture" award, was silent. The first talkie, and the first musical, to win an Oscar was Broadway Melody (1928). The film was a novelty in that it contained sequences shot in a primitive, two-color form of Technicolor (using only red and green). Gone With the Wind was the first all-color winner of the "Best Picture" award.

OSCAR WINNERS – STARS & DIRECTORS

ACTORS AND ACTRESSES WITH MOST OSCAR NOMINATIONS

	Actor/actress/nomination years	Nominations
1	Katharine Hepburn 1932–33*; 1935; 1940; 1942; 1951; 1955; 1956; 1959; 1962; 1967*; 1968*(shared); 1981*	12
2=	Bette Davis 1935*; 1938*; 1939; 1940; 1941; 1942; 1944; 1950; 1952; 1962	10
2=	Jack Nicholson 1969#; 1970; 1973; 1974; 1975*; 1981#; 1983#; 1985; 1987; 1992#	10
2=	Laurence Olivier 1939; 1940; 1946; 1948*; 1956; 1960; 1965; 1972; 1976#; 1978	10
5	Spencer Tracy 1936; 1937*; 1938*; 1950; 1955; 1958; 1960; 1961; 1967	9
6=	Marlon Brando 1951; 1952; 1953; 1954*; 1957; 1972*; 1973; 1989#	8
6=	Jack Lemmon 1955#; 1959; 1960; 1962; 1973*; 1979; 1980; 1982	8
6=	Al Pacino 1972#; 1973; 1974; 1975; 1979; 1990#; 1992*; 1992#	8
6=	Geraldine Page 1953#; 1961; 1962; 1966; 1972; 1978; 1984; 1985*	8
10=	Ingrid Bergman 1943; 1944*; 1945; 1948; 1956*; 1974#; 1978	7
10=	Richard Burton 1952#; 1953; 1964; 1965; 1966; 1969; 1977	7
10=	Jane Fonda 1969; 1971*; 1977; 1978; 1979; 1986; 1981#	7
10=	Greer Garson 1939; 1941; 1942*; 1943; 1944; 1945; 1960	7
10=	Paul Newman** 1958; 1961; 1963; 1967; 1981; 1982; 1986*	7
10=	Peter O'Toole 1962; 1964; 1968; 1969; 1972; 1980; 1982	7

* Won Academy Award
\# Nomination for
   "Best Supporting Actor"
   or "Best Supporting Actress"
** Also won an honorary Oscar in 1985

JACK NICHOLSON
*Although in equal second place
on this list, with 10 nominations,
he has won only two Oscars.*

As the Top 10 shows, a number of actors and actresses have received numerous nominations without actually winning many (or, in Richard Burton's and Peter O'Toole's cases, any) Oscars. Two actresses and two actors tie in first place with totals of eight unsuccessful nominations for "Best Actor," "Best Actress," "Best Supporting Actor," or "Best Supporting Actress": Bette Davis, Katharine Hepburn, Jack Nicholson, and Laurence Olivier. Deborah Kerr was nominated as "Best Actress" and Thelma Ritter six times as "Best Supporting Actress," but neither ever won (although Deborah Kerr won an Honorary Award in 1993). It is clearly worth persevering, however: up to 1992, Al Pacino had been nominated four times as "Best Actor" and twice as "Best Supporting Actor" without winning, but in that year he found himself nominated in both categories and broke his losing streak by winning the "Best Actor" Oscar for *Scent of a Woman*.

"BEST ACTOR" OSCAR WINNERS OF THE 1970s

Actor	Film	Year
George C. Scott	*Patton**	1970
Gene Hackman	*The French Connection**	1971
Marlon Brando	*The Godfather**	1972
Jack Lemmon	*Save the Tiger*	1973
Art Carney	*Harry and Tonto*	1974
Jack Nicholson	*One Flew Over the Cuckoo's Nest*#*	1975
Peter Finch	*Network***	1976
Richard Dreyfuss	*The Goodbye Girl*	1977
John Voight	*Coming Home***	1978
Dustin Hoffman	*Kramer vs Kramer**	1979

*   *Winner of "Best Picture" Oscar*
\#   *Winner of "Best Director," "Best Actress,"
    and "Best Screenplay" Oscars*
** *Winner of "Best Actress" Oscar*

Peter Finch was the first (and so far only) "Best Actor" to be honored posthumously: he died on January 14, 1977 and the award was announced at the 1976 ceremony held on March 28, 1977. He was not the first posthumous winner of any Academy Award, however: that distinction went to Sidney Howard for his screenplay for *Gone With the Wind*. Howard died on August 23, 1939, and on February 29, 1940 the Nobel Prize-winning novelist Sinclair Lewis received the Oscar on his behalf.

The oldest "Best Actor" Oscar winner (and nominee) is Henry Fonda, who was 76 at the time of his 1981 win for *On Golden Pond*. The oldest "Best Actress" Oscar-winner (and also oldest nominee) is Jessica Tandy (for *Driving Miss Daisy*, 1989 Awards), who was in her 80th year at the time of the ceremony. The oldest "Best Supporting Actor" is George Burns, aged 80 (*The Sunshine Boys*, 1975). Ralph Richardson was 82 when he was nominated as "Best Supporting Actor" for his role in *Greystoke: The Legend of Tarzan* (1984), as was Eva Le Gallienne, nominated as "Best Supporting Actress" for her part in *Resurrection* (1980), but the oldest winner in the latter category is Peggy Ashcroft, aged 77, for *A Passage to India* (1984).

TOP 10

"BEST ACTRESS" OSCAR WINNERS OF THE 1970s

Actress	Film	Year
Glenda Jackson	*Women in Love*	1970
Jane Fonda	*Klute*	1971
Liza Minelli	*Cabaret*	1972
Glenda Jackson	*A Touch of Class*	1973
Ellen Burstyn	*Alice Doesn't Live Here Any More*	1974
Louise Fletcher	*One Flew Over the Cuckoo's Nest* **	1975
Faye Dunaway	*Network*#	1976
Diane Keaton	*Annie Hall**	1977
Jane Fonda	*Coming Home*#	1978
Sally Field	*Norma Rae*	1979

* *Winner of "Best Picture" Oscar*
** *Winner of "Best Director," "Best Actor," and "Best Screenplay" Oscars*
# *Winner of "Best Actor" Oscar*

DIANE KEATON
Her "Best Actress" award was for her starring role in Woody Allen's film Annie Hall.

TOP 10

"BEST DIRECTOR" OSCAR WINNERS OF THE 1970s

Director	Film	Year
Franklin J. Schaffner	*Patton**	1970
William Friedkin	*The French Connection**	1971
Bob Fosse	*Cabaret*	1972
George Roy Hill	*The Sting**	1973
Francis Ford Coppola	*The Godfather Part II**	1974
Milos Forman	*One Flew Over the Cuckoo's Nest**	1975
John G. Avildsen	*Rocky**	1976
Woody Allen	*Annie Hall**	1977
Michael Cimino	*The Deer Hunter**	1978
Robert Benton	*Kramer vs Kramer**	1979

* *Winner of "Best Picture" Oscar*

TOP 10

"BEST ACTOR" OSCAR WINNERS OF THE 1980s

Actor	Film	Year
Robert De Niro	*Raging Bull*	1980
Henry Fonda	*On Golden Pond*#	1981
Ben Kingsley	*Gandhi**	1982
Robert Duvall	*Tender Mercies*	1983
F. Murray Abraham	*Amadeus**	1984
William Hurt	*Kiss of the Spider Woman*	1985
Paul Newman	*The Color of Money*	1986
Michael Douglas	*Wall Street*	1987
Dustin Hoffman	*Rain Man**	1988
Daniel Day-Lewis	*My Left Foot*	1989

* *Winner of "Best Picture" Oscar*
# *Winner of "Best Actress" Oscar*

The "Best Actor" Oscar-winners of the 1990s to date are – 1990: Jeremy Irons for *Reversal of Fortune*; 1991: Anthony Hopkins for *The Silence of the Lambs* (which also won "Best Picture" and "Best Actress" Oscars); 1992: Al Pacino for *Scent of a Woman*; 1993: Tom Hanks for *Philadelphia*.

TOP 10

"BEST ACTRESS" OSCAR WINNERS OF THE 1980s

Actress	Film	Year
Sissy Spacek	*Coal Miner's Daughter*	1980
Katharine Hepburn	*On Golden Pond*#	1981
Meryl Streep	*Sophie's Choice*	1982
Shirley MacLaine	*Terms of Endearment**	1983
Sally Field	*Places in the Heart*	1984
Geraldine Page	*The Trip to Bountiful*	1985
Marlee Matlin	*Children of a Lesser God*	1986
Cher	*Moonstruck*	1987
Jodie Foster	*The Accused*	1988
Jessica Tandy	*Driving Miss Daisy**	1989

* *Winner of "Best Picture" Oscar*
# *Winner of "Best Actor" Oscar*

The winners of "Best Actress" Oscars during the 1990s are – 1990: Kathy Bates for *Misery*; 1991: Jodie Foster for *The Silence of the Lambs*; 1992: Emma Thompson for *Howard's End*; 1993: Holly Hunter for *The Piano*.

TOP 10

"BEST DIRECTOR" OSCAR WINNERS OF THE 1980s

Director	Film	Year
Robert Redford	*Ordinary People**	1980
Warren Beatty	*Reds*	1981
Richard Attenborough	*Gandhi**	1982
James L. Brooks	*Terms of Endearment**	1983
Milos Forman	*Amadeus**	1984
Sydney Pollack	*Out of Africa**	1985
Oliver Stone	*Platoon**	1986
Bernardo Bertolucci	*The Last Emperor**	1987
Barry Levinson	*Rain Man**	1988
Oliver Stone	*Born on the Fourth of July*	1989

* *Winner of "Best Picture" Oscar*

The winners of "Best Director" Oscars in the 1990s are – 1990: Kevin Costner for *Dances with Wolves*; 1991: Jonathan Demme for *The Silence of the Lambs*; 1992: Clint Eastwood for *Unforgiven*; 1993: Steven Spielberg for *Schindler's List*.

FILM STARS – ACTORS

TOP 10

TOM CRUISE FILMS

1	*Rain Man*	1988
2	*Top Gun*	1986
3	*The Firm*	1993
4	*A Few Good Men*	1992
5	*Days of Thunder*	1990
6	*Born on the Fourth of July*	1989
7	*Cocktail*	1988
8	*Risky Business*	1983
9	*Far and Away*	1992
10	*The Color of Money*	1986

TOP 10

MICHAEL DOUGLAS FILMS

1	*Fatal Attraction*	1987
2	*Basic Instinct*	1992
3	*The War of the Roses*	1989
4	*The Jewel of the Nile*	1985
5	*Romancing the Stone*	1984
6	*The China Syndrome*	1979
7	*Black Rain*	1989
8	*Wall Street*	1987
9	*Falling Down*	1993
10	*Coma*	1978

TOP 10

ANTHONY HOPKINS FILMS

1	*The Silence of the Lambs*	1991
2	*Bram Stoker's Dracula*	1992
3	*A Bridge Too Far*	1977
4	*Magic*	1978
5	*Howard's End*	1992
6	*The Elephant Man*	1980
7	*Shadowlands*	1993
8	*The Remains of the Day*	1993
9	*The Lion in Winter*	1968
10	*Freejack*	1992

TOP 10

HARRISON FORD FILMS

1	*Star Wars*	1977
2	*Return of the Jedi*	1983
3	*The Empire Strikes Back*	1980
4	*Raiders of the Lost Ark*	1981
5	*Indiana Jones and the Last Crusade*	1989
6	*Indiana Jones and the Temple of Doom*	1984
7	*The Fugitive*	1993
8	*American Graffiti*	1973
9	*Presumed Innocent*	1990
10	*Apocalypse Now*	1979

Harrison Ford is in the fortunate position of having appeared in so many successful films that even if, for example, *Apocalypse Now* were deleted from the Top 10 (since his role in it amounted to little more than a cameo), several similarly profitable films in which he starred could easily replace it, among them *Patriot Games* (1992), *Working Girl* (1988), *Witness* (1985), *Regarding Henry* (1991), and *Blade Runner* (1982). One film organization has recently voted Ford "Box Office Star of the Century."

TOP 10

SEAN CONNERY FILMS

1	*Indiana Jones and the Last Crusade*	1989
2	*The Hunt for Red October*	1990
3	*The Untouchables*	1987
4	*Rising Sun*	1993
5	*Thunderball*	1965
6	*Never Say Never Again*	1983
7	*Goldfinger*	1964
8	*Medicine Man*	1992
9	*Time Bandits*	1981
10	*A Bridge Too Far*	1977

If Sean Connery's fleeting cameo entry in the final two minutes of *Robin Hood: Prince of Thieves* (1991) is taken into account, it would be placed 2nd in the list.

TOP 10

SYLVESTER STALLONE FILMS

1	*Rambo: First Blood 2*	1985
2	*Rocky IV*	1985
3	*Rocky III*	1982
4	*Rocky*	1976
5	*Cliffhanger*	1993
6	*Rocky II*	1979
7	*Tango and Cash*	1989
8	*Cobra*	1986
9	*Demolition Man*	1993
10	*First Blood*	1982

TOP 10

AL PACINO FILMS

1	*The Godfather*	1972
2	*Dick Tracy*	1990
3	*The Godfather Part III*	1990
4	*The Godfather Part II*	1974
5	*Sea of Love*	1989
6	*Scent of a Woman*	1992
7	*Scarface*	1983
8	*Dog Day Afternoon*	1975
9	*Carlito's Way*	1993
10	*Serpico*	1973

TOP 10

JACK NICHOLSON FILMS

1	*Batman*	1989
2	*A Few Good Men*	1992
3	*One Flew Over the Cuckoo's Nest*	1975
4	*Terms of Endearment*	1983
5	*The Witches of Eastwick*	1987
6	*The Shining*	1980
7	*Broadcast News*	1987
8	*Reds*	1981
9	*Easy Rider*	1969
10	*Carnal Knowledge*	1971

TOP 10

CLINT EASTWOOD'S FIRST FILMS

1	*Revenge of the Creature*	1955
2	*Lady Godiva*	1955
3	*Tarantula*	1955
4	*Never Say Goodbye*	1956
5	*The First Traveling Saleslady*	1956
6	*Star in the Dust*	1956
7	*Escapade in Japan*	1957
8	*Ambush at Cimarron Pass*	1958
9	*Lafayette Escadrille*	1958
10	*A Fistful of Dollars*	1964

Eastwood's first roles were as a laboratory technician in *Revenge of the Creature*, the 1955 sequel to *The Creature from the Black Lagoon*; as "First Saxon" in *Lady Godiva*; as the squadron leader of the force that attacks the giant spiders in *Tarantula*; and back to his role as a lab assistant in *Never Say Goodbye*. *The First Traveling Saleslady*, a bizarre Western about a corset-seller, was his first film in the genre that he was to make his own: after a brief excursion as a soldier called Dumbo in *Escapade in Japan*, and his appearance in *Lafayette Escadrille*, a film about First World War flying aces, all the rest of his early films were Westerns – and it was with the "spaghetti Western" that he finally broke through to superstardom.

TOP 10

ARNOLD SCHWARZENEGGER FILMS

1	*Terminator 2: Judgment Day*	1991
2	*Total Recall*	1990
3	*Twins*	1988
4	*Kindergarten Cop*	1990
5	*Predator*	1987
6	*Last Action Hero*	1993
7	*Conan the Barbarian*	1981
8	*Commando*	1985
9	*The Terminator*	1984
10	*The Running Man*	1987

TOP 10

CLINT EASTWOOD FILMS

1	*Every Which Way But Loose*	1978
2	*In The Line of Fire*	1993
3	*Unforgiven*	1992
4	*Any Which Way You Can*	1980
5	*Sudden Impact*	1983
6	*Firefox*	1982
7	*The Enforcer*	1976
8	*Tightrope*	1984
9	*Heartbreak Ridge*	1986
10	*Escape from Alcatraz*	1979

Unforgiven, Eastwood's 1992 multi-Oscar-winning film ("Best Picture," "Director," "Editing," "Supporting Actor"), rapidly made an impact and by the end of the following year had become his third highest-earning film ever, although just overtaken by *In The Line of Fire*.

TOP 10

KEVIN COSTNER FILMS

1	*Robin Hood: Prince of Thieves*	1991
2	*Dances with Wolves*	1990
3	*The Bodyguard*	1992
4	*The Untouchables*	1987
5	*JFK*	1991
6	*Field of Dreams*	1989
7	*The Big Chill*	1983
8	*Bull Durham*	1988
9	*Silverado*	1985
10	*No Way Out*	1987

Costner's acting role in *The Big Chill* was cut, and we see only parts of his body as it is being prepared for a funeral. If this entry is ignored, his 10th most successful film is *Night Shift* (1982). Ten years after his first film, Costner (born January 18, 1955, Lynwood, California) received huge acclaim (and seven Oscars) for *Dances With Wolves*, which was the first film he directed. He followed it with the smash commercial success *Robin Hood: Prince of Thieves*, and is now ranked by *Premiere* magazine as the most powerful actor in Hollywood.

TOP 10

CLINT EASTWOOD DIRECTED FILMS

1	*Unforgiven*	1992
2	*Sudden Impact*	1983
3	*Firefox*	1982
4	*Heartbreak Ridge*	1986
5	*Pale Rider*	1985
6	*The Gauntlet*	1977
7	*Bronco Billy*	1980
8	*A Perfect World*	1993
9	*The Outlaw Josey Wales*	1976
10	*The Rookie*	1990

His directorial debut was of a single scene in *Dirty Harry* (1971). If this were included, it would appear in 6th place.

TOP 10

BRUCE WILLIS FILMS

1	*Look Who's Talking**	1989
2	*Die Hard 2*	1990
3	*Die Hard*	1988
4	*Death Becomes Her*	1992
5	*The Last Boy Scout*	1991
6	*Blind Date*	1987
7	*National Lampoon's Loaded Weapon 1#*	1993
8	*The Bonfire of the Vanities*	1990
9	*Hudson Hawk*	1991
10	*Mortal Thoughts*	1991

* *Voice only*
\# *Uncredited cameo performance*

It is somewhat ironic to consider that the most successful film role of an actor whose screen persona is of a tough-guy should be that of a baby in *Look Who's Talking* – and that consisting only of Willis's dubbed voice. If discounted, either of two other films, *Sunset* (1988) and *In Country* (1989) could be considered as contenders for 10th place, although neither can be regarded as in any sense high-earning films. Willis has also had cameo roles – as himself – in *The Player* (1992) and *National Lampoon's Loaded Weapon 1* (1993).

FILM STARS – ACTRESSES

T O P 1 0

DEMI MOORE FILMS

1	Ghost	1990
2	A Few Good Men	1992
3	Indecent Proposal	1993
4	St. Elmo's Fire	1985
5	About Last Night	1986
6	Young Doctors in Love	1982
7	Blame it on Rio	1984
8	Mortal Thoughts	1991
9	The Seventh Sign	1988
10	One Crazy Summer	1986

DEMI MOORE
Former star of TV soap General Hospital, *Demi Moore (real name Demi Guynes) has appeared in hit films for more than a decade. She has been married to actor Bruce Willis since 1987.*

T O P 1 0

SIGOURNEY WEAVER FILMS

1	Ghostbusters	1984
2	Ghostbusters II	1989
3	Aliens	1986
4	Alien	1979
5	Alien^3	1992
6	Dave	1993
7	Working Girl	1988
8	Gorillas in the Mist	1988
9	The Deal of the Century	1983
10	The Year of Living Dangerously	1982

Sigourney Weaver also had a fleeting minor part in *Annie Hall* (1977). If included, this would appear in 7th position.

T O P 1 0

SHARON STONE FILMS

1	Total Recall	1990
2	Basic Instinct	1992
3	Last Action Hero	1993
4	Sliver	1993
5	Police Academy 4: Citizens on Patrol	1987
6	Action Jackson	1988
7	Above the Law/Nico	1988
8	Irreconcilable Differences	1984
9	King Solomon's Mines	1985
10	He Said, She Said	1991

MICHELLE PFEIFFER
In 1994 Premiere *magazine ranked her in 97th place among the 100 most powerful people in Hollywood.*

T O P 1 0

MICHELLE PFEIFFER FILMS

1	Batman Returns	1992
2	The Witches of Eastwick	1987
3	Scarface	1983
4	Tequila Sunrise	1988
5	Dangerous Liaisons	1988
6	The Age of Innocence	1993
7	Frankie and Johnny	1991
8	The Russia House	1990
9	The Fabulous Baker Boys	1989
10	Married to the Mob	1988

T O P 1 0

KATHLEEN TURNER FILMS

1	Who Framed Roger Rabbit?*	1988
2	The War of the Roses	1989
3	The Jewel of the Nile	1985
4	Romancing the Stone	1984
5	Peggy Sue Got Married	1986
6	The Accidental Tourist	1988
7	Prizzi's Honor	1985
8	Body Heat	1981
9	V.I. Warshawski	1991
10	The Man with Two Brains	1983

* *Speaking voice of Jessica Rabbit; if excluded, the 10th film in which she acted is* Switching Channels *(1988).*

TOP 10
KIM BASINGER FILMS

1	Batman	1989
2	9½ Weeks	1986
3	Never Say Never Again	1983
4	Wayne's World 2	1993
5	The Natural	1984
6	Blind Date	1987
7	Final Analysis	1992
8	No Mercy	1986
9	The Marrying Man	1991
10	My Stepmother is an Alien	1988

TOP 10
DIANE KEATON FILMS

1	The Godfather	1972
2	The Godfather, Part II	1974
3	Father of the Bride	1991
4	The Godfather, Part III	1990
5	Reds	1981
6	Annie Hall	1977
7	Manhattan	1979
8	Looking for Mr. Goodbar	1977
9	Baby Boom	1987
10	Crimes of the Heart	1986

TOP 10
MEG RYAN FILMS

1	Top Gun	1986
2	Sleepless in Seattle	1993
3	When Harry Met Sally	1989
4	Joe Versus the Volcano	1990
5	The Doors	1991
6	Innerspace	1987
7	The Presido	1988
8	Rich and Famous	1981
9	D.O.A.	1988
10	Amityville 3-D	1983

TOP 10
CARRIE FISHER FILMS

1	Star Wars	1977
2	Return of the Jedi	1983
3	The Empire Strikes Back	1980
4	When Harry Met Sally	1989
5	The Blues Brothers	1980
6	Shampoo	1975
7	Hannah and Her Sisters	1986
8	The 'Burbs	1989
9	Soapdish	1991
10	Sibling Rivalry	1990

Along with Mark Hamill and Harrison Ford, Carrie Fisher has had the remarkable good fortune to appear in three of the Top 6 highest-earning films of all time. If she had managed to negotiate a 10 percent stake in just the North American rental income of these three, she would have received more than $50,000,000. Her part in *Shampoo* was very minor; if excluded, her 10th entry would be *Under the Rainbow* (1981).

TOP 10
JODIE FOSTER FILMS

1	The Silence of the Lambs	1990
2	Sommersby	1993
3	The Accused	1988
4	Taxi Driver	1976
5	Freaky Friday	1976
6	Little Man Tate*	1991
7	Alice Doesn't Live Here Any More	1975
8	Candleshoe	1977
9	Tom Sawyer	1973
10	The Hotel New Hampshire	1984

*   Also directed

SILENCE IS GOLDEN
Jodie Foster wins her second "Best Actress" Oscar, for The Silence of the Lambs. *She had previously won for her role in* The Accused.

TOP 10
MELANIE GRIFFITH FILMS

1	Working Girl	1988
2	Pacific Heights	1990
3	One-on-One	1977
4	Shining Through	1992
5	Paradise	1991
6	The Bonfire of the Vanities	1990
7	The Milagro Beanfield War	1988
8	Body Double	1984
9	Something Wild	1986
10	The Harrad Experiment*	1973

*   Appeared as extra only

FILM STARS –

COMEDY

TOP 10

DAN AYKROYD FILMS

1	Ghostbusters	1984
2	Indiana Jones and the Temple of Doom	1984
3	Ghostbusters II	1989
4	Driving Miss Daisy	1989
5	Trading Places	1983
6	The Blues Brothers	1980
7	Spies Like Us	1985
8	Dragnet	1987
9	My Girl	1991
10	Sneakers	1992

TOP 10

DANNY DEVITO FILMS

1	Batman Returns	1992
2	One Flew Over the Cuckoo's Nest	1975
3	Twins	1988
4	Terms of Endearment	1983
5	The War of the Roses*	1989
6	The Jewel of the Nile	1985
7	Romancing the Stone	1984
8	Ruthless People	1986
9	Throw Momma from the Train*	1987
10	Hoffa*	1992

* Also director

DANNY DEVITO
The comedy star has had success as a director as well as in his film roles.

Danny DeVito had a relatively minor role in *One Flew Over the Cuckoo's Nest*. If this is discounted from the reckoning, his 10th most successful film becomes *Other People's Money* (1991).

HORROR STORY
Rick Moranis was an unlikely hero in Little Shop of Horrors.

TOP 10

RICK MORANIS FILMS

1	Ghostbusters	1984
2	Honey, I Shrunk the Kids	1989
3	Ghostbusters II	1989
4	Parenthood	1989
5	Honey, I Blew Up the Kid	1992
6	Brewster's Millions	1985
7	Little Shop of Horrors	1986
8	Spaceballs	1987
9	My Blue Heaven	1990
10	Club Paradise	1986

TOP 10

MEL BROOKS FILMS

1	Blazing Saddles*#	1974
2	Young Frankenstein#	1975
3	The Muppet Movie*	1979
4	Look Who's Talking Too* **	1990
5	Silent Movie*	1976
6	High Anxiety*#	1977
7	Spaceballs*#	1987
8=	Robin Hood: Men in Tights	1993
8=	History of the World – Part I *#	1981
10	To Be or Not to Be*	1983

* Appeared in
 # Directed or co-directed
** Voice only

TOP 10

ROBIN WILLIAMS FILMS

1	Mrs. Doubtfire	1993
2	Hook	1991
3	Good Morning, Vietnam	1987
4	Dead Poets Society	1989
5	Popeye	1980
6	Awakenings	1990
7	The Fisher King	1991
8	Dead Again	1991
9	The World According to Garp	1982
10	Cadillac Man	1990

Robin Williams's voice appears as that of the genie in the 1992 animated blockbuster *Aladdin*. If this were included, its earnings would place it second in the list. If his minor cameo role in *Dead Again* is excluded, his 10th most successful film would be *Toys* (1992).

CLEANING UP
Robin Williams has had amazing success with his role as the housekeeper Mrs. Doubtfire.

T O P 1 0
BILL MURRAY FILMS

1	*Ghostbusters*	1984	6	*Scrooged*	1988
2	*Tootsie*	1982	7	*What About Bob?*	1991
3	*Ghostbusters II*	1989	8	*Meatballs*	1979
4	*Stripes*	1981	9	*Caddyshack*	1980
5	*Groundhog Day*	1993	10	*Little Shop of Horrors*	1986

T O P 1 0
WOODY ALLEN FILMS

1	*Annie Hall* (A, S, D)	1977
2	*Hannah and Her Sisters* (A, S, D)	1986
3	*Manhattan* (A, S, D)	1979
4	*Casino Royale* (A)	1967
5	*Everything You Always Wanted to Know about Sex (But Were Afraid to Ask)* (A, S, D)	1972
6	*What's New, Pussycat?* (A, S)	1965
7	*Sleeper* (A, S, D)	1973
8	*Crimes and Misdemeanors* (A, S, D)	1989
9	*Love and Death* (A, S, D)	1975
10	*Zelig* (A, S, D)	1983

A – *actor*
S – *scriptwriter*
D – *director*

This list includes films which Woody Allen has either written, starred in, or directed. If it were restricted only to films he has directed, *Casino Royale* and *What's New, Pussycat?* would be dropped from the list, and the new 9th and 10th entries would be *Radio Days* (1987) and *Broadway Danny Rose* (1984). *Annie Hall* was the first occasion since 1941 that one individual has been nominated for "Best Picture," "Best Actor," "Best Director," and "Best Screenplay" (the previous nominee was Orson Welles for *Citizen Kane*; he won only for "Best Screenplay," jointly with Herman J. Manciewicz). The film won Allen "Best Picture" and "Best Screenplay" Oscars – which, characteristically, he did not bother to collect.

T O P 1 0
TOM HANKS FILMS

1	*Sleepless in Seattle*	1993
2	*A League of Their Own*	1992
3	*Big*	1988
4	*Turner & Hooch*	1989
5	*Splash!*	1984
6	*Philadelphia*	1993
7	*Dragnet*	1987
8	*Bachelor Party*	1984
9	*Joe Versus the Volcano*	1990
10	*The 'Burbs*	1989

T O P 1 0
EDDIE MURPHY FILMS

1	*Beverly Hills Cop*	1984
2	*Beverly Hills Cop 2*	1987
3	*Coming to America*	1988
4	*Trading Places*	1983
5	*Another 48 Hrs*	1990
6	*The Golden Child*	1986
7	*Boomerang*	1992
8	*Harlem Nights**	1989
9	*48 Hours*	1982
10	*The Distinguished Gentleman*	1992

* *Also director*

Eddie Murphy Raw (1987), which features Murphy live on stage, is one of an elite group of documentary or "non-fiction" films that rank alongside major feature films in terms of their earnings, both from screenings and video sales and rental.

T O P 1 0
WHOOPI GOLDBERG FILMS

1	*Ghost*	1990
2	*Sister Act*	1992
3	*The Color Purple*	1985
4	*Sister Act 2: Back in the Habit*	1993
5	*Made in America*	1993
6	*Soapdish*	1991
7	*National Lampoon's Loaded Weapon 1*	1993
8	*Jumpin' Jack Flash*	1986
9	*Burglar*	1987
10	*Fatal Beauty*	1987

T O P 1 0
STEVE MARTIN FILMS

1	*Parenthood*	1989
2	*The Jerk**	1979
3	*Father of the Bride*	1991
4	*Housesitter*	1992
5	*Planes, Trains and Automobiles*	1987
6	*¡Three Amigos!**	1986
7	*Little Shop of Horrors*	1986
8	*Dirty Rotten Scoundrels*	1988
9	*Roxanne*	1987
10	*Grand Canyon*	1991

* *Also co-writer*

Steve Martin was also one of the many "guest stars" in *The Muppet Movie* (1979). If included, it would appear in 5th place.

BEING A PARENT
Steve Martin appeared as the troubled father in Parenthood.

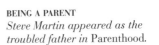

DIRECTORS

T O P 1 0

FILMS DIRECTED BY ACTOR-DIRECTORS

	Film	Year	Director
1	*Pretty Woman*	1990	Gary Marshall
2	*Dances With Wolves*	1990	Kevin Costner
3	*Three Men and a Baby*	1987	Leonard Nimoy
4	*Rocky IV*	1985	Sylvester Stallone
5	*A Few Good Men*	1992	Rob Reiner
6	*Rocky III*	1982	Sylvester Stallone
7	*On Golden Pond*	1981	Mark Rydell
8	*Dick Tracy*	1990	Warren Beatty
9	*Stir Crazy*	1980	Sidney Poitier
10	*Star Trek IV: The Voyage Home*	1986	Leonard Nimoy

Heading this list, *Pretty Woman* director Garry Marshall is the brother of actress-director Penny Marshall, who only just fails to achieve a place in this Top 10, but makes three appearances in the *Top 10 Films Directed by Women*. (Keeping it in the family, she was also once married to Top 10 actor-director Rob Reiner.) Among other actors who have also directed may be numbered Marlon Brando (*One-Eyed Jacks*, 1961), Mel Brooks (*Blazing Saddles*, 1974, *Young Frankenstein*, 1975), Robert de Niro (*A Bronx Tale*, 1993), Danny DeVito (*The War of the Roses*, 1989, *Throw Momma From the Train*, 1987), Clint Eastwood (*Sudden Impact*, 1983, *Unforgiven*, 1992), Mel Gibson (*The Man Without a Face*, 1993), former child-star Ron Howard (*Splash!*, 1984, *Parenthood*, 1989), Eddie Murphy (*Harlem Nights*, 1989), Paul Newman (*Rachel, Rachel*, 1968, *The Effect of Gamma Rays on Man-in-the-Moon Marigolds*, 1972), Jack Nicholson (*Drive, He Said*, 1971, *The Two Jakes*, 1990), Robert Redford (*Ordinary People*, 1980, *A River Runs Through It*, 1992), Burt Reynolds (*The End*, 1978, *Sharky's Machine*, 1981), William Shatner (*Star Trek V: The Final Frontier*, 1989), Orson Welles (*Citizen Kane*, 1941), and Gene Wilder (*The World's Greatest Lover*, 1977, *The Woman in Red*, 1984). British actor-directors include Richard Attenborough (*A Bridge Too Far*, 1977, *Gandhi*, 1982), Kenneth Branagh (*Henry V*, 1989, *Dead Again*, 1991), Terry Jones (*Monty Python's Life of Brian*, 1979, *Monty Python's The Meaning of Life*, 1983), and Laurence Olivier (*Henry V*, 1944, *The Prince and the Showgirl*, 1957). Notable actress-directors are Barbra Streisand (*The Prince of Tides*, 1991, *Yentl*, 1983) and Jodie Foster (*Little Man Tate*, 1991).

T O P 1 0

FILMS DIRECTED OR PRODUCED BY GEORGE LUCAS

1	*Star Wars* (D)	1977
2	*Return of the Jedi* (P)	1983
3	*The Empire Strikes Back* (P)	1980
4	*Raiders of the Lost Ark* (P)	1981
5	*Indiana Jones and the Last Crusade* (P)	1989
6	*Indiana Jones and the Temple of Doom* (P)	1984
7	*American Graffiti* (D)	1973
8	*Willow* (P)	1988
9	*The Land Before Time* (P)	1988
10	*Howard the Duck* (P)	1986

D – director   P – producer

George Lucas made the move from directing to producing after the phenomenal success of *Star Wars*, but he clearly has a Midas touch in both fields, the first six films on this list ranking among the 14 highest-earning of all time. *Howard the Duck* can be mercifully relegated from the list if his uncredited role as executive producer of *Body Heat* (1981) replaces it in 10th position.

T O P 1 0

FILMS WRITTEN OR DIRECTED BY JOHN HUGHES

1	*Home Alone* (S)	1990
2	*Home Alone 2: Lost in New York* (S)	1992
3	*National Lampoon's Christmas Vacation* (S)	1989
4	*Mr. Mom* (S)	1983
5	*National Lampoon's Vacation* (S)	1983
6	*Uncle Buck* (D, S)	1989
7	*Ferris Bueller's Day Off* (D, S)	1986
8	*National Lampoon's European Vacation* (S)	1985
9	*Planes, Trains and Automobiles* (D, S)	1987
10	*The Breakfast Club* (D, S)	1985

D – director   S – scriptwriter

T O P   1 0

FILMS DIRECTED BY WOMEN

	Film	Year	Director
1	Look Who's Talking	1989	Amy Heckerling
2	Sleepless in Seattle	1993	Nora Ephron
3	Wayne's World	1992	Penelope Spheeris
4	Big	1988	Penny Marshall
5	A League of Their Own	1992	Penny Marshall
6	The Prince of Tides	1991	Barbra Streisand
7	Pet Sematary	1989	Mary Lambert
8	National Lampoon's European Vacation	1985	Amy Heckerling
9	Awakenings	1990	Penny Marshall
10	Look Who's Talking Too	1990	Amy Heckerling

OUT OF THIS WORLD
Since the 1970s, Steven Spielberg has enjoyed astronomical success as a director.

T O P   1 0

FILMS DIRECTED BY JOHN LANDIS

1	National Lampoon's Animal House	1978
2	Coming to America	1988
3	Trading Places	1983
4	The Blues Brothers	1980
5	Spies Like Us	1985
6	Three Amigos	1986
7	Twilight Zone – The Movie*	1983
8	An American Werewolf in London	1981
9	Oscar	1991
10	The Kentucky Fried Movie	1977

* Part only; other segments directed by Joe Dante, George Miller, and Steven Spielberg.

T O P   1 0

FILMS DIRECTED BY FRANCIS FORD COPPOLA

1	The Godfather	1972
2	Bram Stoker's Dracula	1992
3	The Godfather, Part III	1990
4	Apocalypse Now	1979
5	The Godfather, Part II	1974
6	Peggy Sue Got Married	1986
7	The Cotton Club	1984
8	The Outsiders	1983
9	Tucker: the Man and His Dream	1988
10	Finian's Rainbow	1968

T O P   1 0

FILMS DIRECTED BY STEVEN SPIELBERG

1	E.T. The Extra-Terrestrial	1982
2	Jurassic Park	1993
3	Jaws	1975
4	Raiders of the Lost Ark	1981
5	Indiana Jones and the Last Crusade	1989
6	Indiana Jones and the Temple of Doom	1984
7	Close Encounters of the Third Kind	1977/80
8	Hook	1991
9	The Color Purple	1985
10	Schindler's List	1993

T O P   1 0

FILMS DIRECTED BY ALFRED HITCHCOCK

1	Psycho	1960		6	Frenzy	1972
2	Rear Window	1954		7	Vertigo	1958
3	North by Northwest	1959		8	The Man Who Knew Too Much	1956
4	Family Plot	1976		9	The Birds	1963
5	Torn Curtain	1966		10	Spellbound	1945

PSYCHO
Anthony Perkins starred as the deranged killer Norman Bates in Psycho *(1960).*

STUDIOS

COLUMBIA
Dominated for many years by Harry Cohn, who founded it in 1924, Columbia was taken over by Coca-Cola and briefly (1986–88) run by British film producer David Puttnam.

TOP 10

COLUMBIA FILMS OF ALL TIME

1	Ghostbusters	1984
2	Tootsie	1982
3	Close Encounters of the Third Kind	1977/80
4	A Few Good Men	1992
5	City Slickers	1991
6	Ghostbusters II	1989
7	Kramer vs Kramer	1979
8	Stir Crazy	1980
9	The Karate Kid Part II	1986
10	A League of Their Own	1992

TOP 10

ORION FILMS OF ALL TIME

1	Dances With Wolves	1990
2	Platoon	1986
3	The Silence of the Lambs	1991
4	Arthur	1981
5	Back to School	1986
6	10	1979
7	Throw Momma from the Train	1987
8	Robocop	1987
9	Amadeus	1984
10	First Blood	1982

MGM
Metro-Goldwyn-Mayer was established in 1924 and became the leading Hollywood studio during the 1930s. Leo the Lion, MGM's familiar logo, was devised by advertising executive Howard Dietz, who based it on the lion featured in the Columbia college magazine. White Shadows of the South (1928) was the first film in which Leo was heard roaring.

TOP 10

MGM FILMS OF ALL TIME

1	Rain Man	1988
2	Gone With the Wind	1939
3	Rocky IV	1985
4	Rocky III	1982
5	Doctor Zhivago	1965
6	The Goodbye Girl	1977
7	War Games	1983
8	Poltergeist	1982
9	Ben Hur	1959
10	Moonstruck	1987

20TH CENTURY-FOX
This studio was formed in 1935 by the merging of William Fox's film production company and studio, which made feature films and Movietone newsreels, and 20th Century Pictures. It was recently acquired by Rupert Murdoch.

TOP 10

20TH CENTURY-FOX FILMS OF ALL TIME

1	Star Wars	1977
2	Return of the Jedi	1983
3	The Empire Strikes Back	1980
4	Home Alone	1990
5	Mrs Doubtfire	1993
6	Home Alone 2	1992
7	The Sound of Music	1965
8	Die Hard 2	1990
9	9 to 5	1980
10	Porky's	1982

TOP 10

TRI-STAR FILMS OF ALL TIMES

1	Terminator 2	1991
2	Rambo: First Blood 2	1985
3	Look Who's Talking	1989
4	Hook	1991
5	Sleepless in Seattle	1993
6	Total Recall	1990
7	Basic Instinct	1992
8	Cliffhanger	1993
9	Steel Magnolias	1989
10	Rambo 3	1988

TOP 10

WARNER BROTHERS FILMS OF ALL TIME

1	Batman	1989
2	Batman Returns	1992
3	The Fugitive	1993
4	The Exorcist	1973
5	Robin Hood: Prince of Thieves	1991
6	Superman	1978
7	Lethal Weapon 3	1993
8	Gremlins	1984
9	Lethal Weapon 2	1989
10	Superman II	1981

PARAMOUNT
After several changes of name, Paramount Pictures appeared in 1933. Following various setbacks, it was rescued from the commercial doldrums in 1972 by its film The Godfather.

TOP 10

PARAMOUNT FILMS OF ALL TIME

1	Raiders of the Lost Ark	1981
2	Indiana Jones and the Last Crusade	1989
3	Indiana Jones and the Temple of Doom	1984
4	Beverly Hills Cop	1984
5	Ghost	1990
6	Grease	1978
7	The Godfather	1972
8	Beverly Hills Cop II	1987
9	Top Gun	1986
10	The Firm	1993

TOP 10

BUENA VISTA/WALT DISNEY FILMS OF ALL TIME

1	Aladdin	1992
2	Pretty Woman	1990
3	Three Men and a Baby	1987
4	Who Framed Roger Rabbit?	1988
5	Honey, I Shrunk the Kids	1989
6	Beauty and the Beast	1991
7	101 Dalmatians	1961
8	Sister Act	1992
9	Snow White and the Seven Dwarfs*	1937
10	The Jungle Book	1967

* Originally released by RKO

TOP 10

UNITED ARTISTS FILMS OF ALL TIME

1	One Flew Over the Cuckoo's Nest	1975
2	Rocky	1976
3	Rocky II	1979
4	Fiddler on the Roof	1971
5	Apocalypse Now	1979
6	Moonraker	1979
7	Thunderball	1965
8	Revenge of the Pink Panther	1978
9	The Spy Who Loved Me	1977
10	Around the World in 80 Days	1956

United Artists was formed in 1919 by actors including Charlie Chaplin and Douglas Fairbanks, together with director D.W. Griffith, to provide an independent means of producing and distributing their films. It never actually owned a studio, but rented production facilities. After many vicissitudes, and a successful run in the 1970s with the consistently successful James Bond films, it was merged with MGM in 1981.

TOP 10

UNIVERSAL FILMS OF ALL TIME

1	E.T. The Extra-Terrestrial	1982
2	Jurassic Park	1993
3	Jaws	1975
4	Back to the Future	1985
5	The Sting	1973
6	Back to the Future, Part II	1989
7	National Lampoon's Animal House	1978
8	On Golden Pond	1981
9	Smokey and the Bandit	1977
10	Twins	1988

RADIO, TV, & VIDEO

TOP 10

LONGEST-RUNNING PROGRAMS ON NATIONAL PUBLIC RADIO

1	*All Things Considered*
2	*National Press Club*
3	*BBC News and Science Magazines*
4	*Weekend All Things Considered*
5	*Marian McPartland's Piano Jazz*
6	*Morning Edition*
7	*Horizons*
8	*NPR Playhouse*
9	*NPR World of Opera*
10	*St. Louis Symphony*

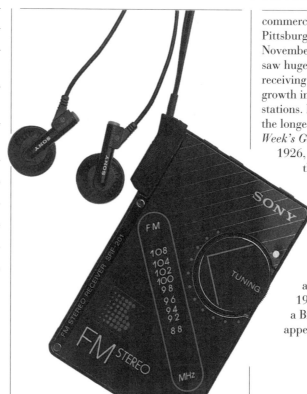

The first known radio program in the US, consisting of two selections of music, the reading of a poem, and a short talk, went out on Christmas Eve, 1906. Broadcast by Reginald Aubrey Fessenden from his experimental radio station in Brant Rock, Massachusetts, the program was heard by radio operators on ships within a radius of several hundred miles. The first commercial radio station was KDKA in Pittsburgh, which started broadcasting on November 2, 1920; the following decade saw huge increases in the sales of radio receiving equipment, matched by a rapid growth in the number of transmitting stations. However, unlike the UK, where the longest-running radio program (*The Week's Good Cause*) started on January 24, 1926, and is still on the air, most of the oldest American programs have been going for less than a quarter of a century. *All Things Considered*, the longest-running National Public Radio program, was first broadcast on May 3, 1971. Nos. 2 to 7 date from the 1970s, and nos. 8 to 10 from the early 1980s. (It is interesting to note that a British radio program from the BBC appears at No. 3 on the NPR list.)

MOST LISTENED-TO RADIO STATIONS IN THE US

	Station	City	Format	Listeners*
1	WRKS-FM	New York	Black	163,300
2	WABC	New York	Talk	147,000
3	WLTW-FM	New York	Soft Adult Contemporary	143,700
4	WCBS-FM	New York	Oldies	133,100
5	WBLS-FM	New York	Black	128,600
6	KFI	New York	Talk	119,800
7	WXRK-FM	New York	Classic Adult Oriented Albums	119,700
8	WPLJ-FM	New York	Contemporary Hit Radio	116,800
9	KOST-FM	Los Angeles	Adult Contemporary	110,200
10	WOR	New York	Talk	105,500

* *Average for listeners aged 12+ listening at any time*

Source: Duncan's American Radio, Inc.

RADIO-OWNING COUNTRIES IN THE WORLD

	Country	Radios per 1,000 population
1	US	2,091
2	Bermuda	1,710
3	UK	1,240
4	Australia	1,144
5	Finland	984
6	New Zealand	902
7	Virgin Islands (USA)	884
8	France	866
9	Sweden	842
10	Canada	828

RADIO FORMATS IN THE US

	Format	Share (%)*
1	Adult Contemporary	16.8
2	News/Talk	16.2
3	Country	12.8
4	Top 40	9.7
5	Urban	8.7
6	Album Rock	8.5
7	Oldies	6.5
8	Spanish	4.8
9	Classic Rock	3.7
10	Adult Standards	3.0

* *Of all radio listening during an average week, 6 am to midnight, Jan–Mar 1994, for listeners aged 12+*

News/Talk radio continues its upward trend, increasing from a 15.4 percent share registered for the same quarter in 1993, mostly at the expense of Adult Contemporary, which slipped from its previous figure of 17.1 percent.

Source: Arbitron

US RADIO STATIONS BY AUDIENCE SHARE

	Station	City	Share (%)*
1	WIVX-FM	Knoxville, Tennessee	32.7
2	WXBQ-FM	Johnson City, Tennessee	28.5
3	WTCR-FM	Huntington, West Virginia	28.1
4	KLLL-FM	Lubbock, Texas	27.7
5	WJBC	Bloomington, Illinois	26.9
6	WFGY-FM	Altoona, Iowa	24.6
7	WWNC	Asheville, North Carolina	24.2
8	WQBE-FM	Charleston, West Virginia	24.1
9	WUSY-FM	Chattanooga, Tennessee	23.9
10	KCCY-FM	Pueblo, Colorado	23.2

* *Of all radio listening for listeners aged 12+*

All the stations listed specialize in country music, with the exception of WJBC, which is a "full service" station, broadcasting talk, news, and middle-of-the-road music. Country music has been growing in popularity – and in radio terms in market share – for the past decade. Many of these stations in America's heartland have ridden that wave of popularity.

Source: Duncan's American Radio, Inc.

TV FIRSTS

THE FIRST TOP 10 LIST BROADCAST ON *LATE NIGHT WITH DAVID LETTERMAN*

THE TOP 10 WORDS THAT ALMOST RHYME WITH "PEAS"

10	Heats	**5**	Lens	
9	Rice	**4**	Ice	
8	Moss	**3**	Nurse	
7	Ties	**2**	Leaks	
6	Needs	**1**	Meats	

Now part of US popular culture, Letterman's "Top 10" list made its bow on September 18, 1985 on NBC-TV's *Late Night With David Letterman* and has endured as one of the most popular features on his show, making the move with him to CBS in 1993 with its nightly inclusion on *The Late Show With David Letterman*. *The Top 10 of Everything* pays tribute to Mr Letterman's contribution to Top 10s by publishing this, his first-ever list.

Source: CBS Broadcast Group

THE CAST OF *DALLAS*
One of the most famous of all TV programs, this long-running saga, telling of the glamorous, violent lives of the Ewings, an oil-rich Texan dynasty, was watched by an estimated 65% of the world's population. Dramatic peaks of the story, such as the shooting of wicked J.R. Ewing and the death of his saintly brother Bobby, were among the most widely viewed moments ever on TV.

TOP 10

FIRST GUESTS ON *THE TONIGHT SHOW* – STARRING JOHNNY CARSON

1	Groucho Marx	Comic actor
2	Joan Crawford	Actress
3	Rudy Vallee	Singer/actor
4	Tony Bennett	Singer
5	Mel Brooks	Comic
6	Tom Pedi	Actor
7	The Phoenix Singers	Vocal trio
8	Tallulah Bankhead	Actress
9	Shelley Berman	Comedian
10	Artie Shaw	Band leader

Originally a two-hour weeknightly show taped in New York, Carson took over *The Tonight Show* from Jack Parr on October 1, 1962, and became America's late-night TV legend for almost three decades, his final show airing on May 22, 1992. Groucho Marx was actually the surprise host for the first 15 minutes of the broadcast, flying in from Hollywood to introduce Carson as the *The Tonight Show*'s new permanent host.

Source: Carson Productions

TOP 10

FIRST COUNTRIES TO HAVE TELEVISION

(*High-definition regular public broadcasting service.*)

	Country	Year
1	UK	1936
2	US	1939
3	USSR	1939
4	France	1948
5	Brazil	1950
6	Cuba	1950
7	Mexico	1950
8	Argentina	1951
9	Denmark	1951
10	Netherlands	1951

TOP 10

LONGEST-RUNNING PROGRAMS ON BRITISH TELEVISION

	Program	First shown
1	*Come Dancing*	Sep 29, 1950
2	*Panorama*	Nov 11, 1953
3	*What the Papers Say*	Nov 5, 1956
4	*The Sky at Night*	Apr 24, 1957
5	*Grandstand*	Oct 11, 1958
6	*Blue Peter*	Oct 16, 1958
7	*Coronation Street*	Dec 9, 1960
8	*Songs of Praise*	Oct 1, 1961
9	*Dr. Who*	Nov 23, 1963
10	*Top of the Pops*	Jan 1, 1964

Only programs appearing every year since their first screenings are listed, and all are BBC programs except the Lancashire soap opera *Coronation Street*. *The Sky at Night*, a popular series on astronomy, has the additional distinction of having had the same host, Patrick Moore, since its first program. Although *The Sooty Show* has been screened intermittently, Sooty, a teddy-bear glove puppet, is the longest-serving TV personality. Several US imports have also enjoyed lasting success; one of the most notable is *Dallas*, which does not make it onto this list but ran from 1978 to 1991.

TOP 10

FIRST PROGRAMS ON BBC TELEVISION

	Time	Program
		Monday November 2, 1936
1	15:02	Opening ceremony by Postmaster General G. C. Tryon
2	15:15	British Movietone News No. 387 (repeated several times during the next few days)
3	15:23	*Variety* – Adele Dixon (singer), Buck and Bubbles (comic dancers), and the Television Orchestra
		(15.31 close; 15.32 Television Orchestra continues in sound only with music.)
4	21:05	Film: *Television Comes to London*
5	21:23	*Picture Page* (magazine program featuring interviews with transatlantic flyer Jim Mollison, tennis champion Kay Stammers, King's Bargemaster Bossy Phelps, and others, ghost stories from Algernon Blackwood and various musical interludes)
6	22:11	Speech by Lord Selsdon, followed by close
		Tuesday November 3, 1936
7	15:04	Exhibits from the Metropolitan and Essex Canine Society's Show – "Animals described by A. Croxton Smith, OBE"
8	15:28	*The Golden Hind* – "a model of Drake's famous ship, made by L. A. Stock, a bus driver"
9	15:46	*Starlight* with comedians Bebe Daniels and Ben Lyon (followed by repeat of items 7 and 8)
10	21:48	*Starlight* with Manuela Del Rio

Although there were earlier low-definition experimental broadcasts, BBC television's high-definition public broadcasting service – the first in the world – was inaugurated on a daily basis on November 2, 1936. During the first three months, two parallel operating systems were in use: the opening programs were thus broadcast twice, first on the Baird system, and repeated slightly later on the Marconi-EMI system.

TEN

US TV FIRSTS

The first president to appear on TV

Franklin D. Roosevelt was seen opening the World's Fair, New York, on April 30, 1939.

The first king and queen televised in the US

The UK's King George VI and Queen Elizabeth were shown visiting the World's Fair on June 10, 1939.

The first televised baseball game

The match between the Brooklyn Dodgers (a major league team from 1930 to 1943) and the Philadelphia Eagles, at Ebbets Field, Brooklyn, New York, was broadcast on August 26, 1939.

The first televised professional football game

Brooklyn played Philadelphia at Ebbets Field in a game shown on October 22, 1939.

The first TV commercial

A 20-second commercial for a Bulova clock was broadcast by WNBT New York on July 1, 1941.

The first soap opera on TV

The first regular daytime serial, DuMont TV network's A Woman to Remember, *began its run on February 21, 1947.*

The first broadcast of a current TV show

NBC's Meet the Press *was first broadcast on November 6, 1947.*

The first televised atomic bomb explosion

An "Operation Ranger" detonation at Frenchman Flats, Nevada, on February 1, 1951, was televised by KTLA, Los Angeles.

The first networked coast-to-coast color TV show

The Tournament of Roses parade at Pasadena, California, hosted by Don Ameche, was seen in color in 21 cities nationwide on January 1, 1954.

The first presidential news conference televised live

President John F. Kennedy was shown in a live broadcast from the auditorium of the State Department Building, Washington, DC, on January 25, 1961. (A filmed conference with President Eisenhower had been shown on January 19, 1955.)

MTV LOGO

Another first on American TV was the inauguration of MTV, the world's first 24-hour music video network, on August 1, 1981. It has largely taken over music programming from the four major US networks.

TOP TV

T O P 1 0

TV-OWNING COUNTRIES IN THE WORLD

	Country	Homes with TV
1	China	103,009,000
2	Former USSR	100,900,000
3	US	94,857,000
4	Brazil	45,567,000
5	Japan	40,667,000
6	Germany	35,379,000
7	UK	22,538,000
8	Indonesia	22,365,000
9	Italy	21,793,000
10	France	20,807,000

Taking population into account, China disappears from the list and the US comes top with 790 sets per 1,000 people.

BIG STARS OF THE SMALL SCREEN
Roseanne, *starring Roseanne Barr and John Goodman, is hugely popular worldwide as well as in the US. Although not in Nielsen's list of shows attracting the 10 biggest audiences, it is still one of the most-watched of all current TV programs.*

T O P 1 0

NIELSEN'S DAYTIME SOAP OPERAS IN THE US, 1993–94

		Households viewing	
	Program	total	%
1	Young and Restless	8,084,000	8.6
2	All My Children	6,204,000	6.6
3	General Hospital	5,828,000	6.2
4	Bold and the Beautiful	5,730,000	6.1
5	As the World Turns	5,452,000	5.8
6=	Days of Our Lives	5,364,000	5.6
6=	One Life to Live	5,264,000	5.6
8	Guiding Light	5,076,000	5.4
9	Another World	3,290,000	3.5
10	Loving	2,538,000	2.7

T O P 1 0

NIELSEN'S DOCUMENTARIES IN THE US, 1993–94

		Households viewing	
	Program	total	%
1	60 Minutes	19,720,000	20.9
2	20/20	19,910,000	14.8
3	Turning Point	13,020,000	13.8
4	48 Hours	10,910,000	11.6
5	Dateline NBC	10,150,000	10.8
6	Now with Tom Brokaw and Katie Curic	10,080,000	10.7
7	Eye to Eye with Connie Chung	9,780,000	10.4
8	Cops 2	7,720,000	8.2
9	Cops	7,060,000	7.5
10	National Geographic on Assignment	6,820,000	7.2

T O P 1 0

NIELSEN'S ANIMATED TV PROGRAMS IN THE US, 1993–94

		Households viewing	
	Program	total	%
1	X-Men	4,700,000	5.0
2	Terrible Thunderlizards	3,984,000	4.2
3	Power Rangers (Saturday)	3,854,000	4.1
4=	Garfield and Friends	3,760,000	4.0
4=	Taz-Mania	3,760,000	4.0
4=	Tiny Toons (Saturday)	3,760,000	4.0
7	Animaniacs	3,384,000	3.6
8=	Batman	3,290,000	3.5
8=	Carmen Sandiego	3,290,000	3.5
8=	Power Rangers	3,290,000	3.5

T O P 1 0

MOST WATCHED PROGRAMS ON PBS TELEVISION*

	Program	Viewers
1	National Geographic Special: The Sharks	24,100,000
2	National Geographic Special: Land of the Tiger	22,400,000
3	National Geographic Special: The Grizzlies	22,300,000
4	Great Moments With National Geographic	21,300,000
5	Best of Wild America: The Babies	19,300,000
6	National Geographic Special: The Incredible Machine	19,000,000
7	The Music Man	18,700,000
8	National Geographic Special: Polar Bear Alert	18,400,000
9	National Geographic Special: Lions of the African Night	18,100,000
10	National Geographic Special: Rain Forest	18,000,000

*As of May 1994

40 YEARS AGO

The most popular networked show of the 1950s was *Arthur Godfrey's Talent Scouts*, which achieved an average Nielsen rating of 32.9 over the decade, just beating *I Love Lucy*. The latter show, which ran continuously on CBS from 1951, was also the first American sit-com to be exported to the UK, where it also achieved a huge following. *You Bet Your Life* was the third most popular, and *Dragnet* the fourth; between December 16, 1951, when *Dragnet* was first broadcast by NBC, and 1958, some 300 episodes were made in black and white (a color series appeared in the late 1960s). *The Ed Sullivan Show* (originally titled *The Toast of the Town*) began its 22-year run on June 20, 1948, and was the TV show on which the Beatles were first presented to a US audience.

T O P 1 0

NIELSEN'S FILMS OF ALL TIME ON PRME-TIME NETWORK TV

	Film	Year released	Broadcast	Rating %*
1	*Gone With the Wind* Pt. 1	1939	Nov 7, 1976	47.7
2	*Gone With the Wind* Pt. 2	1939	Nov 8, 1976	47.4
3=	*Love Story*	1970	Oct 1, 1972	42.3
3=	*Airport*	1970	Nov 11, 1973	42.3
5	*The Godfather, Part II*	1974	Nov 18, 1974	39.4
6	*Jaws*	1975	Nov 4, 1979	39.1
7	*The Poseidon Adventure*	1972	Oct 27, 1974	39.0
8=	*True Grit*	1969	Nov 12, 1972	38.9
8=	*The Birds*	1963	Jan 6, 1968	38.9
10	*Patton*	1970	Nov 19, 1972	38.5

* Of households viewing   © Copyright 1994 Nielsen Media Research

All the films listed are dramas made for theatrical release, but if such productions were included, the controversial 1983 made-for-TV post-nuclear war movie, *The Day After* (screened on November 20, 1983) would rank in 3rd place with a rating of 46.0 percent. It is significant that all the most watched films on TV were broadcast before the dawn of the video era, and attracted substantial audiences to whom this was the only opportunity to see a particular film that they might have missed or wished to see again.

T O P 1 0

NIELSEN'S TV AUDIENCES OF ALL TIME IN THE US

	Program	Date	Households viewing total	%
1	*M*A*S*H* Special	Feb 28, 1983	50,150,000	60.2
2	*Dallas*	Nov 21, 1980	41,470,000	53.3
3	*Roots* Part 8	Jan 30, 1977	36,380,000	51.1
4	Super Bowl XVI	Jan 24, 1982	40,020,000	49.1
5	Super Bowl XVII	Jan 30, 1983	40,500,000	48.6
6	XVII Winter Olympics	Feb 23, 1994	45,690,000	48.5
7	Super Bowl XX	Jan 26, 1986	41,490,000	48.3
8	*Gone With the Wind* Pt. 1	Nov 7, 1976	33,960,000	47.7
9	*Gone With the Wind* Pt. 2	Nov 8, 1976	33,750,000	47.4
10	Super Bowl XII	Jan 15, 1978	34,410,000	47.2

© Copyright 1994 Nielsen Media Research

As more and more households have television sets, the most recently screened programs naturally tend to be watched by larger audiences, which distorts the historical picture. By listing the Top 10 according to percentage of households viewing, we get a clearer picture of who watches what. The last-ever episode of *M*A*S*H* had both the largest number and highest percentage of households watching. The last episode of *Cheers* (broadcast May 20, 1993; 42,360,000 households/ 45.5 percent) only just failed to gain a place in the Top 10.

SUPERBOWL 1982
Bengals' Pete Johnson (top) is stopped by the 49ers 3rd quarter goal line stand.

CABLE TV AND VIDEO

T O P 1 0

FIRST VIDEOS TO TOP THE UK RENTAL CHART

1	*Jaws*	6	*The Jazz Singer*
2	*Star Trek: The Motion Picture*	7	*Monty Python's Life of Brian*
3	*Scanners*	8	*Watership Down*
4	*The Exterminator*	9	*Chariots of Fire*
5	*Superman: The Movie*	10	*Star Wars*

The video rental market in the United Kingdom is notable in that records of rentals have been kept more or less since videos first arrived on those shores. Since the country is among the Top 10 video-owning nations in the world (with the percentage of households possessing VCRs even higher in the UK than in the US), and lists of favorite films tend to be similar in the UK and the US, this list may be seen as representative of the most popular titles in the first years of the video boom. A varied mix headed the rental chart during 1981 and 1982, the early years of the UK video rental industry. *Scanners* and *The Exterminator* were both strictly for adult viewing, while *Watership Down* was an animated family film and *The Jazz Singer* was a musical – one of

the few such ever to reach No. 1. Some of these early chart-toppers occupied the No. 1 position for months on end; the very first of these, *Jaws*, held its position for a never-equalled 17 weeks, *The Jazz Singer* was at No. 1 for 13 weeks, and *Star Trek: The Motion Picture* enjoyed nine weeks of supremacy. Lengthy stays at the top were easier to achieve in the less crowded and less competitive market of the early 1980s – over a decade later, a movie that can hold the No. 1 position for a full month is special indeed, such is the urgency with which box office successes now transfer to the home viewing market.

T O P 1 0

REGIONAL CABLE CHANNELS IN THE US

	Channel	Subscribers*
1	Madison Square Garden Network	4,900,000
2	Prime Ticket	4,200,000
3	Home Sports Entertainment	3,700,000
4	Sunshine Network	3,500,000
5	The California Channel	3,256,000
6	Home Team Sports	2,500,000
7	SportsChannel Chicago	2,245,000
8	KBL Sports Network	2,000,000
9	SportsChannel Philadelphia	1,900,000
10	Cable TV Network of New Jersey	1,700,000

* As of May 1994

Source: Cablevision

T O P 1 0

CABLE DELIVERY SYSTEMS IN US CITIES

	Location	Operator	Subscribers*
1	New York, New York	Time Warner Cable	950,036
2	Long Island, New York	Cablevision Systems	610,717
3	Orlando, Florida	Cablevision Systems	475,684
4	Puget Sound, Washington	Viacom	400,500
5	Phoenix, Arizona	Times Mirror	353,000
6	Tampa/St. Petersburg, Florida	Paragon	327,954
7	San Diego, California	Cox Cable	326,571
8	San Antonio, Texas	KBLCOM	248,980
9	Houston, Texas	Time Warner Cable	240,390
10	Denver suburbs, Colorado	TCI	240,000

* Ranked by locations with most subscribers to one system, as of May 1994

Source: Cablevision

Its purchase of Tele Cable will further enhance the market share of Denver-based TCI (Telecommunications, Inc.), America's largest cable operator (Time Warner Cable is ranked second). Owned by media visionary John Malone, TCI delivers cable TV to more than 11,000,000 homes. The first threat to cable-based systems comes from DirecTV. Owned by GM and Hughes Electronics, it uses DBS (Digital Broadcast Satellite) to deliver high-quality programming via 18-inch satellite dishes, and is aimed initially at un-cabled rural areas where large and expensive dishes have previously been the norm.

NETWORK CABLE
CHANNELS IN THE US

	Channel	Subscribers*
1	ESPN	61,804,000
2	Cable News Network	61,614,000
3	USA Network	61,193,000
4	Nickelodeon	60,929,000
5	TBS Superstation	60,504,000
6	The Discovery Channel	60,468,000
7	TNT	59,975,000
8	C-SPAN	59,800,000
9	MTV	59,457,000
10	Lifetime	58,588,000

* As of May 1994

Numbers 2, 5, and 7 belong to the Atlanta-based Turner Broadcasting System. Their Cartoon Network, launched in 1993, has over 10,000,000 subscribers. ESPN2, also launched in 1993, has 12,600,000.

Source: Cablevision

COUNTRIES WITH MOST VCRs

			1980		1993	
	Country	(1980 ranking)	As % of homes with TV	VCRs	As % of homes with TV	VCRs
1	US	(2)	2.5	1,950,000	70.2	66,560,000
2	Japan	(1)	6.1	1,975,000	74.0	30,095,000
3	Germany	(3)	3.2	775,000	61.5	21,770,000
4	Brazil	(6=)	0.7	100,000	45.4	20,669,000
5	UK	(4)	3.1	580,000	72.6	16,354,000
6	France	(5)	0.8	144,000	64.5	13,417,000
7	Italy	(9)	0.2	30,000	40.6	8,851,000
8	Canada	(6=)	1.3	100,000	64.1	6,955,000
9	Spain	(8)	0.5	48,000	51.7	5,866,000
10	Former USSR	(–)	–	–	5.6	5,648,000
	World total		*1.7*	*7,687,000*	*36.9*	*275,055,000*

The 1980s have rightly been described as the "Video Decade": according to estimates published by *Screen Digest*, the period from 1980 to 1990 saw an increase in the number of video recorders in use in the world of more than 27 times, from 7,687,000 to 210,159,000, while the estimated 1993 total for the UK alone is more than double the entire world total for 1980. Since 1992, more than one-third of all world homes with TV have also had video.

VIDEO CONSUMERS IN THE WORLD

	Country	Rental	Purchase	Total
		Spending per video household (US $)		
1	Netherlands	147.28	116.28	263.56
2	Japan	88.31	110.21	198.52
3	Australia	174.58	13.13	187.71
4	Canada	139.80	35.24	175.04
5	US	116.21	47.85	164.06
6	Ireland	118.06	32.95	151.01
7	Norway	133.20	8.35	141.55
8	New Zealand	89.55	13.43	102.99
9	UK	56.09	37.76	93.85
10	Italy	27.10	62.93	90.03

Based on figures prepared by *Screen Digest* for 1991 (except Australia and Canada, which are for 1990). Total spending per head of population, rather than per household with video, produces a somewhat different picture, with Japan at the top of the list, followed closely by the US, Canada, and Australia. Norway moves up to 5th place and the UK to 6th. Ireland, New Zealand, Germany, and Sweden make up the rest of the list.

VIDEO FAVORITES

TOP 10

BESTSELLING VIDEOS OF 1993 IN THE US

1. *Free Willy*
2. *Aladdin*
3. *The Bodyguard*
4. *Miracle on 34th Street* (colorized version)
5. *Dennis the Menace*
6. *Home Alone 2: Lost in New York*
7. *Homeward Bound*
8. *The Muppet Christmas Carol*
9. *Tom & Jerry: The Movie*
10. *Happily Ever After*

Source: Video Scan

All but one of 1993's bestselling video titles were recent motion picture releases, the exception being *Miracle on 34th Street*, which was made in 1947 and found an appreciative new audience with the release of its computer colorized version. Sentimental family films such as this, others featuring animals (*Free Willy* and *Homeward Bound*), animation (*Aladdin*, *Tom & Jerry: The Movie*, and *Happily Ever After*), comedy, and adventure make up the traditional annual mix of video bestsellers.

TOP 10

BESTSELLING EXERCISE VIDEOS OF 1993 IN THE US

1. *Target Training Total Body Shape Up and Maintenance*
2. *Abs of Steel*
3. *Target Training Stomach*
4. *Lean, Strong & Healthy*
5. *Target Training Hips, Thighs and Buttocks*
6. *Buns of Steel 3*
7. *Sweating to the Oldies* Vol. 3
8. *Abs of Steel 2*
9. *Buns of Steel*
10. *Thighs of Steel*

Source: Video Scan

TOP 10

BESTSELLING MUSIC VIDEOS OF ALL TIME IN THE US

	Artist	Video
1	New Kids On The Block	*Hangin' Tough Live*
2	New Kids On The Block	*Hangin' Tough*
3	New Kids On The Block	*Step By Step*
4	Michael Jackson	*Moonwalker*
5	Garth Brooks	*This Is Garth Brooks*
6	Garth Brooks	*Garth Brooks*
7	Jose Carreras, Placido Domingo, Luciano Pavarotti	*In Concert*
8	Billy Ray Cyrus	*Billy Ray Cyrus*
9	Kid Songs	*A Day At Old MacDonald's Farm*
10	Bruce Springsteen	*Video Anthology 1978–1988*

In a diverse list ranging from children's music to opera, rhythm & blues, rock, and country, the three New Kids' titles are still the only music video releases to sell over 1,000,000 units each in the US.

TOP 10

BESTSELLING VIDEOS OF ALL TIME IN THE UK

(*To March 31, 1994*)

1. *The Jungle Book*
2. *Fantasia*
3. *Beauty And The Beast*
4. *Cinderella*
5. *The Little Mermaid*
6. *Bambi*
7. *Lady And The Tramp*
8. *Peter Pan*
9. *Dirty Dancing*
10. *The Three Tenors Concert*

Disney titles now dominate the bestselling video list, with enormous sales for the limited-period releases in 1992–94 of Disney classics such as *The Jungle Book* (over 4,500,000 sold), *Fantasia* (3,200,000), *Beauty And The Beast* (2,000,000), and *Cinderella* (1,750,000).

TOP 10

MOST RENTED ACTION VIDEOS OF 1994 IN THE US

(*First six months only*)

1. *Cliffhanger*
2. *Demolition Man*
3. *Striking Distance*
4. *Last Action Hero*
5. *Hard Target*
6. *The Program*
7. *True Romance*
8. *The Real McCoy*
9. *Sidekicks*
10. *Menace II Society*

Source: Video Store Magazine

TOP 10

MOST RENTED DRAMA VIDEOS OF 1994 IN THE US

(*First six months only*)

1. *Sleepless in Seattle*
2. *Rising Sun*
3. *Indecent Proposal*
4. *The Man Without a Face*
5. *Dragon: The Bruce Lee Story*
6. *Three of Hearts*
7. *Chaplin*
8. *Lost in Yonkers*
9. *Poetic Justice*
10. *Jack the Bear*

Source: Video Store Magazine

T O P 1 0

BESTSELLING SPORT VIDEOS OF 1993 IN THE US

	Video	Sport
1	Michael Jordan: Air Time	Basketball
2	Leslie Nielsen – Bad Golf	Golf
3	NBA Jam Session	Basketball
4	NBA Rising Stars	Basketball
5	Michael Jordan: Come Fly With Me	Basketball
6	1993 NBA World Championship	Basketball
7	Michael Jordan's Playground	Basketball
8	NFL's 15 Greatest Comebacks	Football
9	NFL Rocks Extreme	Football
10	NFL/100 Great Touchdowns	Football

Source: Video Scan

It is perhaps ironic that in the year that Michael Jordan quit basketball to take up minor league baseball, three of the 10 bestselling sports videos feature him in the sport through which he achieved his fame and fortune.

T O P 1 0

BESTSELLING CHILDREN'S VIDEOS OF 1993 IN THE US

1	Barney & Gang: Waiting 4 Santa	**6**	Barney Rhymes with Mother Goose
2	Mighty Morphin Power Ranger Vol. 1	**7**	Mighty Morphin Power Ranger Vol. 5
3	Mighty Morphin Power Ranger Vol. 4	**8**	Mighty Morphin Power Ranger Vol. 2
4	Barney & Gang: Home Sweet Homes	**9**	Mighty Morphin Power Ranger Vol. 3
5	Barney's Best Manners	**10**	Barney & Gang: Barney in Concert

Source: Video Scan

T O P 1 0

MOST RENTED VIDEOS OF ALL TIME IN THE UK

(To December 31, 1993)

1	Dirty Dancing
2	Crocodile Dundee
3	Basic Instinct
4	Home Alone
5	Sister Act
6	Ghost
7	Pretty Woman
8	The Silence of the Lambs
9	Robocop
10	A Fish Called Wanda

Of these 10 titles, *Sister Act* and *Basic Instinct* were still renting buoyantly in video libraries (the latter 18 months after its original release) in the spring of 1994, and both have the potential to rise higher still in the all-time stakes.

T O P 1 0

MOST RENTED COMEDY VIDEO OF 1994 IN THE US

(First six months only)

1	Dave
2	Made in America
3	Dennis the Menace
4	Son-in-Law
5	Hocus Pocus
6	The Sandlot
7	Rookie of the Year
8	Robin Hood: Men in Tights
9	Cop and a Half
10	National Lampoon's Loaded Weapon

Source: Video Store Magazine

T O P 1 0

MOST RENTED HORROR VIDEOS OF 1994 IN THE US

(First six months only)

1	The Dark Half
2	Jason Goes to Hell: The Final Friday
3	Warlock: The Armageddon
4	The Tommyknockers
5	Children of the Corn 2
6	When a Stranger Calls Back
7	Amityville: A New Generation
8	Dead Alive
9	The Hit List
10	Body Bags

Source: Video Store Magazine

T O P 1 0

MOST-RENTED VIDEO CATEGORIES IN THE US, 1993

1	Comedy
2	Family
3	Drama
4	Adventure
5	Thriller
6	Action
7	Western
8	Erotic thriller
9	Science-fiction
10	Horror

Source: Video Store Magazine

THE COMMERCIAL WORLD

T O P   1 0

PAPER CONSUMERS IN THE WORLD

| | | Annual consumption | | |
| | | | per capita | |
	Country	Total tonnes	lb	kg
1	US	77,502,000	679	308
2	Sweden	2,574,000	659	299
3	Denmark	1,337,000	571	259
4	Japan	29,091,000	518	235
5	Belgium/ Luxembourg	2,345,000	500	227
6	Netherlands	3,322,000	487	221
7	Finland	1,103,000	485	220
8	Switzerland	1,455,000	474	215
9	Germany	16,629,000	459	208
10	Canada	5,583,000	456	207

So much for the "paperless office": the coming of computers, with their relative ease of printing, has increased, rather than reduced, international paper consumption, while the proliferation of junk mail, packaging, and newspaper publishing has contributed to the world's voracious appetite for paper. Currently, the average US citizen consumes the equivalent of five times his own weight in paper annually, and despite various curbs, such as recycling, the United Nations has predicted that by the year 2010 the nation's total demand will have reached 113,422,000 tonnes, or 858 lb/389 kg for each member of the 291,290,000 population projected for that year.

T O P   1 0

FAIRS IN THE US

	Fair	Attendance (1993)
1	State Fair of Texas, Dallas	3,154,772
2	State Fair of Oklahoma, Oklahoma City	1,785,305
3	New Mexico State Fair, Albuquerque	1,681,066
4	Minnesota State Fair, St. Paul	1,601,325
5	Houston (Texas) Livestock Show	1,568,266
6	Western Washington Fair, Puyallup	1,420,037
7	Los Angeles County Fair, Pomona	1,401,876
8	De Mar (California) Fair	1,105,797
9	Colorado State Fair, Pueblo	1,082,018
10	Tulsa (Oklahoma) State Fair	1,027,642

THE WORLD OF WORK

TOP 10

COUNTRIES WITH MOST WORKERS

	Country	Economically active population*
1	China	584,569,000
2	India	314,904,000
3	US	128,458,000
4	Indonesia	75,508,000
5	Russia	73,809,000
6	Japan	65,780,000
7	Brazil	64,468,000
8	Bangladesh	50,744,000
9	Germany	39,405,000
10	Pakistan	33,829,000

* *Excluding unpaid groups, such as students, housewives, and retired people*

TOP 10

EMPLOYERS IN THE US

	Industry	Employees
1	Health services	8,122,000
2	Eating/drinking places	6,503,000
3	Business services	5,898,000
4	Durable goods	3,759,000
5	Transportation	3,665,000
6	Food stores	3,379,000
7	Finance	3,363,000
8	Nondurable goods	2,595,000
9	General merchandise stores	2,435,000
10	Insurance	2,165,000

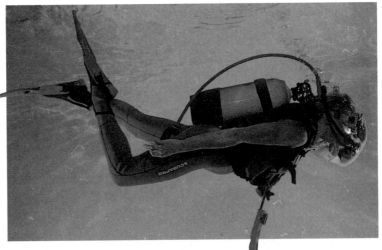

MIXING OIL AND WATER
Divers working in the sea around offshore oil rigs have to contend with a variety of hazards. Even so, diving is not one of the Top 10 most dangerous jobs – perhaps because relatively few people work in this field.

TOP 10

MOST DANGEROUS JOBS IN THE US

	Job	Deaths per 100,000
1	Loggers	129.0
2	Aircraft pilots	97.0
3	Asbestos and insulation workers	78.7
4	Structural metal workers	72.0
5	Electric power line and cable installers and repairers	50.7
6	Firefighters	48.8
7	Garbage collectors	40.0
8	Truck drivers	39.6
9	Bulldozer operators	39.3
10	Earth drillers	38.8

At least 240 people die every working day in the US as a result of accidents at work or from diseases caused by their jobs. All the 10 riskiest jobs, except that of pilots, are "blue-collar" or manual jobs. Among other dangerous jobs that do not quite make the Top 10 are those of miners, taxi drivers, and policemen. Some of these jobs expose workers to several hazards at once; for instance, divers who carry out maintenance and repair tasks on offshore oil-drilling platforms, in places such as the Gulf of Mexico and the North Sea, have to work with heavy or dangerous equipment, in often deep and turbulent seas. The risk attached to most "white-collar" jobs is under 10 per 100,000, with some types of employment being placed extremely low – the chance of death at work among embalmers and librarians, for example, is put at zero.

TOP 10

CITIES WITH THE MOST FEDERAL GOVERNMENT EMPLOYEES

	City	Employees		City	Employees
1	Washington, DC*	389,427	6	Boston, Massachusetts	59,337
2	New York, New York/ Newark, New Jersey	153,617	7	Norfolk, Virginia/ Virginia Beach, North Carolina	53,209
3	Chicago, Illinois	73,414	8	Baltimore, Maryland	49,164
4	Philadelphia, Pennsylvania#	71,846	9	Atlanta, Georgia	45,027
5	Los Angeles, California	68,559	10	San Antonio, Texas	38,049

The total number of civilians employed by the federal government at December 31, 1992 was 2,597,279, including 12,592 in Puerto Rico.

* *Includes employees attached to Washington's federal office but located in Maryland, Virginia, and West Virginia*
\# *Includes employees attached to Philadelphia's federal office but located in New Jersey*

Source: US Office of Personnel Management

COMPANIES AND PRODUCTS

TOP 10

US COMPANIES BY MARKET VALUE

	Corporation	Principal products/ activity	Market value ($)
1	General Electric	Electrical household goods, electronic equipment	89,953,000,000
2	Exxon	Petroleum products	80,550,000,000
3	AT&T	Telecommunications	71,001,000,000
4	Wal-Mart Stores	Department stores	65,221,000,000
5	Coca-Cola	Soft drinks	55,371,000,000
6	Philip Morris	Foodstuffs, beer, cigarettes	49,117,000,000
7	General Motors	Motor vehicles	41,946,000,000
8	Merck	Pharmaceutical products	40,596,000,000
9	Procter & Gamble	Soap and other detergents	39,272,000,000
10	Dupont	Petroleum refining	36,062,000,000

Source: Business Week

AUTOMOTIVE REVOLUTION
The Ford Motor Company, which sold its first car in 1904, was the first to produce automobiles that ordinary people could afford, such as the famous Model T. By the 1920s so many people were buying automobiles that the industry was a mainstay of the US economy.

TOP 10

LARGEST LIFE INSURANCE COMPANIES IN THE US

	Company	Assets ($)
1	Prudential of America	154,779,400,000
2	Metropolitan Life	118,178,300,000
3	Teachers Insurance & Annuity	61,776,700,000
4	Aetna Life	50,896,500,000
5	New York Life	46,925,000,000
6	Equitable Life Assurance	46,624,000,000
7	Connecticut General Life	44,075,500,000
8	Northwestern Mutual Life	39,663,300,000
9	John Hancock Mutual Life	39,146,100,000
10	Principal Mutual Life	35,124,800,000

The huge assets of the major US life insurance companies are greater than the entire gross domestic product of most countries (i.e. the value of the output of all goods and services produced within their borders). Indeed, only 21 of the world's leading industrialized countries have GDPs in excess of the No. 1 company on this list, Prudential of America. The total assets of the Top 50 companies are $1,141,431,900,000, a sum equivalent to approximately one-fifth of the GDP of the whole United States.

Source: Fortune *magazine,* Fortune's Service 500

TOP 10

SOURCES OF IMPORTS TO THE US

	Country	Total value of imports in 1992 ($)
1	Japan	96,483,000,000
2	Canada	75,127,000,000
3	Germany	27,954,000,000
4	Mexico	27,098,000,000
5	China	24,354,000,000
6	Taiwan	24,231,000,000
7	UK	17,331,000,000
8	South Korea	16,325,000,000
9	France	13,272,000,000
10	Singapore	11,062,000,000

Source: US Department of Commerce,
International Trade Administration

TOP 10

GOODS IMPORTED TO THE US

	Product	Total value of imports in 1992 ($)
1	Road vehicles	75,200,000,000
2	Electrical machinery and parts	39,700,000,000
3	Office and ADP machines	36,300,000,000
4	Apparel/clothing/ accessories	31,200,000,000
5	Miscellaneous manufactured articles	28,500,000,000
6	Telecommunications and sound-reproduction equipment	25,800,000,000
7	Power-generating machinery	15,900,000,000
8	Industrial machinery and parts	15,500,000,000
9	Special industrial machinery	11,800,000,000
10	Nonmetallic mineral products	10,100,000,000

Source: US Department of Commerce,
International Trade Administration

TOP 10

EXPORT MARKETS FOR GOODS FROM THE US

	Country	Total value of imports from US in 1992 ($)
1	Canada	80,827,000,000
2	Mexico	34,551,000,000
3	Japan	30,258,000,000
4	UK	20,999,000,000
5	Germany	19,217,000,000
6	France	13,109,000,000
7	Taiwan	12,213,000,000
8	Netherlands	10,601,000,000
9	South Korea	10,240,000,000
10	Singapore	9,047,000,000

Source: US Department of Commerce,
International Trade Administration

TOP 10

GOODS EXPORTED FROM THE US

	Product	Total value of exports in 1992 ($)
1	Transportation equipment	38,600,000,000
2	Road vehicles	37,900,000,000
3	Electrical machinery and parts	37,400,000,000
4	Office and ADP machines	30,900,000,000
5	Miscellaneous manufactured articles	23,200,000,000
6	Industrial machinery and parts	18,800,000,000
7	Power-generating machinery	18,400,000,000
8	Special industrial machinery	17,200,000,000
9	Professional/scientific/ control instruments	14,900,000,000
10	Telecommunications and sound-reproduction equipment	12,300,000,000

Source: US Department of Commerce,
International Trade Administration

TOP 10

COUNTRIES THAT REGISTER THE MOST PATENTS

	Country	Patents
1	US	97,443
2	Japan	92,100
3	Germany	46,520
4	France	38,215
5	UK	37,827
6	Italy	27,228
7	Netherlands	20,346
8	Sweden	18,672
9	Switzerland	18,642
10	Canada	18,332

A patent is an exclusive license to manufacture and exploit a unique product or process for a fixed period. The figures refer to the number of patents actually granted during 1992 – which in most instances represents only a fraction of the patents applied for; the process of obtaining a patent can be tortuous, and many are refused after investigations show that the product is too similar to one that has already been patented. This international list is based on data from the World Intellectual Property Organization.

TOP 10

BANKS WITH GREATEST ASSETS IN THE US

	Bank	Assets ($)
1	CitiCorp	213,701,000,000
2	BankAmerica Corp.	180,646,000,000
3	Chemical Banking Corp.	139,655,000,000
4	NationsBank Corp.	118,059,300,000
5	J.P. Morgan & Co.	102,941,000,000
6	Chase Manhattan Corp.	95,862,000,000
7	Bankers Trust New York Corp.	72,448,000,000
8	Banc One Corp.	61,417,400,000
9	Wells Fargo & Co.	52,537,000,000
10	PNC Bank Corp.	51,379,900,000

Source: Fortune magazine,
Fortune's Service 500

SHOPPING LISTS

TOP 10

LARGEST SHOPPING MALLS IN THE US

	Mall	Gross leasable area (sq ft)*
1	Del Amo Fashion Center, Torrance, California	3,000,000
2	South Coast Plaza/Crystal Court, Costa Mesa, California	2,918,236
3	Mall of America, Bloomington, Minnesota	2,472,500
4	Lakewood Center Mall, Lakewood, California	2,390,000
5	Roosevelt Field Mall, Garden City, New York	2,300,000
6	Gurnee Mills, Gurnee, Illinois	2,200,000
7	The Galleria, Houston, Texas	2,100,000
8	Randall Park Mall, North Randall, Ohio	2,097,416
9	Oakbrook Shopping Center, Oak Brook, Illinois	2,006,688
10=	Sungrass Mills, Sunrise, Florida	2,000,000
10=	The Woodlands Mall, The Woodlands, Texas	2,000,000
10=	Woodfield, Schaumburg, Illinois	2,000,000

* As of June 1994

Gross leasable area is defined as "the total floor area designated for tenant occupancy," and includes square footage occupied by anchor stores.

Source: Blackburn Marketing Services Inc.

TOP 10

RETAILERS IN THE US

	Retailer	Annual sales
1	Sears, Roebuck & Co.	59,101,100,000
2	Wal-Mart Stores	55,483,800,000
3	KMart Corp.	37,724,000,000
4	The Kroger Co.	22,144,600,000
5	J.C. Penney Co., Inc.	19,085,000,000
6	American Stores Co.	19,051,200,000
7	Dayton-Hudson Corp.	17,927,000,000
8	Safeway Stores	15,151,900,000
9	The Great Atlantic & Pacific Tea Co., Inc.	11,592,500,000
10	May Department Stores	11,170,000,000

TOP 10

SUPERMARKET GROUPS WITH MOST OUTLETS IN THE US

	Retailer	No. of outlets
1	The Kroger Co.	2,214
2	The Great Atlantic & Pacific Tea Co., Inc.	1,193
3	Winn-Dixie Stores Inc.	1,164
4	Safeway Inc.	1,103
5	Food Lion Inc.	1,050
6	American Stores Company	930
7	Albertson's, Inc.	656
8	Publix Super Markets Inc.	407
9	The Vons Companies Inc.	346
10	Pathmark Supermarkets General Corp.	147

TOP 10

SPORTS FOOTWEAR RETAILERS IN THE US

	Retailer	Sales (1993)
1	Foot Locker	1,900,000,000
2	The Athlete's Foot	388,000,000
3	Lady Foot Locker	326,000,000
4	Foot/Action	260,000,000
5	The Finish Line	153,000,000
6	Athletic X-Press	95,000,000
7	Athletic Attic	60,000,000
8	Kids Foot Locker	54,000,000
9	Just For Feet	42,000,000
10	Fleet Feet	23,000,000

Figures for all except Nos. 2 and 9 are minimum estimates for sales in 1993; precise amounts may be even greater, and the relentless growth in the US sports footwear market continues: in 1993, total sales of the Top 10 retailers alone accounted for $3,301,000,000, 19 percent up from the $2,777,000,000 of the previous year – which was 35 percent up from1991's $2,051,000,000.

Source: National Sporting Goods Association

TOP 10

SPORTSWEAR RETAILERS IN THE US

	Company	Average 1993 sales per store ($)
1	Sportmart	9,657,143
2	The Sports Authority	9,400,000
3	Sports & Recreation	8,500,000
4	Academy Corp.	8,100,000

	Company	Average 1993 sales per store ($)
5	SportsTown	7,700,000
6	Sport Chalet	7,500,000
7	MVP Sports Stores	5,178,105
8	Olympic Sports	4,700,000

	Company	Average 1993 sales per store ($)
9	Modell's	4,127,000
10	Herman's	3,250,000

Source: Sports Trend Top 100/May 1994

TOP 10

DEPARTMENT STORE CHAINS IN THE US

	Chain	Annual sales ($)
1	Sears, Roebuck & Co., Chicago, Illinois	59,101,100,000
2	Wal-Mart Stores, Bentonville, Arkansas	55,483,800,000
3	KMart, Troy, Michigan	37,724,000,000
4	J.C. Penney, Plano, Texas	19,085,000,000
5	Dayton-Hudson, Minneapolis, Minnesota	17,927,000,000
6	May Department Stores, St. Louis, Missouri	11,170,000,000
7	Woolworth, New York, New York	9,962,000,000
8	Federated Department Stores, Cincinnati, Ohio	7,079,900,000
9	R.H. Macy, New York, New York	6,648,900,000
10	Dillard Department Stores, Little Rock, Arizona	4,883,200,000

TOP 10

DRUG STORE ITEMS IN THE US

(Not including private label and miscellaneous items)

	Product	Annual Sales ($)
1	Prescriptions	38,000,000,000
2	General merchandise	9,978,000,000
3	Food, drink, tobacco products	8,345,000,000
4	General health care	5,969,000,000
5	Toiletries/Beauty care	4,701,000,000
6	Other grocery products	2,344,000,000
7	Cosmetics/Fragrances	1,879,000,000
8	Cough/cold/allergy/sinus remedies	1,590,000,000
9	Internal analgesics	1,097,000,000
10	Oral care products	1,071,000,000

TOP 10

SUPERMARKET GROUPS IN THE US

	Retailer	Annual sales
1	The Kroger Co.	22,145,000,000
2	Safeway Inc.	15,151,900,000
3	American Stores Co.	14,500,000,000
4	Winn-Dixie Stores Inc.	10,831,535,000
5	The Great Atlantic & Pacific Tea Co., Inc.	10,499,465,000
6	Albertson's, Inc.	10,173,676,000
7	Food Lion Inc.	7,195,923,000
8	Publix Super Markets Inc.	6,700,000,000
9	The Vons Companies Inc.	5,600,000,000
10	Pathmark Supermarkets General Corp.	4,340,000,000

TOP 10

SHOPPING STREETS IN THE WORLD

	Street	Location
1	The Ginza	Tokyo, Japan
2	Pedder Street/ Chater Street	Hong Kong
3	East 57th Street	New York, US
4	5th Avenue	New York, US
5	Madison Avenue	New York, US
6	Kaufinger Strasse	Munich, Germany
7	Hohe Strasse	Cologne, Germany
8	Kurfürstendamm	Berlin, Germany
9	Königsallee	Dusseldorf, Germany
10	Königstrasse	Stuttgart, Germany

Based on prime retail rents at end of 1992

TOP 10

DRUG STORE BRANDS IN THE US

	Product	Sales ($)*
1	Tylenol analgesics	327,900,000
2	Revlon cosmetics	220,100,000
3	Cover Girl cosmetics	199,500,000
4	Maybelline cosmetics	149,600,000
5	Advil analgesics	129,400,000
6	L'Oreal cosmetics	123,200,000
7	Lifescan testing kits	121,200,000
8	Robitussin cough remedies	115,400,000
9	Trojan condoms	109,800,000
10	J&J first aid products	98,600,000

* 12 months to March 1994

Source: Towne-Oller & Associates/ Information Resources, Inc.

DUTY-FREE

DUTY-FREE FAVORITES
Cigarettes top the duty-free product sales, ahead of perfumes and other women's fragrances, which have sales of over one and three quarter billion dollars annually.

IN-FLIGHT SHOPPING
International airlines, such as American Airlines, figure prominently as duty-free outlets.

TOP 10

DUTY-FREE PRODUCTS

	Product	Sales (US$)
1	Cigarettes	1,960,000,000
2	Women's fragrances	1,760,000,000
3	Scotch whisky	1,310,000,000
4	Women's cosmetics and toiletries	1,300,000,000
5	Cognac	1,200,000,000
6	Men's fragrances and toiletries	840,000,000
7	Accessories	720,000,000
8	Leather goods (handbags, belts, etc.)	715,000,000
9	Confectionery	710,000,000
10	Jewelry and pearls	520,000,000

In 1992 total world duty-free sales were estimated to have reached $16,000,000,000, of which the Top 10 comprise $11,035,000,000, or 69 percent.

TOP 10

DUTY-FREE FERRY OPERATORS IN THE WORLD

	Ferry operator/country	Annual sales (US$)
1	DSB Ferries (Denmark)	185,000,000
2	Viking Line Ferries (Finland)	180,000,000
3	Stena Line (Sweden)	135,000,000 *
4	Stena Sealink Ferries (UK)	125,000,000 *
5	P & O European Ferries (UK)	110,000,000
6	Silja Line (Finland)	100,000,000
7	Puttgarden-Rödby (Germany)	86,000,000
8	Sweferry/Scandlines (Sweden/Denmark)	85,000,000
9	Scandinavian Seaways (Denmark)	71,200,000
10	Color Line (Norway)	70,500,000

* Estimated

TIME TO BROWSE
Ranking fourth in the world list of duty-free ferry operators, Stena Sealink Ferries are the second largest UK outlet for duty-free goods, ahead of London Gatwick Airport and beaten only by London Heathrow.

TOP 10

DUTY-FREE SHOPS IN THE WORLD

	Shop location	Annual sales (US$)
1	Honolulu Airport	427,000,000
2	Hong Kong Airport	400,000,000
3	London Heathrow Airport	348,000,000
4	Amsterdam Schiphol Airport	262,000,000
5	Paris Charles de Gaulle Airport	257,000,000
6	Tokyo Narita Airport	241,000,000
7	Frankfurt Airport	220,000,000
8	Singapore Changi Airport	200,000,000
9	DSB Ferries (Denmark)	185,000,000
10	Viking Line Ferries (Finland)	180,000,000

Despite the international recession, total global duty-free sales in 1992 increased to $16,000,000,000, of which the Top 10 accounted for about 17 percent. Honolulu is not only the world's top duty-free shop in terms of total annual sales, but also one of the highest in average sales per passenger ($106.94, compared with Heathrow's average of $17.91).

T O P   1 0

DUTY-FREE AIRLINES IN THE WORLD

	Airline/country	Annual sales (US$)
1	Japan Air Lines (Japan)	80,000,000
2	Korean Air (Korea)	75,000,000*
3	British Airways (UK)	64,350,000
4	Scanair (Scandinavia)	59,300,000*
5	Lufthansa (Germany)	54,000,000
6	Conair (Denmark)	48,000,000*
7	Sterling Airways (Denmark)	42,500,000
8	Britannia Airways (UK)	42,000,000
9	Alitalia (Italy)	40,000,000*
10	Swissair (Switzerland)	39,500,000*

Estimated

T O P   1 0

DUTY-FREE AIRPORTS IN THE WORLD

	Shop location	Annual sales (US$)
1	Honolulu Airport	427,000,000
2	Hong Kong Airport	400,000,000
3	London Heathrow Airport	348,000,000
4	Amsterdam Schiphol Airport	262,000,000
5	Paris Charles de Gaulle Airport	257,000,000
6	Tokyo Narita Airport	241,000,000
7	Frankfurt Airport	220,000,000
8	Singapore Changi Airport	200,000,000
9	Copenhagen Airport	152,000,000
10	Osaka International Airport	146,000,000

T O P   1 0

DUTY-FREE SHOPS IN THE US

	Shop location	Annual sales (US$)
1	Honolulu International Airport	427,000,000
2	Los Angeles International Airport	95,000,000
3	John F. Kennedy Airport, New York	45,000,000 *
4	Miami International Airport	42,000,000
5	San Francisco International Airport	36,000,000
6	United Airlines	22,000,000
7	Northwest Airlines	21,500,000
8	American Airlines	21,000,000
9	Delta Airlines	20,000,000
10	Anchorage International Airport	16,300,000

* *Estimated*

T O P   1 0

DUTY-FREE COUNTRIES IN THE WORLD

	Country	Total annual duty- and tax-free sales (US$)		Country	Total annual duty- and tax-free sales (US$)
1	UK	1,130,000,000	6	France	510,000,000
2	US	885,000,000	7	Sweden	495,000,000
3	Denmark	630,000,000	8	Finland	450,000,000
4	Germany	620,000,000	9	Hong Kong	420,000,000
5	Japan	540,000,000	10	Netherlands	330,000,000

DID YOU KNOW

THE BIRTH OF DUTY-FREE

Duty-free sales began in 1951 at Shannon Airport in Ireland, where transatlantic flights stopped to refuel on their way to New York. Dr. Brendan O'Regan is credited with the idea of selling goods to people waiting in the transit lounge (technically not part of Irish soil, and so exempt from local taxes). By the end of the 1950s, airport shops had opened in Amsterdam, Brussels, London Heathrow, and Frankfurt.

MAIL AND TELEPHONES

T O P   1 0

MOST POPULAR TYPES OF GREETING CARDS MAILED IN THE US

	Holiday	Estimated no. sent
1	Christmas	2,700,000,000
2	Valentine's Day	1,000,000,000
3	Easter	160,000,000
4	Mother's Day	150,000,000
5	Father's Day	101,000,000
6	Thanksgiving	40,000,000
7	Halloween	35,000,000
8	St. Patrick's Day	19,000,000
9	Jewish New Year	12,000,000
10	Hanukkah	11,000,000

Some 50 percent of all personal mail is greeting cards. Of these, cards given during the major holidays dominate the market. Greeting cards for these occasions – as well as birthday, anniversary, and graduation cards (81,000,000 alone), and cards for such modern inventions as Secretary's Day (1,600,000) and National Boss Day (1,000,000) – combine to a projected 1994 sales of $5,900,000,000.

T O P   1 0

FIRST CITIES/COUNTRIES TO ISSUE POSTAGE STAMPS

	City/country	Stamps first issued
1	UK	May 1840
2	New York City, US	Feb 1842
3	Zurich, Switzerland	Mar 1843
4	Brazil	Aug 1843
5	Geneva, Switzerland	Oct 1843
6	Basle, Switzerland	Jul 1845
7	US	Jul 1847
8	Mauritius	Sep 1847
9	France	Jan 1849
10	Belgium	Jul 1849

The first adhesive postage stamps issued in the US were designed for local delivery (as authorized by an 1836 Act of Congress) and produced by the City Despatch Post, New York City, inaugurated on February 15, 1842 and later that year incorporated into the US Post Office Department. After a further Act in 1847, the rest of the United States followed suit and the Post Office Department issued its first national stamps: a 5-cent Benjamin Franklin stamp and a 10-cent George Washington stamp, both of which first went on sale in New York City on July 1, 1847. By the time they were withdrawn, 3,712,200 and 891,000 respectively had been issued.

T O P   1 0

OLDEST POST OFFICES IN THE US

	Facility	Zip code	Date first occupied by US Postal Service
1	Galena, Illinois	61036	November 1, 1858
2	Ogdensburg, New York	13669	January 1, 1870
3	Delaware, New Jersey	07833	January 1, 1884
4	Front Street Station, Memphis, Tennessee	38103	June 1, 1887
5	Winstonville, Mississippi	38781	October 1, 1887
6	Savannah, Georgia	31412	June 1, 1889
7	Brooklyn, New York	11201	February 1, 1892
8	Hoboken, New Jersey	07030	January 1, 1893
9	Port Townsend, Washington	98368	June 1, 1893
10	Amenia, New York	12501	January 1, 1894

This list comprises the 10 oldest facilities continuously occupied by the US Postal Service.

Source: U.S. Postal Service, Postal History Department

T O P   1 0

COUNTRIES SENDING AND RECEIVING THE MOST MAIL

	Country	Items of mail handled p.a.
1	US	164,639,561,000
2	Japan	22,723,628,000
3	Russia	21,923,325,000
4	France	21,867,860,000
5	Germany (former West)	17,051,746,000
6	UK	16,412,000,000
7	India	14,626,630,000
8	Ukraine	13,466,000,000
9	Canada	9,004,547,000
10	Italy	8,995,333,000

COUNTRIES WITH THE MOST PUBLIC TELEPHONES

	Country	Telephones
1	US	1,761,407
2	Japan	830,000
3	Italy	406,532
4	Republic of Korea	271,927
5	Brazil	263,643
6	Germany	200,000
7	France	190,497
8	Canada	172,049
9	India	145,577
10	Mexico	125,073
	UK	*110,000*

COUNTRIES THAT MAKE THE MOST INTERNATIONAL PHONE CALLS

	Country	Calls per head p.a.	Total calls
1	US	6.5	1,651,913,000
2	Germany	12.6	1,011,600,000
3	UK	8.3	480,000,000 *
4	Italy	6.9	396,000,000
5	Netherlands	22	334,000,000
6	Switzerland	44.3	304,940,000
7	Canada	11.1	302,500,000 *
8	Japan	2.3	290,000,000
9	Belgium	24.7	243,906,000
10	Hong Kong	40.6	241,023,000

* *Estimated*

COUNTRIES SENDING AND RECEIVING THE MOST MAIL 100 YEARS AGO

	Country	Items of mail handled p.a.
1	US	7,028,000,000
2	Germany	2,488,000,000
3	UK	2,363,000,000
4	France	1,523,000,000
5	Austria	960,000,000
6	Italy	476,000,000
7	Russia	326,000,000
8	Australia	294,000,000
9	Belgium	290,000,000
10	India	274,000,000

Statistics for worldwide mail 100 years ago indicate the extent to which postal services were then developed, and the high numbers of letters and other items per head of certain populations: the US leading the world with 110 per capita, followed by Australia with 82 items, reflecting the importance of long-distance internal mail, and the traffic between immigrants and their homelands.

COUNTRIES WITH THE MOST TELEPHONES

	Country	Telephones
1	US	143,325,389
2	Japan	58,520,000
3	Germany	35,420,843
4	France	29,521,000
5	UK	26,880,000
6	Italy	23,708,388
7	Russia	22,778,601
8	Canada	16,227,000
9	Republic of Korea	15,865,381
10	Spain	13,792,156

It is estimated that there are some 574,860,000 telephone lines in use in the world, of which 234,083,000 are in Europe, 193,053,000 in North and South America, 127,290,000 in Asia, 10,336,000 in Oceania, and 10,098,000 in Africa. It is remarkable that, given its population, the whole of China has only 11,469,100 telephones – fewer than half the total for Italy.

COUNTRIES WITH THE MOST TELEPHONES/100 PEOPLE

	Country	Telephones per 100 inhabitants
1	Sweden	68.43
2	Switzerland	60.83
3	Canada	59.24
4	Denmark	58.30
5	US	56.12
6	Luxembourg	55.07
7	Finland	54.57
8	Iceland	54.28
9	Norway	53.00
10	France	51.52
	UK	*46.75*

Contrasting with the Top 10 countries, where the ratio is around two people per telephone or better, there are many countries in the world with fewer than one telephone per 100 inhabitants. Most of Central and West Africa possesses fewer than one telephone for every 200 people.

FUEL AND POWER

T O P 1 0

COAL CONSUMERS IN THE WORLD

	Country	Consumption 1991 (tonnes)
1	China	1,058,208,000
2	US	806,483,000
3	Germany	469,095,000
4	Russia	395,000,000
5	India	227,921,000
6	Poland	168,783,000
7	South Africa	133,527,000
8	Japan	117,938,000
9	UK	108,247,000
10	Australia	98,881,000

T O P 1 0

COAL PRODUCERS IN THE WORLD

	Country	Annual production (tonnes)
1	China	1,087,406,000
2	US	901,877,000
3	Germany	458,102,000
4	Russia	353,000,000
5	India	224,500,000
6	Australia	214,030,000
7	Poland	209,782,000
8	South Africa	176,174,000
9	Ukraine	135,600,000
10	Kazakhstan	130,315,000

DID YOU KNOW

BURNING RUBBER

In 1993, as an alternative to power stations using conventional fuels such as coal or oil, plants were opened near St. Louis, Missouri, and in Wolverhampton, UK, to burn used tires. With similar targets (7,500,000 and 8,000,000 tires respectively), the plants are designed to produce greater energy efficiency but with reduced sulfur emissions, and, even allowing for the cost of transporting the tires, will save money. The British plant was designed to burn 23 percent of the country's waste tires in its first year of operation and provide electricity to 25,000 homes.

T O P 1 0

COUNTRIES WITH THE GREATEST COAL RESERVES IN THE WORLD

	Country	Reserves (tonnes)
1	Former USSR	265,582,000,000
2	US	240,561,000,000
3	China	114,500,000,000
4	Australia	90,940,000,000
5	Germany	80,069,000,000
6	India	62,548,000,000
7	South Africa	55,333,000,000
8	Poland	41,200,000,000
9	Indonesia	32,063,000,000
10	Kazakhstan	25,000,000,000

T O P 1 0

ELECTRICITY-PRODUCING COUNTRIES

	Country	Production (kw/hr)
1	US	3,079,085,000,000
2	Russia	1,068,000,000,000
3	Japan	888,086,000,000
4	China	677,550,000,000
5	Germany	573,752,000,000
6	Canada	507,913,000,000
7	France	454,702,000,000
8	UK	322,133,000,000
9	India	309,370,000,000
10	Ukraine	279,000,000,000

T O P 1 0

ENERGY CONSUMERS IN THE WORLD

	Country	Annual consumption coal equivalent (tonnes)
1	US	2,481,686,000
2	Former USSR	1,931,301,000
3	China	922,183,000
4	Japan	512,110,000
5	Germany	457,300,000
6	UK	286,525,000
7	Canada	271,975,000
8	India	264,920,000
9	France	222,741,000
10	Italy	209,851,000

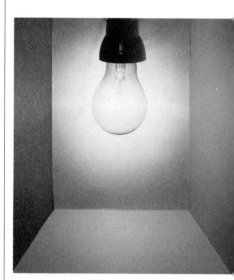

STANDARD ELECTRIC LIGHT BULB
The incandescent light bulb has a tungsten filament that glows yellow-white when electricity is passed through it. This type of bulb is very inefficient, converting only 8 percent of the electric energy to light.

TOP 10
COUNTRIES PRODUCING THE MOST ELECTRICITY FROM NUCLEAR SOURCES

	Country	Nuclear power as % of total power use	Output (megawatt-hours)
1	US	22.3	98,729
2	France	72.9	57,688
3	Japan	27.7	34,238
4	Germany	30.1	22,559
5	Russia	11.8	18,893
6	Canada	15.2	14,874
7	Ukraine	25.0	13,020
8	UK	23.2	12,066
9	Sweden	43.2	10,002
10	South Korea	53.2	7,220
	World total		*323,497*

TOP 10
STATES CONSUMING THE GREATEST AMOUNT OF GASOLINE

	State	Consumption 1992 (gallons)
1	California	13,188,923,000
2	Texas	8,885,758,000
3	Florida	6,457,057,000
4	New York	5,616,855,000
5	Ohio	4,947,546,000
6	Pennsylvania	4,744,271,000
7	Illinois	4,702,150,000
8	Michigan	4,565,031,000
9	Georgia	3,967,794,000
10	North Carolina	3,517,366,000

TOP 10
COUNTRIES WITH THE LARGEST CRUDE OIL RESERVES

	Country	Reserves (barrels)*
1	Saudi Arabia	258,600,000,000
2	Russia	156,700,000,000
3=	Iraq	99,840,000,000
3=	Iran	99,840,000,000
5	Kuwait	92,428,000,000
6	United Arab Emirates	64,747,000,000
7	Venezuela	63,330,000,000
8	Mexico	51,225,000,000
9	Libya	38,190,000,000
10	China	29,600,000,000
	US	*22,845,000,000*

* A barrel contains 42 US gallons

TOP 10
CRUDE OIL PRODUCERS IN THE WORLD

	Country	Production (barrels per annum)
1	Saudi Arabia	2,975,000,000
2	US	2,617,000,000
3	Russia	2,911,000,000
4	Iran	1,220,000,000
5	China	1,061,000,000
6	Mexico	1,009,000,000
7	Venezuela	865,000,000
8	United Arab Emirates	837,000,000
9	Norway	800,000,000
10	Canada	501,000,000

Despite its huge output, the US produces barely half the 4,921,000,000 barrels of oil it consumes every year – an energy consumption that is equivalent to 19 barrels per capita. The average US citizen thus uses one barrel of oil about every 19 days.

TOP 10
COUNTRIES CONSUMING THE MOST OIL

	Country	Consumption 1991 (barrels)
1	US	4,921,000,000
2	Russia	3,700,000,000
3	Japan	1,432,000,000
4	China	905,000,000
5	Germany	667,000,000
6	UK	591,000,000
7	France	555,000,000
8	Saudi Arabia	534,000,000
9	Italy	533,000,000
10	Canada	486,000,000

TOP 10
OIL COMPANIES WITH THE MOST OUTLETS IN THE US*

	Company	No. of outlets
1	Texaco	14,151
2	Citgo	12,531
3	Exxon	9,450
4	Amoco	9,370
5	Shell	8,533
6	Chevron	8,525
7	Mobil	8,230
8	Phillips	7,449
9	BP American	6,600
10	Conoco	4,947

* To September 1992

SAVING THE PLANET

TOP 10

CARBON DIOXIDE EMITTERS IN THE WORLD

	Country	CO_2 emissions (tonnes of carbon) per capita	total
1	US	5.3301	1,345,969,180
2	Former USSR	3.3579	977,396,410
3	China	0.6035	694,153,740
4	Japan	2.4013	297,801,560
5	Germany	3.3131	264,637,260
6	India	0.2226	192,017,500
7	UK	2.7266	157,520,800
8	Canada	4.1518	112,070,740
9	Italy	1.9022	109,856,540
10	France	1.7924	102,104,730

The Carbon Dioxide Information Analysis Center at Oak Ridge, Tennessee, calculates CO_2 emissions from fossil fuel burning, cement manufacturing, and gas flaring. Their findings show that increasing industrialization in many countries has resulted in huge increases in carbon dioxide.

TOP 10

DEFORESTING COUNTRIES IN THE WORLD

	Country	Average annual forest loss in 1980s sq km	sq miles
1	Brazil	36,500	14,100
2	India	15,000	5,800
3	Indonesia	9,200	3,600
4	Colombia	8,900	3,400
5	Mexico	6,150	2,400
6	Zaïre	5,800	2,300
7	Congo	5,260	2,000
8	Ivory Coast	5,100	1,970
9	Sudan	5,040	1,950
10	Nigeria	4,000	1,550

The loss of Brazilian forest at an annual average of 14,100 sq miles/36,500 sq km means that over the decade of the 1980s the total loss was equivalent to the entire area of Germany, or one-and-a-half times the area of the UK.

TOP 10

MOST POLLUTED CITIES IN THE WORLD

(Based on levels of atmospheric sulfur dioxide)

1	Milan, Italy
2	Shengyang, China
3	Tehran, Iran
4	Seoul, South Korea
5	Rio de Janeiro, Brazil
6	São Paulo, Brazil
7	Xian, China
8	Paris, France
9	Peking, China
10	Madrid, Spain

Assessments made by the World Health Authority in the 1980s lacked information from the former Soviet bloc countries, where pollution levels in some areas may be even higher than in the cities mentioned on this list. Many countries have since taken steps to "clean up their acts."

TOP 10

GARBAGE PRODUCERS IN THE WORLD

	Country	Domestic waste per head per annum kg	lb
1	US	864	1,905
2	Canada	625	1,378
3	Finland	504	1,111
4	Norway	473	1,043
5	Denmark	469	1,034
6	Luxembourg	466	1,027
7	Netherlands	465	1,025
8	Switzerland	424	935
9	Japan	394	869
10	UK	357	787

TOP 10

SULFUR DIOXIDE EMITTERS IN THE WORLD

	Country	Annual SO_2 emissions (kg per head)
1	Canada	143
2	US	83
3	UK	65
4	Spain	55
5	Finland	49
6	Ireland	47
7	Belgium	43
8	Denmark	38
9	Italy	35
10	Luxembourg	27

Sulfur dioxide, the principal cause of acid rain, is produced by fuel combustion in factories and power stations. During the 1980s, emissions by all countries declined.

TOP 10

LEAST POLLUTED CITIES IN THE WORLD

(Based on levels of atmospheric sulfur dioxide)

1	Craiova, Poland
2	Melbourne, Australia
3	Auckland, New Zealand
4	Cali, Colombia
5	Tel Aviv, Israel
6	Bucharest, Romania
7	Vancouver, Canada
8	Toronto, Canada
9	Bangkok, Thailand
10	Chicago, US

STATES WITH THE HIGHEST WASTE RECYCLING TARGETS

	State*/target year	Target %
1	Rhode Island (not stated)	70
2	New Jersey (1995)	60
3=	California (2000)	50
3=	Hawaii (2000)	50
3=	Indiana (2001)	50
3=	Iowa (2000)	50
3=	Maine (1994)	50
3=	Massachusetts (2000)	50
3=	Nebraska (2002)	50
3=	New Mexico (2000)	50
3=	New York (1997)	50
3=	Oregon (2000)	50
3=	South Dakota (2001)	50
3=	Washington (1995)	50
3=	West Virginia (2010)	50

* Ten states have not stated their target for recycling

STATES WITH THE MOST SOLID WASTE

	State	recycled	Disposal % incinerated	landfilled	Total (tons per annum)
1	California	11	2	87	44,535,000
2	New York	21	17	62	22,800,000
3	Florida	27	23	49	19,400,000
4	Ohio	19	6	75	16,400,000
5	Texas	11	1	88	14,469,000
6	Illinois	11	2	87	14,140,000
7	Michigan	26	17	57	13,000,000
8	Pennsylvania	11	30	59	8,984,000
9	Indiana	8	17	25	8,400,000
10	North Carolina	4	1	95	7,788,000

* Totals for some states include quantities of industrial waste

Estimates put the total amount of solid waste generated by the entire United States in 1992 at 291,742,000 tons (more than one ton per head of the population), of which the top 10 states were responsible for 169,916,000 tons, or 58 percent. Of this total, an average of 17 percent was recycled, 11 percent incinerated, and 72 percent disposed of by burial in landfill sites. The state recycling the greatest proportion of its solid waste in 1992 was Minnesota, at 38 percent, with Hawaii, Montana, North Carolina, and Wyoming tied for the lowest place at 4 percent.

CITIES COLLECTING AND RECYCLING THE MOST CHEMICALS IN THE US, 1992

	City/State	Chemicals collected (lb) Amount recovered*	Amount recycled#	Total
1	Pascagoula, Mississippi	4,093,574,108	1,749,130	4,095,323,238
2	Deer Park, Texas	407,832,800	27,458	407,860,258
3	Claypool, Arizona	390,075,000	1,715,000	391,790,000
4	Lake Charles, Louisiana	165,552,135	160,128,000	325,680,135
5	El Dorado, Kansas	292,852,030	–	292,852,030
6	Oregon, Ohio	274,857,200	1,034,559	275,891,759
7	Freeport, Texas	263,408,859	1,829,788	265,238,647
8	Savannah, Georgia	260,330,220	139,121	260,469,341
9	Boss, Missouri	110,003,980	143,613,120	253,617,100
10	Whiting, Indiana	28,900	221,338,441	221,367,341

* Recovered onsite
# Sent offsite for recycling

WASTE NOT WANT NOT
These paper logs are made by soaking and compressing old newspapers.

INDUSTRIAL AND OTHER ACCIDENTS

T O P 1 0

WORST EXPLOSIONS IN THE WORLD

(Excluding mining disasters, and terrorist and military bombs)

	Location/incident	Date	Killed
1	Lanchow, China (arsenal)	October 26, 1935	2,000
2	Halifax, Nova Scotia (ammunition ship *Mont Blanc*)	December 6, 1917	1,635
3	Memphis, Tennessee (*Sultana* boiler explosion)	April 27, 1865	1,547
4	Bombay, India (ammunition ship *Fort Stikine*)	April 14, 1944	1,376
5	Cali, Colombia (ammunition trucks)	August 7, 1956	1,200
6	Salang Tunnel, Afghanistan (oil tanker collision)	November 2, 1982	over 1,100
7	Chelyabinsk, USSR (liquid gas beside railway)	June 3, 1989	up to 800
8	Texas City, Texas (ammonium nitrate on *Grandcamp* freighter)	April 16, 1947	752
9	Oppau, Germany (chemical plant)	September 21, 1921	561
10	San José, Cubatao, Brazil (oil pipeline)	February 25, 1984	508

All these "best estimate" figures should be treated with caution, since, as with fires and shipwrecks, body counts are notoriously unreliable.

T O P 1 0

WORST INDUSTRIAL DISASTERS

(Excluding mining disasters, and marine and other transportation disasters)

	Location/incident	Date	Killed
1	Bhopal, India (methyl isocyanate gas escape at Union Carbide plant)	Dec 3, 1984	over 2,500
2	Oppau, Germany (chemical plant explosion)	Sep 21, 1921	561
3	Brussels, Belgium (fire in L'Innovation department store)	May 22, 1967	322
4	Guadalajara, Mexico (explosions after gas leak into sewers)	Apr 22, 1992	230
5	São Paulo, Brazil (fire in Joelma bank and office building)	Feb 1, 1974	227
6	North Sea (Piper Alpha oil rig explosion and fire)	Jul 6, 1988	173
7	New York City (fire in Triangle Shirtwaist Factory)	Mar 25, 1911	145
8	Eddystone, Pennsylvania (munitions plant explosion)	Apr 10, 1917	133
9	Cleveland, Ohio (explosion of liquid gas tanks at East Ohio Gas Co.)	Oct 20, 1944	131
10	Caracas, Venezuela (fuel tank fire)	Dec 19–21, 1982	129

T O P 1 0

MOST COMMON CAUSES OF INJURY AT WORK IN THE US

	Cause	% of total injuries
1	Overexertion	31.3
2	Contact with objects or equipment	27.0
3	Falls	15.0
4	Other/nonclassifiable	13.0
5	Exposure to harmful substances	5.0
6	Repetitive motion	4.0
7	Slips, trips	3.5
8	Transportation accidents	3.0
9	Assaults, violent acts by person	1.0
10	Fires, explosions	0.2

Source: US Department of Labor, Bureau of Labor Statistics

T O P 1 0

MOST COMMON CAUSES OF FATAL ACCIDENTS AT WORK IN THE US

	Cause	% of total injuries		Cause	% of total injuries		Cause	% of total injuries
1	Motor vehicle	35.6	5	Fires/burns	3.2	9	Poison (gas/vapor)	1.3
2	Falls	12.2	6	Air transportation	2.5	10	Other*	33.9
3	Electric current	3.7	7	Drowning	2.4			
4	Poison (liquid/solid)	3.5	8	Water transportation	1.7			

* Includes machinery, being struck by a falling object, railroads, and mechanical suffocation
Source: National Safety Council

WORST FIRES IN THE WORLD

(Excluding sports and entertainment venues, mining disasters, and the results of military action)

	Location/incident	Date	Killed
1	Kwanto, Japan (following earthquake)	September 1, 1923	60,000
2	Cairo, Egypt (city fire)	1824	4,000
3	London Bridge, England	July 1212	3,000 #
4	Peshtigo, Wisconsin (forest)	October 8, 1871	2,682
5	Santiago, Chile (church of La Compañía)	December 8, 1863	2,500
6	Chungking, China (docks)	September 2, 1949	1,700
7	Constantinople, Turkey (city fire)	June 5, 1870	900
8	Cloquet, Minnesota (forest)	October 12, 1918	800
9	Hinckley, Minnesota (forest)	September 1, 1894	480
10	Hoboken, New Jersey (docks)	June 30, 1900	326

 # Burned, crushed, and drowned in ensuing panic

CAUSES OF FATAL INJURIES AT WORK IN THE US

	Event or exposure	Fatalities (1993)
1	Shooting	874
2	Highway collision between vehicles/mobile equipment	652
3	Falls to lower level	530
4	Nonhighway transportation accident (farm/industrial premises)	392
5	Struck by vehicle	361
6	Struck by falling object	345
7	Highway noncollision accident	333
8	Contact with electrical current	324
9	Caught in or compressed by equipment or objects	308
10	Aircraft	280
	Total (incl. others not in Top 10)	**6,271**

Death by shooting (such as the homicide of police and security officers and workers as a result of armed robbery incidents) and highway collisions sadly feature as prominently among the most common causes of occupational fatalities as they do in daily life in modern America. Of the 1993 total, 5,790 victims were men and 481 women – vastly out of proportion to a labor force that comprises some 66,029,000 men and 54,761,000 women.

WORST MINING DISASTERS IN THE WORLD

	Location	Date	Killed
1	Hinkeiko, China	April 26, 1942	1,549
2	Courrières, France	March 10, 1906	1,060
3	Omuta, Japan	November 9, 1963	447
4	Senghenydd, UK	October 14, 1913	439
5	Coalbrook, South Africa	January 21, 1960	437
6	Wankie, Rhodesia	June 6, 1972	427
7	Dharbad, India	May 28, 1965	375
8	Chasnala, India	December 27, 1975	372
9	Monongah, West Virginia	December 6, 1907	362
10	Barnsley, UK	December 12, 1866	361*

A mining disaster at the Fushun mines, Manchuria, on February 12, 1931 may have resulted in up to 3,000 deaths, but information was suppressed by the Chinese government. Soviet security was also responsible for obscuring details of an explosion at the East German Johanngeorgendstadt uranium mine on November 29, 1949, when as many as 3,700 may have died.

* Including 27 killed the following day while searching for survivors

OCCUPATIONS FOR FATAL INJURIES AT WORK IN THE US

	Occupation	Fatalities (1993)
1	Motor vehicle operators	917
2	Construction trades	565
3	Sales occupations	556
4	Executives, administrators, and managers	427
5	Farming operators and managers	409
6	Mechanics and repairers	317
7	Protective service occupations	288
8	Professional specialists	254
9	Construction laborers	218
10	Farm workers	209
	Total (incl. others not in Top 10)	**6,271**

Truck drivers (731) and taxicab drivers and chauffeurs (113) comprise most of the No. 1 category. Outside this list, "Technicians and related support occupations" (167) includes 104 deaths of airplane pilots and navigators.

CHARITIES

FUND-RAISING CHARITIES IN THE US

	Charity	Income ($)
1	Lutheran Social Ministry	1,937,800,000
2	Catholic Charities U.S.A.	1,848,500,000
3	YMCA	1,677,900,000
4	American Red Cross	1,567,800,000
5	Salvation Army	1,398,700,000
6	UNICEF	938,000,000
7	Girl Scouts of the U.S.A.	457,400,000
8	Planned Parenthood	446,000,000
9	United Jewish Appeal	407,600,000
10	United Cerebral Palsy Associations	417,700,000

RELIEF AND DEVELOPMENT CHARITIES IN THE US

	Charity	Program spending (%)*	Income ($)
1	MAP International	95.0	52,600,000
2	Catholic Relief Services	94.6	290,300,000
3	International Rescue Committee	93.5	54,400,000
4	Food for the Hungry	91.4	32,600,000
5	Feed the Children	90.0	88,300,000
6	Mennonite Central Committee	90.0	39,200,000
7	American Red Cross	88.2	1,567,800,000
8	UNICEF	84.9	938,000,000
9	Save the Children Federation	83.5	92,300,000
10	Church World Service	81.5	43,600,000

* *Source for all lists showing percentage used for program spending:*
MONEY, *December 1993*

CONSERVATION CHARITIES IN THE US

	Charity	Program spending (%)	Income ($)
1	World Wildlife Fund	83.7	56,900,000
2	National Wildlife Federation	80.0	86,900,000
3	Nature Conservancy	72.5	274,100,000
4	National Audubon Society	70.9	40,100,000
5	Greenpeace Fund	69.7	47,600,000
6	Humane Society of the US	65.8	26,700,000

	Charity	Program spending (%)	Income ($)
7	Jewish National Fund	64.2	24,300,000
8	North Shore Animal League	61.0	32,300,000

HEALTH CHARITIES IN THE US

	Charity	Program spending (%)	Income ($)
1	AmeriCares Foundation	99.1	100,600,000
2	California Family Planning Council	97.9	41,600,000
3	Northwest Medical Teams International	97.1	34,800,000
4	Project Hope	91.7	87,000,000
5	United Cerebral Palsy Associations	83.5	417,700,000
6	American Heart Association	82.8	289,100,000
7	National Mental Health Association	82.3	69,600,000
8	Muscular Dystrophy Association	79.9	100,300,000
9	National Easter Seal Society	79.0	335,000,000
10	Juvenile Diabetes Foundation	78.4	30,500,000

EDUCATION AND CULTURE CHARITIES IN THE US

	Charity	Program spending (%)	Income ($)
1	Population Council	80.5	44,100,000
2	National Trust for Historic Preservation	78.7	29,200,000
3	United Negro College Fund	74.5	71,100,000
4	Childreach	73.3	30,700,000
5	Junior Achievement	71.3	62,200,000
6	The Cleveland Foundation	57.9	51,100,000
7	Museum Associates	45.6	59,100,000
8	Chicago Community Trust	40.8	62,500,000
9	The Orchestral Association	38.8	68,300,000
10	Armenian General Benevolent Union	30.4	65,000,000

T O P 1 0

CORPORATE FOUNDATIONS BY TOTAL GRANTS, 1992

	Corporate foundation	Grant ($)
1	AT&T Foundation	31,541,713
2	Amoco Foundation	23,702,088
3	US WEST Foundation	21,110,094
4	General Motors Foundation	21,049,433
5	General Electric Foundation	20,790,490
6	GTE Foundation	19,955,883
7	Ford Motor Company Fund	19,297,563
8	Exxon Education Foundation	18,516,516
9	Procter & Gamble Fund	17,577,151
10	Prudential Foundation	15,708,212

Source: Foundation Giving, *4th Edition (1994)*

FOUNDATIONS BY TOTAL GRANTS, 1992

	Foundation	Grant ($)
1	Ford Foundation	263,620,911
2	W.K. Kellogg Foundation	173,158,573
3	Pew Charitable Trusts	143,537,605
4	John D. and Katherine T. MacArthur Foundation	137,000,000
5	Lilly Endowment	118,907,952
6	Robert Wood Johnson Foundation	103,124,020
7	New York Community Trust	100,842,773
8	Andrew W. Mellon Foundation	95,865,156
9	Rockefeller Foundation	93,070,397
10	DeWitt Wallace-Reader's Digest Fund	72,324,761

Source: Foundation Giving, *4th Edition (1994)*

SOCIAL SERVICE CHARITIES IN THE US

	Charity	Program spending (%)	Income ($)		Charity	Program spending (%)	Income ($)
1	United Jewish Appeal	95.0	407,600,000	6	AFS Intercultural Programs	88.0	32,900,000
2	World Opportunities International	94.7	38,700,000	7	Catholic Charities U.S.A.	86.7	1,848,500,000
3	New York Association for New Americans	94.2	58,800,000	8	Christian Relief Services	85.9	37,400,000
4	Neighborhood Centers	93.3	32,900,000	9	Youth for Understanding International Exchange	85.3	24,300,000
5	Catholic Medical Mission Board	90.8	25,600,000	10	Salvation Army	85.0	1,398,700,000

GRANT RECIPIENT ORGANIZATIONS, 1992

	Recipient	Grants ($)		Recipient	Grants ($)
1	Harvard University	41,399,635	7	United Jewish Appeal – Federation of Jewish Philanthropies	23,832,977
2	University of Houston	35,635,600	8	University of Pennsylvania	23,451,411
3	Presbyterian/St. Luke's Medical Center	30,000,000	9	Columbia University	21,346,170
4	United Negro College Fund	28,473,306	10	University of California	21,231,598
5	Stanford University	25,535,667			
6	America 3 Foundation	25,525,000			

Source: Foundation Giving, *4th Edition (1994)*

D I D Y O U K N O W

BAND AID AND USA FOR AFRICA

It is 10 years since they were launched, but their achievement stands out as one of the great success stories of international cooperation and charitable activity: two intimately linked but ephemeral charities have contributed between them almost $200,000,000 to aid African famine relief. The story began in 1984 in the UK; Band Aid, the inspiration of Irish rock star Bob Geldof, raised a total of $144,124,694 in little over seven years, from the time of the launch of its hit single (featuring 36 artists), *Do They Know It's Christmas?*, on December 7, 1984 – which became the bestselling single of all time in the UK – through the July 13, 1985 Anglo-American Live Aid concert (which raised $70,000,000), to its closure in 1992. Inspired by Band Aid's success, the charity USA For Africa was founded by Harry Belafonte. The organization recorded the song *We Are the World*, which featured a host of notable stars, including Lionel Richie, Stevie Wonder, Paul Simon, Diana Ross, Michael Jackson, Bob Dylan, and Ray Charles. The record sold 7,500,000 copies, and royalty earnings plus sales of associated merchandise and other fund-raising activities raised more than $50,000,000.

THE WORLD'S RICHEST

T O P   1 0

HIGHEST-EARNING ENTERTAINERS IN THE WORLD*

MONEY TALKS
Oprah Winfrey has transformed her daytime talk show into a multimillion dollar production company.

	Entertainer	Profession	1992–93 income ($)
1	Oprah Winfrey	TV host/producer	98,000,000
2	Steven Spielberg	Film producer/director	72,000,000
3	Charles M. Schulz	"Peanuts" cartoonist	48,000,000
4	David Copperfield	Illusionist	46,000,000
5	Siegfried & Roy	Illusionists	32,000,000
6	Tom Clancy	Novelist	31,000,000
7	Stephen King	Novelist/screenwriter	28,000,000
8	Xuxa	TV host/rock singer	27,000,000
9	John Grisham	Novelist	25,000,000
10=	Michael Crichton	Novelist	24,000,000
10=	Andrew Lloyd Webber	Composer	24,000,000

* Other than actors and pop stars.   Used by permission of Forbes Magazine

As in the previous year of this survey, Oprah Winfrey maintained her place at the top of the pile. Also firmly established in the list are illusionists David Copperfield and Siegfried & Roy, while the increasing presence of novelists reflects the success of blockbuster movies based on their work – such as Michael Crichton's *Jurassic Park*. If newcomer Xuxa is excluded as a candidate as a result of her dual career as a rock singer, British theatrical producer Cameron Mackintosh ($22,000,000) would join this showbiz elite.

T O P   1 0

HIGHEST-EARNING ROCK STARS IN THE WORLD

	Artist(s)	1992–93 income ($)
1	Guns N' Roses	53,000,000
2	Prince	49,000,000
3=	Garth Brooks	47,000,000
3=	U2	47,000,000
5	Michael Jackson	42,000,000

	Artist(s)	1992–93 income ($)
6	Julio Iglesias	40,000,000
7	Madonna	37,000,000
8=	Eric Clapton	33,000,000
8=	Grateful Dead	33,000,000
10	Billy Ray Cyrus	29,000,000

Used by permission of Forbes Magazine

Forbes Magazine's survey of leading entertainers' income covers a two-year period in order to iron out fluctuations, especially those caused by successful tours. Even so, such is the current importance of global tours that when groups such as the Rolling Stones, Aerosmith, and ZZ Top stop touring, they can find their incomes decline so dramatically that they depart from the reckoning altogether. Pink Floyd's international tour in the 1988–89 financial period, for example, netted a total of $135,000,000, and the group themselves earned $56,000,000, despite which they have since vacated the Top 10. Michael Jackson's income peaked at $125,000,000 in the same period, but has been declining ever since. Hovering just outside the Top 10 are Neil Diamond, Paul McCartney, and Jimmy Buffet, while some former entrants – most notably erstwhile inhabitants of this list's top slot, New Kids on the Block – have now disbanded, and will never be seen in it again.

T O P   1 0

COUNTRIES WITH THE MOST DOLLAR BILLIONAIRES

(People with a net worth of $1,000,000,000 or more)

	Country	Billionaires
1	US	108
2	Germany	46
3	Japan	35
4=	France	9
4=	Hong Kong	9
4=	Switzerland	9
7	Canada	7
8=	Italy	6
8=	Taiwan	6
8=	UK	6

Based on data published in Forbes Magazine.

TOP 10

RICHEST PEOPLE OUTSIDE THE US

	Name	Country	Business	Assets ($)
1	Yoshiaki Tsutsumi	Japan	Property	9,000,000,000 *
2	Family of late Taikichiro Mori	Japan	Property	7,500,000,000
3=	Haniel family	Germany	Food wholesaling	6,200,000,000
3=	Erivan Haub	Germany	Supermarkets	6,200,000,000
5=	Hans and Gad Rausing	Sweden	Packaging	6,000,000,000
5=	Shin Kyuk-ho	Korea	Sweets, retailing	6,000,000,000
7	Theo and Karl Albrecht	Germany	Supermarkets	5,700,000,000
8	Kenneth Thomson	Canada	Publishing	5,400,000,000
9	Emilio Azcarraga Milmo	Mexico	TV, bullrings	5,100,000,000
10	Henkel family	Germany	Consumer products	4,900,000,000

* Some sources suggest a figure as high as $22,500,000,000

Based on data published in Forbes Magazine

TOP 10

RICHEST PEOPLE IN THE US

	Name	Profession/source	Assets ($)
1	Warren Edward Buffett	Textiles, etc.	8,325,000,000
2	William Henry Gates III	Computer software	6,160,000,000
3	John Werner Kluge	Media and cellular telephone	5,900,000,000
4	Sumner Murray Redstone	Movie theaters	5,600,000,000
5	Walton family (five members share $23,000,000,000)	Retail stores	4,600,000,000
6	(Keith) Rupert Murdoch	Publishing, TV, and cinema	4,000,000,000
7	Ted Arison	Cruise liners	3,650,000,000
8	Ronald Owen Perelman	Varied businesses	3,600,000,000
9	Samuel Irving Newhouse, Jr. and Donald Edward Newhouse ($7,000,000,000 shared)	Publishing	3,500,000,000
10	Kirk Kerkorian	Film and other industries	3,100,000,000

Close runners-up in the more-than-two-billion dollars league include former Presidential candidate Henry Ross Perot ($2,400,000,000), the Mars (of Mars Bar fame) family (four members sharing $9,600,000,000), and broadcasting magnate (and husband of Jane Fonda) Ted Turner ($2,200,000,000). Paul G. Allen ($2,900,000,000), cofounder of Microsoft (with Bill Gates), and David Packard ($2,750,000,000) of computer giant Hewlett-Packard are two representatives of the new technology billionaire class.

Used by permission of Forbes Magazine

TOP 10

HIGHEST-EARNING ACTORS IN THE WORLD (1992-93)

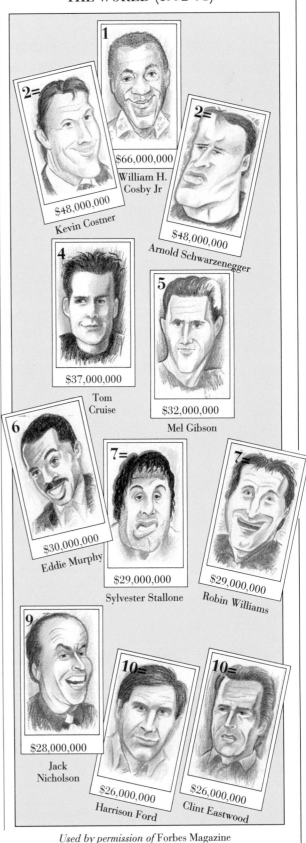

1 $66,000,000 William H. Cosby Jr

2= $48,000,000 Kevin Costner

2= $48,000,000 Arnold Schwarzenegger

4 $37,000,000 Tom Cruise

5 $32,000,000 Mel Gibson

6 $30,000,000 Eddie Murphy

7= $29,000,000 Sylvester Stallone

7= $29,000,000 Robin Williams

9 $28,000,000 Jack Nicholson

10= $26,000,000 Harrison Ford

10= $26,000,000 Clint Eastwood

Used by permission of Forbes Magazine

RICHEST IN THE US

TOP 10

RICHEST PEOPLE IN THE US

	Name(s)	Assets ($)
1	Warren Edward Buffett	8,325,000,000

Buffett was born and still lives in Omaha, Nebraska. His professional career started as a pinball service engineer, after which he published a horse race tip sheet. His diverse business interests include the New England textile company Berkshire Hathaway, which has in turn acquired major stakes in the Washington Post, Coca-Cola, and other companies. In 1992 Buffett was ranked fourth in the Forbes 400, but in 1993 was elevated to first place.

	Name(s)	Assets ($)
2	William Henry Gates III	6,160,000,000

In 1975, at the age of 19, Gates left law school to co-found (with Paul G. Allen, who rates 11th place in this list) the Microsoft Corporation of Seattle, now one of the world's leading computer software companies, and one that has enjoyed phenomenal growth: a $2,000 investment in 1986 was worth nearly $70,000 in 1993. Gates, a self-described "hard-core technoid," was placed in the No. 1 position in 1992.

	Name(s)	Assets ($)
3	John Werner Kluge	5,900,000,000

Founder of the Metromedia Company of Charlottesville, Virginia. He started a radio station and in 1959, with partners, acquired the Metropolitan Broadcasting Company, developing it into Metromedia, a corporation that owns TV and radio stations and cellular telephone franchises and other varied properties. He also owns an 80,000-acre estate and castle in Scotland. Kluge, who was placed as America's richest man in 1989, has diversified his interests into such areas as films (Orion Pictures), printing, and a chain of steak houses.

	Name(s)	Assets ($)
4	Sumner Murray Redstone	5,600,000,000

Redstone built up his own movie theater company, National Amusements, Inc., which now has more than 750 screens across the US, coining the word "multiplex" for his multiscreen movie theater complexes. He has also acquired the film company Viacom.

	Name(s)	Assets ($)
5	Helen Walton, S. Robson Walton, John T. Walton, Jim C. Walton, and Alice L. Walton (shared)	23,000,000,000

Samuel Moore Walton, the founder of Wal-Mart Stores, headed the list of America's richest people for several years. One of the largest retail chains in the US, its stores – which number more than 2,000 – achieved sales of $55,500,000,000 in 1992, the year in which Sam Walton died. His widow Helen and four children share the fortune he created.

	Name(s)	Assets ($)
6	(Keith) Rupert Murdoch	4,000,000,000

Australian-born newspaper tycoon Rupert Murdoch has expanded his News Corporation empire to encompass magazines, book publishing, film (Twentieth Century-Fox), and broadcasting (including Sky satellite TV).

	Name(s)	Assets ($)
7	Ted Arison	3,650,000,000

Born to a shipowning family in Tel Aviv (where he now lives in retirement, while retaining various US business interests, including the Miami Heat basketball team), Arison derives his wealth from his Carnival Cruise Lines fleet of cruise ships, which is the world's largest.

	Name(s)	Assets ($)
8	Ronald Owen Perelman	3,600,000,000

Perelman is a wide-ranging entrepreneur who acquired Revlon, Max Factor, and other cosmetics businesses; he was the former owner of Technicolor, and has professional interests that encompass firms from Marvel Comics and cigars to a camping supply company.

	Name(s)	Assets ($)
9	Samuel Irving Newhouse Jr. and brother Donald Edward Newhouse (shared)	7,000,000,000

The New York City-based Newhouse brothers are owners of America's largest privately owned chain of 29 newspapers with a total daily circulation of 3,000,000, with interests that include cable television and book publishing. Samuel ("Si") Newhouse runs book publisher Random House and magazine publisher Condé Nast, the publisher of Vogue, bought by his father in 1959 as an anniversary gift for his wife ("She asked for a fashion magazine and I went out and got her Vogue"). Donald controls their newspaper group.

	Name(s)	Assets ($)
10	Kirk Kerkorian	3,100,000,000

A newcomer to the Top 10 of the Forbes 400, Kerkorian, the son of an Armenian immigrant fruit farmer, became an Air Force pilot and founder of a charter airline business which he sold in 1966, making a profit of $104,000,000. He later bought and sold (twice) the film studios MGM and United Artists, and retains a large shareholding in motor giant Chrysler.

In 1993 *Forbes Magazine*, which annually surveys the 400 wealthiest people in the US, ranked almost 80 Americans as billionaires – that is, with assets in excess of $1,000,000,000. The *Forbes 400* includes both the inheritors of great family fortunes and self-made individuals. The order of this list is extremely volatile, however; during recent times, particularly, many who made vast fortunes in a short period lost them with even greater rapidity, while stock market falls have led to a decline in the assets of many members of this elite club.

TOP 10

FOOD, DRINK, AND CANDY FORTUNES IN THE US

	Name/main interests	Assets ($)		Name/main interests	Assets ($)
1	Mars family (4 members)/candy and pet food	9,600,000,000	**6**	Busch family/Budweiser beer	1,100,000,000
2	Dorrance family/Campbell's soup	3,450,000,000	**7**	Brown family/liquor	1,000,000,000
3	Edgar Miles Bronfman/Seagram Co.	2,300,000,000	**8**	John Simplot and family/potatoes	950,000,000
4	Bacardi family/liquor	1,400,000,000	**9**	William Wrigley/Wrigley's chewing gum	900,000,000
5	Joan Beverly Kroc/McDonald's	1,350,000,000	**10**	Donald Tyson/food processing	810,000,000

WILLIAM HENRY GATES III

TOP 10
COMPUTER FORTUNES IN THE US

	Name	Main interests	Assets ($)
1	William Henry Gates III	Microsoft	6,160,000,000
2	Paul G. Allen	Microsoft	2,900,000,000
3	David Packard	Hewlett-Packard	2,750,000,000
4	Lawrence J. Ellison	Oracle Corp.	1,600,000,000
5	Gordon Earle Moore	Intel Corp.	1,500,000,000
6	William Redington Hewlett	Hewlett-Packard	1,400,000,000
7	Steven Anthony Ballmer	Microsoft	1,100,000,000
8	Stuart Robert Levine	Cabletron Systems	710,000,000
9	Craig Robert Benson	Cabletron Systems	590,000,000
10=	Alan C. Ashton	WordPerfect Corp.	450,000,000
10=	Bruce W. Bastain	WordPerfect Corp.	450,000,000

TOP 10
CLOTHING AND SHOE FORTUNES IN THE US

	Name/main interests	Assets ($)		Name/main interests	Assets ($)
1	Leslie Herbert Wexner/The Limited	1,600,000,000	5=	Ralph Lauren/Polo/Ralph Lauren	700,000,000
2=	Peter E. Haas Sr., and family/Levi Strauss	1,400,000,000	7	Donald and George Fisher/The Gap	572,000,000
2=	Philip Hampson Knight/Nike	1,400,000,000	8	Bean family/L.L. Bean	550,000,000
4	Nordstrom family/clothing and shoe stores	945,000,000	9	Paul B. Fireman/Reebok International	525,000,000
5=	Gore family/Gore-Tex	700,000,000	10	Gary Campbell Comer/Land's End	430,000,000

TOP 10
PUBLISHING FORTUNES IN THE US

	Name/main interests*	Assets ($)
1	Samuel I. and Donald Newhouse Condé Nast/Random House	7,000,000,000
2	Keith Rupert Murdoch/News Corp.	4,000,000,000
3	William Ziff Jr./Ziff-Davis	1,500,000,000
4	Chandler family/Times Mirror	1,200,000,000
5	Donald Joyce Hall/Hallmark Cards	900,000,000
6	Walter Annenberg/Triangle	800,000,000
7	Helen Kinney Copley/Copley Press newspapers	650,000,000
8	Pulitzer family/newspapers	640,000,000
9	McGraw family/McGraw-Hill	600,000,000
10	Graham family/*Washington Post*/*Newsweek*	565,000,000

* *Several entrants also have interests in broadcasting and other media.*

TOP 10
STORE FORTUNES IN THE US

	Name/main interests	Assets ($)
1	Walton family/Wal-Mart Stores	23,000,000,000
2=	Charles Feeney/Duty Free Shoppers	800,000,000
2=	Meijer family/supermarkets	800,000,000
4	Jenkins family/Publix Super Markets	755,000,000
5	Bernard Marcus/Home Depot	690,000,000
6	Wilmot family/Wilmorite shopping centers	660,000,000
7	William Cafaro and family/shopping malls	630,000,000
8	Leonard Samuel Skaggs Jr./American Stores Co.	560,000,000
9	Arthur Blank/Home Depot	530,000,000
10	Schottenstein family Value City/American Eagle	525,000,000

Published by courtesy of *Forbes Magazine*.

THE WORLD OF WEALTH

TOP 10
COINS AND NOTES IN CIRCULATION IN THE US*

	Denomination	Total value ($)	Units in circulation
1	penny	171,000,000	171,000,000,000
2	dime	2,679,000,000	26,790,000,000
3	quarter	918,800,000	22,970,000,000
4	nickel	923,500,000	18,470,000,000
5	$1 bill	5,800,000,000	5,800,000,000
6	$20 bill	76,329,978,740	3,816,498,937
7	$100 bill	215,686,572,500	2,160,000,000
8	$5 bill	6,816,046,705	1,363,209,341
9	$10 bill	13,064,823,100	1,310,000,000
10	$50 bill	41,854,246,000	837,084,920

* As of December 1993

At number 11 is the $2 bill with a total of $967,452,780/483,726,390 units in circulation. The number of coins minted annually is declining for each denomination, and Congress began discussing the withdrawal of the penny in 1994. Some of the paper money taken out of circulation is now recycled by Crane & Co., Inc. (who make paper for US currency) in their distinctive stationery paper, "Old Money."

TOP 10
RICHEST PLACES IN THE US

	Place	Type	Population	Average household income ($)
1	Bloomfield Hills, Michigan	City	4,288	150,001
2	King's Point , New York	Village	4,843	140,838
3	Old Westbury, New York	Village	3,897	137,518
4	Saddle River, New Jersey	Borough	2,950	135,662
5	Hunters Creek Village, Texas	City	3,954	134,961
6	Village of Indian Hill, Ohio	City	5,383	132,244
7	Atherton, California	Town	7,163	130,734
8	Lloyd Harbor, New York	Village	3,343	130,720
9	Blackhawk, California	Town	6,199	129,135
10	Belle Meade, Tennessee	City	2,830	125,459

US Department of Commerce, Bureau of the Census 1989 figures indicate that the richest places in the US are all within the population range of 2,500–9,999. The richest city with a population over 50,000 is West Bloomfield, Michigan, with a median family income of $68,661.

TOP 10
COUNTRIES WITH MOST CURRENCY IN CIRCULATION 100 YEARS AGO

	Country	Total currency in circulation (US $)
1	US	2,142,000,000
2	France	2,104,000,000
3	India	960,000,000
4	Germany	900,000,000
5	UK	845,000,000
6	Russia	720,000,000
7	China	700,000,000
8	Italy	510,000,000
9	Austria	460,000,000
10	Spain	390,000,000

It is interesting to consider that, as a result of inflation during the past century, there are now individuals in these countries who, on paper at least, own more than the entire country's money supply in the 1890s. There is today in excess of $1,000,000,000,000 in circulation in the US.

TOP 10
COUNTRIES IN WHICH IT IS EASIEST TO BE A MILLIONAIRE

	Country	Currency unit	Value of 1,000,000 units in $
1	Zaïre	Zaïre	0.16
2	Poland	Zloty	51.65
3	Turkey	Lira	87.18
4	Vietnam	Dông	95.43
5	Guinea-Bissau	Peso	203.18
6	Croatia	Dinar	228.34
7	Mozambique	Metical	248.65
8	Cambodia	Riel	282.19
9	Somalia	Shilling	389.95
10	Indonesia	Rupiah	481.78

Runaway inflation in many countries has reduced the value of their currencies to such an extent as to make them virtually worthless. With an exchange rate running at 13,710,079 Zaïre to the US dollar, total assets of just 16 cents will qualify one as a Zaïrese millionaire.

TOP 10
COUNTRIES WITH THE HIGHEST INFLATION

	Country	Annual inflation rate (%)
1	Zaïre	4,129.2
2	Brazil	2,146.3
3	Romania	255.2
4	Zambia	187.2
5	Turkey	66.1
6	Uruguay	54.1
7	Peru	48.6
8	Kenya	45.8
9	Ecuador	45.0
10	Venezuela	38.1

These figures are for 1993 and indicate the rise in consumer prices over the previous year, as calculated by the International Monetary Fund (except for Zaïre, where the latest available figure is for 1992, on 1991). Certain countries have markedly improved their rate. Peru's is down from an annual rate of 3,399 percent in 1989.

TOP 10

GOLD PRODUCERS IN THE WORLD

	Country	Annual production (tonnes)
1	South Africa	619.5
2	US	336.0
3	Australia	247.2
4	Former USSR	244.0
5	Canada	150.9
6	China	127.0
7	Brazil	74.7
8	Papua New Guinea	61.8
9	Indonesia	46.3
10	Ghana	41.4
	World total	2,216.5

As reported by Gold Fields Mineral Services Ltd's *Gold 1994*, after experiencing a temporary decline, world-dominating gold producer South Africa saw its output up again in both 1992 and 1993. Australia's output has increased dramatically over recent years: the country's record annual production had stood at 119 tonnes since 1903, but in 1988 it rocketed to 152 tonnes, and in 1992 for the first time overtook that of the former Soviet Union.

TOP 10

RICHEST AND POOREST COUNTRIES IN THE WORLD

Richest Country	GDP*		Poorest Country	GDP*
Switzerland	33,515	1	Mozambique	72
Luxembourg	30,950	2	Tanzania	96
Japan	26,919	3	Somalia	100
Bermuda	26,600	4	Ethiopia	116
Sweden	25,487	5	Uganda	164
Finland	24,396	6	Bhutan	177
Norway	24,151	7	Nepal	178
Denmark	23,676	8	Afghanistan	195
US	22,560	9=	Cambodia and Myanmar (Burma)	199
Iceland	22,362	10		

* GDP per capita (US $)

TOP 10

LARGEST POLISHED GEM DIAMONDS IN THE WORLD

	Diamond/(last known whereabouts or owner)	Carats
1	"Unnamed Brown" (De Beers)	545.67
2	Great Star of Africa/Cullinan I (British Crown Jewels)	530.20
3	Incomparable/Zale (auctioned in New York, 1988)	407.48
4	Second Star of Africa/Cullinan II (British Crown Jewels)	317.40
5	Centenary (De Beers)	273.85
6	Jubilee (Paul-Louis Weiller)	245.35
7	De Beers (sold in Geneva, 1982)	234.50
8	Red Cross (sold in Geneva, 1973)	205.07
9	Black Star of Africa (unknown)	202.00
10	Anon (unknown)	200.87

The highest price paid for a polished diamond sold at auction is $12,760,000, paid by Robert Mouwad for an 11-sided pear-shaped 101.84-carat diamond now known as the *Mouwad Splendour*, at Sotheby's, Geneva, on November 14, 1990. The $880,000 paid at Christie's, New York, on April 28, 1987 for a 0.95 purplish-red stone is equivalent to a record $926,315.79 per carat. *The Incomparable*, No. 3 in the list, holds the world record for the highest failed bid – $13,200,000, when offered at auction at Christie's, New York, on October 19, 1988, which was insufficient to reach the reserve price set by its vendors.

TOP 10

LARGEST UNCUT DIAMONDS IN THE WORLD

	Diamond	Carats
1	Cullinan	3,106.00

The largest diamond ever found, it was cut into 105 separate gems, the most important of which are now among the British Crown Jewels.

| 2 | Braganza | 1,680.00 |

All trace of this enormous stone has been lost.

| 3 | Excelsior | 995.20 |

The native worker who found this diamond (in 1893 – in a shovelful of gravel at the South African Jagersfontein Mine) hid it and took it directly to the mine manager, who rewarded him with a horse, a saddle, and £500.

| 4 | Star of Sierra Leone | 968.80 |

Found in Sierra Leone on St Valentine's Day, 1972, the uncut diamond weighed 8 oz/225 g and measured 1½ x 2½ in/4 x 6.5 cm.

| 5 | Zale Corporation "Golden Giant" | 890.00 |

Its origin is so shrouded in mystery that it is not even known from which country it came.

| 6 | Great Mogul | 787.50 |

When found in 1650 in the Gani Mine, India, this diamond was presented to Shah Jehan, the builder of the Taj Mahal.

| 7 | Woyie River | 770.00 |

Found in 1945 beside the river in Sierra Leone.

| 8 | Presidente Vargas | 726.60 |

Discovered in the Antonio River, Brazil, in 1938, it was named after the then president.

| 9 | Jonker | 726.00 |

In 1934 Jacobus Jonker, a previously unsuccessful diamond prospector, found this massive diamond after it had been exposed by a heavy storm.

| 10 | Reitz | 650.80 |

Like the Excelsior, *the* Reitz *was found in the Jagersfontein Mine in South Africa, in 1895.*

The weight of diamonds is measured in carats (derived from *qīrāt*, the Arabic name for the carob bean, which grows on the *Ceratonia siliqua* tree and is remarkable for its consistent weight of 0.2 gram). There are about 142 carats to the ounce. Fewer than 1,000 rough diamonds weighing more than 100 carats have been recorded.

SWEET TEETH

SWEET-CONSUMING NATIONS IN THE WORLD

	Country	chocolate	Annual consumption (lb per head) other sweets	total
1	Netherlands	18.10	12.52	30.62
2	Denmark	15.24	14.09	29.33
3	Switzerland	22.12	6.39	28.51
4	UK	16.36	11.40	27.76
5	Belgium/Luxembourg	16.82	10.72	27.54
6	Ireland	14.66	12.74	27.40
7	Norway	17.40	9.63	27.03
8	Germany	14.49	12.52	27.01
9	Sweden	12.24	11.57	23.81
10	Austria	16.14	6.28	22.42
	US	10.28	7.58	17.86

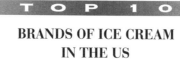

BRANDS OF ICE CREAM IN THE US

	Brand	Sales ($)*
1	Private label	715,500,000
2	Good Humor-Breyers	346,700,000
3	Dreyer's/Edy's	156,700,000
4	Häagen-Dazs	150,400,000
5	Ben & Jerry's	117,200,000
6	Blue Bell	114,300,000
7	Borden	61,200,000
8	Marigold (Kemps)	47,900,000
9	Turkey Hill	42,900,000
10	Wells' Blue Bunny	30,700,000

* *Year to March 27, 1994*
Source: Dairy Foods Magazine

COCOA-CONSUMING NATIONS IN THE WORLD

	Country	Total cocoa consumption (tonnes)
1	US	593,300
2	Germany	264,200
3	UK	180,400
4	France	159,800
5	Japan	110,800
6	Brazil	81,200
7	Italy	73,200
8	Spain	60,000
9	Belgium/Luxembourg	57,300
10	Canada	49,300

Cocoa is the principal ingredient of chocolate, and its consumption is therefore closely linked to the production of chocolate in each consuming country. Like coffee, the consumption of chocolate occurs mainly in the West and in more affluent countries. Since some of the Top 10 consuming nations also have large populations, the figures for cocoa consumption per head present a somewhat different picture, dominated by those countries with a long-established tradition of manufacturing high-quality chocolate products.

COCOA-CONSUMING NATIONS IN THE WORLD (PER HEAD)

	Country	Total consumption kg	lb	oz
1	Belgium/ Luxembourg	5.500	16	12
2	Switzerland	4.821	10	10
3	Iceland	4.100	9	1
4	Germany	3.279	7	4
5	Austria	3.267	7	3
6	UK	3.118	6	14
7	Norway	2.914	6	7
8	France	2.785	6	2
9=	Denmark	2.488	5	8
9=	Italy	2.488	5	8

T O P 1 0

BRANDS OF CANDY IN THE US

	Brand	Sales 1993 ($)
1	M&M's	185,881,472
2	Brach's	181,870,852
3	Hershey	169,958,497
4	Reese's	152,339,870
5	Snickers	122,144,324
6	Hershey Kisses	119,178,840
7	Kit Kat	61,144,354
8	Butterfinger	51,361,624
9	Milky Way	48,005,216
10	Lifesavers	46,340,416

Source: Information Resources Inc.

The figures given in this list, and those provided for the other US brands on these pages, cover only sales through grocery stores. Total sales of some brands through drug stores, mass merchandisers, and other outlets (vending machines, gas stations, etc.) may amount to more than double these figures.

T O P 1 0

BRANDS OF FROZEN YOGURT IN THE US

	Brand	Sales ($)*
1	Private label	94,200,000
2	Dreyer's/Edy's	72,300,000
3	Marigold (Kemps)	60,600,000
4	Good Humor-Breyers	59,900,000
5	Ben & Jerry's	44,000,000
6	Colombo	27,000,000
7	Häagen-Dazs	26,800,000
8	Crowley	21,200,000
9	Turkey Hill	18,500,000
10	Dannon	16,700,000

* Year to March 27, 1994
Source: Dairy Foods Magazine

T O P 1 0

BESTSELLING BEN & JERRY'S ICE CREAM FLAVORS

1	Chocolate Chip Cookie Dough
2	Cherry Garcia
3	Chocolate Fudge Brownie
4	New York Super Fudge Chunk
5	English Toffee Crunch
6	Chocolate Fudge Brownie Frozen Yogurt
7	Chunky Monkey
8	Cherry Garcia Frozen Yogurt
9	Wavy Gravy
10	Mint With Cookies

Grateful Dead founder Jerry Garcia is believed to be the only rock musician ever to have two bestselling ice cream flavors named in his honor.

T O P 1 0

BESTSELLING HÄAGEN-DAZS ICE CREAM FLAVORS

1	Vanilla
2	Pralines and Cream
3	Cookies and Cream
4	Belgian Chocolate
5	Strawberry
6	Vanilla Chocolate Fudge
7	Choc Choc Chip
8	Cookie Dough Dynamo
9	Caramel Cone Explosion
10	Macadamia Nut Brittle

When Reuben Mattus created a range of high-quality ice creams in 1961, he chose a meaningless but Danish-sounding name to emphasize the rich, creamy nature of his product. His three flavors (vanilla, chocolate, and coffee) were sold through New York delicatessens. Today Häagen-Dazs shops across the US and Europe offer as many as 20 different flavors of ice cream.

T O P 1 0

ICE CREAM CONSUMERS IN THE WORLD

	Product	Production per capita (US pints)
1	US	46.80
2	New Zealand	39.87
3	Australia	32.64
4	Sweden	30.09
5	Canada	27.18
6	Norway	26.65
7	Belgium/Luxembourg	25.60
8	Israel	23.76
9	Italy	22.46
10	Denmark	20.69

Global statistics for ice cream consumption are hard to come by, but this list presents recent and reliable International Ice Cream Association estimates for per capita production of ice cream and related products (frozen yogurt, sherbert, water ices, etc.) – and since only small amounts of such products are exported, consumption figures can be presumed to be similar. In 1992 US production of all ice cream products was put at a remarkable 1,492,517,000 US gallons.

FOOD – WORLD

CALORIE-CONSUMING NATIONS IN THE WORLD

	Country	Average daily per capita consumption
1	Ireland	3,952
2	Belgium/Luxembourg	3,925
3	Greece	3,775
4	Former East Germany	3,710
5	Bulgaria	3,695
6	US	3,642
7	Denmark	3,639
8	Hungary	3,608
9	France	3,593
10	Former Czechoslovakia	3,574
	World average	*2,697*

A Calorie is a unit of heat (defined as the amount of heat needed to raise one kilogram of water 1° Celsius in temperature). Calories are used by nutritionists as a means of expressing the energy-producing value of foods. The Calorie requirement of the average man is 2,700 and of a woman 2,500. Inactive people need less, while those engaged in heavy labor might have to consume much more, perhaps even double this amount of energy. Calories that are not consumed as energy turn to fat – which is why Calorie-counting is one of the key aspects of most diets. The high Calorie intake of certain countries, measured over the period 1988–90, reflects the high proportion of starchy foods, such as potatoes, bread, and pasta, in the national diet. In many Western countries the high figures simply reflect over-eating – especially since these figures are averages that include men, women, and children, suggesting that large numbers in each country are greatly exceeding them. While over-eaters in the West guzzle their way through 30 percent more than they need, with those in every country in Europe (except Sweden) consuming more than 3,000 Calories per head, the Calorie consumption in Bangladesh and some of the poorest African nations falls below 2,000. In the Congo it is 1,760 – less than half that of the nations in the world Top 10.

MEAT-EATING NATIONS IN THE WORLD

	Country	Consumption per head per annum		
		kg	lb	oz
1	US	116.9	257	11
2	Australia	104.0	229	5
3	New Zealand	100.8	222	3
4	Canada	98.6	217	6
5	Hong Kong	98.0	216	2
6	Hungary	97.5	215	0
7	France	96.6	213	0
8	Argentina	92.0	202	13
9	Austria	90.3	199	2
10=	Germany	90.2	198	14
10=	Spain	90.2	198	14

Figures compiled by the Meat and Livestock Commission show a huge range of meat consumption around the world, from the nations featured in the Top 10 to very poor countries such as India. Meat-eating reflects factors such as wealth; in general, the richer the country, the more meat is eaten (although in recent years concern about healthy eating in many Western countries has resulted in a deliberate decline in consumption). Availability is another significant factor – New Zealand's consumption of lamb is one of the world's highest, at 84 lb/ 38.1 kg per head. Culture also plays a role – as a result of dietary prohibitions very little pork is eaten in the Middle East, and the Japanese eat only 91 lb/ 41.5 kg of meat, but larger quantities of fish than many other nations.

CONSUMERS OF KELLOGG'S CORN FLAKES

(Based on per capita consumption)

1	Ireland
2	UK
3	Australia
4	Denmark
5	Sweden
6	Norway
7	Canada
8	US
9	Mexico
10	Venezuela

In 1894 the brothers Will Keith and Dr. John Harvey Kellogg were running their "Sanatorium," a health resort in Battle Creek, Michigan. Attempting to devise healthy food products for their patients, they experimented with wheat dough that they boiled and passed through rollers. By accident, they discovered that if the dough was left overnight it came out as flakes, and when these were baked they turned into a tasty cereal. The Kellogg brothers started making their new product on a small scale, providing cereal by mail order to former patients. In 1898 they replaced wheat with corn, thereby creating the Corn Flakes we know today. Will Keith left the Sanatorium in 1906 and set up a business manufacturing Corn Flakes with his distinctive signature on the packet. The cereal was first exported to England in 1922, along with All Bran and, in 1928, Rice Krispies, and Corn Flakes remains Kellogg's bestselling product. The company's corn mill in Seaforth, Liverpool, is Europe's largest and processes 1,000 tons of grain a day. The Kellogg Company, which in 1994 celebrated the centenary of the invention of Corn Flakes, achieves annual sales in 130 countries that are worth in excess of $6,000,000,000. The business is today regarded as such a dominant force worldwide that the importance of the Kellogg brand is rated second in the world, after Coca-Cola.

T O P 1 0

HEINZ PRODUCTS IN THE WORLD

1 Ketchup

2 Baby food

3 Tuna

4 Frozen potatoes

5 Soup

6 Weight Watchers'
frozen entrées and desserts

7 Cat food

8 Sauces and pastes

9 Baked beans

10 Dog food

Henry John Heinz, the founder of the gigantic food processing and canning empire that bears his name, was born in Pittsburgh, Pennsylvania in 1844, of German immigrant parents. In 1869 he formed a partnership with a family friend, L.C. Noble, selling horseradish in clear glass jars (previously green glass disguised the dishonest practice of packing the horseradish out with turnip), beginning the Heinz reputation for quality and integrity. Their products were also sold on their lack of artificial flavorings and colorings, long before these factors became a matter for general concern. Heinz & Noble steadily added other lines, including pickles. In 1876, with his brother John and cousin Frederick, H.J. formed the firm of F. & J. Heinz. One of their first products was ketchup – a staple product in every American household, but one previously made on a domestic scale, a task that involved the whole family stirring a cauldron over an open fire for an entire day.

The business was sufficiently well-established by 1886 for the Heinz family to visit Europe, and H.J. sold the first Heinz products in Britain to Fortnum & Mason, the upmarket Piccadilly emporium, astonishing them by his audacity at entering the store through the front door, rather than the tradesman's entrance. The first branch office in London was opened in 1895, by which time the company had become H.J. Heinz & Co.

Why "57 Varieties"? In 1896, traveling on the New York Third Avenue El, H.J. saw a sign advertising "21 Styles" of shoe. "It set me to thinking," he later recalled. "I said to myself, 'We do not have styles of products, but we do have varieties of products.' Counting how many we had, I counted well beyond 57, but '57' kept coming back into my mind . . . 58 Varieties or 59 Varieties did not appeal to me at all – just '57 Varieties.' " Henry went straight to his printers where he designed the first "Heinz 57" advertisement.

T O P 1 0

CONSUMERS OF HEINZ BAKED BEANS IN THE WORLD

	Consumer	Sales (cans per annum)*		Consumer	Sales (cans per annum)*
1	UK	550,000,000	6	Singapore	520,000
2	Sweden	2,460,000	7	NAAFI, Germany	430,000
3	West Africa	1,780,000	8	Spain	420,000
4	Bahrain	770,000	9	Greece	300,000
5	Dubai, UAE	580,000	10	Kuwait	190,000

* Based on 1 lb/450g can.

These figures are not a mistake: the United Kingdom really does munch its way through 550,000,000 cans of Heinz baked beans a year – equivalent to 10 cans for every inhabitant, and 224 times as many as the next most important international market, Sweden (where the annual consumption is just 0.28 cans per head).

Of all their "57 Varieties," baked beans are Heinz's most famous product. They were originally test-marketed in the North of England in 1901, and imported from the US up until 1928 when they were first canned in the UK. The slogan "Beanz Meanz Heinz" was invented in 1967 over a drink in the Victoria pub in Mornington Terrace by Young and Rubicam advertising agency executive Maurice Drake.

In 1995 H. J. Heinz will celebrate the centenary of baked bean production and of opening the company's first London office.

T O P 1 0

SUGAR-CONSUMING NATIONS IN THE WORLD

	Country	Consumption per head per annum kg	lb
1	Cuba	89.2	196.7
2	Swaziland	67.1	147.9
3	Singapore	65.3	144.0
4	Israel	59.9	132.1
5	Costa Rica	59.2	130.5
6	Iceland	58.6	129.2
7	Netherlands	57.9	127.7
8	Fiji	56.2	123.9
9	Austria	55.1	121.5
10	Hungary	54.1	119.3
	US	29.3	64.5

Each citizen of Cuba, the world's leaders in the sweet-tooth stakes, would appear to consume a quantity equal to a 2.2 lb/1 kg bag of sugar every four days.

FOOD – US

TOP 10

FOOD COMPANIES IN THE US

	Company	Main products	Annual sales ($)
1	Philip Morris	Cheese, cereals, beer	50,261,000,000
2	Conagra	Frozen foods, processed meats, potato products	21,519,000,000
3	Sara Lee	Bakery goods, processed meats	14,580,000,000
4	IBP	Beef and pork	11,671,000,000
5	Archer Daniels Midland	Refined oils, food additives	9,811,000,000
6	General Mills	Cereals, flour, cake mixes, dessert items	8,135,000,000
7	Ralston Purina	Bakery goods, pet food	7,902,000,000
8	H.J. Heinz	Ketchup, baby food, pickles	7,103,000,000
9	CPC International	Sweeteners, corn oil, mayonnaise, pasta, peanut butter	6,738,000,000
10	Borden	Pasta, sauce, snacks, dairy produce, grocery items	6,700,000,000

TOP 10

FOOD AND DRINK ADVERTISERS IN THE US

	Company	Adspend ($)*
1	Kelloggs	101,782,800
2	McDonald's	100,354,700
3	Budweiser	62,632,400
4	Kraft	58,960,100
5	General Mills Cereals	58,891,000
6	Coke/Diet Coke	55,057,000
7	Pizza Hut	44,323,700
8	Miller Beer	43,266,200
9	Post Cereals	41,011,900
10	Burger King	40,055,900

*First quarter of 1994
Source: Advertising Age

TOP 10

FAST FOOD CHAINS IN THE US

	Chain*	Revenue ($)#
1	McDonald's	23,587,000,000
2	KFC	7,100,000,000
3	Burger King	6,700,000,000
4	Pizza Hut	6,300,000,000
5	Wendy's	3,924,000,000
6	Taco Bell	3,720,000,000
7	Hardee's	3,550,000,000
8	Dairy Queen	2,400,000,000
9=	Subway	2,200,000,000
9=	Domino's Pizza	2,200,000,000

* Excluding fast-food contractors such as ARA Services and Marriott Management Services, which would otherwise appear at numbers 8 and 9
# Worldwide, 1993

McDonald's staggering worldwide sales include $9,400,000,000 in revenue from its 4,710 overseas outlets, scattered throughout some 80 countries. The chain is adding between 600 and 700 new sites in foreign countries each year and is expecting overseas revenue to top domestic volume by the turn of the century.

Source: Restaurants & Institutions: The Top 400 List

TOP 10

BRANDS OF FRANKFURTER IN THE US

	Brand	Sales ($)*
1	Oscar Mayer	249,200,000
2	Ball Park	130,900,000
3	Private label	113,700,000
4	Kahn's	52,000,000
5	Bryan	47,900,000
6	Hygrade	43,400,000
7	Bar S	39,400,000
8	Ekrich	37,700,000
9	Armour Star	36,000,000
10	Louis Rich	35,400,000

Year to March 12, 1994

The involvement of superstar athletes (boxer George Foreman and former basketball star Michael Jordan respectively) in promoting the two leading brands of frankfurter helped boost their substantial lead over other varieties on the market.

Source: Advertising Age/A.C. Nielsen

TOP 10

BRANDS OF POTATO CHIP IN THE US

	Brand	Sales ($)*
1	Lay's	417,200,000
2	Ruffles	361,700,000
3	Pringles	161,700,000
4	Private label	149,700,000
5	Eagle Thins	131,700,000
6	Wise	52,300,000
7	Eagle Ripples	47,600,000
8	Keebler O'Boisies	46,900,000
9	Utz	36,600,000
10	Herr's	35,300,000

Year to March 12, 1994
Source: Advertising Age/A.C. Nielsen

TOP 10

BRANDS OF PRETZEL IN THE US

	Brand	Sales ($)*
1	Rold Gold	93,600,000
2	Snyders of Hanover	75,500,000
3	Private label	40,200,000
4	Nabisco Mr. Phipps	36,400,000
5	Mister Sally	30,500,000
6	Eagle	27,200,000
7	Bachman	26,200,000
8	Keebler	20,400,000
9	Combos	19,900,000
10	Quinlan	12,100,000

Year to March 12, 1994
Source: Advertising Age/A.C. Nielsen

TOP 10

GUM BRANDS IN THE US

	Brand	Sales 1993 ($)
1	Wrigley's Extra	108,288,122
2	Trident	76,372,560
3	Carefree	73,746,912
4	Wrigley's Doublemint	39,397,616
5	Freedent	36,320,686
6	Wrigley's Big Red	25,086,000
7	Wrigley's	22,593,408
8	Wrigley's Juicy Fruit	21,305,330
9	Dentyne Cinn A Burst	19,077,312
10	Bubblicious	15,117,924

* *Through grocery stores only – total sales of some brands through drug stores, mass merchandisers, and other outlets (vending machines, gas stations, etc.) may more than double these figures.*
Source: Information Resources Inc.

TOP 10

BRANDS OF POPCORN* IN THE US

	Brand	Sales ($)#		Brand	Sales ($)#
1	Orville Redenbacher	243,700,000	4	Private label	69,800,000
2	Betty Crocker Pop-Secret	170,700,000	5	Pop Weaver's	39,600,000
3	Golden Valley	85,600,000	6	Jolly Time	32,900,000
			7	Newman's Own	9,300,000
			8	Jiffy Pop	9,000,000
			9	Cousin Willie's	8,900,000
			10	Pop-Rite	8,000,000

* *Unpopped only*
# *Year to April 9, 1994*

Unpopped popcorn, which buyers prepare at home (usually in a microwave) now outsells ready-popped varieties.

Source: Advertising Age/A.C. Nielsen

ALCOHOL

BEER-DRINKING NATIONS IN THE WORLD

	Country	Annual consumption per head liters	pints
1	Germany	142.7	251.1
2	Former Czechoslovakia	135.0	237.6
3	Denmark	125.9	221.6
4	Austria	123.7	217.7
5	Ireland	123.0	216.5
6	Luxembourg	116.1	204.3
7	Belgium	111.3	195.9
8	New Zealand	109.5	192.7
9	Hungary	107.0	188.3
10	UK	106.2	186.9

Perhaps surprisingly, despite its position as the world's leading producer of beer, the US is ranked only 13th in terms of consumption (153.8 pints/87.4 liters per head).

LARGEST BREWERIES IN THE WORLD

	Brewery	Country	Annual sales liters	pints
1	Anheuser-Busch, Inc.	US	10,430,000,000	18,354,223,790
2	Heineken NV	Netherlands	5,350,000,000	11,174,431,550
3	Miller Brewing Co.	US	5,260,000,000	11,016,053,780
4	Kirin Brewery Co. Ltd.	Japan	3,240,000,000	5,701,599,720
5	Foster's Brewing Group	Australia	3,050,000,000	5,367,246,650
6	Companhia Cervejaria Brahma	Brazil	2,530,000,000	4,452,175,090
7	Groupe BSN	France	2,500,000,000	4,399,382,500
8	Coors Brewing Co.	US	2,370,000,000	4,170,614,610
9	South Africa Breweries Ltd.	South Africa	2,270,000,000	3,994,639,310
10	Companhia Antarctica Paulista	Brazil	2,000,000,000	3,519,506,000

WINE PRODUCERS IN THE US

	Vintner	Total production 1993 (gallons)
1	E & J Gallo	330,000
2	Canandaigua Wine Company	186,300
3	Grand Metropolitan	112,000
4	Vie-del Company	59,200
5	The Wine Group	56,000
6	JFJ Bronco	43,800
7	Delicato	40,000
8	Golden State Vintners	35,660
9	F. Korbel	34,000
10	Robert Mondavi	18,760

Source: Wines & Vines

CHAMPAGNE IMPORTERS IN THE WORLD

	Country	Consumption per head (75 cl bottles)	Bottles imported
1	Germany	0.189	15,190,026
2	United Kingdom	0.259	14,649,105
3	United States	0.044	10,847,429
4	Switzerland	1.064	7,269,607
5	Belgium	0.631	6,265,211
6	Italy	0.106	6,025,848
7	Netherlands	0.125	1,907,693
8	Japan	0.008	1,015,069
9	Australia	0.053	918,282
10	Spain	0.022	873,282

One of the most telling measures of the economic recession in recent years has been the consumption of champagne. In 1991 most countries' imports of champagne declined – that of the United Kingdom by 34 percent from the 1990 figure, relegating it from the first place it had held for many years (and which it regained in 1992 and lost again in 1993). France, the domestic market for champagne, consumed 152,669,094 bottles in 1993 – equivalent to 2.70 bottles per head. World champagne exports increased by seven percent in 1993 – a sign that the recession is ending?

TOP 10

BREWERIES IN THE US

	Brewery	1992 market share (%)
1	Anheuser-Busch	46.1
2	Miller Brewing Company	22.4
3	Coors	10.4
4	Stroh	7.5
5	G. Heileman	5.3
6	S&P Industries	4.4
7	Genesee	1.2
8	Latrobe Brewing	0.5
9	Pittsburgh Brewing	0.3
10	Hudepohl-Schoenling	0.2

Source: Beverage Marketing Corporation

TOP 10

BRANDS OF IMPORTED BEER IN THE US

	Brand	Country	1992 market share (%)
1	Heineken	Germany	23.2
2	Corona	Mexico	11.6
3	Molsen Golden	Canada	10.1
4	Becks	Germany	9.9
5	LaBatt's	Canada	6.0
6	Amstel Light	Holland	4.5
7	Tecate	Mexico	3.5
8	Moosehead	Canada	3.3
9	Foster's	Australia	2.7
10	Dos Equis	Mexico	2.6

TOP 10

MOST EXPENSIVE BOTTLES OF WINE EVER SOLD AT AUCTION

	Wine	Price ($)
1	Château Lafite 1787 Christie's, London, December 5, 1985	140,700

The highest price ever paid for a bottle of red wine resulted from the bottle having been initialed by the third US President, Thomas Jefferson. It was purchased by Christopher Forbes and is now on display in the Forbes Magazine Galleries, New York.

	Wine	Price ($)
2	Château d'Yquem 1784 Christie's, London, December 4, 1986	58,500

The highest price ever paid for a bottle of white wine.

	Wine	Price ($)
3	Château Lafite Rothschild 1832 (double magnum) International Wine Auctions, London, April 9, 1988	40,300
4	Château Lafite 1806 Sotheby's, Geneva, November 13, 1988	36,100
5	Château Lafite 1811 (tappit-hen – equivalent to three bottles) Christie's, London, June 23, 1988	33,600
6	Château Lafite 1822 Sold at a Heublein Auction, San Francisco, May 28, 1980	31,000
7	Château Margaux 1784 (half-bottle) Christie's, at Vin Expo, Bordeaux, France, June 26, 1987	29,500

The highest price ever paid for a half-bottle.

	Wine	Price ($)
8	Château Lafite Rothschild 1806 Sold at a Heublein Auction, San Francisco, May 24, 1979	28,000
9	Château d'Yquem 1811 Christie's, London, December 1, 1988	25,200
10	Château Lafite Rothschild 1811 International Wine Auctions, London, June 26, 1985	16,000

On April 25, 1989, No. 7 (also initialed by Thomas Jefferson), then with an asking price of $500,000, was smashed by a waiter's tray while on display at a tasting in the Four Seasons restaurant, New York. A little of the wine was salvaged, but was declared virtually undrinkable.

TOP 10

WINE-DRINKING NATIONS IN THE WORLD

	Country	Liters per head per annum	Equiv. 75 cl bottles
1	France	66.8	89.1
2	Portugal	62.0	82.7
3	Luxembourg	60.3	80.4
4	Italy	56.8	75.7
5	Argentina	52.4	69.9
6	Switzerland	48.7	64.9
7	Spain	34.3	45.7
8	Austria	33.7	44.9
9	Greece	32.4	43.2
10	Hungary	30.0	40.0
	US	*7.7*	*10.3*

TOP 10

WINE-PRODUCING COUNTRIES IN THE WORLD

	Country	Annual production (tonnes)
1	France	6,522,000
2	Italy	6,380,000
3	Spain	3,472,000
4	Former USSR	1,800,000
5	US	1,545,000
6	Germany	1,340,000
7	Argentina	1,150,000
8	South Africa	930,000
9	Romania	750,000
10	Portugal	724,000
	World total	*28,825,000*

SOFT SELL

TOP 10

READY-TO-DRINK TEA BRANDS IN THE US

	Brand	1993 market share (%)
1	Snapple	25.1
2	Lipton	21.6
3	Nestea	14.9
4	Arizona	12.6
5	Ssips	3.4
6	Tetley	2.5
7	Mistic	1.4
8	Celestial Seasoning	0.3
9=	Best Health	0.2
9=	White Rock	0.2

Source: Beverage Marketing Corporation

The latest soft drink fad in the US, ready-to-drink iced tea is the most popular new nonalcoholic beverage of the 1990s.

TOP 10

TEA-DRINKING NATIONS

	Country	Annual consumption per head			
		kg	lb	oz	cups*
1	Ireland	3.00	6	10	1,320
2	UK	2.56	5	9	1,126
3	Turkey	2.25	4	15	990
4	Qatar	2.02	4	7	889
5	Hong Kong	1.96	4	5	862
6	Iran	1.69	3	12	744
7	Syria	1.54	3	6	678
8	New Zealand	1.51	3	5	664
9	Tunisia	1.46	3	4	642
10	Egypt	1.38	3	1	607
	US	0.33		12	145

* Based on 440 cups per 2 lb 3 oz/1 kg

Despite the British passion for tea, during recent years the UK's consumption has lagged behind that of Ireland. Qatar's tea consumption has also dropped from its former world record of 8 lb 12 oz/3.97 kg (1,747 cups) per head. At the other end of the scale, Thailand's figure of 0.4 oz/0.01 kg (4 cups) is one of the lowest.

TOP 10

COFFEE-DRINKING NATIONS

	Country	Annual consumption per head			
		kg	lb	oz	cups
1	Finland	12.26	27	0	1,839
2	Sweden	11.29	24	14	1,694
3	Denmark	11.13	24	9	1,670
4	Norway	10.29	22	11	1,544
5	Netherlands	10.08	22	4	1,512
6	Austria	9.23	20	6	1,385
7	Switzerland	8.65	19	1	1,298
8	Germany	8.04	17	12	1,206
9	Belgium/Luxembourg	5.88	12	15	882
10	France	5.87	12	15	881
	US	4.24	9	6	836

* Based on 150 cups per 2 lb 3 oz/1kg

The total coffee consumption of many countries declined during the 1980s. That of Belgium and Luxembourg, for example, went down by almost 70 percent, from 15 lb 13 oz/7.17 kg (1,076 cups) in 1986 to 5 lb 0 oz/2.27 kg (341 cups) in 1990, but has recently risen again. That of both Finland and Sweden has remained high, however – the average Finn drinks more than five cups of coffee a day.

TOP 10

SOFT DRINK CONSUMERS IN THE WORLD

	Country	Consumption per head p.a.	
		liters	pints
1	Switzerland	105.0	221.9
2	Barbados	81.4	179.0
3	Bahamas	75.0	158.5
4	US	74.7	157.9
5	Australia	73.9	156.2
6	Germany	72.0	152.2
7	Canada	69.3	146.5
8=	Belgium	65.0	137.4
8=	Japan	65.0	137.4
10	Singapore	61.4	129.8

TOP 10

COCA-COLA CONSUMERS IN THE WORLD

1	Iceland
2	US
3	Mexico
4	Australia
5	Norway
6	Germany
7	Canada
8	Spain
9	Argentina
10	Japan

This ranking is based on consumption per capita in these countries – although the actual volumes are secret. The figures for many small countries are distorted by the influx of large numbers of tourists, but since Iceland is not noted for the size of its tourist industry, the surprising conclusion must be that Icelanders drink huge quantities of Coke!

TOP 10

CONSUMERS OF PERRIER WATER

1	France
2	US
3	UK
4	Belgium/Luxembourg
5	Canada
6	Germany
7	Middle East*
8	Hong Kong
9	Switzerland
10	Greece

* *Various countries*

In 1903 St. John Harmsworth, a wealthy Englishman on a tour of France, visited Vergèze, a spa town near Nîmes. Its spring, Les Bouillens (which was believed to have been discovered by the Carthaginian soldier Hannibal in *c*.218 BC), was notable for the occurrence of carbon dioxide which is released from the surrounding rock, permeating through the water and making it "naturally sparkling." Harmsworth recognized the potential for selling the spa water and proceeded to buy the spring, naming it after its former owner, Dr Louis Perrier, a local doctor, and bottling it in distinctive green bottles – said to have been modeled on the Indian clubs with which he exercised. The company was sold back to the French in 1948 (and in 1992 the firm was bought by the Swiss company Nestlé). Perrier water has maintained a reputation as a popular beverage in sophisticated circles. In 1960 in *For Your Eyes Only* Ian Fleming even has James Bond drink it – "He always stipulated Perrier…". In the late 1970s a combination of increased health consciousness and ingenious advertising and marketing enabled Perrier to broaden its appeal and to achieve its world dominance of the burgeoning mineral water business. Perrier is now drunk in 145 countries around the world, and its name has become virtually synonymous with mineral water.

TOP 10

FRUIT DRINK COMPANIES IN THE US

	Company	1993 market share (%)
1	Coca-Cola Foods	19.2
2	Tropicana	13.1
3	Ocean Spray	9.8
4	Proctor & Gamble	5.4
5	Welch's	3.8
6=	Dole	2.5
6=	Veryfine	2.5
8	Tree Top	1.9
9=	Del Monte	1.7
9=	Mott's USA	1.7

Proctor & Gamble has shed many of its fruit drink lines, and its 1993 market share was achieved through the sales of just two successful brands: Hawaiian Punch and Sunny Delight.

Source: Beverage Marketing Corporation

TOP 10

DRINK ITEMS CONSUMED IN THE US

	Drink	Consumption*
1	Coffee	260
2	Milk	221
3	Carbonated soft drinks (regular)	177
4	Tea	114
5	Carbonated soft drinks (low calorie)	70
6	Beers and ales	59
7	Citrus fruits and juices	57
8	Regular fruit drinks	54
9	Non-citrus juices and nectars	25
10	Low calorie fruit drinks	11

* *Average in grams per day per individual*

This Top 10, which is based on a two-year study (1989–1991) conducted by the Agricultural Research Service, covers all widely consumed drinks other than water.

TOP 10

BOTTLED WATER BRANDS IN THE US

	Brand	% of 1993 market		Brand	% of 1993 market
1	Arrowhead	7.4	6	Ozarka	2.3
2	Poland Spring	4.9	7	Deer Park	2.1
3	Sparklets	4.8	8	Perrier	2.0
4	Evian	4.7	9=	Mountain Valley	1.8
5	Hinckley-Schmitt	3.5	9=	Great Bear	1.8

TOP 10

SOFT DRINK BRANDS IN THE US

	Drink	1993 market share (%)		Drink	1993 market share (%)
1	Coca-Cola Classic	19.3	6	Mountain Dew	4.3
2	Pepsi	16.1	7	Sprite	3.9
3	Diet Coke	9.8	8	7-Up	2.9
4	Diet Pepsi	6.2	9	Caffeine Free Coke	2.2
5	Dr. Pepper	5.3	10	Caffeine Free Pepsi	1.3

Source: Beverage Marketing Corporation

TRAVEL & TOURISM

TOP 10

MOST EXPENSIVE CARS EVER SOLD AT AUCTION

	Car/auction	Price ($)
1	1962 Ferrari 250 Gran Turismo Berlinetta Competition GTO Sotheby's, Monte Carlo, 1990	12,000,000
2	1931 Bugatti Royale Type 41 Chassis "41.141" Christie's, London, 1987	8,100,000
3	1929 Bugatti Royale Chassis "41.150" William F. Harrah Collection Sale, Reno, Nevada, 1986	6,400,000
4	1962 Ferrari 250 GTO The Auction, Las Vegas, Nevada, 1991	5,500,000
5	1960 Ferrari Dino 196SP Christie's, Monaco, 1990	4,800,000
6	1957 Aston-Martin DBR2 Christie's, Monaco, 1989	4,500,000
7	1934 Alfa Romeo Tipo B Monoposto Christie's, Monaco, 1989	4,100,000
8	1934 Mercedes-Benz 500K Special Roadster Sotheby's, Monaco, 1989	3,160,000
9	Alfa Romeo Tipo 8C Corto 2300 Spyder Christie's, Monaco, 1989	2,700,000
10	John Lennon's 1965 Rolls-Royce Phantom V Sotheby's, New York, 1985	2,299,000

Among the costliest cars sold privately are two purchased in 1989: the only surviving 1967 original ex-factory team Ferrari 330P4 sports prototype, bought by a Swiss collector for $9,000,000, and another 1962 Ferrari 250 GTO, one of only 36 made, bought by a Japanese collector for over $13,000,000.

TOP 10

EXPORT MARKETS FOR ROLLS-ROYCE AUTOMOBILES

1	US
2	Japan
3	Germany
4	Hong Kong
5	France
6	Singapore
7	Switzerland
8	Saudi Arabia
9	United Arab Emirates
10	Belgium

1909 ROLLS-ROYCE 40/50 "SILVER GHOST"
Since its first cars appeared at the beginning of the 20th century, the Rolls-Royce company has had a reputation for excellence. Because of the high-quality craftsmanship and the cars' relative rarity, Rolls-Royces are favored by rich and powerful people worldwide.

THE PROGRESSION OF HOLDERS OF THE LAND SPEED RECORD, 1900–90

(As at the first year of each decade, 1900–90)

Year	Driver	Country	Vehicle	Date	km/h	mph
1900	Camille Jenatzy	Belgium	*Le Jamais Contente*	Apr 29, 1899	105.879	65.790
1910	Barney Oldfield	US	*Blitzen*	Mar 16, 1910	211.267	131.275
1920	Tommy Milton	US	*Duesenberg*	Apr 27, 1920	251.106	156.030
1930	Henry Segrave	UK	*Golden Arrow*	Mar 11, 1929	372.476	231.446
1940	John Cobb	UK	*Railton*	Aug 23, 1939	595.039	369.740
1950	John Cobb	UK	*Railton-Mobil Special*	Sep 16, 1947	634.396	394.196
1960	John Cobb	UK	*Railton-Mobil Special*	Sep 16, 1947	634.396	394.196
1970	Gary Gabelich	US	*The Blue Flame*	Oct 23, 1970	1,014.511	630.388
1980	Gary Gabelich	US	*The Blue Flame*	Oct 23, 1970	1,014.511	630.388
1990	Richard Noble	UK	*Thrust 2*	Oct 4, 1983	1,019.468	633.468

T O P 1 0

BESTSELLING ROLLS-ROYCE AND BENTLEY CARS

	Model	Years manufactured
1	Silver Shadow I (short wheel-base)	1965–76
2	Silver Shadow II	1977–81
3	Silver Spirit	1980–91
4	Silver Spur	1980–92
5	Silver Ghost (British)	1907–25
6	Bentley VI	1946–52
7	Bentley Turbo R	1985–93
8	Rolls-Royce 20/25 HP	1929–36
9	Rolls-Royce Corniche Convertible	1971–87
10	Bentley S1 (short wheel-base)	1955–59

The term "bestselling" used in the context of Rolls-Royce and Bentley is substantially different from that applied to mass-market cars. To put it into perspective, the US giant General Motors produces about 100,000 cars every two weeks, which is more than the entire output of Rolls-Royce since the company started in 1904. A total of 16,717 of the No. 1 bestselling Silver Shadow were sold in its 11 years of production, while the Silver Ghost, in production for nearly 20 years, sold 6,173 of the British model (fewer than General Motors produces in a single day), with a further 1,703 cars made under licence in the US in the five years from 1921.

MOTOR VEHICLES

TOP 10

VEHICLE-OWNING COUNTRIES IN THE WORLD

	Country	Cars	Commercial vehicles	Total
1	US	142,955,623	45,416,312	188,371,935
2	Japan	37,076,015	22,838,608	59,914,623
3	Germany	37,609,165	3,093,621	40,702,786
4	Italy	28,200,000	2,521,000	30,721,000
5	France	23,810,000	5,020,000	28,830,000
6	UK	22,744,142	3,685,141	26,429,283
7	Former USSR	17,000,000	7,500,000	24,500,000
8	Canada	13,061,084	3,744,012	16,805,096
9	Spain	12,537,099	2,615,033	15,152,132
10	Brazil	12,283,914	921,011	13,204,925
	World total	*456,032,819*	*139,273,829*	*595,306,648*

World motor vehicle ownership has increased more than fourfold from the 1960 total of 126,954,817. Of the present world total, some 224,435,987 are in Europe, 219,498,039 in North America, 100,063,770 in Asia, 25,154,275 in South America, 14,321,597 in Africa, and 11,832,980 in Oceania. The ratio of people to vehicles has escalated from 23 in 1960 to 8.8 today. In car-conscious and affluent countries the ratio is much higher: 1.3 people per vehicle in the US and 2.1 in the UK. San Marino, uniquely, claims the equivalent of one vehicle per person. The biggest disparities naturally occur in the least developed economies, with 905 people per vehicle in Ethiopia, 897 in Bangladesh, 190 in India, and 188 in China.

TOP 10

COUNTRIES PRODUCING THE MOST MOTOR VEHICLES

	Country	Cars	Commercial vehicles	Total
1	Japan	9,378,694	3,120,590	12,499,284
2	US	5,663,284	4,038,218	9,701,502
3	Germany	4,863,721	330,221	5,193,942
4	France	3,329,490	438,310	3,767,800
5	Spain	1,790,615	331,272	2,121,887
6	Canada	1,024,739	943,758	1,968,497
7	South Korea	1,306,752	422,944	1,729,696
8	Italy	1,476,627	209,860	1,686,487
9	UK	1,291,880	248,453	1,540,333
10	Former USSR	930,000	600,000	1,530,000
	World total	*34,764,844*	*12,612,490*	*47,377,334*

TOP 10

CAR MODELS IN THE US

	Make/model	Total 1993 sales ($)
1	Ford Taurus	360,448
2	Honda Accord	330,030
3	Toyota Camry	299,737
4	Chevrolet Cavalier	273,617
5	Ford Escort	269,034
6	Honda Civic	255,579
7	Saturn	229,356
8	Chevrolet Lumina	219,683
9	Ford Tempo	217,644
10	Pontiac Grand Am	214,761

* Includes imports

FORD TAURUS

T O P   1 0

MOTOR VEHICLE MANUFACTURERS IN THE WORLD

	Production company	Country	Cars	Commercial vehicles	Total
1	General Motors	US	4,968,659	1,666,076	6,634,735
2	Ford Motor Company	US	3,452,039	1,686,321	5,138,360
3	Toyota	Japan	3,597,179	914,040	4,511,219
4	Volkswagen	Germany	2,921,481	166,952	3,088,433
5	Nissan	Japan	2,333,276	692,483	3,025,759
6	PSA (Peugeot-Citroën)	France	2,257,454	209,773	2,467,227
7	Renault	France	1,705,821	298,416	2,004,237
8	Honda	Japan	1,765,403	143,361	1,908,764
9	Fiat	Italy	1,636,838	261,717	1,898,555
10	Chrysler	US	660,200	1,014,089	1,674,289
	World total		*34,655,650*	*11,840,781*	*46,496,431*

Figures are for 1991 production worldwide in all companies owned by the manufacturers, as compiled by the American Automobile Manufacturers Association. The Japanese companies Mazda and Mitsubishi actually produced more cars than Chrysler (1,250,714 and 1,103,606 respectively – the only other companies in the world to produce more than 1,000,000), but Chrysler's huge commercial vehicle production provides the company with a place in the Top 10. Japanese companies produced 15,381,180 vehicles, North American manufacturers 13,381,180, and western European companies 11,912,416. In response to the world economic recession, most companies produced fewer vehicles in 1991 than in 1990 – a drop of almost 2,000,000 in total.

T O P   1 0

CAR MANUFACTURERS IN NORTH AMERICA

	Company	US	Production Canada	Total (1992)
1	Ford	922,488	214,804	1,137,292
2	Chevrolet	647,227	230,162	877,389
3	Lincoln-Mercury	411,090	151,495	562,585
4	Honda	458,254	104,123	562,377
5	Pontiac	561,940	19	561,959
6	Buick	427,915	97,764	525,679
7	Toyota	345,752	68,092	413,844
8	Oldsmobile	395,974	–	395,974
9	Dodge	263,539	22,705	286,244
10	Chrysler-Plymouth	259,121	16,022	275,143

Based on group totals, General Motors (which encompasses Buick, Cadillac, Chevrolet, Pontiac, and Oldsmobile) is the largest manufacturer by a considerable margin, with US and Canadian production of 2,794,235; Ford's total (Ford plus Lincoln-Mercury), by comparison, is 1,699,877. The output of both Honda and Toyota has increased steadily, and two other Japanese companies, Nissan and Mazda (171,404 and 167,940 cars respectively), are only just outside the Top 10.

T O P   1 0

IMPORTED CARS IN THE US

	Manufacturer	Country	Total 1992 sales
1	Toyota	Japan	418,661
2	Honda	Japan	293,127
3	Nissan	Japan/Spain	274,353
4	Mazda	Japan	169,007
5	General Motors	Belgium/ Finland/ Germany/ Spain	93,917
6	Hyundai	South Korea	91,564
7	Mitsubishi	Japan/Australia	90,980
8	Volkswagen/ Audi	Germany/ Belgium/Spain	87,949
9	Volvo	Sweden/ Netherlands/ Belgium	67,916
10	BMW	Germany	65,693

ROADS AND PUBLIC TRANSPORTATION

COUNTRIES DRIVING ON THE LEFT

	Country	Total vehicles registered
1	Japan	57,914,623
2	UK	26,429,283
3	Australia	9,649,500
4	South Africa	5,324,749
5	India	4,667,749
6	Indonesia	3,001,508
7	Thailand	2,727,509
8	Malaysia	2,400,000
9	New Zealand	1,867,649
10	Nigeria	1,400,000

While more countries drive on the right than on the left, there are 42 countries in the world that drive on the left, including the UK and most members of the British Commonwealth. The last country in Europe to change over from driving on the left to the right was Sweden, on September 3, 1967. There are innumerable explanations for keeping to the left, one being that it is common practice, especially among sword-wearing riders, to mount a horse from the left, and it is then simplest to remain on the left. Similarly, riding on the left facilitates right-handed sword defense against approaching riders. This does not explain, however, why other nations perversely drive on the right.

STATES WITH THE MOST LICENSED DRIVERS

	State	Female drivers	Male drivers	Total
1	California	9,466,000	10,763,000	20,229,000
2	Texas	5,543,000	5,918,000	11,461,000
3	New York	4,896,000	5,524,000	10,420,000
4	Florida	4,762,000	5,075,000	9,837,000
5	Pennsylvania	3,893,000	4,176,000	8,069,000
6	Ohio	3,747,000	3,835,000	7,582,000
7	Illinois	3,670,000	3,799,000	7,469,000
8	Michigan	3,251,000	3,279,000	6,530,000
9	New Jersey	2,686,000	3,058,000	5,744,000
10	Virginia	2,337,000	2,383,000	4,720,000
	US total	*83,353,000*	*88,155,000*	*171,508,000*

The percentage of female drivers has risen steadily from 40.31 in 1964 to 48.60 in 1992. Just nine states (Connecticut, Iowa, Kansas, Louisiana, Maine, Nebraska, Tennessee, North Carolina, and South Carolina) buck the national pattern and have more female than male drivers, while one state – Utah – has identical numbers (541,000 women and 541,000 men).

SWEDEN CHANGES SIDES

On September 3, 1967 Sweden, the last country in mainland Europe to drive on the left, switched sides. The operation, involving over 2,000,000 vehicles, 105,490 miles/169,770 km of roads, and all of the road signs, took four years' planning and a massive publicity campaign. At 1:00 am every vehicle on the road in Sweden stopped and moved gingerly to the opposite side, starting off again at 6:00 am – on the right.

TOP 10

STATES WITH THE GREATEST ROAD NETWORKS

	State	Total length* km	miles
1	Texas	472,048	293,317
2	California	270,978	168,378
3	Illinois	219,925	136,402
4	Kansas	215,097	133,655
5	Minnesota	208,606	129,622
6	Missouri	195,413	121,424
7	Michigan	189,130	117,520
8	Pennsylvania	187,952	116,788

	State	Total length* km	miles
9	Ohio	183,180	113,823
10	Iowa	181,190	112,586

* Interstate, rural, and urban
Source: Federal Highway Administration

US Department of Transportation figures show that Texas has not only the greatest road network overall but also the greatest length of interstate highways (3,229 miles/5,197 km). The District of Columbia has the shortest road network (1,102 miles/1,773 km).

TOP 10

COUNTRIES WITH THE LONGEST ROAD NETWORKS

	Country	km	miles
1	US	6,365,590	3,955,394
2	India	1,970,000	1,224,101
3	France	1,551,400	963,995
4	Brazil	1,448,000	899,745
5	Japan	1,111,974	690,949

	Country	km	miles
6	China	1,029,000	630,391
7	Canada	884,272	549,461
8	Russia	879,100	546,247
9	Australia	837,872	520,629
10	Germany	466,305	289,748

TOP 10

LONGEST HIGHWAYS IN THE US

	Highway	km	Total length miles
1	US-20	5,415	3,365
2	US-6	5,229	3,249
3	US-30	5,020	3,119
4	US-50	4,889	3,038
5	I-80	4,649	2,889
6	I-90	4,649	2,784
7	US-60	4,422	2,748
8	US-70	4,390	2,728
9	US-2	4,253	2,643
10	US-1	4,173	2,593

Source: Federal Highway Administration

The Interstate road system commenced with the introduction of the 1956 Highway Act, after which "I" shields began appearing on new highways that ran through more than one state. An Interstate differs from a US Route in that it is a full freeway, with no "Stop" signs - although some older US Routes still retain a few.

TOP 10

MOST COMMON TYPES OF LOST PROPERTY ON PUBLIC TRANSPORTATION

NEW YORK TRANSIT AUTHORITY		LONDON TRANSPORT (1992-93)
Backpacks	1	Books, checkbooks and credit cards
Radios/Walkmans	2	"Value items" (handbags, pocketbooks, wallets, etc.)
Eyeglasses	3	Clothing
Wallets and pocketbooks	4	Umbrellas
Cameras	5	Cases and bags
Keys	6	Keys
Attaché cases	7	Eyeglasses
Watches	8	Cameras, electronic articles and jewelry
Shoes	9	Gloves (pairs)
Jewelry	10	Gloves (odd)

Although the New York Transit Authority does not keep itemized records in the same meticulous detail as London Transport (which encompasses London's buses and "Tube" trains), a comparison of the ranking of the two lists reveals both interesting similarities (keys feature at No. 6 in both lists) and differences (where are the umbrellas in the New York version?). In the London list, books have figured in the No.1 position for several years, but changes in fashion have meant that hats, once one of the most common lost items, no longer even warrant a separate category, while often expensive electronic calculators, laptop computers, and mobile phones are now lost in increasing numbers in both London and New York. A June 1994 auction of NYTA's unclaimed property included such bizarre items as five wheelchairs (prompting the thought that healers are at work in the New York subways), while false teeth and artificial limbs are among the stranger items lost in recent years in both cities. London's weird list includes a skeleton, a box of glass eyes, breast implants, an outboard motor, a complete double bed, a theatrical coffin, a stuffed gorilla, and an urn containing human ashes (the latter was never claimed and the ashes were ceremoniously scattered in a flowerbed in a nearby park). This is chicken-feed, however, when compared with the plethora of odd items left on Japanese trains in a single year, among which were 500,000 umbrellas, $15,000,000 in cash, 29 small dogs, one live snake in a bag, 150 sets of false teeth, and 15 urns containing ashes of the dead.

ON THE RIGHT TRACK

TOP 10

LONGEST RAILROAD PLATFORMS IN THE WORLD

	Station	Platform length m	ft
1	State Street Center Subway, Chicago, Illinois, US	1,067	3,500
2	Khargpur, India	833	2,733
3	Perth, Australia	762	2,500
4	Sonepur, India	736	2,415
5	Bournemouth, England	720	2,362
6	Bulawayo, Zimbabwe	702	2,302
7	New Lucknow, India	686	2,250
8	Bezwada, India	640	2,100
9	Gloucester, England	624	2,047
10	Jhansi, India	617	2,025

TOP 10

LONGEST RAILROAD NETWORKS IN THE WORLD

	Country	Total rail length km	miles
1	US	270,312	167,964
2	Canada	93,544	58,126
3	Russia	87,180	54,171
4	India	61,950	38,494
5	China	54,000	33,544
6	Germany	45,468	28,253
7	Australia	40,478	25,152
8	France	34,568	21,480
9	Argentina	34,172	21,233
10	Brazil	28,828	17,913

US rail mileage grew fast in the 19th century, but has declined steadily since 1916.

TOP 10

FIRST COUNTRIES WITH RAILROADS

	Country	First railway established
1	UK	1825
2	US	1834
3=	Belgium	1835
3=	Germany	1835
5=	Canada	1836
5=	Russia	1836
7=	Austria	1837
7=	France	1837
9=	Italy	1839
9=	Netherlands	1839

Although there were earlier, horse-drawn railroads, the UK had the first steam service.

TOP 10

FASTEST RAILROAD JOURNEYS IN THE WORLD

	Journey	Train	Distance km	Speed (km/h)
1	Massy – St. Pierre, France	TGV 8501	206.7	245.6
2	Hiroshima – Kokuru, Japan	27 Nozomi	192.0	230.4
3	Madrid – Ciudad Real, Spain	4 AVE	170.7	217.9
4	Hannover – Göttingen, Germany	23 ICE	99.4	192.4
5	Skövde – Alingsås, Sweden	X2000 421	99.2	175.1
6	Doncaster – Grantham, UK	InterCity 225	81.2	171.1
7	Rome – Florence, Italy	Cristoforo Colombo	261.9	163.7
8	Philadelphia, PA – Wilmington, DE	Metroliner	50.6	159.8
9	Toronto – Dorval, Canada	Metropolis	520.9	145.4
10	St. Petersburg – Moscow, Russia	ER200	649.9	130.4

This list comprises the fastest journey for each country; all have other similarly – occasionally equally – fast services.

TOP 10

BUSIEST AMTRAK RAILROAD STATIONS IN THE US

	Station	Boardings (1993)
1	New York-Penn	6,026,202
2	Philadelphia-30th St.	3,384,950
3	Washington-Union	3,376,534
4	Chicago-Union	2,512,921
5	Los Angeles-Union	1,139,083
6	Baltimore-Penn	1,052,419
7	Boston-South	818,591
8	Wilmington (Delaware)	630,331
9	San Diego*	628,335
10	Newark-Penn	558,528

The only station on the list not to have commuter train services (though it will by October 1994)

Source: National Association of Railroad Passengers

TRAIN A GRANDE VITESSE
The current world rail speed record is held by the French TGV, which on May 18, 1990 clocked 320.0 mph/515.0 km/h.

ATTER-DAY LABYRINTH
Trains run 24 hours a day, 365 days a year, n most of the New York subway routes. This etwork is among the oldest and longest ubway systems in the world.

TOP 10

OLDEST SUBWAY SYSTEMS IN THE WORLD

	City	Year in which system was opened
1	London	1863
2=	Budapest	1896
2=	Glasgow	1896
4	Boston	1897
5	Paris	1900
6	Wuppertal	1901
7	Berlin	1902
8	New York	1904
9	Philadelphia	1907
10	Hamburg	1912

DID YOU KNOW

THE FIRST SUBWAYS

A century ago, on March 28, 1895, work began on America's first subway, Tremont Street, Boston, a two-mile track that was opened on September 1, 1897. The first subway trains were steam powered and ran on London's Metropolitan Line, which had opened in 1863. A special device absorbed the smoke so passengers did not suffocate. These first lines were made by the "cut-and-cover" method of digging trenches and arching them over, and in built-up areas by tunneling. Only when deep tunneling, electric motors, electric lights, and elevators or escalators were invented could the service could be electrified; this happened in the 1890s, and spread to the US and the rest of the world.

TOP 10

LONGEST SUBWAY NETWORKS IN THE US

	City	Opened/ extended	No. of stations	Total track length km	miles
1	Washington, DC	1976/93	86	612	380
2	New York	1904/1968	461	370	230
3	Chicago	1943/1983	142	156	97
4	San Francisco	1972	34	115	71
5	Boston	1897/1980	51	70	43
6	Philadelphia	1907	68	63	39
7	Cleveland	1955/1968	18	47	29
8	Atlanta	1979	20	41	25
9	Miami	1984	20	33	21
10	Baltimore	1983	9	22	14

A 17 mile/27-km subway is under construction in Honolulu and scheduled for opening in 1997. Several Canadian cities (Toronto, Montreal, and Vancouver) have subways, and certain other US cities, such as Los Angeles and Detroit, have relatively short sytems.

TOP 10

LONGEST SUBWAY NETWORKS IN THE WORLD

	City	Built	Stations	Total track length km	miles
1	Washington, DC	1976–1993	86	612	380
2	London	1863–1979	272	430	267
3	New York	1904–1968	461	370	230
4	Paris (Metro & RER)	1900–1985	430	301	187
5	Moscow	1935–1979	115	225	140
6	Tokyo	1927–1980	192	218	135
7	Berlin	1902–1980	134	167	104
8	Chicago	1943–1953	142	156	97
9	Copenhagen	1934	61	134	83
10	Mexico City	1969–1982	57	125	78

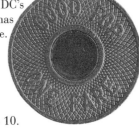

The extension of Washington, DC's subway, completed in 1993, has lifted it from 10th to 1st place. Other underground systems being developed include Seoul, Korea, currently 72 miles/116 km long, and due to gain 21 miles/33 km, which will put it into the Top 10.

LAND TRANSPORTATION DISASTERS

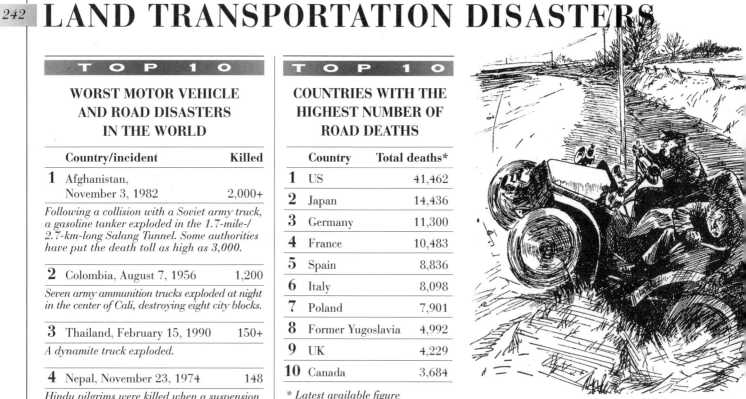

TOP 10

WORST MOTOR VEHICLE AND ROAD DISASTERS IN THE WORLD

Country/incident	Killed
1 Afghanistan, November 3, 1982	2,000+

Following a collision with a Soviet army truck, a gasoline tanker exploded in the 1.7-mile-/ 2.7-km-long Salang Tunnel. Some authorities have put the death toll as high as 3,000.

2 Colombia, August 7, 1956	1,200

Seven army ammunition trucks exploded at night in the center of Cali, destroying eight city blocks.

3 Thailand, February 15, 1990	150+

A dynamite truck exploded.

4 Nepal, November 23, 1974	148

Hindu pilgrims were killed when a suspension bridge over the Mahahali River collapsed.

5 Egypt, August 9, 1973	127

A bus drove into an irrigation canal.

6 Togo, December 6, 1965	125+

Two trucks collided with dancers during a festival at Sotouboua.

7 Spain, July 11, 1978	120+

A liquid gas tanker exploded in a camping site at San Carlos de la Rapita.

8 Gambia, November 12, 1992	c.100

A bus plunged into a river when its brakes failed.

9 Kenya, early December 1992	nearly 100

A bus carrying 112 skidded, hit a bridge, and plunged into a river.

10= Lesotho, December 16, 1976	90

A bus fell into the Tsoaing River.

10= India, March 16, 1988	90

In the state of Madhya Pradesh, the driver of a bus carrying a wedding party lost control and crashed while trying to change a tape cassette.

The worst-ever racing car accident occurred on June 11, 1955 at Le Mans, France, when, in attempting to avoid other cars, French driver Pierre Levegh's Mercedes-Benz 300 SLR went out of control, hit a wall, and exploded in midair, showering wreckage into the crowd and killing a total of 82 (*see also* The 10 Worst Disasters at Sports Venues).

TOP 10

COUNTRIES WITH THE HIGHEST NUMBER OF ROAD DEATHS

	Country	Total deaths*
1	US	41,462
2	Japan	14,436
3	Germany	11,300
4	France	10,483
5	Spain	8,836
6	Italy	8,098
7	Poland	7,901
8	Former Yugoslavia	4,992
9	UK	4,229
10	Canada	3,684

* Latest available figure

TOP 10

LEAST BAD YEARS FOR ROAD FATALITIES IN THE US

	Year	Total fatalities*
1	1899	26
2	1900	36
3	1901	54
4	1902	79
5	1903	117
6	1904	172
7	1905	252
8	1906	338
9	1907	581
10	1908	751

* Deaths occurring within 30 days of accident

From 1899, when the recording of road deaths began, the annual toll has risen at a fairly steady rate, retreating marginally due to restrictions on driving during the Depression years and in the Second World War, before accelerating to their 1972 peak. Fatalities exceeded 10,000 for the first time in 1918, 20,000 in 1925, 30,000 in 1930, 40,000 in 1963, and 50,000 in 1966. It has been calculated that from 1899 to 1993, a total of 2,820,487 people died on the road – more than the present population of Chicago.

TOP 10

WORST YEARS FOR ROAD FATALITIES IN THE US

	Year	Fatalities per 100,000,000 VMT*	Total fatalities#
1	1972	4.3	54,589
2	1973	4.1	54,052
3	1969	5.0	53,543
4	1968	5.2	52,725
5	1970	4.7	52,627
6	1971	4.5	52,542
7	1979	3.3	51,093
8	1980	3.3	51,091
9	1966	5.5	50,894
10	1967	5.3	50,724

* Vehicle Miles of Travel
 # Deaths occurring within 30 days of accident

Although 1972 was the worst year on record for total fatalities, it is important to take into account the progressive increases in population and numbers of vehicles on the road, so the ratio of fatalities to vehicle miles of travel is more significant. This has steadily declined since 1921, the year it was first recorded, when there were 24.1 deaths per 100,000,000 VMT. By 1993 this figure had plunged to 1.7 per 100,000,000 VMT.

TOP 10

WORST RAILROAD DISASTERS IN THE US

Incident	No. killed
1 July 9, 1918, Nashville, Tennessee	101

On the Nashville, Chattanooga and St. Louis Railway, a head-on collision resulted in a death-toll that remains the worst in US history, with 171 injured.

Incident	No. killed
2 November 2, 1918, Brooklyn, New York	97

A subway train was derailed in the Malbone Street tunnel.

3= August 7, 1904, Eden, Colorado	96

A bridge washed away during a flood smashed Steele's Hollow Bridge as the "World's Fair Express" was crossing.

3= March 1, 1910, Wellington, Washington	96

An avalanche swept two trains into a canyon.

5 February 6, 1951, Woodbridge, New Jersey	84

A Pennsylvania Railroad commuter train crashed while speeding through a sharply curving detour.

Incident	No. killed
6 August 10, 1887, Chatsworth, Illinois	82

A trestle bridge caught fire and collapsed as the Toledo, Peoria & Western train was passing over. As many as 372 were injured.

7 December 29, 1876, Ashtabula, Ohio	80

A bridge collapsed in a snowstorm and the Lake Shore train fell into the Ashtabula River. The death toll may have been as high as 92.

8= September 6, 1943, Frankford Junction, Pennsylvania	79

Pennsylvania's worst railway accident (since that at Camp Hill on July 17, 1856 when two trains crashed head-on, resulting in the deaths of 66 school children on a church picnic outing).

8= November 22, 1950, Richmond Hill, New York	79

A Long Island Railroad commuter train rammed into the rear of another, leaving 79 dead and 363 injured.

8= July 15, 1864, Shohola, Pennsylvania	74

A troop train with Confederate prisoners-of-war collided head-on with a coal train.

TOP 10

STATES WITH THE FEWEST AND THE MOST MOTOR VEHICLE FATALITIES

FEWEST

	State	Total fatalities (1993)
1	District of Columbia	57
2	Rhode Island	74
3	North Dakota	89
4	Vermont	110
5	Delaware	111
6	Alaska	118
7	Wyoming	120
8	New Hampshire	121
9	Hawaii	134
10	South Dakota	140

MOST

	State	Total fatalities (1993)
1	California	4,163
2	Texas	3,037
3	Florida	2,635
4	New York	1,781
5	Pennsylvania	1,529
6	Ohio	1,482
7	Michigan	1,408
8	Georgia	1,394
9	Illinois	1,392
10	North Carolina	1,389

While they have the greatest number of motor vehicle deaths, most of the states appearing in the "Most" Top 10 are also among the nation's foremost vehicle users, and if this is taken into account have fatality rates below the national average. The highest rates actually occur in states with relatively few vehicles, including Alaska, Arkansas, Mississippi, Nevada, and New Mexico. Connecticut and Massachusetts have the lowest rates of all.

TOP 10

WORST RAIL DISASTERS IN THE WORLD

Incident	Killed
1 June 6, 1981, Bagmati River, India	c.800

The carriages of a train plunged off a bridge near Mansi when the driver braked, apparently to avoid hitting a sacred cow. Although the official death toll was 268, many claim that the train was so overcrowded that the actual figure was in excess of 800.

2 June 3, 1989, Chelyabinsk, Russia	up to 800

Two passenger trains on the Trans-Siberian railway, laden with vacationers were destroyed by exploding liquid gas from a nearby pipeline.

3 January 18, 1915, Guadalajara, Mexico	600+

A train derailed on a steep incline, but details of the disaster were suppressed.

4 December 12, 1917, Modane, France	573

A troop-carrying train was derailed. It has been claimed that the train was overloaded – 1,000 may have died.

5 March 2, 1944, Balvano, Italy	521

A heavily-laden train stalled in the Armi Tunnel, and many were asphyxiated.

6 January 3, 1944, Torre, Spain	500+

A collision and fire in a tunnel.

7 April 3, 1955, near Guadalajara, Mexico	c.300

A night express carrying hundreds of vacationers plunged into a ravine.

8 September 29, 1957, Gambar, near Montgomery, Pakistan	250–300

A collision between an express and an oil train.

9 February 1, 1970, near Buenos Aires, Argentina	236

A collision between an express and a standing commuter train.

10 December 23, 1933, Pomponne near Lagny, France	230

A collision in fog between an express and two stationary trains.

WATER TRANSPORTATION

ROYAL LINER
The British liner Queen Elizabeth II, *launched by HM Queen Elizabeth II in 1967, is still in service today.*

THE PROGRESSION OF THE WORLD'S LARGEST LINERS IN SERVICE

Ship	Gross tonnage	Years in service
Great Eastern	18,914	1858–88
Oceanic	17,274	1899–1914
Baltic	23,884	1904–33
Lusitania*	31,550	1907–15
Mauretania	31,938	1907–35
Olympic	45,300	1911–35
Titanic*	46,232	1912
Imperator/ Berengaria#	52,022	1913–38
Vaterland/ Leviathan#	54,282	1914–38
Bismarck/Majestic/ Caledonia#	56,621	1922–39
Normandie/ Lafayette*#	79,301/83,102**	1935–42
Queen Mary	80,774/81,237**	1936–67
Queen Elizabeth	83,673/82,998**	1938–72
France/Norway#	66,348/76,049**	1961–
Sovereign of the Seas	73,192	1987–

* Sunk
\# Renamed
** Tonnage altered during refitting

FIRST SHIPS LAUNCHED BY HM QUEEN ELIZABETH II

	Ship	Location	Date launched
1	HMY Britannia	Clydebank, Scotland	Apr 16, 1953
2	SS Southern Cross	Belfast, Northern Ireland	Aug 17, 1954
3	SS Empress of Britain	Govan, Scotland	Jun 22, 1955
4	HMS Dreadnought	Barrow, England	Oct 21, 1960
5	SS British Admiral	Barrow, England	Mar 17, 1965
6	Queen Elizabeth II	Clydebank, Scotland	Sep 20, 1967
7	HMS Sheffield*	Barrow, England	Jun 10, 1971
8	The Royal British Legion Jubilee#	Henley-on-Thames, England	Jul 17, 1972
9	HMS Invincible	Barrow, Scotland	May 3, 1977
10	HMS Lancaster	Scotstoun, Scotland	May 24, 1990

* Sunk May 10, 1982 after being struck by an Exocet missile during the Falklands Conflict.
\# Lifeboat

LARGEST OIL TANKERS IN THE WORLD

	Ship	Year built	Country	Deadweight tonnage
1	Jahre Viking	1979	Japan	564,650
2	Kapetan Giannis	1977	Japan	516,895
3	Kapetan Michalis	1977	Japan	516,423
4	Nissei Maru	1975	Japan	484,276
5	Stena King	1978	Taiwan	457,927
6	Stena Queen	1977	Taiwan	457,841
7	Kapetan Panagiotis	1977	Japan	457,062
8	Kapetan Giorgis	1976	Japan	456,368
9	Sea Empress	1976	Japan	423,677
10	Mira Star	1975	Japan	423,642

The 1,504-ft/485.45-m *Jahre Viking* (formerly called *Happy Giant* and *Seawise*) is the longest vessel ever built. It was extensively damaged during the Iran-Iraq War, but was salvaged, refitted, and relaunched in 1991.

TOP 10

LARGEST PASSENGER LINERS IN THE WORLD

	Ship	Year	Country built in	Passenger capacity	Gross tonnage
1	*France/Norway* (renamed)	1961	France	2,565	76,049
2=	*Majesty of the Seas*	1992	France	2,766	73,937
2=	*Monarch of the Seas*	1991	France	2,764	73,937
4	*Sovereign of the Seas*	1987	France	2,600	73,192
5=	*Sensation*	1993	Finland	2,634	70,367
5=	*Ecstasy*	1991	Finland	2,634	70,367
5=	*Fantasy*	1990	Finland	2,634	70,367
8=	*Crown Princess*	1990	Italy	1,590	69,845
8=	*Regal Princess*	1991	Italy	1,900	69,845
10	*QEII*	1969	Scotland	1,877	69,053

After the fire and capsizing of the *Queen Elizabeth* in Hong Kong harbor (January 9, 1972) and her eventual scrapping, the *France*, later renamed *Norway*, remained the largest passenger vessel in service until the *Sovereign of the Seas* was launched. This ship held the record only until 1990, however, when *Norway* was considerably enlarged during a refit, this regaining her preeminence as the world's largest passenger liner afloat. However, *Norway*, although currently in No. 1 position on this list, is due to be outstripped by the 77,000-tonne *Sun Princess*, currently being built at the Fincantieri shipyard in Monfalcone, Italy, for service with P&O's subsidiary, Princess Cruises. This liner will be joined by another, as yet unnamed, of about 100,000 tonnes – and hence the world's largest liner – which is scheduled for construction in the same yard. It will be 935 ft/285 m long and have a passenger capacity of 2,600.

TOP 10

YEARS FOR BOAT SALES IN THE US

	Year	Total sales ($)
1	1988	17,900,000,000
2	1989	17,100,000,000
3	1987	16,500,000,000
4	1986	14,500,000,000
5	1990	13,700,000,000
6	1985	13,300,000,000
7	1994	12,900,000,000 *
8	1984	12,300,000,000
9	1993	11,300,000,000
10	1991	10,600,000,000

* Projected figure

National Marine Manufacturers Association estimates for total retail sales of boats, services and parts reveal that after climbing steadily during the 1980s, the business experienced a dramatic slump in revenue as a result of the recession and the 10 percent luxury tax on expensive boats imposed in 1990 by President Bush. By 1992, sales had dipped to $10,300,000,000, but have begun to rise again, perhaps mirroring the nation's move out of recession.

TOP 10

SHIPPING COUNTRIES IN THE WORLD

	Country	No. of ships	Total GRT*
1	Panama	5,564	57,618,623
2	Liberia	1,611	53,918,534
3	Greece	1,929	29,134,435
4	Japan	9,950	24,247,525
5	Cyprus	1,591	22,842,009
6	Bahamas	1,121	21,224,164
7	Norway	785	19,383,417
8	Russia	5,335	16,813,761
9	China	2,501	14,944,999
10	Malta	1,037	14,163,357

* GRT or Gross Registered Tonnage is not the actual weight of a ship but its cubic capacity (1 ton = 100 cubic feet). Deadweight tonnage is the weight a ship can carry when fully laden. This list includes only ships of more than 100 GRT.

Liberia held the record for many years, but has recently been overtaken by Panama. The United States is in 11th place with 5,646 ships totaling 14,086,825 GRT, and the UK lies in 26th place with 1,532 ships/4,116,868 GRT, its shipping fleets having steadily declined in recent years. The world total now comprises 80,655 vessels with a total GRT of 457,914,808 tonnes. Norway's low ship/GRT ratio results from the Norwegian International Shipregister's principally recording the country's larger tonnage, chiefly oil tankers.

TOP 10

COUNTRIES WITH THE LONGEST INLAND WATERWAY NETWORKS

(Canals and navigable rivers)

	Country	Total length km	miles
1	China	138,600	86,122
2	Former USSR	113,500	70,526
3	Brazil	50,000	31,069
4	US#	41,009	25,482
5	Indonesia	21,579	13,409
6	Vietnam	17,702	11,000
7	India	16,180	10,054
8	Zaïre	15,000	9,321
9	France	14,932	9,278
10	Colombia	14,300	8,886

 # Excluding Great Lakes

MARINE DISASTERS

SINKING THE UNSINKABLE
The collision of the supposedly unsinkable British liner Titanic *with an iceberg was one of the worst marine disasters ever in peacetime.*

DID YOU KNOW

AMERICA'S WORST SHIPPING DISASTER

The end of the Civil War and the assassination of Lincoln in April 1865 eclipsed news of the sinking of the *Sultana*, the worst shipping catastrophe in American history. In the chaos following the ending of the war, the 1,700-ton Mississippi paddle-steamer was carrying far more than its legal limit of 376. Burdened with more than 2,500 passengers and crew, including many former prisoners of war traveling north to be repatriated, her primitive steam engines were struggling to propel the enormous and unaccustomed load. During the night of April 27, while most of those on board lay asleep, first one, then two further boilers exploded, tearing the vessel apart in an instant and setting the wreckage on fire. Although other ships raced to the scene and rescued many of the survivors, Memphis customs officials were later to estimate that 1,547 had died in the explosion, or as a result of fire or drowning; other authorities have put the figure even higher, but it is clear that more lost their lives on the *Sultana* than on the more famous *Titanic* less than 50 years later.

T O P   1 0

WORST PRE-20TH-CENTURY MARINE DISASTERS

	Incident	Killed
1	Spanish Armada – Military conflict and storms combined to destroy the Spanish fleet in the English Channel and elsewhere off the British coast, August to October 1588.	*c.*4,000
2=	British fleet – Eight ships sunk in storms off Egg Island, Labrador, Canada, August 22, 1711.	*c.*2,000
2=	*St. George*, *Defence*, and *Hero* – British warships stranded off the Jutland coast, Denmark, December 4, 1811.	*c.*2,000
4	*Sultana* – A Mississippi River steamboat destroyed by a boiler explosion near Memphis, April 27, 1865 – the US's worst ever marine accident, although the official death toll may be an underestimate.	1,547
5	*Capitanas* – Twin Spanish treasure vessels sunk in a hurricane off the Florida coast, July 31, 1715.	*c.*1,000
6	*Royal George* – British warship wrecked off Spithead, August 29, 1782, the worst ever single shipwreck off the British coast.	*c.*900
7	*Princess Alice* – Pleasure steamer in collision with *Bywell Castle* on the Thames near Woolwich, September 3, 1878.	786
8	*Queen Charlotte* – British warship burnt in Leghorn harbor, March 17, 1800.	*c.*700
9=	*Ertogrul* – Turkish frigate wrecked off the Japanese coast, September 19, 1890.	587
9=	*Utopia* – British steamer collided with British warship *Amson* off Gibraltar, March 17, 1891.	576

T O P   1 0

WORST OIL TANKER SPILLS OF ALL TIME

	Tanker/location	Date	Spillage (tonnes approx.)
1	*Atlantic Empress* and *Aegean Captain*, Trinidad	Jul 19, 1979	300,000
2	*Castillio de Bellver*, Cape Town, South Africa	Aug 6, 1983	255,000
3	*Olympic Bravery*, Ushant, France	Jan 24, 1976	250,000
4	*Showa-Maru*, Malacca, Malaya	Jun 7, 1975	237,000
5	*Amoco Cadiz*, Finistère, France	Mar 16, 1978	223,000
6	*Odyssey*, Atlantic, off Canada	Nov 10, 1988	140,000
7	*Torrey Canyon*, Scilly Isles, UK	Mar 18, 1967	120,000
8	*Sea Star*, Gulf of Oman	Dec 19, 1972	115,000
9	*Irenes Serenada*, Pilos, Greece	Feb 23, 1980	102,000
10	*Urquiola*, Corunna, Spain	May 12, 1976	101,000

It is estimated that an average of 2,000,000 tonnes is spilled into the world's seas every year. All these accidents were caused by collision, grounding, fire, or explosion. Military action has caused worse tanker oil spills: during the Gulf War tankers sunk in the Persian Gulf spilled more than 1,000,000 tonnes of oil. The *Exxon Valdez* grounding in Alaska on March 24, 1989 spilled about 35,000 tonnes, but resulted in major ecological damage.

WORST MARINE DISASTERS OF THE 20TH CENTURY

	Incident	Approx no. killed
1	*Wilhelm Gustloff* The German liner, laden with refugees, was torpedoed off Danzig by a Soviet submarine, *S-13*, January 30, 1945. The precise death toll remains uncertain, but is in the range of 5,348 to 7,700.	up to 7,700
2	Unknown vessel An unidentified Chinese troopship carrying Nationalist soldiers from Manchuria sank off Yingkow, November 1947.	6,000+
3	*Cap Arcona* A German ship carrying concentration camp survivors was bombed and sunk by British aircraft in Lübeck harbor, May 3, 1945.	4,650
4	*Lancastria* A British troop ship sunk off St. Nazaire, June 17, 1940.	4,000+
5	*Yamato* A Japanese battleship sunk off Kyushu Island, April 7, 1945.	3,033
6	*Dona Paz* The ferry *Dona Paz* was struck by oil tanker MV *Victor* in the Tabias Strait, Philippines, December 20, 1987.	3,000+
7	*Kiangya* An overloaded steamship carrying refugees struck a Japanese mine off Woosung, China, December 3, 1948.	2,750+
8	*Thielbeck* A refugee ship sunk during the British bombardment of Lübeck harbor in the closing weeks of the Second World War, May 1945.	2,750
9	*Arisan Maru* A Japanese vessel carrying American prisoners-of-war was torpedoed by a US submarine in the South China Sea, October 24, 1944.	1,790+
10	*Mont Blanc* A French ammunition ship collided with Belgian steamer *Imo* and exploded, Halifax, Nova Scotia, December 6, 1917.	1,600

Due to a reassessment of the death tolls in some of the Second World War marine disasters, the most famous of all, the sinking of the *Titanic* (the British liner that struck an iceberg in the North Atlantic on April 15, 1912 and went down with the loss of 1,517 lives), no longer ranks in the Top 10. However, the *Titanic* tragedy remains one of the worst ever peacetime disasters.

WORST SUBMARINE DISASTERS

(Excluding those as a result of military action)

	Incident	Killed
1	*Le Surcourf* – A French submarine accidentally rammed by a US merchant ship, *Thomas Lykes*, in the Gulf of Mexico on February 18, 1942.	159
2	*Thresher* – A three-year-old US nuclear submarine, worth $45,000,000, sank in the North Atlantic, 220 miles/350 km east of Boston on April 10, 1963.	129
3=	*Thetis* – A British submarine sank on June 1, 1939 during trials in Liverpool Bay, with civilians on board. Her captain and two crew members escaped. *Thetis* was later salvaged and renamed *Thunderbolt*. On March 13, 1943 she was sunk by an Italian ship with the loss of 63 lives.	99
3=	*Scorpion* – This US nuclear submarine was lost in the North Atlantic, 250 miles/400 km southwest of the Azores, on May 21, 1968. The wreck was located on October 31, of that year.	99
5	*I-67* – A Japanese submarine that foundered in a storm off Bonin Island to the south of Japan in 1940.	89
6=	*Ro-31* – A Japanese submarine lost off Kobe, Japan, on August 21, 1923 when a hatch was accidentally left open as she dived. There were only five survivors.	88
6=	Unnamed Soviet November Class submarine – lost 70 miles/110 km off Land's End, UK, on April 12, 1970.	88
8=	*I-63* – This Japanese submarine sank on February 2, 1939 after a collision in the Bungo Suido (between Kyushu and Shikoku, Japan). Six crew members were saved.	81
8=	*Dumlupinar* – A Turkish submarine lost in collision with a Swedish freighter on April 4, 1953, with five survivors.	81
10	HMS *Affray* – A British submarine lost on April 17, 1951 in Hard Deep, north of Alderney, Channel Islands.	75

THE FIRST TO FLY

TOP 10

FIRST MANNED BALLOON FLIGHTS*

1 November 21, 1783

François Laurent, Marquis d'Arlandes, and Jean-François Pilâtre de Rozier took off from the Bois de Boulogne, Paris, in a hot-air balloon designed by Joseph and Etienne Montgolfier. This first-ever manned flight covered a distance of about 5½ miles/9 km in 23 minutes, landing safely near Gentilly. (On June 15, 1785 de Rozier and his passenger were killed near Boulogne when their hydrogen balloon burst into flames during an attempted Channel crossing, making them the first air fatalities.)

2 December 1, 1783

A crowd of 400,000 watched as Jacques Alexandre César Charles and Nicholas-Louis Robert made the first-ever flight in a hydrogen balloon. They took off from the Tuileries, Paris, and traveled about 27 miles/43 km north to Nesle in about two hours. Charles then took off again alone, thus becoming the first solo flier.

3 January 19, 1784

La Flesselle, a 131-ft-/40-m-high Montgolfier hot-air balloon named after its sponsor, the local Governor, ascended from Lyons piloted by Pilâtre de Rozier with Joseph Montgolfier, Prince Charles de Ligne, and the Comtes de La Porte d'Anglefort, de Dampierre, and de Laurencin – and the first aerial stowaway, a man called Fontaine, who leaped in as it was taking off.

4 February 25, 1784

Chevalier Paolo Andreani and the brothers Augustino and Carlo Giuseppi Gerli (the builders of the balloon) made the first-ever flight outside France, at Moncuco near Milan, Italy.

5 March 2, 1784

Jean-Pierre François Blanchard made his first flight in a hydrogen balloon from the Champ de Mars, Paris, after experimental hops during the preceding months.

6 April 14, 1784

A Mr Rousseau and an unnamed 10-year-old drummer boy flew from Navan to Ratoath in Ireland, the first ascent in the British Isles.

7 April 25, 1784

Guyton de Morveau, a French chemist, and L'Abbé Bertrand flew at Dijon.

8 May 8, 1784

Bremond and Maret flew at Marseilles.

9 May 12, 1784

Brun ascended at Chambéry.

10 May 15, 1784

Adorne and an unnamed passenger took off but crash-landed near Strasbourg.

* The first 10 flights of the ballooning pioneers all took place within a year. Several of the balloonists listed also made subsequent flights, but in each instance only their first flights are included.

Joseph and Etienne Montgolfier conducted the first *unmanned* hot-air balloon test in the French town of Annonay on June 5, 1783 . They were then invited to demonstrate it to Louis XVI at Versailles. On September 19, 1783 it took off with the first-ever airborne passengers – a sheep, a rooster, and a duck.

After the first 10 manned flights, the pace of ballooning accelerated rapidly. On June 4, 1784 a Monsieur Fleurant took as his passenger in a flight at Lyons a Mme Elisabeth Thiblé, an opera singer, who was thus the first woman to fly (the Marchioness de Montalembert and other aristocratic ladies had ascended on May 20, 1784, but in a tethered balloon). On August 27, James Tytler (known as "Balloon Tytler"), a doctor and newspaper editor, took off from Comely Gardens, Edinburgh, achieving an altitude of 350 ft/107 m in a ½-mile/0.8-km hop in a homemade balloon – the first (and until Smeath in 1837, the only) hot-air balloon flight in the UK. On September 15, watched by a crowd of 200,000, Vincenzo Lunardi ascended from the Artillery Company Ground, Moorfields, London, flying to Standon near Ware in Hertfordshire, the first balloon flight in England. (An attempt the previous month by a Dr Moret ended with the balloon catching fire and the crowd rioting.) Lunardi went on to make further flights in Edinburgh and Glasgow. On October 4, 1784 James Sadler flew a Montgolfier balloon at Oxford, thereby becoming the first English pilot.

TOP 10

FIRST PEOPLE TO FLY IN HEAVIER-THAN-AIR AIRCRAFT

1 Orville Wright (1871–1948), US

On December 17, 1903 at Kitty Hawk, North Carolina, Wright made the first-ever manned flight in his Wright Flyer I. It lasted 12 seconds and covered a distance of 120 ft/37 m.

2 Wilbur Wright (1867–1912), US

On the same day, Orville's brother made his first flight in the Wright Flyer I (59 sec) covering a distance of 852 ft/260 m.

3 Alberto Santos-Dumont (1873–1932), Brazilian

At Bagatelle, Bois de Boulogne, Paris, Santos-Dumont made a 197-ft/60-m hop on October 23, 1906 in his clumsy No. 14-bis.

4 Charles Voisin (1882–1912), French

Voisin made a short 6-second hop of 197 ft/60 m at Bagatelle on March 30, 1907 in a plane built by himself and his brother Gabriel to the commission of Léon Delagrange.

5 Henri Farman (1874–1958), British, later French

Farman first flew on October 7, 1907, and by October 26 had achieved 2,530 ft/771 m.

6 Léon Delagrange (1873–1910), French

On November 5, 1907 at Issy-les-Moulineaux, France, Delagrange flew his Voisin-Delagrange 1 (see 4) for 40 seconds over 1,640 ft/500 m in.

7 Robert Esnault-Pelterie (1881–1957), French

On November 16, 1907 at Buc, France, he first flew his REP 1 (55 sec; 1,969 ft/600 m).

8 Charles W. Furnas (1880–1941), US

On May 14, 1908 at Kitty Hawk, Wilbur Wright took Furnas, his mechanic, for a spin in the Wright Flyer III (29 sec; 1,969 ft/600 m). Furnas was thus the first passenger in the US.

9 Louis Blériot (1872–1936), French

On June 29, 1908 at Issy, France, Blériot flew his Blériot VIII for 50 seconds, over 2,297 ft/500 m; on July 25, 1909 he became the first to fly across the English Channel.

10 Glenn Hammond Curtiss (1878–1930), US

On July 4, 1908 at Hammondsport, New York, Curtiss flew an AEA June Bug (1 min 42.5 sec; 5,090 ft/1,551 m), the first "official" flight in the US watched by a large crowd.

T O P 1 0

FIRST FLIGHTS OF MORE THAN ONE HOUR

	Pilot	Location	Duration			Date
			hr	min	sec	
1	Orville Wright	Fort Meyer, US	1	2	15.0	Sep 9, 1908
2	Orville Wright	Fort Meyer, US	1	5	52.0	Sep 10, 1908
3	Orville Wright	Fort Meyer, US	1	10	0.0	Sep 11, 1908
4	Orville Wright	Fort Meyer, US	1	15	20.0	Sep 12, 1908
5	Wilbur Wright	Auvours, France	1	31	25.8	Sep 21, 1908
6	Wilbur Wright	Auvours, France	1	7	24.8	Sep 28, 1908
7	Wilbur Wright*	Auvours, France	1	4	26.0	Oct 6, 1908
8	Wilbur Wright	Auvours, France	1	9	45.4	Oct 10, 1908
9	Wilbur Wright	Auvours, France	1	54	53.4	Dec 18, 1908
10	Wilbur Wright	Auvours, France	2	20	23.2	Dec 31, 1908

First-ever flight of more than one hour with a passenger (M.A. Fordyce)

The first pilot other than one of the Wright Brothers to remain airborne for longer than an hour was Paul Tissandier, who on May 20, 1909 flew for 1 hr 2 min 13 sec at Pont-Lond, near Pau, France. He was followed by Hubert Latham, an Anglo-French aviator, who on June 5, 1909, at Châlons, France, flew an *Antoinette IV* for 1 hr 7 min 37 sec, and by Henry Farman (July 20, 1909, at Châlons), with a flight of 1 hr 23 min 3.2 sec duration, Roger Sommer (who broke Wilbur Wright's record on August 7, 1909 with a flight of 2 hr 27 min 15 sec), and Louis Paulhan. The first flight lasting over an hour in the UK was by Samuel Franklin Cody (an American, but later a naturalized British citizen, and the first person in the UK to fly), in London on September 8, 1909; the flight lasted 1 hr 3 min 0 sec.

T O P 1 0

FIRST TRANSATLANTIC FLIGHTS

1 May 16–27, 1919*
Trepassy Harbor,
Newfoundland to Lisbon, Portugal
US Navy/Curtiss flying boat *NC-4*

Lt.-Cdr. Albert Cushing Read and a crew of five (Elmer Fowler Stone, Walter Hinton, James Lawrence Breese, Herbert Charles Rodd, and Eugene Saylor Rhoads) crossed the Atlantic in a series of hops, refueling at sea.

2 June 14–15, 1919
St. John's, Newfoundland to Galway, Ireland
Twin Rolls-Royce-engined converted Vickers Vimy bomber

British pilot Capt. John Alcock and Navigator Lt. Arthur Whitten Brown achieved the first non-stop flight, ditching in Derrygimla bog after their epic 16 hr 28 min journey.

3 July 2–6, 1919
East Fortune, Scotland to Roosevelt Field, New York
British *R-34* airship

Major George Herbert Scott and a crew of 30 (including the first-ever transatlantic air stowaway, William Ballantyne) made the first east–west crossing. It was the first airship to do so and, when it returned to Pulham, England on July 13, the first to complete a double crossing.

4 March 30–June 5, 1922
Lisbon, Portugal to Recife, Brazil
Fairey IIID seaplane *Santa Cruz*

Portuguese pilots Admiral Gago Coutinho and Commander Sacadura Cabral were the first to fly the South Atlantic in stages, though they replaced one damaged plane with another.

5 August 2–31, 1924
Orkneys, Scotland to Labrador, Canada
Two Douglas seaplanes, *Chicago* and *New Orleans*

Lt. Lowell H. Smith and Leslie P. Arnold in one biplane and Erik Nelson and John Harding in another set out and crossed the North Atlantic together in a series of hops via Iceland and Greenland.

6 October 12–15, 1924
Friedrichshafen, Germany to Lakehurst, New Jersey
Los Angeles, a renamed German-built *ZR 3* airship

Piloted by its inventor, Dr. Hugo Eckener, with 31 passengers and crew.

7 January 22–February 10, 1926
Huelva, Spain to Recife, Brazil
Plus Ultra, a Dornier Wal twin-engined flying boat

The Spanish crew – General Franco's brother Ramón with Julio Ruiz De Alda, Ensign Beran, and mechanic Pablo Rada – crossed in stages.

8 February 8–24, 1927
Cagliari, Sardinia to Recife, Brazil
Santa Maria, a Savoia-Marchetti S.55 flying boat

Francesco Marquis de Pinedo, Capt. Carlo del Prete, and Lt. Vitale Zacchetti crossed in stages as part of a goodwill trip to South America from Fascist Italy.

9 March 16–17, 1927
Lisbon, Portugal to Natal, Brazil
Dornier Wal flying boat

Portuguese flyers Sarmento de Beires and Jorge de Castilho took the route via Casablanca.

10 April 28–May 14, 1927
Genoa, Italy to Natal, Brazil
Savoia-Marchetti flying boat

A Brazilian crew of João De Barros, João Negrão, Newton Braga, and Vasco Cinquini set out on October 17, 1926, flying in stages via the Canaries and Cape Verde Islands.

* All dates refer to the actual Atlantic legs of the journeys; some started earlier and ended beyond their first transatlantic landfalls.

AVIATION AND AIRPORTS

TOP 10

BUSIEST AIRPORTS IN THE WORLD

	Airport	City/country	Terminal passengers per annum*
1	Chicago O'Hare	Chicago, Illinois	64,441,087
2	DFW International	Dallas/Fort Worth, Texas	51,943,567
3	LA International	Los Angeles, California	46,964,555
4	London Heathrow	London, UK	44,964,000
5	Tokyo-Haneda International	Tokyo, Japan	42,638,852
6	Hartsfield Atlanta International	Atlanta, Georgia	42,032,988
7	San Francisco International	San Francisco, California	31,789,021
8	Stapleton International	Denver, Colorado	30,877,180
9	Frankfurt	Frankfurt, Germany	30,183,000
10	J.F. Kennedy International	New York, New York	27,760,912

* *International and domestic flights*

CHICAGO O'HARE
Like the other six US airports in the world's ten busiest, O'Hare handles mainly domestic passengers. Only JFK sees enough international flights to put it in the international Top Ten.

TOP 10

BUSIEST INTERNATIONAL AIRPORTS IN THE WORLD

	Airport	City/country	International passengers per annum
1	London Heathrow	London, UK	38,246,000
2	Frankfurt	Frankfurt, Germany	23,814,000
3	Charles de Gaulle	Paris, France	22,444,000
4	Hong Kong	Hong Kong	22,060,000
5	Tokyo/Narita	Tokyo, Japan	19,022,000
6	London Gatwick	Gatwick, UK	18,688,000
7	Schiphol	Amsterdam, Netherlands	18,607,000
8	Singapore International	Singapore	17,087,000
9	J.F. Kennedy International	New York, New York	15,110,000
10	Zurich	Zurich, Switzerland	12,008,000

TOP 10

SCHEDULED AIRLINES WITH THE MOST PILOT DEVIATIONS, 1992

	Airline	Scheduled flight hours	Pilot deviations
1	American	1,921,972	52
2	US Air	1,194,058	30
3	Delta	1,694,292	27
4	United	1,531,780	26
5	Continental	943,243	15
6	Northwest	1,049,034	14
7	TWA	519,308	10
8	Southwest	422,512	7
9	America West	312,939	3
10	Federal Express*	369,720	2

* *Cargo carrier classified as scheduled airline*

A "pilot deviation" is defined as "the actions of a pilot that may result in the violation of a Federal Aviation Regulation or a North American Aerospace Air Defense Identification Zone Tolerance." Remarkably, none of these deviations led to a single fatality during 1992.

Source: National Transportation Safety Board

TOP 10

BUSIEST AIRPORTS IN THE US

	Airport	Total enplaned passengers (1993)
1	Chicago O'Hare, Illinois	29,133,604
2	Dallas/Fort Worth (Regional), Texas	24,655,922
3	Hartsfield Atlanta, Georgia	22,294,571
4	Los Angeles, California	18,456,714
5	Denver, Colorado	14,328,068
6	San Francisco, California	14,003,254
7	Phoenix, Arizona	11,294,603
8	Detroit, Michigan	11,027,172
9	Newark, New Jersey	10,965,362
10	Minneapolis, St. Paul, Minnesota	10,377,577

Source: Federal Aviation Authority

AIRLINES IN THE US

	Airline	Enplaned passengers (1993)
1	Delta	80,416,268
2	American	75,175,859
3	United	63,027,704
4	US Air	52,982,127
5	Northwest	39,592,069
6	Southwest	37,636,098
7	Continental	35,334,709
8	Trans World	17,964,791
9	America West	14,710,610
10	Alaska	6,157,673

The total includes passengers enplaned for US scheduled and nonscheduled flights. The total number of enplaned passengers on all US such flights in 1993 was 468,313,029.

Source: Federal Aviation Authority

COMPLAINTS AGAINST AIRLINES IN THE US

	Complaint	Total (1992)
1	Flight problems (cancellations, delays, etc)	1,624
2	Baggage	752
3	Refunds	721
4	Customer service (cabin service, meals, etc)	695
5	Ticketing/boarding	680
6	Fares	573
7	Oversales/bumping	265
8	Advertising	54
9	Smoking	25
10	Tours	12

Source: Federal Aviation Authority

CONCORDE
The only supersonic passenger aircraft, Concorde flies at twice the speed of sound.

AIRLINES IN THE WORLD

	Airline/country	Aircraft in service	Passenger-miles flown per annum*
1	Aeroflot (Russia)	103	85,250,982,700
2	American Airlines (US)	552	77,003,085,500
3	United Airlines (US)	462	75,943,470,300
4	Delta Airlines (US)	444	58,979,784,700
5	British Airways (UK)	228	41,504,468,500
6	Continental Airlines (US)	386	39,172,478,000
7	Northwest Airlines (US)	321	35,550,001,900
8	US Air (US)	454	35,549,529,100
9	TWA (US)	206	34,546,042,900
10	JAL (Japan)	98	34,296,669,900

* Total distance traveled by aircraft of these airlines multiplied by number of passengers carried

Departure gates and Eurolounge

LONDON HEATHROW
With nearly 45 million passengers annually, of whom 85 percent are on international flights, Heathrow is among the busiest of the world's airports.

AIRLINE-USING COUNTRIES

	Country	Passenger-miles flown per annum*
1	US	456,825,124,000
2	Russia	149,627,380,000
3	UK	65,243,337,000
4	Japan	62,448,407,000
5	France	32,877,982,000
6	Canada	29,275,895,000
7	Germany	26,244,266,000
8	Australia	25,350,073,000
9	Singapore	19,635,324,000
10	Netherlands	18,042,128,000

* Total distance traveled by aircraft of national airlines multiplied by number of passengers carried

AIR DISASTERS

DOWN IN FLAMES
The Hindenburg *was the ultimate in luxury air travel, but the explosion of the airship, which contained 7,000,000 cubic feet/200,000 cubic meters of hydrogen gas, put an end to plans to expand the use of lighter-than-air craft.*

T O P 1 0

FIRST AIRCRAFT FATALITIES

	Name	Nationality	Location	Date
1	Lt. Thomas Etholen Selfridge	American	Fort Myer, Virginia	Sep 17, 1908
2	Eugène Lefèbvre	French	Juvisy, France	Sep 7, 1909
3	Captain Ferdinand Ferber	French	Boulogne, France	Sep 22, 1909
4	Antonio Fernandez	Spanish	Nice, France	Dec 6, 1909
5	Aindan de Zoseley	Hungarian	Budapest, Hungary	Jan 2, 1910
6	Léon Delagrange	French	Croix d'Hins, France	Jan 4, 1910
7	Hubert Leblon	French	San Sebastián, Spain	Apr 2, 1910
8	Hauvette-Michelin	French	Lyons, France	May 13, 1910
9	Thaddeus Robl	German	Stettin, Germany	Jun 18, 1910
10	Charles Louis Wachter	French	Rheims, France	Jul 3, 1910

Following the Wright Brothers' first flights in 1903, the first four years of powered flying remained surprisingly accident-free. Although there had been many fatalities in the early years of ballooning and among pioneer parachutists, it was not until 1908 that anyone was killed in an airplane. On September 17, at Fort Myer, Virginia, Orville Wright was demonstrating his Type A *Flyer* to the US Army. On board was a passenger, 26-year-old Lieutenant Thomas Etholen Selfridge of the Army Signal Corps. At a height of just 75 feet/ 23 m, one of the propellers struck a wire, sending the plane out of control. It crash-landed, injuring Wright and killing Lt. Selfridge, who thus became powered flying's first victim.

T O P 1 0

WORST AIRSHIP DISASTERS IN THE WORLD

	Incident	killed
1	April 3, 1933, off the Atlantic coast of the US	73

US Navy airship Akron *crashed into the sea in a storm, leaving only three survivors in the world's worst airship tragedy.*

	Incident	killed
2	December 21, 1923, over the Mediterranean	52

French airship Dixmude, *assumed to have been struck by lightning, broke up and crashed into the sea; wreckage, believed to be from the airship, was found off Sicily 10 years later.*

	Incident	killed
3	October 5, 1930, near Beauvais, France	50

British airship R101 *crashed into a hillside leaving 48 dead, with two dying later, and six saved.*

	Incident	killed
4	August 24, 1921, off the coast near Hull, UK	44

Airship R38, *sold by the British Government to the US and renamed USN ZR-2, broke in two on a training and test flight.*

	Incident	killed
5	May 6, 1937, Lakehurst, New Jersey	36

German Zeppelin Hindenburg *caught fire when mooring.*

	Incident	killed
6	February 21, 1922, Hampton Roads, Virginia	34

Roma, *an Italian airship bought by the US Army, crashed killing all but 11 men on board.*

	Incident	killed
7	October 17, 1913, Berlin, Germany	28

German airship LZ18 *crashed after engine failure during a test flight at Berlin-Johannisthal.*

	Incident	killed
8	March 30, 1917, Baltic Sea	23

German airship SL9 *was struck by lightning on a flight from Seerappen to Seddin, and crashed into the sea.*

	Incident	killed
9	September 3, 1915, mouth of the River Elbe, Germany	19

German airship L10 *was struck by lightning and plunged into the sea.*

	Incident	killed
10=	September 9, 1913, off Heligoland	14

German navy airship L1 *crashed into the sea, leaving six survivors out of the 20 on board.*

	Incident	killed
10=	September 3, 1925, Caldwell, Ohio	14

US dirigible Shenandoah, *the first airship built in the US and the first to use safe helium instead of inflammable hydrogen, broke up in a storm, scattering sections over many miles of the Ohio countryside.*

T O P 1 0

WORST AIR DISASTERS IN THE WORLD

	Incident	Killed
1	March 27, 1977, Tenerife, Canary Islands	583

Two Boeing 747s (Pan Am and KLM, carrying 364 passengers and 16 crew and 230 passengers and 11 crew respectively) collided and caught fire on the runway of Los Rodeos airport after the pilots received incorrect control-tower instructions.

2	August 12, 1985, Mt. Ogura, Japan	520

A JAL Boeing 747 on an internal flight from Tokyo to Osaka crashed, killing all but four on board in the worst-ever disaster involving a single aircraft.

3	March 3, 1974, Paris, France	346

A Turkish Airlines DC-10 crashed at Ermenonville, north of Paris, immediately after takeoff for London, with many English rugby supporters among the dead.

4	June 23, 1985, off the Irish coast	329

An Air India Boeing 747 on a flight from Vancouver to Delhi exploded in midair, perhaps as a result of a terrorist bomb.

5	August 19, 1980, Riyadh, Saudi Arabia	301

A Saudia (Saudi Arabian) Airlines Lockheed Tristar caught fire during an emergency landing.

6	July 3, 1988, off the Iranian coast	290

An Iran Air A300 airbus was shot down in error by a missile fired by the USS Vincennes.

7	May 25, 1979, Chicago, Illinois	275

The worst air disaster in the US occurred when an engine fell off a DC-10 as it took off from Chicago O'Hare airport and the plane plunged out of control, killing all 273 on board and two on the ground.

8	December 21, 1988, Lockerbie, Scotland	270

Pan Am Flight 103 from London Heathrow to New York exploded in midair as a result of a terrorist bomb, killing 243 passengers, 16 crew, and 11 on the ground in the UK's worst-ever air disaster.

9	September 1, 1983, Sakhalin Island, off the Siberian coast	269

A Korean Air Lines Boeing 747 that had strayed into Soviet airspace was shot down by a Soviet fighter.

10	April 26, 1994, Nagoya airport, Japan	262

A China Airlines Airbus A300-600R, on a flight from Taipai, Taiwan, stalled and crashed while landing at Nagoya airport, Japan.

Three further air disasters have resulted in the deaths of more than 250 people: on July 11, 1991 a DC-8 carrying Muslim pilgrims from Mecca to Nigeria crashed on takeoff, killing 261; on November 28, 1979 an Air New Zealand DC-10 crashed near Mount Erebus, Antarctica, while on a sightseeing trip, killing 257 passengers and crew; and on December 12, 1985 an Arrow Air DC-8 crashed on takeoff at Gander, Newfoundland, killing all 256 on board, including 248 members of the 101st US Airborne Division.

T O P 1 0

WORST AIR DISASTERS IN THE US

	Incident	Killed
1	May 25, 1979, Chicago, Illinois	275

An American Airlines DC-10 crashed on takeoff from Chicago O'Hare airport after an engine fell off, killing all 273 on board and two on the ground in the world's worst single aircraft disaster to date; as a result, all DC-10s were temporarily grounded.

2	August 16, 1987, Romulus, Michigan	156

A Northwest Airlines McDonnell Douglas MD-80 crashed onto a road following an engine fire after takeoff from Detroit. A girl aged four was the only survivor.

3	July 19, 1982, Kenner, Louisiana	154

A Pan American Boeing 727 crashed after takeoff from New Orleans for Las Vegas, killing all on board (138 passenger and the crew of eight) and eight on the ground.

4	September 25, 1978, San Diego, California	144

A Pacific Southwest Boeing 727 collided in the air with a Cessna 172 light aircraft killing 135 in the airliner, two in the Cessna and seven on the ground.

5	December 16, 1960, New York	135

A United Air Lines DC-8 with 77 passengers and a crew of seven and a TWA Super Constellation with 39 passengers and four crew collided in a snowstorm. The DC-8 crashed in Brooklyn killing eight on the ground; the Super Constellation crashed in Staten Island harbor, killing all on board.

6	August 2, 1985, Dallas-Ft. Worth Airport, Texas	133

A Delta Airlines TriStar crashed when a severe down-draft affected it during landing.

7	June 30, 1956, Grand Canyon, Arizona	128

A United Airlines DC-7 and a TWA Super Constellation collided in the air, killing all on board both in the worst civil aviation disaster to that date.

8	June 24, 1975, JFK Airport, New York	113

An Eastern Air Lines Boeing 727 on a flight from New Orleans crashed while attempting to land in a storm.

9	September 4, 1971, Mount Fairweather, Alaska	109

An Alaska Airlines Boeing 727 crashed in a storm as it approached Juneau Airport.

10	July 19, 1989, Sioux City, Iowa	107

A United Air Lines DC-10 crashed en route from Denver to Chicago after an engine explosion.

The 1988 Lockerbie crash (see The 10 Worst Air Disasters in the World) is the US' worst air disaster outside US territory. Before that, the worst was the crash of a chartered Arrow Air DC-8 during take-off from Gander, Newfoundland on December 12, 1985. All 256 on board were killed, including 248 members of the 101st US Airborne Division. The most potentially disastrous domestic incident took place on July 28, 1945 when a US Army B-25 bomber crashed into the 78th and 79th floors of the Empire State Building, hurling blazing wreckage completely through the building. The crew of three and 11 office workers were killed and a further 25 people were injured.

US TOURISM

TOP 10

COUNTRIES OF ORIGIN OF TOURISTS TO THE US

	Country*	Annual visitors
1	Japan	3,950,000
2	UK	2,980,000
3	Germany	1,710,000
4	Mexico	1,530,000
5	France	860,000
6	Italy	640,000
7	Brazil	490,000
8	China	480,000
9	Australia	470,000
10	Netherlands	390,000

* *Excluding Canada*

TOP 10

TRAVEL AGENCIES IN THE US

	Agency	Air sales 1993 ($)
1	American Express	4,300,000,000
2	Carlson	1,950,000,000
3	Thomas Cook	1,632,000,000
4	Rosenbluth	1,300,000,000
5	Maritz	915,000,000
6	US Travel	852,883,000
7	IVI	680,000,000
8	Omega World Travel	352,000,000
9	World Travel Partners	306,000,000
10	Wagonlit	282,000,000

Source: Business Travel News

Thomas Cook, at No. 3, is actually a British company. The founder, Thomas Cook, invented the package tour in the mid-19th century, when he began to organize excursions by railroad for working people; from these beginnings his business grew to become the best-known travel company in the world.

TOP 10

HISTORIC HOUSES IN THE US

1	Graceland, Memphis, Tennessee
2	Isabella Stewart Gardner Museum, Boston, Massachusetts
3	Gallier House Museum, New Orleans, Louisiana
4	Bonnet House, Ft. Lauderdale, Florida
5	Falling Water, Mill Run, Pennsylvania
6	Victoria Mansion, Portland, Maine
7	Melrose, Natchez, Mississippi
8	Bayou Bend, Houston, Texas
9	Olana, Hudson, New York
10	Gamble House, Pasadena, California

TOP 10

ART MUSEUMS IN THE US

	Art museum	Annual visitors
1	National Gallery of Art, Washington, DC	7,500,000
2	Metropolitan Museum of Art, New York	3,700,000
3	Art Institute of Chicago	1,800,000
4	Museum of Modern Art, New York	1,600,000
5	Hirshhorn Museum and Sculpture Garden, Washington, DC	1,300,000
6	Detroit Institute of Art	1,000,000
7	Museum of Fine Arts, Boston	894,000
8	Los Angeles County Museum of Art	880,000
9	Whitney Museum of Art, New York	837,000
10	Museum of Fine Arts, Houston	631,000

FINAL RESTING PLACE?
Graceland, in Memphis, the palatial former home of Elvis Presley, attracts 600,000 visitors a year – more than any other historical house in the US. Many people come to pay their respects at Elvis's grave – that is, if they believe that he is really dead . . .

T O P   1 0

AMUSEMENT PARKS IN THE US

	Park	No. of visitors (1993 estimate)
1	The Magic Kingdom of Walt Disney World, Lake Buena Vista, FL	12,000,000
2	Disneyland, Anaheim, CA	11,400,000
3	EPCOT at Walt Disney World	10,000,000
4	Disney-MGM Studios at Walt Disney World	8,000,000
5	Universal Studios Florida, Orlando, FL	7,400,000
6	Universal Studios Hollywood, Universal City, CA	4,950,000
7	Sea World of Florida, Orlando, FL	4,500,000
8	Sea World of California, San Diego, CA	4,000,000
9	Knott's Berry Farm, Buena Park, CA	3,700,000
10	Cedar Point, Sandusky, OH	3,600,000

T O P   1 0

ZOOS IN THE US

	Zoo	Annual visitors
1	Lincoln Park Zoo, Chicago	4,000,000
2	San Diego Zoo	3,500,000
3	National Zoo, DC	3,000,000
4=	St. Louis Zoo	2,300,000
4=	International Wildlife Conservation Center, Bronx, New York	2,300,000
6=	Brookfield Zoo, Chicago	2,000,000
6=	Houston Zoo	2,000,000
8	Milwaukee Zoo	1,800,000
9	Los Angeles Zoo	1,700,000
10	Cincinnati Zoo	1,500,000

A NATIONAL TREASURE
The National Gallery of Art (above) and the Hirschhorn Museum and Sculpture Garden are both part of the Smithsonian Institution, Washington, DC. The Smithsonian encompasses centers of excellence in many areas of human endeavor, including the visual and performing arts, the sciences, and technology.

T O P   1 0

MOST VISITED STATES

	State	Annual visitors		State	Annual visitors
1	California	6,192,000	6	Washington	2,108,000
2	New York	5,382,000	7	Arizona	1,982,000
3	Texas	5,032,000	8	Nevada	1,267,000
4	Florida	3,853,000	9	Massachusetts	1,253,000
5	Hawaii	2,203,000	10	Michigan	1,172,000

Of the Top 10, the order of the states most visited by overseas tourists differs somewhat, with Washington, DC, which is 11th overall, moving up to 5th place, and Illinois (12th overall) into 9th, replacing Washington and Michigan.

T O P   1 0

LEAST VISITED STATES

	State	Annual visitors		State	Annual visitors
1	Mississippi	58,000	6	Kansas	76,000
2	Rhode Island	61,000	7	Alaska	111,000
3	Arkansas	65,000	8	Oklahoma	117,000
4	Delaware	68,000	9	Iowa	118,000
5	Nebraska	69,000	10	South Dakota	125,000

WORLD TOURISM

T O P 1 O

COUNTRIES WITH MOST TOURISTS

	Country	Annual arrivals/ departures
1	France	58,500,000
2	US	45,500,000
3	Spain	36,054,000
4	Italy	26,974,000
5	Hungary	22,500,000
6	Austria	19,474,000
7	UK	17,855,000
8	Mexico	17,587,000
9	Germany	15,950,000
10	Canada	15,400,000

Spain has been dislodged from its former No. 1 position in this list, while, as a result of the recent military conflict in the Balkans, former Yugoslavia, a country which once featured prominently in the Top 10 (in 2nd place a decade ago), had by 1992 plummeted to 62nd place with just 700,000 intrepid tourists.

T O P 1 O

CRUISE SHIP VISITS

	Country	Annual arrivals
1	Bahamas	2,020,000
2	Mexico	1,629,000
3	US Virgin Islands	1,215,000
4	Puerto Rico	891,000
5	Spain	826,000
6	St Martin	502,000
7	Jamaica	490,000
8	Korea	481,000
9	Cayman Islands	475,000
10	Martinique	417,000

The cruise vessel business is the most rapidly growing sector of the travel industry, with a compound annual growth rate of almost 10 percent over the past 12 years. In 1992 a total of 130 ships served the US and Canadian market alone, sailing particularly from Miami and other ports in Florida, and serving some 3,500,000 passengers.

THE LOUVRE
The Musée du Louvre – home to the Mona Lisa *– contains one of the world's most important art collections. It was originally constructed in 1190 as a fortress to protect Paris from Viking raids, and was first opened to the public in 1793, following the Revolution.*

T O P 1 O

DESTINATIONS OF JAPANESE TOURISTS

	Country	Trips (%)
1	US	28.0
2	Korea	12.2
3	Hong Kong	10.6
4	Singapore	7.5
5	Taiwan	6.9
6=	Germany	5.6
6=	Italy	5.6
8	China	5.4
9	Guam	4.9
10	Thailand	4.7

In recent years tourism by Japanese nationals has become one of the most important contributors to the international travel industry. Japanese subjects are especially welcomed by the retail trade as the highest spending per head of any travelers. Almost 12,000,000, some 10 percent of the entire population, went abroad in 1992, and it is predicted that, by the year 2005 their expenditure and that of Germany, another major overseas spending nation, will together exceed that of the current world leader, the United States.

EIFFEL TOWER
When the Eiffel Tower was erected for the Universal Exhibition of 1889, it was meant to be a temporary addition to the Paris skyline. In fact, it outraged many Parisians who felt it was an eyesore. The world's tallest building until New York's Empire State Building was completed in 1931, the Eiffel Tower has become the symbol of Paris.

T O P 1 O

OVERSEAS DESTINATIONS MOST FEARED BY THE BRITISH

	Country	% fearing		Country	% fearing
1	Bosnia	86	6	Nicaragua	40
2	Iraq	80	7	Colombia	35
3	Iran	67	8	Russia	33
4	Libya	61	9	Egypt	32
5	El Salvador	46	10	Bolivia	30

This list is based on a survey conducted among British vacationers by the Home and Overseas Insurance Company, which insures one in three British vacationers. The survey also reported that, following reports of robbery and violence in Florida and other US resorts, 21 percent included the United States among their "most feared." Most European countries, other than Russia, are considered 99–100 percent safe. This compares with just 16 percent who said they feared traveling in Péru, a country which is included on the US State Department's "no go" list, and 14 percent who believed that China and India were unsafe. Of Western European countries, Britons placed Germany at the head of their list – although their fear of visiting the country may be allied more to their concerns about the rate of exchange between the Deutsche Mark and Sterling than to any perceived danger.

TOP 10
TOURIST EARNERS

	Country	Annual receipts ($)
1	US	53,861,000,000
2	France	25,000,000,000
3	Spain	22,181,000,000
4	Italy	21,577,000,000
5	UK	13,683,000,000
6	Austria	13,250,000,000
7	Germany	10,982,000,000
8	Switzerland	7,650,000,000
9	Hong Kong	6,037,000,000
10	Mexico	5,997,000,000

TOP 10
TOURIST SPENDERS

	Tourist country of origin	Annual expenditure ($)
1	US	39,872,000,000
2	Germany	37,309,000,000
3	Japan	26,837,000,000
4	UK	19,831,000,000
5	Italy	16,617,000,000
6	France	13,910,000,000
7	Canada	11,265,000,000
8	Netherlands	9,330,000,000
9	Taiwan	7,098,000,000
10	Austria	6,895,000,000

TOP 10
TOURIST ATTRACTIONS IN FRANCE

	Attraction	Annual visitors
1	Euro Disney	11,000,000
2	Pompidou Centre, Paris (art and culture center)	8,262,513
3	Eiffel Tower, Paris	5,757,357
4	Parc de La Villette, Paris (City of Science)	5,300,000
5	Musée du Louvre, Paris	4,900,000
6	Versailles Palace	4,211,000
7	Musée d'Orsay, Paris	3,000,000
8	Les Invalides, Paris (museums, Napoleon's tomb)	1,212,271
9	Parc Astérix (theme park)	1,100,000
10	Chenonceaux Château, Loire Valley	850,000

France's newest Top 10 tourist attraction, Euro Disney, created in the French countryside at a cost of $4,000,000,000, opened to the public on April 12, 1992. Despite attaining its annual target of 11,000,000 visitors it has been beset with financial problems, losing more than $930,000,000 in 1993.

TOP 10
TRAVEL SHOPPERS

	Country of origin	Average spend per head ($)*
1	Japan	389.83
2	Korea	360.00
3	Australia	340.91
4	Qatar	312.50
5	South Africa	300.00
6	Norway	260.00
7	Kuwait	250.00
8	New Zealand	237.50
9	Israel	216.67
10	Oman	200.00
	US	190.48

* *Shopping during travel overseas, including duty-free purchases*

Shopping by international travelers was reckoned to be worth $50,000,000,000 in 1992. The US was the greatest beneficiary, with earnings of some $5,600,000,000, followed by France ($3,350,000,000) and the UK ($3,250,000,000). The country receiving the highest average spend per traveler was the United Arab Emirates, with an estimated $848.38.

SPORTS & GAMES

T O P 1 0

LONGEST-STANDING CURRENT OLYMPIC RECORDS

	Event	Winning time/distance	Competitor/ nationality	Date when record was set
1	Men's long jump	29 ft 2½ in/8.90 m	Bob Beamon (US)	Oct 18, 1968
2	Men's javelin	310 ft 3½ in/94.58 m	Miklos Nemeth (Hun)	Jul 25, 1976
3	Women's shotput	73 ft 6¼ in/22.41 m	Ilona Slupianek (GDR)	Jul 24, 1980
4	Women's 800 meters	1 min 53.43 sec	Nadezhda Olizarenko (USSR)	Jul 27, 1980
5	Women's 4 x 100 meters relay	41.60 sec	GDR	Aug 1, 1980
6	Men's 1500 meters	3 min 32.53 sec	Sebastian Coe (UK)	Aug 1, 1980
7	Women's marathon	2 hr 24 min 52 sec	Joan Benoit (US)	Aug 5, 1984
8	Men's 800 meters	1 min 43.00 sec	Joaquim Cruz (Bra)	Aug 6, 1984
9	Decathlon	8,847 points	Daley Thompson (UK)	Aug 9, 1984
10	Men's 5000 meters	13 min 05.59 sec	Said Aouita (Mor)	Aug 11, 1984

Bob Beamon's record-breaking jump in 1968 is regarded as one of the greatest achievements in athletics. He was aided by Mexico City's rarefied atmosphere, but to add a staggering 21¾ ins/55.25 cm to the old record, and win the competition by 28½ ins/72.39 cm, was no mean feat. Beamon's jump of 29 ft 2½ ins/8.90 m was the first beyond both 28 and 29 feet (8.53 and 8.84 m). The next 28 ft/8.53 m jump in the Olympics was not until 1980, 12 years later. The "unbeatable" world record was finally broken during the 1991 World Championships in Tokyo, by American Mike Powell.

Roger Bannister (UK)
Oxford, England
May 6, 1954
3:59.4

John Landy (Aus)
Turku, Finland
Jun 21, 1954
3:58.0

Derek
Ibbotson
London,
England
Jul 19, 1
3:57.2

TOP 10

FASTEST MEN ON EARTH

	Athlete/nationality	Venue	Date	Time (sec)
1	Leroy Burrell (US)	Lausanne	Jul 6, 1994	9.85
2	Carl Lewis (US)	Tokyo	Aug 25, 1991	9.86
3	Leroy Burrell (US)	Tokyo	Aug 25, 1991	9.88
4=	Dennis Mitchell (US)	Tokyo	Aug 25, 1991	9.91
4=	Davidson Ezinwa (Nig)	Azusa	Apr 11, 1992	9.91
6	Linford Christie (UK)	Tokyo	Aug 25, 1991	9.92
7=	Calvin Smith (US)	Colorado Springs	Jul 3, 1983	9.93
7=	Mike Marsh (US)	Walnut	Apr 18, 1992	9.93
9=	Jim Hines (US)	Mexico City	Oct 14, 1968	9.95
9=	Frankie Fredericks (Nam)	Tokyo	Aug 25, 1991	9.95

The fastest-ever 100 meters, with wind assistance, was at Indianapolis on July 16, 1988, when Carl Lewis was timed at 9.78 seconds, but he had the benefit of winds measuring 17 feet/5.2 meters per second.

TOP 10

LONGEST LONG JUMPS

	Athlete/nationality	Location	Date	ft	in	m
1	Mike Powell (US)	Tokyo	Aug 30, 1991	29	4	8.95
2	Bob Beamon (US)	Mexico City	Oct 18, 1968	29	2½	8.90
3	Robert Emmiyan (USSR)	Tsakhadzor	May 22, 1987	29	0	8.86
4=	Carl Lewis (US)	Indianapolis	Jun 19, 1983	28	10	8.79
4=	Carl Lewis (US)	New York*	Jan 27, 1984	28	10	8.79
6=	Carl Lewis (US)	Indianapolis	Jul 24, 1982	28	9	8.76
6=	Carl Lewis (US)	Indianapolis	Jul 18, 1988	28	9	8.76
8	Carl Lewis (US)	Indianapolis	Aug 16, 1987	28	8½	8.75
9	Larry Myricks (US)	Indianapolis	Jul 18, 1988	28	8	8.74
10	Carl Lewis (US)	Seoul	Sep 26, 1988	28	7	8.72

Indoors

THE PROGRESSION OF THE WORLD MILE RECORD SINCE THE FIRST SUB-FOUR-MINUTE MILE

Herb Elliott (Aus)
Dublin, Ireland
Aug 6, 1958
3:54.5

Peter Snell (NZ)
Wanganui, New Zealand
Jan 27, 1962
3:54.4

Peter Snell (NZ)
Wanganui, New Zealand
Nov 17, 1964
3:54.1

Michel Jazy (Fra)
Rennes, France
Jun 9, 1965
3:53.6

Jim Ryun (US)
Berkeley, US
Jul 17, 1966
3:51.3

Jim Ryun (US)
Berkeley, US
Jun 23, 1967
3:51.1

John Walker (NZ)
Gothenburg, Sweden
Aug 12, 1975
3:49.4

Filbert Bayi (Tan)
Kingston, Jamaica
May 17, 1975
3:51.0

Sebastian Coe (UK)
Oslo, Norway
Jul 17, 1979
3:49.0

Steve Ovett (UK)
Oslo, Norway
Jul 1, 1980
3:48.8

Sebastian Coe (UK)
Zurich, Switzerland
Aug 19, 1981
3:48.53

Steve Ovett (UK)
Koblenz, Germany
Aug 26, 1981
3:48.40

Sebastian Coe (UK)
Brussels, Belgium
Aug 28, 1981
3:47.33

Steve Cram (UK)
Oslo, Norway
Jul 27, 1985
3:46.32

Noureddine Morcelli (Alg)
Rieti, Italy
Sep 5, 1993
3:44.39

260

BASEBALL

TEAMS WITH THE MOST WORLD SERIES WINS

	Team*	Wins
1	New York Yankees	22
2=	Philadelphia/Kansas City/ Oakland Athletics	9
2=	St. Louis Cardinals	9
4	Brooklyn/Los Angeles Dodgers	6
5=	Boston Red Sox	5
5=	Cincinnati Reds	5
5=	New York/San Francisco Giants	5

	Team*	Wins
5=	Pittsburgh Pirates	5
9	Detroit Tigers	4
10=	St. Louis/ Baltimore Orioles	3
10=	Washington Senators/ Minnesota Twins	3

* Teams separated by / indicate changes of franchise and are regarded as the same team for Major League record purposes.

Major League baseball started in the U S with the forming of the National League in 1876. The rival American League was started in 1901, and two years later Pittsburgh, champions of the National League, invited American League champions Boston to take part in a best-of-nine games series to establish the "real" champions. Boston won 5–3. The following year the National League champions, New York, refused to play Boston and there was no World Series. However, it was resumed in 1905 and has been held every year since. It has been a best-of-seven games series since 1905, with the exception of 1919–21, when it reverted to a nine-game series.

PLAYERS WITH THE HIGHEST CAREER BATTING AVERAGES

	Player	At bat	Hits	Average*
1	Ty Cobb	11,429	4,191	.367
2	Rogers Hornsby	8,137	2,930	.360
3	Joe Jackson	4,981	1,774	.356
4	Ed Delahanty	7,502	2,591	.345
5=	Billy Hamilton	6,284	2,163	.344
5=	Tris Speaker	10,208	3,515	.344
5=	Ted Williams	7,706	2,654	.344
8	Willie Keeler	8,585	2,947	.343
9=	Dan Brouthers	6,711	2,296	.342
9=	Harry Heilmann	7,787	2,660	.342
9=	Babe Ruth	8,399	2,873	.342

* Calculated by dividing the number of hits by the number of times a batter was "at bat".

OLDEST STADIUMS IN MAJOR LEAGUE BASEBALL

	Stadium	Home club	Year built
1=	Tiger Stadium	Detroit Tigers	1912
1=	Fenway Park	Boston Red Sox	1912
3	Wrigley Field	Chicago Cubs	1914
4	Yankee Stadium	New York Yankees	1923
5	Cleveland Stadium	Cleveland Indians	1931*
6	Mile High Stadium	Colorado Rockies	1948#
7	County Stadium	Milwaukee Brewers	1953
8	Candlestick Park	San Francisco Giants	1960
9	Dodger Stadium	Los Angeles Dodgers	1962
10	Shea Stadium	New York Mets	1964

* First used for baseball in 1933
 # First used for baseball in 1993

Each stadium has a unique history, but the Yankee Stadium is particularly notable for its association with Babe Ruth, the best-known name in baseball. The Stadium was built during the early 1920s to hold the huge crowds that he attracted, and was known as "The House Babe Built" because the revenue he brought in financed its construction.

LARGEST MAJOR LEAGUE BALLPARKS

(By capacity)

	Stadium	Home club	Capacity
1	Mile High Stadium	Colorado Rockies	76,100
2	Anaheim Stadium	California Angels	64,593
3	Veterans Stadium	Philadelphia Phillies	62,382
4	Candlestick Park	San Francisco Giants	62,000
5	The Kingdome	Seattle Mariners	59,702
6	Jack Murphy Stadium	San Diego Padres	59,022
7	Three Rivers Stadium	Pittsburgh Pirates	58,727
8	Yankee Stadium	New York Yankees	57,545
9	Busch Stadium	St Louis Cardinals	56,227
10	Dodger Stadium	Los Angeles Dodgers	56,000

Stadium capacities vary constantly, some being adjusted according to the event: Veterans Stadium, for example, holds fewer for baseball games than for football. Baseball's newest ballpark, Jacobs Field, home of the Cleveland Indians, was opened on April 4, 1994 and has a capacity of 42,400.

BADGE OF HONOR
Shown here is the emblem of the New York Mets, who have been a major league team since 1962.

TOP 10

PLAYERS WHO PLAYED THE MOST GAMES IN A CAREER

	Player	Games		Player	Games
1	Pete Rose	3,562	6	Willie Mays	2,992
2	Carl Yastrzemski	3,308	7	Rusty Staub	2,951
3	Hank Aaron	3,298	8	Brooks Robinson	2,896
4	Ty Cobb	3,034	9	Robin Yount	2,856
5	Stan Musial	3,026	10	Dave Winfield	2,850

TOP 10

PLAYERS WHO ACHIEVED THE MOST RUNS IN A CAREER

(Regular season only, excluding World Series)

	Player	Runs		Player	Runs
1	Ty Cobb	2,245	6	Stan Musial	1,949
2=	Babe Ruth	2,174	7	Lou Gehrig	1,888
2=	Hank Aaron	2,174	8	Tris Speaker	1,881
4	Pete Rose	2,165	9	Mel Ott	1,859
5	Willie Mays	2,062	10	Frank Robinson	1,829

TOP 10

SALARIES IN MAJOR LEAGUE BASEBALL IN 1994

	Player	Team	Salary ($)*
1	Bobby Bonilla	New York Mets	6,300,000
2	Ryne Sandberg#	Chicago Cubs	5,975,000
3	Joe Carter	Toronto Blue Jays	5,500,000
4	Rafael Palmeiro	Baltimore Orioles	5,406,603
5	Carl Ripken Jr.	Baltimore Orioles	5,400,000
6	Robert Alomar	Toronto Blue Jays	5,333,334
7	Jack McDowell	Chicago White Sox	5,300,000
8	Jimmy Key	New York Yankees	5,250,000
9	Kirby Puckett	Minnesota Twins	5,200,000
10	Roger Clemens	Boston Red Sox	5,155,250

* *Figures include base salary and prorated signing bonuses as of opening day*
\# *Retired midseason*

THE TEN

FIRST PLAYERS TO HIT FOUR HOME RUNS IN ONE GAME

	Player/club	Date
1	Bobby Lowe, Boston	May 30, 1884
2	Ed Delahanty, Philadelphia	Jul 13, 1896
3	Lou Gehrig, New York	Jun 3, 1932
4	Chuck Klein, Philadelphia	Jul 10, 1936
5	Pat Seerey, Chicago	Jul 18, 1948
6	Gil Hodges, Brooklyn	Aug 31, 1950
7	Joe Adcock, Milwaukee	Jul 31, 1954
8	Rocky Colavito, Cleveland	Jun 10, 1959
9	Willie Mays, San Francisco	Apr 30, 1961
10	Mike Schmidt, Philadelphia	Apr 17, 1976

The only other players to score four homers in one game are Bob Horner, who did so for Atlanta on July 6, 1986, and Mark Whitten, for St. Louis, on September 7, 1993.

THE TEN

FIRST PITCHERS TO THROW PERFECT GAMES

	Player	Match	Date
1	Lee Richmond	Worcester *v* Cleveland	Jun 12, 1880
2	Monte Ward	Provident *v* Boston	Jun 17, 1880
3	Cy Young	Boston *v* Philadelphia	May 5, 1904
4	Adrian Joss	Cleveland *v* Chicago	Oct 2, 1908
5	Charlie Robertson	Chicago *v* Detroit	Apr 30, 1922
6	Don Larson*	New York *v* Brooklyn	Oct 8, 1956
7	Jim Bunning	Philadelphia *v* New York	Jun 21, 1964
8	Sandy Koufax	Los Angeles *v* Chicago	Sep 9, 1965
9	Catfish Hunter	Oakland *v* Minnesota	May 8, 1968
10	Len Barker	Cleveland *v* Toronto	May 15, 1981

* *Larson's perfect game was, appropriately, in the World Series*

Fourteen pitchers have thrown perfect games; that is, they have pitched in all nine innings, dismissing 27 opposing batters, and without conceding a run. The last player to pitch a perfect game was Kenny Rogers, for Texas against California, on July 28, 1994.

BASKETBALL

BIGGEST ARENAS IN THE NBA

	Arena/location	Home team	Capacity
1	Charlotte Coliseum, Charlotte, North Carolina	Charlotte Hornets	23,698
2	The Palace of Auburn Hills, Auburn Hills, Michigan	Detroit Pistons	21,454
3	The Coliseum, Richfield, Ohio	Cleveland Cavaliers	20,273
4	Meadowlands Arena, East Rutherford, New Jersey	New Jersey Nets	20,029
5	The Alamodome, San Antonio, Texas	San Antonio Spurs	20,500
6	Delta Center Arena, Salt Lake City, Utah	Utah Jazz	19,911
7	Madison Square Garden, New York	New York Knicks	19,763
8	America West Arena, Phoenix, Arizona	Phoenix Suns	19,023
9	Target Center, Minneapolis, Minnesota	Minnesota Timberwolves	19,006
10	US Air Arena, Landover, Maryland	Washington Bullets	18,756

The Chicago Bulls and the Cleveland Cavaliers will move into new stadiums for the 1994–95 season – the United Center (21,500 capacity) and the Gateway Arena (20,750) respectively. The smallest arena is the 12,888 capacity Memorial Coliseum, home of the Portland Trailblazers. The largest ever NBA stadium was the Louisiana Superdome used by Utah Jazz from 1975 to 1979, which was capable of holding crowds of 47,284.

POINTS AVERAGES IN AN NBA SEASON

	Player	Club	Season	Average
1	Wilt Chamberlain	Philadelphia	1961–62	50.4
2	Wilt Chamberlain	San Francisco	1962–63	44.8
3	Wilt Chamberlain	Philadelphia	1960–61	38.4
4	Elgin Baylor	Los Angeles	1961–62	38.3
5	Wilt Chamberlain	Philadelphia	1959–60	37.6
6	Michael Jordan	Chicago	1986–87	37.1
7	Wilt Chamberlain	San Francisco	1963–64	36.9
8	Rick Barry	San Francisco	1966–67	35.6
9	Michael Jordan	Chicago	1987–88	35.0
10=	Elgin Baylor	Los Angeles	1960–61	34.8
10=	Kareem Abdul-Jabbar	Milwaukee	1971–72	34.8

HIGHEST-EARNING PLAYERS IN THE NBA, 1993–94

	Player	Team	Earnings ($)
1	David Robinson	San Antonio Spurs	5,740,000
2	John Williams	Cleveland Cavaliers	4,570,000
3	Vlade Divac	Los Angeles Lakers	4,133,000
4=	Robert Parish	Boston Red Sox	4,000,000
4=	Ron Harper	Los Angeles Clippers	4,000,000
6	Sam Perkins	Seattle Supersonics	3,587,000
7	Benoit Benjamin	New Jeresey Nets	3,575,000
8	Patrick Ewing	New York Knicks	3,525,000
9	Danny Ferry	Cleveland Cavaliers	3,543,000
10	Brad Daugherty	Cleveland Cavaliers	3,541,000

KAREEM ABDUL-JABBAR
In his 20-year career Abdul-Jabbar, shown here playing for the LA Lakers, appeared in more games than any other NBA player. His total points score is still unequaled.

TOP 10

TEAMS WITH THE MOST NBA TITLES

	Team*	Titles
1	Boston Celtics	16
2	Minnesota/Los Angeles Lakers	11
3=	Chicago Bulls	3
3=	Philadelphia/ Golden State Warriors	3
3=	Syracuse Nationals/ Philadelphia 76ers	3
6=	Detroit Pistons	2
6=	New York Knicks	2
8=	Baltimore Bullets	1
8=	Houston Rockets	1
8=	Milwaukee Bucks	1
8=	Rochester Royals#	1
8=	St Louis Hawks**	1
8=	Seattle Supersonics	1
8=	Portland Trail Blazers	1
8=	Washington Bullets	1

Basketball is one of the few sports that can trace its exact origins. It was invented by Dr. James Naismith at Springfield, Massachusetts, in 1891. Professional basketball in the US dates to 1898, but the National Basketball Association (NBA) was not formed until 1949, when the National Basketball League and Basketball Association of America merged. The NBA consists of 27 teams split into Eastern and Western Conferences. At the end of an 82-game regular season, the top eight teams in each Conference play off and the two Conference champions meet in a best-of-seven final for the NBA Championship.

* *Teams separated by / indicate change of franchise: they have won the championship under both names.*
# *Now the Sacramento Kings*
** *Now the Atlanta Hawks*

TOP 10

PLAYERS TO HAVE PLAYED MOST GAMES IN THE NBA AND ABA

	Player	Games played
1	Kareem Abdul-Jabbar	1,560
2	Moses Malone*	1,438
3	Robert Parish*	1,413
4	Artis Gilmore	1,329
5	Elvin Hayes	1,303
6	Caldwell Jones	1,299
7	John Havlicek	1,270
8	Paul Silas	1,254
9	Julius Erving	1,243
10	Dan Issel	1,218

* *Still active*

The ABA (American Basketball Association) was established as a rival to the NBA in 1968 and survived until 1976. Because many of the sport's top players "defected," their figures are still included in this list.

TOP 10

POINTS-SCORERS IN AN NBA CAREER

(*Regular season games only*)

	Player	Total points		Player	Total points
1	Kareem Abdul-Jabbar	38,387	6	John Havlicek	26,395
2	Wilt Chamberlain	31,419	7	Alex English	25,613
3	Moses Malone*	27,360	8	Jerry West	25,192
4	Elvin Hayes	27,313	9	Dominique Wilkins*	24,019
5	Oscar Robertson	26,710	10	Adrian Dantley	23,177

* *Active at end of 1993–94 season*

If points from the ABA were also considered then Abdul-Jabbar would still be number one, with the same total. The greatest points-scorer in NBA history, he was born as Lew Alcindor but adopted a new name when he converted to the Islamic faith in 1969. The following year he turned professional, playing for Milwaukee. His career spanned 20 seasons before he retired at the end of the 1989 season. Despite scoring an NBA record 38,387 points he could not emulate the great Wilt Chamberlain by scoring 100 points in a game, which Chamberlain achieved for Philadelphia against New York at Hershey, Pennsylvania on March 2, 1962. Chamberlain also scored 70 points in a game six times, a feat Abdul-Jabbar never succeeded in rivaling.

TOP 10

MOST SUCCESSFUL NBA COACHES

	Coach	Games won*
1	Red Auerbach	938
2	Lenny Wilkens#	926
3	Jack Ramsay	864
4	Dick Motta	856
5	Bill Fitch	845
6	Cotton Fitzsimmons	805
7	Don Nelson#	803
8	Gene Shue	784
9	John Macleod	707
10	Pat Riley#	701

* *Regular season games only.* # *Still active* •

Pat Riley (coached the LA Lakers from 1981 to 1990; now coaches the New York Knicks) has the best percentage record with 701 wins from 973 games (a 0.7204 percent success rate).

CAR RACING

T O P 1 0

FASTEST WINNING SPEEDS OF THE INDIANAPOLIS 500

	Driver*	Car	Year	Speed km/h	mph
1	Arie Luyendyk (Neth)	Lola-Chevrolet	1990	299.307	185.984
2	Rick Mears	Chevrolet-Lumina	1991	283.980	176.457
3	Bobby Rahal	March-Cosworth	1986	274.750	170.722
4	Emerson Fittipaldi (Bra)	Penske-Chevrolet	1989	269.695	167.581
5	Rick Mears	March-Cosworth	1984	263.308	163.612
6	Mark Donohue	McLaren-Offenhauser	1972	262.619	162.962
7	Al Unser, Jr.	March-Cosworth	1987	260.995	162.175
8	Tom Sneva	March-Cosworth	1983	260.902	162.117
9	Gordon Johncock	Wildcat-Cosworth	1982	260.760	162.029
10	Al Unser	Lola-Cosworth	1978	259.689	161.363

* From the US unless otherwise stated

The current track record, set by Emerson Fittipaldi in the 1990 qualifying competition, is 225.301 mph/362.587 km/h.

INDY 500 CUP
The winner of the Indy 500 is awarded this highly decorated cup, which is adorned with portraits of past champions.

T O P 1 0

WINNERS OF THE INDIANAPOLIS 500 WITH THE HIGHEST STARTING POSITIONS

	Driver	Year	Starting position
1=	Ray Harroun	1911	28
1=	Louis Meyer	1936	28
3	Fred Frame	1932	27
4	Johnny Rutherford	1974	25
5=	Kelly Petillo	1935	22
5=	George Souders	1927	22
7	L.L. Corum and Joe Boyer	1924	21
8=	Frank Lockart	1926	20
8=	Tommy Milton	1921	20
8=	Al Unser, Jr.	1987	20

Of the 75 winners of the Indianapolis 500, 44 have started from a position between 1 and 5 on the starting grid. The Top 10 is of those winners who have started from farthest back in the starting line-up.

T O P 1 0

MONEY-WINNERS AT THE INDIANAPOLIS 500, 1994

	Driver*	Chassis	Prize money ($)
1	Al Unser Jr.	Mercedes	1,373,813
2	Jacques Villeneuve	Ford Cosworth	622,713
3	Bobby Rahal	Ilmor VB-D	411,163
4	Jimmy Vasser	Ford Cosworth	295,163
5	Michael Andretti	Ford Cosworth	245,563
6	Eddie Cheever	Mercedes	238,563
7	Bobby Gordon	Ford Cosworth	227,563
8	Teo Fabi	Ilmor VB-D	216,563
9	Brian Herta	Ford Cosworth	212,213
10	John Andretti	Ford Cosworth	191,750

The first Indianapolis 500, known affectionately as the "Indy," was held on May 30, 1911 and won by Ray Harroun. Then, as today, the race, over 200 laps of the 2¼-mile Indianapolis Raceway, formed part of the Memorial Day celebrations. Prize money in 1994 totaled $7,864,800. Roberto Guerrero, who finished in 33rd (last) position, having completed only 20 of the 200 laps, still earned $143,912.

* From the US unless otherwise stated

T O P 1 0

NASCAR MONEY-WINNERS OF ALL TIME

	Driver*	Total prizes ($)		Driver*	Total prizes ($)
1	Dale Earnhardt	20,362,376	6	Harry Gant	8,184,519
2	Bill Elliott	13,918,144	7	Rickey Rudd	8,030,985
3	Darrell Waltrip	13,110,818	8	Geoff Bodine	7,887,153
4	Rusty Wallace	10,167,556	9	Richard Petty	7,757,964
5	Terry Labonet	8,300,950	10	Bobby Allison	7,102,233

T O P 1 0

FASTEST WINNING SPEEDS OF THE DAYTONA 500

	Driver*	Car	Year	Speed km/h	mph
1	Buddy Baker	Oldsmobile	1980	285.823	177.602
2	Bill Elliott	Ford	1987	283.668	176.263
3	Bill Elliott	Ford	1985	277.234	172.265
4	Richard Petty	Buick	1981	273.027	169.651
5	Derrike Cope	Chevrolet	1990	266.766	165.761
6	A.J. Foyt	Mercury	1972	259.990	161.550
7	Richard Pett	Plymouth	1966	258.504	160.627 #
8	Davey Allison	Ford	1992	257.913	160.260
9	Bobby Allison	Ford	1978	257.060	159.730
10	LeeRoy Yarborough	Ford	1967	254.196	157.950

*   All winners from the US   #   Race reduced to 495 miles/797 km

First held in 1959, the Daytona 500 is raced every February at the Daytona International Speedway, Daytona Beach, Florida. One of the most prestigious races of the NASCAR season, it covers 200 laps of the 2½-mile high-banked oval circuit.

T O P 1 0

CART* DRIVERS WITH MOST RACE WINS

	Driver	Wins
1	A.J. Foyt	67
2	Mario Andretti	52
3	Al Unser	39
4	Bobby Unser	34
5=	Michael Andretti	29
5=	Rick Mears	29
7	Johnny Rutherford	27
8	Roger Ward	26
9	Gordon Johncock	25
10=	Ralph DePalma	24
10=	Bobby Rahal	24
10=	Al Unser Jr.	24

*   Championship Auto Racing Teams

T O P 1 0

DRIVERS WITH THE MOST WINSTON CUP TITLES

	Driver	Years	Titles
1	Richard Petty	1964–79	7
2	Dale Earnhardt	1980–93	6
3=	Lee Petty	1954–59	3
3=	David Pearson	1966–69	3
3=	Cale Yarborough	1976–78	3
3=	Darrell Waltrip	1981–85	3

	Driver	Years	Titles
7=	Herb Thomas	1951–53	2
7=	Tim Flock	1952–55	2
7=	Buck Baker	1956–57	2
7=	Ned Jarrett	1961–65	2
7=	Joe Weatherly	1962–63	2

The Winston Cup is a season-long series of races organized by the National Association of Stock Car Auto Racing, Inc (NASCAR). Races take place over enclosed circuits such as the Daytona speedway, and are among the most popular motor races in the US. The series started in 1949 as the Grand National series, but changed its style to the Winston Cup in 1970 when it became sponsored by the R.J. Reynolds tobacco company, the manufacturers of Winston cigarettes. Cale Yarborough is the only driver to win three successive titles. He, and all the other drivers in the Top 10, are from the US.

RACING INTO HISTORY
Ray Harroun, in his Marmon Wasp, speeds down the home straight to win the very first Indianapolis 500, in 1911.

FOOTBALL

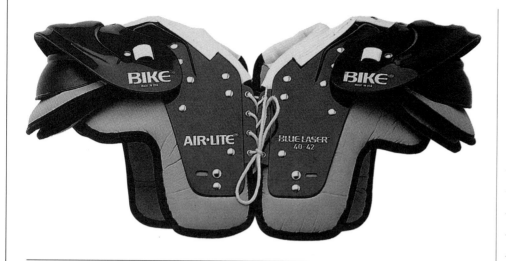

MOST SUCCESSFUL COACHES IN AN NFL CAREER

	Coach	Games won
1	Don Shula	327
2	George Halas	325
3	Tom Landry	270
4	Curly Lambeau	229
5	Chuck Noll	209
6	Chuck Knox	189
7	Paul Brown	170
8	Bud Grant	168
9=	Steve Owen	153
9=	Joe Gibbs	153

BIGGEST WINNING MARGINS IN THE SUPER BOWL

	Winners	Runners-up	Year	Score	Margin
1	San Francisco	Denver	1990	55–10	45
2	Chicago	New England	1986	46–10	36
3	Dallas	Buffalo	1993	52–17	35
4	Washington	Denver	1988	42–10	32
5	LA Raiders	Washington	1984	38–9	29
6	Green Bay	Kansas City	1967	35–10	25
7	San Francisco	Miami	1985	38–16	22
8	Dallas	Miami	1972	24–3	21
9=	Green Bay	Oakland	1968	33–14	19
9=	New York Giants	Denver	1987	39–20	19

The closest Super Bowl was in 1991 when the New York Giants beat the Buffalo Bills 20–19. Scott Norwood missed a 47-yard field goal 8 seconds from the end of time to deprive the Bills of their first-ever Super Bowl win.

COLLEGES WITH THE MOST BOWL WINS

	College	Wins
1	Alabama	26
2	University of Southern California (USC)	23
3	Oklahoma	20
4=	Penn State	18
4=	Tennessee	17
6	Georgia Tech	17
7	Texas	16
8	Georgia	15
9=	Mississippi	14
9=	Nebraska	14

POINTS-SCORERS IN AN NFL SEASON

	Player	Team	Year	Points
1	Paul Hornung	Green Bay	1960	176
2	Mark Moseley	Washington	1983	161
3	Gino Cappelletti	Boston	1964	155*
4	Chip Lohmiller	Washington	1991	149
5	Gino Cappelletti	Boston	1961	147
6	Paul Hornung	Green Bay	1961	146
7	Jim Turner	New York Jets	1968	145
8=	John Riggins	Washington	1983	144
8=	Kevin Butler#	Chicago	1985	144
10	Tony Franklin	New England	1986	140

Bowl games are end-of-season college championship games, played at the end of December or beginning of January each year. The "Big Four" Bowl games are: Rose Bowl, Cotton Bowl, Sugar Bowl, and Orange Bowl. The Rose Bowl, one of college football's great occasions, dates to 1902, when the leading Eastern and Western teams met at Pasadena as part of the Tournament of Roses floral celebration, which was first held in 1890 and by the turn of the century had become a major attraction. Originally called the "East–West Bowl," it became known as the Rose Bowl when the 100,000-plus capacity Rose Bowl stadium was opened in 1923.

Including a two-point conversion   # *The only rookie in the Top 10*

MOST SUCCESSFUL TEAMS

(Based on two points for a Super Bowl win, and one for runner-up)

	Team	Wins	Runners-up	Points
1	Dallas Cowboys	4	3	11
2=	Pittsburgh Steelers	4	0	8
2=	San Francisco 49ers	4	0	8
2=	Washington Redskins	3	2	8
5=	Miami Dolphins	2	3	7
5=	Oakland/Los Angeles Raiders	3	1	7
7=	Buffalo Bills	0	4	4
7=	Denver Broncos	0	4	4
7=	Green Bay Packers	2	0	4
7=	Minnesota Vikings	0	4	4
7=	New York Giants	2	0	4

LARGEST NFL STADIUMS

	Stadium	Home team	Capacity
1	Memorial Coliseum	Los Angeles Raiders	92,488
2	Pontiac Silverdrome	Detroit Lions	80,500
3	Rich Stadium	Buffalo Bills	80,290
4	Cleveland Stadium	Cleveland Browns	80,098
5	Arrowhead Stadium	Kansas City Chiefs	78,067
6	Giants Stadium	New York Giants/Jets	76,891
7	Mile High Stadium	Denver Broncos	76,273
8	Tampa Stadium	Tampa Bay Buccaneers	74,314
9	Joe Robbie Stadium	Miami Dolphins	73,000
10	Sun Devil Stadium	Phoenix Cardinals	72,608

The smallest NFL stadium is the Robert F. Kennedy Stadium, home of the Washington Redskins, with a capacity of 55,672.
Between 1946 and 1979 the capacity of the Los Angeles Memorial Coliseum was 92,604 – the largest-ever capacity of any stadium in the NFL.

THE WILL TO WIN
Walter Payton, shown here in the NFL play-off between the Chicago Bears and the Washington Redskins, has achieved more touchdowns than almost any other player; he is very narrowly beaten by Jim Brown.

PLAYERS WITH THE MOST TOUCHDOWNS IN AN NFL CAREER

	Player	Touchdowns
1	Jim Brown	126
2	Walter Payton	125
3	Jerry Rice	124
4	John Riggins	116
5=	Marcus Allen	113
5=	Lenny Moore	113
7	Don Hutson	105
8	Steve Largent	101
9	Franco Harris	100
10	Eric Dickerson	96

MOST SUCCESSFUL RUSHERS IN AN NFL CAREER

	Player	Total yards gained rushing
1	Walter Payton	16,726
2	Eric Dickerson	13,168
3	Tony Dorsett	12,739
4	Jim Brown	12,312
5	Franco Harris	12,120
6	John Riggins	11,352
7	O.J. Simpson	11,236
8	Ottis Anderson	10,273
9	Earl Campbell	9,407
10	Marcus Allen	9,309

If figures from the All-American Football Conference (1946–49) are taken into account, Joe Perry would rank 9th with 9,723 yards.

GOLF – THE MAJORS

T O P 1 0

PLAYERS TO WIN THE MOST MAJORS IN A CAREER

	Player/ nationality	British Open	US Open	Masters	PGA	Total
1	Jack Nicklaus (US)	3	4	6	5	18
2	Walter Hagen (US)	4	2	0	5	11
3=	Ben Hogan (US)	1	4	2	2	9
3=	Gary Player (SA)	3	1	3	2	9
5	Tom Watson (US)	5	1	2	0	8
6=	Harry Vardon (UK)	6	1	0	0	7
6=	Gene Sarazen (US)	1	2	1	3	7
6=	Bobby Jones (US)	3	4	0	0	7
6=	Sam Snead (US)	1	0	3	3	7
6=	Arnold Palmer (US)	2	1	4	0	7

The four Majors are the British Open, US Open, US Masters, and US PGA. The oldest is the British Open, first played at Prestwick in 1860 and won by Willie Park. The first US Open was at the Newport Club, Rhode Island, in 1895 and won by Horace Rawlins, playing over his home course. The US PGA Championship, probably the least prestigious of the four Majors, was first held at the Siwanoy Club, New York. Jim Barnes beat Jock Hutchison by one hole in the match-play final. It did not become a stroke-play event until 1958. The youngest of the Majors is the Masters, played over the beautiful Augusta National course in Georgia. Entry is by invitation only and the first winner was Horton Smith. No man has won all four Majors in one year.

T O P 1 0

LOWEST WINNING TOTALS IN THE US OPEN

	Player*	Year	Venue	Score
1=	Jack Nicklaus	1980	Baltusrol	272
1=	Lee Janzen	1993	Baltusrol	272
3	David Graham (Aus)	1981	Merion	273
4=	Isao Aoki	1980	Baltusrol	274
4=	Payne Stewart	1993	Baltusrol	274
6=	Jack Nicklaus	1967	Baltusrol	275
6=	Lee Trevino	1968	Oak Hill	275
8=	Ben Hogan	1948	Riviera	276
8=	Keith Fergus	1980	Baltusrol	276
8=	Lon Hinkle	1980	Baltusrol	276
8=	Tom Watson	1980	Baltusrol	276
8=	George Burns	1981	Merion	276
8=	Bill Rogers	1981	Merion	276
8=	Greg Norman	1984	Winged Foot	276
8=	Fuzzy Zoeller#	1984	Winged Foot	276

All from the US unless otherwise stated   # *Won after play-off*

T O P 1 0

HIGHEST-EARNING GOLFERS ON THE PGA TOUR

	Player/nationality	Winnings ($)*
1	Greg Norman (Aus)	12,294,509
2	Bernhard Langer (Ger)	11,211,053
3	Tom Kite (US)	10,700,602
4	Fred Couples (US)	10,607,527
5	Nick Faldo (Eng)	10,374,569
6	Severiano Ballesteros (Spa)	9,525,297
7	Lee Trevino (US)	9,497,703
8	Masashi Ozaki (Jap)	9,347,744
9	Ian Woosnam (Wales)	9,309,488
10	David Frost (SA)	9,113,871

* *Cumulative winnings*

T O P 1 0

LOWEST WINNING SCORES IN THE US MASTERS

	Player*	Year	Score
1=	Jack Nicklaus	1965	271
1=	Raymond Floyd	1976	271
3	Ben Hogan	1953	274
4=	Severiano Ballesteros (Spa)	1980	275
4=	Fred Couples	1992	275
6=	Arnold Palmer	1964	276
6=	Jack Nicklaus	1975	276
6=	Tom Watson	1977	276
9=	Bob Goalby	1968	277
9=	Johnny Miller	1975	277
9=	Gary Player (SA)	1978	277
9=	Ben Crenshaw	1984	277
9=	Ian Woosnam (UK)	1991	277
9=	Raymond Floyd	1992	277
9=	Bernhard Langer (Ger)	1993	277

* *All from the US unless otherwise stated*

The Masters is the only Major played on the same course each year, at Augusta, Georgia.

T H E   T O P

LOWEST FOUR-ROUND TOTALS IN THE PGA CHAMPIONSHIP

	Player*	Year	Score
1	Bobby Nichols	1964	271
2=	David Graham (Aus)	1979	272
2=	Ben Crenshaw	1979	272
2=	Raymond Floyd	1982	272
2=	Jeff Sluman	1988	272
2=	Paul Azinger	1993	272
2=	Greg Norman	1993	272
8=	Lee Trevino	1984	273
8=	Nick Faldo (UK)	1993	273

All from the US unless otherwise stated

T O P · 1 0

MOST FREQUENTLY USED COURSES FOR THE BRITISH OPEN

	Course	First used	Last used	Times used
1=	Prestwick	1860	1925	24
1=	St. Andrews	1873	1990	24
3	Muirfield	1892	1992	14
4	Royal St George's, Sandwich	1894	1993	12
5	Hoylake	1897	1967	10
6	Royal Lytham	1926	1988	8
7	Royal Birkdale	1954	1991	7
8=	Musselburgh	1874	1889	6
8=	Royal Troon	1923	1989	6
10	Carnoustie	1931	1975	5

The only other courses to have staged the Open are Turnberry (three times), Deal (twice), Prince's, Sandwich (once), and Royal Portrush (once) – the only Irish course to play host to Britain's only Major. The Carnoustie course in 1968 was the longest ever used for the Open, measuring 7,252 yd/6,592 m.

T O P   1 0

LOWEST FOUR-ROUND TOTALS IN THE BRITISH OPEN

The first time the Open Championship was played over four rounds of 18 holes was at Muirfield in 1892 when the amateur Harold H. Hilton won with scores of 78, 81, 72, and 74 for a total of 305. Since then the record has kept falling. At Turnberry in 1977 Tom Watson and Jack Nicklaus decimated British Open records with Watson winning by one stroke with a championship record 268. It remained unbeaten for 16 years until Australia's Greg Norman became the first champion to shoot four rounds under 70 when he won with a 267 at Royal St George's, Sandwich in 1993.

TOM WATSON
With more than $6,000,000 in career earnings, five British Open wins, and success in the US Open and Masters, Tom Watson can rightly be labeled one of the most feared opponents faced by today's players.

	Player/nationality	Venue	Year	Total
1	Greg Norman (Aus)	Sandwich	1993	267
2	Tom Watson (US)	Turnberry	1977	268
3=	Jack Nicklaus (US)	Turnberry	1977	269
3=	Nick Faldo (UK)	Sandwich	1993	269
5=	Nick Faldo (UK)	St Andrews	1990	270
5=	Bernhard Langer (Ger)	Sandwich	1993	270
7	Tom Watson (US)	Muirfield	1980	271
8=	Ian Baker-Finch (Aus)	Royal Birkdale	1991	272
8=	Nick Faldo (UK)	Muirfield	1992	272
8=	Corey Pavin (US)	Sandwich	1993	272
8=	Peter Senior (Aus)	Sandwich	1993	272

The lowest individual round is 63, which has been achieved by seven golfers: Mark Hayes (US), Turnberry 1977; Isao Aoki (Jap), Muirfield 1980; Greg Norman (Aus), Turnberry 1986; Paul Broadhurst (UK), St. Andrews 1990; Jodie Mudd (US), Royal Birkdale 1991; Nick Faldo (UK), Sandwich 1993; and Payne Stewart (US), Sandwich 1993. Hubert Green (1980), Tom Watson (1980), Craig Stadler (1983), Christy O'Connor Jr. (1985), Seve Ballesteros (1986), Rodger Davis (1987), Ian Baker-Finch (1990 and 1991), Fred Couples (1991), Nick Faldo (1992), Raymond Floyd (1992), Steve Pate (1992), Wayne Grady (1993), and Greg Norman (1993) have all recorded rounds of 64. A further 23 men have registered rounds of 65; the first to do so was Henry Cotton at Sandwich in 1934. Experts regard Cotton's second round 65 as one of the finest in the interwar era of Championship golf. He had already opened with a 67, and thus became the first man to shoot two sub-70 rounds in the Open. His 65 lowered the Open record of 67 set by Walter Hagen at Muirfield in 1929. Cotton went on to become the first British winner of the Open for 11 years when he beat South Africa's Sid Brews by five strokes with a then record total of 283, which was not surpassed until 1977.

HORSE AND HARNESS RACING

HARNESS-RACING DRIVERS OF ALL TIME

MOST WINS

	Driver	Wins
1	Herve Filion	14,084
2	Carmine Abbatiello	7,100
3	Michael Lachance	6,740
4	John Campbell	6,308
5	Walter Case, Jr.	6,144
6	Dave Magee	5,889
7	"Cat" Manzi	5,877
8	Walter Paisley	5,712
9	Joe Marsh, Jr.	5,649
10	Ron Waples	5,648

MONEY WON

	Driver	Winnings ($)
1	John Campbell	118,951,088
2	Herve Filion	80,668,478
3	Bill O'Donnell	78,765,711
4	Michael Lachance	70,083,387
5	Ron Waples	54,451,262
6	Carmine Abbatiello	49,315,634
7	"Cat" Manzi	46,197,533
8	Doug Brown	45,462,774
9	Buddy Gilmour	43,934,107
10	Jack Moiseyev	43,670,264

Although Bill O'Donnell is third in the all-time money-winning list, he is in 20th place in the list of race wins, with 4,830.

MONEY WINNING JOCKEYS IN A CAREER

	Jockey	1st places	Total winnings ($)
1	Laffit Pincay, Jr.	8,055	177,071,603
2	Chris McCarron	5,919	166,817,558
3	Angel Cordero, Jr.	7,057	164,526,217
4	Pat Day	5,990	135,153,578
5	Ed Delahoussaye	5,191	129,485,541
6	Bill Shoemaker	8,833	123,375,524
7	Jorge Velasquez	6,611	122,043,875
8	Gary Stevens	3,426	105,631,307
9	Eddie Maple	4,115	94,082,886
10	Jerry Bailey	3,060	88,052,685

MONEY-WINNING HORSES IN A HARNESS-RACING CAREER

TROTTERS

	Horse	Winnings ($)
1	Peace Corps	4,907,307
2	Ourasi	4,010,105
3	Mack Lobell	3,917,594
4	Reve d'Udon	3,611,351
5	Ideal du Gazeau	2,744,777
6	Vrai Lutin	2,612,429
7	Grades Singing	2,607,552
8	Embassy Lobell	2,566,370
9	Napoletano	2,467,878
10	Sea Cove	2,466,355

PACERS

	Horse	Winnings ($)
1	Nihilator	3,225,653
2	Artsplace	3,085,083
3	Presidential Ball	3,021,363
4	Matt's Scooter	2,944,591
5	On The Road Again	2,819,102
6	Beach Towel	2,570,357
7	Western Hanover	2,541,647
8	Precious Bunny	2,281,142
9	Jake and Elwood	2,273,187
10	Jate Lobell	2,231,187

Harness racing is one of the oldest sports in the US, its origins going back to the Colonial period, when many races were held along the turnpikes of New York and the New England colonies. After growing in popularity in the 19th century, the exotically titled governing body, the National Association for the Promotion of the Interests of the Trotting Turf (now the National Trotting Association) was founded in 1870. This sport, widespread in the US, is also popular in Australia and New Zealand, and, increasingly, elsewhere around the world.

It has enjoyed a following in the UK since the 1960s, when a trotting track was opened at Prestatyn, North Wales. Harness-racing horses pull a jockey on a two-wheeled "sulky" (introduced in 1829) around an oval track. Unlike thoroughbred racehorses, Standardbred harness-racing horses are trained to trot and pace, but do not gallop. A trotter is a horse whose diagonally opposite legs move forward together, while a pacer's legs are extended laterally and with a "swinging" motion. Pacers usually travel faster than trotters.

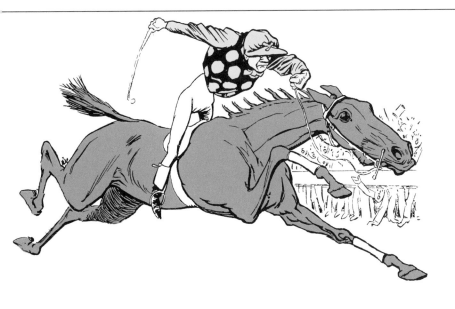

JOCKEYS IN THE US TRIPLE CROWN RACES

	Jockey	K	P	B	Total
1	Eddie Arcaro	5	6	6	17
2	Bill Shoemaker	4	2	5	11
3=	Bill Hartack	5	3	1	9
3=	Earle Sande	3	1	5	9
5	Jimmy McLaughlin	1	1	6	8
6=	Angel Cordero, Jr.	3	2	1	6
6=	Pat Day	1	3	2	6

	Jockey	K	P	B	Total
6=	Chas Kurtsinger	2	2	2	6
6=	Ron Turcotte	2	2	2	6
10=	Ed Delahoussaye	2	1	2	5
10=	Lloyd Hughes	0	3	2	5
10=	Johnny Loftus	2	2	1	5
10=	Willie Simms	2	1	2	5

K – *Kentucky Derby*
P – *Preakness Stakes*
B – *Belmont Stakes*

The US Triple Crown consists of the Kentucky Derby, Preakness Stakes, and Belmont Stakes. Since 1875 only 11 horses have won all three races in one season. The only jockey to complete the Triple Crown twice is Eddie Arcaro on Whirlaway in 1941 and on Citation in 1948.

FASTEST WINNING TIMES OF THE KENTUCKY DERBY

	Horse	Year	Time min	sec
1	Secretariat*	1973	1	59.4
2	Northern Dancer	1964	2	00.0
3	Spend a Buck	1985	2	00.2
4	Decidedly	1962	2	00.4
5	Proud Clarion	1967	2	00.6

	Horse	Year	Time min	sec
6=	Lucky Debonair	1965	2	01.2
6=	Affirmed*	1978	2	01.2
8	Whirlaway*	1941	2	01.4
9=	Middleground	1950	2	01.6
9=	Hill Gail	1952	2	01.6
9=	Bold Forbes	1976	2	01.6

* *Triple Crown winner*

America's best-known race, the Kentucky Derby, is run over 1¼ miles of the Churchill Downs track in Louisville, Kentucky, on the first Saturday each May. It was inaugurated in 1875 and between then and 1895 the race was run over 1½ miles. Eddie Arcaro and Bill Hartack, each with five wins, have been the most successful jockeys and the top trainer, with six wins, is Ben A. Jones. The slowest time for the current 1¼-mile distance was in 1908, when Stone Street won in 2 mins 15.2 secs.

JOCKEYS IN THE BREEDERS CUP

	Jockey*	Years	Wins
1=	Ed Delahoussaye	1984–93	7
1=	Laffit Pincay, Jr.	1985–93	7
3	Pat Day	1984–91	5
4=	Chris McCarron	1985–92	5
4=	José Santos	1986–90	5
4=	Pat Valenzuela	1986–92	5
7	Angel Cordero, Jr.	1985–89	4
8=	Craig Perrett	1984–90	3
8=	Randy Romero	1987–89	3
10=	Jerry Bailey	1991–93	2
10=	Pat Eddery (Ire)	1985–91	2
10=	Walter Guerra	1984–85	2
10=	Freddy Head (Fra)	1987–88	2

10=	Mike Smith	1992–93	2
10=	Gary Stevens	1990–93	2
10=	Yves St. Martin (Fra)	1984–86	2
10=	Jorge Velasquez	1985	2

* *All American unless otherwise stated*

Held at a different venue each year, the Breeders Cup is an end-of-season gathering staged in October or November. Seven races are run during one day, with the season's best throughbreds competing in each category. There is $10 million in prize money, with $3,000,000 going to the winner of the day's senior race, the Classic.

ICE HOCKEY

TOP 10

TEAMS WITH THE MOST STANLEY CUP WINS

	Team	Wins
1	Montreal Canadiens	24
2	Toronto Maple Leafs	11
3	Detroit Red Wings	7
4	Ottawa Senators	6
5=	Boston Bruins	5
5=	Edmonton Oilers	5
7=	Montreal Victorias	4
7=	Montreal Wanderers	4
7=	New York Islanders	4
7=	New York Rangers	4
10=	Chicago Black Hawks	3
10=	Ottawa Silver Seven	3

The Stanley Cup trophy was first presented in 1893 by Sir Frederick Arthur Stanley, then Governor General of Canada. It was won by the Montreal Amateur Athletic Association. In 1914 the Cup was contested by the champions of the National Hockey Association (formed 1910; became the National Hockey League (NHL) in 1917) and the Pacific Coast Hockey Association (formed 1912). The two groups continued to play each other until the PCHA disbanded in 1926. Since then the NHL play-offs have decided the Cup finalists.

TOP 10

POINTS-SCORERS IN AN NHL CAREER
(*Regular season only*)

	Player	Seasons	Goals	Assists	Total points
1	Wayne Gretzky	15	803	1,655	2,458
2	Gordie Howe	26	801	1,049	1,850
3	Marcel Dionne	18	731	1,040	1,771
4	Phil Esposito	18	717	873	1,590
5	Stan Mikita	22	541	926	1,467
6	Bryan Trottier	18	524	901	1,425
7	John Bucyk	23	556	813	1,369
8	Guy Lafleur	17	560	793	1,353
9	Gilbert Perreault	17	512	814	1,326
10	Mark Messier	15	478	838	1,316

TOP 10

ASSISTS IN AN NHL CAREER
(*Regular season only*)

	Player	Seasons	Assists		Player	Seasons	Assists
1	Wayne Gretzky	16	1,747	6	Bryan Trottier	18	901
2	Gordie Howe	26	1,049	7	Ray Bourque	14	877
3	Marcel Dionne	18	1,040	8	Phil Esposito	18	873
4	Paul Coffey	14	934	9	Bobby Clarke	15	852
5	Stan Mikita	22	92	10	Mark Messier	15	838

TOP 10

POINTS-SCORERS IN STANLEY CUP PLAY-OFF MATCHES

	Player	Total points
1	Wayne Gretzky	346
2	Mark Messier	259
3	Jari Kurri	222
4	Glenn Anderson	207
5	Bryan Trottier	184
6	Jean Beliveau	176
7	Denis Potvin	164
8=	Mike Bossy	160
8=	Gordie Howe	160
10	Bobby Smith	155

TOP 10

GOALSCORERS IN AN NHL CAREER
(*Regular season only*)

	Player	Seasons	Goals
1	Wayne Gretzky	15	803
2	Gordie Howe	26	801
3	Marcel Dionne	18	731
4	Phil Esposito	18	717
5	Bobby Hull	16	610
6	Mike Gartner	15	607
7	Mike Bossy	10	573
8	Guy Lafleur	16	560
9	John Bucyk	23	556
10	Jarri Kurri	13	555

TOP 10

GOALTENDERS IN AN NHL CAREER
(*Regular season only*)

	Goaltender	Seasons	Games won
1	Terry Sawchuk	21	435
2	Jacques Plante	18	434
3	Tony Esposito	16	423
4	Glenn Hall	18	407
5	Rogie Vachon	16	355
6	Gump Worsley	21	335
7	Harry Lumley	16	332
8	Billy Smith	18	305
9	Andy Moog	14	303
10	Turk Broda	12	302

TOP 10

GOALSCORERS IN AN NHL SEASON

	Player	Team	Season	Goals
1	Wayne Gretzky	Edmonton Oilers	1981–82	92
2	Wayne Gretzky	Edmonton Oilers	1983–84	87
3	Brett Hull	St. Louis Blues	1990–91	86
4	Mario Lemieux	Pittsburgh Penguins	1988–89	85
5=	Phil Esposito	Boston Bruins	1970–71	76
5=	Alexander Mogilny	Buffalo Sabres	1992–93	76
5=	Teemu Selanne	Winnipeg Jets	1992–93	76
8	Wayne Gretzky	Edmonton Oilers	1984–85	73
9	Brett Hull	St. Louis Blues	1989–90	72
10=	Wayne Gretzky	Edmonton Oilers	1982–83	71
10=	Jari Kurri	Edmonton Oilers	1984–85	71

TOP 10

BEST-PAID PLAYERS IN THE NHL, 1993–94

	Player	Team	Salary ($)
1	Wayne Gretzky	Los Angeles Kings	8,366,000
2=	Eric Lindros	Philadelphia Flyers	3,500,000
2=	Patrick Roy	Montreal Canadiens	3,500,000
4	Steve Yzerman	Detroit Red Wings	3,214,520
5=	Doug Gilmour	Toronto Maple Leafs	3,000,000
5=	Mario Lemieux	Pittsburgh Penguins	3,000,000
7	Mark Messier	New York Rangers	2,533,000
8	Ray Bourque	Boston Bruins	2,500,000
9	Pierre Turgeon	New York Islanders	2,350,000
10	Pat Lafontaine	Buffalo Sabres	2,217,202

Salaries take into account base salary and deferred payments. Signing bonuses are not included.

TOP 10

WINNERS OF THE HART TROPHY

	Player	Years	Wins
1	Wayne Gretzky	1980–89	9
2	Gordie Howe	1952–63	6
3	Eddie Shore	1933–38	4
4=	Bobby Clarke	1973–76	3
4=	Howie Morenz	1928–32	3
4=	Bobby Orr	1970–72	3
7=	Jean Beliveau	1956–64	2
7=	Bill Cowley	1941–43	2
7=	Phil Esposito	1969–74	2
7=	Bobby Hull	1965–66	2
7=	Guy Lafleur	1977–78	2
7=	Mark Messier	1990–92	2
7=	Stan Mikita	1967–68	2
7=	Nels Stewart	1926–30	2

The Hart Trophy, presented to the player "adjudged to be the most valuable to his team during the season," has been awarded every year since 1924; the winner is selected by the Professional Hockey Writers' Association. The trophy is named after Cecil Hart, the former manager/coach of the Montreal Canadiens, and the first winner was Frank Nighbor of Ottawa.

TOP 10

BIGGEST NHL ARENAS

	Stadium	Home team	Capacity
1	Thunderdome, Tampa	Tampa Bay Lightning	28,000
2	Olympic Saddledrome, Calgary	Calgary Flames	20,130
3	Joe Louis Sports Arena, Detroit	Detroit Red Wings	19,275
4	Meadowlands Arena, East Rutherford	New Jersey Devils	19,040
5	Madison Square Garden, New York	New York Rangers	18,200
6	US Air Arena, Landover	Washington Capitals	18,130
7	Northlands Coliseum, Edmonton	Edmonton Oilers	17,503
8	San Jose Arena, San Jose	San Jose Sharks	17,500
9	The Spectrum, Philadelphia	Philadelphia Flyers	17,380
10	The Pond of Anaheim	Mighty Ducks	17,250

The 10th position on this list was previously occupied by the Chicago Stadium, home of the Chicago Black Hawks (capacity:17,317), but this stadium was demolished at the end of the 1993–94 season. The smallest arena is the Ottawa Civic Centre, home of the Ottawa Senators, which has a capacity of 10,585.

LAWN TENNIS

T O P 1 0

WINNERS OF MEN'S GRAND SLAM SINGLES TITLES

	Player/ nationality	A	F	W	US	Total
1	Roy Emerson (Aus)	6	2	2	2	12
2=	Bjorn Borg (Swe)	0	6	5	0	11
2=	Rod Laver (Aus)	3	2	4	2	11
4=	Jimmy Connors (US)	1	0	2	5	8
4=	Ivan Lendl (Cze)	2	3	0	3	8
4=	Fred Perry (UK)	1	1	3	3	8
4=	Ken Rosewall (Aus)	4	2	0	2	8
8=	René Lacoste (Fra)	0	3	2	2	7
8=	William Larned (US)	0	0	0	7	7
8=	John McEnroe (US)	0	0	3	4	7
8=	John Newcombe (Aus)	2	0	3	2	7
8=	William Renshaw (UK)	0	0	7	0	7
8=	Richard Sears (US)	0	0	0	7	7
8=	Mats Wilander (Swe)	3	3	0	1	7

A – *Australian Open*   F – *French Open*
W – *Wimbledon*   US – *US Open*

T O P 1 0

WINNERS OF WOMEN'S GRAND SLAM SINGLES TITLES

	Player/nationality	A	F	W	US	Total
1	Margaret Court (*née* Smith) (Aus)	11	5	3	5	24
2	Helen Wills-Moody (US)	0	4	8	7	19
3=	Chris Evert-Lloyd (US)	2	7	3	6	18
3=	Martina Navratilova (Cze/US)	3	2	9	4	18
5	Steffi Graf (Ger)	4	3	5	3	15
6	Billie Jean King (*née* Moffitt) (US)	1	1	6	4	12
7	Maureen Connolly (US)	1	2	3	3	9
8=	Suzanne Lenglen (Fra)	0	2	6	0	8
8=	Molla Mallory (*née* Bjurstedt) (US)	0	0	0	8	8
8=	Monica Seles (Yug)	3	3	0	2	8

A – *Australian Open*   F – *French Open*
W – *Wimbledon*   US – *US Open*

In 1988 Steffi Graf accomplished the rare feat of achieving a gold medal in the Olympics as well as winning the Grand Slam.

T O P 1 0

PLAYERS WITH THE MOST WIMBLEDON TITLES

	Player/nationality	Years	Singles	Doubles	Mixed	Total
1	Billie Jean King (*née* Moffitt) (US)	1961–79	6	10	4	20
2	Elizabeth Ryan (US)	1914–34	0	12	7	19
3	Martina Navratilova (Cze/US)	1976–93	9	7	2	18
4	Suzanne Lenglen (Fra)	1919–25	6	6	3	15
5	William Renshaw (UK)	1880–89	7	7	0	14
6=	Louise Brough (US)	1946–55	4	5	4	13
6=	Lawrence Doherty (UK)	1897–1905	5	8	0	13
8=	Helen Wills-Moody (US)	1927–38	8	3	1	12
8=	Reginald Doherty (UK)	1897–1905	4	8	0	12
10=	Margaret Court (*née* Smith) (Aus)	1953–75	3	2	5	10
10=	Doris Hart (US)	1947–55	1	4	5	10

Billie Jean King's first and last Wimbledon titles were both in the ladies' doubles. The first, in 1961, as Billie Jean Moffitt, was with Karen Hantze when they beat Jan Lehane and Margaret Smith 6–3, 6–4. When Billie Jean won her record-breaking 20th title in 1979 she partnered Martina Navratilova to victory over Betty Stove and Wendy Turnbull. Two of the foremost male player William Renshaw's titles were in the doubles in 1880 and 1881, then known as the Oxford University Doubles Championship, but which are now regarded as having full Wimbledon championship status. William and his twin brother Ernest won 22 titles between them. The Doherty brothers' dominance of world tennis began with Reginald, known as "Big Do," winning the 1897 Wimbledon singles title. For the next eight years Reginald and Lawrence reigned supreme, winning a total of 25 titles.

TOP 10

PLAYERS WITH MOST US SINGLES TITLES

	Player/nationality	Years	Titles
1	Molla Mallory (née Bjurstedt)	1915–26	8
2=	Richard Sears	1881–87	7
2=	William Larned	1901–11	7
2=	Bill Tilden	1920–29	7
2=	Helen Wills-Moody	1923–31	7
2=	Margaret Court (Aus)*	1962–70	7
7	Chris Evert-Lloyd	1975–82	6
8	Jimmy Connors	1974–83	5
9=	Robert Wrenn	1893–97	4
9=	Elisabeth Moore	1896–1905	4
9=	Hazel Wightman (née Hotchkiss)	1909–19	4
9=	Helen Jacobs	1932–35	4
9=	Alice Marble	1936–40	4
9=	Pauline Betz	1942–46	4
9=	Maria Bueno (Bra)	1959–66	4
9=	Billie Jean King	1967–74	4
9=	John McEnroe	1979–84	4
9=	Martina Navratilova	1983–87	4

All players are from the US unless otherwise stated

* *Includes two wins in Amateur Championships of 1968 and 1969 which were held alongside the Open Championship*

TOP 10

GRAND SLAM TITLES BY AMERICANS SINCE THE SECOND WORLD WAR

	Name	Singles	Doubles	Mixed doubles	Total
1	Martina Navratilova*	18	31	5	54
2	Billie Jean King (née Moffitt)	12	17	11	40
3	Doris Hart	6	14	15	35
4	Louise Brough	6	9	15	30
5	Margaret Osborne duPont	6	16	7	29
6=	Chris Evert-Lloyd	18	3	–	21
6=	Darlene Hard	3	13	5	21
8=	Shirley Fry	4	12	1	17
8=	John McEnroe	7	9	1	17
10	Vic Seixas	2	5	8	15

* *Navratilova won two of her titles before becoming a US citizen. She defected to the US on September 6, 1975.*

TOP 10

PLAYERS WITH MOST FRENCH CHAMPIONSHIP SINGLES TITLES

	Player/nationality	Years	Titles
1	Chris Evert-Lloyd (US)	1974–86	7
2	Bjorn Borg (Swe)	1974–81	6
3	Margaret Court (née Smith) (Aus)	1962–73	5
4=	Henri Cochet (Fra)	1926–32	4
4=	Helen Wills-Moody (US)	1928–32	4
6=	René Lacoste (Fra)	1925–29	3
6=	Hilde Sperling (Ger)	1935–37	3
6=	Yvon Petra (Fra)	1943–45	3
6=	Ivan Lendl (Cze)	1984–87	3
6=	Mats Wilander (Swe)	1982–88	3
6=	Monica Seles (Yug)	1990–92	3
6=	Steffi Graf (Ger)	1987–93	3

The French Championship was inaugurated in 1891 but was a "closed" tournament for French Nationals only until 1925 when it went open to players from other countries. The list is of winners since that year. Prior to 1925, Max Decugis won 8 titles.

MARTINA NAVRATILOVA
Her tally of nine championship titles put her at the top of the Wimbledon singles list.

TOP 10

PLAYERS WITH MOST AUSTRALIAN CHAMPIONSHIP SINGLES TITLES

	Player/nationality	Years	Titles
1	Margaret Court (née Smith)	1960–73	11
2=	Nancy Bolton (née Wynne)	1937–51	6
2=	Roy Emerson	1961–67	6
4	Daphne Akhurst	1925–30	5
5=	Pat Wood*	1914–23	4
5=	Jack Crawford	1931–35	4
5=	Ken Rosewall	1953–72	4
5=	Evonne Cawley (née Goolagong)	1974–77	4
5=	Steffi Graf (Ger)	1988–94	4
10=	Joan Hartigan	1933–36	3
10=	Adrian Quist	1936–48	3
10=	Rod Laver	1960–69	3
10=	Martina Navratilova (US)	1981–85	3
10=	Mats Wilander (Swe)	1983–88	3
10=	Monica Seles (Yug)	1991–93	3

All players are from Australia unless otherwise stated

* *Men's singles*

WATER SPORTS

T O P 1 0

LARGEST SPECIES OF FRESHWATER FISH CAUGHT IN THE US

	Species	Angler/location/year	Weight kg	g	lb	oz
1	White sturgeon	Joey Pallotta III, Benicia, California, 1983	212	28	468	0
2	Alligator gar	Bill Valverde, Rio Grande, Texas, 1951	126	55	279	0
3	Blue catfish	George A. Lijewski, Cooper River, South Carolina, 1991	49	62	109	4
4	Chinook salmon	Les Anderson, Kenai River, Arkansas, 1985	44	18	97	4
5	Lake sturgeon	James Michael DeOtis, Kettle River, Montana, 1986	41	91	92	4
6	Flathead catfish	Mike Rogers, Lake Lewisville, Texas, 1982	41	46	91	4
7	Big skate	Scotty A. Krick, Humboldt Bay, Eureka, California, 1993	41	28	91	0
8	Bigmouth buffalo	Delbert Sisk, Bussey Brake, Bastrop, Louisiana, 1980	31	98	70	5
9	Smallmouth buffalo	Jerry L. Dolezal, Lake Hamilton, Arkansas, 1984	31	20	68	8
10	Striped landlocked bass	Hank Ferguson, O'Neull Forebay, San Luis, California, 1992	30	75	67	8

T O P 1 0

LARGEST SPECIES OF SALTWATER FISH CAUGHT IN THE US

	Species	Angler/location/year	Weight kg	g	lb	oz
1	Tiger shark	Walter Maxwell, Cherry Grove, South Carolina, 1964	807	41	1,780	0
2	Pacific blue marlin	Jay W. Debeaubien, Kaaiwi Point, Kona, Hawaii, 1982	624	15	1,376	0
3	Great hammerhead shark	Allen Ogle, Sarasota, Florida, 1982	449	52	991	0
4	Dusky shark	Warren Girle, Longboat Key, Florida, 1982	346	55	764	0
5	Jewfish	Lynn Joyner, Ferdinanda Beach, Florida, 1961	308	45	680	0
6	Giant sea bass	James McAdam Jr., Anacapa Island, California, 1968	255	74	563	8
7	Bull shark	Phillip Wilson, Dauphin Island, Alabama, 1986	222	26	490	0
8	Warsaw grouper	Steve Haeusler, Gulf of Mexico, Destin, Florida, 1985	197	92	436	12
9	Lemon shark	Colleen D. Harlow, Buxton, North Carolina, 1988	183	71	405	0
10	Bigeye Atlantic tuna	Cecil Browne, Ocean City, Maryland, 1977	170	46	375	8

T O P 1 0

OLYMPIC ROWING NATIONS

	Country	Medals gold	silver	bronze	Total
1	US	30	22	16	65
2	West Germany	21	15	15	51
3	East Germany	33	7	8	48
4	USSR/CIS	12	20	12	44
5	UK	18	15	6	39
6	Italy	12	11	9	32
7	Romania	10	10	7	27
8	France	4	13	9	26
9	Canada	7	8	9	24
10	Switzerland	4	7	9	20

A member of the winning United States eights team at the 1924 Paris Olympics was Benjamin Spock, who later became famous as the "baby expert" and author of the bestselling book *The Common Sense Book of Baby and Child Care*.

THE TOP

MARK SPITZ GOLD MEDALS

Event	Time min:sec
100 meters freestyle	0:51.22
200 meters freestyle	1:52.78
100 meters butterfly	0:54.27
200 meters butterfly	2:00.70
4 x 100 meters freestyle relay	3:26.42
4 x 200 meters freestyle relay	7:35.78
4 x 100 meters medley relay	3:48.16

Spitz holds the record for winning the most gold medals at one Games – seven in 1972, which is the most by any competitor in any sport. His gold medals came in the above events and, remarkably, all were won in world record-breaking times.

T O P 1 0

MOST SUCCESSFUL OLYMPICS SWIMMING COUNTRIES

	Country	gold	silver	bronze	Total
1	US	215	164	134	513
3	E. Germany	40	34	25	99
5	USSR (CIS)	24	32	37	93
7	Hungary	26	22	17	65
9	Japan	15	18	17	50

	Country	gold	silver	bronze	Total
2	Australia	39	34	41	114
4	Germany/ W. Germany	22	31	42	95
6	UK	18	22	29	69
8	Sweden	13	20	21	54
10	Canada	10	15	17	42

Medals*

* Including those awarded for diving and water polo

T O P 1 0

OLYMPIC SWIMMING GOLD MEDAL WINNERS

	Swimmer/nationality	Years	Gold medals*
1	Mark Spitz (US)	1968–72	9
2=	Matt Biondi (US)	1984–92	8
2=	Kristin Otto (GDR)	1988	6
4=	Charles Daniels (US)	1904–08	5
4=	Johnny Weissmuller (US)	1924–28	5
4=	Don Schollander (US)	1964–68	5
7=	Henry Taylor (UK)	1906–08	4
7=	Pat McCormick (US)	1952–56	4
7=	Murray Rose (Aus)	1956–60	4
7=	Dawn Fraser (Aus)	1956–64	4
7=	Roland Matthes (GDR)	1968–72	4
7=	Kornelia Ender (GDR)	1976	4
7=	John Naber (US)	1976	4
7=	Vladimir Salnikov (USSR)	1980–88	4
7=	Greg Louganis (US)	1984–88	4
7=	Krisztina Egerszegi (Hun)	1988–92	4

* Including those awarded for diving

T O P 1 0

MEN'S WORLD WATER-SKIING TITLE WINNERS

	Skier/nationality	Overall	Slalom	Tricks	Jump	Total
1	Patrice Martin (Fra)	3	0	4	0	7
2	Sammy Duval (US)	4	0	0	2	6
3=	Alfredo Mendoza (US)	2	1	0	2	5
3=	Mike Suyderhoud (US)	2	1	0	2	5
3=	Bob La Point (US)	0	4	1	0	5
6=	George Athans (Can)	2	1	0	0	3
6=	Guy de Clercq (Bel)	1	0	0	2	3
6=	Wayne Grimditch (US)	0	0	2	1	3
6=	Mike Hazelwood (UK)	1	0	0	2	3
6=	Ricky McCormick (US)	0	0	1	2	3
6=	Billy Spencer (US)	1	1	1	0	3

SPORTING MISCELLANY

HIGHEST-EARNING SPORTSMEN IN THE WORLD IN 1993

	Name	Sport	Salary/winnings	Income (US $) Other*	Total
1	Michael Jordan	Basketball	4,000,000	32,000,000	36,000,000
2	Riddick Bowe	Boxing	23,000,000	2,000,000	25,000,000
3	Ayrton Senna	Motor racing	14,000,000	4,500,000	18,500,000
4	Alain Prost	Motor racing	12,000,000	4,000,000	16,000,000
5	George Foreman	Boxing	12,500,000	3,300,000	15,800,000
6	Shaquille O'Neal	Basketball	3,300,000	11,900,000	15,200,000
7	Lennox Lewis	Boxing	14,000,000	1,000,000	15,000,000
8	Cecil Fielder	Baseball	12,400,000	300,000	12,700,000
9	Jim Courier	Tennis	3,600,000	9,000,000	12,600,000
10	Joe Montana	American football	5,000,000	6,500,000	11,500,000

Some $32,000,000 of list-leader Michael Jordan's "other income" is reckoned to come from his sponsorship deal with sports footwear manufacturer Nike. Boxing is the sport perhaps most affected by success and failure, its volatile rewards exemplified by the fates of boxers such as George Foreman (who plunged from 4th highest earner in 1991 to 19th in 1992, but bounced back at No. 5 in 1992). Several other sports stars did not make the Top 10 in 1993, but still earned total incomes in excess of $7,000,000. Among them were golfers Arnold Palmer, Jack Nicklaus, and Greg Norman.

* *From sponsorship and royalty income from endorsed sporting products.*
Used by permission of Forbes Magazine

NIELSEN'S TV AUDIENCES OF ALL TIME FOR SPORTS EVENTS IN THE US

	Program	Date	Households viewing total	%
1	Super Bowl XVI (San Francisco v Cincinnati)	Jan 24, 1982	40,020,000	49.1
2	Super Bowl XVII (Washington v Miami)	Jan 30, 1983	40,500,000	48.6
3	XVII Winter Olympics	Feb 23, 1994	45,690,000	48.5
4	Super Bowl XX (Chicago v New England)	Jan 26, 1986	41,490,000	48.3
5	Super Bowl XII (Dallas v Denver)	Jan 15, 1978	34,410,000	47.2
6	Super Bowl XIII (Dallas v Pittsburgh)	Jan 21, 1979	35,090,000	47.1
7=	Super Bowl XVIII (LA Raiders v Washington)	Jan 22, 1984	38,800,000	46.4
7=	Super Bowl XIX (San Francisco v Miami)	Jan 20, 1985	39,390,000	46.4
9	Super Bowl XIV (LA Rams v Pittsburgh)	Jan 20, 1980	35,330,000	46.3
10	Super Bowl XXI (Giants v Denver)	Jan 25, 1987	40,030,000	45.8

Copyright © 1994 Nielsen Media Research

INDIVIDUAL OLYMPIC GOLD MEDAL WINNERS

Ray Ewry (US) 1900–08

Paavo Nurmi (Fin) 1920–28

Carl Lewis (US) 1984–88
Ville Ritola (Fin) 1924–28

Martin Sheridan (US) 1906–08
Harrison Dillard (US) 1948–52

Archie Hahn (US) 1904–06
Alvin Kraenzlein (US) 1900

Erik Lemming (Swe) 1906–12
James Lightbody (US) 1904–06

Hannes Kolehmainen (Fin) 1912–20
Al Oerter (US) 1956–68

Jesse Owens (US) 1936

Mal Shepp (U) 1908–

Myer Prinstein (US) 1900–06

1 10 medals
2 9 medals
3 6 medals
4= 5 medals
6= 4 medals

TOP 10

FASTEST WINNING TIMES OF THE IDATAROD DOG SLED RACE

	Winner	Year	Time day	hr	min	sec
1	Martin Buser	1994	10	13	02	39
2	Jeff King	1993	10	15	30	15
3	Martin Buser	1992	10	19	17	15
4	Susan Butcher	1990	11	01	53	28
5	Susan Butcher	1987	11	02	05	13
6	Joe Runyan	1989	11	05	24	34
7	Susan Butcher	1988	11	11	41	40
8	Susan Butcher	1986	11	15	06	00
9	Rick Swenson	1981	12	08	45	02
10	Rick Mackey	1983	12	14	10	44

The race, which has been held annually since 1973, stretches from Anchorage to Nome, Alaska, the course following an old river mail route and covering 1,158 miles/ 1,864 km. Idatarod is a deserted mining village along the route, and the race commemorates an emergency operation in 1925 to get medical supplies to Nome following a diphtheria epidemic. Rick Swenson has won the race a record five times. Susan Butcher has won it four times (men and women compete together on equal terms).

TOP 10

WORST DISASTERS AT SPORTS VENUES

(20th century only)

	Location/disaster	Date	No. killed
1	Hong Kong Jockey Club (stand collapse and fire)	Feb 26, 1918	604
2	Lenin Stadium, Moscow, Russia (crush in soccer stadium)	Oct 20, 1982	340
3	Lima, Peru (soccer stadium riot)	May 24, 1964	320
4	Sinceljo, Colombia (bullring stand collapse)	Jan 20, 1980	222
5	Hillsborough, Sheffield, UK (crush in soccer stadium)	Apr 15, 1989	96
6	Le Mans, France (racing car crash)	Jun 11, 1955	82
7	Katmandu, Nepal (stampede in soccer stadium)	Mar 12, 1988	80
8	Buenos Aires, Argentina (riot in soccer stadium)	May 23, 1968	73
9	Ibrox Park, Glasgow, Scotland (barrier collapse in soccer stadium)	Jan 2, 1971	66
10	Bradford Stadium, UK (fire in soccer stadium)	May 11, 1985	56

TOP 10

PARTICIPATION SPORTS, GAMES, AND PHYSICAL ACTIVITIES IN THE US

	Activity	No. participating
1	Walking	64,000,000
2	Swimming	61,400,000
3	Bicycle riding	53,972,000
4	Fishing	51,200,000
5	Camping	42,700,000
6	Bowling	41,300,000
7	Exercising with equipment	41,300,000
8	Basketball	29,600,000
9	Billiards/pool	29,400,000
10	Aerobic exercise	24,900,000

A survey of participation sports conducted by the National Sporting Goods Association in 1993 showed that baseball as a participation (in contrast to spectator) sport scored relatively low in the US (16,700,000), being beaten by softball (17,900,000). Soccer (10,300,000) showed a 3.2 percent increase on the previous year's survey, while football (14,700,000) gained 9.1 percent. Golf, boating, volleyball, and running/jogging each had over 20,000,000 devotees, while hunting with firearms had 18,500,000 followers.

TOP 10

HIGHEST-EARNING FILMS WITH SPORTING THEMES

	Film	Sport
1	*Rocky IV* (1985)	Boxing
2	*Rocky III* (1982)	Boxing
3	*Rocky* (1976)	Boxing
4	*A League of Their Own* (1992)	Baseball
5	*Rocky II* (1979)	Boxing
6=	*Days of Thunder* (1990)	Stock car racing
6=	*White Men Can't Jump* (1992)	Basketball
8	*Chariots of Fire* (1973)	Track
9	*Field of Dreams* (1989)	Baseball
10	*The Main Event* (1979)	Boxing

The boxing ring dominates Hollywood's most successful sports-based epics, which are led by superstar Sylvester Stallone's *Rocky* series. Baseball is a popular follow-up, both in the films represented in the Top 10 and in others just outside, including *The Natural* (1984), *Bull Durham* (1988), and *Major League* (1989). Stock car racing, women's baseball, and basketball are all unique as the sporting themes of successful films.

Fanny Blankers-Koen (Hol) 1948

Betty Cuthbert (Aus) 1956–64

asse Viren (Fin) 1972–76

Emil Zatopek (Cze) 1948–52

Bärbel Wöckel (GDR) 1976–80

TOYS AND GAMES

MOST EXPENSIVE TOYS EVER SOLD AT AUCTION BY CHRISTIE'S EAST, NEW YORK

	Toy/sale	Price ($)*
1	"The Charles," a fire hose reel made by American manufacturer George Brown & Co, c1875 December 1991	231,000
2	Märklin fire station December 1991	79,200
3	Horse-drawn double-decker tram December 1991	71,500
4	Mikado mechanical bank December 1993	63,000

	Toy/sale	Price ($)*
5	Märklin Ferris wheel June 1994	55,200
6	Girl skipping rope mechanical bank June 1994	48,300
7	Märklin battleship June 1994	33,350
8	Märklin battleship June 1994	32,200
9=	Bing keywind open phaeton tinplate automobile December 1991	24,200

	Toy/sale	Price ($)*
9=	Märklin fire pumper December 1991	24,200

* *Including 10% buyer's premium*

The fire hose reel at No.1 in this list is the record price paid at auction for a toy other than a doll. Models by the German tinplate maker Märklin, regarded by collectors as the Rolls-Royce of toys, similarly feature among the record prices of auction houses in the UK and other countries, where high prices have also been attained.

HIGHEST-SCORING WORDS IN SCRABBLE

Word/play	Score
1 QUARTZY	
(i) Play across a triple-word-score (red) square with the Z on a double-letter-score (light blue) square	164
(ii) Play across two double-word-score (pink) squares with Q and Y on light blue squares	162
2= BEZIQUE	
(i) Play across a red square with either the Z or the Q on a light blue square	161
(ii) Play across two pink squares with the B and second E on two light blue squares	158
2= CAZIQUE	
(i) Play across a red square with either the Z or the Q on a light blue square	161
(ii) Play across two pink squares with the C and E on two light blue squares	158
4= ZINKIFY	
Play across a red square with the Z on a light blue square	158
5= QUETZAL	
Play across a red square with either the Q or the Z on a light blue square	155
5= JAZZILY	
Using a blank as one of the Zs, play across a red square with the nonblank Z on a light blue square	155
5= QUIZZED	
Using a blank as one of the Zs, play across a red square with the nonblank Z or the Q on a light blue square	155

Word/play	Score
8= ZEPHYRS	
Play across a red square with the Z on a light blue square	152
8= ZINCIFY	
Play across a red square with the Z on a light blue square	152
8= ZYTHUMS	
Play across a red square with the Z on a light blue square	152

All the Top 10 words contain seven letters and therefore earn the premium of 50 for using all the letters in the rack. Being able to play them depends on there already being suitable words on the board to which they can be added. In an actual game, the face values of the perpendicular words to which they are joined would also be counted, but these are discounted here as the total score variations would be infinite.

Scrabble was invented in the US during the Depression, by a jobless architect, Alfred Butts. It was developed in the late 1940s by James Brunot, who chose the name *Scrabble* after rejecting several others already in use for other products. By 1953 over 1,000,000 sets had been sold. Versions in languages other than English have different ratios of letters, appropriate to each language. For example, in Dutch, there are 18 Es, 10 Ns, and two Js, while the German game has 119 rather than 100 letters, and players have eight letters rather than seven on their racks.

BESTSELLING TOYS OF 1993 IN THE US

	Toy	Manufacturer
1	Barney the Dinosaur	The Lyons Group
2	Hollywood Hair Barbie	Mattell
3	Batman	Kenner
4	Jurassic Park	Kenner
5	Genesis	Sega
6	Super Nintendo Entertainment System	Nintendo
7	Littlest Pet Shop	Kenner
8	Magic Tea Party	Playskool
9	G.I. Joe	Hasboro
10	Teenage Mutant Ninja Turtles	Playmates

The 1990s have already proved to be boom years for toy sales in the US. A long period of only steady growth averaging some two percent a year brought the industry to total 1991 sales of $15,150,000,000, but in 1992 this rocketed by an unprecedented 12 percent to almost $17,000,000,000, an expansion that continued in 1993, with character merchandising maintaining its grip on the market. It can confidently be predicted that the mega-selling Mighty Morphin Power Rangers products, derived from the cult Japanese TV series, will continue this trend in 1994.

TOP 10

MOST EXPENSIVE TEDDY BEARS SOLD AT AUCTION IN THE UK

Bear/sale	Price (£)*
1 "Happy," dual-plush Steiff Teddy bear, 1926 Sotheby's, London, September 19, 1989	55,000

Although Happy's value was originally estimated at £700–£900, competitive bidding pushed the price up to the world record, when the bear was bought by collector Paul Volpp.

2 "Eliot," a blue Steiff bear, 1908 Christie's, London, December 6, 1993	49,500

Eliot was produced as a sample for Harrods, but was never manufactured commercially.

3 Black Steiff Teddy bear, c.1912, Sotheby's, London, May 18, 1990	24,200
4 "Alfonzo," a red Steiff Teddy bear, c.1906–09 Christie's, London, May 18, 1989	12,100

This bear was once owned by Princess Xenia of Russia.

Bear/sale	Price (£)*
5 Rod-jointed Steiff apricot plush Teddy bear, c.1904 Sotheby's, London, May 9, 1991	11,770
6 Black Steiff Teddy bear, c. 1912, Phillips, London, October 19, 1990	8,800
7 Apricot-colored Steiff Teddy bear, c.1904, Sotheby's, London, January 31, 1990	7,700
8= White plush Steiff Teddy bear, c. 1904, Sotheby's, London, January 31, 1990	6,050
8= White plush Steiff Teddy bear, c.1905, Sotheby's, London, May 18, 1990	6,050
10 White plush Steiff Teddy bear, c. 1920, Sotheby's, London, January 22, 1991	4,620

* Prices include buyer's premium.

Teddy bears have become highly valued items in international auction houses such as Sotheby's and Christie's. Their story begins in the early 1900s; it is said that, while on a hunting trip, US President Theodore ("Teddy") Roosevelt refused to shoot a young bear, and this became the subject of a famous cartoon by Clifford K. Berryman, published in the *Washington Post* on November 16, 1902. Immediately afterward, Morris Michtom, a New York shopkeeper (and later founder of the Ideal Toy and Novelty Company) made stuffed bears and – with Roosevelt's permission – began advertising them as "Teddy's Bears." At about the same time, Margarete Steiff, a German toymaker, began making toy bears, exporting them to the US to meet the demand "Teddy's Bears" had created. In 1903 Steiff's factory made 12,000 bears; by 1907 the figure had risen to 974,000. Steiff bears, recognizable by their distinctive ear tags, are still made and are sold internationally, but the early ones are the most prized among collectors, with the result that all the Top 10 are Steiffs.

GRIN AND BEAR IT
Arctophily, or Teddy bear collecting, is an increasingly serious hobby.

TOP 10

MOST LANDED-ON SQUARES IN MONOPOLY®

1	Illinois Avenue
2	Go
3	B & O Railroad
4	Free Parking
5	Tennessee Avenue
6	New York Avenue
7	Reading Railroad
8	St. James Place
9	Water Works
10	Pennsylvania Railroad

Monopoly® is a registered trademark of Parker Brothers division of Tonka Corporation, USA.

Monopoly was patented on February 7, 1936. It had been devised in Philadelphia during the Depression by Charles Darrow, an unemployed heating engineer. Darrow's streets were derived from those of the New Jersey resort Atlantic City – it is said, because he dreamed of going there, but could not afford the fare. There were already several real estate board games around, such as The Landlord's Game, patented in 1904 by Elizabeth Magie, which, like Monopoly, had a "Go to Jail" square, and Finance, which featured "Chance" and "Community Chest" cards. However, none of the earlier prototypes was commercially successful, and Darrow's version, with its subtle balance of skill and luck, was the first property game that was fun to play. His sales in 1934 rocketed to 20,000, and he entered into a licensing arrangement with Parker Brothers. Darrow rapidly became a millionaire, devoting the rest of his life to travel and the cultivation of rare orchids.

Monopoly is now available in 23 languages and in 34 countries. Around the world, either the Atlantic City board is used (as in Japan and Venezuela) or the British (in Australia and India), while various national editions are based on cities such as Athens, Hong Kong, Tel Aviv, Oslo, and Dublin. Whatever the city, all versions use local currency, so it may be played with South African rand, Peruvian sols, or Austrian schillings. Since 1935 over 100,000,000 sets have been sold, making Monopoly the bestselling copyrighted game of all time.

INDEX

ACKNOWLEDGMENTS

Special thanks to Caroline Ash for her continuing assistance in compiling *The Top 10 of Everything*, to Luke Crampton, Ian Morrison, and Dafydd Rees for their work on this edition, and to the following individuals and organizations who kindly supplied the information to enable me to prepare many of the lists:

Richard Braddish, Ludo Craddock, Paul Dickson, Greg Fielden, Christopher Forbes, Darryl Francis, Monika Half, William Hartston, Duncan Hislop, Robert Lamb, Barry Lazell, Dr Benjamin Lucas, Dr Jacqueline Mitton, Giles Moon, Sir Tim Rice, Adrian Room, Rocky Stockman MBE, Carey Wallace, Tony Waltham

AB Research, Academy of Motion Picture Arts and Sciences, *Advertising Age*, AFL-C1O, AGB Group, Agricultural Research Service, Airport Operators Council International, American Correctional Association, American Forestry Association, American Hotel/Motel Association, *American Karaoke Magazine*, American Kennel Club, Inc., American Society of Association Executives, American Veterinary Medical Association, Amusement and Music Operators Association, *Amusement Business Magazine*, Arbitron, Art Institute of Chicago, Art Sales Index, Association of British Investigators, Automobile Association, BBC Written Archives, Ben & Jerry's, Beverage Marketing Corporation, *BioCycle*, Blackburn Marketing Services, Inc., Bonhams, Boy Scouts of America, British Airports Authority, British Allergy Foundation, British Astronomical Society, British Broadcasting Corporation, British Cave Research Association, British Interplanetary Society, British Library, British Rail, Bureau of Engraving & Printing, Bureau of Justice Statistics, Business Publications Audit, *Business Travel News*, *Business Week*, *Cablevision*, Cadbury Schweppes Group, Cameron Mackintosh Ltd, Carbon Dioxide Information Analysis Center/Greg Marland/Tom Boden, Carson Productions, Cat Fancier's Association, CBS Broadcast Group, Center for the American Woman and Politics, Central Intelligence Agency, Central Statistical Office, Chairman of the Joint Chiefs of Staff, Champagne Bureau, Championship Auto Racing Teams (CART), Channel Swimming Association, Christie's East, Christie's London, Christie's South Kensington, Civil Aviation Authority, *Classical Music*, Coca-Cola Great Britain and Ireland, The College of William and Mary, *Criminal Statistics England & Wales*, CSG Information Services, *Dairy Foods Magazine*, Dateline, Daytona 500, De Beers, Death Penalty Information Center, Diamond Information Centre, Duncan's American Radio, Inc., *Entertainment Business*, Entertainment Data, Inc., Federal Aviation Authority, Federal Bureau of Investigation, Feste Catalogue Index Database/Alan Somerset, Fine Arts Museum, Boston, Food and Agriculture Organization of the United Nations, *Forbes Magazine*, Forestry Commission, *Fortean Times*, Fortune, *Foundation Giving*, Gallup, Generation AB, Girl Scouts of USA, Geological Museum, Gold Fields Mineral Services Ltd, H.J. Heinz Co Ltd, Häagen-Dazs UK, Hallmark, Home and Overseas Insurance Company, Indianapolis 500, Infoplan, Information Resources, Inc., International Cocoa Organization, International Coffee Organization, International Dairy Foods Association, International Game Fish Association, International Ice Cream Association, International Monetary Fund, International Tea Committee, International Union of Geological Sciences Commission, *International Water Power and Dam Construction Handbook*, International Wine Auctions, The Jockey Club, Kellogg Company of Great Britain, Lloyds Register of Shipping, London Theatre Record, London Transport Lost Property, Magazine Publishers of USA, MARC Europe, The Masters, Meat and Livestock Commission, Metropolitan Museum of Art, New York, Metropolitan Opera House, New York, Michigan Department of Natural Resources, Modern Languages Association of America, *Money*, MORI, Motor Vehicle Manufacturers Association of the United States, Inc., MRIB, Museum of the Moving Image, NASA,

National Association for Stock Car Auto Racing (NASCAR), National Association of Chain Drug Stores, National Association of Railroad Passengers, National Basketball Association (NBA), National Blood Transfusion Service, National Center for Educational Statistics, National Center for Health Statistics, National Climatic Data Center, National Collegiate Athletic Association (NCAA), National Football League (NFL), National Gallery, Washington, DC, National Hockey League (NHL), National Marine Manufacturers Association, National Maritime Museum, National Oceanic and Atmospheric Administration, National Park Service, *National Petroleum News*, National Public Radio, National Safety Council, National Solid Waste Management Association, National Sporting Goods Association, National Transportation Safety Board, New York Transit Authority, A.C. Nielsen, Nielsen Media Research, Nobel Foundation, Nonprescription Drug Manufacturers Association, North American Breeding Bird Survey, Nuclear Engineering International, Ordnance Survey, *Outside*, Overstreet Publications, Inc., Oxford University Press, Parker Brothers, PBS, Pet Food Institute/Frosty Paws, PGA Tour, Inc., Phillips West Two, Phobics Society, *Playthings*, Produktschap voor Gedistilleerde Dranken, *Publishers Weekly*, Pullman Power Products Corporation, *Railway Gazette International*, Really Useful Group, Relate, *Restaurants & Institutions*, Rolls-Royce Motor Cars, Royal Aeronautical Society, Royal College of General Practitioners, Royal Opera House, Covent Garden, Royal Society for the Prevention of Cruelty to Animals, Scout Association, *Screen Digest*, Shakespeare Birthplace Trust, Siemens AG, Social Security Administration, Sotheby's London, Sotheby's New York, *Spaceflight*, *Sporting News*, Standard Rate & Data Service, Sugar Bureau, Taylors of Loughborough, Thoroughbred Racing Associations, Towne-Oller & Associates/Information Resources, Inc., Trebor Bassett, Tree Register of the British Isles, *UBS Phillips & Drew Global Pharmaceutical Review*, United Nations, United States Trotting Association (USTA), *USA Today*, US Bureau of the Census, US Department of Agriculture, US Department of Agriculture, Forest Service, US Department of Commerce, International Trade Administration, US Department of Justice, US Department of Justice/FBI, *Uniform Crime Statistics*, US Department of Labor, US Department of the Interior, National Register of Historic Places, US Department of Transportation, Federal Highway Administration, US Department of Transportation, National Highway Traffic Safety Administration, US Fish and Wildlife Service, US Geological Survey, US Immigration and Naturalization Service, US Mint, US Office of Personnel Management, US Postal Service, Postal History Department, US Travel and Tourism Administration, *Variety*, *Video Scan*, *Video Store Magazine*, *Wines & Vines*, World Association of Girl Guides and Girl Scouts, World Health Organization, World Intellectual Property Organization, *World of Travel Shopping*

PICTURE CREDITS

t = top; c = centre; b = bottom; l = left; r = right

The J Allan Cash Photolibrary: 102l
American Airlines: 207t
Bassano & Vandyk Portrait Studios: 63tr; 64br
British Library: 68 tr; 122 bl
British Museum: 222b
Bruce Coleman Ltd./Johnny Johnson: 26cl;/Jeff Foott Productions 37bl
Channel Four Television: 193br
Christie's Images: 156tl
Mary Evans Picture Library: 2bl; 8br; 62bl; 86tr; 162bl; 164c; 246tr; 252tl
Ford's Photographic Dept.: 236b
Ronald Grant Archive: 1br; 166br; 167tr; 168br; 170bl; 187bl; 188tl; 188tr; 189c; 189cl
Greenpeace/Hodson: 200tr
Robert Harding Picture Library: 16bl; 20bl; 113bc; 136tc;/G. Hellier: 112tr;/M.J. Howell: 108bl

The Hulton Deutsch Collection: 3br; 60tl; 61r; 71tr; 122bc
IBM UK Ltd.: 200cla
Image Bank: 15br; 159tr; 237tr; /Walter Bibikow: 214; /Gary Cralle: 116t; /Steve Dunwell: 250cl; /Romilly Lockyer: 251bc; /Colin Bell: 254bl
Impact/Marc Henley: 97tc
The Imperial War Museum: 84br; 85cr
International Brotherhood of Teamsters: 56cra
Kobal Collection: front cover cl; 168br; 171cr; 172br
Magnum Photos Ltd./Elliot Erwin: 68tl; /Burt Glinn: 70bl; /George Rodger: 87b; /Danny Lyon: 80bl; /Mike Nichols: 238tl; /Stuart Franklin: 253b
Memorial Museum of Cosmonautics, Moscow: 14bc; 15tr
MTV Networks Europe: 193br
Musee d'Orsay, Paris: 132c
Museo Archeologico di Napoli: 25b
NASA: 10cb; 10tl
National Maritime Museum: Title page; 64tl; 65b; 88r; 247br
National Motor Museum, Beaulieu: 234br; 235b
The Nature Conservancy: 216 cr
Pennsylvania State University Public Information/G.Grieco: 115tl
Pictor International: 92tr; 204br; 254bc; 255tr
Range/Bettmann: 123br; 202b;/UPI: 81tl; 127br; 195br; 264tr; 265b; 267br
Rex Features Ltd.: front cover tr; 3tr; 24tl; 58tl; 76cl; 82bc; 114cl; 126tr; 138cl; 142br; 143tr; 144l; 148tl; 150tr; 151tc; 151bl; 153tl; 154c; 154cr; 155cr; 174bc; 178bc; 179tr; 182tr; 182bl; 183br; 184cl; 184c; 184br; 185br; 187tr; 190tr; 192cl; 218tl; 220tr; 220bl; 243; 244tr; /L. Goldsmith: 194tl; /D. Hogan: 152bc; SIPA Press/R. Trippett 220 tl
Riverside Press: 77br
Royal Artillery Historical Trust, London: 83br
Royal Geographical Society: 65cr
Royal Marines Museum, Portsmouth: 48tc
The Science Museum: 9cr; 249c
Science Photo Library: /NASA: 23tr; /Tony Buxton: 26tr
Sotheby's: 135tc; 157b; 280c
Sporting Pictures (UK) Ltd.: front cover br; 258tl; 258tra; 258trb; 262br; 265tr; 269bl; 270cb; 272tr; 275tr; 280tc
Stena Sealink: 207bl
Text 100/Microsoft 221 tl
Tony Stone Images: 110tr; 206tr; /S. Climpson: 105bl; /Val Corbett: 105bl; /J. Ortner: 103t
World Scout Bureau: 57bc
WPLJ New York: 191bl

ADDITIONAL PHOTOGRAPHY

Geoff Brightling, John Bulman, Jane Burton, Martin Cameron, Peter Chadwick, Andy Crawford, Brian Deff, Philip Dowell, Mike Dunning, David Exton, Neil Fletcher, Philip Gatwood, Steve Gorton, Bob Guthany, Chas Hawson, Steven Hayward, J. Heseltine, Ed Ironside, Colin Keates, Roland Kemp, Dave King, Cyril Lauscher, Andrew McRobb, Cameron MacKintosh, Roy Moller, Steven Oliver, Brian Pitkin, Laurence Pordes, Tim Ridley, Dave Rudkin, Philippe Sebert, Rodney Shackill, Karl Shone, Chris Stevens, James Stevenson, Clive Streeter, Kim Taylor, Mathew Ward, Richard Ward, Dan Wright, Jerry Young

ILLUSTRATIONS

Paul Collicutt, Janos Marffy, Richard Ward, Dan Wright

DORLING KINDERSLEY WOULD LIKE TO THANK:

Heather McCarry, Katie John, Ellen Woodward, Antonia Cunningham, Colette Connolly, Andrea Horth, Dingus Hussey, Josephine Buchanan, Lynne Brown

PICTURE RESEARCH

Valya Alexander
Additional US picture research: Becky Halls

INDEX

Patricia Coward